The Reign of Philip the Fair

THE REIGN OF PHILIP THE FAIR

By Joseph R. Strayer

PRINCETON UNIVERSITY PRESS
PRINCETON, NEW JERSEY

Copyright © 1980 by Princeton University Press
Published by Princeton University Press, Princeton, New Jersey
In the United Kingdom: Princeton University Press, Guildford, Surrey

All Rights Reserved
Library of Congress Cataloging in Publication Data will be found
on the last printed page of this book

Designed by Bruce Campbell
This book has been composed in Linotype Janson

Clothbound editions of Princeton University Press books are
printed on acid-free paper, and binding materials are chosen
for strength and durability

Printed in the United States of America by Princeton
University Press, Princeton, New Jersey

Contents

List of Illustrations

Preface

This book has been a long time aborning. My interest in the subject goes back to the 1930s, when I had completed a monograph and edited a text dealing with the administration of Normandy under St. Louis. It seemed reasonable to go on and trace the development of French institutions during the rest of the century. I discovered, however, that although most of the sources on the reign of St. Louis had been published, there were relatively few sources for the time of Philip III and abundant, but unpublished, sources for the reign of Philip the Fair. Grants from Princeton University and from the Social Science Research Council made it possible for me to spend about 18 months in France between 1935 and 1937. During this period I took notes on most of the financial documents later edited by Robert Fawtier, on the Chancery Registers, and on other material in the Bibliothèque Nationale and the Archives Nationales. My monograph on taxation under Philip the Fair, published in *Studies in Early French Taxation* in 1939, was the result of this research.

As with many other scholars, my work was interrupted by the war. A heavy teaching load and equally heavy administrative responsibilities, plus some intermittent work for the government, left little time for research. These burdens did not lessen at the end of the war; in fact, I spent more than a year in government service in 1953-1954. Only in 1955 was I able to begin the work that I should have done ten years earlier. The time was not entirely lost, however, because it was during these years that Fawtier began publication of the *Comptes royaux*, followed by the *Inventaire analytique* of the Chancery Registers. These magnificent works of scholarship made it far easier to find, verify, and compare the references to governmental activities that I had recorded, often imperfectly, in my notes.

After 1955 there were other reasonable and unreasonable causes for delay. I did not want to spend all my time on Philip, as this would have led to a narrow and distorted view of the significance of the reign. Work on the Crusades brought me back into the days of St. Louis, who was a rather different person from his grandson; work on England under the Edwards showed me that there were alternatives to the French pattern of government;

and work on early feudalism provided an instructive contrast to thirteenth-century social and political conditions. When I did turn to Philip's reign I came to the conclusion that we needed to know more about the personnel of government. I began to compile a card catalogue of all the men who had worked for Philip, from members of the Council and the Parlement down to *prévôts* and foresters. It took time to prepare this catalogue, and even more time to keep it up-to-date, since important new works, such as Jean Favier's *Cartulaire et actes d'Enguerran de Marigny*, kept appearing. (I regret that Favier's recent book on Philip appeared after this study went to press.) It was also necessary to visit departmental and municipal archives in France to fill in gaps in my earlier research (again I must thank Princeton University for including travel grants in the stipend for my professorship). My articles on "Viscounts and Viguiers under Philip the Fair," "Pierre de Chalon," and "Italian Bankers and Philip the Fair" and my monograph on *Les gens de justice du Languedoc sous Philippe le Bel* were byproducts of this activity.

Another difficulty was caused by a change in my appraisal of the character and abilities of the king. I had begun my work with the belief—held by many earlier historians—that Philip had been a weak ruler dominated by aggressive and unscrupulous bureaucrats. It was only as I became familiar with the early, less spectacular years of the reign that I began to feel that Philip had formed his basic ideas about kingship and about the policies that a king of France should pursue long before he had a Flote, a Nogaret, or a Marigny to advise him. Philip had an acute, probably too acute, sense of his royal dignity. He would not make stirring speeches to crowds or engage in debates with emissaries of popes and kings, but he was determined to preserve his rights and to secure acknowledgment of his sovereignty throughout the realm. This attitude and these policies were evident by 1290, when Philip was still working with ministers and with a structure of government inherited from his father. New policies were not foisted on the king by his ministers; rather, the king gave his ministers the heavy task of imposing his new policies on the Church, the barons, and the common people. The number of royal officials increased because there was more work to be done. The "unscrupulous bureaucrats" were unscrupulous because Philip demanded that they find money for his wars or secure recognition of his sovereignty in autonomous regions such as the Gévaudan or border regions such as the Lyonnais. They were not noticeably corrupt, and, with the exception of Marigny, they were not trying to build bureaucratic empires that they could control.

If these hypotheses were to be accepted, then obviously the whole question of policy making and policy implementation had to be rethought. Granted that the king laid down the general lines of policy, how much attention did he pay to detail? To take a specific case, Philip certainly wanted taxes, but who worked out the specific types of taxation that were used during the reign? Philip wanted to build up the authority and prestige of his High Court of Parlement, but who was responsible for the changes in procedures and jurisprudence that made the Parlement more effective in the latter years of the reign? Or, to take an entirely different kind of problem, royal agents in the provinces clearly used some discretion in carrying out the directives that came down from Paris; they delayed, or compromised, or at times simply ignored royal mandates. At times the delays and the compromises were specifically authorized by higher authority, notably when it was a question of collecting taxes; but even then, one must wonder whether there had been warnings from local agents not to push too hard. At other times, provincial officials may have been more zealous than the king in asserting royal supremacy; they might be rebuked, but they also might so discourage a local lord or prelate that he would abandon some of his rights. How many of the *paréages* in the south were planned in Paris and how many were the result of steady pressure by local officials?

There are no very satisfactory answers to any of these questions, but it took some time to reach this rather disheartening conclusion. Philip's government was not highly structured, though it was certainly less informal than that of St. Louis. Nevertheless, personal relationships at which we can only guess and ad hoc decisions about which we are ill-informed probably played as great a role in decision making and in administration as formal consultations and permanent bureaus. This conclusion made it important to investigate again the careers of the second- and third-level men who worked for Philip—the *rapporteurs* of the Parlement, the collectors of subsidies, the paymasters of the armies, for example. These men may have influenced policy more than we realize, and they were certainly the ones who implemented it. It has taken some time to discover even tentative patterns of recruitment, training, and promotion for these officials.

Behind these uncertainties, however, a few facts are clear. The reign of Philip the Fair marks the culmination of the medieval French monarchy. Royal power reached a point that was not surpassed, and often not equaled, during the rest of the fourteenth century. The basic structure of central and local government inherited from Philip Augustus and St. Louis was perfected and institutionalized. The bureaucracy increased in size and improved its professional techniques. Philip was the first French king to impose general taxes, and he was surprisingly successful in this innovation. His tax of 1304 produced more money than any tax levied during the next half century.[1]

Philip's success in imposing taxes illustrates another important aspect of his reign. He had no standing army and only a rudimentary police force. Taxes could be collected only with the assent, implied or formal, of the people and communities of the realm. That assent was not always easy to obtain. There was always a certain amount of bargaining and at times open resistance. However, a large majority of the king's subjects did pay, even those in recently acquired provinces, such as the county of Toulouse. The king's ministers had developed the concept that the Kingdom of France was a body politic that must be preserved and defended at all costs.[2] This concept, proclaimed in official documents and in unofficial works of propaganda, was widely accepted. During the thirteenth century there had been a gradual transfer of loyalty to the king at the expense of local dynastics and of the Church.[3] This transfer made possible the building of a French state. The reign of Philip the Fair marked the point when

---

[1] John Bell Henneman, *Royal Taxation in Fourteenth Century France: The Development of War Financing 1322-1356* (Princeton, 1971), p. 309.

[2] J. R. Strayer, "Defense of the Realm, and Royal Power in France," first published in *Studi in onore di Gino Luzzatto* (Milan, 1949), I, 291-96, reprinted in *Medieval Statecraft and the Perspectives of History: Essays by Joseph R. Strayer*, ed. John F. Benton and Thomas N. Bisson (Princeton, 1970), pp. 296-99, and "France: The Holy Land, the Chosen People, and the Most Christian King," first published in Theodore K. Rabb and Jerrold E. Siegel, eds., *Action and Conviction in Early Modern Europe: Essays in Memory of E. H. Harbison* (Princeton, 1969), pp. 8-14, reprinted in *Medieval Statecraft*, pp. 308-13. (Further references to these articles will cite page numbers in *Medieval Statecraft*.)

[3] See the articles cited in note 2 above, and also "The Laicization of French and English Society in the Thirteenth Century," first published in *Speculum*, xv (1940), 80-85, reprinted in *Medieval Statecraft*, pp. 256-64 (further references to this article will cite page numbers in *Medieval Statecraft*).

the balance of loyalty definitely swung toward the secular sovereign state. From the political point of view, this shift marks the transition from the medieval to the modern period.

It should be clear from what I have been saying that this is a history of the reign of Philip the Fair, not a history of France in the time of Philip the Fair. I have tried to explain how very considerable increases in the power of the royal government and in the effectiveness and complexity of the administration were achieved. I have also considered how these changes affected the possessing classes and how they were made acceptable, or at least tolerable, to the politically conscious part of the population. I have not discussed the political theories or the theological controversies of the learned because they had little influence on events, much less than they were to have in the latter part of the fourteenth century. A few slogans like "defense of the realm" had far more effect than the books of Egidius Romainus or even the pamphlets of Pierre du Bois. Hatred of the Inquisition was a much more dangerous force in Languedoc than the rather confused writings of Olivi. The University of Paris was neither the center of unrest that it had been earlier nor the power in ecclesiastical policy that it was to become later.

For rather different reasons I have said little about economic history. I have suggested in earlier articles that the French economy was stagnant, if not declining, by Philip's reign, but there were no dramatic changes between 1285 and 1314. For most classes, the standard of living remained about the same. It was the government that did most to shake the economy, through heavy and unprecedented taxation and through manipulation of the currency. As I said in my article on the "Costs and Profits of War," the long-run effect of these acts was to transfer wealth from the productive to the unproductive sectors of the economy, but these effects were not fully felt in Philip's time.

While this is certainly a political-administrative history, I hope that it is a little more than that. There were interesting people in Philip's day, not least Philip himself, and I hope that some of them come to life. There is more evidence available about public opinion, or at least the opinion of the possessing classes, than for earlier reigns, and it is interesting to see how this opinion was formed and manipulated. Philip's *superioritas* was not quite sovereignty, and the *regnum* (which all subjects were bound to preserve) was not quite the State, but the concept of the sovereign state could easily grow out of these words, which were used repeatedly in his propaganda. In the same way, Philip was not the founder of the French bureaucracy, nor did he bring it to the degree of complexity that it later achieved. Nevertheless, the shift from ad hoc committees and temporary appointments to continuing organizations (for example, the Chambre des Comptes) and long-term appointments (for example, receivers, *juges-mages*) took place in his reign and marked a profound change in the French administrative system. The French state that began to emerge in the time of Philip the Fair was the model for many other European states. Given the importance of the state in recent history, it is worth spending some time in tracing its origin.

One advantage in spending many years working on a single topic is that I could receive assistance from so many of my students and friends. For several years the University provided me with undergraduate research assistants, who helped to prepare the card catalogue of royal officials. I did not give a seminar on Philip the Fair every year, but I did so often enough for several generations of graduate students to make important contributions to my work. I must give special thanks to Professor John Benton, now of the California Institute of Technology, who prepared an excellent research study of Philip's relations with the Empire, to Professor Thomas Bisson, now of the University of California at Berkeley, who found valuable materials for me in the archives of Languedoc, and to Dr. Elaine Robison who made an analysis of the cases reported in the *Olim*. Dr. Jan Rogozinski's thesis on the "Lawyers of Lower Languedoc" was helpful in studying the administration of justice in that region, and Dr. Teofilo Ruiz wrote a paper on "Reaction to Anagni" (now published in *Catholic Historical Review*, LXV, [1979], 385-401) that threw new light on an old problem.

My colleagues in other universities have been equally helpful. Charles H. Taylor, long a professor at Harvard University, gave me some useful criticisms of the first draft of my "Taxation under Philip the Fair" and, by associating this monograph with his own remarkable work on "Towns and War Subsidy, 1318-1319," made it possible to publish a study of awkward length in book form (*Studies in Early French Taxation*). Professor Elizabeth A. R. Brown of Brooklyn College, who is working on many problems dealing with the reign of Philip the Fair, has generously let me read some of the essays that she is preparing for publication; my debt to her will be evident in my footnotes. Professor John Henneman of the University of Iowa, by allowing me to read the manuscripts of his two excellent books on French taxation in the fourteenth century, helped me to work out some problems on financial organization.

My debt to French scholars is enormous; the bibliography will show how impossible it would have been to write this book if they had not produced so many scholarly monographs and published so many important documents. I owe special thanks to the late Robert Fawtier, membre de l'Institut, who greatly facilitated my work in the Archives Nationales and whose own publications saved me countless hours of work on the Chancery Registers and financial manuscripts, to to Philippe Wolff, membre de l'Institut, who helped me to find and to use essential documents in the archives of the southern departments. I must also thank the hundreds of archivists and librarians who made it possible for me to work, year after year, in their depositories. I have sometimes felt guilty about how much help I have asked from them and how little I have done in return. I hope that this book will give some evidence that their kindness was not entirely wasted.

One final note: in spite of the excellence of the analysis of the Chancery Registers prepared under Fawtier's direction, I have preferred to cite the documents as they appear in the JJ series in the Archives Nationales. This is because Fawtier occasionally omits a small detail that is important for my work, and because at times we disagree on the reading of a proper noun. For all ordinary purposes Fawtier's work is completely satisfactory, and since he always gives document and folio number, my references can easily be verified in his book. However, when I cite a long series of documents in which details are of no great importance (for example, the acts in favor of Edward II in 1313), the references are to Fawtier's publication. I have followed the same rule in citing documents in departmental and municipal archives, especially since some of the earlier *inventaires* are not very accurate. Unfortunately, some documents are mentioned in the inventories that cannot now be found in their proper places in the archives; in such cases the only possible reference is to the printed inventory. There are also some archives (for example, the municipal archives of Pézenas) that have not been completely classified; here one can only give approximate location by *layette* and *liasse*.

My wife has had to live with Philip for forty years, which is longer than his subjects did, and at times she must have found him as annoying as they did. She has spent lonely hours while I was buried in archives and libraries and tedious hours in reading and correcting early drafts of some of the chapters. This book is dedicated to her.

A Note on French Monetary Units

The French, like most of their neighbors, reckoned money in pounds (l.), shillings (s.), and pence (d.). 12 d. = 1 s.; 20 s. = 1 l.

There were two monetary systems in France, one for the old royal domain (*parisis*), the other for newly acquired territories (*tournois*). These terms are abbreviated as p. and t. Paris money was worth more than Tours money: 4 l.p. = 5 l.t.

Pennies and half-pennies were actual coins. For a brief period a coin called the *gros tournois* was roughly equal to 1 s.t., but its value increased through exchange operations and through governmental manipulations, at times to 30 or even 36 d.t. There was no coin equivalent to a pound.

The government kept its financial records consistent by leaving the figures on the book unchanged, while altering the number of actual coins that were paid out or collected. Thus a man who was owed 3 s.t. might be paid with 3 *gros tournois* early in the reign and with 1 *gros tournois* later on. Conversely, if he owed the king 3 s.t. he would pay 3 *gros* t. in the early period and 1 *gros* t. later. In periods of war, when expenditures greatly exceeded receipts, it was obviously to the king's advantage to pay in overvalued coins.

Abbreviations

A.D.	Archives Départementales
A.N.	Archives Nationales
B.M.	Bibliothèque Municipale
B.N.	Bibliothèque Nationale
C.R.	Robert Fawtier and François Maillard, eds., *Comptes royaux 1285-1314*, 3 vols., Recueil des historiens de la France, Documents financiers, III (Paris, 1953-1956)
C.R. Maillard	François Maillard, ed., *Comptes royaux (1314-1328)*, 2 vols., Recueil des historiens de la France, Documents financiers, IV (Paris, 1961)
H.F.	*Recueil des historiens des Gaules et de la France*, ed. Martin Bouquet et al., 24 vols. (Paris, 1738-1904)
Hist. litt.	*Histoire littéraire de la France* (Paris, 1733-)
H.L.	Claude de Vic and Jean-Joseph Vaissette, *Histoire générale de Languedoc, avec des notes et les pièces justificatives*, rev. ed. by A. Molinier et al., 16 vols. (Toulouse, 1872-1905)
J.T.C.	Jules Viard, ed., *Les journaux du Trésor de Charles IV le Bel* (Paris, 1917)
J.T.P.	Jules Viard, ed., *Les journaux du Trésor de Philippe IV le Bel* (Paris, 1940)
M.G.H.	*Monumenta Germaniae Historica* (Berlin, (1826-)
Mignon	Robert Mignon, *Inventaire d'anciens comptes royaux dressé par Robert Mignon sous le règne de Philippe de Valois*, ed. Charles-Victor Langlois, Recueil des historiens de la France, Documents financiers, I (Paris, 1899)
Olim	*Les Olim, ou registres des arrêts rendus par la cour du roi . . .*, ed. Arthur Beugnot, 3 vols. in 4 parts (Paris, 1839-1848)
Ord.	*Ordonnances des roys de France de la troisième race . . .*, ed. Eusèbe-Jacob de Laurière et al., 22 vols. (Paris, 1723-1849)

The Reign of Philip the Fair

FIG. 1. Administrative Map of France under Philip IV. Most of the towns shown were the seats of royal *bailliages* and *sénéchaussées* or of major dependent fiefs, including appanages. Names in parentheses are those of administrative districts ruled directly by agents of the king.

I. The King and His Family*

Philip the Fair is a hard man to get to know. His contemporaries were puzzled by him, and later historians have found him no easier to understand. Very formal, very conscious of his royal dignity, he seems always screened off from the world by his chief ministers and his bureaucrats. There are almost no anecdotes about him: the Vicar of God, the high priest of the religion of monarchy[1] seldom revealed his human side. Yet there was a human side. He was capable of deep affection and sudden flashes of anger; he was loyal to his friends; he showed stubborn courage in times of adversity; and he had strong, if peculiar, convictions about morality and religion.

It is a great deal easier to think of Philip as a symbol of monarchy than to understand Philip as a man. Most French writers of the early fourteenth century tended to believe that Philip was dominated by evil counsellors who ruled in his name. This is the story of Yves of St. Denis,[2] of Geoffroi of Paris,[3] and even of such an ardent supporter of the monarchy as Pierre du Bois.[4] Bishop Bernard Saisset made many indiscreet remarks, but the one that stung most and has been longest remembered is his comparison of Philip with the owl: "the handsomest of birds which is worth absolutely nothing . . . such is our king of France, who is the handsomest man in the world and who can do nothing except to stare at men."[5] Foreign chronicles, such as the Italian

---

* An earlier version of this chapter, "Philip the Fair—A 'Constitutional' King," appeared in the *American Historical Review*, LXII (1956), 18-32, and was reprinted in *Medieval Statecraft*, pp. 195-212 (further references to this article will cite page numbers in *Medieval Statecraft*).

[1] The phrase comes from Robert Fawtier, *L'Europe occidentale de 1270 à 1380*, pt. I (Vol. VI, pt. I of Gustave Glotz, ed., *Histoire générale* [Paris, 1940]), p. 301.

[2] Heavy taxes and alteration of the currency were "consiliariorum suorum monitu magis quam proprio ejusdem regis instinctu" (*Recueil des historiens des Gaules et de la France*, ed. Martin Bouquet et al., 24 vols. [Paris, 1738-1904], XXI, 205 [hereafter cited as *H.F.*]).

[3] Ibid., XXII, 97, 99, 119.

[4] The king had made some unwise decisions, "non motu priprio sed ducente suo consilio" Pierre du Bois, *De recuperatione terre sancte*, ed. Charles-Victor Langlois [Paris, 1891], p. 120; cf. pp. 123-24).

[5] Pierre Dupuy, *Histoire du différend d'entre le pape Boniface VIII et*

Villani and the Fleming Gilles le Muisis, also believed that Philip was a figurehead.[6] Even Boniface VIII, in listing Philip's offenses in the bull *Ausculta fili*, thought it wise to insert some lines attacking the king's evil counsellors, though he added that this was no excuse and that the king bore full responsibility for allowing such men to have power.[7] The Aragonese writer who said that Philip was a masterful ruler, emperor, pope, and king rolled into one was an exception.[8]

Modern historians have been less willing to write off Philip as a nonentity. The Germans, who see Philip as the originator of the French drive to the east, are especially emphatic on this point. Heinrich Finke, Robert Holtzmann, Fritz Kern, and Karl Wenck all agree that Philip gave consistency and strength to French policy during his reign.[9] The English historian T.S.R. Boase warns against "believing that so much of France was created . . . with no central guiding will."[10] French scholars, who should know the facts best, are less certain. Edgard Boutaric believed in Philip's leadership and personal responsibility, but he wrote at the very beginning of serious scholarly investigation of the period. Charles-Victor Langlois felt that the problem was insoluble, but his discussion does not do much to convince the reader that Philip was a strong king. Georges Digard, without taking a very definite stand, tended to ascribe responsibility to the "counsellors of the king," to the "court," and to Pierre Flote rather than to

---

Philippes le Bel . . . (Paris, 1655), p. 643. That the simile hurt is shown by the fact that it is mentioned several times in royal documents dealing with the bishop's imprisonment (ibid., pp. 656, 660).

6 Karl Wenck, *Philipp der Schöne von Frankreich—seine Persönlichkeit und das Urteil der Zeitgenossen* (Marburg, 1905), pp. 28-29.

7 Dupuy, p. 51. Boniface, like the chroniclers, suggested that the king's agents were feathering their own nests and that they used royal authority to oppress the people.

8 Heinrich Finke, "Zur Charakteristik Philipps des Schönen," *Mitteilungen des Instituts für Osterreichische Geschichtsforschung*, XXVI (1905), 209: "pus el es rey et papa et emperader." See also Finke, *Papsttum und Untergang des Templerordens*, 2 vols. (Münster, 1907), II, 123. Dino Compagni (*Cronica*, ed. Isidoro del Lungo [Florence, 1902], bk. 3, chap. 23, p. 174) felt that Philip was responsible for French policy toward the Church.

9 Finke, "Charakteristik," pp. 219-21; Robert Holtzmann, *Wilhelm von Nogaret* (Freiburg-im-Breisgau, 1898), p. 213; Fritz Kern, *Die Anfänge der französischen Ausdehnungspolitik bis zum Jahre 1308* (Tübingen, 1910), pp. 45, 95, 114; Wenck, *Philipp der Schöne*, pp. 49 ff.

10 T.S.R. Boase, *Boniface VIII* (London, 1933), p. 68.

Philip.[11] On the other hand Robert Fawtier, who knew the documents of the reign better than any other historian, had no doubt that Philip controlled and directed his government. He admitted that some measures may have been initiated by members of the Council rather than by the king, but he was sure that Philip always knew and approved of what was done in his name.[12]

More opinions on both sides of the question could be found, but this is not a problem that can be settled by accumulating authorities. Medieval writers are not very reliable in such matters; many were ill-informed, and all were influenced by the convention that blamed evil advisers for unpopular royal acts. Modern writers may be better informed but can be misled by other conventions: that great events must be the result of deliberate policy, and that such policies must be imposed by a single man—the chief minister or the king. In all the discussion there has been too much arguing from effect to cause and too much concentration on a few striking, and therefore exceptional, events. It may be worthwhile to shift ground and to ask some simple, preliminary questions. What do we know about Philip as a man? In what ways was he influenced by his closest relatives—his father, his wife, his brothers, his children? How did he handle the routine work of government, the minor problems that take up the largest part of the time of any political leader? If we can answer these questions, we may be able to form a better judgement about Philip's influence on the major events of the reign.

We begin with a typical uncertainty: we do not know the exact date of Philip's birth. The place—Fontainebleau[13]—is certain,

<hr/>

[11] Edgard Boutaric, *La France sous Philippe le Bel* (Paris, 1861), pp. 415 ff.; Charles-Victor Langlois, *St. Louis, Philippe le Bel et les derniers Capétiens directs* (Vol. III, pt. 2 of E. Lavisse, *Histoire de France* [Paris, 1911]), pp. 119-23; Georges Digard, *Philippe le Bel et le Saint-Siège de 1285 à 1304*, 2 vols. (Paris, 1936), I, 284, 286, 305, II, 75, 93. In an earlier work, *Le Règne de Philippe III le Hardi* (Paris, 1887), pp. 11-12, Langlois was fairly sure that Philip the Fair's policies were determined by his counsellors.

[12] "On peut donc laisser à Philippe le Bel la responsabilité des événements de son règne. Il est vraisemblable qu'il n'a pas eu l'initiative de toutes les mesures qui ont été prises en son Conseil, mais ces mesures ont été prises par des hommes qu'il avait choisis. Il ne leur a fait aucune opposition; rien n'autorise à croire qu'il n'en a pas compris l'esprit ou la portée" (Fawtier, *L'Europe occidentale*, p. 299). Finke, *Papsttum*, I, 94-95, comes to the same conclusion: "er war ein selbständiger, für seiner Handlungen verantwortlicher Charakter. . . . Er leitet die Aktionen ein, oft nur mit einigen wenigen Worte, das übrige wird seinen Raten uberlassen. . . ."

[13] *H.F.*, XXI, 42, 695.

and some scholars have thought that the year was 1267, though two chroniclers put it in 1268.[14] The difference is not very important; by French custom the heir to the throne came of age at 14, and everywhere in medieval Europe youths of 17 or 18 had to assume heavy responsibilities. Philip was married and knighted in 1284;[15] by the standards of his day he was a young man, not a boy. But it is well to remember that he was still a young man when he became king, although in the documents and writings of the reign he always seems to be middle-aged.

He may have been a very unhappy young man; certainly he had suffered some painful experiences. His mother, Isabella of Aragon, died in 1270 while returning from the disastrous crusade against Tunis. Only three years old at the time, Philip may have remembered little of her, but no one took her place, certainly not his stepmother. He had no Blanche of Castile as St. Louis had had, no Marguerite of Provence as his father had had—both strong, even domineering women, but women who could give their sons some feeling of security, some ties to an earlier generation. In 1274 Philip III remarried. His new wife, Marie de Brabant, was lively and amusing, a patroness of poets, and something of a political intriguer. It was only natural that when she produced a new brood of royal children she preferred her own offspring to those of her predecessor. The preference, however, seems to have become somewhat extreme. The stories about her plots to put her own children in the place of the sons of Isabella of Aragon are certainly untrue, but it is significant that when Philip's elder brother Louis died in 1276 enough people believed that the queen had caused his death to create a scandal. Philip III had to go to considerable trouble to track down rumormongers, and he would not have done so if he had not been worried about his wife's reputation.[16] At the very least, there must have been some bad feeling between Marie and her stepchildren. Although the queen lived many years after the death of her husband, Philip the Fair had as little to do with her as possible. Favors for Marie de Brabant were rare during his reign, and the few grants that she did receive were warranted by members of the Council and not—as in the case of those for other members of the royal family—by the king.[17] It is also evident that the young Philip

[14] Ibid., xx, 428, xxii, 199.   [15] Ibid., xxiii, 103.
[16] Langlois, *Philippe III*, pp. 22 ff., discusses the death of young Louis and the charges against Marie.
[17] See note 55 below.

felt very close to his mother's Aragonese relatives, even when his affection conflicted with his father's policy. The death of Louis made Philip heir to the throne. Whether he lamented his brother more than he rejoiced in his new eminence is a matter for speculation. Philip clearly was very fond of his younger brother Charles; he may have felt the same way about Louis. But, as usual, we have no evidence about Philip's state of mind.

If young Philip disliked his stepmother, his relationship with his father may have been troubled. Unfortunately, Philip III, like his son, left few evidences of personal feelings in contemporary records.[18] Statements by either Philip about the other are proper, formal, and cold—which may prove nothing except the limitations of Chancery language. Philip III did his duty by his heir; he gave the boy a good education and arranged a brilliant marriage for him. The marriage may have been more successful than the education: Philip the Fair loved his wife, but although he was literate, he showed no great love of learning.[19]

If Philip III really persuaded Egidius Romanus to act as his son's tutor, he made an excellent choice, but it is very doubtful that Egidius had a close personal relationship with the boy. The great Augustinian scholar dedicated his *De regimine principum* to the young prince about 1280, and Philip spoke of Egidius in warm and friendly terms when he became king.[20] But Egidius was a busy man as a scholar and as an official of his order; he could not have had time to supervise the details of Philip's education. This was probably the task of a young clerk, Guillaume d'Ercuis, and there is no evidence to show that Egidius planned the course of study.

[18] Langlois, *Philippe III*, pp. 5-10, thinks the king was formal and not very intelligent.

[19] Wenck, *Philipp der Schöne*, pp. 10-19, argues that Philip was well educated and had intellectual interests because nine authors dedicated books to him. But this list includes Pierre du Bois, who received no sign of favor, and Raymond Lull, who had no influence. Philip probably did want Jean de Meung's translation of Boethius (a standard text for rulers) and Guillaume de Nangis's histories (useful for checking on past policies), but this does not make him an intellectual.

[20] In 1293 Philip made a grant to the Augustinians "ob favorem potissimum dilecti et familiaris nostri fratri Egidii Romani" (Richard Scholz, *Die Publizistk zu Zeit Philipps des Schönen* [Stuttgart, 1903], pp. 37-38). A little later (1295) Egidius became archbishop of Bourges, certainly with royal approval, though Philip may have regretted the choice later, when Egidius strongly supported papal authority.

One wonders whether an adolescent, busy in his own way as Egidius was in his, ever read or had read to him the long and often ponderous treatise of Egidius. If he did, he would have been taught that kings are above positive law, though bound by natural law, that it is better to be ruled by a king than by positive law, which may be defective, but that kings must rule for the common good. An unjust king is a tyrant and loses his right to rule, though Egidius points out that the rule of a tyrant may be preferable to the anarchy of rebellion.[21] These doctrines fit well with Philip's later actions, but it seems unlikely that a king of France at the end of the thirteenth century needed a learned treatise to be reminded of his power. And as far as we can judge by the memorials addressed to Philip the Fair by his officials, he preferred short, pithy tracts to long scholarly works.

The influence of Egidius on Philip was intermittent and perhaps not very great. The influence of Guillaume d'Ercuis, who, as Philip himself said, taught the young prince "letters," was continuous and long-lasting. Guillaume was probably not much older than his pupil; he took his master's degree in or shortly before 1285, when he would have been in his twenties, and he died about the same time as the king, soon after July 1314. He was neither noble nor rich, but he remained on close and friendly terms with Philip all his life and was rewarded by a series of lucrative benefices. As canon of Laon, Senlis, and Reims and archdeacon of Thiérache, his net income in 1308 was about 783 *livres parisis* (l.p.), more than that of many high royal officials. He was a royal notary until about 1302, and he kept the title of king's clerk until his death. In 1311 Philip saw to it that Guillaume received a dispensation from residence in all of his benefices so that he could continue to live in Paris.[22]

---

[21] See Egidius Columna seu Romanus, *De regimine principum* (Rome, 1607), bk. III, pt. 2, chap. 29, pp. 532-33 ("melius est regi rege quam lege"; the king should be "supra iustitiam legalem"), bk. III, pt. 2, chap. 12, pp. 482-84 (kings rule for the common good; if they do not, they are tyrants); but cf. bk. III, pt. 2, chap. 34, p. 549 (sometimes even tyrants should be obeyed to avoid disorder). By 1301 Egidius, in his *De ecclesiastice potestate*, was taking a strongly pro-papal position: all power comes from the pope, who wields both the temporal and the ecclesiastical sword. Note that in the *De regimine*, bk. II, pt. 2, chap. 8, p. 309, Egidius warned Philip against lawyers: "omnes legiste sunt quasi quidam ideote politici." This is one piece of advice that Philip rejected.

[22] On Guillaume d'Ercuis see Léopold Delisle's excellent study in *Histoire*

Guillaume was one of the few private persons of the period who left a fairly complete record of his income and expenditures. The document tells a good deal about the man. Prudent and thrifty, he had a surplus to his credit in all but one or two years. He amassed a considerable fortune, most of which he bequeathed as an endowment for a chapel he had built on his manor at Ercuis. He was a competent clerk, not a great scholar or administrator; he never rose very high in the royal service, even though he had the favor of the king. He bought books, including a set on Roman law, but he sold the three volumes of the *Digest* soon after he had acquired them, and nothing indicates that he was particularly interested in legal studies. In short, he was a man of limited abilities, careful about money, likable enough to get on with people of different ranks and interests, conventionally pious, but most unlikely to have had new and stimulating ideas. His interest in keeping accurate accounts may have taught Philip to pay somewhat more attention to financial problems than other rulers did; otherwise, his influence would have been in favor of accepting the world as it was. In estimating Philip's character it is well to remember that this essentially conservative man was one of his closest associates for many years.

The last year of the reign of Philip III began with a political triumph and ended in disaster. On 28 August 1284 young Philip married Jeanne, heiress of the kingdom of Navarre and the county of Champagne. Jeanne had been brought up in the French court, and the marriage had been arranged before Philip became heir to the throne; the fact that he was to be the next king increased its significance. Navarre had some strategic importance but produced little income; Champagne was even more important strategically and was immensely wealthy. The annexation of Champagne to the royal domain reduced the number of great semi-independent fiefs to four: Flanders, Brittany, Aquitaine, and Burgundy. A potential threat to the old royal domain was removed, a potential opening to the east was acquired, and royal revenues were substantially increased. Both Philips could rejoice in these prospects. The younger one had another reason for rejoicing. Jeanne had a gentle and sympathetic character; she gave Philip the affection that had so long been denied him. And he was devoted to her. Still in his thirties at the time of her death in 1305,

littéraire de la France (Paris, 1733-), XXXII, 154-71 (hereafter cited as *Hist. litt.*). See also Wenck, *Philipp der Schöne*, p. 4.

he never seriously considered remarrying, though he could have
gained considerable financial and political advantages through a
second marriage—after all, he was the greatest catch in western
Europe. Very few of his contemporaries missed such an opportunity.

While the wedding festivities were going on, Philip III was
completing his plans for an invasion of Aragon. The complicated
story of the political events that led to this war has been discussed
elsewhere. Here it is only necessary to say that Peter of Aragon
had taken advantage of a revolt in Sicily to seize the island, that
the king of Sicily (and Naples) was Charles of Anjou, brother of
St. Louis and uncle of Philip III, that the pope, offended by the
attack on a papal fief, had excommunicated Peter, proclaimed a
crusade against him, and offered the crown of Aragon to Philip
III's second son, Charles of Valois, and that the French court,
after some hesitation, had accepted the offer.[23] This decision put
the young Philip in a cruel dilemma. He did not like the idea of
attacking his mother's relatives; on the other hand, he could not
be disloyal to his father or to his brother. The Catalan chroniclers report that Philip opposed the attack on Aragon, but they
are not very reliable. Better evidence of his feelings is shown by
the fact that he is said to have exchanged messages with Peter of
Aragon during the war[24] and by his obvious lack of interest in
continuing hostilities after his father's death.

If Philip had in fact opposed the crusade, events proved him
right. The only French success was the capture of Gerona after
a long siege. But by the time Gerona fell, the crusaders had been
cut off from their supply base at Rosas by the naval victories of
Peter's admiral, Roger de Loria, and sickness was appearing in
the army. Retreat was necessary, and on the retreat Philip III
became mortally ill. Again the Catalan chroniclers tell a plausible
story of a secret agreement between Peter and the younger Philip
whereby the French were not to be harassed if they left the
country promptly. Such an agreement does not seem to have
been necessary. The French were leaving as quickly as they

---

[23] See my "Crusade against Aragon," *Speculum*, xxviii (1953), 102-13
(reprinted in *Medieval Statecraft*, pp. 107-21), and the works cited in the
notes to this article. (Further references to this article will cite page numbers in *Medieval Statecraft*.)

[24] See ibid., n. 1. A curious poem denouncing a King Philip says that
he trusts Spaniards too much ("Aragon es," *Bulletin de la Société de l'Histoire de France*, 2d ser., 1 [1857-1858], 198).

could, and Peter had nothing to gain by provoking a desperate rear-guard action or by angering the younger Philip, who had, at the very least, been more friendly to Aragon than his father. Philip III barely survived the crossing of the Pyrenees; he died at Perpignan on 5 October 1285. Philip IV—Philip the Fair, as he was to be called—was now king. He inherited a losing war, a large debt, and an insecure frontier with Aragon.[25] Whatever his relations with his father had been, it must have been a shock to have had to assume power so suddenly. Philip III was not an old man; he might well have lived 10 or 15 years longer. Philip the Fair could have expected to learn his trade of kingship gradually, in his wife's lands of Navarre and Champagne and in his father's court and council. The burden was thrust upon him with no warning and little preparation.

There is some reason for thinking that Philip was embittered by the events of 1285. That he gave up his father's policy of intervention in the affairs of the Spanish kingdoms proves little. The policy had been a failure, and any sensible man would have abandoned it. That he refused to take much interest in the problems of his Angevin cousins of Naples is more striking. The Capetian family had been extraordinarily close, and the Angevin branch had always been able to rely on the help of Louis IX and Philip III. That Philip was seeking new advisers by the 1290s is also significant. Old age and death accounted for some of these changes, but the break was sharper than it had been in 1270. Even men who kept their rank moved around. Almost every *bailli* and seneschal was assigned to a new province in 1286-1287 or in 1289. And Philip knew exactly what he was doing: he was careful to keep in office Eustache de Beaumarchais, seneschal of Toulouse and virtual viceroy of the south, at a time when he was moving other men to new positions.

The surest indication that Philip the Fair was repudiating his father's policies can be seen in his unwillingness to follow the leadership of the Church. He seldom accepted the advice of the pope on political questions; he had no use for crusades against opponents of papal policies. The old alliance of the papacy and

[25] Loans for the war were being repaid as late as 1293-1294, and in one case, as late as 1306 ("Crusade against Aragon," nn. 48, 49). Threats of attacks came from Aragon up to 1290 (Claude de Vic and Jean-Joseph Vaissette, *Histoire générale de Languedoc, avec des notes et les pièces justificatives*, rev. ed. by A. Molinier et al., 16 vols. (Toulouse, 1872-1905), x, *preuves*, 230, 237, 242-43, 248 [hereafter cited as *H.L.*]).

the French monarchy had been seriously strained. If it were to continue, it must continue on terms laid down by the king. What was good for France was good for the Church, and a pope who could not understand this simple fact was in danger. It is an over-simplification to say that the Crusade against Aragon led to the attack on Boniface VIII at Anagni, but there was certainly a connection between the two events.

Going further into the realm of speculation, how had Philip's entire youthful experience affected his character? Doubtless the boy had had a lonely life and had suffered a series of shocks, but was there anything unusual in this? At all levels of society mothers died young, fathers remarried, stepmothers were not always kind to the children of their predecessors, parents were too busy to pay much attention to their offspring, young men had to assume the responsibility of adults while still in their teens. Philip was not unique in his misfortunes, though he may well have thought he was. One does get a feeling that loneliness and the absence of affection made him withdrawn, uncomfortable in large public meetings, perhaps a little insecure,[26] eager to hide his real self behind the mask of kingship. His strong attachment to the few people with whom he had been intimate as a boy, such as his brother Charles and his teacher Guillaume d'Ercuis, his devotion to his wife, his remarkable loyalty to members of his inner group of councillors, such as Guillaume de Nogaret, all suggest that Philip was a man who longed for close personal relationships but who could have them with very few people. For the rest of the world he was the image on the great seal, enthroned alone in his royal glory.

Philip's education, both formal and informal, had tended to make him conservative. His father had been satisfied to continue the policies of Louis IX,[27] and Philip the Fair was brought up in the same tradition. It was a strongly religious tradition, and Philip the Fair was a pious Christian, as far as he understood piety. He did all the right things: he founded or added to the endowments of churches; he attended mass and went to confession regularly; he made a pious end.[28] Though conscious of the

[26] This is the opinion of Elizabeth A. R. Brown in her article on Philip in *Encyclopedia Britannica*, 15th ed., 1974, s.v. "Philip IV the Fair of France."
[27] Langlois, *Philippe III*, pp. 9-10.
[28] See Elizabeth A. R. Brown, "Royal Salvation and the Needs of State in Late Capetian France," in William C. Jordan, Bruce McNab, and Teofilo F. Ruiz, eds., *Order and Innovation in the Middle Ages: Essays in Honor of Joseph R. Strayer* (Princeton, 1976), pp. 368-69, 374, 544n, 545n, 553n.

evils of the Inquisition, he decided in the end to support it rather than risk the spread of heresy. In the crisis that followed the defeat at Courtrai his requests for prayers and for divine intervention seem completely sincere.[29] But Philip's piety was conventional and limited; it is doubtful that he ever went beyond formal observances to true religious experience.

Philip the Fair also learned another religion at his father's court —the religion of monarchy. This religion made a deeper impression on him than Christianity; or, to put it in his terms, Christianity obviously supported the religion of monarchy. The king of France was the Vicar of God, the chief supporter of the Church. He was anointed with oil that had been sent down from Heaven; he could cure the sick; he had inherited the insignia and the holy mission of Charlemagne. He was the greatest king in Christendom, subject to no temporal authority.[30] To oppose such a king was not only evil, it was sacrilegious.

Philip understood and practiced this religion rather better than he did Christianity. Recognition of the dignity and majesty of the king of France came first, but once the king's preeminence had been acknowledged, then he was bound by the obligations of his royal faith. The chief duty of the high priest of the religion of royalty was to dispense justice, and Philip insisted more on his right to make final decisions in lawsuits than on any of his other powers. His ideas of justice were sometimes as legalistic as his ideas of Christianity were ritualistic, but Philip and his High Court often came nearer the ideal of true justice than did feudal lords and petty bureaucrats.

For Philip there could be no conflict between his two religions. If a conflict emerged, it was obviously produced by evil, probably heretical men. No true believer could fail to see that the interests of the French monarchy and the interests of the Church were identical. The Flemings were heretics, and Boniface VIII was a heretic, because they opposed the French monarchy, which was the pillar of the Church.[31]

Philip was worried about his unfulfilled crusade vow and his financial exactions, including manipulations of the currency.

[29] A.N., JJ 36, fols. 81v, 82, nos. 187, 189. It must be admitted, however, that Philip wanted financial aid as well as prayers from his clergy.

[30] See my "France: The Holy Land, the Chosen People, and the Most Christian King," pp. 302-3, and the authorities cited in the notes to these pages.

[31] Ibid., p. 309. As Nogaret put it in a tract printed by Dupuy (p. 241),

A wryly amusing story illustrates the way in which Philip combined his two religions. Since early in the reign Philip had been hearing complaints against the excessive zeal of the Inquisition in the dioceses of Toulouse, Albi, and Carcassonne. By 1301 the agitation had reached such a dangerous level that Philip sent two of his trusted agents, the vidame of Amiens and Richard Leneveu (later bishop of Béziers), to investigate. As the guardian of true justice, the king was shocked by the stories he heard. He managed to persuade the Church to dismiss the Inquisitor of Toulouse, and in 1303 he went south to clear up the problem. He might have imposed a salutary reform on what had become a perverted institution, but the leaders of the protest insulted him by their vehement language and over-familiar behavior. Philip rebuffed them, and was even more offended when the rebuff led to a silly and hopeless conspiracy. Lack of respect for the king proved that there must be lack of respect for the faith. Philip had to protect both of his religions, and so he abandoned his efforts to check and reform the Inquisition.[32]

Philip was brought up in a royal court, and any court of the 1270s was an aristocratic court, peopled with counts and barons, knights and squires. There were clerks and commoners to do the dirty work of keeping accounts and writing up reports of trials, but Philip would have had little to do with such people. He had to be trained as a knight, to learn the arts of war and of the chase. He was never a great fighter, but he was fond of hunting (too fond, in the opinion of some of his subjects),[33] and as king he obviously enjoyed the company of noble members of his Household, who had few administrative duties but who could set a proper tone for the court. It is well to remember that Philip was in many ways "a baron of his times."[34] He had a proper respect for the role of the great lords of the realm and for the dignity and rights of men of noble birth. This respect explains some of the curious contradictions in his policy. He would take extreme measures to secure acknowledgment of his rights as

France was a "venerabilem partem ecclesie sancte Dei ac principalem columnam sustentionis ecclesie Romane. . . ."

[32] The story is told by Langlois, *St. Louis*, pp. 201-5; *H.L.*, IX, 228, 257, 264, 277-79; Henry Charles Lea, *History of the Inquisition in the Middle Ages*, 3 vols. (New York, 1888), II, 77-90. For some of the key documents, see *H.L.*, X, cols. 273, 275-76, 278-81, 379, 382-85, 418, 428.

[33] The poem cited in note 24 above says that Philip is always hunting and never thinking.

[34] Fawtier, *L'Europe occidentale*, p. 325.

suzerain, but once he had obtained that recognition he would return almost everything that he had seized to the once rebellious but now repentent vassal. This is the story of the duchy of Aquitaine, of the county of Foix, even, to some degree, of the county of Flanders. Philip's reluctance to evict feudal lords was in part just plain common sense; his government simply could not have administered all of France directly. But there was more than expediency in his policy; there was a feeling that men of noble birth had an inalienable claim to a decent income and some rights of local government.

This, then, was the young man who became king of France in October 1285. Proud, conscious of his dignity, sure of the destiny of his family, perhaps somewhat less sure of himself, withdrawn and with few close friends, only adequately educated and probably only moderately intelligent, respectful of tradition but irritated by the way in which respect for tradition had led his father into trouble—what influence could such a man have on the fate of France? Would his personal weaknesses, his shyness, his lack of experience, his conservatism and respect for things as they were make him simply a figurehead? Was he to be a ruler who merely presided over the workings of a bureaucracy that would almost automatically strengthen royal government and unite France? Or would his pride, his belief in the religion of monarchy, his insistence that his unique position as king of France be recognized by all make him a ruler who would determine all major policies and deliberately begin the building of a sovereign state?

The first acts of the new reign suggest that Philip the Fair immediately took responsibility for basic policy. It took some time to find new advisers, but long before they had emerged there was a marked change in objectives. Foreign adventures were abandoned. It was made clear that the essential tasks of the government were not to support French princes in Spain and Italy but to make sure that the king's authority was respected everywhere within the boundaries of France. As a corollary, those boundaries were to be defined as carefully and as widely as possible. This was basic policy long before new men such as Flote, Nogaret, and Enguerran de Marigny became prominent, and it remained basic policy throughout the reign. The principle was laid down clearly in the controversy with the church of Chartres in 1289,[35] and it was equally evident in the dispute with

---

[35] In a letter to the archbishop of Sens and the bishop of Auxerre, who

Edward I of England in 1293. The fact that the dispute led to an unnecessary war shows how seriously Philip took his theory of suzerainty. It also shows that the young king could make a very risky decision without urging from his advisers. No one has ever been able to blame the war of 1294-1297 on anyone but Philip.[36] Efforts to increase respect for royal authority were an old and almost inevitable part of bureaucratic tradition, but expensive wars were not. Nor was the avoidance of foreign entanglements a part of the bureaucratic tradition, at least not as that tradition had been expressed in the policies of Philip's father. Even under Philip the Fair there were plenty of royal councillors who urged participation in crusades or intervention in Italy.[37] Concentration on internal affairs was a distinguishing feature of the reign, and it is hard to see how anyone but the king himself could have maintained such concentration over so many years.

There is also a style closely associated with the policy, a style that had not been evident in the acts of the reign of Philip III. Certainly one should not suppose that the king dictated word for word the letters written in his name, but he must have approved the content, the general line of argument, and the tone. Once again, we find as early as 1289 a style that persists throughout the reign, a style that is sarcastic, biting, based on legalistic arguments. There are passages in the letters of 1289 to the bishop of Auxerre and the archbishop of Sens that could have been written by Nogaret, but Nogaret was an obscure provincial lawyer in 1289. In this letter Philip complains that the pope, "perhaps suspicious of his youth," warns him "out of paternal affection" to cease the attacks that he was falsely alleged to have made against the rights and liberties of the church of Chartres. Philip goes on to thank the pope for his eagerness to admonish him so quickly on mere hearsay and adds that he must have done so "out of special zeal and deep charity."[38] The letter continues

---

were charged by the pope to settle the dispute between the chapter of Chartres and the royal *prévôt*, Philip wrote (ca. September 1289): "pro nostris debitis exigendis, nullum et nullius judicis territorium, dummodo non sacrum sed prophanum, infra fines regni nostri exemptum a nostra jurisdictione recognoscimus . . ." (Digard, II, 249).

[36] Fawtier, *L'Europe occidentale*, pp. 317-18.

[37] For an example of the majority of the Council favoring a crusade, see Jakob Schwalm, "Beiträge zur Reichsgeschichte des 14. Jahrhunderts," *Neues Archiv*, XXV (1900), 565-66.

[38] Digard, II, 247-48.

with legal arguments, including the one cited above that no one and no lands within the boundaries of the realm could be exempt from royal jurisdiction. It seems reasonable to believe that some of these phrases, especially the one about taking advantage of his youth, came from the king himself. Moreover, the style and tone of this letter are typical of letters written in the king's name during the remaining 25 years of the reign. They are also typical of propaganda tracts written during the great struggles with the Church, tracts that were certainly meant to please the king as well as to persuade his subjects.

The argument that Philip the Fair had direct control of the government is strengthened by the fact that there was no other source of power. The royal family can be ruled out immediately. The only member of the family who was active during the entire reign was Charles of Valois, and Philip had no illusions about Charles's ability. He was fond of Charles; he gave him money for his adventures, but he carefully avoided any deep commitment to Charles's attempts to establish himself in Italy or in Constantinople, and his support for Charles's candidacy as German emperor was minimal.[39] He would accept Charles's recommendations for minor favors to his friends,[40] but he never took Charles's advice on major appointments or policies. That Charles resented his exclusion from power is suggested by his vicious attacks on Marigny and other royal councillors after the king's death. Philip's half brother, Louis of Evreux, was treated with respect and given an adequate, though not very large, lordship. He sat in the Council, was given nominal command of armies, and was rather useful as a diplomat. He had, however, little influence on policy.

The queen, Jeanne of Champagne-Navarre, lived through the most critical years of the reign, but although her husband loved her as a woman and was willing to help her friends and prosecute her enemies, he did not take her advice on major decisions. The best illustration of his attitude appears in the affair of the men of Languedoc and the Inquisition, mentioned above. Jeanne seems to have sympathized with the opponents of the Inquisition. They hailed her as a "new Esther" and gave her costly presents. When Philip felt that his royal dignity had been affronted and became

[39] Joseph Petit, *Charles de Valois* (Paris, 1900), chaps. 3 and 4, esp. pp. 55-56, 57, 125.
[40] On Charles's request, the king ennobled a man of Cahors (A.N., JJ 45, fol. 86, no. 92) and an Italian was naturalized (JJ 46, fol. 122v, no. 219).

disgusted with the anti-Inquisition groups, he forced the queen to return the presents.[41] It is likely that Edward I hoped that Jeanne would mollify Philip in the quarrel over Aquitaine in 1293; if so, he was disappointed. One may wonder whether Jeanne's inability to influence her husband is reflected in some of the passages of Joinville's *Life of St. Louis*. Joinville says explicitly that the book was composed at the request of the queen. It was, of course, only natural for her to encourage her own seneschal of Champagne to dictate his reminiscences, but she may also have hoped to persuade her husband to follow more closely in the footsteps of his grandfather. Joinville at least makes some unflattering comparisons between St. Louis and "the present king." If Jeanne encouraged this criticism, it had little effect, and in any case she died before the book was completed.

As for his children, Philip could not have been influenced by his young sons until the latter part of his reign. At that time the oldest boy, Louis, the titular king of Navarre, is mentioned in some documents, but only *pro forma*. The two younger sons, Philip and Charles, appear less often. None of them had any influence on royal policy or any real authority in the provinces that they held. Hugues de la Celle administered Poitou and La Marche, though Philip was count of Poitiers and Charles of La Marche. Louis, who had inherited Champagne and Navarre, had a little more independence, but he was surrounded by men who had been his father's servants. Thus his Chancellor was Pierre de Grez, a king's clerk who became bishop of Auxerre; his *bailli* of Chaumont in 1308-1309 and guard of the fairs of Champagne in 1311 was Jean de Vannoise, who was *prévôt* of Paris from 1310 to early 1311 and a collector of subsidies for Philip in 1314; and his governor of Navarre (1297-1306, 1314-1316) was Alfonse de Rouvrai, a king's knight who was seneschal of Beaucaire between 1292 and 1295 and seneschal of Carcassonne from 1310 to 1312.[42] It should also be noted that although the three princes had all been married (in 1305, 1307, and 1308, respectively), none of them was knighted at the time of marriage, as Philip the Fair had been. Even Louis, the heir to the throne,

---

[41] Langlois, *St. Louis*, p. 203; H.L., x, col. 418.
[42] For Pierre de Grez see below, p. 94. On Jean de Vannoise, see H.F., xxiv, *169, 171; A.N., JJ 47, fol. 38v, no. 59; Robert Mignon, *Inventaire d'anciens comptes royaux dressé par Robert Mignon sous le règne de Philippe de Valois*, ed. Charles-Victor Langlois (Paris, 1899), no. 1629. For Alfonse de Rouvrai, see Strayer, *Les Gens de justice du Languedoc sous Philippe le Bel* (Toulouse, 1970), pp. 51, 101.

was not knighted until the spring of 1313. Of course the young men could have played a political role without being knighted, but the fact that Philip put off the ceremony suggests that he was not anxious to have them recognized as fully adult participants in the affairs of the kingdom.

Another sign that relations between Philip and his sons were not very close is the scandalous affair of the king's daughters-in-law. In the last year of his reign, Philip accused the wives of Louis and Charles of adultery and blamed young Philip's wife for concealing the misconduct of her sisters-in-law. With no firsthand evidence, it is impossible to be sure of their guilt, though Philip must have been completely convinced before he made the case a public scandal. No attempt was made to hush up the affair; the lovers of the princesses were executed with atrocious tortures in the market square at Pontoise, while the ladies were put in prison. Jeanne, the wife of the younger Philip, proved her innocence and was released, but the other two died in captivity.[43]

It is difficult to understand why Philip chose to inflict such open humiliation on his sons. He was certainly shocked; he had led a chaste life himself, and whatever faults could be found in his court, promiscuity was not one of them. He was inclined to believe the worst of everyone, as he showed in his relations with Boniface VIII and in the case of the Templars. His piety may have made him feel that the royal family should set an example of upright behavior and that adultery by a member of the family deserved spectacular punishment. Whatever his reasons, his behavior indicates a lack of close affection between father and sons.

It may be that Philip felt closer to his daughter, Isabella. A story, to which Langlois gave some credence, relates that it was Isabella who first suggested to the king that her sisters-in-law were guilty of misconduct. Certainly Philip kept in close touch with her after she married Edward II of England,[44] and when Edward visited Paris in 1313 Philip granted his son-in-law a long series of favors, usually with a remark that Isabella had joined her husband in making the requests.[45] But even here, paternal

[43] Langlois, St. Louis, pp. 212-16.

[44] F. D. Blackley and G. Hermansen, eds., The Household Book of Queen Isabella (Edmonton, 1971), pp. xix, 90, 91. Guillaume, cantor of Milly, an experienced royal clerk (see Mignon, nos. 673, 693, 1300, 2543, 2545, etc.), was assigned to Isabella's household to act as a liaison agent with her father.

[45] See 30 letters in A.N., JJ 49, revoking fines and other penalties imposed on towns and subjects of Edward in Aquitaine. The letters appear

affection and reason of state indicated identical courses of action. By 1303, if not earlier, Philip had decided that he needed to be on good terms with England in order to have a free hand in dealing with the papacy, Flanders, and the western German princes. Favors to Isabella were necessary for political as well as for family relationships.

If we rule out the royal family as an alternate source of power, then the only other group that could have made policy was the bureaucracy. But here we must distinguish between the provincial bureaucrats and the men who worked in the central agencies of government in Paris. Local officials, such as *baillis* and seneschals, receivers and provincial judges, made thousands of decisions each year, and these decisions, in the long run, might have added up little by little into definite policies. But the work of local officials was reviewed and often reversed by the Council in one or another of its aspects (Parlement, Chambre des Comptes, the Chancery staff, or the Council itself acting as an advisory body). One might then argue that the Council made policy, but several facts militate against this theory. The composition of the Council was completely at the king's discretion. There was no guarantee that a man who was called "king's councillor" would be called to every or, indeed, to any meeting at which the king sought advice. There were no permanent assignments to any commission (such as the Parlement) or to any field of work (such as foreign affairs or finance). We should not be dazzled by the reputation of a Flote, a Nogaret, or a Marigny. One should consider first of all that these men were picked by the king, not foisted on him by the workings of an impersonal bureaucratic machine. Most provincial judges never reached Paris, and of the handful that did, only Nogaret became Keeper of the Seals.[46] Many chamberlains profited financially from their close association with Philip; but of all the chamberlains, Marigny was the only one who became a principal adviser of the king. The king made these men, and they had only such authority as

---

in several groups from fol. 27v, no. 50, to fol. 47v, no. 111. All are dated July 1313 at Poissy. It was on the occasion of this visit that Isabella is supposed to have discovered the scandal in the royal family. See Langlois, *St. Louis*, pp. 213-14.

[46] Strayer, *Gens de justice*, pp. 21-22. There were several hundred royal judges in Languedoc during Philip's reign, most of whom were highly trained professionals. Only 10 or 11 were ever called to Paris; of this group, Nogaret was the only one who held an important office.

the king chose to give them. That authority was limited; it would be a mistake to think that any of Philip's councillors acted as a sort of prime minister. Nogaret was called to Paris before Flote died; at the height of Marigny's prominence, Nogaret was still Keeper of the Seals. There were always other councillors who had independent mandates to deal with specific problems, such as negotiating with foreign countries or raising money. In fact, responsibility was so widely divided that it would have been impossible to have had a consistent policy unless one man supervised and coordinated the work of the Council. The one man, the only man, who could have done this was the king.

A strong proof that Philip did coordinate the work of government comes from a new procedure adopted by the Chancery clerks during the reign. Given the number of men who were clamoring for royal gifts and offices and the number of councillors who had access to the king, it is not surprising that there are instances of letters that were obtained surreptitiously, of conflicting promises made by the king and members of the Council,[47] of contradictory royal charters.[48] Such confusion was irritating and humiliating. To avoid the appearance of these unauthorized or conflicting letters the rule was gradually established that every document issued in the king's name must carry at the bottom the name of the notary who wrote it and the name of the official who ordered it written.[49] The earliest examples of this practice come from the 1290s;[50] by 1314 most documents are so authenticated. What is even more helpful to the historian is that the scribes who copied royal letters into the registers of the last years of the reign included in their copies the names of the notaries and of the officials who ordered the letters written. This means that we have hundreds of cases in which we know precisely who took the responsibility for a certain act of government.

Most of the documents that appear in the registers deal only with trivial matters—amortizations, approval of farms made by

---

[47] *Les Olim, ou registres des arrêts rendus par la cour du roi . . .*, ed. Arthur Beugnot, 3 vols. in 4 pts. (Paris, 1839-1848), II, 497, 547, III, 815; A.N., J 317, no. 50, J 1046, JJ 38, no. 29, JJ 42A, no. 1.

[48] *Olim*, II, 444.

[49] Octave Morel, *La grande chancellerie royale* (Paris, 1900), pp. 154-66, 209-311.

[50] A.N., J 178B, nos. 48 (1292), 51 (1294), 55 (1297), 56 (1299). Morel, p. 160, gives as his earliest example J 162, no. 9 (1292). Arthur Giry, *Manuel de diplomatique* (Paris, 1925), p. 761, says that he found some examples from as early as 1286, but he gives no reference.

local officials, exchanges of property, gifts, acts of pardon and of grace. This has its advantages. We can be sure that we are watching the normal operations of government, not extraordinary procedures invented for great occasions. And it is at least a reasonable supposition that the men who worked steadily on these routine matters would be well informed about the kingdom, well versed in administrative procedures, well acquainted with all important members of the court, and hence influential in making major decisions.

A rough tabulation of the names on these documents during the last eight years of the reign yields interesting results. First of all, a rather large number of men—at least 32—had authority to order letters written in the king's name. Not all of them were very active. The great lords of the Council, men such as the counts of Valois and Saint-Pol, seldom commanded letters. On the other hand, about 15 names appear again and again. Purely numerical comparisons among this group would be meaningless, since the record is incomplete, and some letters are more important than others. It is clear, however, that there was a certain amount of specialization. For example, Philippe le Convers ordered most of the letters dealing with forests; Hugues de la Celle was the expert on the Saintonge-Poitou area; Guillaume de Marcilly and Guillaume Cocatrix were given the task of buying land and houses to make room for the extension of the royal palace. Others seem to have had more general interests. In this group Nogaret, as Keeper of the Seals, and Marigny, as financial expert, are conspicuous but not unique. They were no busier than some of their colleagues. Marigny, for example, warranted fewer letters than did Philippe le Convers. Nor did these men have exclusive power in any field; Marigny, for all his expertise in finance, was far from being the only councillor to deal with matters of income and expenditure. Once again it is evident that there was no chief minister and no collective action by the Council as a whole.[51] If there was any direction to this activity at all, it must have come from the king.

This conclusion is supported by the fact that the king was far more active in commanding letters than all of his councillors put together. Of about 939 letters,[52] 440 bear the notation "per domi-

---

[51] There are a few exceptions to this rule, such as acts warranted by the Chambre des Comptes or "Per Cameram." But these letters comprise less than 1 percent of the total.

[52] An exact total cannot be given; some acts are duplicated, incomplete,

num regem." Subtracting the anonymous warrants by the Chambre des Comptes and the Parlement (about 50), about half of a very ordinary batch of letters were ordered by the king alone. Most pardons, most amortizations, most gifts to churches and royal favorites were ordered by the king, but letters in all of these categories were also warranted by members of the Council.[53] Although most acts dealing with the royal family were ordered by the king, this was not always the case. Of a series of marriage contracts involving the Valois branch of the family, three were warranted by the lord of Chambli and Philippe le Convers, one by the Keeper of the Seals, and only two by the king.[54] Favors for the dowager queen, who was not on good terms with her stepson, were usually ordered by members of the Council.[55] On the other hand, although the king did not always act in cases where he might be expected to have done so, he frequently took responsibility for approving farms of the royal domain, exchanges of property between subjects, and marriage contracts of quite ordinary people—all routine acts that could have been accomplished by any councillor.[56]

It might be argued that these mentions of the king are purely formal, that he was merely approving acts that had been decided on by others. But if this were true, it would be difficult to explain why the Chancery clerks thought there was a difference between letters ordered by the king and those ordered by members of the Council. It would also be difficult to explain why most of the letters warranted "per dominum regem" were written by a single notary, Maillard, and why Maillard seldom prepared letters for anyone else. If Philip's warrant were mere form, any notary could have written the document; only if the king took a personal interest would he need a personal scribe.

Moreover, there is some reason for believing that letters or-

---

or canceled. But such acts are rare, and whether they are eliminated or included, the overall pattern does not change.

[53] Most pardons not by the king are by the chancellor (A.N., JJ 46, nos. 134, 238, JJ 50, no. 78), but some are by Marigny (JJ 46, nos. 29, 151). It was fairly common for members of the Council to order letters of amortization (cf. JJ 45, nos. 104, 108, 202, JJ 47, nos. 37, 46, 90). For gifts to churches see JJ 47, nos. 19, 132, JJ 48, no. 42, JJ 49, no. 40; for gifts to intimates of the king, JJ 47, no. 89, JJ 48, nos. 36, 75.

[54] A.N., JJ 49, nos. 58, 59, 71, 114, 229, 254.

[55] A.N., JJ 47, no. 37, JJ 49, nos. 19, 120.

[56] A.N., JJ 45, no. 121, JJ 47, no. 42, JJ 48, no. 127 (farms); JJ 47, no. 14, JJ 49, nos. 73, 193 (exchanges); JJ 46, no. 30, JJ 49, no. 221 (marriages).

dered by the Keeper of the Seals sometimes reflected a personal command by the king. On at least two occasions Philip sent a private letter to Nogaret ordering him to prepare letters under the great seal.[57] There is also an interesting case in which two letters ordered by the king were canceled, apparently because they lacked some details, and replaced by a fuller letter ordered by the Keeper of the Seals.[58] Here the Keeper probably took the king's letters as warrants for the preparation of his own. Finally, we have a few cases in which the scribe noted that the Keeper told him that the king had ordered the letter written.[59] Even if only a few of the letters ordered by the Keeper of the Seals were actually commanded by the king, it would still raise the proportion of letters in which the king took a personal interest to well above 50 percent of the total.

To sum up, the impression given by this material is that the king controlled and directed the routine work of the government. He was the one who assigned tasks to his councillors, and he reserved the right to act directly and personally in any matter that interested him. There were too many councillors, and responsibility was too evenly divided among them, for any single minister to dominate the government. At the very least, the king was busier than any member of his Council; he was informed about a great variety of matters, and he made many decisions. Certainly Philip was not the lazy king who, according to some chroniclers, did nothing but hunt, nor yet the stupid king described by Bernard Saisset who understood nothing and only stared at people.

This king who took such interest in the small details of government cannot have been indifferent to greater affairs. If no one councillor was given full responsibility for handling routine business, it is difficult to believe that any councillor had unlimited power in making important decisions. We may therefore place more confidence in the scattered notes in the *Olim*, which show the king intervening in cases that came before the Parlement, making decisions, ordering punishments, suspending sentences, reversing previous acts, and directing that inquests be

[57] Holtzmann, pp. 265 (an order to Nogaret, 5 April 1308, to seal a charter granting land to the king's son Charles), 272 (orders to seal letters to the *baillis* of Sens and Auvergne).

[58] A.N., JJ 48, fols. 58v, 59 (unnumbered), fol. 59, no. 102.

[59] A.N., JJ 49, no. 145: "per dominum Regem, ut dicitis."

held.[60] We may also believe that the rare references in financial documents to direct intervention by the king would be more numerous if we had fuller records.[61] And we can be reasonably sure that the king who intervened in both judicial and financial business was Philip the Fair in person, not some vague group of ministers acting in his name.

It seems clear that Philip directed and controlled ordinary operations of government. This raises a strong presumption that he also directed and controlled the government when it made major policy decisions. But presumption is not proof, and it is precisely in this area that Philip seems to be screened most completely by his ministers. His opinions and wishes are never expressed; it is the ministers who make the accusations against Boniface VIII and against the Temple, who draw up the lawsuits that nag the king of England and the count of Flanders into war, who prepare the way for the annexation of Lyon and other imperial territories by adroit diplomacy and propaganda. It is precisely on such matters that the foreign ambassadors complain that they can never get a personal interview with the king, that Philip will answer only with and through his Council.[62]

Even here there are two cases that suggest that Philip made the final decisions. The first is the report of the discussion in the Council following the arrest of Bishop Bernard Saisset.[63] There

[60] *Olim*, II, 311, 404, 485, III, 626, 891 (king makes decisions in Parlement); II, 590, III, 542, 622, 705 (king modifies punishments or reverses sentences); III, 222, 879, 891 (king orders inquests made).

[61] In a list of difficult points in the accounts of All Saints 1298, two are marked "loquendum cum rege" (B.N., ms. lat. 9018, no. 47). An accusation against Betin Caucinel, a master of the royal mints, suggests that Philip took a personal interest in having accounts carefully checked: "quar d'unes de vos simples bailliees, sire, voulez que vostre conseill sache la verité, que le vous puent valoir, et voulez savoir se li baillez en rente bon conte et louial" (Charles-Victor Langlois, ed., "Notices et documents relatifs à l'histoire de France au temps de Philippe le Bel," *Revue historique*, LX [1896], 327).

[62] Philip refused to discuss a marriage treaty because "ibi non erat suum consilu," and he refused to speak with envoys of Aragon about the Val d'Aran because "non essent ibi presentes illi de suo consilio qui debebant huic negocio interesse" (Heinrich Finke, ed., *Acta Aragonensia*, 3 vols. [Berlin, 1908-1922], I, 455, 462). It should be noted that in each case Philip had good reasons for wishing to evade an interview. There was little to be gained by a marriage alliance with Aragon, and Philip had trouble in deciding what to do about the Val d'Aran (see below, pp. 27-31).

[63] *Gallia Christiana in provincias ecclesiasticas distributa*, 16 vols. (Paris, 1717-1865), XIII, cols. 107-15.

was a long argument between clerical and lay members over the treatment of the bishop. The churchmen naturally wanted to be lenient, while the laymen were angry and urged severe punishment. Philip had to intervene repeatedly, and although the speeches ascribed to him probably do not give his exact words, it is clear that he made the final decisions in a badly divided Council. He was willing to proceed with the case, but he wanted it done with as little scandal as possible—a policy that pleased neither faction.

Thus Philip made the decision that was to lead to the final quarrel with Boniface VIII. We can only speculate about the king's role during the acute stages of the quarrel. The formal approval given in his name to the acts of Nogaret could cover anything from mere acquiescence to active participation. But it has often been pointed out that once Boniface was dead, Philip could have settled the whole dispute quickly and on favorable terms by sacrificing Nogaret. Nogaret himself seems to have feared this, since he begged the king to maintain his cause.[64] Philip accepted the responsibility; only when Nogaret was absolved on easy terms did he make a final settlement.[65] Yet this settlement was reached during a period when Marigny was rising to prominence. Marigny was the only one of Philip's principal councillors who had not been involved in some way in the quarrel with Boniface. Doubtless he wanted to wind up the affair and get on with current business. But it is hard to see why Marigny, or any other leading member of the Council, should have tried to get better terms for Nogaret than had been proposed earlier. There must have been some rivalry among Philip's advisers, and Nogaret certainly believed that he needed the king's support. It is doubtful that anyone else could have saved him from severe penalties. On the other hand, it is difficult to see why Philip should have been so anxious to protect Nogaret if he felt that Nogaret was entirely responsible for the difficulties that followed Anagni. Only if Philip had made the policy was it his duty to protect a minister who had merely acted as an agent.

The case of the Val d'Aran is less well known than that of Anagni, but the remarkable collection of documents preserved in the Archives of the Crown of Aragon makes it possible to follow the French decision-making process in great detail.[66] Superfi-

---

[64] Holtzmann, pp. 131, 137, 253.   [65] Ibid., pp. 163, 201-6.
[66] Juan Reglá Campistol, *Francia. La Corona de Aragon y la Frontera Pirenaica. Le luche por el Valla de Arán*, 2 vols. (Madrid, 1951), is the most

cially, it looks as if Philip threw all responsibility on his Council. Yet if we examine the documents closely, we shall see that no decision could be made until the king had studied the record carefully, that he twice rejected the opinions of influential members of his Council, and that in the end he relied on the advice of a very minor member of his administration, even though that advice was strongly opposed by Nogaret.

The facts about the case were as simple as the negotiations were complex. The Val d'Aran lies on the French side of the Pyrenees; in it are the sources of the Garonne. It had been part of the old kingdom of Aquitaine and had at one time been held by the count of Comminges, who was a vassal of the count of Toulouse. On the other hand, the Val had been subject to the king of Aragon throughout the thirteenth century, and probably earlier. The Val was seized by Eustache de Beaumarchais, seneschal of Toulouse, in November 1283. The French at that time were beginning to plan a war against Aragon, though the actual campaign did not begin until 1285. Eustache seized the Val to protect the French flank and to block a possible counterinvasion through the Val down the Garonne to Toulouse.[67]

When peace was finally restored after the collapse of the crusade of 1285, it was agreed that France should return all Aragonese lands taken during the war. But the Val d'Aran was not returned, on the grounds that it had been seized before the war began and that it was not really an Aragonese possession. James II of Aragon protested, and in 1289 the Val was turned over to the king of Majorca, a close relative of both James and Philip, to hold until the rival claimants had settled their dispute.[68]

Philip was in no hurry to act, perhaps because he knew that he had a bad case. James kept pressing him, but no action of any consequence occurred until 1308. In that year Charles of Valois, anxious to obtain Aragonese support for his futile attempt to restore the Latin Empire in Constantinople, put some pressure on Philip to give up the Val. He was so sure of his influence on his brother that he wrote a very optimistic letter to the queen of Aragon, assuring her that Philip would soon accept the Aragonese claim.[69] But although Philip was fond of Charles and was

---

complete publication of these documents. But Finke, ed., *Acta Aragonensia*, I, 159-60, 452 ff., has some useful additional material.

[67] Reglá, I, 65-66; Langlois, *Philippe III*, pp. 146-47.

[68] Reglá, II, doc. no. 10.

[69] "Tres chiere suer, encores vos faisons nous savoir, que tenons pour

generous in giving him money for his schemes, he had little
respect for Charles's political sense. A few months after the hope-
ful letter to the queen, Charles had to apologize profusely to
James of Aragon. Philip, he said, had been persuaded by his advisers that he should keep the Val. Charles could not force the
king and Council to change their minds.[70]

What had actually happened was that Philip had sent three
able, but second-rank, officials (the seneschal of Toulouse, the
seneschal's lieutenant, and Gérard de Courtonne, a lawyer-diplo-
mat) to investigate the problem.[71] It was almost certainly this
group that drew up a remarkable document stating the French
case in the strongest possible terms.[72] Geography, history, and
public law all proved that the Val d'Aran had been and should
remain a French possession. It lay on the French side of the
mountains; it had been subject to French lords; no king of France
(who was emperor in his kingdom) could surrender a part of
the realm; de facto possession by others could not extinguish
royal rights. Philip firmly believed in these principles. As we
shall see, they were invoked in other crises by other royal officials. If they became common arguments in official documents, it
must have been because they pleased the king. Thus it is not
surprising that Philip rebuffed Charles of Valois and maintained
his claim to the Val.

What is surprising is that in 1312 Philip changed his mind.
He probably did so because he needed support at the Council of
Vienne, and the Val d'Aran was of little value compared with
what could be gained by suppressing the Order of the Temple.
Whatever the reason, he agreed to allow a bipartite commission
to discuss who had *possessed* the Val before Eustache de Beaumarchais seized it.[73] By emphasizing the question of possession,

---

certain que monseigneur li rendra le val si il le li requiert" (Carl Wil-
lemsen, "Der Kampf um das Val d'Aran," *Spanische Forschungen der
Görresgesellschaft. Erste Reihe. Gesammelte Aufsätze zur Kulturgeschichte
Spaniens*, 6 Band, p. 157).

[70] Reglá, II, doc. no. 40.

[71] Ph. Lauer, "Une enquête au sujet de la frontière française dans le
Val d'Aran sous Philippe le Bel," *Comité des travaux historiques et scientifiques. Bulletin de la section de géographie*, XXXIV (1919), 24. Gérard
eventually became bishop of Soissons and an influential member of the
Council.

[72] Published by Lauer, pp. 29-31; summarized by Reglá, II, 52, 55. The
legal arguments in this report will be discussed in detail in Chapter V.

[73] Reglá, II, 59, 70.

as opposed to property, Philip threw away his best arguments. He made certain that he would lose his case by appointing as his chief commissioner Yves de Loudéac, a man who either already believed in or was soon convinced of the justice of the Aragonese claims. Yves was a southerner, a doctor of law, a former judge of Toulouse, and by 1312 a member of the Parlement and a councillor of the king.[74] His career was an almost exact copy of that of Nogaret, yet he disliked Nogaret and opposed his policies —a warning that we should not assume that the *légistes* spoke with a single voice. It was Yves who described Nogaret in a single biting phrase as "a body without a soul, who cares nothing about anyone's rights but only wants to increase the wealth of the king of France."[75]

There was a certain amount of procedural bickering when the commissioners met. The French could not give in too easily without ruining their reputation as diplomats; they even found it necessary to tell the Aragonese that Philip would defend the Val as he would Paris.[76] But from the beginning the Aragonese were on excellent terms with Yves de Loudéac, and they soon became convinced that he would support their claims.[77] He agreed readily to reduce a long list of questions to a simple inquiry: Did Aragon hold the Val before the war? A long string of witnesses proved that the kings of Aragon had held the Val. This was enough for Yves; he saw no use in further argument and agreed that a joint report clearly favoring Aragon should be sent to the two kings.[78] After this report, and only after it, Yves received a handsome present from Aragon. It was not unusual for medieval and renaissance diplomats to receive such presents, and Yves had made all of his important decisions before accepting any gifts. But he felt a little guilty about the present and asked that it be kept secret.[79]

[74] Strayer, *Gens de justice*, pp. 180-81.

[75] Willemsen, p. 217: "ipse timet de Guillelmo de Nogareto qui est corpus sine anima, quia non curet de iure alicuius nisi de impingando erarium domini regis Francie."

[76] Ibid., p. 108: "intelleximus quod rex Francis habet ita cordi, ut et sui dicunt, deffendere dictam vallem sicut deffenderet civitatem Parisiensum. . . ."

[77] Ibid., p. 207: "magister Yuo de Laudunaco, qui preexcellit alium [the other French commissioner, the dean of Cassel] et est devotus vestre regie majestati. . . ."

[78] Reglá, II, 153, 156, 160, 211.

[79] Yves said to one of the Aragonese commissioners, "quod in facto

The final stage of the settlement is especially helpful in illustrating the way in which Philip reached decisions. It was agreed that he should examine the report in person with five councillors.[80] The five were probably Valois, Gilles Aicelin (archbishop of Rouen), the count of Saint-Pol, Nogaret (or Nogaret's shadow, Guillaume de Plaisians), and Philip's eldest son Louis, king of Navarre in his mother's right. These at least were the men to whom James of Aragon wrote in February 1313, saying that he had proved his case and urging them to persuade Philip to yield gracefully.[81] (He had written to Philip himself in almost the same terms.)[82] Now this was a very evenly balanced group: Valois had long supported the Aragonese claim; the archbishop was noted for his sense of justice and independent spirit;[83] the count of Saint-Pol seldom took a decided position on matters of policy; and Nogaret and Plaisians were strongly opposed to surrendering the Val. Louis of Navarre probably had no influence and was sent a letter only out of courtesy, as heir apparent and nominal ruler of a kingdom bordering on the Val. Nogaret died on 11 April 1313,[84] but he must have made his position clear before his death, and in any case Plaisians was there to present Nogaret's argument. Yet on 26 April Philip issued an order to surrender *possession* of the Val d' Aran to Aragon.[85] He reserved the question of *property*,[86] but nothing ever came of this, and the Val d'Aran has remained Spanish ever since.

To sum up, the Council as a whole never acted on the matter of the Val d'Aran. Charles of Valois, who was both a member of the Council and the blood relative for whom the king felt the greatest affection, could not make Philip act before he was ready. Nogaret, chancellor in all but name, could not keep the king

vallis faceret omnia que posset," but he would not take a gift until the business was finished (Willemsen, pp. 216, 217).

[80] Reglá, II, 260-68 (17 October 1312).

[81] Ibid., II, docs. nos. 17-20 (26 February 1313).

[82] Lauer, p. 31 (26 February 1313).

[83] Franklin J. Pegues, *The Lawyers of the Last Capetians* (Princeton, 1962), pp. 95-97.

[84] In reporting Nogaret's death, the Aragonese envoy added, "ex quo negocium nostrum multum credimus prosperare" (Willemsen, p. 187; also in Finke, ed., *Acta Aragonensia*, I, 463). Nogaret had been much interested in the question of the Val d'Aran; documents concerning it were in his possession at the time of his death (Charles-Victor Langlois, ed., "Les Papiers de Guillaume de Nogaret et de Guillaume de Plaisians au Trésor des Chartes," *Notices et extraits*, XXXIX, pt. 1 [1909], 211 ff.).

[85] Reglá, II, docs. nos. 27, 30.   [86] Ibid., II, docs. nos. 58, 61.

from acting when he was ready. Written reports seem to have influenced Philip more than verbal arguments—and the decisive reports were prepared by councillors of the second rank, Gérard de Courtonne and Yves de Loudéac. No one has ever suggested that Gérard and Yves dictated the policy of Philip the Fair.

No other case is so well documented, but the preference for written documents and the division of responsibility among many councillors appears again and again. Few men could have had easier access to the king than Nogaret, yet when Nogaret felt in danger he wrote to Philip and did not rely entirely on oral persuasion. The annexation of Lyon was surely one of Philip's major objectives, and here again the way toward annexation was smoothed by carefully prepared written arguments.[87] Philip sent out *enquêteurs* not only to squeeze money out of his subjects and to assert royal rights, but also to prepare written reports on specific problems.[88] In fact, one of the striking features of the reign is the increase in the number and length of official and semiofficial documents.

As for division of responsibility, negotiations with the papacy show constant changes in the composition of the French missions, overlapping groups of envoys, and direct control by the king. For example, in 1302 Philip had three sets of envoys in Rome.[89] In 1310 there were again three French missions at the curia, much to the confusion of Clement V, who felt that at least two of the envoys were contradicting each other.[90] In 1304 Philip sent Geoffroi du Plessis to the conclave at Perugia with secret documents on the affair of Boniface VIII. Even Nogaret received copies of the documents only at a later date, and the Council as a whole was not supposed to see them.[91] Only the king could have coordinated and directed the activities of such envoys.

[87] Pierre Bonnassieux, *De la réunion de la Lyon à la France* (Lyons, 1875), pp. 88-90, 148.

[88] For example, a commission sent to determine the boundary between the *sénéchaussées* of Beaucaire and Carcassonne, 1302-1303 (*C.R.*, I, no. 13906).

[89] Edgard Boutaric, ed., "Notices et extraits de documents inédits relatifs à l'histoire de France sous Philippe le Bel," *Notices et extraits*, xx, pt. 2 (1861), 146.

[90] Edgard Boutaric, *Clement V, Philippe le Bel et les Templiers* (Paris, 1874), pp. 59-60.

[91] Charles-Victor Langlois, "Geoffroi du Plessis, protonotaire de France," *Revue historique*, LXVII (1899), 75-76. Even after Philip's death, Geoffroi hesitated to surrender these documents and did so only by direct personal order of the new king.

Philip was a busy man; he may have been too busy. The trivial nature of some of the letters that he warranted and the unimportance of some of the judicial cases in which he intervened suggest that he may have been at times unwilling to delegate authority. On the other hand, attention to detail did not keep him from formulating broad general policies, and by attending to details he kept himself extraordinarily well informed about the affairs of the realm. Philip controlled his government because he worked hard at his job. He had many able advisers, but he made the final decisions.

If Philip made the decisions, why then did so many of his contemporaries think that he was a figurehead? Largely, I think, because Philip on important occasions insisted on consulting his ministers and usually let them announce his decisions.

This pattern of behavior was caused in part, but only in part, by personal peculiarities. Shy, withdrawn, unable to mix easily with ordinary people, very conscious of his royal dignity, Philip preferred to avoid the rough-and-tumble of public debate and to let others explain and expound his policies. The sacred mysteries of the religion of monarchy were not to be revealed to the profane; there must be intermediaries between the Vicar of God and his subjects. Philip was also convinced—and most political theorists of the time would have agreed with him—that, leaving aside matters of dignity, it was still necessary and proper to consult his councillors before making a final decision. After all, he was the grandson of St. Louis, as his contemporaries never tired of reminding him, and a good king like St. Louis did not act on his own whims or make decisions in haste. He was always surrounded by "prud'hommes" who advised and informed him; he took counsel before acting. St. Louis had held a council in the midst of the battle of Mansourah; Philip held councils in the midst of his political battles. But once the formality of asking counsel had been observed, a good king made—and took responsibility for—his decisions. St. Louis had remained in the Holy Land in spite of the opposition of a large part of his Council. Philip was equally free to accept or reject the opinions of his advisers.

In an article written some years ago I said that Philip wanted to be a "constitutional" king.[92] Several scholars have objected to

92 "Philip the Fair," pp. 209-10.

this adjective,[93] and it is true that if we believe that a king is a constitutional monarch only when he is restrained by independent, external forces, then Philip cannot be described by such a phrase. But if we take "constitutional" in McIlwain's sense, that is, a body of laws and precedents that binds the conscience of the ruler even if it cannot be enforced by external agencies,[94] then Philip was a "constitutional" king. He was not an unfettered despot; he had to give at least an appearance of legality to all his actions. The strongest, most highly developed and most popular branch of his government was the judicial system. In Philip's own concept of sovereignty, respect for his authority as supreme and final judge was a basic ingredient.[95] If he had obviously and openly broken the law, then he would have destroyed his position as guardian and interpreter of the law.

Therefore Philip tried to govern his realm through a well-established system of courts that followed, and when necessary interpreted or even established, rules of law. When he took actions that went beyond the traditional powers of the French monarchy he always sought legal justification for his behavior and the consent, tacit or expressed, of those who were affected by his decisions. Thus he called large general assemblies to hear explanations of his policy toward Boniface and the Templars. He sought approval of his taxes (perhaps the greatest innovation of his reign) from local assemblies or provincial Church councils.[96] When he annexed the Lyonnais and imposed an onerous treaty on Flanders, he insisted that agents be sent to obtain the consent of the communities of each province to the terms of the final settlements.[97] At the very least, consent satisfied Philip's desire to remain within the limits of legality. Often, of course,

[93] Notably Bryce Lyon, "What Made a Medieval King Constitutional?" in T. A. Sandquist and M. R. Powicke, eds., *Essays in Medieval History Presented to Bertie Wilkinson* (Toronto, 1969), pp. 157 ff.

[94] C. H. McIlwain, *The Growth of Political Thought in the West* (New York, 1932), pp. 128, 132-33, 136.

[95] In a very generous agreement (1307) recognizing the rights of the bishop of Mende, Philip expressly reserved "nostra majori superioritate ac superiori ressorto" (Jean Roucaute and Marc Saché, eds., *Lettres de Philippe le Bel relatives au pays de Gévaudan* [Mende, 1897], p. 179). This is typical of all such agreements; see below, pp. 247-48.

[96] Joseph R. Strayer and Charles H. Taylor, *Studies in Early French Taxation* (Cambridge, Mass., 1939), pp. 25-28, 46, 51-52, 67.

[97] Bonnassieux, pp. 96-105; Frantz Funck-Brentano, *Philippe le Bel en Flandre* (Paris 1897), pp. 513-15.

consent had political advantages as well; it certainly facilitated the collection of taxes and strengthened the king's hand in the struggle with Boniface VIII.

Philip wanted to be well informed and well advised. He regularly consulted his officials and seldom acted in haste or without some color of reason. This is not to say that he was the model of a just and wise ruler. His will was stronger than his intelligence; he could be led astray by the very intensity of his belief in the Christian faith and the French monarchy. His piety was as narrow as it was deep; if his own conscience could be satisfied by appropriate forms and phrases, he often failed to realize what consequences his acts might have for others. His faith in the mission of the French monarchy was so broad that it tended to blot out any other considerations—the interests of Western Christendom as a whole, or the rights and welfare of his subjects. He sought moral and legal justification for all his acts, but he had a tendency to believe that in any dispute right must be on his side and that opposition was therefore inexcusable. He had real respect for custom and for law, but he could be easily satisfied that due process had been observed. If the proper legal forms had been used in a suit to establish royal rights of jurisdiction, if a plausible case had been made for the annexation of a border territory, if an assembly had given official support to his policy, he was not apt to ask for further investigation.

Royal officials knew of these weaknesses and sought to exploit them. Their interest clearly lay in extending royal power, and if they could achieve this end by playing on the king's piety and pride in the French monarchy, they naturally did so. Thus the king was told repeatedly that it was his duty as a Christian ruler to persevere in the charges against Boniface VIII and against the Temple. Philip was undoubtedly influenced by this pressure, just as any ruler, no matter how strong, is influenced by the advice of his immediate subordinates. It is even probable that his tactics were altered by the advice that he received. For example, his growing caution in the last years of the reign may reflect Marigny's worries about finance, just as his aggressiveness in the period 1297-1302 may owe something to Flote's impetuous nature. (On the other hand, the young, energetic king may have sought out an aggressive minister, and the tired, middle-aged ruler may have looked for a cautious adviser.) But influence on tactics does not mean that royal officials determined basic strategy.[98] Some of Philip's officials had served his father; many of them served his sons; and a surprisingly large number still held high positions in the early years of Philip VI. But the reign of Philip the Fair was not like the reigns of his father, his sons, or his nephew. It had a quality all its own, more emphatic and more dramatic.

Philip could be hesitant at times, as in the affair of the Val d'Aran or in the prosecution of his claims in Aquitaine after the 1290s. More often, he was persistent and patient, applying steady pressure until his opponents caved in. This was the way in which he reduced the independence of the southern bishops and the pattern he followed in annexing the city of Lyon. But when he was deeply concerned or deeply annoyed, he would take extraordinary risks. Anagni was one—what would have happened if Boniface had lived for a year or two after the attack? The denunciation of his daughters-in-law was another, and in this case we know what happened—a lack of male heirs and a succession problem that poisoned French politics for half a century. Philip was not always prudent, any more than he was always just. But he usually knew what he wanted, and it was his desires that gave the period from 1285 to 1314 its special flavor. He never blamed his councillors for his mistakes, another sign that he felt responsible for major decisions. As he said on his deathbed, if he had received bad advice it was because he had asked for it.[99] It is only fair to add that he was also responsible for the very real achievements of the reign. He was industrious, persistent, and usually skillful in judging political situations. He drove his people hard and used up some of the reservoir of good will that St. Louis had accumulated. But he left behind him a France that was better administered, more unified, and more conscious of its identity than it had been before.

[98] Jean Favier, "Les légistes et le gouvernement sous Philippe le Bel," *Journal des Savants* (1969), pp. 104-6, would disagree with this statement. We are in accord on two points: Philip always consulted his Council on important matters, and he made the final decisions. But M. Favier believes that Philip usually accepted the advice of the dominant minister, Nogaret or Marigny.

[99] Charles Baudon de Mony, "La Mort et les funerailles de Philippe le Bel d'après un compte rendu à la cour de Majorque," *Bibliothèque de l'Ecole des Chartes*, LVIII (1897), 12: "ipsetmet erat causa mali consilii sui." At the same time, he took full blame for his financial exactions and the manipulation of the currency; see note 28 above.

II. The King and His Officers

Social and Geographic Origins of the King's Servants

T housands of men served Philip the Fair during his long reign. He needed a large group of expert officials in Paris, an even larger group to administer his possessions and protect his rights in the provinces, and a considerable number of *enquêteurs* and commissioners to maintain close relations between central and local authorities. He also needed an "unlimited multitude" (as it seemed to contemporary writers) of sergeants, forest guards, purchasing agents, master workmen, and local collectors of royal revenues to make sure that his orders were obeyed, his revenues received, his armies supplied, and his estates kept in good condition.

The last-named group was the most numerous and the one that had the closest, and often the most abrasive relations with the mass of the population. Unfortunately, this is also the group about which we have the least information. In the royal accounts these men are usually anonymous. The sergeants of the watch of Paris, the forest guards of Poitou, the keeper of the castle of Bellencombre in Normandy are simply items in a list of expenditures, not identifiable individuals. Sergeants and guards might be named when they became involved in lawsuits, and revenue collectors were often named when accounts were being audited, but the names at best indicate only the birthplace or residence of an agent. About all that can be said of the vast majority of these petty officials is that most of them were natives of the region where they were employed, that they were not very well paid[1] but had the great advantage of steady, year-round employment, and that they had a reputation for being somewhat overzealous in enforcing the king's rights and somewhat too willing to take bribes.

The local collectors or subcollectors of royal revenues were a

---

[1] For example, in 1299 sergeants of the watch in Paris received 1 s.p. a day (*C.R.*, 1, no. 1438); a forest guard in Vermandois had only 6 d.p. a day (no. 1923); the watchman and porter of Tours had 8 d.p. a day (no. 3002), as did the porters of Chinon (no. 3002). In the same year foresters, jailers, sergeants, porters, and watchmen in Toulouse received 12 d.t. (about 10 d.p.), 10 d.t., or 8 d.t. a day (nos. 11912-14). Of course, many of these men had free lodging and other perquisites.

little less obscure and of a somewhat higher class than other subordinate agents of the king. Many of them, especially those who collected money from the Church, were members of the clergy; others were well-to-do bourgeois or leading men in their parishes. For most of them, revenue collecting was not a career. The work was intermittent, and the remuneration was not enough to compensate for the difficulties and risks involved.[2] The collectors who did remain in royal service usually worked outside their own provinces at one time or another and had wider responsibilities than men who dealt only with their own neighbors.[3] On the whole, the collectors of royal revenues seem to have been fairly honest. They might be accused of asking too much for the king, but few of them were charged with taking money for themselves.

Even at the level of the local collectors, however, it is difficult to move beyond broad generalizations; there is not enough information to justify statistical analysis. Above this level, however, more precision is possible. The careers of about a thousand men who worked for Philip the Fair can be traced in some detail. These men fall into four fairly distinct groups:

1. *High officials based in Paris*, or, if they were on missions in the provinces, with direct access to the king and Council. These would be the men who made the judgements in the Parlement, who were Treasurers or Masters of Accounts, who held high positions in the Household, who were heads of missions sent to the pope or other great personages, who commanded large military forces, who were responsible for investigations or adminis-

---

[2] The only remuneration mentioned in the accounts is for "expenses," and these were often questioned. Many collectors wound up owing money to the king. For example, two brothers of Narbonne, Bonat Constantin and Raymond Joan (probably bankers), owed 425 l.t. in 1310 on their account for the tenth of Narbonne of 1304 (Mignon, no. 785; *C.R.*, I, no. 6557); Pons Boton, a wealthy citizen of Béziers, owed 1,727 l.t. in 1302 on his account for the subsidy of 1297 (Mignon, no. 1426; *C.R.*, III, no. 29111).

[3] For example, Bertaud Mahiel of Pont-Audemer, who collected loans, tenths, and subsidies in the 1290s in Champagne, Brittany, and finally in Caen and the Cotentin, became *bailli* of the Cotentin and then of Gisors in 1308-1309 (*H.F.*, XXIV, *153; Mignon, nos. 1151, 740, 1400). Guillaume Arrenart of Chartres, *scolasticus* of Lisieux, began as a collector in Vermandois in 1299; he was a councillor and sat in the Parlements of Louis X and Philip V (Mignon, no. 1347; Jules Viard, ed., *Les journaux du Trésor de Philippe IV le Bel* [Paris, 1940], nos. 2803-5 [hereafter cited as *J.T.P.*]; *H.F.*, XXIV, *168). More evidence about the collectors may be found below, pp. 157-64.

trative supervision in wide areas (for example, general *enquêteurs* in Languedoc, a general Master of Waters and Forests, the general supervisor of customs dues). These men were often called counsellors in a broad sense,[4] and many of them were members of the Council, however narrowly it be defined. There are about 150 officials in this category.

2. *The supporting staff in Paris*—clerks, notaries, *rapporteurs* in the Parlement, lesser Household officials. These men had good opportunities for advancement, and many of them entered the highest group toward the end of Philip's reign or during the reigns of his sons. Others, however, remained obscure, so that there are satisfactory data for only about 125 men of this group.

3. *High-ranking provincial officials*—seneschals, *baillis*, the *juges-mages* of the south, local masters of forests, masters of mints, general collectors of subsidies and of payments by the Church, castellans of key fortresses (for example, Carcassonne), commanders of occupied or recently annexed territories (for example, the captain of Montreuil, the rector of Montpellier, the *gardeur* of Lyon). This is a large group (a few more than 200) and a key group in the administration. Careers were long, and often distinguished; 33 of the men who held these positions eventually sat in the Council and the Parlement or became Treasurers or Masters of Accounts. This represents an overall promotion rate of 15 percent; for *baillis* and seneschals the rate was even higher, about 18 percent.

4. Finally, *lower-ranking local officials*—the viscounts of Normandy, the *viguiers* of Languedoc, the *prévôts* of the old royal domain, the district judges of the Midi, royal procurators and advocates, lesser castellans and keepers of forests, and the receivers of *bailliages* and *sénéchaussées*. (It may seem strange to put receivers in this group, but in spite of the potential power of their position, they actually had little authority and not much hope for promotion. They were more important and better paid in the south than in the north, but even in the south the Italians,

---

[4] Pierre de Chalon, who was the head of the customs service, was given the title of councillor by the king in 1311, though he was almost never at court. See A.N., JJ 42A, no. 132, and my "Pierre de Chalon and the Origins of the French Customs Service," in *Festschrift Percy Ernst Schramm*, 2 vols. (Wiesbaden, 1964), I, 334-39 (reprinted in *Medieval Statecraft*, pp. 232-38; further references to this article will cite page numbers in *Medieval Statecraft*).

who held many of the receiverships, were pure technicians, and only a few of the French receivers had any influence. In general, the official who imposed a tax was more important than the receiver who merely counted and disbursed the money.)[5] These lower-ranking officials were very numerous, but there are usable data for only about 500 of them. Naturally, the longer a man served and the more successful he was, the better are the chances of knowing something of his career. Statistics on this group should therefore be used with caution. It is not meaningful, for example, to count the number of promotions of *prévôts*, viscounts, and *viguiers* because there are too many gaps in the list. It can be said nevertheless that promotion was not infrequent. *Prévôts*, viscounts, and *viguiers* could become *baillis* and seneschals;[6] district judges could become *juges-mages*, and men who reached these high provincial offices could go on to Paris.[7] On the other hand, it is clear that some local officials were not eager for long careers in royal service. Many receivers held office less than five years. A large number of the early receivers were Italians, mere deputies of Lombard bankers and not really members of the French bureaucracy, but some French-born receivers showed no more liking for the job. Many judges in the south served only briefly or intermittently.[8] Some officials who did stay in royal service apparently wanted only part-time work, like Robert le Parmentier, who was briefly receiver of Senlis in 1305 but who shifted

[5] On the receivers see below, pp. 112-20, and my "Italian Bankers and Philip the Fair," in D. Herlihy, R. S. Lopez, and V. Slessarev, eds., *Economy, Society, and Government in Medieval Italy: Essays in Memory of Robert L. Reynolds* (Kent, Ohio, 1969), pp. 113-21 (reprinted in *Medieval Statecraft*, pp. 239-47; further references to this article will cite page numbers in *Medieval Statecraft*).

[6] Strayer, "Viscounts and Viguiers under Philip the Fair," *Speculum*, XXXVIII (1963), pp. 247, 249-51 (reprinted in *Medieval Statecraft*, pp. 221, 223-24; further references to this article will cite page numbers in *Medieval Statecraft*). See also L. Carolus-Barré, "Les baillis de Philippe III le Hardi," *Annuaire-Bulletin de la Société de l'Histoire de France* (1966-1967), pp. 162, 160, 209-10, 224. The *baillis* Gautier Bardin, Gilles de Compiègne, Jean de Montigny, and Pierre Saimel all began their careers as *prévôts*.

[7] Four *juges-mages* of Beaucaire first served as local judges (Strayer, *Gens de justice*, pp. 54, 56, 58, 60); 10 or 11 southern judges were called to Paris (ibid., 21-22). Many *baillis* eventually sat in the Parlement; see Carolus-Barré, "Baillis de Philippe III."

[8] Strayer, *Les gens de justice*, pp. 22-23 and Appendix. A good example is Gauvain des Bonconseils, an eminent lawyer of Toulouse, who was *juge-mage* of Agenais in 1296, of Toulouse from 1298 to 1300, and of Périgord for a short period in 1309 (ibid., pp. 168-69).

to the less demanding but reasonably profitable position of keeper of the seal of Senlis.[9] In short, at this level—a level far above that of sergeant, forest guard, or subcollector, but below that of *bailli* or seneschal—there was a large pool of talented and capable men that could be tapped for many kinds of government service. Only a small number of these men, however, became more or less permanent members of the administration.

Some generalizations can be made that apply to all four groups, though they fit the lower-level officials less well than those in higher ranks. In the first place, there was remarkable continuity in the personnel of the French administrative services. Naturally, the intimate advisers of the king changed with each reign, but the experts in law and finance, the administrators of the provinces, and the clerks and notaries and accountants who supported these higher officials continued their careers without interruption. Of the highest-ranking group, 42 had served Philip's father, and 52 served his sons; 3 (or perhaps 4) of these 94 men were in the administration before 1285 and continued after 1314. To put it in other terms, in the early years of Philip's reign at least one-third of his high-ranking officials had had previous experience in important posts, and a third of the men who held high posts during his reign continued to hold these or similar positions after his death. It is not surprising that the median length of service for this group as a whole was about 25 years.

As might be expected, the curve for the supporting staff at Paris is less symmetrical. These would have been younger men, less apt to be noticed in the records of the time of Philip III and more likely to have survived Philip the Fair. It is certain that at least 15 of them served before 1285; there may well have been more. The figure at the other end of the reign is impressive: 53 members of the supporting staff worked for one or more of the three kings who followed Philip. Of these, 20 (or 21) were promoted to higher office either late in Philip's reign or in the reign of his sons. Again, the median length of service was about 25 years. This group of well-trained, experienced civil servants was one of the most important legacies that Philip left to his successors.

Among the high-ranking local officials the pattern is more like

---

[9] On Parmentier's career see: *C.R.*, 1, nos. 4748, 4782, 4807, 4832 (receiver); A.N., JJ 45, no. 206, JJ 46, no. 59, K 38, no. 8, and B.N., ms. fr. 20334, nos. 6, 9, 15, 39, 70 (keeper of the seal of Senlis, 1310-1312).

that of the leading men at Paris. Of the *baillis* and seneschals, 32 had held office under Philip III—and, in two cases, under St. Louis—while 43 continued in government service after the death of Philip the Fair. Of those in other positions (mainly judges and masters of forests), at least 9 had served Philip III, and 25 served after the death of Philip the Fair. The totals then would be 41 in office before 1285 and 68 continuing after 1314. Median length of service was a little lower than that of the first two groups, only about 20 years.

The evidence is too incomplete to justify a numerical analysis of the careers of lower-ranking local officials. What data exist suggest that there was a good deal of continuity even in this group. At least a quarter of these men had either served Philip's father or went on to serve his sons. As usual, there are more names on the post-1314 list than on the pre-1285 one, but with this group the built-in bias of the data is especially apt to lead to distortion. There are so few financial records for the reign of Philip III that it is almost impossible to tell who were the judges, *prévôts*, and viscounts at that time. With Philip the Fair, this information becomes relatively abundant, and it is very likely that many men who first appear after 1285 were actually in office before that date. On the other hand, there was a striking increase in the number of lesser officers under Philip the Fair. To give only two examples, receivers were instituted in all provinces, and royal procurators, who had held only ad hoc appointments, were given permanent commissions. If there were more officials, then more of them would survive the death of the king who appointed them.

For the reasons already given, and also because of the prevalence of intermittent and part-time employment at the local level, it is impossible to make an estimate of the median length of service of these lower-ranking officials. There is fairly good evidence about the receivers—the vast majority served less than 10 years and about one-third served less than 5 years—but, as noted above, the receivers were not typical. It is also clear that the majority of the southern judges served for relatively short periods; but again, these highly skilled professionals were not typical of the lesser bureaucracy on a whole. Neither their income nor their status depended on continuous service to the king; they could hold a judgeship for a year or two, retire to private practice, and receive another judgeship 5 or 10 years later. At the other extreme were the men who became career civil servants. They also are exceptional cases, usually men who had been rapidly promoted to the higher positions and who therefore had good reason to remain in the king's service.[10] An official like Simon de la Salle, doctor of laws, who was willing to remain in the minor position of king's advocate in the ecclesiastical court of Sens for some 30 years, was even more exceptional.[11] Moreover, while Simon was paid a reasonably good yearly salary (80 l.t.) it is doubtful that he spent all his time working for the king. One wonders whether lesser bureaucrats who could not practice their profession on the side were as likely to stay in royal service for two or three decades.

A second characteristic of the royal bureaucracy was the predominance of officeholders from the old royal domain. This was nothing new: it was an almost unavoidable consequence of the rapid expansion during the thirteenth century of the area ruled directly by the king. The king did not know, and was not sure that he could trust, the leading men of Normandy or of Languedoc; he preferred to draw his officials from regions that had long been subject to the crown. This prejudice, very marked under St. Louis, was somewhat attenuated by the time of Philip the Fair, but even as late as the reign of Philip of Valois there was a clear preference for men from the old domain, and especially for those who came from the northeastern *bailliages*.[12]

Of the high officials in the central government, 84 came from the old domain (63 from Paris and the northeast), 15 from Normandy, 9 from Languedoc, 9 from the Burgundy-Mâconnais region, 6 from Champagne, 5 from Auvergne, 5 from the Anjou-Poitou area, and 4 from Brittany. There were 8 foreigners, of whom 5 were Italians. The increase in the number of Normans is significant and is repeated at other levels. Philip's marriage to the heiress of Champagne explains the choice of officials from that county; in fact, it is a little surprising that there were so few of them. The groups from Languedoc and Auvergne were not large, but it was something of an innovation to have any high-ranking officials from these areas.

[10] Guillaume de Plaisians, for example, served only two or three years as a provincial judge before being called to Paris. Yves de Loudéac was judge of Toulouse for six years before he became a member of the Parlement and an ambassador. On these men see the Appendix to my *Gens de justice*.

[11] *C.R.*, I, nos. 351, 2232, 5250; Jules Viard, ed., *Les journaux du Trésor de Charles IV le Bel* (Paris, 1917), nos. 2644, 2730 (hereafter cited as *J.T.C.*).

[12] Raymond Cazelles, *La société politique et la crise de la royauté sous Philippe de Valois* (Paris, 1958), pp. 269-72.

Mere numbers, of course, can be somewhat misleading. It is true that the routine work of government was carried on largely by men from the old domain. But when one thinks of the men who probably had the greatest influence on Philip, it is surprising to see how many came from other provinces or even from regions not subject to the crown. Pierre Flote and Guillaume de Plaisians probably were born in Dauphiné (though Flote had connections with Auvergne and Plaisians with Languedoc); the Guidi brothers (Biche and Mouche) were Italians, as was Betin Caucinel, Philip's chief adviser on the coinage; Guillaume de Nogaret came from Languedoc and Gilles Aicelin from Auvergne; Enguerran de Marigny, probably the most powerful of all Philip's ministers, was a Norman. It would appear that Philip was a little suspicious of the old families of the Ile de France and Picardy, who had enjoyed almost a monopoly of high positions in the French government, and that he wanted to weaken the "old boy" network by bringing in new men. The new men were much more dependent on the king's favor, much less bound by old traditions, much more willing to accept innovations in policy. Socially, Philip preferred the company of the old nobility that had served his ancestors; politically, he wanted the assistance of able men, regardless of rank or place of origin.

This interpretation of his choice of officials is quite compatible with the fact that the less important officials in Paris came almost entirely from the old domain—83 as opposed to 29 from other regions (the place of origin of 13 is unknown). The Normans, 12 in all, were the only large group from a recently acquired province. Only 6 men came from Auvergne and Languedoc; the others were scattered among Brittany, Champagne, and Burgundy. These minor officials were technicians, not advisers or decision makers. It was obviously easier to recruit them in Paris or in nearby districts. Why seek a notary or an accountant in Languedoc when there were plenty of capable men living no more than 20 or 30 miles from the capital? Conversely, why should a man who had a satisfactory position in Toulouse or Montpellier want to take a minor post in Paris? The northern origins of the supporting staff in Paris did have some long-run influence on the composition of the upper level of officialdom, since some 20 of these minor officers were eventually promoted. But few of those promoted ever reached positions where they could influence policy.

With the *baillis* and seneschals we return to a distribution not unlike that for the higher officials in Paris—74 from the old domain (55 of these from the Ile de France and Picardy), 17 from Normandy, 11 from Champagne, 9 from Languedoc, 7 from the Burgundy area, 5 from Auvergne, 1 from the Lyonnais, and 1 from Flanders. Once again there is a significant increase in the number of Normans. On the other hand, the apparent increase for Champagne is deceptive. It is largely due to the fact that when Philip took over Champagne he tended to retain or to name men of the county as *baillis* of Troyes, Meaux, Vitry, and Chaumont.

For the high-ranking local officials as a whole, the picture is distorted by including *juges-mages*, judges of appeal, and lieutenants of seneschals. Most, though not all, of these men came by necessity from Languedoc. Few northerners had mastered the Romanized law of the south, and when a seneschal needed a lieutenant it was only sensible to pick a local noble or lawyer. With this exception, the distribution is about the same as for *baillis* and seneschals alone: 96 men from the old domain, 5 from Auvergne, 11 from Burgundy, 16 from Champagne, 2 from Flanders, 42 from Languedoc, 20 from Normandy, 1 each from Forez, the Lyonnais, and Poitou, 2 Italians, and 27 unknown. The old domain still had the largest share, but Philip was showing more confidence than his predecessors in men from Normandy and Languedoc.

This impression is strengthened when we look at the lower-level local officials. Less than half of those who can be identified came from the old domain. At least 50 were Normans and more than 100 were natives of Languedoc. The problem of staffing law courts in the region of the written law accounts for the large number in the latter group; most of these men were *viguiers*, district judges, or procurators. Champagne also had somewhat more than its share of local offices, especially in fiscal administration. The other provinces had about the same proportion of low-ranking officers that they had at higher levels. The one really striking difference is the large number of Italians in local administration. They served mostly as receivers or minters, and they were more numerous in the first half of the reign than they were at the end,[13] but they played a significant role in the southern *sénéchaussées*.

There was obviously some tendency to let natives take care of the minor affairs of their own provinces, but this was not

[13] Strayer, "Italian Bankers and Philip the Fair," pp. 244-47.

allowed to go to dangerous extremes. There were viscounts in Normandy who came from the old domain, *viguiers* and judges in Languedoc who were northerners,[14] and receivers in Champagne who were Italians.[15] Conversely, men from Normandy, Languedoc, and Champagne served outside their own provinces, most often as collectors of lay and ecclesiastical taxes. In short, there was always enough of a mixture so that there was no danger that a province could be semiautonomous, administered only by its own inhabitants. The government seems to have worried less about this risk at the lower level than it did about positions such as *bailli*, seneschal, and *juge-mage*, where there was a rule—not always enforced[16]—that a man could not hold high office in his own home district. But the basic principle was never entirely forgotten, not even for minor jobs.

Finally, it is possible to make some generalizations about the social origins of the king's servants. They can be classified as noble, clergy, and nonnoble. The last term is preferable to bourgeois, even though it is likely that most of the nonnobles were actually members of the bourgeoisie. But for many men, including even such an important official as Nogaret, it is difficult to prove actual membership in the community of a privileged town or city. The clergy, of course, included many men of noble birth, such as Gilles Aicelin, but too often the sources mention only rank in the Church and say nothing of family origins.

Roughly speaking, the higher the official rank, the greater the preponderance of nobles and upper-level clergy (cathedral dignitaries, archdeacons, and bishops). Thus, of the leading officials in Paris, at least 73 were clergy: 28 were or became bishops, 35 were canons, deans, archdeacons, and the like, 4 were abbots or priors; only 10 are called simply king's clerk or clerk. There were 53 nobles, including great nobles, such as the counts of Artois and Saint-Pol, and only 20 nonnobles. It is significant that at least 4 of the latter group were ennobled soon after they reached high rank. As might be expected, the supporting staff was largely

---

[14] See Strayer, "Viscounts and Viguiers" and *Gens de justice*, pp. 58, 82, 83, 105, 141, for northerners who held judgeships in the south.

[15] D. Ozanam, "Les receveurs de Champagne," in *Recueil . . . Clovis Brunel* (Paris, 1955), II, 343-45.

[16] Jean Marti was moved from the position of *juge-mage* of Beaucaire to the position of *juge-mage* of Toulouse because he was a "native," but several of his predecessors had also been inhabitants of the *sénéchaussée* (Strayer, *Gens de justice*, p. 61). Normans frequently held Norman *bailliages*.

clerical (in both senses of the word): 78 clergy, 10 nobles, 33 nonnobles (of whom 2 were ennobled), and 2 doubtful.

At the highest provincial levels, the figures are somewhat distorted by the requirement that seneschals had to be nobles and that clerics could not be *baillis*, seneschals, or judges with criminal jurisdiction. Thus, of 131 men who were *baillis* or seneschals (8 of these held both positions), 71 were nobles and 60 nonnobles (one of the latter was ennobled). For the *baillis* alone, however, the proportions are quite different: 35 nobles (including the 8 who became seneschals) and 60 nonnobles (including the one who was ennobled). For all high-level provincial positions the figures are 100 nobles, 89 nonnobles (of whom 4 were ennobled), and 16 clerics.

Lower-level provincial officials were, for the most part, nonnoble laymen. There was a fairly large group of clerics involved in the collection of lay subsidies and payments by the Church, but they did not have a monopoly of this work. As a rough estimate, if all lower-level positions are counted, there were about two laymen for every cleric. Nobles usually held only the more honorific positions of castellans, viscounts, *viguiers*, and keepers of forests. But nonnobles also could hold these positions, so that the total number of nobles in lower-level provincial posts was quite low, probably no more than 15 percent of the total. On the other hand, the nobles had a much better chance of promotion than clerics or nonnobles; about 10 percent of them became *baillis*, seneschals, or members of the high-ranking group of officials at Paris. For the other two classes, the chance of promotion was only about 1 percent.

How were these thousands of servants of the king chosen? Obviously the ruler himself knew personally only a small number of those who exercised power in his name. He had intimate contacts with the serving members of his (or the queen's) Household, and somewhat more formal contacts with the men who sat in the Council, the Parlement, and the Treasury or the Chambre des Comptes. He probably knew most of the *baillis* and seneschals. He certainly knew the bishops and the more important abbots of the north, but he may not have been as well acquainted with the southern prelates. (One wonders, for example, whether he had ever talked to Bernard Saisset before Bernard became bishop of Pamiers.) All these men could recommend their relatives, their friends, and their dependents for jobs in the government. To take a famous example, Enguerran de Marigny probably owed his first appointment, in the household of the queen, to his cousin Nicolas de Fréauville, who was at the time the king's confessor and who later became archbishop of Rouen and a cardinal.[17] As Marigny rose in rank he carried his family and his clerks with him. One of his brothers became archbishop of Sens, another bishop of Beauvais. Two of his clerks gained high offices. Geoffroi de Briançon was made one of the Treasurers, and Michel de Bourdenay a *Maître des Comptes*.[18] Not all of the king's councillors were able to push their clients so high, but the remarkable continuity in the personnel of the central administrative services is due in part to the effects of patronage. Sons, nephews, and clerks of men who had held high office under Philip III held high office under his son, and the relatives and dependents of these men in turn served Philip's successors.

The same process can be observed at other levels. Renaud Barbou, *bailli* of Rouen from 1275 to 1287, was succeeded after a brief interval by his son (*bailli*, 1291-1298). Simon de Montigny (or Montagny), *bailli* of Orléans for more than 20 years (1296-1316), was certainly a relative and probably a son of Jean de Montigny, who held various *bailliages* from 1284 to 1299 and then became a member of the Council.[19] Sanche de la Charmoye, *Maître des Comptes* by 1304, had as a clerk in 1298 his nephew Amaury. Amaury was a clerk of accounts by 1307 and became *Maître des Comptes* after the death of Philip the Fair.[20] Sanche also had a son, Jean, who entered Marigny's service and who in 1316 was a clerk of the Chambre des Comptes.[21] Raoul de Courjumelles, *juge-mage* of Beaucaire (1305-1308), was related to Mathieu de Courjumelles, judge of Quercy (1306-1317) and later a *rapporteur* in the Parlement.[22] Or, to take a case of patronage rather than family influence, Pons d'Aumelas, *juge-mage* of Rouergue, then of Toulouse, and finally a member of the Parlement, was aided at several crucial points in his career by Bérenger Frédol, bishop of Maguelonne, who eventually became a cardinal.[23]

---

[17] Jean Favier, *Un conseiller de Philippe le Bel. Enguerran de Marigny* (Paris, 1963), p. 63.

[18] Ibid., pp. 28-31, 79-80, 99.

[19] Carolus-Barré, "Baillis de Philippe III," pp. 155-99, 211.

[20] Favier, *Marigny*, p. 231; *J.T.P.*, nos. 481, 1324, 5860; *J.T.C.*, no. 436.

[21] Favier, *Marigny*, p. 21; Robert Fawtier, ed., *Comptes du Trésor (1296, 1316, 1384, 1477)* (Paris, 1936), no. 774. See below, p. 185.

[22] Strayer, *Gens de justice*, pp. 58, 141.

[23] Charles-Victor Langlois, "Pons d'Aumelas," *Bibliothèque de l'Ecole*

Although these examples could be multiplied, the importance of family connections and the influence of well-placed patrons should not be exaggerated. Not all sons of royal officials wanted to enter the service of the king, and not all clerks of great men were qualified for important positions. Moreover, a considerable number of jobs were not very desirable; to be a receiver or a tax collector brought small rewards and serious financial risks. Some of the king's ablest servants lost interest in working for him when they were promoted to bishoprics. For example, Richard Leneveu, who had been a very active, even aggressive *enquêteur-réformateur*, did practically nothing for the king after he was made bishop of Béziers in 1305. Thus there was a constant search for new men to fill posts in a rapidly growing bureaucracy.

The *baillis* and the seneschals must have played an important role in recruiting men for royal service. They would have known the substantial people of their districts, men who could be used as tax collectors, *prévôts*, viscounts, *viguiers*, castellans, and judges. They must have made most of the recommendations that led to promotions from lower to higher rank in provincial government. Itinerant royal commissioners may also have played a part in this process. The result was a small but steady flow of able men into the upper ranks of the bureaucracy.

It is also possible that the title of king's clerk or king's knight was used as a means of attracting men into government service or of persuading them to remain in service after they had taken on a temporary job. Even in the time of Philip VI it is not entirely clear what these titles meant or how they were conferred,[24] and the obscurity is even greater in the reign of Philip the Fair. Certainly the king acted directly and of his own knowledge in some cases, for example, in making Biche and Mouche king's knights. But Philip could not possibly have known the hundreds of obscure country gentlemen, lawyers, and clerks who became knights and clerks of the king. They must have been named on the recommendation of *baillis*, seneschals, and royal commissioners. This would have been especially likely in Languedoc. A district judge or a *viguier* was not a very conspicuous person, yet 17 judges and 10 (possibly 12) *viguiers* were made king's clerks

---

des Chartes, LII (1891), 259-64, 673-76; Strayer, *Gens de justice*, pp. 149-50. Pons also acted as a lawyer for Nogaret.

[24] Cazelles, pp. 314-22. By the time of Philip V we find formal appointments of men as king's clerks; cf. A.N., JJ 54A, nos. 45, 47, 94, 129.

or king's knights.[25] On the other hand, the 38 local revenue collectors who were called king's clerks (very few nobles engaged in this work) were in closer contact with Paris than southern judges and may have been recommended by officials in the central financial administration.

These titles were not conferred lightly. Only about half of the *juges-mages* were king's clerks or king's knights. What is even more surprising, some seneschals and *baillis* of noble birth never became king's knights. At the other extreme were men who had the title but who did little or no work for the king, such as Guillaume de Chanac, who may have helped to impose one tax but who does not appear again in royal service. Guillaume should have been a good choice; he was related to the Maumont family, many of whom were king's clerks or king's knights, and he was a *légiste*.[26] Philip the Fair liked to have plenty of lawyers in reserve, but he received little help from this one. On the whole, however, naming men as king's knights and king's clerks was a successful way of recruiting and retaining officials of high quality. The promotion rate for these men was unusually high. At the lower level of local office, where the overall rate of promotion was only about 1 percent, king's clerks and king's knights had about a 33 percent chance of promotion. Clearly they were a carefully selected group.

There remain some cases in which patronage or appointment by local agents of the king played a part, but in which promotion was so rapid that Philip himself must have intervened directly in order to speed up the normal pattern of advancement. Some of Philip's most influential officials—Pierre Flote, Biche and Mouche, Guillaume de Nogaret—fall into this category. These men had several things in common. All came from regions outside the normal recruiting area for royal officials. All were given unusual authority in the central government. And all were selected for rapid advancement during the crises caused by the Anglo-French war of 1294-1297.

The last point is probably the most important. In Chapter I it was suggested that Philip began to develop a policy of his own during the early 1290s, a policy of strongly asserting royal rights against the Church and against his greatest vassals, the king of

[25] Strayer, "Viscounts and Viguiers," pp. 247-48; *Gens de justice*, pp. 37-38 and Appendix.
[26] A.N., JJ 42A, no number, fols. 91-91v, JJ 48, no. 221, fol. 132, JJ 50, no. 52, fol. 38.

England and the count of Flanders. He had retained his father's administrative staff, but he was not close to his father's advisers. He must have felt that he needed advice and support, especially as the war against England proved to be more expensive and less profitable than he had hoped. Drastic financial measures had to be taken and difficult decisions had to be made. This is the point at which Philip would feel that he needed new men who would help him to carry out his far-reaching and sometimes dangerous policies.

For purely financial problems, the obvious course was to turn to the Italians. Philip may have been aware that his adversary, Edward I, was being financed by the Riccardi. In any case, he would have known about the activities of the Italian bankers in Paris and in the county of Champagne. He certainly had to find men who could handle the vastly increased revenues and expenditures of the French crown. Why he selected the Guidi (Biche and Mouche) for this task is not entirely clear. Perhaps they had been more honest than some of the other Italians. Renier Accorre, for example, who had been receiver of Champagne, was fined and imprisoned in 1293.[27] Biche and Mouche, who were already working for the king in 1289,[28] never lost his confidence. They were general receivers by 1291 and, for a brief period in 1295, Treasurers of France.[29] Their overall control of French finance ended with the establishment of the Treasury of the Louvre at the end of 1295,[30] but they remained trusted servants and advisers of the king until they died (in 1306 and 1307, respectively). They were frequently employed as ambassadors, and they helped to organize the attack on Boniface VIII at Anagni.

Apparently Philip valued above all else the organizing ability of the Guidi. The Guidi bank, which was staffed with relatives and dependents of the two brothers,[31] was a power in itself, and

[27] On Renier see Henri d'Arbois de Jubainville, *Histoire des ducs et comtes de Champagne*, 7 vols. (Troyes, 1859-1869), IV, pt. 2, pp. 466-68; Ozanam, p. 343; and *C.R.*, II, nos. 15281, 15299. He had been receiver of Champagne from 1274 to 1288.

[28] A.N., J 938, no. 23.

[29] Mignon, nos. 2065, 2092; *Ord.*, I, 326.

[30] Borrelli de Serres, *Recherches sur divers services publics du XIIIe au XVIIe siècle*, 3 vols. (Paris, 1895-1909), III, 15-20.

[31] Many agents of Biche and Mouche are mentioned in Mignon; see nos. 534, 1138, 1356, 2061, 2099, 2102, 2109, etc. Their brother Colin (or Nicolo) was apparently not active in France after the 1290s, but their nephews Thotus and Vanna Guidi remained in royal service for many years (Mignon, nos. 847, 1979, 1980; *C.R.*, II, no. 17210; *J.T.C.*, col. 16, n. 2).

Biche and Mouche were able to secure the cooperation of most of the Lombards doing business in France (for example, the Falconieri).[32] When the king needed financial agents in the provinces,[33] loans or tallages from the Lombards,[34] or taxes on Italian trade,[35] he turned to Biche and Mouche. Once the crisis caused by the outbreak of war in 1294 had been eased, the king was able to build up his own corps of financial administrators and therefore had less need of the Italians. The rapid rise of Biche and Mouche had been tied to the first great emergency of the reign; they played a lesser, though still significant, role in the next crisis, the confrontation with Boniface VIII.

Pierre Flote was a younger son of a noble family of Dauphiné, but he also had close connections with the Aicelins of Auvergne. According to an old tradition, the great lawyer Gilles Aicelin was a nephew of Pierre; certainly the two were related in some fashion. Gilles was the brother of a cardinal (Hugh Aicelin), a councillor of Philip the Fair by 1288, and archbishop of Narbonne by 1290.[36] He was obviously in a position to recommend Pierre Flote to the king. Pierre had shown his ability as a lawyer and councillor of the dauphin of Viennois from 1283 to 1289; Philip may have known something of his work there, since he was already interested in acquiring Lyon, which bordered on Dauphiné. In any case, in 1289 Philip bought Pierre's services by giving him the castle and lordship of Ravel in Auvergne,[37] a holding that was very close to the Aicelin lands. Pierre rose rapidly in the king's service. He sat in the Parlement of Toulouse in 1291 and was a king's knight by 1293, when he was one of the officials sent to Agen to summon the king of England to appear at Paris.[38] He played an important role in providing men and supplies for the war in Aquitaine.[39] But he reached the peak of his power only

[32] *J.T.P.*, nos. 275, 281, 397, 599, etc.

[33] Mignon, nos. 101, 103, 106, 107, 2054, 2059, 2066, 2078, 2084, etc.

[34] Ibid., nos. 2073, 2076; *Olim*, III, 336; Frantz Funck-Brentano, "Document pour servir à l'histoire des relations de la France et l'Allemagne," *Revue historique*, XXXIX (1889), 333.

[35] *Ord.*, I, 326.   [36] Pegues, pp. 90-92.

[37] Actually, Philip gave Pierre a rent of 250 l.t. a year, which was immediately exchanged for the lordship of Ravel. Philip III had bought Ravel in 1283 for 1,220 l.(t.?). *C.R.*, III, nos. 28723, 28779.

[38] Pegues, pp. 88-89; *Olim*, II, 13, 19.

[39] In December 1293 the seneschal of Périgord-Querey wrote the king that "circa munitionem et apparatum senescallie mee insisto vigilanti animo, prout possum, et juxta consilium domini P. Flote., qui procul dubio ferventi animo anhelat et incessanter intendit ac studet summopere ad cus-

in the confused period that followed the end of major military operations against the English. The threat to cancel royal taxes on the Church, posed by the bull *Clericis laicos*, had to be met; a truce with England had to be arranged; negotiations to ward off a war with Flanders had to be undertaken. Flote was deeply involved in all these affairs and proved especially successful in dealing with the pope. He was rewarded by being made Keeper of the Seals (in effect, chancellor) in April 1298. In this capacity he was primarily responsible for the accusations against Bishop Bernard Saisset and for the propaganda war against Boniface VIII that followed Saisset's arrest. He was still Keeper of the Seals when he was killed in the battle of Courtrai in 1302.

Nogaret's career was somewhat more normal than those of the Guidi or of Pierre Flote. He was not a foreigner; he was well known, at least in his own province, and he had obtained some training in a middle-level job. But even Nogaret was promoted very rapidly—much more rapidly, for example, than Marigny, who began as a very minor official in the queen's household and received his first important position only after six (possibly even nine) years of service. The difference probably lies in the fact that Marigny's career began only after the king had found a group of capable assistants and presumably no longer felt a pressing need for new men.

Nogaret had to overcome more obstacles than most of his colleagues. He was not noble; his family was so undistinguished that it is impossible to be entirely sure of his birthplace or his relationship to other men of the same name.[40] His enemies claimed, probably falsely, that his father had been condemned for heresy, but the accusation would have been pointless if the family had been well known. Nevertheless, if undistinguished, the family was not poor; there was enough money to send Guillaume to the University of Montpellier, where he pursued the long course of study that led to a doctorate in law. Nogaret must have done well; by 1287 he was a member of the Faculty of Law at Montpellier. This was an eminent group of men,[41] and Nogaret

---

todiendum utilitatem et honorem regie majestatis . . ." (*Olim*, II, 24). For examples of his activity see *C.R.*, I, nos. 7681, 7699, 7700, 7730-32, and *H.L.*, x, col. 296.

[40] Louis Thomas, "La vie privée de Guillaume de Nogaret," *Annales du Midi*, XVI (1904), 161-98, was fairly sure that he was born in S. Félix de Caraman, as was Robert Holtzmann, p. 10. But direct proof is lacking.

[41] Strayer, *Gens de justice*, pp. 15-17, 56.

must have been a fairly conspicuous figure in Lower Languedoc. Like other professors of law, he was asked to take part in arbitrations and negotiations of contracts, some of which touched on the interests of the royal government. One of these affairs was the sale in 1293 by the bishop of Maguelonne of his small part of the town of Montpellier to Philip the Fair. Nogaret did not initiate this transaction; rather, the bishop (Bérenger Frédol) seems to have wanted to rid himself of a holding that involved him in endless bickering with the king of Majorca, who held the larger part of the town. But the sale did go through quickly and smoothly; if this was owing to Nogaret's skill, the king had reason to be gratified.[42] Still, there was no need to be excessively grateful. Philip did not gain full control of the commerce and wealth of the town, and officials of the king of Majorca resisted every effort of the French government to increase its authority in the section they administered. The acquisition of Lyon a few years later was a far more important addition to the kingdom of France, and the man who was largely responsible for the annexation, Thibaud de Vassalieu, never received an important office.

By the standards of the period Nogaret was sufficiently rewarded by receiving the title of king's clerk and the office of *juge-mage* of Beaucaire. This was a normal appointment; a good many professors of law (including two of Nogaret's colleagues on the Faculty of Montpellier) became *juges-mages*, though few of them kept the position very long. It was an honorable post, but it paid very little (only 160 l.t. a year in Beaucaire);[43] a good lawyer could make much more in private practice. Nogaret was not unique in holding the office for less than two years (from 1293 to the fall of 1295); he was unique in being called to a high position in Paris after so short an apprenticeship. Even Guillaume de Plaisians, who had the advantage of having been a student under Nogaret, had to serve more than two years as a *juge-mage* before his old master could bring him to Paris.

Why Philip suddenly decided that he wanted Nogaret as one of his advisers is hard to determine. The king was certainly trying to build up a staff of men with legal training—Gilles Aicelin, Pierre de Belleperche, Pierre Flote—to help defend his widening claims to authority over all men and all lands in the realm, but there were many men at Montpellier or at Toulouse who were

---

[42] Alexandre Germain, *Histoire de la commune de Montpellier*, 3 vols. (Montpellier, 1851), II, 96 ff.; Holtzmann, p. 14.

[43] *C.R.*, I, no. 14008.

as qualified as Nogaret. Some scholars have thought that Flote asked for Nogaret, and this is not impossible. Flote may well have known or heard of Nogaret, since they had both been practicing lawyers in the south, but there is no evidence to show that Flote made the recommendation. Alfonse de Rouvrai, who was seneschal of Beaucaire from 1292 to 1295, may have been consulted. He was well regarded by the king; he was later appointed seneschal of Carcassonne and served as governor of Navarre for many years. He must have had a good opinion of Nogaret, since he had appointed, or at least accepted, him as *juge-mage*. It is also possible that Brémond de Montferrier had some influence. Brémond had been a colleague of Nogaret's on the Faculty of Law and had served briefly as *juge-mage* (1287-1291). He was probably the most eminent lawyer in Montpellier at the time, and it seems clear that efforts were being made to attach him permanently to the service of the king.[44] He preferred to remain in private practice, but he may have softened his refusal by recommending an able substitute.

The most likely patron of all, however, was Bérenger Frédol, bishop of Maguelonne. It is certain that he later secured promotion for Pons d'Aumelas, and he could have done as much for Nogaret. He had known Nogaret at least since 1292, when he intervened with the Faculty of Law to secure special treatment for Pons d'Aumelas on his doctoral examination,[45] and he may have been as grateful to Nogaret for facilitating the sale of his Montpellier holdings as the king was for their acquisition. Moreover, a Raimond Frédol was a professor of law at Montpellier at the time of the Aumelas examination,[46] and he could have told the bishop about the technical abilities of his colleague Nogaret. A recommendation by Bérenger Frédol would have carried a great deal of weight.

Once Nogaret reached Paris, he had much the same sort of career as Pierre Flote. He was employed as a commissioner to enforce royal rights, especially in Champagne. He sat in the Parlement and in Council. By 1299 he was king's knight instead of king's clerk,[47] as happened to several other lawyers who preferred a secular to an ecclesiastical career.[48] He aided Pierre Flote

---

[44] Strayer, *Gens de justice*, p. 55.   [45] See note 23 above.

[46] Alexandre Germain, ed., *Cartulaire de l'Université de Montpellier*, 2 vols. (Montpellier, 1890-1912), I, no. 22.

[47] Holtzmann, p. 16.

[48] A somewhat similar case is that of Aimeri du Cros, who was at first

in the dispute over Bernard Saisset; when Flote was killed, he took charge of the propaganda war against Boniface VIII and led the attack on the pope at Anagni. He continued to press charges against the memory of the pope until the final settlement of the case in 1312, but this was far from being his only occupation. He was responsible for the expulsion of the Jews and the confiscation of Jewish property in 1306; he took the lead in pressing the accusations that led to the suppression of the Order of the Temple; as Keeper of the Seals from September 1307 to his death in April 1313 he was involved in all important internal and external affairs of the kingdom. The peak of his power came in the period between the death of Flote in 1302 and the rise of Marigny to high favor with the king (roughly 1307-1308). But Nogaret had been a royal official during all the great crises of the reign, and in some of those crises he played the leading role.

To repeat, most of Philip's high officials came from the old royal domain. On the other hand, the most conspicuous and the most influential advisers of the king were outsiders; Italians and men of the south in the troubled years from 1294 to 1303, and the Norman Marigny in the last, and almost as difficult, years of the reign. Here is one more proof that Philip controlled his government. A self-perpetuating bureaucracy would not have chosen a Flote or a Marigny as its leader, and a bureaucracy that dominated the king would not have accepted his rapid promotion of men who had not come up through the ranks.

The Rewards of Office

How did Philip the Fair persuade so many men to serve him? In some cases, doubtless, there was more compulsion than persuasion, especially when it was a matter of finding local collectors of taxes or tenths from the Church. The thousands of men who collected the aid for knighting Louis (X) in 1313-1314 cannot all have been volunteers.[1] But the professionals, the men who served for 10, 20, or 30 years, did so of their own free will. It would have been unwise, even if it had not been impossible, to force

---

a king's clerk and a district judge and later became a king's knight and seneschal of Carcassonne (Strayer, *Gens de justice*, p. 11).

---

[1] There were 322 collectors in the viscounty of Paris, excluding the city itself (B.N., ms. Clairembault 228, pp. 929 ff.).

a man to take an office of any importance. There must have been inducements, both financial and psychological.

The most obvious financial inducement was a salary. The pay scale for royal officials was no higher than it had been in St. Louis's day, but it was still high enough to be attractive. A skilled workman in the 1290s could make 12 to 18 d.t. a day.[2] If he worked 360 days a year (which of course he did not), he would make 18 to 27 l.t. a year. Lower-ranking royal officials were paid on a daily basis, but every day in the year was counted.[3] Even those who had as little as 2 s.t. a day were far better off than a workman, who would be lucky if he drew wages for 250 days in a year. Higher officials were paid on a yearly basis: 60 to 100 l.t. a year for viscounts, 100 to 150 l.t. a year for *juges-mages*, 365 to 700 l.t. a year for *baillis* and seneschals.[4] A salary of 700 l.t. was literally a princely income; the king could acquire the friendship and support of a man like the count of Luxembourg for a *fief-rente* of 500 l. a year.[5] At the other extreme were castellans of small places at 2 s.t. a day, a few *viguiers* of unimportant dis-

[2] For example, in Toulouse in 1294 carpenters were paid 16 d.t. or 18 d.t. a day and roofers were paid 18 d.t. a day, but ordinary laborers were paid only 6 d.t.; see *C.R.*, I, nos. 9738, 9759, 9760, 9765, 9771.

[3] A sergeant-at-arms in Sens was paid 5 s. a day for the terms of Candlemas and Ascension 1305—228 days, including all holidays (*C.R.*, I, no. 5235); wages in the *bailliage* of Caen from 1 May to 1 November 1297 were paid for 184 days (no. 7081). Wages for various minor officials in Toulouse run from 5 s. 6 d.t. a day to 8 d.t. a day (nos. 9825-33), the total per day being 4 l. 20 d.t., for the year, 1,490 l. 13 s. 4 d.t. Everyone was paid for 365 days.

[4] See Strayer, "Viscounts and Viguiers," p. 219, and *Gens de justice*, pp. 32-33, for viscounts and judges. In 1299 *baillis* drew only 16 s.p. or 20 s.t. a day (*C.R.*, I, nos. 2824, 3079); wages were the same in 1305 (nos. 4388, 4995, 5320, 6331). The *bailli* of Caen, who had had 400 or 500 l.t. a year under Philip III, was cut back to 365 l.t. in 1292 (Strayer, *Administration of Normandy under St. Louis* [Cambridge, Mass., 1932], p. 120, and *C.R.*, I, no. 6889). The seneschal of Poitou had 500 l.t. a year in 1294 (*C.R.*, I, no. 7454); the seneschal of Saintonge had 365 l.t. (no. 7651), which was later raised to 500 l.t. (no. 7865); the seneschal of Toulouse had 700 l.t. a year, including "robes" (no. 10232); the seneschal of Rouergue had 400 l.t. (no. 10497). In 1299 the seneschal of Toulouse again was paid 700 l.t. (no. 12336), and the seneschal of Rouergue, 400 l.t. (no. 12626). In 1303 the seneschal of Beaucaire received 600 l.t., plus 100 l.t. for "robes" (no. 14007).

[5] Bryce D. Lyon, *From Fief to Indenture* (Cambridge, Mass., 1957), p. 213. The dauphin of Vienne also was given a fief of 500 l. Of course, both men had other sources of income, but 500 l. a year was enough to influence their policies.

tricts who might draw as little as 20 or 30 l.t. a year, and judges and procurators in areas where the king had little direct jurisdiction, who were paid 5 to 30 l.t. a year.[6] These poorly paid positions, however, were usually part-time jobs, as is shown by the fact that a man might hold several judgeships at the same time.[7] Some of them were sinecures that did not require residence. Marigny was made castellan of Issoudun in 1298 to supplement his very small salary (18 l.p. a year) in the queen's household;[8] he certainly never performed any duties at Issoudun. And even a castellan who did reside in his castle had free lodging, and probably free board.

Salaries in Paris are more difficult to determine. They were lower when an official was with the king, because he was fed (and often lodged) at the king's expense;[9] they rose when the official was not at court. The men who were based in Paris were frequently sent on missions throughout France and on embassies to foreign countries, for which they received travel allowances instead of their regular salaries. Finally, the *gens des comptes* often drew on their salary accounts as they needed money, with-

---

[6] See *C.R.*, I, nos. 2552, 5924, 6947, 8215, 9829, 12833-34, for castellans at 2 s.t. a day; many had only 1 s. or even only 6 d.t. a day (nos. 10816-17, 12836, 12837). See *C.R.* I, nos. 11643, 13653, 13694, 13849, 12797, for *viguiers* at 20 to 30 l.t., and one at 18 d.t. a day; nos. 13760, 13676, 13851, for judges paid 5 or 10 l.t. a year; nos. 12322-25, for procurators at 25 l.t. a year. Receivers in the south were better paid than other low-ranking officials. In Toulouse they had 5 s. 6 d.t. a day in 1294 and 1299 (*C.R.*, I, nos. 9827, 11907). Elsewhere the usual rate was 5 s.t. a day (Auvergne, *C.R.*, I, nos. 8834, 8981; Carcassonne, no. 12810), which was rounded off to 100 l.t. a year in Auvergne in 1299 (no. 10695) and in Beaucaire in 1303 (no. 14009). In 1307 it was ruled that the regular pay for a receiver in Carcassonne was to be 5 s.t. a day (*C.R.*, II, no. 16510 and n.). But in 1299 a receiver in Paris was paid only 18 d.p., or a little less than 2 s.t. a day (*C.R.* I, nos. 1211, 1604). The receiver of Champagne, who was responsible for four *bailliages*, was paid 500 l.t. a year in 1317 (Ozanam, p. 340), but this was an exception, perhaps because the office had been established by the last count of Champagne and not by the king.

[7] Aimeri du Cros held four judgeships at one time (Strayer, *Gens de justice*, pp. 115-16); Hugues de la Porte was a royal procurator and at the same time judge of Calvisson and Lunel (ibid., p. 29).

[8] Favier, *Marigny*, pp. 57-58.

[9] For example, Guillaume Courteheuse, king's knight, had to explain in 1309 that he was entitled to his full salary of 10 s.p. a day for work in the Parlement even when he was with the king, "quoniam non comedit in curia nec aliquem habuit ibi" (*J.T.P.*, no. 5996). Pierre de Blanot was paid 10 s.p. a day for work in the Parlement of 1306, except for 41 days when he drew only 4 s.p. because he was "cum rege" (ibid., no. 5976).

out stating the total for the year.[10] Nevertheless, there is enough information to determine the base salaries for a wide range of officials.

The most striking fact about Paris salaries is that most of them were no higher than those of provincial officials. The Treasurers were paid 600 l.p. a year in 1297, 1298, and 1299.[11] This would be 750 l.t., only slightly more than the salary of the seneschal of Toulouse. Pierre Flote, Keeper of the Seals, was paid only 500 l.t. in 1298 and 1299,[12] no more than the seneschal of Poitou. At the height of his power, Marigny in 1314 received 2 l.p. a day—730 l.p., or over 900 l.t. a year[13]—but Marigny was a special case. Renaud Barbou, a member of the Council in 1299, received 500 l.p. for the year, as did Jean de Montigny (or Montagny), a permanent member of the Parlement.[14] Etienne de Chanlistre, Robert de Resignies, Ansel de l'Isle, Raoul de Breuilli, and Pierre de Blanot, all listed as members of the Council, were paid only 10 s.p. a day in 1299—182 l. 10 s.p., if they worked through the year.[15] This was less than a bailli's salary. Betin Caucinel and Jean Dimer, who held the immensely important positions of Masters of the Monies, received 200 l.p. a year, still less than the pay of a bailli.[16] Even Oudard de Chambly, a favorite and a chamberlain of the king, had only 20 s.t. a day (365 l.t. a year), the exact equivalent of the usual salary of a bailli.[17] (It is true that he was promised this pay for life, which is more than a bailli could expect.) Curiously enough, the highest salary recorded in the Journal of the Treasury was the 3 l.p. a day (1,095 l.p. a year) paid to Thibaud, bishop of Dol.[18] Thibaud never had the fame of a Flote

[10] Ibid., nos. 627, 1223, 1324, 2273.

[11] Ibid., nos. 616, 2776. The rate was the same in 1315-1316 (Fawtier, ed., *Comptes du Trésor*, nos. 785, 786, 792).

[12] *J.T.P.*, nos. 1903, 3748. He also had a pension of 200 l.t. a year from the Dauphin of Viennois.

[13] Ibid., no. 6080. Note that this was for service out of court; he would have been paid less when with the king.

[14] Ibid., nos. 2462, 4127.

[15] Ibid., nos. 1928, 2181, 2255, 2433, 4065, 4084, 4457. No. 4877 shows that these men were knights of the Council, 1297-1300.

[16] Ibid., nos. 635, 4716 (250 l.t.–200 l.p.), 5435; Fawtier, ed., *Comptes du Trésor*, no. 360.

[17] *J.T.P.*, no. 3485.

[18] Ibid., nos. 3484, 4041; Fawtier, ed., *Comptes du Trésor*, no. 84. Thibaud held the seals in 1296. The count of Saint-Pol, Butler of France, drew 25 s.p. a day when with the king and 3 l.p. a day when out of court in 1296 (Fawtier, ed., *Comptes du Trésor*, no. 439). By 1322 Pierre de Chalon, the

or a Marigny, but he was an elder statesman and a long-time servant of Philip III. He knew all the precedents, and he could keep any part of the machinery of government going (for example, by running the Chancery when Guillaume de Crépy was absent or ill). Thibaud, however, received none of the gifts, over and above salary, that were bestowed on younger men who had a closer personal relationship with the king.

The vast majority of the men who served in Paris were paid only 5 s.p. a day if they were clerks, and 10 s.p. a day if they were knights. The difference was based on the fact that almost all the clerks had benefices that would bring their annual income up to or above that of the knights. But it is striking to see men who sat in Parlement or who acted as *enquêteurs* or general collectors of taxes being paid at a rate no better than that of Norman viscounts or southern judges. Philippe le Convers (or de Villepreux), godson and favorite of the king, Richard Leneveu, later bishop of Béziers, Pierre de Latilly, later Keeper of the Seals and bishop of Châlons-sur-Marne—all drew only 5 s.p. a day at a time when they were making decisions that affected hundreds of the king's subjects or collecting and disbursing thousands of pounds.[19] Pierre de Belleperche was paid 10 s.p. a day,[20] unlike the other clerks, but he was a famous lawyer and could certainly have made even more in private practice. As for the knights, they could have made almost as much by serving in the army (10 s.t. a day instead of 10 s.p., a 25 percent difference), and they would have had almost as good a chance of receiving gifts and pensions. An income of 225 l.t. a year was larger than that of many minor nobles, but it was not riches.

The great advantage of serving in Paris was not the salary but the increased chance of receiving gifts, pensions, and (for the clerks) benefices. Provincial officials were not completely barred from such rewards, especially if they became involved in military operations, but the rain of favors was heavier in Paris. Norman viscounts and southern judges may have been paid as well as men who worked in the Parlement of Paris, but they seldom received pensions or gifts.[21] The *baillis* and seneschals fared a little better,

---

expert on important and export dues, had 3 l.t. a day for life (P. Gras, "Les évêques de Chalon," *Mémoires de la Société pour l'histoire du droit et des institutions des anciens pays bourguignons* . . . , xv [1953], 20).

[19] *J.T.P.*, nos. 2466, 3182, 4541.   [20] Ibid., no. 2383.

[21] Some royal procurators in Languedoc received pensions of 20 to 50 l.t. a year, and one was given confiscated lands worth 700 l.t. (Strayer,

especially if they had served in the provinces for long periods. Thus Pierre Saimel, who had begun as *bailli* of Amiens in 1281 and who died as *bailli* of Tours in 1303, was given a life pension of 100 l.t. in 1298 while he was *bailli* of Rouen.[22] Gautier Bardin, a *bailli* for over 30 years, was given an estate and a life pension of 100 l.t.[23] Alfonse de Rouvrai, seneschal of Beaucaire and then longtime governor of Navarre, was granted a life pension of 300 l.t. in 1300.[24] (Note that this gift came after Nogaret had gone to Paris; it reinforces the suggestion that Alfonse, as seneschal of Beaucaire, had recommended his *juge-mage* to the king; Nogaret would then have been repaying a favor.) Jean d'Arrablay, who was a seneschal from 1291 to 1313, received a pension of 200 l.t. before 1298, but he promptly sold it to a chamberlain.[25] Somewhat later, perhaps after Jean had been called to Paris in 1313, Philip gave him another pension of 300 l.t.[26]

Such gifts, however, were minor compared with what the king's servants in Paris could expect. They not only received numerous grants of money and pensions, but they were also in a position to have these gifts converted into landed estates, often on very advantageous terms. There were times when it seems that the chief business of everyone at court was exchanging property with one another and with the king. There is no need to repeat Thomas's description of the way in which Nogaret built up his lordship in the region of Beaucaire[27] or Favier's masterly account of the formation of Marigny's even larger lordship in Normandy;[28] suffice it to say that both men were very skillful in trading pensions for land. Flote was persuaded to join the royal bureaucracy by the gift of a pension of 250 l.t., which he promptly exchanged for the seigneury of Ravel in Auvergne.[29] This was only a beginning. The dauphin of Vienne had given

---

Gens de justice, pp. 34-37). Many judges were able to acquire land on advantageous terms, but they did not receive gifts or pensions.

[22] Charles-Victor Langlois, "Registres perdus des archives de la Chambre des Comptes de Paris," *Notices et extraits*, XL (1916), App. II ("Le livre rouge"), no. 673.

[23] *C.R.*, I, no. 895; B.N., ms. fr. 26961.

[24] *J.T.P.*, no. 4759.

[25] Langlois, "Registres perdus," App. II, nos. 28, 177; *J.T.P.*, nos. 916, 1851, 2715.

[26] Langlois, "Registres perdus," App. II, no. 902; Fawtier, ed., *Comptes du Trésor*, no. 1053.

[27] See Thomas, pp. 161-68.   [28] Favier, *Marigny*, pp. 33-53.

[29] *C.R.*, III, nos. 28723, 28779.

him a pension of 200 l.t. by 1298.[30] After his untimely death in 1302 his son (also a royal official) was given 400 l.(t.?) a year, in recognition of the elder Flote's services.[31] It is very likely that this was a continuation of a pension to his father. In any case, by 1317 Guillaume Flote was so wealthy that he was included in the list of a dozen or so men who were suspected of having taken undue advantage of the king's generosity.[32]

Some less well-known officials did equally well for themselves. Etienne de Suisy, a very active royal clerk who became Keeper of the Seals after Flote's death, was given a valuable manor and a pension of 500 l.t. When he became a cardinal in 1305, all his gifts from the king were commuted into a pension of 1,000 l.p.[33] The chamberlains, who were closely attached to the person of the king, were also generously rewarded. The Chambly family, especially, acquired almost as much land as Marigny. They also figure prominently on the list of those whose acquisitions were investigated in 1317.[34] Philippe le Convers, the converted Jew who was the protégé and godson of Philip the Fair, also profited from his close personal relationship with the king. He had known Philip at least since 1285, and he had been educated at Philip's expense. His wages for serving in the Parlement in 1299 were only 5 s.p. a day,[35] but he accumulated benefices and acquired rents on the Treasury that made him a rich man. It must be said that he worked hard for his income; he was the Council's expert on forest affairs, and he spent much time in the field. But he was also one of the most successful land speculators in the court, building up an estate at Léry in Normandy that was worth over 1,000 l.t. a year. (The exact value is doubtful, for when he sold Léry to the queen in 1318, he received lands, rents, and cash that would have brought in much more than 1,000 l.—but he was accused of having been paid twice.)[36]

Finally, to mention a few officials who never became very prominent: Gilles de Remi, a royal notary, had a pension of 50 l.t.; Geoffroi du Temple, king's clerk and collector of Church taxes, had a pension of 30 l.t.; Jean de Lillers, a Treasury clerk, was given a pension of 100 l.t.; Etienne de Chanlistre, a knight who served in several meetings of the Parlement, drew 40 l.p. a

---

[30] *J.T.P.*, nos. 1903, 3748.
[31] Langlois, "Registres perdus," App. II, no. 349.
[32] Ibid., pp. 107-8.   [33] Ibid., App. II, nos, 813, 819, 825.
[34] Ibid., pp. 107-8, 111-12.   [35] *J.T.P.*, no. 2466.
[36] Pegues, pp. 132-34, 137-38.

year; Jean de St. Just, a Treasury clerk who later was a Master of
Accounts, had 100 l.t. a year.[37] Other names could be cited, but
these examples are enough to show that minor officials, as well as
the great men of the Council, had a reasonable chance of receiving pensions in addition to their salaries.

Philip the Fair seems to have felt that the salary scale at Paris
was a little too low. In addition to granting pensions, he made
cash gifts from time to time to men who had rendered special
services. For example, Nogaret was given 200 l.p. in 1298, and
Jean de Montigny and Renaud Barbou, both hard-working members of the Parlement, were given 200 l.p. apiece in the same
year.[38] Pierre de Blanot, also a useful member of the Parlement,
received 300 l.t. in 1301, as did the eminent lawyer, Pierre de
Belleperche.[39] The easiest way to reward clerks was to give them
an extra benefice, but if one were not available, then a single gift
or a temporary pension could be used as a substitute. Thus
Geoffroi du Plessis was given 300 l.t. a year in 1307 until he was
suitably provided for,[40] and Guillaume Bonnet, who was to become bishop of Bayeux in 1306, received a temporary pension of
300 l.p. a year shortly before his promotion.[41] Usually, however,
it was not difficult to find additional benefices for clerks who
enjoyed the king's favor. The case of Philip's old tutor, Guillaume
d'Ercuis, who drew about 783 l.p. from his four benefices, has
already been mentioned.[42] It is not surprising that Philippe le
Convers was named to so many prebends and archdeaconries that
it is difficult to tell exactly what positions he held at any one
time.[43] But the best example of all is Pierre de Chalon, the man
who established the French customs service.[44] Not only did he
draw a pension of 500 l.t. a year, but he was also archdeacon of
Autun and canon of Langres, Chalon, Mâcon, Beauvais, Lyon,
and Aigueperse.[45] It was no great gain for him when, in his old
age, he became bishop of Chalon.

[37] Langlois, "Registres perdus," App. II, nos. 254, 432, 732; *J.T.P.*, nos.
399, 1518, 4760.
[38] *J.T.P.*, nos. 3368, 4315.   [39] Ibid., nos. 5444, 5529.
[40] Ibid., no. 5907. Philippe de Mornay, a king's clerk who eventually
became a member of the Grand'Chambre, had a pension of 90 l.p. a year
"donec provideatur" in 1305 (*C.R.*, I, no. 5660).
[41] Langlois, "Registres perdus," App. II, no. 693.
[42] See above, Chapter I, p. 8.
[43] Pegues, p. 134; *J.T.P.*, col. 109, n. 3.
[44] See above, note 18.
[45] Langlois, "Registres perdus," App. II, nos. 1066, 1067. According to
Gras, p. 20, he was also dean of Beaune and treasurer of Avallon.

Considering that the clergy formed the largest group of Philip's high officials, it is easy to see how important to the king was control of Church benefices. The prospect of receiving lucrative archdeaconries and prebends drew able men into royal service, men who would not have been attracted by the relatively modest salaries that were offered for work in the Parlement, the Chancery, and the financial departments. For those who distinguished themselves, there was always the prospect of a bishopric or even a cardinalate. Over one-third of the clergy who served in high office reached episcopal rank. This was not always financially advantageous, since a bishop normally drew no salary from the king. But exceptions could be made, as in the case of the bishop of Dol, who received the abnormally high salary of 3 l.p. a day to supplement the meager income of his diocese. Other bishoprics were better endowed, and episcopal status conferred benefits that could not be measured in monetary terms. A bishop ranked with the greater nobles of the kingdom. Pierre de Latilly, who was one of Philip's chief financial agents and who succeeded Nogaret as Keeper of the Seals, stood even higher; as bishop of Châlons-sur-Marne he was one of the peers of the realm. Moreover, although all royal officials of any standing were able to obtain some favors for their relatives, bishops had unusual opportunities to aid their families and dependents. For example, Pierre de Mornay, bishop of Orléans (later Auxerre), was one of Philip the Fair's most competent diplomats. Of his three nephews, Etienne became the Chancellor of Charles of Valois and Keeper of the Seals under Louis X, Pierre was abbot of St. Laumer, and Philip, who was an archdeacon in the diocese of Soissons, served in the Parlement in various capacities from 1309 to 1325.[46] And it should not be forgotten that Flote, Nogaret, and Marigny were all aided in their early careers by prelates who were their relatives or their friends.

What has been said of the bishops applies to other royal officials; financial awards alone do not fully explain their willingness to devote long years of arduous labor to the service of the king. Philip's agents were accused of many things, but seldom of being lazy. The lesser men had the tedious work of preparing the innumerable letters, court records, accounts, and registers that were essential for all branches of the administration. The greater officials had to check through this mass of written material, discuss it in lengthy meetings, travel constantly through the kingdom to

---

[46] Pegues, pp. 121-23; *J.T.P.*, col. 879, n. 1.

make sure that the king's orders were being carried out, or go on embassies to foreign countries. We have a list of the documents that Nogaret and Plaisians had in their possession at the time of their deaths in 1313;[47] they concerned almost every aspect of royal government. Other high officials, such as Marigny and Latilly, must have had similar collections. One wonders when they found time to master these records when one looks at the frequent entries for their travel expenses—long and uncomfortable journeys to Flanders, to Languedoc, to Germany, and to Rome. It might be financially rewarding to build up a lordship at the king's expense, but few officials were able to relax and enjoy life on their country estates. Nogaret spent very little time at his seigneury of Tamarlet, and Flote was seldom in residence at Ravel. Marigny, whose Norman estates were close to Paris, probably visited his properties more frequently; at least he carried out a fairly elaborate building program at Mainneville, Plesis, and Ecouis.[48] But even Marigny spent most of his time at Paris or on missions for the king.

It is not surprising that many of these busy men died in office—Nogaret and Plaisians, Biche and Mouche, Oudart de la Neuville (councillor and member of the Parlement), Pierre Saimel, *bailli* of Tours, Philippe de Bois-Archambaud, seneschal of Beaucaire, Simon Briseteste, seneschal of Carcassonne, Guichard de Marzi, seneschal of Toulouse, or, to take the clearest case of a death caused by overwork, Raoul des Courjumelles, *juge-mage* of Beaucaire, who died shortly after completing, with extraordinary speed and accuracy, the great survey of royal and episcopal holdings in the Gévaudan.[49] Nor is it surprising that there were a number of early retirements. What is surprising is that so many men survived and that so many were willing to remain in office for three or four decades. Salaries and pensions, gifts and graft are not enough to account for these long professional careers. The psychic rewards of officeholding were great and should not be underestimated.

The most important psychic reward came from association, however tenuous, with the king. Some of the charisma of the French monarchy was imparted to anyone who served the king; outsiders were constantly reminded that these men were king's sergeants, king's valets (the first title given to Biche and Mouche), king's panetiers (for example, Géraud Chauchat, receiver of Au-

---

[47] Langlois, ed., "Papiers de Nogaret et Plaisians," pp. 211 ff.
[48] Favier, *Marigny*, pp. 49-53.   [49] Strayer, *Gens de justice*, p. 58.

vergne), *king's* clerks or knights, *king's* familiars or councillors. Men who had these titles were received with deference and respect; even the greatest nobles could not mistreat them with impunity. Since the vast majority of the king's servants were non-nobles, younger sons of nobles, or, at best, lords of petty seigneuries, this sharp rise in status was a strong attraction. It would have been the chief attraction if the higher status had been made hereditary. But Philip shared the social prejudices of the old aristocracy; he did not wish to dilute the ranks of the nobility. Compared with later kings, he ennobled comparatively few of his bourgeois officials, and he never even thought of giving his chief ministers the title of count or duke. (Think of what Marigny could have become under the Bourbons!) Again, although there were administrative families, sons did not automatically inherit their fathers' offices. They did have greater opportunities than other men, but they had to prove their ability. Thus the best way to preserve newly acquired high status was to build up the family estates, which explains the frantic scramble for land by officials at all levels of the bureaucracy. But this brings us back to the financial, not the psychic, rewards of service to the king.

Another incentive was the desire for power. This is a strong force; men have always been willing to sacrifice ease, comfort, and even wealth in order to achieve power. Philip's agents had the authority of the king behind them. They could give orders to counts and bishops; they could collect vast sums of money from all classes of society; they could investigate the activities and determine the rights of nobles, clergy, and communes. Their acts could be reversed only by higher officials or by the king himself. This was a heady experience for the commoners and petty nobles who comprised the majority of Philip's officials. It is not surprising that many of them became ruthless and arrogant. But the power lent to them by the king was returned to him with interest. Royal officials (with the possible exception of Marigny) were not trying to create independent islands of authority for themselves. Rather, they sought to please the king by increasing his income and extending his rights. If they succeeded in making the king more powerful, then he would have more power to delegate to them. Outright graft was not very common in the higher levels of the administration because large-scale corruption would have weakened the interlocking power structure on which everyone depended. The most oppressive acts of Philip's officials—Latilly's foray through Languedoc in 1297 to raise money by recovering alleged royal rights,[50] the manipulation of the coinage, the expulsion of the Jews, the attack on the Order of the Temple—were all for the king's profit and did not directly enrich his servants. Once the money was in the Treasury it might of course be diverted to the king's officers through sloppy accounting or through solicitations of gifts and pensions. But power was an end in itself, not an immediate source of wealth.

Some men seem to have accepted office in the government because it gave them an opportunity to use their professional talents at their highest level. This would be true of certain lawyers, such as Pierre de Belleperche and Gilles Aicelin, men who were primarily scholars but who had the urge (not unknown today) to see their theoretical knowledge put to practical use. It may have been true of some of the southern *juges-mages* who accepted the office only in their later years, after they had reached the top of their profession, men like Clément de Fraissé of Beaucaire or Gauvain des Bonsconseils of Toulouse.[51] It may even have been true of Nogaret and Plaisians. Certainly ambition was the main driving force for both men; nevertheless, both had a vision of a greater French state that was not shared by many of their contemporaries in the south. Nogaret was ready to "die for his fatherland"—not a common phrase in the early fourteenth century[52]—and Plaisians emphatically asserted that the king was sovereign over all men and all property in the realm.[53] If they really believed in these ideas, then their only place was in royal service.

Other officials left no such explicit statements of their beliefs, but it seems likely that a man with a taste for administration found himself happier governing a province rather than his own small lordship and that a man who had some skill in financial operations enjoyed dealing with the revenues of a kingdom rather than the income of a family business. Certainly the clerks who

[50] This mission produced an extraordinary number of complaints against Latilly's highhanded methods; see A.N., J 896, nos. 9, 25, 29, 34, J 1024, no. 38, J 1029, no. 2; J 1031, nos. 7, 8, J 1033, nos. 9, 10, 11; J 1034B, nos. 46, 47. Latilly's career, however, was not damaged; he became Keeper of the Seals and bishop of Châlons.

[51] Strayer, *Gens de justice*, pp. 59, 168.

[52] Dupuy, p. 297. On the newness of the idea see Ernst H. Kantorowicz, *The King's Two Bodies: A Study in Mediaeval Political Theology* (Princeton, 1957), pp. 232-72 ("Pro patria mori").

[53] "Mémoire relatif au paréage de 1307," ed. Abel Maisonobe, *Bulletin de la Société d'Agriculture, Industrie, Sciences et Arts du Département de la Lozère* (Mende, 1896), p. 521.

kept the records of the Chancery, the Parlement, and the Treasury took pride in their work; it was carefully done and checked and rechecked for accuracy. Even the little receipts prepared for soldiers receiving wages for service in the army were neat and legible documents. These clerks could be rewarded by promotion to higher office, but, promoted or not, they were professionals, not amateurs. They had an *esprit de corps* that led, later in the fourteenth century, to the establishment of the great "companies" of parlementarians and *gens des comptes*.

Finally, service to the monarch could bring the greatest reward of all, the hope of eternal salvation, coupled with the perpetuation of one's memory among men. Not all the money wheedled out of the king was spent in acquiring fine homes and valuable estates. A considerable amount was used to endow pious foundation. Marigny, perhaps the greediest of all the king's men, richly endowed his collegiate church at Ecouis.[54] Renaud Barbou the elder (*bailli* and then councillor under Philip the Fair) and Renaud Barbou the younger (also a *bailli*) gave even more to build and maintain a hospital for the blind at Chartres.[55] Philippe le Convers founded a hospital for the poor in his native village;[56] Pierre de Belleperche left an endowment that produced 175 l.t. rent for eight vicarages at Villeneuve-sur-Allier.[57]

Especially interesting are the colleges at Paris founded by officials of Philip the Fair. Queen Jeanne had set the example with the College of Navarre; Gilles Aicelin started what became an even more famous institution, the Collège de Montaigu.[58] Guillaume Bonnet, bishop of Bayeux, who had served in the Parlement and who was deeply involved in the affair of the Templars, founded the Collège de Bayeux.[59] Gui de Laon, treasurer of the Sainte Chapelle, who was often employed in financial administration, and Raoul de Presles, a king's clerk and lawyer, founded the Collège de Laon.[60] Raoul seems to have had a real interest in education; he revived, rebuilt, and gave a rent of 10 l.p. to the grammar school in his native village of Presles.[61] This is one of the earliest examples of an endowment for a secondary school. Geof-

---

[54] Favier, *Marigny*, p. 51.
[55] Carolus-Barré, "Baillis de Philippe III," pp. 156-57, 159.
[56] A.N., JJ 59, fol. 178v, no. 339, JJ 60, fol. 119, no. 186.
[57] A.N., JJ 44, fol. 68, no. 108.   [58] *Hist. litt.*, xxxii, 500.
[59] A.N., JJ 45, fol. 50, no. 66; *Gallia Christiana*, xi, col. 371.
[60] A.N., JJ 49, fol. 119v, no. 257. See also Pegues, p. 160.
[61] A.N., JJ 52, fol. 3v, no. 10.

froi du Plessis, often used as an ambassador to Popes Boniface VIII and Clement V, also accumulated revenues to endow a college,[62] though it did not take form until after Philip's death.

These are only the most striking among the numerous examples of pious gifts. Clerks were donors more often than laymen, even though there were no more clerks than laymen in the upper levels of the bureaucracy. But the clerks did not have sons and daughters to provide for and could afford to be more generous.[63] It is also true that most of the gifts were no larger than those regularly made by any decent person of moderate wealth, but it is interesting to note that this convention was followed by the employees of a supposedly anticlerical administration. No more than their master did Philip's agents feel that there was any conflict between strengthening the monarchy and supporting the Christian faith. One final example will illustrate all these points. Pierre du Bois, that famous opponent of ecclesiastical jurisdiction, gave a rent of 7 l. 15 s.t. to the cathedral chapter of Coutances in 1307.[64] Yet Pierre was only a local procurator who was never promoted and who never received gifts or pensions. Zeal for the monarchy kept him in government service and led him to write his pamphlets suggesting ways of increasing royal power. Hope for salvation led him to establish an endowment whose capital value was greater than his annual salary.

Policy Makers and Technicians

To argue, as I did in Chapter I, that Philip the Fair determined basic French policy throughout his reign is not to say that his officials had no influence on policy. Philip needed and sought advice on many occasions. There had to be a great deal of experimentation in some areas, especially when innovations such as general taxation were introduced. It is unlikely that Philip alone invented all the different ways of raising money that were tried out during his reign. In other areas a considerable amount of

[62] A.N., JJ 49, fol. 22, no. 34, JJ 50, fol. 56v, no. 84.

[63] Hugues de Bouville, one of the king's chamberlains, was considerably less generous than Pierre de Belleperche. He gave less than 30 l.p. of rent to found two chaplaincies, plus tithes and grain that could not have been worth more than 10 or 15 l.p. a year. The Bouvilles were wealthy but had large families. See A.N., JJ 46, fol. 113v, no. 199, JJ 47, fol. 28v, no. 44, JJ 49, fol. 57, no. 132.

[64] A.N., JJ 38, fol. 98v, no. 228.

technical knowledge was required. Philip certainly wanted the Parlement to be recognized as a court that had final jurisdiction over all inhabitants of the realm, but he did not make the decisions through which the Parlement implemented this principle. Philip had an active foreign policy, but, except for the brief raid into Catalonia in 1285, he never visited a foreign country. He depended on his envoys for information about the leadership, resources, and goals of potential enemies or allies. Thus there were a number of men in his entourage who had influence on policy, men whom the king trusted as advisers or respected for their special knowledge or technical ability.

It is not difficult to identify these men; it is difficult to determine which men influenced what policy. Generally speaking, there was very little specialization at the highest levels; the same man could be an ambassador, sit in the Parlement, impose general taxes, act as a *Maître des Comptes*, and be sent out to the provinces to enforce royal orders and preserve royal rights. The eminent lawyer Pierre de Belleperche served in all these capacities,[1] as did Pierre de Latilly, who was Keeper of the Seals (1313-1314).[2] But so did much less conspicuous men, such as Jean de la Forêt and Yves de Loudéac.[3] This mixture of duties was caused

---

[1] L. Perrichet, *La grande chancellerie de France* (Paris, 1912), p. 524. Pierre de Belleperche was sent on embassies to Flanders, England, and the pope (*Hist. litt.*, xxv, 351-58). He sat in the Parlements of 1296, 1298, 1303, and many others (*Ord.*, XII, 353-57; *Olim*, II, 422-23, III, 126), was a *Maître des Comptes* in 1304 and collected a tenth in 1306 (Perrichet, pp. 524, 528), and was frequently sent to the meetings of the Norman Exchequer and the Grands Jours of Troyes *J.T.P.*, nos. 2585, 3494, 3737, 5529). He was Keeper *ad interim*, 1305-1307.

[2] Latilly was ambassador to Clement V in 1305 and to Henry VII in 1310 (Georges Lizerand, *Clement V et Philippe IV le Bel* [Paris, 1910], pp. 45, 182). He sat in the Parlement (Charles-Victor Langlois, ed., *Textes relatifs à l'histoire du Parlement* [Paris, 1888], pp. 178, 179), was one of the most active collectors of money for the king in the 1290s (Pegues, pp. 112-19), and was an *enquêteur* in Languedoc (see the entries under his name in Mignon's *Inventaire*).

[3] Jean was sent to England in 1298 to protest breaches of the Anglo-French truce, to England and Scotland in 1299, and to Rome in 1301 *J.T.P.*, nos. 1231, 3334, 3808, 5462). He certainly served in the Parlement of 1299 and probably in the one of 1298 (ibid., nos. 4529, 2518). He was very active as a collector of war subsidies in Carcassonne in 1297; see *H.L.*, x, cols. 341, 345, and *C.R.*, II, nos. 14956, 14973, 14987. He was an *enquêteur* in Sens and Orléans in 1302 (Mignon, nos. 2655, 2658). On Yves, see Strayer, *Gens de justice*, pp. 180-81. He was the chief negotiator in the affair of the Val d'Aran, was a *rapporteur* in the Parlement, 1309-1313, collected

in part by the fact that the king's Household, Court, and Council had not yet separated into clearly differentiated bodies.

The Court was the most general of these terms; it included everyone who held an office in the central government, and it could be cited as the authority for almost any action taken in the king's name. For example, in the Journals of the Treasury many payments are warranted "per cedulam curie." This does not mean that the *curia*, as a collective body, discussed these matters. At most, it would mean that an ad hoc committee (the *curia in compotis*) had acted. At the very end of the reign, when Marigny had full control of royal finance, it could mean that Marigny alone had approved the payment (as he was authorized to do by the ordinance of January 1314). At other times the *curia* is primarily a court of justice; a decision of the Parlement is a decision of the *curia*. A nice example occurs in a case of 1291 concerning the municipal accounts of Rouen. The accounts were investigated by "aliquos de nostro concilio"; they gave a full report to the Council; the accounts were approved "per curie nostre judicium"; and this judgement was recorded in the *Olim*.[4]

Thus titles meant little, and, at the upper level, permanent assignment to one type of work was never considered. The chamberlains were technically Household officials, but, as the case of Marigny shows, they could be given many other duties. A man could be an official member of the Council and never attend a meeting for many years, though he had heavy responsibilities for the eastern frontier of the kingdom (the case of Pierre de Chalon).

Departments of government had not yet been organized. The Parlement was only the *curia* acting in its judicial capacity, the Chambre des Comptes was just ceasing to be an ad hoc committee of the *curia*, and the Council itself was composed of whatever men the king wanted to consult on any particular matter. Lesser officials—notaries in the Chancery or in the Parlement, clerks of accounts, or provincial judges—might specialize, but the king's closest advisers had to have competence in many fields. It may be that Philip felt that lack of specialization at the higher levels of the bureaucracy worked to his advantage. It left him free to

the aid for marrying the king's daughter in Périgord, and was an *enquêteur* in Périgord, 1309-1310.

4 See Jules Viard, "La cour au commencement du XIVᵉ siècle," *Bibliothèque de l'Ecole des Chartes*, LXXVII (1916), 3-16. The Rouen case is *Olim*, II, 326-27.

choose any man for any job—for example, to use the obscure Yves de Loudéac to settle the affair of the Val d'Aran instead of picking Nogaret, who had higher rank and was just as well informed about the problem.[5] This practice also slowed down the growth of the great corporations of officials, which were to limit the freedom of choice of his successors. Philip could remain in overall control of policy because no one could claim to have exclusive knowledge of or complete responsibility for any field of government. At the very end of the reign Philip slipped a little and concentrated too much power in the hands of Marigny; the result was a serious, if temporary, crisis of the monarchy.

All this is understandable, but it does not ease the problem of determining the influence of specific men on specific policies. Titles and official positions are of no help. The chamberlains were close to the king and had many opportunities to influence him, but there is all the difference in the world between chamberlains like the Chambly, who used their influence chiefly to enrich themselves, and a chamberlain like Marigny, who certainly did not fail to enrich himself but who used his influence to affect French financial and foreign policy. The great officers of the crown were by tradition the closest advisers of the king, but again there is a great difference between the Chambrier of France, Robert, duke of Burgundy, whose advice was certainly heeded but who could not often be present at meetings of the Council and the Parlement, and the Butler of France, Gui, count of Saint-Pol, who was always busy with details of administration (notably at the time of the arrest of Bernard Saisset) and with the government of occupied Flanders.[6] The Keeper of the Seals (in effect, the chancellor) was a key man in the administration, since all important documents passed through his hands, but the early Keepers (Pierre Chalou, 1282-1290, and Jean de Vassoigne, 1291-1292) seem to have had little influence, perhaps because they had been inherited from the previous reign. After 1292 all the Keepers belonged to the inner group of advisers (Guillaume de Crépy, 1293-1298, Etienne de Suisy, 1302-1307, and Pierre de Latilly, 1313-1314), and two were very powerful, Pierre Flote, 1298-1302, and Guillaume de Nogaret, 1307-1313. An acting Keeper, such as Thibaud, bishop of Dol, who substituted for the ailing Guillaume de Crépy in 1296-1297, could have great influence, but Thibaud would have had influence in any case. He was

[5] See above, p. 29.
[6] Gallia Christiana, XIII, cols. 109, 115; Mignon, nos. 2543, 2544, 2559.

one of the most experienced men in the government (he had served Philip III) and an expert on the work of the Parlement. The same could be said of Pierre de Belleperche, who acted for Etienne de Suisy after Etienne became a cardinal in December 1305. Pierre was probably the most learned lawyer in the Parlement and a man who had performed many services for the king; holding the seals added nothing to his power. One could also argue that Nogaret had less influence after he became Keeper than in the period 1303-1307, when he was in charge of implementing royal policy toward the Church. Nogaret was made Keeper to carry out the attack on the Templars. (Pierre de Belleperche, the acting Keeper, probably did not want to become involved in what was a very messy and laborious affair.) But except for the process against the Temple, Nogaret did nothing after he was Keeper that he had not done before, and in the last years of his keepership Nogaret had less influence on policy than did Marigny. In short, the Keeper of the Seals was not necessarily the leader of the administration, and he might not be a very influential member of the administration. The title by itself gave little power; power came from the favor of the king.

There is thus a sharp difference between the position of the Keeper under Philip the Fair and that of the Chancellor under the Valois. Both were heads of the Chancery, the royal secretariat, and thus had as their primary duty the supervision of the clerks who prepared and validated documents issued in the king's name. But the Chancellor had not only a higher title—he ranked as one of the great officers of state—but also greater power. He was the head of the whole administration and of the High Court of Parlement. It was precisely because earlier Chancellors had been too powerful that the office had been left vacant since the time of Philip Augustus. It is typical of Philip the Fair that, although many of the reasons for fearing a powerful Chancellor were no longer valid, he did not give the title to any of his officials. This is perhaps the clearest example of his unwillingness to concentrate authority in the hands of even his most trusted advisers.

Just as the Keeper was important because of his personality, not his office, so the Chancery clerks of Philip the Fair were not very influential, in contrast to their position in later reigns. They were competent technicians, rather more specialized than the clerks in other agencies, and promotion was slow, if it came at all. The career of Ami d'Orléans is typical. He was a Chancery clerk at least as early as 1301, but he became a *maître des requêtes* only in 1318—and at that, he was luckier than many of his colleagues. One must admire the diligence and accuracy of these clerks, but one wonders why they were willing to spend so many years in such tedious work. At least they had job security and reasonably high pay.[7]

The Treasurers were more specialized than other high officials, and, perhaps for that reason, seem to have had less influence on policy. The only exceptions would be Biche and Mouche Guidi, and their greatest influence came before their brief term as Treasurers in 1295. They certainly advised the king on ways of raising money for the war in Aquitaine, notably in arranging the enormous loans that were collected in 1294-1295.[8] Yet even in this period their advice was not always taken. They had argued against manipulating the currency, but Philip instead listened to an obscure Paris minter, Thomas Brichart,[9] and it was precisely in 1295 that he began the process of inflation that culminated in 1303. After 1295, when Philip either had Frenchmen as Treasurers or (briefly) used the Temple as his bank (1303-1307), the influence of the Guidi on financial policy declined. They were still close advisers of the king, and they or their agents still collected some of the royal revenues, but they were used more for negotiations with the cardinals, with Italian cities, and with German princes than as experts on taxation. During this period there were no large loans and no important sales-taxes, both of which were ideas that probably came from the Italians. Instead, Philip relied on overvaluing the currency (definitely contrary to the advice of the Guidi), on tenths granted by the clergy, and on subventions based on the principle that all subjects were bound to contribute to the defense of the realm. These subventions were justified by arguments developed by French officials and political theorists; the Guidi brothers contributed little to the formulation of either the policy or the theory.

Of the other Treasurers, both those who served from 1295 to 1303 and those who served from 1307 to 1314, only Guillaume de Hangest (1296-1303, 1307-1311) seems to have had much in-

---

[7] On these last two paragraphs see Morel, pp. 5-11, 60-63, and Perrichet, pp. 519-47 (p. 545 for Ami).

[8] Mignon, nos. 1111, 1113, 1114, 1117, 1120, 1122, 1125-33, 1138-46, 1152-58, 1161, 1162.

[9] Adolphe Vuitry, *Etudes sur le régime financier de la France avant la Révolution de 1789*, new ser., 2 vols. (Paris, 1883), I, 185-86.

fluence. He was a former *bailli*, an active member of the Parlement, and a trusted councillor of the king.[10] Simon Festu played a leading role in the intrigues against Bishop Guichard of Troyes, but this was more a matter of factional politics than of national policy.[11] The others, Pierre La Reue (1295-1303), Henri, abbot of Jouy (1296-1303), Renaud de Roye (1307-1311), Geoffroi de Briançon (1309-1315), Gui Florent (1310-1316), and Guillaume du Bois (1311-1314),[12] were primarily technicians. Renaud de Roye, for example, spent his whole career as a Household and Treasury officer, and Geoffroi de Briançon had been one of Marigny's clerks. Moreover, by 1312 Marigny was gaining control of all financial operations, a control that was officially sanctioned by the ordinance of 19 January 1314.[13] No Treasurer could have much influence on policy when Marigny could approve or disapprove all expenditures.

The Masters of the Monies seem to have been primarily technicians, men who knew how to run or supervise the royal mints. They could advise the king on ways to increase his income from coinage, but they did not make the final decisions on manipulating the currency. These were matters of high policy, to be decided by the king in Council, after consultation with representatives of leading towns or negotiations with the clergy and the nobles.[14] Even Betin Caucinel, who was the most influential Master, does not seem to have been a policy maker. A note that he sent to the king (probably before 1300) deals only with the problems of the export of silver and the use of foreign coins, and an anonymous accusation against him charges him with dishonesty rather than bad advice.[15] And when the inflated currency was suddenly re-

[10] On Guillaume as Treasurer see Borrelli de Serres, *Recherches*, III, 21-24, 47; for his work in the Parlement, *Olim*, II, 397, 412, 597, A.N., J 427, no. 17, B.N., ms. Moreau 217, fol. 250.

[11] See Abel Rigault, *Le procès de Guichard, évêque de Troyes* (Paris, 1896), pp. 23, 41-43, and the Appendix to Chapter IV below. As Borrelli de Serres points out (*Recherches*, III, 47), Festu was Treasurer for less than three years (1307-1309).

[12] For these dates see Borrelli de Serres, *Recherches*, III, 21-24, 47-48.

[13] For one of the many commentaries on this ordinance see Favier, *Marigny*, pp. 103-6.

[14] *Ord.*, I, 408, 383, 406, 548 (this last entry is a consultation in 1314 of the deputies of 43 towns); Strayer and Taylor, pp. 99-102 (consultation of the prelates in 1303).

[15] A. Grunzweig, "Les incidences internationales des mutations monétaires de Philippe le Bel," *Le Moyen Age*, LIX (1953), 118, thinks that the note proves that Betin favored overvaluing the currency. The evidence seems

stored to its old value in 1306, it was the pressure of the prelates and barons that forced the change, not the advice of Betin.[16]

Keepers of the Seals, Treasurers, and Masters of the Monies at least had specific duties (though they could be used for other purposes) and determinable terms of office (though they might be just as influential before or after their terms as during them). However, there is not even this modest degree of certainty about the Parlement or the Council. The king called whom he would to the High Court, which was the Council in Parlement; its composition shifted from term to term, and even from case to case. There could be over 60 people present for one decision and fewer than 10 for another.[17] Duties were assigned at the beginning of each session, but the lines were not strictly observed. For example, the *rapporteurs* were usually subordinate to the judges of the Chamber of Enquêtes and thus to the judges of the Chamber of Pleas (later the Grand'Chambre), but both Nogaret and Hugues de la Celle acted as *rapporteurs* at a time when they were judges.[18] The Council was even more fluid; the king took advice from those who were concerned with or who had special knowledge of a problem. Its size varied with the importance of the occasion and the urgency of the case. To give only two examples, the Council at Senlis in 1301 that discussed the charges against Bernard Saisset was heavily loaded with prelates, including the

unconvincing; export of precious metals was regularly forbidden, whatever the state of the currency, for example, in 1289, when there was no thought of changing the value of the coinage (*Ord.*, XI, 365). For the accusation see Langlois, "Notices et documents," p. 327. On Betin Caucinel, who founded a French noble family, see Camille Piton, *Les Lombards en France et à Paris*, 2 vols. (Paris, 1891-1892), I, 114-19.

[16] See, for example, a letter of two merchants to their partner in Siena, 17 June 1305: "E sapiate ch'e baroni i prelati di Francia sono fermi che la buona muneta sia, e vogliono ch'ella corra piue tosto, e molto n'ano parlate innanzi a re" (C. Paoli and E. Piccolomini, eds., *Lettere volgari del secolo XIII* [Bologna, 1871], p. 71). These merchants were well informed; they were greatly concerned about the proposed change, but they never mention Betin (or any of the other Masters of the Monies).

[17] The king, 5 bishops, the duke of Burgundy, the count of Ponthieu, the abbot of Moissac, and more than 60 others gave a judgement against the lord of Montaigu, 21 May 1290 (*Olim*, II, 361). A ruling on the custody of money from papal grants was made by 13 men, 26 November 1296 (ibid., 397-98), and a minor case was decided by 3 men in October 1303 (but 2 of the 3 were Pierre de Belleperche and Jean de Montigny, very influential councillors) (ibid., III, 126).

[18] Nogaret reported in 1306 and 1307 (*Olim*, III, 179, 184, 223); Hugues reported in 1306 (ibid., 186, 195).

archbishop of Auch, who hardly ever appeared at Court but who was Saisset's neighbor.[19] The Council of January 1314 that gave complete control of royal finance to Marigny was composed largely of financial officers (though the king's sons and brothers and the great officers of the crown were also present).[20]

In these circumstances it is meaningless to say that a man was a member of the Council or a member of the Parlement. One must ask what meetings of either body he attended and how important were the problems discussed in his presence. Unfortunately, this information is lacking in most cases. And even when it is known that a man was present, there is no way of estimating his influence. This is especially true of the great nobles, who were not involved in the day-to-day operations of government and who therefore have left little record of their interests and policies. Gaucher de Châtillon, who was an army commander (Constable after 1302), presumably was aware of the need for taxation in 1303, but did Louis of Evreux understand the problem or influence the decision?[21] Yet both men were at the Council that accepted the tax. Judging by what happened after Philip's death, Charles of Valois can hardly have been enthusiastic about the decision to give Marigny control of the finances of the kingdom, but both he and Louis of Navarre (who was at least morally responsible for Marigny's later execution) were present when the decision was made. Robert of Burgundy was a loyal and helpful supporter of Philip, but he does not seem to have been a policy maker. Gui, count of Saint-Pol, was frequently at court and was certainly trusted by Philip, but what kind of advice did he give the king?

This lack of information about the attitudes of the great lords is especially troublesome because these were the men with whom Philip felt most comfortable, the men who had the best opportunity to influence him in private and unofficial conversations.[22] It may be that all students of the reign have overestimated the influence of the professional bureaucrats, because they are the

[19] *Gallia Christiana*, XIII, cols. 107-15.

[20] Borrelli de Serres, *Recherches*, III, 54. The great officers were the count of Clermont (Chambrier), the count of Saint-Pol (Butler), the Marshal (Jean de Grez), and a chamberlain (Mathieu de Trie).

[21] *Ord.*, I, 408. Béraud de Mercoeur, also an army commander, was at this meeting. He would not have had much expertise in taxation.

[22] Favier, "Les légistes," pp. 97-98, quite rightly stresses the importance of Gaucher de Châtillon, Gui de Saint-Pol, and Jean de Grez, all nobles and army commanders.

men who have left some record of their opinions, either in words or through their administrative actions. On the other hand, it may be that the great nobles were satisfied with their position in the social life and ceremonies of the court, with grants of privileges and land that they received from the king, and, if they were ambitious, with army commands. In any case, when one looks for specific instances of influence on Philip's policies, one has to concentrate on the bureaucrats rather than on the nobles.

During most of the reign we cannot say with certainty who advised the king on his foreign policy or on his financial program. Nor can we be sure who were the legal experts who perfected the techniques and developed the jurisprudence of the Parlement. It is possible, however, to make some reasonable guesses, and, on a few decisions, to speak with certainty.

In foreign policy, it is hard to see any principal councillor until the first quarrel with Boniface VIII. The war with England was completely Philip's responsibility, and the war with Flanders was not the result of any single decision. Given Philip's convictions about the proper relationship between the king of France and his vassals, and the equally strong desire of the count of Flanders to preserve a semi-independent status, the Flemish war was probably as inevitable as any war could be. It is possible that some nobles welcomed an opportunity to gain military distinction and that some bureaucrats were eager to demonstrate the king's supremacy, but no one had to push very hard to start a war. The quarrel with Boniface was different. There were many decisions to be made, many opportunities for compromise, many risks to be accepted or avoided. The most hazardous decision of all, to let the quarrel with the pope and the war with Flanders reach a climax at the same time, has traditionally been ascribed to Flote's influence. There is probably some truth in this, but Nogaret carried on the same policies after Flote's death in 1302, which looks as if the king were picking advisers who could implement his policies rather than being unduly influenced by unscrupulous councillors. After all, Philip had taken a fairly stiff position toward the Church before either Flote or Nogaret was very prominent. Moreover, neither Flote nor Nogaret had full power in some areas of foreign policy. Flote was only one of several men who negotiated the truces and the final peace with England, and Nogaret certainly did not have a free hand in the negotiations that led to peace with Flanders in 1305. The settlement with England, which was one of the real successes of Philip's foreign policy, was worked out primarily by Pierre de Mornay, bishop of Auxerre, and Pierre de Belleperche.[23] The same two men, with Gilles Aicelin, archbishop of Narbonne, were responsible for much of the negotiating with Flanders.[24]

The election of Clement V and the treaty of Athis with Flanders (both in 1305) put an end to the feverish diplomatic activity that had begun in 1293. For a while, the chief problems were the annexation of Lyon, attempts to influence the election of German kings, the condemnation of the Temple, and the clearing up of the results of the attack on Anagni. Nogaret was certainly concerned with these affairs (and especially with the last two), but as an excommunicate he could not deal directly with the pope, and no one else can be said to have been a principal adviser on foreign policy. It was only at the end of the reign, with the revival of difficulties with Flanders, that Marigny emerged as the king's chief councillor in diplomacy as well as in finance. He certainly directed policy toward Flanders; he played a leading role in settling disputes with the papacy over Temple property and the charges against Boniface VIII, and he was concerned with German affairs.[25] But, as had been true throughout the reign, relations with the Spanish kingdoms were handled by a separate group of second-level officials, such as Yves de Loudéac,[26] and Philip seems to have made his own policy on Germany. At least Marigny was rather pointedly excluded from an interview in which the king sent word to the pope that his candidate for the German throne was Philip of Poitiers.[27]

In short, once more we see Philip carefully dividing responsibility among a number of councillors. There was no foreign minister, though at the end of the reign Marigny came close to having the powers of a foreign minister. Even Marigny, however, could scarcely be called a specialist in foreign affairs. Men like Gui de la Charité, Plaisians, Gilles Aicelin, and Pierre de Mornay

23 For Pierre de Mornay, see the account in *Hist. litt.*, xxv, 356, xxxii, 480; for Pierre de Belleperche, ibid., xxv, 355-56, xxxii, 480, 486. Gilles Aicelin also helped to draw up the final treaty. The first, and most important step, the truce of Vyve-Saint-Bavon was the work of Guillaume de Mâcon, bishop of Amiens, Pierre de Mornay, and three great lords; its prolongation was arranged by Guillaume of Amiens, Pierre de Mornay, Gilles Aicelin, Pierre Flote, and four lords. See Funck-Brentano, *Philippe le Bel en Flandre*, pp. 267-71.

24 Funck-Brentano, *Philippe le Bel en Flandre*, pp. 492, 501.

25 Favier, *Marigny*, pp. 186-88.   26 See above, p. 29.

27 Schwalm, "Reichsgeschichte," pp. 564-66.

were sent on diplomatic missions, but they had many other duties; they did not form a permanent corps of ambassadors. In any case, policy was not made by ambassadors; it was determined in the Council. The men who were sent on embassies were councillors in the broad sense of the word, and it is very likely that they were present at the meetings where their instructions were prepared, although this cannot be proved. Philip certainly sought the advice of experts, and on some rare occasions we know what that advice was—Nogaret's pleas to keep pressing charges against Boniface VIII, the consultations on the Val d'Aran, the discussion about a successor to Henry VII. How much influence this advice had, we shall never know; the king made and took responsibility for final decisions.

General and frequent taxation was one of the chief innovations of Philip's reign, but it is impossible to discover the chief advisers on tax policy. Collecting taxes (or tenths from the clergy) seems to have been a sure road to royal favor, and it was a road taken by many men. Most of the leading officials in Paris and many high-ranking local officials (even judges)[28] collected taxes at one time or another, but collecting a tax does not prove that the collector suggested imposing the tax. This is the chief weakness of Franklin Pegues's argument that Pierre de Latilly was a principal adviser on tax policy.[29] Pierre did collect or supervise the collection of a wide variety of imposts, but so did Raoul Rousselet (later bishop of Laon)[30] and the relatively unknown Corraud de Crépy.[31] The consent of the Council to taxation is mentioned several times, but the names of the councillors are seldom given, and even when they are, the information is not very enlightening. Thus the Council of October 1303, which accepted a very heavy

[28] See Strayer, *Gens de justice*, pp. 103, 142.

[29] Pegues, pp. 118-19.

[30] Raoul collected a subsidy in Carcassonne in 1300, sought out money owed the king in Agennais in 1299-1300, and seized Jewish property in Périgord-Quercy in 1306 (Mignon, nos. 1341, 1949, 2161). He was concerned with enforcing the ordinances on forbidden money in Beaucaire in 1301 and 1305 (*H.L.*, x, col. 375; A.N., K 166, no. 95; B.N., ms. lat. 9192, fols. 73, 74). He collected a subsidy in Britanny in 1303 (A.N., J 241, no. 23) and one in the county of Foix in 1305 (*H.L.*, ix, 283).

[31] Corraud collected loans for the Gascon war in 1295, a tenth on the churches of Paris and Meaux in 1297-1298, a fiftieth in Chartres in 1296, a fiftieth in Orleans in 1300, and a subsidy in Poitou in 1303 and in 1304 (Mignon, nos. 1119, 718-20, 1296, 1297, 1504, 1540). He was sent to seize Jewish property in Beaucaire in 1306 (A.N., JJ 48, fol. 126v, no. 213). He also attended several meetings of the Parlement.

and carefully planned tax, had only three professional members: Gilles Aicelin, Pierre de Mornay, bishop of Auxerre, and Jean de Montrelet, bishop of Meaux. None of these prelates had had much experience in finance. The other members were great lords: the duke of Burgundy, the counts of Valois, Evreux, and La Marche, Jean de Chalon-Arlay, and the army commanders Gaucher de Châtillon and Béraud de Mercoeur.[32] These were imposing names, but it seems unlikely that such a Council had much to do with determining the form and amount of the tax to be imposed, although the great lords of the Council may have suggested moderating impositions on the nobility. Moreover, one must distinguish between the officials who provided reasons for levying a tax and those who decided how much had to be raised and who should pay. Justification for taxation followed a common form that was used in all the crises of the reign. To defend and preserve the unity of the kingdom of France was the duty of all inhabitants of the realm. This was closely connected with preservation of the faith, since opponents of the king were wicked, evil, oath-breakers and suspect of heresy, or excommunicates.[33] This language could be used about Jews and Templars as well as about Flemings, and it could have been written by a dozen different men—Flote, Nogaret, Plaisians, Latilly, Richard Leneveu, Raoul Rousselet, to name a few. As a matter of fact, it could have been written before any of these councillors were prominent; the first general taxes for the war of Aquitaine were based on the idea of a universal obligation to defend the realm.[34] The lawyers of the Council were able to put the argument in striking form, but this does not mean that they worked out the ways in which it was to be applied. As a matter of fact, Flote, Nogaret, and Plaisians had very little to do with the details of fiscal administration. It is striking to see how few records dealing with financial matters are among the documents collected by Nogaret and Plaisians.[35] This

---

[32] *Ord.*, I, 408.

[33] See the sources cited in my articles "Defense of the Realm," pp. 296-98, and "France," pp. 305-8. A nice example of this kind of royal propaganda may be found in Dom Jean Leclerq, "Un sermon prononcé pendant la Guerre de Flandre," *Revue du Moyen Age Latin*, I (1945), 165-72. See especially p. 170: "Pax regis est pax regni, pax regni est pax ecclesie, scientie, virtutis et justitie. . . . Igitur qui contra regem invehitur, laborat contra totam ecclesiam, contra doctrinam catholicam, contra sanctitatem et justitiam. . . ."

[34] Strayer and Taylor, pp. 44-48.

[35] Langlois, ed., "Papiers de Nogaret et Plaisians," pp. 211 ff. Nogaret did

lack of financial expertise may be one reason why Nogaret gradually lost ground to Marigny. Latilly had more experience with collecting taxes than any other lawyer, but this experience came largely before 1300, and he was not primarily concerned with finance during the period when he had the greatest influence on the government. In fact, none of the Keepers (Latilly's final official position) were tax experts; rather, they were most active in the Parlement and in diplomacy.

To put the problem another way, basic tax policies were worked out between 1294 and 1304, a period that corresponds closely with the period in which Philip took control of the Treasury away from the Temple and entrusted it to his own officials (1295-1303). During the brief return of the Treasury to the Temple (1303-1307) there were no innovations, nor were there any significant changes after the downfall of the Temple in 1307. In fact, general taxation was much less frequent and much less productive from 1304 to 1314 than it had been from 1294 to 1304. But between 1294 and 1304 no one man stands out as an expert on taxation.

It looks as if Philip, shocked by the tremendous and unexpected expenses of the war with England, decided that he had to raise large sums of money quickly and realized that the Temple could not do the job. He turned first to Biche and Mouche; the large loan they collected in 1294-1295 eased the immediate emergency. At the same time, he asked some of his advisers to prepare a rough budget for meeting the expenses of the war. The document is anonymous, but it includes the idea of a general tax on property.[36] Philip may very well have thought of this himself. He must have known that Edward I was collecting large sums from a tax on personal property in England; it was logical to use and expand this kind of a levy in France. Once the principle was determined, Philip could leave details to his technical experts, the Treasurers and the clerks of accounts. They could estimate how much money was needed and how much might be produced by various types of taxes. It is significant that in all the grumbling

---

have the documents dealing with protests against the marriage aid of 1309, but this, I think, was because they raised legal points that might have had to have been settled in the Parlement, not because he was an expert on finance. For a contrary opinion see Elizabeth A. R. Brown, *Customary Aids and Royal Finance* (forthcoming), chap. 5.

[36] Funck-Brentano, "Document," pp. 333-34. An earlier edition by Boutaric, in *Notices et extraits*, xx, pt. 2 (1861), is less accurate.

about taxation, no one minister was ever blamed for the policy. Biche and Mouche were accused (wrongfully) of inflating the currency but not of advising property taxes or hearth taxes.

Where the king's councillors did play a significant role was in modifying the tax structure to make it more acceptable to the king's subjects. They tied it more and more closely to the idea of universal obligation for military service. The earliest taxes were simply for "defense," with no specific connection between the amount of money demanded and the amount of personal service that might (theoretically) be owed. By 1302, however, a change had taken place. The taxes of 1302, 1303, and the last and most productive of the great taxes, the subvention of 1304, were all based on the principle of commutation of military service. Everyone was summoned, but most subjects were allowed to buy their way out. In 1304 nobles were to provide one mounted soldier or pay 100 l. for each 500 l. of income; nonnobles were to support six foot soldiers for each group of 100 hearths.[37] Such arrangements strengthened the king's legal position and were probably worked out by the lawyers of the Council—which ones, we shall never know. It is likely that the same men suggested giving wide discretionary powers to local collectors, allowing them to change property taxes to hearth taxes or to take lump sums instead of using actual assessments.

After 1305, peace with Flanders and the election of a friendly pope (Clement V) gradually lessened financial pressures. Clement was generous in granting tenths from the clergy, Flanders was paying a war indemnity (though reluctantly and slowly), and the royal domain was producing large revenues. Philip may have been somewhat chastened by recent narrow escapes. The Flemings had come very close to defeating him, and if Boniface VIII had survived Anagni, there might have been a dangerous confrontation with the Church. Moreover, there had been strong and sometimes violent opposition to taxation. Philip certainly realized that it was unwise to impose new taxes until resentment had died down, and, as Professor Brown has suggested, he may have felt some remorse for his earlier exactions.[38] Thus during the period

---

[37] *Ord.*, I, 383-408. Later, subjects of nobles were allowed to provide only four soldiers per 100 hearths, or only two if the peasants were *taillables haut et bas* (ibid., 391). Nobles who failed to send fully armed mounted men still had to pay 100 l. for every 500 l. of income. On this shift in the form of taxation see Strayer and Taylor, pp. 56-67.

[38] Elizabeth A. R. Brown, "Taxation and Morality in the Thirteenth and

from 1305 to 1314 royal policy was to raise money in ways that were not too offensive to the propertied classes and to avoid, as far as possible, excessive expenditures.

This policy could be implemented in many different ways by the king's advisers. The good administrators improved the organization and increased the revenues of the bureaus for which they had chief responsibility. For example, Philippe le Convers brought the administration of the royal forests to a new level of efficiency.[39] Philippe had a solid foundation on which to build, since the basic principles of forest administration had been laid down in the time of St. Louis.[40] Pierre de Chalon, who organized the customs service, had a more difficult task, since he had no precedents for his operations. It is not surprising that he was unable to raise much money, but at least he was able to bring in several thousand pounds a year from a source that had previously produced nothing.[41] The clerks of accounts carefully scrutinized the records of the war years and usually found arrears in collectors' accounts or overpayment of expenses. Certainly they did not recover all this money for the king, but, equally certainly, they gained something. Biche and Mouche had stood high in the king's favor to the very end of their lives, but their heirs had to pay substantial sums to clear their accounts.[42]

It is well to stress the work of the technicians, for it has been overshadowed by such spectacular events as the expulsion of the Jews and the overthrow of the Temple. Nogaret almost certainly suggested both moves. He was an adventurer, not a financier; a sudden coup against an unpopular minority was more to his liking than trying to find new, permanent, and acceptable sources of revenue. In both cases he could count on the king's narrow piety for support and on his own ability to manipulate public opinion

---

Fourteenth Centuries: Conscience and Political Power and the Kings of France," *French Historical Studies*, VIII (1973), 17-19.

[39] Pegues, pp. 128-32. Pegues mentions several other forest administrators but omits Etienne de Bienfaite, who was very active in the north (A.N., JJ 50, fol. 58v, no. 93; *J.T.P.*, no. 553n; Mignon, no. 2240; *C.R.*, II, no. 15652; Fawtier, ed., *Comptes du Trésor*, no. 362), and Bertaud de Borest, master of the forests of Languedoc from April 1309 to 1318 (A.N., JJ 48, fols. 80v-81v, no. 133; *C.R.*, II, nos. 14190 ff.; *C.R.* Maillard, I, nos. 1397-99, 4627).

[40] Strayer, *Administration of Normandy*, pp. 73-80.

[41] See above, "Social and Geographic Origins of the King's Servants," note 4.

[42] Mignon, nos. 2048, 2116; A.N., JJ 40, fol. 15, no. 32, JJ 46, fol. 67, no. 89.

for final success. But it should be noted that these were one-shot operations that could not be repeated and that they did not produce large sums of money in any one year. Attacking the Jews had the immediate political advantage of diverting attention from the crisis caused by the sudden revaluation of the currency. In the first years after the expulsion, the confiscations may have produced 50,000 l.t. a year; after 1310 the process of selling Jewish goods and collecting debts owed to the Jews dragged on with diminishing returns.[43] Settling the accounts of the Temple with the king and assessing the costs of administering Temple property (which were the only legitimate ways of making a profit from the abolition of the Order) took even longer.[44] Nogaret may also have suggested trying to expand to all subjects the aid for marrying the king's daughter,[45] another project that brought in money rather slowly. Altogether, his expedients may have done more harm than good, since they used up the time of a large number of capable administrators who might otherwise have been working on more profitable tasks.

The last years of the reign were the period in which Marigny was the chief adviser on finance. He may have been as unscrupulous as Nogaret, but he had a great deal more sense about money. His downfall was caused by the fact that when the old quarrel with Flanders broke out again in 1313, he did not want to wage an all-out, and therefore expensive war. He preferred negotiation, and so he was accused of treason. Taxation could not be wholly avoided, but it was kept at a low level. Some money was coming in from the aid for knighting the king's eldest son (which

[43] By 1310 the king had received about 87,193 l.t. from Toulouse and about 104,430 l.t. from Champagne (Strayer and Taylor, p. 10). This, however, was "weak money"; by 1310 it was worth only 63,873 l.t. (cf. Mignon, no. 2170), or about 16,000 l.t. a year. Moreover, these were districts in which there were large amounts of Jewish property; others produced much less—for example, only 2,455 l.t. weak for Bourges, 4,300 l.t. (weak?) for Tours, and 16,888 l.t. weak for Rouen (ibid., nos. 2137, 2139, 2145). Sales of Jewish goods were still going on in 1314 (A.N., JJ 49, fol. 70, no. 164; JJ 50, fol. 49v, no. 67). The king even had to let two Jews enter France temporarily to identify their creditors (A.N., JJ 49, fol. 70, no. 164). See Mignon, nos. 2133, 2155, 2156, 2170-72, for efforts to squeeze more money from Jewish goods after 1310. Very little was received.

[44] The final settlement came only in 1318 (A.N., JJ 56, fol. 60, no. 142).

[45] At least he had documents about the aid among his papers; see Langlois, ed., "Papiers de Nogaret et Plaisians," nos. 128, 186. On the slow collection of the aid see below, pp. 108, 154, and Elizabeth A. R. Brown, *Customary Aids and Royal Finance*, chap. 5.

had been requested before the war began) and from the war taxes of 1313 and 1314, but both of these taxes were suspended when a truce with Flanders was made (though Philip was very reluctant to do so in 1314). They produced almost nothing in 1313 and relatively little in 1314.[46] If the suspension of these taxes was the result of Marigny's advice, then he had a good deal to do with establishing the rule of *cessante cause*, that is, taxation ends when the emergency ends. Although the idea was not new —French prelates had included it in their grants of tenths in the 1290s[47]—it had never before been effectively invoked, and it was to cause many problems for the successors of Philip the Fair.[48]

Great advances were made in the organization and in the jurisprudence of the Parlement during Philip's reign, but, as usual, it is hard to identify the individuals who were responsible for these developments. Certainly the technicians—the *greffier*, Pierre de Bourges,[49] clerks of the Council, like Jean le Duc,[50] notaries and *rapporteurs* like Gilles de Rémi[51]—had much to do with improving recordkeeping and procedure. Down to 1300, or even a little later, the Parlement was full of men who had served Philip III—Gilles

[46] Strayer and Taylor, pp. 81-82, 86-87.

[47] Ibid., pp. 26-28.

[48] Elizabeth A. R. Brown, "Cessante Causa and the Taxes of the Last Capetians: The Political Applications of a Philosophical Maxim," *Studia Gratiana*, xv (1972), 567-87. As Professor Brown points out, Philip had accepted the principle in 1302 and in 1304, but since the war did not end, the taxes did not cease.

[49] See the account of the career of Pierre de Bourges by A. Grün in his "Notice sur les Archives du Parlement de Paris," which appears in Edgard Boutaric, ed., *Actes du Parlement de Paris*, 2 vols. (Paris, 1863-1867), I, lxxv-lxxxii.

[50] Jean served in the Parlements of 1286, 1296, and 1307 (Langlois, ed., *Textes*, pp. 129, 163, 178). He had worked on *enquêtes* in 1285 (and probably earlier) and was in the Parlements of 1293 and 1298-1299 (*J.T.P.*, col. 48, n.1, nos. 4529, 2324). In 1291 he was to sit every day to hear "requêtes" (*Ord.*, I, 320), and he was in the Chamber of Pleas in or about 1296 (ibid., xii, 353). The Parlement sent him to hear the testimony of the bishop of Dol in 1292 (*Olim*, ii, 355). He was an *enquêteur* in Languedoc in 1290 (*H.L.*, x, col. 251), in Anjou in 1294 (A.N., J 178, no. 51), in the *prévôté* of Paris in 1296 (Fawtier, ed., *Comptes du Trésor*, nos. 384, 405), and in Périgord in 1303 (*Olim*, ii, 464).

[51] Gilles was a notary, 1301-1321 (Perrichet, p. 546), and a *rapporteur* in 1306 and 1309 (*Olim*, iii, 200, 357) and under Philip V, according to Paul Lehugeur, *Histoire de Philippe le Long, Roi de France*, Vol. ii, *Le mechanisme du gouvernement* (Paris, 1931), p. 194. For more information about the *rapporteurs* see below, pp. 214-18.

Camelin, Gilles Lambert, Guillaume de Crépy, Jean de Montigny, Renaud Barbou the elder, Robert d'Harcourt (bishop of Coutances), Thibaud de Pouancé (bishop of Dol), to name only the most important. These men were on the whole conservative and inclined to respect precedents (though not unwilling to expand them). When Philip's own men became more numerous and more prominent in the Parlement one might have expected a change in tone. But Flote, Nogaret, Plaisians, and Latilly were busy with many other duties. They often sat in the Parlement, but its jurisprudence was not their chief concern. Gilles Aicelin had a more judicial temperament and was probably more concerned about his work in the Parlement, but he also was involved in other affairs, notably the attack on the Temple. Of all of Philip's stable of lawyers, Pierre de Belleperche was probably the ablest jurisprudent, and he took some part in the work of the Parlement. But less well-known figures, such as Jean d'Auxois, who became bishop of Troyes, and Gui de la Charité, bishop of Soissons, were at least as active. So, for that matter, was the layman Hugues de la Celle, whose main job was to watch over the king's interests in Saintonge but who frequently appeared in the Parlement.[52]

On the whole, the Parlement was not a policy-making body. It enforced, interpreted, and at times modified policy, but the great men who sat in the Council in Parlement also sat in the Council out of Parlement, where basic decisions were made. It was much easier to experiment with innovations in finance and administration by using the informal procedures of the Council rather than by using the increasingly rigid procedures of the Parlement. For example, the decision to try to collect the aid for marrying the king's eldest daughter from inhabitants of the realm who were not the king's immediate vassals was a decision of the king in Council. The enforcement of this decision was left to royal commissioners, who made the best bargains they could with local communities, subject, of course, to the approval of the king and his advisers.[53] Only as a last resort was the Parlement

---

[52] Hugues appears at a judgement of 5 June 1311 (*Olim*, III, 610), in the Parlement list of ca. 1307 (Langlois, ed., *Textes*, p. 179), and as the judge who announced the court's decision, 13 May 1316 (*Olim*, III, 1053). Other references to his work in the Parlement are *Olim*, III, 173, 185, 194 (1306), and Paul Guilhiermoz, *Enquêtes et procès* (Paris, 1892), p. 366 (n.d., but in the time of Pierre de Bourges).

[53] *Olim*, II, 508. The general policy was laid down in a letter sent by Philip to all *baillis* in 1309: try to persuade men not directly subject to the king to

asked to decide cases concerning the aid,[54] probably because the king's rights were not entirely clear, and hard and fast decisions would have blocked the policy of obtaining money through well-timed compromises.

The lack of a clear distinction between the Parlement and the Council is illustrated by a document of 1297. Philip, ready to begin the occupation of Flanders, gave full powers to seven men left behind in Paris to carry on the work of the government.[55] Technically, they were acting for the Council, but they were all closely identified with the work of the Parlement, especially Oudard de la Neuville, Jean de Montigny, and Gilles Lambert, dean of St. Martin of Tours. Pierre de Mornay, bishop of Auxerre, and Guillaume de Crépy, the Keeper, had had wider responsibilities than the others and were accustomed to making administrative decisions. Even with these men as leaders, however, no very important decisions were made. The committee dealt with problems in the collection of subsidies and other financial business, and its composition suggests that it was also meant to deal with legal problems, especially since the Parlement did not meet that year. In either case, it was a committee for current affairs, not a policy-making body.

Some cases were so important that the names of the men present at the decision were recorded. Unfortunately, these lists give little indication of leadership. Thus in 1298 a case involving the

---

make an "aimable et convenable composicion"; if not, have them send proctors with full power to the Parlement (but even then there may be a possibility that the king's people will "accorder amiablement avec eulz"). This policy was reaffirmed in letters of 15 October to the collectors of the aid in Périgord, Quercy, Saintonge, and Angoulême (A.N., JJ 42A, fols. 97-98). Many towns made deals with the king's men rather than go to court; for example, Carcassonne paid 2,000 l.t. (*H.L.*, x, col. 473), and Rouen promised 30,000 l.t., both for the aid and to regain its monopoly of navigation on the lower Seine (A.N., JJ 41, fol. 90, no. 152). For other examples see Elizabeth A. R. Brown, *Customary Aids and Royal Finance*, chap. 5.

[54] See *Olim*, II, for a ruling against the Norman prelates (p. 502), a ruling in favor of Italian merchants and bankers (but delayed until 1313) (p. 607), and for cases in which a postponement was granted and no decision made (pp. 514, 515, 589). See also Brown, *Customary Aids and Royal Finance*, chap. 5; *Olim*, II, 508.

[55] M. Jusselin, "Les 'Presidenz à Paris' au temps des derniers Capétiens," *Bibliothèque de l'Ecole de Chartes*, XCII (1931), 277-79. The two men not mentioned in my discussion of the text were Jean, canon of Bayeux (Jean de Chevry, later bishop of Carcassonne), and a very obscure canon, Etienne de Limoges.

interpretation of a royal charter was heard by 38 men.[56] Here
there was a real merger of Council and Parlement. The counts of
Aumâle, Dammartin, and Dreux and the chamberlains were obviously councillors, not legal experts. Jean le Duc, Oudard de la
Neuville, Guillaume de Nogaret (at this early stage of his career),
and Pierre de Belleperche were just as clearly valued primarily
as lawyers. Jean de la Forêt was both an authority on Norman
law and a collector of subsidies. Gilles Aicelin, Robert d'Harcourt, Jean de Montrelet, Philippe le Convers, Richard Leneveu,
to name only a few of the others, were expert in law and influential in policy. With such a mixture, who made the decision?
Aicelin and Belleperche were the most famous lawyers; on the
other hand, the case turned on rights of inheritance under a northern custom that may have been better understood by Jean de la
Forêt or Robert d'Harcourt.

Two years earlier a decision about the custody of tenths and
other levies on the clergy granted by the pope was witnessed
by an entirely different group. It naturally included men with
financial expertise, such as the Treasurers (Henri, abbot of Jouy,
and Guillaume de Hangest), a *Maître des Comptes* (Jean Clersens), and Mouche. But Gui de Saint-Pol, the Butler, was also
present, as were Bishop Thibaud of Dol, Pierre Flote, Geoffroi
du Temple, and Jean de Montigny.[57] The last four were very
active in the work of the Parlement. Yet it seems likely that the
decision to accept the arrangement about custody of payments
by the clergy was made by the financiers and not by the legal
experts, and that it was as much an act of the Council as of the
Parlement. Even in 1311, when the structure of the Parlement
had become somewhat more rigid, the list of 24 men present at
a judgement gives no clues about the leadership. Eminent men
such as Hugues de la Celle and Gilles Aicelin appear next to
second-level officials such as Jean de Roye and Philippe de Bla-
veau, and the list ends with the counts of Valois and Saint-Pol,
the bishop of Coutances (Robert d'Harcourt), and the king![58]
Finally, a list of 13 officials who were to judge *enquêtes* in 1313

---

[56] *Olim*, II, 422-23.   [57] Ibid., pp. 397-98.
[58] Ibid., III, 608-10. The official Parlement list of 1307 does show the preeminence of Gilles Aicelin, but Nogaret and the Constable, who also are
given high rank, had little to do with the Parlement; see Langlois, ed.,
Textes, pp. 178-81. Langlois was unsure of the date, but in the document
Nogaret is already Keeper (22 September 1307), and Robert de Fouilloy,
who has no title, became bishop of Amiens on or before 12 September 1308.

when the Parlement was not sitting was headed by Guillaume de Plaisians, but the other members of the group were professional civil servants, men who were executors, not makers, of policy (even though some of them were called councillors at times). Seven of them had been *baillis* or seneschals (Alfonse de Rouvrai, Guillaume de Hangest the younger, Jean d'Arrablay, Louis de Villepreux, Pierre de Dicy, Pierre le Féron, and Renaud de Ste. Beuve), and at least four had had long experience in the Parlement (Bernard du Mèz, Guillaume Courteheuse, Pierre de Blanot, and Pierre de Dicy).[59] Granted that they were not going to judge cases of the first importance during the vacations and that only 5 were members of the Grand'Chambre (the others were in the Chambre des Enquêtes), these men are probably a fairly good example of the group that did the bulk of the work of the Parlement. This list, then, like most of the others, leads one to the conclusion that leadership of the Parlement depended more on experience and technical skill than on membership in the inner circle of royal advisers. The Parlement did its job well because, although it always included some policy makers, it was not dominated by them.

Among the men who were most trusted by the king were the *enquêteurs-réformateurs*. The *enquêteurs* (they usually worked in pairs) had practically viceregal (though temporary) powers in the districts to which they were sent. They represented the person of the king himself; they were to do what the king would have done if he could have been present.[60] They could take any steps necessary to regain royal rights and income; they could demand the cooperation of all local authorities; they could fine, dismiss, or even (in one case) execute royal officials whom they thought were inefficient, oppressive, or corrupt.[61] Appeals from

[59] Langlois, ed., *Textes*, p. 198.

[60] See the commission to Nogaret and J. de Gressia for Senlis, 22 October 1302: "et, cum in singulis locis et partibus regni nostri hujus modi exequi regimen nequeamus, exemplo decemur et urgente necessitate compellimur determinatis provinciis certas deputare personas que, quoad ipsis est, regalis virtute potencie, defectum nostre suppleant absencie corporalis nostrasque in execucione justicie vices gerant" (A.N., JJ 36, fol. 12, no. 38). A similar commission was given to the *enquêteurs* for Beaucaire, 27 October 1302 (H.L., x, *preuves*, col. 414).

[61] Pierre Roche, judge of Minervois, was condemned and dismissed by the *enquêteurs* in 1309 (H.L., x, *preuves*, col. 539), pardoned by Philip the Fair in 1314, and condemned again (on basically the same charges) by the *enquêteurs* in 1318 and executed (A.N., JJ 59, fols. 180-84, nos. 343, 344).

their decisions were discouraged and were not numerous. When they were allowed, they usually went to the Parlement, and an outright reversal of an *enquêteur*'s decision was rare, though some cases were sent back for further hearings.[62] Since many *enquêteurs* were already involved in the work of the Parlement, their colleagues would naturally have tended to support them, but decisions of *enquêteurs* who were not connected with the Parlement seem to have been equally respected. Another check on the *enquêteurs* was that some of their acts, such as accepting fines for pardons or for encroachments on royal rights and payments for sales or exchanges of royal property, had to be ratified by the king. In most of these cases, however, the ratification seems to have been a routine act of the Chancery in which the king took no personal interest.[63]

Given their enormous power and virtual independence of higher authority, one would have expected the *enquêteurs* to be among the most powerful men in the country. But if one looks at the list that Jean Glénisson compiled in 1946,[64] and at the additions to that list that have been made possible by recent publications, one finds many unfamiliar names and many officials who were clearly of secondary importance. Apparently, if the

[62] In 1305 the Parlement ruled that no appeal was allowed from the decision of an *enquêteur*, but an aggrieved subject could proceed "per viam supplicationis" (*Olim*, III, 153). The results, however, were about the same. Thus in this case the decision was reversed, and in two other cases the *enquêteurs* were reversed after a new *enquête* (ibid., pp. 231, 237, 522). Jean d'Auxois and Nicolas de Luzarches, who had to cover all of Languedoc in 1305-1306, were particularly vulnerable because they had to work through deputies, who did not have the standing of an *enquêteur*. Nevertheless, their acts through deputies were upheld five times (ibid., pp. 301, 307, 381, 520, 801) and reversed only once (ibid., p. 361). The one case in which the Parlement really seemed to be annoyed with the *enquêteurs* came in 1313, when a patently unjust decision of Guillaume des Buissons, king's clerk, and Philippe de St. Verain, king's knight (*enquêteurs* in Auvergne, 1308 to some date in 1314), was completely reversed and the petitioner told that he could sue the two officials for damages (ibid., p. 788). This may have hurt their careers; they were replaced as *enquêteurs* in 1314 (Mignon, p. 365), and I have found no trace of them after this date.

[63] See Robert Fawtier, et al., eds., *Registres du Trésor des Chartes*, Vol. I, *Le règne de Philippe le Bel* (Paris, 1958), Index, s.v. "enquêteurs-réformateurs." Most, but not all, of the 45 entries deal with *enquêteurs* as I would define them, and there is no indication that there was any review of the acts sent to Paris.

[64] Jean Glénisson, "Les enquêteurs-réformateurs de 1270 à 1328" (thèse dactylographé, Ecole des Chartes, Paris, 1946).

district to be visited were not seriously disturbed, the king would name as *enquêteurs* respectable clergymen and worthy knights who had little connection with the government. If there was more unrest and widespread complaints about royal policies, the *enquêteurs* would come from Paris and almost always would have some connection with the Parlement. But even in such cases the men who were selected were usually at a fairly early stage in their careers. Nogaret was never an *enquêteur* after 1302, nor Latilly after 1303. Raoul Rousselet and Hugues de la Celle reached the peak of their careers only after Philip's death. Gilles Camelin had been an *enquêteur* under Philip III, but, even though he remained influential under Philip the Fair, he never again served as an *enquêteur*. Some powerful members of the Council—Flote, Plaisians, Marigny, Pierre de Belleperche, Gilles Aicelin—were never *enquêteurs*. It was a job for young men, coming men; it demanded too much physical effort for the old and too much time for the leaders of the Council.

A few statistics will support these generalizations. Approximately 73 men served as *enquêteurs* under Philip the Fair. It is impossible to give a precise number; the names are missing for the *bailliage* of Orléans in 1295,[65] and there is doubt as to whether some commissioners had the full powers of an *enquêteur*. For example, in 1298 Pierre de Latilly and Raoul de Breuilly made a vigorous and much-resented enquiry into lost or usurped royal rights in the south.[66] This was normally part of an *enquêteur's* work, but they did not investigate royal officials, as *enquêteurs* should have done. At the other extreme, Robert, duke of Burgundy, had extraordinary powers as lieutenant of the king in Toulouse in 1287 and "pro custodia et tuitione regni" in Beaucaire

[65] Charles-Victor Langlois, "Doléances recueillies par les enquêteurs de S. Louis et les derniers Capétiens directs," *Revue historique*, c (1909), 70-78.

[66] Adolphe Baudouin, ed., *Lettres inédites de Philippe le Bel* (Paris, 1887), nos. 145, 168-70 (these last three deal with abuse of power by royal officials, but this is a side issue); Mignon, no. 2393; *Cartulaire de Notre-Dame de Prouille*, 2 vols. (Paris, 1907), I, 74, 75, 86; A.N., J 1031, nos. 7-8, J 1033, nos. 9-11, J 1024, no. 38, J 1029, no. 2, J 1034B, nos. 46, 47, J 896, nos. 9, 25, 29, 34. Another doubtful case is the mission of Alain de Lamballe, bishop of St. Brieuc, and Aimeri du Cros, seneschal of Carcassonne in 1314 (A.N., JJ 50, fol. 1, no. 1, fol. 3v, no. 2, fol. 6, no. 3, fol. 17, no. 18, fol. 66, no. 99). All their work dealt with taking fines for amortization and new acquisitions by towns and a monastery, but they were once called "commissarii generales pro . . . reformatione patrie" (fol. 6, no. 3). This must have been a scribal error.

in 1294,[67] but he was something more than an *enquêteur*. Fortunately, these doubtful cases are not numerous and have little influence on the statistical pattern.

The group of 73 divides almost evenly between officials stationed in Paris (36) and men from the provinces (37). Each group can be subdivided. The *enquêteurs* from Paris included some influential councillors, such as Alain de Lamballe, Nogaret, Gui de la Charité, Hugues de la Celle, Jean de Picquigny, Latilly, and Raoul Rousselet, and some experts in the work of the Parlement, such as Bernard du Mès, Etienne de Chanlitre, Lambert de Waissi, and Oudard de la Neuville. On the other hand, the notary Jean du Temple, the clerk Goulard de May, Master Robert Foison, the knights Jean de Melun and Pierre de Ste. Croix did not have particularly distinguished careers, though they all had some connection with the Parlement. Very roughly, about half of the *enquêteurs* chosen from officials working in Paris were men who could have been consulted by the king on difficult problems. The other half were useful subordinates who could be trusted to keep the machinery of government running. Of course, the categories did not remain stable. Philippe de Mornay, for example, who was not prominent under Philip the Fair, was far more important under Philip V, while Geoffroi de Vendôme interrupted a promising career to become a councillor of Charles of Valois. Nevertheless, the proportion seems to have remained about the same overall.

The *enquêteurs* who came from the provinces were most often local notables, usually knights and often men connected with well-known families. Thus Guillaume Aicelin acted in Rouergue in 1296-1297, Gautier de Joinville in Carcassonne in 1302-1303, and Gérard de Maumont (a king's clerk) in Normandy in 1313. There were also eight abbots and three other members of the clergy. In most cases, but not all, the local notable was paired with a man sent from the king's court. Another, more dangerous way of getting *enquêteurs* who had both local knowledge and experience in government was to appoint men who were or who recently had been local royal officials. There were ten such *enquêteurs*: six had been *baillis* or seneschals, two had been receivers, one was a castellan who was clearly on the road to promotion, and one was an experienced Norman viscount.[68] Sur-

[67] *H.L.*, x, cols. 205, 293.

[68] The *baillis* or seneschals were Alfonse de Rouvrai, Bertrand Agasse, Guillaume de Mussy, Guillaume de Rivière, Henri de Hans, and Jean de

prisingly enough, three of the seneschals—Alfonse de Rouvrai, governor of Navarre, Bertrand Agasse, seneschal of Saintonge, and Henry de Hans, seneschal of Agenais—were actually in office when they were named as *enquêteurs* in their own districts.[69] Since one of the chief duties of an *enquêteur* was to investigate the conduct of local officials, these men, in effect, were being asked to investigate themselves. Probably no harm was done, since each had a very high-ranking colleague—Gui de la Charité for Agenais, Hugues de la Celle for Saintonge (and Poitou), and Miles de Noyers for Navarre. Perhaps the seneschals were appointed simply to give the chief *enquêteur* the advice of someone who knew local problems and customs. Nevertheless, these cases show how very free the king was to select anyone he pleased and how little correlation there was between high status at court and appointment as an *enquêteur*.

One final test gives somewhat more conclusive results. During Philip's reign about 28 of his officials became bishops. (It is impossible to be precise: for example, Bertrand de Bordes of Albi, later a cardinal, and Jean de Comines of Le Puy had both accomplished some missions for the king, but they can scarcely be called royal officials. Thibaud de Pouancé of Dol and Guillaume de Mâcon of Amiens both worked for Philip but were bishops before 1285.) When cathedral chapters had some freedom of election they would presumably choose men who seemed to have influence with the king. When the pope made the appointment, he was not likely to select a royal official except at the king's request. These 28 bishops, therefore, should all have been high-ranking administrators and trusted advisers of the king. By and large this is true, but Philip could have personal as well as political reasons for supporting a candidate for the episcopacy. Egidius Romanus had supervised the king's education but could scarcely be called a royal official (in fact, he was clearly hostile to the policy of the government during the quarrels with Boni-

---

St. Verain. For their careers see Delisle's list in the introduction to Vol. xxiv of *H.F.* The receivers were Arnoul Mellin (Crécy; Mignon, no. 128) and the Templar Raoul de Gisy (Champagne; Mignon, no. 86). The castellan was Jean l'Archévêque (also *viguier* of Toulouse), and the viscount was Geoffroi d'Anisy of Bayeux; on these men see my "Viscounts and Viguiers," pp. 218, 223, 227, 252.

[69] Glénisson, App. I, nos. 15, 40, 45; A.N., JJ 41, fols. 111-12, no. 198 (Bertrand Agasse); *H.F.*, xxiv, *269 (Alfonse de Rouvrai), *220 (Henri de Hans).

face VIII). Yet Philip welcomed his appointment as archbishop
of Bourges in 1295. Robert d'Harcourt, who became bishop of
Coutances in 1291, was a useful member of the Parlement, but
it may have been more important that he was also a member of
a great Norman noble family. The Frédol were friendly and
helpful to Philip but could hardly be called his servants; three
members of this powerful southern clan were bishops of Béziers
(and two of these became cardinals).

It was also true that the king could not always be sure that
the pope (even a very friendly pope like Clement V) would
accept his candidates. In 1308 Philip apparently wanted Jean
d'Auxois, a very active collector of subventions and an *enquêteur*,
as bishop of Auxerre. He had to settle for Pierre de Grez, a perfectly respectable king's clerk, Chancellor of Louis of Navarre,
and brother of Marshal Jean de Grez, but a man who had done
much less work for the king than had his rival.[70] It was not until
1314 that Jean d'Auxois received his reward, the bishopric of
Troyes. Pierre de Laon had even worse luck; Philip tried but
failed to have him chosen bishop of Orléans in 1312, and Pierre
died before he had another chance.[71] Even more striking, though
with a happier ending, is the case of Etienne de Suisy. Recommended to Tournai in 1300, he aroused such opposition that the
pope instead named a great noble, Guy of Auvergne-Boulogne.[72]

[70] Pierre worked on the charges against Guichard in 1303, worked with
Pierre de Belleperche in 1298, sat in the Parlement of 1300, and was sent
on a mission for the king in 1301 (Rigault, pp. 31-32; *J.T.P.*, nos. 974, 2382,
4664, 5130). But according to Petit, *Charles de Valois*, pp. 59, 104, 316,
343, Pierre also worked for Charles of Valois before he became bishop. In
short, he was a first-rate Paris lawyer, and the king was not his only client.
Jean d'Auxois, on the other hand, worked almost full time on subsidies,
on gaining support for the Council against Boniface, on Jewish affairs, as
an *enquêteur*, and in Parlement; see *J.T.P.*, nos. 4762, 5659, 5888, Mignon,
nos. 1343, 2059, 2677, Georges Picot, ed., *Documents relatifs aux Etats
Généraux sous Philippe le Bel* (Paris, 1901), pp. 324-26; *H.L.*, x, cols. 446,
447. The statement that the king preferred to have Jean rather than Pierre
become bishop is based on *Gallia Christiana*, xii, 313, where the king asked
Jean to be executor of the will of Pierre de Mornay, late bishop of Auxerre,
and on *J.T.P.*, no. 5942, which states that Philip sent Alain de Lamballe,
one of his ablest clerks, to Auxerre in 1308 to see about the election of the
bishop.
[71] Lizerand, *Clément V*, p. 473. For Pierre's career see André Guillois,
Recherches sur les maîtres des requêtes de l'hôtel des origines à 1350 (Paris,
1909), pp. 229-30.
[72] A.N., J 345B, no. 113. See A. Herbomez, *Philippe le Bel et les Tour-*

Etienne's standing at the court is sufficiently demonstrated by the fact that he became Keeper in 1302. He had his revenge in 1305 when Clement V made him a cardinal.

In short, the list of king's clerks who became bishops does not correspond exactly with the list of the most influential clerical members of the government. Nevertheless, a list that includes the names of five Keepers or acting Keepers (Pierre Chalou of Orléans, Jean de Vassoigne of Tournai, Pierre de Belleperche of Auxerre, Gilles Aicelin of Narbonne, and Pierre de Latilly of Châlons), one Treasurer (Simon Festu of Meaux), and such influential councillors as Giles Camelin of Rennes, Gui de la Charité of Soissons, Guillaume Bonnet of Bayeux, Pierre de Mornay of Orléans and Auxerre, and Richard Leneveu of Béziers has some significance. Rigault thought that Jean de Montrelet of Meaux was as important as any of the men just named,[73] and three of Philip's younger bishops—Alain de Lamballe of St. Brieuc, Raoul Rousselet of St. Mâlo and Laon, and Robert de Fouilloy of Amiens —were clearly rising to power during the latter part of the reign, though they reached the peak of their careers only under Philip's sons.

Although the other bishops were not as conspicuous, none of them was entirely negligible. They all attended the Parlement on some occasions, and five of them served as *enquêteurs*. Some of them had special duties that kept them away from court. Thus Pierre de Grez of Auxerre had an early career not unlike that of many other royal officials. When he was named to the commission that was to investigate the charges against Bishop Guichard de Troyes, he sat with two other king's clerks who were also to become bishops, Richard Leneveu (Béziers, 1305) and Robert de Fouilloy (Amiens, 1308).[74] These two men continued to work in the central government, but Pierre became Chancellor of Louis of Navarre in 1308. As such, he was in a position to protect Philip's interests in a county that theoretically belonged to his son. Jacques de Boulogne, like Pierre de Grez, was not deeply involved in the affairs of the court after becoming bishop of Thérouanne in 1287, but he was helpful in gaining support for the king among the clergy of Flanders after Philip occupied most

---

naisiens (Brussels, 1892 [extracted from *Bulletin de la commission royale d'histoire de Belgique*, 5th ser., III]), p. 31.

[73] Rigault, p. 30.   [74] Ibid., pp. 31-32.

of the county in 1297.[75] And while Pierre de la Chapelle-Taillefer, who had been bishop of Carcassonne and then of Toulouse, did not work directly for Philip after he became a cardinal, it was certainly helpful to have him in the College.

Perhaps the most accurate conclusion would be that the royal officials who became bishops were drawn from the abler members of the bureaucracy, that most of them had some expertise in law or in finance, that about half of them played important roles in executing royal policy, and that six of them (Pierre de Mornay, Pierre de Belleperche, Gilles Aicelin, Pierre de Latilly, Gui de la Charité, and perhaps Richard Leneveu)[76] helped to make policy. This is not very precise, but it is more than can be done for other categories of royal servants.

It is difficult to sum up this discussion, but the difficulty may indicate the conclusion. Philip had many able administrators but no hierarchically organized ministries (except, perhaps Eaux et Forêts and the customs service). He had many councillors but no permanent, or even semipermanent, inner council or secret council. There was very little specialization at the highest levels; men trained as lawyers acted as collectors of taxes, and men who had been primarily administrators acted as judges in the Parlement. There were exceptions to this rule: Gilles Aicelin and Pierre de Belleperche had little to do with finance, and the Treasurers were not often concerned with the routine work of the Parlement. But on most occasions the king felt free to use any man for any job. He also felt quite free to consult with any of his subjects on any problem. The Council was not composed exclusively of professional civil servants; it included prelates and nobles whom the king liked or wished to influence. It could reflect the opinion of the possessing classes rather than the advice of the bureaucracy, as in the case of the reform of the coinage in 1306.

In these circumstances one can make only tentative statements about the king's principal advisers. Early in his reign Philip was naturally working with the men whom he had inherited from his father—Robert of Burgundy, Pierre de Mornay, Thibaud de

[75] Funck-Brentano, *Philippe le Bel en Flandre*, p. 277.

[76] Richard served in the Parlement of 1298 (*J.T.P.*, no. 3182), but he spent most of his time on various missions outside of Paris. Two of these missions were so important that he must have enjoyed the king's confidence; the investigation of the Inquisition (*H.L.*, IX, 228, 257, X, col. 418), and an inquiry into the charges against Bernard Saisset (Dupuy, pp. 628-32).

Pouancé, Gilles Camelin, Robert d'Harcourt, Renaud Barbou, and the like. He respected these men and treated them well, but, if only because of the age difference, he could not have felt very close to them. The first high officials who were wholly his own were Biche and Mouche, who reached the peak of their influence in financial affairs about 1295. They remained on good terms with Philip and were useful advisers on foreign affairs until their deaths in 1306-1307, but they never again controlled the royal revenue as they had in 1294 and 1295. Just about the time that the Guidi brothers began to lose influence, other men who had recently been recruited or promoted by Philip the Fair became more conspicuous. Pierre de Mornay had served Philip III, but he became prominent only after 1285; Digard thought that Pierre and Robert of Burgundy were the leading councillors in the early 1290s.[77] Gilles Aicelin entered the king's service before 1290. Pierre de Latilly, Pierre Flote, Pierre de Belleperche, and Guillaume de Nogaret appear for the first time as royal agents in the 1290s. These men had all had legal training, but all were used in many capacities—as ambassadors, administrators, and, in the case of Latilly, as collector of taxes. By 1300 Pierre Flote was the most powerful member of this group (at least he spoke most frequently and most vehemently for the king), but Gilles Aicelin and Pierre de Mornay were not far behind, and Pierre de Belleperche was rising rapidly. Nogaret and Latilly reached the peak of their influence only after Flote's death in 1302.

By and large, Philip kept this team as long as he could. Pierre de Mornay and Pierre de Belleperche died after the crisis years were over (1306 and 1308, respectively); Nogaret and his chief aid, Guillaume de Plaisians, both passed away in 1313; Gilles Aicelin and Pierre de Latilly survived the king. There was no great effort to bring in new blood, as there had been in the 1290s. Philip had a group of well-trained, middle-level officials who were capable of handling routine business, and there was no real crisis between 1305 and the very end of the reign. Many of these middle-level men became prominent under Philip's sons, and even before 1314 Hugues de la Celle, Raoul Rousselet, and Robert de Fouilloy were clearly moving toward the top. Yet during Philip's reign one can hardly place them at the level of a Nogaret or a Pierre de Mornay.

[77] Digard, I, 105. The pope apparently thought that these were the two men who had the greatest influence with Philip in 1290.

An obvious reason for the failure to replace the men who had had key roles in the period 1295-1305 was the spectacular rise of Marigny. By 1314 he was officially in charge of the finances of the kingdom and unofficially in charge of French relations with Flanders and with the pope. No one, not even Flote, and certainly not Nogaret, had had such power. Marigny by 1313-1314 was nearer to being a prime minister than anyone else who ever served Philip the Fair. Moreover, he made a greater effort than most other royal officials to surround himself with subordinates who were his men rather than the king's. Flote may have brought in Nogaret, and Nogaret probably brought in Plaisians, but neither Flote nor Nogaret tried to control a key section of the government through protégés. Other high officials found jobs for their relations, but again without seeking to build up a family enclave. But in 1314 Marigny controlled the Chambre des Comptes through one of his clerks (Michel de Bourdenay), the Treasury through another (Geoffroi de Briançon), and banking and foreign exchange through his associate Thote Gui.[78] If Marigny had lived, he might have created a "ministry" (almost in the modern sense of the word), although it is doubtful that he could have gained control of the Parlement. His execution led to the disgrace of his followers and a reversion to more normal methods of government. At the same time, Pierre de Latilly was driven from public life by false accusations of contriving the death of Philip the Fair. Probably Latilly had worked too closely with Marigny to escape being involved in the latter's downfall. Gilles Aicelin was left as the only survivor of those who had been Philip's principal advisers, and Gilles was old, tired, and apparently disgusted with the accusations against his colleague Latilly.[79] He appeared at court from time to time but was not very active between 1314 and his death in 1318.

On the other hand, the death or retirement of Philip's most influential officials opened the road to a large and very competent group of younger men. Four of them have already been mentioned: Raoul Rousselet, Alain de Lamballe, Robert de Fouilloy, and Hugues de la Celle. Others, less powerful but still influential, were Denis de Sens, Dreux de la Charité, Gérard de Cortonne

[78] Favier, *Marigny*, pp. 21, 29, 100, 103, 104, 124-25.

[79] Pegues, pp. 70-71. The Butler, Gui de Saint-Pol, who had been the most active of the great officers of the crown, was in much the same situation as Gilles Aicelin. He attended court but was not influential; he died in 1319.

(bishop of Soissons), Guillaume Arrenard, Guillaume Flote, Jean de Forgetes, Philippe de Mornay, and Guillaume Courteheuse. A glance at the very full lists of members of the Parlements of 1316 shows the preponderance of men who had served Philip the Fair.[80] Even the new favorites, such as Henri de Sully (and eventually, in the time of Philip of Valois, Miles de Noyer), had worked for Philip, though they had been less active than the men mentioned above. Earlier in this chapter I estimated that about one-third of Philip's high- and middle-ranking officials continued to serve his sons, often in higher positions than they had held before 1314. The fact that there were so many capable and experienced officials explains why it was so easy to replace the men who disappeared between 1313 and 1318. The king had a wide choice; there were several hundred clerks and laymen who could handle almost any job. He picked the ones whom he respected for their intellectual and personal qualities, those who were most sympathetic with his ideas, and, during the period of disputed successions, those who were most likely to have support from the princes of the blood and the great nobles. Philip the Fair did not have to worry much about the last qualification, but otherwise he had followed the same rules. He picked Gilles Aicelin because he respected his ability, even though Aicelin at times disagreed with him. He picked Flote and Nogaret because they carried out his policies energetically. He picked Marigny first, in all likelihood, because he found him an agreeable companion, and then because he discovered that Marigny was an excellent administrator. Certainly the style of royal policy was affected by such choices; Aicelin and Marigny were more cautious than Flote and Nogaret. Whether the content of policy was much altered is another matter. Philip knew what he wanted, he could probably have achieved most of his objectives with an entirely different group of advisers.

[80] *Olim*, III, 1051-55, II, 624-25; Boutaric, ed., *Actes du Parlement*, II, 145-46.

III. The King and the Administration of the Realm

This chapter deals with the changes in administrative structures that were made necessary by the king's policies. Philip was not consciously trying to systemize or to expand the French administrative system, but he could not achieve his objectives without making, or approving, some important innovations. Thus the growing importance of extraordinary, as opposed to domain, revenues forced changes in both the provincial and the central financial system, culminating in the establishment of the Chambre des Comptes. At the same time, the emphasis on the king's judicial sovereignty required an increase in the number of judges, the introduction of procurators, and the growing professionalization of the Parlement. Philip did not create the French medieval bureaucracy; he built on precedents that went back for many generations. Nor did Philip make the bureaucracy as complex and as rigid as it later became. He did make it more professional, more structured, and, to some extent, more independent of temporary shifts in the political atmosphere. The great Companies of permanent, practically hereditary officials that were so important in the Old Regime were not entirely wrong when they traced their origins back to events in Philip's reign.

Local Administration

ADMINISTRATIVE DISTRICTS

The basic units of administration in France were the *bailliages* of the north and the *sénéchaussées* of the south. The northern *bailliages* fell into three groups. First in most official lists came the *bailliages* of "France," that is, the old royal domain. They were Paris (called a *prévôté* but actually a *bailliage*), Senlis, Vermandois, Amiens, Sens, Orléans, Bourges, Tours, and Mâcon. (Lille, at first a military district, became a *bailliage* after the "transport of Flanders," but Mignon listed it as "terra foranea" and not as a *bailliage* of France.) Then there were the Norman *bailliages*: Rouen, Caux, Caen, Cotentin, and Gisors-Verneuil. Finally,

Champagne had Troyes-Meaux, Vitry, and Chaumont. The *séné-chaussées* were Poitou, Saintonge, Auvergne (called a *bailliage* but always listed with the *sénéchaussées*), Périgord-Quercy, Rouergue, Toulouse, Carcassonne, Beaucaire, and, after 1310, Lyon. (The kingdom of Navarre, the county of Bigorre, and the county of Burgundy were considered "foreign.")

These districts were far from including all of France, but many *baillis* and seneschals had "ressort" over the lands of neighboring nobles. This meant that they transmitted and at times enforced royal orders, collected subventions for defense, protected people who were appealing to the king, and in general tried to ensure that the great barons and semi-independent bishops conformed to royal policy. Thus the *bailli* of Tours supervised collection of the subventions of Tours, Anjou, Maine, and Brittany,[1] and the seneschal of Carcassonne imposed payments on the county of Foix.[2] The seneschal of Beaucaire was responsible for the Vivarais,[3] and the *bailli* of Mâcon for Lyon.[4] The *baillis* of Amiens and Vermandois, either in person or through their agents, executed the king's orders in the county of Flanders.[5] This system meant that the power and importance of a royal official had no direct correspondence to the size and wealth of the territory he administered. The royal domain in Périgord-Quercy was small, but the seneschal of Périgord-Quercy was also responsible for maintaining the king's authority in the duchy of Aquitaine.[6] On the other side of the kingdom the *bailli* of Chaumont, the poorest district of Champagne, represented the king in his dealings with the clergy and people of Toul.[7] Therefore, these apparently minor offices were often held by distinguished members of the bureaucracy, such as Jean d'Arrablay and Guillaume de Hangest. On the other hand, the *bailliage* of the Cotentin, which was equally poor but had no external jurisdiction, usually went to elderly men on the edge of retirement.[8]

---

[1] Subventions from Brittany and Anjou were filed under the heading "baillivia Turonensis" (Mignon, nos. 1187, 1242, 1244, 1303, 1305, 1378).

[2] *H.L.*, IX, 174.

[3] Fritz Kern, ed., *Acta Imperii Angliae et Franciae (1267-1313)* (Tübingen, 1911), no. 45.

[4] Bonnassieux, pp. 65, 72.

[5] Funck-Brentano, *Philippe le Bel en Flandre*, pp. 113, 124-25, 163, 167.

[6] The "day" of the king of England in the Parlement is the "day" of the seneschal of Périgord (*Olim*, II, 46-47).

[7] Kern, ed., *Acta Imperii*, nos. 62, 68, 140, 141.

[8] Strayer, "Viscounts and Viguiers," pp. 223-24.

Each *bailliage* and *sénéchaussée* was divided into smaller districts—*prévôtés* in the old domain, in Saintonge-Poitou, in Auvergne, and in Champagne, viscounties in Normandy, and *baylies*, *viguieries*, and *jugeries* in the south. Except for the viscounties, the meaning of each of these terms varied so greatly that it is almost impossible to define them. A viscounty was a distinct financial and judicial unit; it had its own court and rendered its own separate accounts. The viscount was a professional officer; many viscounts were promoted to the rank of *bailli*.[9] A *prévôté* could be anything from a mere accounting unit to a quite effective branch of local government. Some *prévôtés* were fragments of the old domain, farmed for 20 or 30 pounds;[10] others included valuable rights of justice, tolls, and market dues as well as land.[11] A *prévôt* of St. Quentin could play an important role in royal policy in Flanders;[12] a *prévôt* of Péronne could become a *bailli*.[13] Men of this sort could be quite useful in local administration, but the majority of *prévôts* never reached this level.

The south presents an even more complicated picture. Toulouse, Carcassonne, Rouergue, and Périgord-Quercy were divided into *baylies*.[14] These *baylies*, farmed to local men, were like *prévôtés* in including land, tolls, and low justice, but they remained mere farms. The men who held them could thwart policy through inefficiency or bring the government into disrepute by oppressing the peasants, but they were not makers or executors of policy except on a very small scale.

There was a *viguier* in the city of Toulouse, but he had only limited jurisdiction. The really important local official in the *sénéchaussée* was the judge. There was a judge in the city itself and at least five (sometimes six or seven) local judges,[15] each of whom presided over a fairly well-defined district called a *jugerie*.

[9] Ibid., pp. 223-25.

[10] *C.R.*, I, nos. 1009 (Grange worth 25 l. a year), 1020 (Dollot, a little less than 18 l.), 1125 (Le Bourgneuf, 14 l.).

[11] Income from Péronne included rents, *péage*, and profits of justice (*C.R.*, I, nos. 4006-7); the *prévôt* of Melun accounted for rents, cens, sales-tax, and profits of justice (nos. 4111-13).

[12] Funck-Brentano, *Philippe le Bel en Flandre*, pp. 124-25.

[13] Carolus-Barré, "Baillis de Philippe III," pp. 169, 224.

[14] See below, p. 135. Beaucaire had *baylies*, but they were not numerous after 1285.

[15] Strayer, *Gens de justice*, pp. 177-94; "Viscounts and Viguiers," p. 216. See *C.R.*, I, nos. 9526-35, for an account of the profits of justice of the *viguier* of Toulouse.

These districts did not coincide with the *baylies*, which were much more numerous, so that in Toulouse the administration of justice and financial administration were almost completely separated. Rouergue had four local judges, much less important than those of Toulouse; Périgord-Quercy had one (for Cahors and its region).

Carcassonne and Beaucaire were divided into *vigueries*. There were 7 or 8 of these districts in Carcassonne and about 13 in Beaucaire; the numbers varied as additions were made to and lands were granted from the royal domain.[16] (In the extreme north of Beaucaire, where the nearly independent areas of Vivarais and Velay needed special attention, there was a *bailli*, subordinate to the seneschal of Beaucaire but much more powerful than a *viguier*.)[17] Basically, the *viguerie* was a military, financial, and judicial unit. The *viguiers* had primarily police and defense duties; many of them were also castellans.[18] Revenues were collected by other officers, and there was usually one local judge for each *viguerie*.[19] Sometimes a judge held several judgeships when the king held little land and few rights in a district.[20] On the whole, however, there was a closer correspondence between judicial and financial administrative districts in Carcassonne and Beaucaire than in Toulouse.

Auvergne, on the border between north and south, was unlike any other district. It was called a *bailliage* but was listed with the *sénéchaussées*. Most of Auvergne was divided into *prévôtés*, but a large area in the south was formed into a *bailliage* of the Mountains of Auvergne. This was not a real *bailliage*; its accounts were included in the accounts of Auvergne proper and the *bailli* (or *custos*, as the head of the district was called at times) was not a member of the upper bureaucracy.[21] Yet the *bailliage* of the Mountains was more than a *prévôté*, for it included several towns (Aurillac, St. Flour), and the *bailli* had police powers over a large

---

16 Strayer, "Viscounts and Viguiers," p. 219.

17 P. Fournier, *Le royaume d'Arles et Vienne 1138-1378* (Paris, 1891), p. 263; Kern, *Anfänge*, p. 112.

18 Strayer, "Viscounts and Viguiers," p. 217.

19 See the Appendix to Strayer, *Gens de justice*, for judges of Beaucaire and of Carcassonne.

20 Ibid., pp. 29-30.

21 *C.R.*, I, nos. 8578-92, 10540-51. The *custos* was paid only 5 s.t. a day (nos. 8707, 10603), no more than many castellans. For Delisle's list of the *baillis* of the Mountains see *H.F.*, XXIV, *209.

area. The nearest parallel would be the *bailli* of upper Beaucaire, though the latter had more power and responsibility.[22] The units described thus far are the ones that regularly appear in royal accounts. This neat picture is blurred, however, by the existence of castellanies. Much of France, especially in the north, was divided into castellanies, which were rather clearly defined geographical districts. In royal registers and in the acts of lay and ecclesiastical lords, lands and revenues are said to lie in such and such a castellany. For the nobles, especially those of middle rank, the castellany could be an administrative unit. This does not seem true of the royal domain. For example, Poissy and Pontoise were both *prévôtés*, but loans for the Gascon war were said to be collected in the castellanies of Poissy and Pontoise.[23] The dowager queen Marie assigned rents on the *prévôtés* or castellanies of Mantes, Paci, Anet, Nogent-le-Roi, and Bréval.[24] Niort, in Poitou, appears in one account both as a castellany and as a *prévôté*, and it is the mayor of Niort, not a castellan, who acts in the castellany.[25] These combinations do not prove, of course, that a castellany and a *prévôté* with identical names had exactly the same boundaries. What they do prove is that in the royal domain in the north the castellany did not have separate institutions and officers; it was administered by the same men who administered the *prévôtés*. The lands acquired from Flanders were described as the castellanies of Lille, Douai, and Béthune; there was general agreement about the boundaries of the castellanies proper, but bitter arguments about dependencies of and enclaves within these districts.[26] In any case, the transition from military occupation to civilian administration was slow; it was only after Philip's death that Douai and Orchies were incorporated into the *bailliage* of Lille (Béthune was given to Mahaut d'Artois). Meanwhile, the principal representative of royal authority there, Baudouin de Longwez, was called governor and not castellan.[27]

In the south there were many castellans—far too many, in the

---

[22] See above, note 17. Delisle gives a list of these *baillis* in *H.F.*, xxiv, *243.

[23] *C.R.*, i, nos. 292, 3762 n. 2, 3888, ii, nos. 19056, 19117.

[24] Lands formerly in the *prévôté* and castellany of Boiscommun were attached to the castellany and *prévôté* of Lorris (A.N., JJ 49, fol. 11, no. 19; cf. JJ 49, fol. 54v, no. 125). The unit of jurisdiction in this document is clearly the *prévôté*; the lands are specifically exempted from the jurisdiction of the *prévôt* of Boiscommun.

[25] *C.R.*, ii, nos. 7251, 7353, 7377.

[26] Funck-Brentano, *Philippe le Bel en Flandre*, pp. 627-28.

[27] Mignon, nos. 141, 142, 144.

opinion of the central government, which tried to reduce their numbers. The castellans, however, had no jurisdiction, and the castellany seldom appears as a geographical district.[28] The most important exception was the castellany of Montréal in the *sénéchaussée* of Carcassonne. This district accounted separately at the level of a *viguerie*,[29] and the castellan of Montréal, as one of the great men of the *sénéchaussée*, was frequently called to the seneschal's council.[30]

France was full of towns of all sizes, from great commercial centers such as Rouen, Toulouse, or Narbonne, to places that were nothing more than large villages with a few artisans and traders. Some towns had extensive rights of self-government; others had none at all. Size had nothing to do with this difference. Paris, by far the largest town, was governed directly by royal officials; little places in the south, such as Fons in Quercy or Ondes in the Toulousain, had their consulates. The degree of self-government also varied, but the essential element was the recognition of the town as a corporation that could sue and be sued in the person of its officials or legally constituted procurators. Such towns also had elected or co-opted officials, courts with varying degrees of jurisdiction (usually most extensive on the criminal side), limited rights to make local ordinances, which dealt mainly with trade, building regulations, food supply, and the like, and carefully controlled powers to impose local taxes for such things as repair of bridges or fortifications and for legal expenses (including the heavy fines imposed by the royal government). No town in the realm, not even the great towns of Flanders, was entirely independent, as many Italian towns were. Only the Flemish towns had jurisdiction that extended out into the countryside; the most that the ordinary French town could claim was control of the suburban area that lay within a mile or two of its walls. Even within the walls, certain enclaves—usually quarters held by a monastery or a cathedral chapter—were exempt from the jurisdiction of the town governments.

[28] Jean d'Arrablay was sent in 1297 to reduce the number of castellans in Saintonge-Poitou, Gascony, and Périgord (A.N., J 307, no. 4). Castellans in Toulouse had no jurisdiction (J 329, no. 43, para. 16).

[29] *C.R.*, 1, nos. 12688, 12706, 12714, 12801.

[30] A.N., JJ 46, fol. 2, no. 3, JJ 49, fol. 83v, no. 195, JJ 50, fol. 17, no. 18, fol. 51, no. 75, fol. 64, no. 99. In general, the southern castellans were more influential in local government than those of the north, but they seldom had a jurisdiction of their own. For castellans as forest officers see below, p. 131.

Large or small, privileged or not, the towns had to be treated as distinct administrative entities. They had their own rules about landholding and inheritance, problems about the organization and regulation of trade and crafts, and requirements for fortfications and other public works. They produced revenues different from those of purely agricultural areas, for example, market dues, sales-taxes, payments connected with the use or verification of weights and measures. They developed strong corporate feeling; they could, for example, resist royal demands for taxation far more effectively than peasants living in scattered villages. This resistance was most effective when the king was not the immediate lord of the town, as in the cases of Montpellier (held by the king of Majorca) and the Flemish towns. But even Paris, which was ruled directly by the king, could bargain its way out of a sales-tax and create its own machinery for collecting a substitute payment.[31]

To some extent this desire of the towns to run their own affairs was helpful to the king. He did not have to recruit additional officials to handle the details of municipal affairs and he probably received as much money from bourgeois collectors of revenues, who may have cheated but who knew their town, as he would have from honest but uninformed collectors brought in from outside. Except for Flanders and, on one occasion, Carcassonne, the towns were loyal to the king. They might riot, but they did not rebel. Again with the exception of Flanders, the leaders of the towns were well-to-do bourgeois who wanted peace and security. They could profit from the king's favor, and a considerable number of them entered royal service. One of the worst riots of the reign was in Rouen; yet citizens of Rouen became *baillis* and viscounts.[32]

The king could not administer all the towns directly, any more than he could have administered all the realm directly. He needed town governments to ease the burden just as he needed baronial governments. He could not, however, trust either barons or towns completely, and he trusted the towns rather less than

---

[31] Boutaric, "Documents inédits," pp. 22-25. For a description of the way in which the city organized the collection of its payments see K. Michaëlsson, *Le livre de la taille de Paris: l'an 1296* (Göteborg, 1958), p. iv.

[32] A notable example was Jean de Saint-Liénart, who served as mayor of Rouen, 1269-1270 and 1284-1285, as *bailli* of Caen, 1293-1295, and as *prévôt* of Paris; see Carolus-Barré, "Baillis de Philippe III," p. 231. Geoffroi Avice (mayor, 1292-1293) became viscount of Rouen in 1298 and *bailli* of the Cotentin in 1305; see my "Viscounts and Viguiers," pp. 224-25.

the barons. *Baillis* and seneschals kept a close watch on the towns and intervened whenever they thought that a town was disobeying royal orders or following policies that the king could not approve. In the old domain the *prévôts*, especially the salaried and career-minded ones, also kept a careful eye on the towns. Smaller communities, where the *prévôt* was simply a businessman who farmed certain royal revenues, were less closely supervised, but there was less danger that they would get into mischief. There were many possible varieties of royal control. Perhaps the most complicated was at Rouen, which had its own mayor and council, and also a royal *bailli*, a royal viscount, and the Viscounty of the Water. The latter was in effect a *prévôté* that collected duties on all imports by land and by water (wine was the source of the largest part of the revenue). The Viscounty of the Water could be farmed as a whole, farmed in separate blocks, or administered by royal officials.[33] The archbishop and chapter of Rouen also had extensive rights of jurisdiction in the city. The Normans were traditionally fond of lawsuits; they needed to be at Rouen, where there were so many overlapping rights that litigation was inevitable. It was at times difficult for the *bailli* to know whom he should support.

Narbonne, at the other end of the realm, was also difficult to administer. The archbishop and the hereditary viscount of the town each had their own jurisdictions, and the king was trying to build up a jurisdiction of his own at the expense of the other two. Such divisions of authority were not rare in the south. Montpellier had been like Narbonne: one part of the city was held by the king of Majorca, the other by the bishop of Maguelonne, who ceded his rights to Philip the Fair. Elsewhere, a monastery might control the *bourg* that had grown up around its buildings while the rest of the town was ruled by another lord. Such divisions encouraged the interventions of royal officials and often led to *paréages* or sales of rights to the king.

The royal government did not become deeply involved in disputes among burgesses about the selection of town officials. An exception would be the condemnation of the governing clique of Périgueux in 1309, when other citizens claimed that recent elections had been rigged.[34] It should be noted, however, that the

---

[33] The basic book on the Viscounty of the Water is Charles de Beaurepaire, *De la vicomté de l'eau de Rouen* (Paris, 1856). See chapter 3 on the farming of the viscounty.

[34] *Olim*, III, 366.

towns in this *sénéchaussée* were resisting Philip's request for an aid for marrying his daughter, and royal officials may have been glad to have an excuse to inflict a heavy fine on the consuls. On the other hand, the government was annoyed by towns that tried to arrogate power to themselves. By far the most common source of friction was the hostility of townsmen to ecclesiastical jurisdictions and their resentment of exemptions of clerks in minor orders from municipal justice and taxation. On the whole, local royal officials sympathized with this feeling, but the central government tried to hold it within reasonable limits[35] and was very severe when urban resentment of clerical privileges led to rioting.[36] There were also disputes about the extent and nature of the jurisdiction of municipal courts. Like everyone else who had rights of justice, town officials tried to expand these rights to include as wide an area and as many people as possible. Disputes over such matters were usually settled by the king or by the Parlement rather than by local royal officials, and the towns were reasonably successful in defending their claims.[37]

When it came to collecting subventions and aids, local officials were deeply involved in negotiations with the towns. A town could scarcely deny that it should furnish money for the defense of the realm, but it could propose changes in the form and the amount of the tax.[38] The aids for marrying the king's daughter or knighting the king's son were a different matter. It was not at all clear that the marriage aid was a general obligation, and

[35] Baudouin, ed., *Lettres inédites*, nos. 11 (77), 12 (75), 28 (76), for royal mandates ordering consuls of Toulouse to respect the privileges of clerks. (The numbers in parentheses are repetitions of the preceding mandate.)

[36] Laon lost all of its rights of self-government and was fined 30,000 l.p. in 1295 for breaking into the cathedral, seizing two squires who had taken sanctuary there, and killing one of them. The fine was collected, but communal rights were restored in 1297, perhaps because it was too much trouble to keep a royal *gardiator* there (*Olim*, II, 384; *J.T.P.*, no. 949 and n. 3; Mignon, nos. 1897, 1898).

[37] See Baudouin, ed., *Lettres inédites*, nos. 142, 157, 160, 165, for royal mandates concerning the justice of the consuls of Toulouse. *Olim*, II, 317, 383, 398, 429, 431, 445 (vi), 523, 555-56, are a few of the cases in which the Parlement upheld the rights of communes. In the abstract of my paper on "La clientèle du Parlement de Paris," read at the Journées internationales de Rouen in 1974 (published in *Revue historique de droit français et étranger* [1975], 160), I showed that the confidence of the bourgeoisie in the Parlement grew during Philip's reign; after 1300, about 31 percent of the pleaders were bourgeois.

[38] Strayer and Taylor, pp. 50-52, 54, 67-68.

many towns refused to pay—with varying success. The league of towns of Quercy managed to delay and on the whole to block collection, while in Saintonge-Poitou a forceful seneschal raised a considerable amount of money.[39] There was also opposition to the aid for knighting Louis of Navarre, and again many towns escaped paying.[40]

Payments for amortization irritated the towns, but they were usually assessed and collected by special commissioners.[41] On the other hand, the ordinances on the currency, which were especially annoying to businessmen, were enforced by the *baillis* and seneschals.[42] The towns in the royal domain could do little but grumble, though it is significant that the one serious riot in Paris during Philip's reign was caused by the revaluation of the currency in 1306.[43] It is also significant that Philip found it helpful to consult town representatives on monetary policy in 1308, 1313, and 1314.[44] Towns that had a powerful noble as their immediate lord could usually count on him to protest, as in the cases of the Flemish towns and Majorcan Montpellier.[45] The protests were rejected, but royal officials found it difficult to enforce the ordinances on money in these districts.

To sum up, the town governments were useful in local administration. They were fairly easily controlled by royal officials, with the notable and almost disastrous exception of the towns of Flanders. They lacked the strength to prevent rioting, but this meant that they also lacked the strength to rebel (Flanders is again an obvious exception). Town governments that could not keep order could be suspended by the king and governed directly by royal officers. There was no resistance to such takeovers, only persistent pleas for restoration of old privileges. Usually, after a period of penance, the forfeited rights were restored. This was done partly because the king could demand large sums of money for reviving the old municipal government, partly because there was a feeling in high circles that forfeitures ought to be restored

---

[39] See above, p. 84.

[40] See above, pp. 84-85, and Brown, *Customary Aids and Royal Finance*, chap. 6.

[41] See below, pp. 398-99.　　　　[42] *Ord.*, I, 324, 347, 389, 430, XI, 365.

[43] See below, p. 396.　　　　[44] See below, Chapter VI, note 21.

[45] Funck-Brentano, *Philippe le Bel en Flandre*, pp. 137-38, 153-54, 158; B.N., ms. lat. 9192, fols. 59, 62, 71v, 72v, 74, 75v, 82v; *H.L.*, x, col. 519. Léon Ménard, *Histoire civile, ecclésiastique et littéraire de la ville de Nismes*, 7 vols. (1744-1758), I, *preuves*, 142, published two of Philip's letters ordering enforcement in Montpellier of the ordinances on money.

after a reasonable length of time, and partly because town governments did save time and expense in carrying some of the burden of local administration.

The towns were useful in another way, which can scarcely be called administrative, but which certainly aided the central government. The great assemblies that heard charges against Boniface VIII and the Temple and the request for a subvention for the Flemish campaign of 1314 were supposed to include representatives of ordinary inhabitants and subjects of the kingdom,[46] as well as nobles and clergymen. The *baillis* and seneschals were told to summon men from the "communities" of the realm, or, in 1308, from the "communities" and "locis insignibus." This left a good deal of leeway to the *baillis* and seneschals who did the summoning, especially in 1308. Nevertheless, the cardinals in 1302 clearly believed that most of the delegates came from chartered towns; they addressed their letter of protest to the mayors, *échevins, jurés,* consuls, and communities of the cities and towns of France.[47] Even in 1308, when it is certain that delegates came from what we would call unincorporated villages,[48] the largest number received their powers from mayors, consuls, or other officials of chartered towns.[49] It is difficult to see how it could have been otherwise. There was no regular machinery for summoning procurators from the semirural areas, as was shown by the variety of devices adopted by royal officials in 1308. Moreover, the assemblies were primarily exercises in propaganda, and it was much more important to influence the bourgeoisie than the peasants. The towns had more money; they could make more trouble; they were better informed and both needed and could understand the explanations given by the king's officials. The towns were one of the principal targets in Philip's attempts to influence the opinion of the possessing classes, and the fact that towns had regular procedures for choosing representatives in lawsuits made it easy for them to choose representatives who would meet with the king and hear and support his proposals. Some confusion resulted when communities that did not normally have the power to name procurators were summoned. The

---

[46] Picot, pp. 1, 6, 22, 26 (for 1303), pp. 490, 491 (1308). The letters of 1303 were addressed primarily to the towns, but "incole" are twice mentioned. In 1308 towns and "loci insignes" were summoned. In 1314 only men from the cathedral cities appeared. (*H.F.,* xx, 691).

[47] Picot, p. 22.   [48] Ibid., pp. liv-lv.

[49] Ibid., pp. liv-lv, and the *Table des documents,* pp. 851-58.

delegates might then be chosen by a royal official or the local agent of the immediate lord; they might also be named in a town meeting attended, at least in theory, by all adult males.[50] By and large, however, the pattern of representation was set by the chartered towns, the communes of the north, and the consulates of the south. If they had not existed, it would have been impossible to have convoked the great assemblies of the reign.

LOCAL ADMINISTRATIVE OFFICIALS

The key man in local administration throughout Philip's reign was the *bailli* or seneschal. He was ultimately responsible for every action in his district that touched the interests of the king—keeping the peace and defending the borders, arresting malefactors and seeing that the law courts performed their functions properly, collecting revenues and maintaining revenue-producing properties in proper condition, enforcing royal ordinances, and putting into effect the numerous mandates that ordered transfers of land, establishment of rents, compromises over jurisdiction, and enforcement of decisions of the Parlement. He was the highest judge and the final administrative authority; appeals from his decisions ran only to the Parlement or to the king and Council. The seneschals and *baillis* were capable men, as is shown by the fact that they were often promoted to positions in the central administration.[51] Even the most capable men, however, must have found it difficult to keep up with their work.[52] The average size of their districts was larger than that of a modern department, and travel would have consumed much of their time, even if they had never left their bailiwicks. But they were also required to attend sessions of the Council or the Parlement, carry orders and admonitions to great lords like the count of Flanders or the duke of Aquitaine, and go to regional meetings, such as the Exchequer of Normandy or the Grands Jours of Champagne. They needed help, and during Philip's reign they got it.

One of the most desirable innovations was the establishment of a receiver (or treasurer) in each district.[53] The *baillis* and

[50] Picot, pp. liv-lv; cf. pp. 646-59 for examples of all these procedures.

[51] See above, p. 38.

[52] In 1294-1295 the seneschal of Beaucaire noted in his register 191 orders from the king (E. Martin-Chabot, ed., *Les archives de la cour des comptes, aides et finances de Montpellier* [Paris, 1907], pp. 16-46).

[53] *J.T.P.*, pp. vii-x, gives names of some of the receivers for the period

seneschals had always needed assistance in preparing their accounts and in handling the money that they took in or paid out;
their clerks had usually taken care of much of this work. A clerk
like Master Richard du Fay, who was active in the *bailliage* of
Rouen in the last decades of the reign of St. Louis, was almost
as important a figure in administering the domain lands as the
bailli himself.[54] But although a clerk might make leases and prepare accounts, the final responsibility lay with the *bailli*, who
had to justify his expenditures and was liable for any deficits.[55]
Only in the 1290s did accounts begin to be rendered in the name
of a receiver rather than in the name of a *bailli* or seneschal.

The change began, as might have been expected, in the south.
Whereas by Philip's reign, *baillis* and seneschals had almost identical functions, and men could be shifted back and forth between
the two offices, the seneschal had originally been one of the great
officers of a feudal court (for example, the seneschal of Poitou),
and the first *baillis* were simply working members of the administration. The seneschal was almost always a noble, sometimes a
noble of considerable importance (for example, Bertrand Jourdain de l'Isle Jourdain, seneschal of Beaucaire, 1304-1309), whereas the *bailli* could be of bourgeois origin. The social difference
was marked by the difference in pay: *baillis* regularly received
365 l.t. a year; seneschals, 500 to 700 l.t.[56] The seneschals, who
worked in the recently acquired and still imperfectly assimilated
lands of the south had greater military responsibilities than the
baillis; they had to guard the unsettled borders with Aquitaine
and the Spanish kingdoms and the turbulent region of the Massif
Central. In short, by birth and by the nature of their duties they
were less apt to be expert in financial matters than the *baillis*. In
his famous description of the good *bailli*, Philippe de Beaumanoir
emphasizes the need for financial skill: the *bailli* must know how
to keep accurate accounts; he must increase the income from the
lands of his lord.[57] Such advice would have been beneath the

---

1298-1301. Mignon's lists (nos. 67-108) cover a longer period but are incomplete and do not always distinguish receivers from seneschals and
baillis.

[54] Strayer, *Administration of Normandy*, pp. 98-99.

[55] A document published by Langlois in *Revue historique*, LX (1896),
327, says that Philip wanted to know "se li baillez en rende bon conte et
louial."

[56] See above, Chapter II, "The Rewards of Office," note 4.

[57] Philippe de Beaumanoir, *Coutumes de Beauvaisis*, ed. Amédée Salmon

dignity of a seneschal like Eustache de Beaumarchais (Toulouse, 1272-1294), who was a virtual viceroy in southwestern France. Thus it is not surprising that we hear of a treasurer of Toulouse under Philip III and perhaps of a receiver of Carcassonne at about the same time. This treasurer of Toulouse was still in office in 1286 and seems to have had responsibility for revenues in Rouergue and part of Beaucaire as well as for Toulouse. There was also a receiver of Auvergne by 1288.[58] Champagne, which had many small *bailliages*, had had a single receiver since about 1240;[59] Philip the Fair, as husband of Jeanne of Champagne, was perhaps more familiar with this precedent than with the one in the south. In any case, early in his reign, he began to establish receivers throughout the *bailliages* and *sénéchaussées*. Biche and Mouche, who were given extraordinary financial powers in the period between 1288 and 1296, were receivers of Toulouse by 1288 and of Carcassonne and Champagne by 1290.[60] In 1291 they also had responsibility for Rouergue and Périgord-Quercy.[61] Obviously, they could not act directly in all those districts, and the bulk of the work was performed by their deputies. There was a receiver for Paris in 1292, in Vermandois by 1294, and in all the other *bailliages* of France, plus Poitou and Auvergne, at least by 1296.[62] It is more difficult to observe the emergence of receivers in Normandy. Men who certainly were receivers are not always given

---

(Paris, 1899-1900), para. 20: "cil est bons bailli en qui main la terre son seigneur croist. . . . Et si li convient mout qu'il sache bien conter, car c'est uns des plus grands perieus qui soit en l'office du baillif que d'estre negligens ou peu soigneus de ses contes."

[58] See Langlois, *Philippe III*, p. 327 and n., A.N., J 421, and *C.R.*, II, nos. 15474-79, for the account of the treasurer of Toulouse for late 1285–July 1286; see *C.R.*, II, no. 15576, for the treasurers of Toulouse for 1287-1288. For Auvergne see below, n. 93.

[59] Ozanam, p. 335.

[60] *C.R.*, II, no. 16556; Borrelli de Serres, *Recherches*, III, 13; Mignon, no. 2678; Ozanam, p. 343; B.N., ms. Doat 155, fol. 247; Martin-Chabot, ed., *Les archives de la cour des comptes de Montpellier*, no. 463.

[61] Borrelli de Serres, II, 13. For later years see *C.R.*, I, nos. 8834 (Quercy, 1293-1294), 8985 (Toulouse, 1293-1294), 10267 (Rouergue, 1293-1294).

[62] Nicolas Brussel, *Novel examen de l'usage général des fiefs*, 2 vols. (Paris, 1727), I, 475-77, and *C.R.*, II, no. 15072 (Paris, 1292; Amiens, 1296; Orléans, 1296); *J.T.P.*, no. 106 and n. 4 (Vermandois, 1294), no. 418 (Bourges, 1298); Mignon, p. 247, "Compoti receptarum balliviarum ac senescalliarum ubi prius non fuerant receptores," and, under this rubric, nos. 1971 (Sens, 1296), 1973 (Senlis, before 1299), 1974 (Vermandois, 1294); *C.R.*, III, no. 30199 (Poitou, Orléans, Tours, Bourges, and Auvergne, May 1296).

the title (especially when accounting in the Exchequer), but by 1298 there was a receiver in each Norman *bailliage*.[63]

The institution of receivers throughout France started on an ad hoc basis but was formalized in 1296. An entry in Mignon speaks of accounts of receivers "ubi prius non fuerant receptores," and five of these appear first in 1296. There is also a list of receivers for each *bailliage* or *sénéchaussée*, probably from 1296, since Mouche is still responsible for Champagne, and certainly no later than 1297, since all but two are mentioned in the Journal of the Treasury early in 1298, which means that they must have been in office at least in the latter part of 1297. This document also shows that the general use of receivers was a new idea, since five "visiteurs des receveurs" were appointed: Jean Clersens, a clerk of the *Chambre aux Deniers*; the clerk of Renaud Barbou, who was a Master of the Chamber; the clerk of the acting Keeper (Thibaud de Pouancé, bishop of Dol); Jean de Dijon, a royal notary; and Jean de "Castro Censorii," a collector of tenths. These were minor officials, but all except the last represented great men. Clearly, the court wanted to keep track of the experiment. The results must have been satisfactory, for we hear nothing more of "visitors" of the receivers.[64]

As with most new offices, the precise duties and competence of the receiver were not established immediately. He must have been rather independent in Champagne, where there was only one receiver and three or four *baillis* and where the receiver was paid more than a *bailli* (500 l.t., as opposed to 365 l.t. in 1317).[65] At the other extreme was Normandy, where the receivers were clearly subordinate to the *baillis* and accounted only in the name of their superiors. As late as 1309 an ordinance specifically stated that the *baillis* were responsible for the revenues of their *bailliage*.[66] This is not surprising. The Norman *baillis* had been concerned

---

[63] *J.T.P.*, nos. 101 (Rouen), 688 (Gisors-Verneuil), 725 (Caen), 755 (Cotentin), 3467 (Caux).

[64] Mignon, p. 247. The list of receivers is in B.N., ms. fr. 25992, no. 48. The names of the receivers are sometimes deformed, but are recognizable. They can be found in the references given in notes 62 and 63, and in *J.T.P.* The "visitors" are also in Viard's index to *J.T.P.*

[65] Ozanam, p. 340. Southern receivers were paid 100 l.t. a year (*C.R.*, I, nos. 10695, 11907, 14009), a salary equal to that of some of the *juges-mages*, but the receiver of Paris had only 18 d.p. a day, about 37 l.t. a year (*C.R.*, I, no. 1604).

[66] *J.T.P.*, no. 3467 (the *bailli* of Caux accounts for his receiver); see also *Ord.* I, 464, art. 15.

with financial duties even before the French conquest of 1204, and their viscounts collected a large part of the revenues of the royal domain. When a single viscount had to account for a gross revenue of 4,937 l.t. for one term,[67] it is easy to see that a receiver would not have much to do.

Elsewhere, it is difficult to see a consistent pattern. In the *bailliage* of Tours there were local receivers, perhaps one for each *prévôté*,[68] which would have diminished the importance of the receiver-general. In the *bailliages* of France, except for Paris, where the *bailli* and the receiver rendered a joint account,[69] the *bailli* alone accounted, perhaps because the *prévôts* in this region received a substantial part of the royal revenues and the *bailli* was responsible for the *prévôts*. The same system was followed in Auvergne, also a land of *prévôtés*.[70] But in the region where Biche, Mouche, and their deputies had been made responsible for collecting revenues the receivers rendered the accounts. This was true of Périgord-Quercy, of Rouergue, and of Toulouse in 1294 and 1299.[71] In the case of Toulouse, it is clear that the receivers presented the accounts in Paris.[72] Beaucaire, which had not been included in the great southern receivership given to Biche and Mouche, was a little different. The one full account (1302-1303) that has survived was rendered in the names of both the seneschal and the receiver, although only the receiver and his staff seem to have made the journey to present the account.[73] In the list of debts of the 1290s there is a clear distinction between payments owed by the account of the seneschal of Beaucaire and those owed by the account of the receivers.[74] The evidence for Carcassonne is the least satisfactory of that for all the *sénéchaussées*, but in the account of 1302-1303 a large deficit (877 l.t.) caused by heavy military expenses was said to be owed to the receivers, and the receivers rendered the account in Paris.[75] On the other

[67] *C.R.*, II, no. 17503. A viscounty could have its own receiver (*J.T.P.*, no. 3960 [Mortain]).

[68] *C.R.*, I, nos. 3078, 3109, 3111, 3113-19, 3129, 3133.

[69] Ibid., nos. 1211 (1299), 4234 (1305).   [70] Ibid., no. 10498.

[71] Ibid., nos. 8834, 10729 (Périgord-Quercy); nos. 10267, 12377 (Rouergue); nos. 8986, 10867 (Toulouse).

[72] Ibid., nos. 10086, 12338. The second entry is conclusive; expenses for the clerk of the seneschal are crossed out, and expenses of the clerks of the receiver for going "ad compotos" are substituted.

[73] Ibid., nos. 13122, 14012.

[74] Ibid., II, nos. 15001, 15004-5, 15029, 15076-89, 15106.

[75] Ibid., I, no. 13106.

hand, the seneschal of Carcassonne had his own (partial?) account in 1296-1297.[76]

The autonomy and the responsibility of a receiver might vary not only with the official terms of his appointment but also with his own background and that of the *bailli* or seneschal whom he served. Most of the early receivers were Italians associated with the great banking companies of the Tuscan towns. They were not career officials; they served relatively short terms and had little influence on decisions made by their superiors. Renier Acorre, receiver of Champagne from 1274 to 1288, is an apparent exception, but he was a holdover from the time of Count Henry III, and he ended his career in prison, probably for malversation.[77] Members of the Guidi family had long and successful careers, but the most successful of them, Biche and Mouche, gradually moved out of their receiverships. By 1298 they were mainly concerned with foreign affairs. Their nephew, Thotus Guidi, was responsible for collecting the indemnity promised by the treaty of Athis and for other Flemish revenues from 1307 to 1332. He was called receiver of Lille and Béthune in 1310 and receiver of Flanders in 1311-1312. He was also master of the mint of Tournai from 1310 into the reign of Philip VI. Vanna Guidi, brother of Thotus, was also working on the Flanders account in the years 1315-1330.[78] But the receiver of Flanders was not doing the work of a receiver of Rouen, much less that of a receiver of Toulouse.

As Philip gradually replaced Italian with French receivers,[79] the office became more important and attractive, at least in the south. The northern receivers, often working under *baillis* of bourgeois origin who knew a good deal about accounting and with viscounts and *prévôts* who handled their own subordinate accounts, were never very important. Even the receiver of Paris, Hervé de la Trinité, who served at least 11 years (1294-1305), was paid only 18 d.p. a day and had no significant duties except to keep his accounts.[80] It is true that he was an elderly man (he

[76] Ibid., II, nos. 15372, 15406.

[77] He was fined 15,000 l.t. (Ozanam, p. 343; C.R., II, nos. 15281, 15299).

[78] Funck-Brentano, *Philippe le Bel en Flandre*, p. 522; Mignon, nos. 144, 146, 1979, 1981, 2004; C.R., II, nos. 17210, 27557 (the last entry is for the mint). Cf. *J.T.C.*, col. 16, and Cazelles, p. 278, for the later careers of Thotus and Vanna Guidi.

[79] There were no Italian receivers in Champagne after 1305 (Strayer, "Pierre de Chalon," pp. 245-47; Ozanam, pp. 344-45).

[80] Mignon, no. 67; *J.T.P.*, nos. 558, 5170; C.R., I, nos. 1604, 4234. For Hervé as a notary of the Châtelet see L. Carolus-Barré, "L'organization de

had been a notary of the Châtelet in the 1270s), but other receivers in the north were equally inconspicuous. Thus Robert le Parmentier, receiver of Senlis in 1305, was guard of the seal of Senlis from 1310 to 1312.[81] He probably made as much (or more) out of this office as he did out of the receivership, and the work was probably easier.

The situation was different in the south, where the seneschals seem to have relied more on their receivers. Many of these receivers were natives of the region, but some came from Paris; most of them had local influence, and some had distinguished administrative careers. To give an example of a man of moderate importance, Arnaud de Proboleno, a citizen of Cahors, was a professional receiver (Rouergue, 1305, 1317; Périgord-Quercy, 1309-1311, 1317; Toulouse, 1315-1316).[82] The receivership of Périgord-Quercy turned into a family job; Jean de Proboleno held the position from 1324 to 1340 and was succeeded by Marcus de Proboleno.[83] Arnaud also collected subsidies in Périgord-Quercy and Toulouse in 1314 and 1315 and acted as adviser to the seneschals of Périgord-Quercy and Toulouse on settlements of claims of the crown against private persons.[84]

A much more distinguished man was Gérard Baleine of Figéac, receiver of Périgord-Quercy from 1296 to at least 1299, and perhaps later.[85] The exact dates are hard to establish because during the war with England he was also receiver for the part of Périgord that lay in the duchy of Aquitaine, and at times he was even

---

la jurisdiction gracieuse à Paris," *Le Moyen Age*, LXIX (1963), 427. He was still a notary in 1301, so he could not have spent all his time on his work as receiver.

[81] *C.R.*, I, nos. 4748, 4782, 4835 (as receiver); A.N., JJ 45, fol. 119v, no. 206, JJ 46, no. 59, K 38, no. 8, B.N., ms. fr. 20334, nos. 6, 9, 15, 39, 70 (keeper of the seal of Senlis). Note that, like Hervé, he was in effect a notary.

[82] Mignon, nos. 99, 100, 101, 107; *Cartulaire de Prouille*, I, 247; A.N., JJ 46, fol. 65v, no. 88, JJ 50, fol. 10v, no. 8, JJ 54A, fol. 8, no. 112, J 1030, no. 5; A.D. Aveyron, G 641.

[83] G. Dupont-Ferrier, ed., *Gallia Regia ou l'état des officiers royaux des bailliages et des sénéchaussées de 1328 à 1515*, 6 vols. (Paris, 1942-1965), IV, no. 17300.

[84] Mignon, nos. 1635, 1682, 1685; A.N., JJ 46, fol. 65v, no. 88, JJ 50, fol. 10v, no. 8.

[85] Mignon, nos. 99, 107; *C.R.*, I, no. 10729; B.N., ms. Doat 176, fol. 275v; J.T.P., no. 4626; G. Lacoste, *Histoire générale de Quercy*, 2 vols. (Cahors, 1883-1886), II, 417 (this last document dated in April 1304).

called receiver of Gascony.[86] He was deeply involved in the finances of the Gascon war as a paymaster for troops, ships, and supplies, and he collected subsidies in 1297, 1302, and 1304.[87] He amassed a small fortune, not all of it honestly, and, though not of noble birth, he became a king's knight.[88] Trouble caught up with him in 1306. An ominous note in Nogaret's papers says that the case against Gérard was "sufficienter probatus."[89] Gérard admitted that he owed the king 15,000 l.t. and surrendered his castle of Almont and other lands in Quercy.[90] It is likely that Gérard had obtained Almont illicitly; it was part of the land given to the count of Périgord in exchange for the viscounties of Auvillars and Lomagne, an exchange that Gérard's brother Pierre (receiver of Périgord-Quercy, 1304) had helped to arrange.[91] Gérard was not completely disgraced; he kept his title of king's knight and his lordship over some lands,[92] but he was not employed again.

Another southern receiver who had a longer, if less prosperous, career than Gérard Baleine was Géraud Chauchat of Clermont. A member of one of the great banking families of his city, he began his career by handling various banking transactions for the famous Cepperello Diotaiuti, who was receiver of Auvergne in 1288-1290.[93] Géraud himself had become receiver at least by 1295, and he kept the job until he died in 1311.[94] He collected subsidies and took Jewish goods in 1306.[95] He received a hereditary rent of 100 l.t. a year in 1305, in addition to his salary of

[86] Mignon, nos. 113, 118; A.N., J 307, no. 41; B.N., ms. Clairembault 210, no. 20, ms. Doat 176, fol. 192.

[87] Mignon, nos. 1338, 1547, 2263, 2311, 2339, 2349, 2354, 2380, 2395, 2477; H.L., x, col. 431.

[88] Gérard's brother Pierre, though not noble, was allowed in 1310 to hold noble land (A.N., JJ 47, fol. 11, no. 15). But Gérard had become a king's knight by 1308 (JJ 44, fol. 70v, no. 114).

[89] Langlois, ed., "Papiers de Nogaret et Plaisians," no. 524.

[90] A.N., J 392 no. 9, J 295, no. 48, K 166, no. 104, JJ 44, fol. 70v, no. 114.

[91] A.N., JJ 38, fol. 47v, no. 114, JJ 45, fols. 56v-58v, no. 86.

[92] A.N., JJ 41, fol. 84v, no. 143.

[93] M. Boulet, "Les Gayte et les Chauchat de Clermont," Revue d'Auvergne, xxviii, xxix, xxx (1911-1913); C. Paoli, "Documenti di ser Ciappeleto," Giornale storico della letterature Italiana, v (1885), 344, 348, 352-53, 359.

[94] Olim, ii, 385; C.R., iii, no. 30109; J.T.P., nos. 707, 2360, 4684; Mignon, nos. 98, 302, 1422, 2680; A.N., J 1046, no. 19; Fawtier, ed., Comptes du Trésor, no. 262.

[95] Mignon, nos. 1422, 1546 (subsidies), no. 2159 (Jews); A.N., JJ 37, no. 75; Fawtier, ed., Comptes du Trésor, no. 262 (subsidies).

100 l.t. as receiver.[96] He was allowed to hold noble land by an act of Philip the Fair in 1304, and he held two "castles" of the bishop of Clermont.[97] Like several other southern receivers, his office eventually passed to his son Louis.[98]

A final example of a powerful receiver is Geoffroi Cocatrix, burgess of Paris and receiver of Rouergue (1300) and Toulouse (1301-1303).[99] However, he became so involved in other affairs, such as acting as paymaster for the armies of Aquitaine and of Flanders,[100] that he could not have had much time for his work in Toulouse. He was regularly assisted, and was eventually supplanted, by Nicolas d'Ermenonville, who came from a village near Chartres. Nicolas was coreceiver, receiver, or treasurer of Toulouse from 1301 to 1316, and he was also twice called receiver of Rouergue.[101] He had, like Geoffroi Cocatrix, worked on payments for the Gascon war.[102] (It is noticeable that the receivers who seem most important were all involved in obtaining supplies and paying army wages.) Nicolas was well rewarded for his long service; he had a rent of 100 l.t. on the Treasury from the count of Armagnac and a gift of forfeited lands worth 39 l.t. a year. He died in debt to the king, however, and his rent was confiscated, but Philip V restored it to his son in 1321.[103]

To return to Geoffroi Cocatrix, he went on to great things after his brief experience as a receiver. He was one of the three controllers of exports from 1305 to 1314;[104] he took fines from the Lombards, brought up land for the royal palace, enforced the ordinance about money in 1313, and became master of the Chambre aux Deniers (1309) and eventually of the Chambre des Comptes (1315).[105] Councillor and "familiar" of the king, he had

[96] A.N., JJ 37, fol. 20, no. 51; C.R., I, no. 10695.

[97] *Gallia Christiana*, XII, *Instrumenta*, 92; Boulet, "Les Gayte et les Chauchat," *Revue d'Auvergne*, XXIX (1912), 257.

[98] *J.T.P.*, no. 707n.

[99] Ibid., nos. 4682, 4684, 4937, 5808; Mignon, no. 100.

[100] *J.T.P.*, nos. 4683-84; Mignon, nos. 2513-14, 2585; A.N., JJ 39, fol. 117, no. 244. See below, p. 167.

[101] Mignon, nos. 100, 101, 1636, 2459; *J.T.P.*, nos. 4683, 5891; A.N., JJ 44, fol. 37, no. 66, JJ 45, fol. 86v, no. 134, JJ 47, fol. 29v, no. 45, J 1030, no. 5, J 392, no. 214; B.N., ms. fr. 2356, fol. 90, ms. fr. 25697, no. 37, ms. fr. 25992, nos. 92-107; C.R. Maillard, I, nos. 1463, 4756.

[102] Mignon, nos. 2265, 2459-67; *J.T.P.*, nos. 1123, 1571, 4683.

[103] A.N., JJ 47, fol. 29v, no. 45, JJ 40, fol. 87v, no. 168, JJ 60, fol. 8, no. 20; Fawtier, ed., *Comptes du Trésor*, no. 942.

[104] *Ord.*, I, 424, XI, 422; Mignon, nos. 2009, 2016.

[105] *J.T.P.*, no. 19 and n.; Favier, *Marigny*, pp. 231-32; *Ord.*, I, 524n.

the most notable career of any receiver. It should be noted, however, that as receiver he did much of his work through a colleague and that he gained promotion not because he was a capable local official but because he helped to mobilize and distribute resources from all parts of the kingdom for two great wars.

The administration of justice would have seemed to St. Louis or to Beaumanoir a more important duty of the *baillis* and seneschals than the collection or disbursement of royal revenues. Philip the Fair might not have agreed; he certainly sent out more men from the center to make sure that money owed him was collected than he sent to examine the judicial activities of his local officials. Even the *enquêteurs*, who were supposed to see that wrongs were righted and justice done, at times became absorbed in the search for overlooked sources of royal income.[106] Yet, whatever the priorities, the administration of justice was an essential part of the duties of the king's local representatives, and the burden increased steadily during the reign. If private war, feuds, and riots were to be discouraged, there had to be courts that were ready to act. A good many lawsuits were simply the continuation of private war and family feuds by legal means, and if legal remedies were not available, reversion to violence was likely. If the king's ordinances were to be obeyed, they had to be enforced in local courts. If the king's sovereignty was expressed in terms of his right to be final judge in all secular affairs, then cases had to be transferred from private courts to royal courts. The *baillis* and seneschals needed help in handling their judicial business.

As in the case of finance, the development of a corps of legal experts began earlier and went farther in the south than in the north. The seneschals, who were all northerners at first, and largely northerners even under Philip the Fair, did not understand the "written law" of the south. Custom, of course, was an important part of southern law, but it was a different custom from that of the old domain or of Normandy. The differences increased with the growth of a class of lawyers trained in Roman law. These "légistes" were especially numerous in the court of the seneschal, which heard appeals from lower courts. Thus a legal adviser, the "seneschal's judge," began to act as the real head of the seneschal's court, and by the time of Philip the Fair the seneschal's judge was regularly given the title of *juge-mage*. At

[106] See above, pp. 89-90.

about the same time, local administrators, such as the *viguiers* of Beaucaire and Carcassonne, also turned over their judicial duties to men who had special competence in the law.[107] In Toulouse there was only one *viguier*; he kept some jurisdiction in the city itself, but most of the *sénéchaussée* was divided into *jugeries*, each with its own judge.[108] Rouergne and Périgord-Quercy were slower to make these changes; the title of *juge-mage* was not consistently used in these districts in the early part of Philip's reign, and there were fewer subordinate judges (only one in Périgord-Quercy).[109] It is true that both the population and the royal domain in these *sénéchaussées* were smaller than in Toulouse, Carcassonne, and Beaucaire, but there were also fewer men trained in the written law.

The judges of Languedoc not only relieved the seneschals of most of their judicial responsibilities; they were also members of their councils. Even in Paris the distinction between the king's Court of Parlement and the king's Council was not always very clear, and the *curia* of a seneschal combined both functions. Almost any administrative act could have legal consequences, so the judges were consulted on many problems of local government—assignment or exchange of lands, grants of rights to village or urban communities, establishment of boundaries between districts.[110] Next to the seneschals, they were the most important men in the governments of Languedoc. Some of them reached higher office than any seneschal, for example, Guillaume de Nogaret and Guillaume de Plaisians (both former *juges-mages* of Beaucaire).[111] Yves de Loudéac, *juge-ordinaire* of Toulouse, and

[107] Robert Michel, *L'administration royale dans la sénéchaussée de Beaucaire au temps de Saint Louis* (Paris, 1910), pp. 47-48, 58-59, 93-94.

[108] Strayer, *Gens de justice*, pp. 177-94. Toulouse also had judges of appeal (ibid., pp. 172-74). District judges in Toulouse were supposed to hold office for only one year and then move to another "judicatura" (A.N., J 329, no. 43). This rule was not enforced in Toulouse, but it was applied in Beaucaire in the 1290s, though there were exceptions.

[109] Strayer, *Gens de justice*, pp. 139-42 (Périgord-Quercy), 151-59 (Rouergue).

[110] The *juge-mage* of Toulouse was consulted on an ordinance made for the town of Beaumont-en-Lomagne (ibid., p. 39); for other examples see Fawtier et al., eds., *Registres*, I, nos. 233, 405, 948, 975, 1044, etc. *H.L.*, x, col. 390, is an example of a very full council, with the *juge-mage* of Beaucaire and four district judges in attendance. Two judges and a former *juge-mage* advised the seneschal of Beaucaire on establishing the boundary between Beaucaire and Carcassonne (*C.R.*, I, no. 13906).

[111] Strayer, *Gens de justice*, pp. 56-58.

Gérard de Courtonne, *juge-ordinaire* of Nîmes, worked in the Parlement and were sent on important diplomatic missions.[112] Sicard de Lavaur, *juge-mage* of Toulouse (1286-1294) and of Carcassonne (1296-1303), preferrd to end his career in papal rather than in royal service, but as *juge-mage* he was one of the most influential men in Languedoc.[113]

Outside the region of written law there were almost no professional judges. The *prévôts* had what was essentially police-court jurisdiction. They could try criminal cases, although noble defendants wanted to have their cases heard in a higher court,[114] but they could not judge suits about noble land or rights annexed to land. The viscount had a court, but its jurisdiction was specifically limited to minor cases.[115] And as both *prévôts* and viscounts were concerned primarily with collecting royal revenues, they did not have much time to perfect their skill as judges. They usually sought the advice of leading men of the neighborhood, which probably improved the quality of their decisions but did not persuade their superiors to increase the jurisdiction of their courts. In spite of limitations placed upon them, the *prévôts* were very active in prosecuting offenses against the king or breaches of the peace—too active in the opinion of many people[116]—but they were still required to leave the most difficult cases to their superiors.

The one exception to this rule was in Paris, and even there it was only a partial exception. The *prévôt* of Paris actually ranked as a *bailli*, but he also had many of the duties of a *prévôt*, including that of keeping order in the largest city in the kingdom. As a *bailli* he had to supervise and hear appeals about the conduct of all the lesser *prévôts* in the region around Paris. Finally, contracts made before and sealed by a royal official could be enforced

---

[112] Ibid., pp. 82, 180; see also above, p. 28.

[113] Strayer, *Gens de justice*, pp. 102 , 168.

[114] H. Gravier, "Essai sur les prévôts royaux," *Revue historique de droit français et étranger*, XXVII (1903), 649-53, 661-64. The charter of Louis X for Berri forbids *prévôts* to hear cases involving nobles (André Artonne, *Le mouvement de 1314 et les chartes provinciales de 1315* [Paris, 1912], p. 189, art. 17).

[115] E. J. Tardif, *Coutumiers de Normandie*, Vol. II, *La summa de legibus Normannie* (Rouen and Paris, 1896), pp. 143-44; Strayer, *Administration of Normandy*, p. 25.

[116] See Artonne, pp. 172, 200 (Amiens and Vermandois), 192 (Berri), and *Ord.*, I, 574 (Champagne), for complaints against the excessive zeal of the *prévôts*.

in royal courts. Naturally, there were many such contracts in Paris; as the *prévôt*'s court gained experience in this field, people from other districts began to register their acts in Paris. There was simply too much work for one man and a few assistants to handle, and the *prévôt*'s court—the Châtelet—had become a large and vigorous organization long before the time of Philip the Fair. It had nearly 200 sergeants to enforce its orders, a staff of at least 60 notaries, and two auditors who regularly acted as judges.[117] Nevertheless, the officers of the Châtelet did not have the influence or the prestige of the southern judges. Although they played an important role in keeping the peace and settling disputes in and around Paris, they were overshadowed by the great men of the king's court, and they were not given significant promotions. The case of Hervé de la Trinité has already been mentioned. A long-time notary of the Châtelet, he was made receiver of Paris at wages lower than those of most southern district judges. The Châtelet produced no Nogarets and not even a Yves de Loudéac.

Thus, except in Paris, the *baillis* had relatively little help with their judicial responsibilities. Their assizes were the only really effective courts in the northern provinces. Assizes were supposed to be held six times a year, according to the reform ordinance of 1303.[118] It is doubtful that any *bailli* was able to meet this requirement, but in 1312 there were at least four assizes (February, May, September, and December) in the *bailliage* of Caen, three held by the *bailli* and one by his lieutenant.[119]

Baillis and seneschals had used lieutenants to help them with their judicial and administrative duties before the time of Philip the Fair,[120] but the practice seems to have become more frequent after 1285. The central government was worried by this procedure and tried to check it in one of the clauses of the reform ordinance of 1303. *Baillis*, seneschals, and other officials were to use lieutenants as little as possible; if they had to be appointed, they should be good men of the region, not lawyers or men who belonged to local cliques. Seneschals and *baillis* were responsible for

[117] *Olim*, II, 587; *Ord.*, I, 532; Carolus-Barré, "L'organization de la jurisdiction gracieuse à Paris," pp. 425-31.
[118] *Ord.*, I, 362, art. 26.
[119] *H.F.*, XXIV, *142. Cf. H. Waquet, *Le bailliage de Vermandois* (Paris, 1919), pp. 47-49, who finds about the same frequency in Vermandois.
[120] Strayer, *Administration of Normandy*, p. 21; Michel, p. 48 and *pièce just.* no. 36.

the acts of their lieutenants.[121] This ordinance was only partially observed. Lieutenants were not permanent officials; in fact, they were not necessarily officials of any rank but only personal representatives of the seneschals and *baillis*. They were named for specific tasks and had no continuing powers. Nevertheless, in the south lieutenants served so frequently and performed so many duties that they might as well have been recognized as permanent employees of the state.

Two examples will illustrate this point. Géraud de Sabanac, king's clerk and doctor of both laws (so much for the rule forbidding lawyers), was lieutenant of the seneschal of Périgord-Quercy at various dates between 1291 and 1314. He helped to arrange the transfer of lands and rents to the count of Périgord, was a collector of the aid for the marriage of the king's daughter, and made *enquêtes* for the seneschal and the judge of Cahors. Under Philip V he was frequently named as *iudex datus* to hear appeals from legal decisions made in his *sénéchaussée*.[122]

Lambert de Thury, lord of Saissac, was called lieutenant of the seneschal of Carcassonne in 1292, 1297, 1298, 1299, 1303, 1304, and 1308-1309. He was regent of the *sénéchaussée* in 1298, when the seneschal was acting as governor of Gascony.[123] He frequently served as a member of the seneschal's council, perhaps as early as 1281, certainly in the period 1303-1308.[124] Because he was not a lawyer, he did not act as a judge (though he did take part in the condemnation of the consuls of Carcassonne for treason in 1305),[125] but he was a collector of subsidies and helped to value portions of the royal domain that were to be sold or exchanged.[126]

Men such as these added more or less permanent strength to the personnel at the disposal of a seneschal or a *bailli*. On the other hand, when an official already holding a full-time position —a viscount, a castellan, a *viguier*, or a *juge-mage*—was named as lieutenant, he could not be expected to do more than preside

---

[121] *Ord.*, I, 361, art. 22.   [122] Strayer, *Gens de justice*, p. 145.
[123] *H.L.*, IX, 165, H.F., XXIV, *256, *257, J. A. Mahul, ed., *Cartulaire et archives des communes de l'ancien diocèse . . . de Carcassonne*, 7 vols. (Paris, 1857-1885), IV, 460, 590, VI¹, 284 (as lieutenant); Mahul, V, 338 (as lieutenant); A.M., Albi, FF 7, FF 10, FF 13 (lieutenant in 1297 and 1298).
[124] Lambert in 1281 witnessed a sentence "in consistorio civ. Carc. domini Regis" (A.D. Aude, II E no. 2). See also Mahul, VI¹, p. 11; A.N., JJ 44, fol. 51v, no. 82.
[125] *H.L.*, IX, 283.
[126] He was also involved in an *enquête* on the Val d'Aran in 1308 (*C.R.*, I, no. 12683, II, no. 16452; A.N., JJ 42A, fol. 112v, no. 110).

in a court or conduct a brief investigation before returning to his regular duties. There was no net gain in the time available for financial or judicial administration.

Another group of officials, the king's procurators and advocates, took some of the responsibility for making decisions that affected the king's interests from the shoulders of the *baillis* and seneschals. On the other hand, as professional lawyers they complicated administrative procedures. The permanent, salaried procurator had scarcely existed before Philip's time, although the practice of obtaining legal advice before taking an action that might diminish the king's revenues or rights had certainly been known. Nevertheless, even in the south, where there were more formalities than in the north, the first procurators were appointed by the seneschals on an ad hoc basis and did not act in the king's name. This was certainly the case in Beaucaire and in Périgord-Quercy,[127] and in Rouergue the Parlement ruled that no procurator had a sufficient mandate before 1312. This may have been a mistake, since there was a salaried procurator in Rouergue from 1293 on, but it shows how slowly the office developed.[128] As for Toulouse, the picture is clouded by the activity of Gilles Camelin, who certainly did the work of a procurator from 1272 to 1289 but who was much more than a procurator. He protected the king's rights throughout Languedoc, advised kings and seneschals, and ended his career as a member of the Parlement and as bishop of Rennes.[129]

Beyond the region of the written law procurators and royal advocates were needed to protect the king's interests in ecclesiastical courts, courts whose procedure was different enough from that of a lay court to require the presence of an expert in law. As in the south, the first appointments were made by the *baillis* for specific cases. For example, in the accounts of Auvergne for 1289 there is an entry for a clerk who acted as procurator in a dispute with the bishop of Clermont over regalia and coinage.[130]

---

[127] Strayer, *Gens de justice*, pp. 94 (three procurators "a senescallo dumtaxat constituebantur"), 142.

[128] Ibid., pp. 159-60. Cf. *Olim*, III, 1126. The "defensor Regis" of Rouergue was paid 20 l.t. for the year 1293-1294 (*C.R.*, I, no. 10494).

[129] Strayer, *Gens de justice*, pp. 195-96. For his service in the Parlement see Langlois, ed., *Textes*, pp. 122, 129; *Ord.*, I, p. 320. He became bishop of Rennes, 11 February 1299 (*J.T.P.*, no. 3131).

[130] "Jacobo Granerii clerico, procuratori causarum regalie et monete" was paid 10 l.t. (Paoli, p. 364). There were also advocates to protect the king's rights "in curia ecclerie," also paid 10 l.t.

By 1300, however, salaried procurators or advocates practiced in the ecclesiastical courts of Bourges, Orléans, Sens, and Troyes,[131] not to mention the famous Pierre du Bois, advocate for the king in the ecclesiastical courts of the Cotentin in the early 1300s.[132] Master Laurent Herout was royal procurator in the *bailliage* of Caen in 1295 and 1296, but this appears to have been an ad hoc appointment, since his usual assignments were to collect subsidies and fines for amortization.[133] On the other hand, the royal procurator and royal advocate for Normandy, who are mentioned in 1305 and in 1310, seem to have been professional lawyers, as was probably the case with Master Yves, royal procurator in Britanny about 1313.[134]

Procurators and advocates of the north have been discussed together because there is little information about their activities and because they did not play a very important role in local administration. They did little to help the *bailli* in his judicial responsibilities. In the south, however, both procurator and advocate were regular members of the seneschal's council and were consulted whenever actions were taken whose legality or utility to the king could be questioned. To give just one example, the Templars of Pézenas were allowed to acquire rights of high justice only after consultations with the king's advocate, the procurator, the *juge-mage* acting as lieutenant of the seneschal, and three other judges.[135] The advocates—or patrons of the king's cases, as they were often called—were better educated (many of them were doctors of law) and better paid than the procurators.[136] As often happens, they did less work and were less concerned with minor problems than their professional inferiors. They were eminent lawyers and their salary was a sort of retaining fee. They could argue cases for the king (though examples of this activity are rare), but their main responsibility was to give legal advice when it was needed by a seneschal or a *juge-mage*.

In addition to the judges, advocates, procurators, and receivers

---

131 Strayer, *Gens de justice*, p. 41, n. 115.

132 See Langlois's edition of du Bois, *De recuperatione*, pp. vii-xii.

133 *Olim*, II, 378, 402 (as procurator); Mignon, nos. 1344, 1843, *J.T.P.*, no. 3, A.N., JJ 38, fol. 37, no. 65, A.D. Calvados, H 5 (as collector).

134 Strayer, *Gens de justice*, p. 41, n. 115.

135 A.N., JJ 37, fol. 1, no. 1. See my *Gens de justice*, pp. 39-40, for other examples.

136 Strayer, *Gens de justice*, pp. 28, 29.

who worked with and under the seneschals and *baillis*, there were also local royal agents who were practically autonomous, the mint masters and the Masters of the Forests. The mint masters were not involved in the affairs of their district; they reported directly to the Treasury in Paris.[137] Although in times of war the mint masters might be asked to transfer money directly to a receiver for paying troops,[138] the receivers' superiors (*baillis* and seneschals) had no control over the mint masters' operations and no claim on their income. It is interesting to note that some of the most active mints (Montreuil-Bonnin, Sommières, and Toulouse) were in the south and that another set of mints ran down the eastern frontier (St. Quentin, Tournai, Troyes, and Mâcon). Operations in Rouen seem to have been relatively unimportant, and Paris was erratic, producing large numbers of coins in some years and very few in others. This pattern may be explained by the fact that the great wars were in the south and east and that it was easier to send money to armies from nearby mints. It is also true that such silver mines as there were lay in the south and that silver from exchange operations could be obtained most easily from towns on the trade routes to the Low Countries and to Italy.

The Masters of the Forests were in a rather different position. Whereas the mint masters controlled only the few buildings in which they worked, the Masters of the Forests were responsible for thousands of acres in every *bailliage* or *sénéchaussée*. A mint master needed no outside assistance to do his work; the Masters of the Forests had to obtain information from local officials to establish the location and estimate the value of woods that were included in grants to or exchanges with members of the clergy or the nobility.[139] Also, since the largest income from the forests was produced by sales of wood, and since payments for the right to cut wood were spread over several years, the *bailli* or seneschal usually had the duty of collecting these payments. "Vende boscorum" was a common heading in the accounts of *baillis* and seneschals. The clearest case is in 1300, when Etienne de Bienfaite, a Master of the Forests, sold a large amount of wood in the forest of Breteuil. He notified the *bailli* of Gisors of the terms of the sale and told him to collect the money; a letter from the king

[137] *J.T.P.*, nos. 21, 23, 31, etc.; *C.R.*, II, nos. 27527, 27535, 27539, etc.
[138] See, for example, *J.T.P.*, nos. 559, 638, 1005, 1138.
[139] See Jean Favier, ed., *Cartulaire et actes d'Enguerran de Marigny* (Paris, 1965), no. 24; A.N., JJ 46, fol. 97v, no. 168, JJ 48, fol. 109, no. 189.

repeated this order.[140] In some districts "vende boscorum" included payments made by private persons for permission to sell
their wood; in Normandy the two kinds of payment were clearly
distinguished, but the *bailli* was responsible for both.[141] Fines for
forest offenses were also at times accounted for by *baillis*.[142]

The exact relationship between the forest administration and
the local representatives of the king is not at all clear. The forest
administration was well established by the middle of the thirteenth century, and under Philip the Fair it was strengthened
through the efforts of Philippe le Convers (or de Villepreux), the
king's godson and one of his most influential ministers.[143] Philippe
le Convers was sometimes called general *enquêteur* for the forests,
and he ordered most of the letters in the royal registers dealing
with forest affairs. At about the same time that he was taking
over general responsibility for the forests, the Masters of the Forests, who had existed earlier, seem to have been given more extensive powers. There were Masters for Normandy, a Master for
Champagne (and Paris?), and Masters for Languedoc; each group
had jurisdiction over areas far larger than that of a *bailliage* or
a *sénéchaussée*.

Many of the Masters ranked socially with, or even above, the
baillis and seneschals. Etienne de Bienfaite of Normandy was a
king's knight, held the great fief of Orbec, frequently attended
the Exchequer, and sat in the Parlement of 1307. He worked
mainly in Normandy, but he also made leases in the *bailliage* of
Orléans and accounted for the king's fisheries in the 1290s (probably before he was a Master of Forests).[144] He was certainly a
Master of Forests in November 1300, when he notified the *bailli*
of Gisors of a sale of wood in Breteuil, and he remained a Master
until his death late in 1312.[145]

Geoffroi le Danois had been *bailli* of Gisors (1307-1308) but
was a Master of Forests by 5 August 1309. He served exclusively
in Normandy, at least until the end of December 1312. In 1313
he was sent to enforce the ordinances on money in Normandy.

[140] *C.R.*, II, no. 15652.

[141] Strayer, *Administration of Normandy*, pp. 73, 78-9; *C.R.*, I, nos. 1691-
99, 2155-59, 4632, 4661, 6814-23, etc.

[142] *C.R.*, I, nos. 1684, 5509.   [143] Pegues, pp. 128-31.

[144] A.N., JJ 35, fol. 42v, no. 74; *J.T.P.*, no. 5182 (for Orbec), nos. 2567,
3496, 4651 (Exchequer); Langlois, ed., *Textes*, p. 179 (Parlement); *C.R.*,
I, no. 2495, and Mignon, no. 2234 (fisheries).

[145] Mignon, no. 2240.

In 1316 he was drawing the sizable pension of 100 l.p., more of a reward than most *baillis* ever received.[146]

To take a southern Master, Bertaud de Borest was at first in charge of forest sales in Poitou and Saintonge (as Etienne de Bienfaite had been in Normandy).[147] He was commissioned, with Jean Pilet, as Master of the Forests of Languedoc on 13 April 1309. This commission is in a fuller form than others that have survived. The Masters' authority extended throughout the *sénéchaussées* of Toulouse, Périgord, Carcassonne, and Beaucaire. They could sell wood and pasturage, assess fines for offenses in the forest, and force debtors to pay what they owed. All justiciars and officers of the king were to obey their orders. Bertaud and Jean were to pay the forest sergeants, but they themselves were to be paid their wages of 160 l.t. a year by the treasurer of Toulouse and to account to the receivers of each *sénéchaussée*.[148] (One such account, to the receiver of Carcassonne for 1312-1313, has survived in part.)[149] It should be noted that Bertaud's powers could also be exercised in Saintonge; the seneschal there was ordered in 1311 to pay for a wood that Bertaud, Master of Forests of Languedoc, had bought.[150]

Bertaud's activity as Master can be traced through the royal registers and accounts from 1309 to 1316.[151] His career and the terms of his commission illustrate the problem of the relationship between a Master and a seneschal. Bertaud had authority in many districts, and he held office longer than most of the seneschals with whom he worked. He was responsible only to Philippe le Convers and Philippe's staff in Paris. Yet he was less well paid than a seneschal and was dependent on a receiver for his salary. He accounted and probably sent in his receipts through receivers, without whose support he could not have operated. Although there were many chances for friction here, none have been recorded.

---

[146] *H.F.*, xxiv, *125, Picot, p. 598 (as *bailli*); A.N., JJ 41, fol. 69, no. 118, JJ 46, fol. 97v, no. 168, JJ 47, fol. 20v, no. 34, JJ 48, fol. 109, no. 189 (forests); *H.F.*, xxiv, *154 (money); Fawtier, ed., *Comptes du Trésor*, no. 754 (pension).

[147] Guérin, ed., *Archives historique du Poitou*, xiii, no. 206.

[148] *H.L.*, x, cols. 504-6.

[149] *C.R.*, ii, nos. 24190 ff. Mignon, no. 2259, had seen this and other accounts from 1309 to 1312.

[150] A.N., J 181, no. 59.

[151] A.N., JJ 48, fol. 80v, no. 133, fol. 90, no. 160; *C.R.* Maillard, i, nos. 1397, 4626-27, ii, nos. 15637-77.

Finally, there is the curious case of Guillaume de Saint-Marcel, of Provins. He was, until the very end of his career, associated with Philippe le Convers, but he certainly did not have the power or prestige (or, for that matter, the income) of his colleague. He was guard of the fairs of Champagne in 1301 and, with Philippe, collected fines for the subvention of 1302 from the towns of Reims and Châlons.[152] By September 1303 he and Philippe were *enquêteurs* of the forests. One of their accounts for 1304-1305 has survived. They worked together in Champagne (perhaps because Guillaume was also *gruyer* of Champagne), but Philippe alone took care of Norman problems. Philippe was paid the standard wages of a clerk of the king's court, 10 s.p. a day, while Guillaume received only 4 s. 5 d.p.[153] They were still *enquêteurs* in 1307, but by 1308 they were Masters of the Forests of Languedoc (Saintonge and Poitou were included under this heading, which was unusual), with full power to hire, punish, and dismiss all forest officers, including castellans.[154] Perhaps by virtue of this commission Philippe and Guillaume named Bertaud de Borest and Jean Pilet as Masters of the Forests of Languedoc in 1309.[155] After 1309 Guillaume worked mainly in the north and especially in Champagne,[156] and by 1317 he was called Master of the Forests of Champagne, overseer of all *gruyers* and guards of these forests. He already had a pension of 100 l.p.; in 1317 he was promised 10 s. a day for life, in or out of office. He was still Master of the Forests in 1322.[157]

Here again we have the paradox of a man of low rank—Guillaume never became even a *valletus regis*—drawing a low salary, who could still give orders on certain matters to seneschals and *baillis*. Guillaume certainly owed a great deal to the patronage of Philippe le Convers. He presumably did not make forest policy but merely took care of details that Philippe had no time to handle. Nevertheless, with one of the most powerful men in Paris behind him, Guillaume would not have met much opposition if he had interfered with local administrators. As far as the record shows, however, Guillaume never became involved in a serious dispute with other officials during his long years of service.

---

[152] A.D. Aube, *Inventaire*, sér. G, II, 103; Mignon, no. 1436.

[153] *C.R.*, I, nos. 6534-41; A.N., JJ 59, fol. 332, no. 603, JJ 37, fol. 22, no. 58.

[154] A.N., JJ 42A, fol. 74, no. 26.

[155] *H.L.*, x, col. 504; *C.R.* Maillard, II, no. 15673.

[156] A.N., JJ 49, fol. 33, no. 69 (forest of Fontainebleau, 1313), JJ 47, fol. 46v, no. 75 (Champagne, 1311).

[157] A.N., JJ 54A, fol. 24, no. 263, JJ 56, fol. 12v, no. 42; *J.T.C.*, no. 386.

Lesser forest officials—castellans (who were often in charge of a forest), foresters, verderers, and forest sergeants—were also in an anomalous situation. They were paid by the seneschal or *bailli* of their district (as all accounts show), and the Parlement of 1291-1292 specifically ordered them to obey the *baillis*.[158] On the other hand, most of them (and even some sergeants) were appointed by the king,[159] and they were subject, at least for disciplinary purposes, to the Masters and *enquêteurs* of the forest. There would seem to have been some possibility of conflict caused by this division of authority, but none of any importance has been recorded.

The forest service had enough local resources—personnel, income, housing—so that it did not put a very heavy burden on seneschals, *baillis*, and receivers. Its requests for administrative assistance were predictable and did not vary greatly from year to year. Far more annoying and time-consuming were the men who might be called deputies on special missions. The *enquêteurs-réformateurs* could, in theory, suspend all ordinary activities of local officials while hearing complaints about their behavior. In practice, they worked on only a few officials at a time,[160] but if a group of sergeants, a *prévôt*, a viscount, or a judge were busy defending themselves, they could not perform their normal duties. Seneschals and *baillis* were usually investigated only after they left office, but this must have caused some trouble to their successors. And if, as often happened, the *enquêteurs* were ordered to recuperate royal rights,[161] this would add to the work of local officials, if only because they would have to collect the sums due.

Besides the *enquêteurs* with general powers, there were men sent out for the sole purpose of collecting or increasing royal revenue. The most annoying of these were the collectors of fines for amortization; not only did they make work, but they also stirred up resentment and occasional lawsuits.[162] Collectors of

---

[158] *Olim*, II, 328.

[159] The king named the castellan-forester of Benon (A.N., JJ 42A, fol. 74, no. 27); Masters and guards of forests were to be appointed by the Council, 1303 (*Ord.* I, 360, art. 14); sergeants in forests of the *bailliage* of Rouen were appointed by the king (*C.R.*, II, nos. 15586-99). In 1287-1288 the king appointed a castellan and 19 minor officials in Carcassonne (Martin-Chabot, ed., *Les archives de la cour des comptes de Montpellier*, pp. 64-65).

[160] For examples see Langlois, "Enquêteurs," pp. 63-86, and Strayer, *Gens de justice*, pp. 105, 118-19, 194.

[161] See above, pp. 89-90.　　　　[162] See below, pp. 397-99.

subsidies for war and of tenths on the clergy also put extra burdens on local authorities. A *bailli* might be asked to help impose or collect a tax; a seneschal might become involved in a long argument with a magnate like the king of Majorca (lord of Montpellier) or the count of Foix as to whether a tax should be paid at all.[163] And although the collectors were reasonably efficient, there were almost always arrears, which the local administrators had to dig out and send to Paris in later years.[164] These were the big problems, but some of the little ones must have been almost as irritating—advancing money to cover expenses of the deputies on mission, finding them lodging and office space, replacing horses that were lamed or had died, providing an escort when work had to be done in an unruly district. It was good policy for the king to remind his local representatives that they were entirely at the disposal of the central government, but sometimes they must have wished that the reminders did not come so frequently.

Another problem in local administration was that the seneschal or *bailli* did not have full control over his subordinates. In fact, the tendency to define and formalize the powers and authority of secondary officials tended to weaken the chain of command in the *bailliages* and *sénéchaussées*. When the receiver was simply a clerk of the *bailli* or seneschal, he was much more of a subordinate than when he was appointed from Paris. The seneschal's judge or ad hoc procurator was more dependent on the seneschal than a *juge-mage* or procurator who received a commission directly from the king. Viscounts, *viguiers*, and salaried *prévôts* were also chosen by the central government.[165] Their terms of office did not correspond with those of their superiors, and in many cases they had had more experience than a newly arrived seneschal or *bailli*. They could not easily be disciplined or removed from office; usually they were punished only by the *enquêteurs* or by the king or one of his agencies in Paris (such as the Chambre des Comptes). Doubtless, the recommendation of a well-regarded seneschal or *bailli* carried some weight, and

---

[163] Mignon, nos. 1258, 1280, 1290, 1328, 1331, 1348, etc.; *H.L.*, x, cols. 400-402, 405 (troubles with the king of Majorca and the count of Foix).

[164] Mignon, nos. 1276, 1335, 1349, 1359, 1413; *J.T.P.*, nos. 4394, 4410, 4768, 4920, 4960, etc.

[165] *Ord.*, I, 476. The king gave the *gens des comptes* power to discharge such officers if they were unworthy (1310). See the long string of transfers, replacements, and appointments made by Philip V in early 1317 (A.N., JJ 54A passim).

in 1290 Philip specifically told the seneschal of Carcassonne that he could fire men appointed by royal letters.[166] Nevertheless, a viscount or *viguier* who held office for 10, 20, or even 30 years must have been rather independent.[167]

Castellans who were not mere caretakers were usually named by the king; many of them were also in charge of a forest, so that they had a double claim to autonomy.[168] On the other hand, in 1311 the king ordered the Chambre des Comptes to reduce the number of castellans and to turn over many castles to seneschals, *baillis*, viscounts, and simple foresters.[169] This act, if fully implemented, would have given increased authority to the chief administrative officers of a province.

The central government not only named middle-level local officials directly; it also felt free to use them outside of the districts where they were supposed to do their work. To give only a few examples, Geoffroy d'Anisy, viscount of Bayeux, was sent in 1299, with Raoul Rousselet, to investigate complaints against collectors of a clerical tenth in the *bailliage* of Tours.[170] Simon de Courceaux, *prévôt* of Orléans (earlier of Melun), was sent, also in 1299, "ex parte Regis" to press the *baillis* of Champagne to enforce the ordinances about money.[171] Sicard de Lavaur, *juge-mage* of Carcassonne, collected tenths and subsidies and was a member of a mission sent to Rome in 1297.[172] Mathieu de Courjumelles, judge of Cahors, was also used as a collector of subsidies and as an ambassador to the pope in 1310.[173] Even a rather undistinguished man, Nicolas de Pont-Audemer, a king's advocate in Normandy, was summoned to Lyon in 1305 when Philip was having his first interview with Clement V. He was absent from Normandy for 135 days.[174] Such absences must have caused some problems in local administration.

At the lowest level, that of *prévôts* and *bayles* who farmed their offices, control by *baillis* and seneschals was somewhat greater. Royal ordinances forbade the employment of men of

---

[166] See note 165 above. The letter to the seneschal is in *H.L.*, x, col. 248. It is significant that the seneschal had to be reassured on this point.

[167] Strayer, "Viscounts and Viguiers," pp. 226-27.

[168] The castellan of Issoudun was appointed by the king (*Ord.*, 1, 360, art. 14; Favier, *Marigny*, pp. 57-58), and the king appointed a castellan-forester of Benon (A.N., JJ 42A, fol. 74, no. 27).

[169] *Ord.*, 1, 476-77.   [170] Ibid., 332, n. f.

[171] *C.R.*, 1, nos. 3257-60.   [172] Strayer, *Gens de justice*, p. 103.

[173] Ibid., pp. 141-42.

[174] A.N., JJ 45, fol. 69, no. 99; *C.R.*, 1, nos. 6727-28.

bad reputation, and the farm was for a brief period, usually for
only three years.[175] Thus it should have been easy to get rid of
oppressive, incompetent, or dishonest *prévôts*. A grim story from
Auvergne, however, shows that a high royal official, the seneschal of Beaucaire, had no illusions about the difficulty of removing a bad *prévôt*. The seneschal had been asked by the *bailli* of
Auvergne to turn over certain men accused of an attack on a
church. The seneschal refused, because men whom he had surrendered earlier had been imprisoned by a *prévôt* of Auvergne
and had been treated so badly that some of them had died. He
offered to hold an *enquête* on the accused men in his *sénéchaussée*.
The *bailli* could send a deputy to the hearing if he wished, but
the seneschal flatly refused to turn over anyone to the *bailli* without consulting the king.[176]

It is evident from the accounts of the *bailliage* that at this time
the *prévôtés* of Auvergne were farmed rather than held by appointed royal officers.[177] It should have been possible to replace
the unjust *prévôt*, at least when his lease expired. Yet this was
the one remedy for a bad situation that was not even suggested
by the seneschal. Apparently it was easier to appeal to the king
than to dismiss a *prévôt*.

The *prévôts* of the old royal domain were not accused of such
serious offenses, at least to judge from the charges brought against
them by the *enquêteurs*.[178] They were, on the whole, jealous
defenders of the king's rights and revenues, and, on the basis of
the same *enquêtes*, quite capable of acting on their own without
orders from their *bailli*. The *prévôts* were severely criticized by
the leaders of the protests of 1314 for interfering with the jurisdiction of the nobles, for taking excessive fines, and for having
too many sergeants (who, of course, had to be paid off with fees
and bribes).[179] In Artois the inhabitants said that, because of the
sergeants, "tout li pays en est gastés, exillés, et reubés."[180] The
strongest criticism was of the *prévôts* who farmed their offices;
in Amiens, Vermandois, and Berri the leaguers asked that the
sale of *prévôtés* be forbidden.[181] This suggests that the paid *pré-*

---

[175] *Ord.*, I, 360, art. 19; Gravier, pp. 551-53.
[176] *H.L.*, x, col. 304 (8 September 1294).
[177] Paoli, p. 364. (Two *prévôtés* could not be farmed and had *custodes*.)
See for later years *C.R.*, I, nos. 8168, 8562, 10521 (*prévôtés* that could not
be farmed), but nos. 8529 ff., bidding was usually intense.
[178] Gravier, pp. 815-17; Langlois, "Enquêteurs," pp. 70-78.
[179] See above, notes 114 and 116.   [180] Artonne, p. 200.
[181] Ibid., pp. 173, 192, 199.

vôts, who were public officials, not private contractors, had a better record. They certainly were preferred by the king's subjects.

The *bayles* had as bad a reputation as the *prévôts*, perhaps worse, since they were almost always farmers. As Yves Dossat pointed out, Alfonse de Poitiers was so concerned about their behavior that he put in *superbaiuli* to supervise and discipline the *bayles*.[182] This experiment was apparently unsuccessful; the *superbaiuli* appear in Rouergue and Toulouse in a few accounts of the 1290s, but only as collectors of small amercements and confiscations.[183] They disappear entirely after 1299.

The abandonment of the experiment with the *superbaiuli* did not end the problem of supervising the *bayles*. The worst fault of the *bayles*, in the eyes of the central government, was not their abuse of power but their failure to pay for their farms. Thus four *bayles* of Toulouse were heavily in debt to the king in the early 1290s, and one is said to have fled.[184] There was also trouble in Périgord-Quercy at the same time, where three *bayles* owed 210 l.t., 340 l.t., and 286 l.t., respectively.[185] The seneschals made a considerable effort to farm the *baylies* (in 1292-1293 and 1298-1299 the seneschal of Toulouse sent sergeants and trumpeters throughout his *jugeries* to announce the farming),[186] and they probably hired men to administer *baylies* only when there had been financial problems with previous farmers. Yet in 1302-1303 four *baylies* in Carcassonne had to be given to *custodes*, who were paid 12 d.t., 14 d.t., or 15 d.t. a day,[187] which suggests that there had been defaults in payments there. At the same time, the *enquêteurs* in Carcassonne and Périgord-Quercy amerced six *bayles* for unspecified offenses. Since the sums ran only from 8 l.t. to 30 l.t., it seems likely that these men were guilty of financial abuses rather than criminal behavior.[188] In any case, some

---

[182] Yves Dossat, "Une tentative de réforme administrative dans la sénéchaussée de Toulouse en 1271," *Bulletin philologique et historique (jusqu'à 1610) du Comité des travaux historiques et scientifiques* (1964), pp. 505-7.

[183] Ibid., p. 514. To his references may be added *C.R.*, I, nos. 10733 (as late as 1299), 12440-50, II, no. 16900.

[184] *C.R.*, II, nos. 14635, 14714, 14754, 14815.

[185] Ibid., nos. 14591, 14592, 14598.   [186] Ibid., I, nos. 10040-41, 12037-41.

[187] Ibid., nos. 12796, 12798, 12811-914. The last-named, the *custos* of the *baylie* of Olangues, had been appointed by royal letters in 1300; he served until 1 March 1303, "tunc fuit sibi officium interdictum." Something peculiar had happened in this *baylie*, but no explanation is given.

[188] Ibid., nos. 12735, 12798 (the *bayle* of Sault, 11 l.t.; he was a paid *bayle*, not a farmer, so pay was no guarantee of honesty), 12740 (*bayle* of

local official was needed to protect the king's interests and to make sure that all royal income was collected. The appointment of a procurator for each *jugerie* of Toulouse and a *clavier* (treasurer) for each *viguerie* of Carcassonne may have been an attempt to meet this need. The procurator had somewhat wider responsibilities than the *clavier*, but the pay was the same in many cases (25 l.t. a year), and both the *jugerie* and the *viguerie* were small enough districts so that misbehavior of a *bayle* should have been obvious to the new officials.

In any case, the coincidence in time between the disappearance of the *superbaiuli* and the general use of local procurators and *claviers* is striking. The district judges of Toulouse may have occasionally named an ad hoc procurator before 1298, but in 1298 five local procurators were named "de speciali mandato domini senescalli."[189] Most of the *claviers* of Carcassonne were instituted "per dominos magistros" on 1 March 1306, though the *clavier* of Béziers had taken office on 1 September 1305.[190] Unfortunately, few accounts survive for either of these *sénéchaussées* in the period immediately after the procurators and *claviers* were named. There was still a procurator in each *jugerie* of Toulouse in 1322[191] and a *clavier* in each *viguerie* of Carcassonne in 1317, so presumably they had been useful. The *claviers'* financial responsibilities were heavy in 1317; each one was to prepare a record "de omnibus redditibus, firmis, censibus et aliis juribus" that the king had in his *viguerie* and to send a paper copy to his seneschal and a parchment copy to the Chambre des Comptes.[192] The seneschals would certainly have had better control over the *bayles* after such documents were available, far better than they could have had if they had tried to use the badly organized and outdated list of the *domania* of Carcassonne, which had obviously been the basis for checking the accounts of the *sénéchaussée* down

---

Peyriac, 8 l.t.), 12741 (*bayle* of Pennautier, 8 l.t.)—all these in Carcassonne. In Périgord-Quercy the fines were larger, and two *bayles* had lost their office. Ibid., nos. 10778 (*bayle* of Almont, 30 l.t., removed), 10781 (*bayle* of Montcuq, 20 l.t., removed), 10789 (a new *bayle* of Almont, 10 l.t.).

189 Ibid., nos. 12316, 12322-34. The procurator of Villelongue was appointed early in 1297 (nos. 12322-23).

190 Ibid., II, nos. 16471, 16475, 16479.

191 *C.R.* Maillard, I, nos. 1561-66.

192 Ibid., nos. 5203-19. The registers were certainly prepared, and they were expensive documents—101 l.t. for Montréal, 80 l.t. for the Cabardès, 44 l.t. for Carcassonne.

to 1317.[193] Many entries in the old list went back to the 1280s; corrections had been made during the next 30 years, and a few additional items had been added as late as 1317 and 1318.[194] However, the entries were not always arranged by *vigueries*, and it is hard to see how anyone could have checked on the work of a single local official. If the *claviers'* reports had survived (we know that they were finished because they were paid for), they would have been a magnificent source for the history of the region in the early fourteenth century.

The situation in Beaucaire is less clear. Robert Michel found evidence of a large number of *bayles* there in the reign of St. Louis,[195] but they scarcely appear in the account of the *sénéchaussée* for 1302-1303. Although there was a *clavier* at Aigues-mortes in the 1270s, the institution never really took hold in Beaucaire. Only a few *claviers* are named, and one *clavier* was also a *viguier*, which seems a complete misunderstanding of the purpose of the office.[196] By 1312 a few *bayles* appear in the accounts of Beaucaire, but they certainly did not collect all the revenues of the *sénéchaussée*. On the contrary, the *viguiers* had ceased to be paid officials and were farming their *vigueries*,[197] and for sums no larger than those rendered by many *bayles*. To the people of Languedoc, this hardly seemed to be an improvement. They requested in 1315 that neither *vigueries* nor *baylies* be farmed (note that they were now assimilating the two offices), but Louis X merely promised that he would consider the problem.[198] Farming out offices, especially when they included no extensive rights of justice, was too convenient a way of collecting revenue for the monarchy to abandon it.

To sum up, local administration became more structured under Philip the Fair than it had been earlier. Old, rather informal arrangements for aiding the seneschals and *baillis* in their work were superseded by the appointment of full-time subordinates. The seneschal's judge became a *juge-mage*; the ad hoc procurator became a government official; the *baillis'* or seneschals' clerks for financial business became or were replaced by receivers. The number of sergeants, forest guards, messengers, and other assistants to local administrators increased (far too much, in the

[193] *C.R.*, III, nos. 29002-403.   [194] Ibid., nos. 29343, 29348.
[195] Michel, pp. 83-85.
[196] Strayer, "Viscounts and Viguiers," pp. 229-30.
[197] Ibid., p. 230. See *C.R.*, II, nos. 17578, 17596.
[198] *Ord.*, I, 555, art. 10.

opinion of the public), so there was more manpower to do the work that had to be done.

Whether there was enough manpower to handle all the new duties imposed on local officials is another matter. Philip's ordinances for restricting exports of certain commodities, regulating the currency, and imposing fines for amortization had precedents, but he was far more active in developing these policies than his predecessors, and these were precisely the policies that aroused general opposition. General taxation had no precedents, and it stirred up even more opposition. The chief collectors of taxes were not local administrators, but they depended on local administrators for assistance, especially when there was open resistance to their demands. Collectors of supplies for the armies also required local assistance and were also likely to cause vehement and sometimes violent protests. The Parlement at Paris was doubtless more popular than the agents of the central financial offices, but the Parlement also made many demands on the time of local officials, asking for information, ordering the enforcement of its decrees, and allowing, if not encouraging, appeals from local courts. In the region of written law, where the influence of men who had studied civil law was steadily growing, the length and complexity of court proceedings increased. Appeals became more frequent. Even when they were disallowed, arguments on quashing them took time, and when they were allowed, the case had to be heard again. Apparently simple cases before local judges could drag on for years, and really complicated ones, such as the suit between the king and the bishop of Mende over rights in the Gévaudan, lasted for decades. In these long, drawn-out cases new seneschals, new judges, and their lieutenants had to go back over the record and familiarize themselves with the facts.[199] Since royal sovereignty was expressed in terms of the all-embracing authority of the king's courts, these were duties that could not be neglected; but they took a great deal of time.

Life was a little simpler for the northern *baillis* because the law of the north was simpler. Lawsuits could be settled more

[199] See, for example, A.M., Albi, FF 10, for arguments about appeals from the temporal court of the bishop which began in 1289 and were ready for final decision only in 1297. The roll is yards long. The case involved two seneschals of Carcassonne and two of their lieutenants, the *juge-mage* and two of his lieutenants, the *viguier* of Albi, the judge of Albi, and the king's procurator and advocate. And this was just the preliminary pleading; the final arguments and decision are lost.

rapidly, and appeals were less frequent, except in Paris, where the proximity of the Parlement made it easy to move cases from the *prévôt*'s court to the higher jurisdiction. In Normandy, however, a considerable number of cases went from the *baillis* to the Exchequer, which the *baillis* had to attend, and in Champagne the Grands Jours played somewhat the same role as the Exchequer. Also, if the judicial work of officials in the north was less exacting than that of those in the south, their financial responsibilities were greater. The receivers of the north (except for the receiver of Champagne) were lesser men than the Chauchats or Balènes of the South, and the *baillis* were more involved in the work of accounting. Here again, the Norman *baillis* were especially burdened. They had to attend not only the judicial Exchequer but also the meetings of the financial Exchequer, and even then their accounts could be questioned by the *gens des comptes* in Paris.

Altogether, one has an impression (it can be nothing more) that many local administrators were overworked. They were blamed for their inefficiency and their slowness in carrying out orders from the center, but it is hard to see how they could have accomplished much more than they did. Some of them were doubtless incompetent, but the long careers and fairly frequent promotions of these men suggest that the government was engaging the most capable local administrators it could find. Constant intervention from Paris and the presence in every district of men who were directly responsible to the king and not to the *bailli* or seneschal probably caused as much inefficiency and delay as any weaknesses of the chief local officials.

One problem that the central government did not have to worry about was the loyalty of its chief subordinates. No *bailli* or seneschal, not even one who governed the same region for a decade or more, ever showed any signs of trying to thwart royal policy, much less of trying to obtain power for himself. This was owing first of all to the old traditions of transferring higher officials from one province to another at fairly frequent intervals and of allowing no one to hold office in his native district. This second rule was broken at times, but not often enough to cause any problems. The regular appearance of commissioners sent out from Paris, although it must have been a nuisance, made serious acts of disobedience impossible. Conversely, local officials (sometimes rather minor officials) were regularly summoned to Paris to explain their financial reports or to justify their judicial decisions. Failure to obey the king's orders could bring stern letters of rebuke.²⁰⁰ This careful supervision did not prevent a considerable amount of corruption (especially among lower-level officials) and some oppressive actions (especially against the poorer classes and against the Church), but it kept corruption and oppression within tolerable limits. Even at the end of the reign, when complaints against local officials formed an important part of the protests of the provincial leagues, no sweeping changes in local administrative personnel were made, perhaps because they did not seem necessary. Comparisons are dangerous, but both the loyalty and the honesty of local administrators seem to have been greater under Philip than during the troubled times of John the Good.

This is not to say that French local administration in the reign of Philip the Fair was entirely effective. It did hold the country together; it produced a certain amount of income for the king; and it prevented serious outbreaks of violence. But it also had many weaknesses. It intervened only sporadically and on special occasions in the lands of the great nobles. This did no harm when it was a question of Burgundy or Brittany; their dukes were loyal supporters of Philip and were willing to follow his policies if due respect was paid to their high positions and their own interests. The rulers of Aquitaine and Flanders, on the other hand, were always resentful when neighboring seneschals and *baillis* intervened in their affairs. Usually a direct order from the king was necessary to secure compliance with the citations and summonses issued by his officials, and, as the great wars of the reign demonstrated, even a royal command was not always obeyed. Friendly or hostile, the four great fiefs were not really included in the French administrative system. Lands held by other nobles (and by some of the bishops) had varying degrees of autonomy, but in even the least-privileged fiefs there could be delays in carrying out the orders of royal officials. The same could be said of many of the towns. In short, the effectiveness of the local administrative system varied widely from region to region and within each region. No royal policy could be put into effect uniformly and simultaneously.

²⁰⁰ Strayer, "Philip the Fair," pp. 198-99. For example, a *bailli* of Caen was threatened with confiscation of his goods if he did not do justice to a king's clerk (B.N., ms. fr. 25697, no. 28); a seneschal was told that he would be punished if he did not observe the rights of the consuls of Cahors (A.N., J 341, no. 8). Cf. *H.L.*, x, col. 236; *Ord.*, 1, 434.

Other weaknesses have already been mentioned. Some local officials, even of very low rank, were appointed directly by the king. Philip certainly did not know all these men personally, but they must have been recommended by someone at court, and it could have been difficult for a seneschal or *bailli* to discipline a subordinate who had a powerful patron. Many *prévôts* and almost all *bayles* farmed their offices. As long as they paid the sums due at the appointed times they were not closely supervised in their dealings with peasants and petty bourgeois—the vast majority of the population. A notoriously oppressive or inefficient man might be amerced, but he was seldom removed from office. A contract was a contract: a man who had bought a job was entitled to the profits of that job until his term of office expired. The greatest weakness in the system was not that *prévôts* and *bayles* disobeyed specific orders (after all, there were fees for serving a summons or seizing property) but that they evaded or enforced half-heartedly the general rules laid down by the central government on such matters as privileges of the clergy or the use of foreign currencies. Seneschals and *baillis* often were blamed for the actions (or the failures to act) of subordinates over whom they had only very loose control.

In fact, when one looks at the weaknesses of French local administration the real question to be asked is how it functioned as well as it did. It had two strengths that compensated, to some extent, for the weaknesses. First, the higher-ranking local officials —*baillis*, seneschals, most of the judges, many of the collectors, viscounts, and *viguiers*—were highly competent and extraordinarily hard-working men. Second, as noted above, the central government kept close watch over the work of local administrators. Accounts were carefully audited—slowly, to be sure—but in the end even the most insignificant expenditures had to be justified and the smallest debts paid. The Parlement heard appeals from, and often reversed, the decisions of local courts. The king and the Council could intervene directly in local administration, ordering certain actions, suspending or forbidding others. The *enquêteurs* and other delegates from Paris may not have redressed many grievances, but they kept the king informed about local conditions. Supervision from Paris was most effective at the higher levels of local government; it scarcely touched the world of the *bayles* and the *prévôts*. But it was effective where, from the king's point of view, it was most necessary for it to be effective. It prevented large-scale embezzlement and checked ac-

tions that might unnecessarily antagonize the rich and the powerful. It ensured, as far as was possible in a country so diverse as
France, uniformity in the implementation of royal policy. This
is about as much as could have been expected, and this, on the
whole, is what Philip got.

Financial Administration

The financial machinery that Philip the Fair inherited from his
father and grandfather was reasonably effective in handling the
ordinary revenues and expenses of the crown. Most of the king's
income down to 1285 came from the royal domain, that is, from
the lands and forests, mills, tolls, market dues, profits of justice,
and payments for privileges in areas that were directly administered by royal agents. This income was fairly easy to estimate
several years in advance because most of the domain was leased
(sometimes for long terms) to inhabitants of the domain. Nobles,
clergy, well-to-do peasants, and members of the bourgeoisie paid
annual rents for the land and bought the right to cut wood in
the forests (usually for a period of several years). Mills and other
monopolies were also leased, often by men who were farming
nearby land. Tolls, market dues, and profits of (low) justice
were collected by *prévôts*, who farmed their offices for three-
year terms; these leases were frequently renewed. Thus the chief
duty of the *baillis* and seneschals, who were responsible by 1285
for domain revenues, was to find out where the king's revenue-
producing properties lay, who held them, and whether the yearly
rents had been paid. Obviously, there had to be a description of
the domain for each *bailliage* or *sénéchaussée*, and some of these
have survived. The most elegant and best arranged is the description of the royal domain in the *bailliage* of Rouen, which was
prepared in the 1260s.[1] If the reports prepared by the *claviers*
of Carcassonne in 1317 had not been lost,[2] we would have an
even more complete description of a southern district.

   There was, of course, casual revenue that came from the
domain—reliefs, wardships, forfeitures, amercements and the like
—but this seldom added up to any large sum. Presumably a competent local official would know about most of these sources of
income, although he would have to be notified from Paris about

[1] Strayer, *The Royal Domain in the Bailliage of Rouen* (Princeton, 1936;
2d ed., London, 1976).
[2] *C.R.* Maillard, I, nos. 5203, 5205, 5207, 5209, 5214.

amercements and forfeitures imposed by the king's court. He would also, of course, have to be notified about decreases in the domain—gifts, exchanges, forgiveness of fines, and restoration of forfeitures—but there would not be many of these in any one year in any one district. By and large, income from the domain was fairly stable down to about 1290, and the changes that did occur favored the king. Norman revenues certainly increased,[3] and the accounts of the king with the Temple suggest that other regions were also turning in more money.[4]

Local expenses were also fairly predictable down to 1290. Wages of castellans, forest officers, sergeants, and doorkeepers and salaries of higher officials did not vary greatly; if anything, there was a general decrease under Philip III[5] and a decrease in the salaries of baillis in the early years of Philip the Fair.[6] On the other hand, the number of minor officials increased, so that there was no net saving. "Feoda et elemosine" was a category that was almost bound to expand; each new king gave grants to his favorite churches and his favorite courtiers. The death of courtiers with life pensions and the extinction of families that had hereditary rents diminished the burden somewhat, but the Church never died, and new courtiers took the place of old ones. Nevertheless, the increase in any given year was not great enough to unbalance local accounts seriously. The figure for "Opera"— repairs to castles, mills, market halls, and the like—did not run high, though of course it fluctuated more than other expenses. Administrative costs—travel, messengers, food for prisoners, payments to executioners—were low, especially in the north (travel to Paris from the south was of course more expensive). These administrative costs increased later in the reign of Philip the Fair, but never enough to be a real burden.

No very elaborate machinery was needed to handle the finances of the domain. Baillis and seneschals, after deducting local expenses, sent their net income to the Temple at Paris, which acted as the king's banker. The king was only one of the Temple's

[3] Strayer, Administration of Normandy, p. 55.

[4] Léopold Delisle, Mémoire sur les opérations financières des Templiers (Paris, 1889), pp. 118-24; Fawtier, ed., Comptes du Trésor, pp. xlvi-l. Overall income reported by the Temple increased from 1286 to 1290: for example, 209,321 l. at All Saints 1286; 250,136 l. at All Saints 1289; 378,916 l. at All Saints 1290. Not all of this income came from the domain, since a tenth was being collected, but the yield of a tenth was more or less constant. Thus the domain must have contributed most of the increase.

[5] Strayer, Administration of Normandy, p. 53.

[6] Ibid., App. III; see also above, p. 56.

clients, though of course his account was by far the largest. The Temple kept a careful record of these deposits, noting the source of each payment and crediting the sum to the king. At the end of each accounting period (Candlemas, Ascension, and All Saints) it struck a balance—so much received for the king's account, so much spent by the king's order, so much left to the credit of the king, or so much owed by the king to the Temple.[7] These were awkward accounting periods, first, because they were uneven and variable in length (since Ascension is a moveable feast), and, second, because they did not coincide with the accounting periods of Normandy (Michaelmas and Easter) or of the south (where the fiscal year began on 24 June, the feast of St. John the Baptist). They would have been utterly useless for budgetary purposes, but no one was yet thinking in terms of budgets. They were acceptable and useful only for bank statements.

The Treasurer of the Temple and his assistants were skilled in accounting, but they took no responsibility for the completeness or the accuracy of the work of the collectors of royal revenue. They would know that a *bailli* had sent in a certain number of pounds; they would not know whether this represented all or only a part of what he owed. *Baillis* and other collectors of revenue sent their money to the Temple, but their accounts went to the *curia*. There they were examined and then approved (or corrected) at special meetings of the *curia*—the *curia in compotis* —which were held in the Temple at the end of each accounting term.[8] These sessions were attended by some of the great men of the Council[9] and lasted for only a few days.[10] Detailed studies of

[7] Delisle, *Templiers*, pp. 118-32; Fawtier, ed., *Comptes du Trésor*, pp. xlvi-liv.

[8] Borrelli de Serres, *Recherches*, I, 303-4, 320.

[9] In 1289 the king heard his accounts at Creil (Delisle, *Templiers*, pp. 121-22). Present were: the papal legate; Charles of Valois; the duke of Burgundy; the Constable (the lord of Nesle); the lord of Harcourt (Jean); the bishop of Orléans (Pierre de Mornay); the dean of Tours (Gilles Lambert); the lord of Montmorenci (Mathew, chamberlain); Guillaume d'Harcourt (*maître d'hôtel* of the king); Arnoul de Wisemale (a Templar and also a *maître d'hôtel*); Renaud Barbou (ex-*bailli* of Rouen and a member of the Council); Pierre and Oudard de Chambly (chamberlains); and Hugues de Bouville (another chamberlain). The last four were financial experts, and Oudard became a permanent member of the Chambre aux deniers (Borrelli de Serres, *Recherches*, I, 313, 314, 317). The two *maîtres d'hôtel* also had financial experience. On the other hand, one cannot imagine Valois or Robert of Burgundy spending much time on accounting problems.

[10] Borrelli de Serres, *Recherches*, I, 306, 313.

all the accounts that had come in over a period of several months could not have been made at such meetings. The *curia* could resolve difficult questions and give general approval of decisions made by underlings, but the real work had to be done by financial experts who were on duty throughout the year.

A nice example of the way in which the *curia in compotis* did its work was a balancing of accounts between the king and the duke of Burgundy at Candlemas 1299. The duke was too great a man to deal only with technicians; some of the leading men of the Council had to be present. At the same time, the accounts were rather complicated. The duke had been receiving for the king the revenues of the county of Burgundy; he had also been spending money for the king in the county. He was, in fact, in a position not very different from that of a *bailli*, except that he had to be treated with more respect. The accounts were heard by the bishop of Dol (the senior member of the Council), the abbot of Jouy (Treasurer), Pierre La Reue (Treasurer), Renaud Barbou (a leader in the Parlement), Jean Clersens and Jean de Lillers (clerks of accounts), "et plusieurs autres clers de comptes."[11] It is perfectly apparent, however, that all the real work had been done before the meetings, perhaps by the anonymous clerks who came at the end of the list of men present. The bishop, Renaud Barbou, and the two Treasurers could give only formal approval to the work of the experts.

These experts, who were known as clerks of accounts by the time of Philip the Fair, must have appeared at least as early as the reign of St. Louis.[12] As Borrelli de Serres pointed out, by 1268 someone in Paris was preparing checklists of items for which the *baillis* of Normandy and the old domain were to account in their next reports.[13] These lists were revised frequently, and it is evident from the marks on them that they were compared with the *baillis'* accounts. Obviously, some group in Paris had been going over old accounts, adding new items as information came in, and thus preparing themselves to check the work of the *baillis*. Such a group must have been composed of the early clerks of accounts.

The clerks of accounts also helped to prepare for and took part

[11] B.M., Dijon, ms. 1105. I must thank M Jean-Pierre Redoutey of the University of Besançon for calling this manuscript to my attention and for sending me photostats of the first section.
[12] Borrelli de Serres, *Recherches*, 1, 312-16.
[13] Ibid., 108 ff., 136-37; Strayer, *Administration of Normandy*, pp. 33-34.

in the sessions of the financial Exchequer of Rouen, which audited Norman accounts twice a year. Normandy had a much more advanced financial administration when it was annexed in 1204 than did the old domain, and the Norman Exchequer continued to function as a nearly autonomous body. It was supervised by a delegation sent down from the *curia in compotis*, and this delegation in turn was advised by the clerks of accounts. The checklists already mentioned were prepared by these clerks, some of whom were specialists in Norman affairs. Thus Eudes de Lorris, dean of Orléans, and Etienne de Montfort, dean of St. Aignan of Orléans, attended the meetings of the Exchequer regularly from 1252 to 1270, and Nicolas d'Auteil was placed on the council of regency in 1270 "propter scacarios et propter compotos Templi et alios compotos nostri."[14] This was a useful experience; Norman accounts of the first half of the century were clearer and better arranged than those of the old domain, and it seems likely that clerks sent from Paris could learn something from Norman methods.

As far as the domain was concerned, then, income and expenses were predictable, fairly easy to check, and reasonably stable during the early years of Philip's reign. This stability is especially evident in the case of the Norman *bailliages*, which had a long tradition of good fiscal administration. Thus the Michaelmas Exchequer turned in 56,677 l.t. in 1286, 56,389 l.t. in 1289, 81,717 l.t. in 1290, and 58,551 l.t. in 1291. The Easter Exchequer produced 59,842 l.t. in 1287, 60,225 l.t. in 1290, and 65,747 l.t. in 1291. For some reason 1292 was a bad year, yielding only 42,440 l.t. at Easter and 44,397 l.t. at Michaelmas. The revenues of the *prévôtés* also stayed within a fairly narrow range, which is not surprising, since they were farmed for three-year periods. Income from the *bailliages* of France fluctuated more widely, but even the *bailliages* show some consistency: at All Saints 1289, 1290, and 1291 they were credited with 75,026 l.p., 74,602 l.p., and 72,011 l.p., respectively.[15]

If domain income was fairly stable and predictable, the expenses of the king and the central government were not. Using the accounts cited above, total expenses charged to the king by the Temple varied from a minimum of 111,073 l.p. at Ascension 1292 to a maximum of 355,772 l.p. at Candlemas 1290. (I exclude

<hr/>

[14] Borrelli de Serres, *Recherches*, I, 314; *Gallia Christiana*, XI, 38.

[15] For all the figures in this paragraph see Delisle, *Templiers*, pp. 118-30, or Fawtier, ed., *Comptes du Trésor*, pp. xlvi-liv.

the figure of 421,542 l.p. at Candlemas 1293 because 264,353 l.p. of this went to Biche and Mouche for unknown reasons, perhaps as repayment of loans.) Household expenses varied from about 34,000 l.p. a term to 72,000 l.p. a term, with a median of 46,000 l.p. a term. There was no steady increase, and a high expenditure was often followed by a low one. The largest amounts spent by the king were summed up under the heading "magne partes," which meant, roughly, all nonrecurring expenses, as opposed to the Household, "feoda et elemosine," or "dona." Even this category did not grow steadily; it was lower in 1292 than in 1290.

There is every reason to suppose that the Temple accounts do not include all royal income and expenditure. Nevertheless, a man's balance with his banker tells something of his financial position. Philip owed the Temple considerable sums of money at times, but during his first years the debts were always paid off promptly. At All Saints 1292, the year before the war with England began, the Temple owed Philip 106,000 l.p.[16] He was clearly living within his means during those years of peace.

He was living within his means, but he was not living exclusively on the income from the domain. Most of the extraordinary levies for the Crusade against Aragon (the aid for knighting Philip, the gifts from the towns, and loans) had long been spent; in fact, there was now a deficit in this account, since loans had to be repaid out of current income—31,607 l.t. at Candlemas 1288.[17] But the tenth imposed on the Church for the war ran until 1288 and was then renewed for three years, so that until 1292 Philip could count on about 260,000 l.t. a year from this source.[18] Without this resource he would have been running a deficit over the period, though not a very large one in most years.

Nevertheless, it was clear by 1292 that changes had to be made in the financial operations of the monarchy. The king could no longer expect the domain to produce enough revenue to meet his needs; nor could he continue to rely on a few expert clerks or chamberlains (who had many other duties) to handle his finances. He may have begun to feel that he needed his own Treasury instead of banking with the Temple. Until Philip's time, royal finance was not very different from that of any other great lord; it was based on lordship rather than sovereignty. The count of

[16] Delisle, *Templiers*, p. 130; Fawtier, ed., *Comptes du Trésor*, p. liv.
[17] Delisle, *Templiers*, pp. 151, 154-60.
[18] Ibid., pp. 120, 123-29. Note declining income in 1292.

Flanders had an older, and perhaps better system of accounting than did the king of France, and the Church had a better idea of the income of the clergy than the king had of the income of the nobility. It is only under Philip that one can begin to speak of "public finance," and even then the term is a little premature.

That Philip was worrying about his finances in the early 1290s is shown by two facts that have already been mentioned: the appointment of receivers to take over some of the financial duties of seneschals and *baillis*, and the growing reliance on the financial expertise of Biche and Mouche. The loss of income from the tenth was one shock, and the decrease in domain revenue in 1292, not only in Normandy but also in other districts, was another.[19] If Philip was already considering the possibility of conflict with England over Aquitaine in 1292, he had even more reason to be concerned.

Whatever the reason, in 1292 Philip made a great effort to increase his income. One of his first steps was to impose a sales-tax on the northern towns, and perhaps elsewhere. Many towns were already paying such a tax (Aigues-Mortes since the time of St. Louis), and most of those that had not paid before bought off the tax for annual lump-sum contributions. Paris, for example, agreed to pay 10,000 l.t. a year for ten years.[20] As this example shows, income from the sales-tax did not amount to much in any one year, though it certainly produced as much as the net income of two or three of the *bailliages* of the old domain. At the same time, the *sénéchaussées* of Saintonge and Poitou agreed to pay a *fouage* at the high rate of 6 s.t. a hearth each year for six years in return for the expulsion of the Jews from the region. (Edward I had expelled the Jews from Gascony in 1290, and Charles II of Sicily had done the same in Anjou and Maine in 1288, so that Saintonge-Poitou, lying between these provinces, may have been overrun by refugees.) This was a profitable operation. Judging by existing accounts, it increased the income from each *sénéchaussée* each term by at least 50 percent[21] and yielded about 4,500 l.t. a year in Poitou and 5,000 l.t. a year in Saintonge (these totals are doubtless

---

19 Borrelli de Serres, *Recherches*, II, 490 and App. A, sec. v.

20 Strayer and Taylor, pp. 12-13.

21 The *fouage* in Poitou produced 750 l.t. a year in 1293-1294, when net revenue for two terms was 1,589 l.t. (*C.R.*, I, nos. 7303, 7388); the *fouage* produced 2,500 l.t. the next term, when the net revenue was 5,025 l.t. (nos. 7452, 7559). In Saintonge a *fouage* for half a year produced 3,200 l.t. (nos. 7567, 7643, 7738); gross income for All Saints was 7,643 l.t. and net was 1,306 l.t.

incomplete).[22] An annual increase in income of nearly 10,000 l.t. a year was certainly welcome, but even by peacetime standards, it was a very small fraction of total expenditures. Finally, in 1292-1293 Philip, through Biche and Mouche, tallaged the Lombards. This tallage produced either 141,000 l.t. or 152,000 l.t. (Mignon's figures differ in the two entries).[23]

The sales-tax, the *fouage*, and the tallage are important because they show that the king and his advisers saw the need for additional income before the financial crisis caused by the war in Gascony. They also saw that income could be increased only by extraordinary measures; no reforms in the administration of the domain could make any significant difference. As a result, by 1294, when the occupation of Aquitaine was causing large expenses, they were ready to act. A *fouage* of 6 s.t. a hearth was imposed in Languedoc, technically, perhaps, as a substitute for the general obligation to defend that part of the realm, but in fact as a tax that might be bought off by lump-sum payments but that could not easily be redeemed by actual service. Even a great lord like the count of Foix, who could have supplied (and later did supply) troops for the war, was asked for money instead of service.[24] In the same year the king decided to bypass the pope and called provincial councils of the French Church, which were persuaded to grant a tenth for two years.[25] These precedents were followed in the succeeding years. Laymen paid taxes on personal property—a hundredth in 1295, a fiftieth in 1296, and another fiftieth in 1297.[26] There were protests by nobles and clergy, and the taxes were often commuted, especially in the south, for lump-sum payments or for hearth taxes. The greater nobles were conciliated by being given a share of the taxes,[27] but the taxes *were* collected and produced large sums. Meanwhile, the French Church was asked to renew and increase its grant. This move was blocked by Boniface VIII in the bull *Clericis laicos*, but this was only a temporary respite. By 1297 Philip had put enough pressure on the pope to make him withdraw his prohibition against grants for defense, and the French clergy conceded a double tenth, which was renewed in 1298.[28]

---

[22] The *fouage* of Poitou for six years produced 27,000 l.t. (*C.R.*, II, no. 14414); the *fouage* of Saintonge yielded 32,778 l.t. for six years (no. 14484).
[23] Mignon, nos. 2073, 2076.   [24] Strayer and Taylor, pp. 44-46.
[25] Ibid., pp. 25-28.   [26] Ibid., pp. 46-52.
[27] Ibid., pp. 47-50.
[28] See below, pp. 254-55, and Strayer and Taylor, pp. 29-31.

The degree to which the government had become dependent on extraordinary sources of income is shown by an interesting document, drawn up about 1296, which explained how the expenses of the Gascon war could be met.[29] The list starts with 200,000 l.t. in the Treasury. Some, but not all, of this money could have come from the domain. But this sum is dwarfed by other estimates: 189,000 l.t. from the tenth paid by the clergy, plus 60,000 l.t. from the Order of Cîteaux (which made a separate grant), and an unestimated sum from the tenth in Languedoc; 315,000 l.t. from the hundredth, plus 35,000 l.t. from a fiftieth in Champagne; another unestimated sum from the subsidy of Toulouse, Beaucaire, and Carcassonne; and 60,000 l.t. from commutation of the sales-tax in Paris, Châlons, Reims, Laon, and Tournai (this must have represented several years' income). The Lombards were to pay 65,000 l.t., perhaps for arrears of the tallage of 1292, although a fine on the Riccardi (who were in financial difficulties) is specifically mentioned. In addition, the Lombards had agreed in 1295 to pay a sales-tax on transactions among themselves in France; this is estimated as worth 16,000 l.t. a year, though later records suggest that it produced only about 13,000 l.t.[30] Tallage and fines of the Jews were supposed to yield 225,000 l.t. Treasury accounts of the 1290s suggest that this figure was much too high; 100,000 l.t. for the period Candlemas–All Saints 1292 is the largest revenue recorded, and it undoubtedly included tallages from 1291.[31]

The largest item in the estimate is loans—200,000 l.t. from Biche, Mouche, and other Italians, 630,000 l.t. from rich burgers, and 50,000 l.t. from prelates and royal officials. There was a precedent for this: Philip III had borrowed something on the order of 150,000 l.t. for the Crusade against Aragon,[32] and, according to Mignon, much of this had been repaid by early 1288,[33] so that a new loan was possible. Nevertheless, force was used to obtain loans in some districts, and elsewhere men preferred to make small gifts to the king rather than loans, which might never be

---

[29] Funck-Brentano, "Document," pp. 326-48.

[30] Strayer and Taylor, p. 11.

[31] Ibid., p. 18; Fawtier, ed., *Comptes du Trésor*, p. xxxi; Mignon, no. 2113.

[32] Strayer, "Crusade against Aragon," p. 113.

[33] Either 31,530 l.t. or 31,607 l.t. of loans was repaid by the account of Candlemas 1288 (N.S.) (Mignon, no. 1171 [note error in date; it must have been 1288]; Delisle, *Templiers*, nos. 242, 272-87). Large sums were repaid in the period 1291-1294 (cf. *C.R.*, I, nos. 6122, 7380-85, 8129-38, 8280-84, 9955-80).

repaid. Thus in Saintonge-Poitou gifts came to 44,910 l.t. and loans to only 5,666 l.t.[34] Most of the loans and gifts were collected in 1295, and if Mignon's figures can be trusted (they check out perfectly in the one case where we have an original roll), the total came to at least 632,000 l.t., even with no entries for Mâcon, Périgord, Rouergue, Toulouse, Carcassonne, and Beaucaire.[35]

The loan was a great success, but it could not be repeated. For one thing, repayments were slow; indeed, it is hard to think of any time between 1295 and 1314 when Philip had 880,000 l.t. to spare. Even favored creditors, such as the nuns of Prouille, were repaid relatively promptly (14 October 1298) only by charging the debt against what they owed for tenths and amortization.[36] There was a real effort to repay loans in 1301 (a year in which military expenses were low), but there was a clear preference for creditors who had transferred their rights to the mendicant orders[37] (or, in one case, to a king's valet)[38] and for executors of the estates of dead creditors, who would presumably use some of the money for pious purposes.[39] The same pattern is seen in loans repaid in 1305; all go to the Franciscans of Issoudun, and one of the donors had already died.[40] The figures are very incomplete, but they do not suggest massive repayments up to 1305. In short, Philip did not repudiate his debts, but he certainly was in no hurry to repay them. Given prevailing rates of interest, an interest-free loan that ran for ten years or more was about the same as a gift to the king. Moreover, the heaviest taxes came in the years after 1295, which would have been another deterrent to floating large loans. Some effort was made in 1302 and 1304 to obtain loans, especially from royal officials, and Philip continued to borrow money until the end of his reign, but never again on

[34] Strayer and Taylor, pp. 19-20; Mignon, nos. 1126, 1159. The high figure for gifts in Saintonge was noted in a partial list of loans there (C.R., II, nos. 18233, 18278). The latter entry reads "sachez que il a trop plus de don que de prest."

[35] Mignon, nos. 1105-70. The total amount of loans in C.R., II, nos. 18279-633 (20,064 l.p.), is exactly the figure given by Mignon, no. 1134. The incomplete general roll of loans in C.R., II, nos. 1863 ff., does not fit Mignon at all; Fawtier (C.R., III, lv) thought it was written ca. 1290, so it would probably be a list of loans for the Aragon war.

[36] J.T.P., no. 1294.

[37] Ibid., nos. 4611, 4879, 5263, 5691, 5692, 5712, 5804.

[38] Ibid., no. 4615.   [39] Ibid., nos. 5479, 5705, 5799.

[40] C.R., I, no. 6122.

the scale of 1295.[41] The French financial system was not yet capable of operating with a large floating debt.

One inconspicuous item in the estimate of 1296, 60,000 l.t. from "weak money," proved to be more useful than loans in meeting Philip's needs. At All Saints 1296 the slightly debased and greatly overvalued currency was already yielding 101,435 l.t.[42] By 1298 the process had gone further; Borrelli de Serres estimates that for the fiscal year from St. John's 1298 to St. John's 1299 coinage produced more than 1,200,000 l.t.[43] Of course, to continue making a profit from coinage Philip had to "weaken" the money steadily, since prices rose with the overvaluation of the currency. When a *gros tournois*, originally considered the equivalent of 12 pence, was declared to be the equivalent of 36 pence, the person who received the coin was getting no more silver than he had before (actually a little less, since there had been some reduction in the silver content of the coin as well). But if silver valued at 12 pence was now valued at 36 pence, then a measure of grain valued at 12 pence would eventually be paid for by the coin officially valued at 36 pence. Fortunately for the king, it took prices some time to adjust to his manipulation of the currency, and until the adjustment had taken place he could reap a profit by reissuing his coins at inflated values. Fortunately again for the king, the salaries, pensions, and wages he paid did not increase at all. Army wages, the largest single item in royal expenses, remained at the same level, though the size of the army increased and Philip had some difficulties in paying his troops in 1303.[44] Philip, however, was getting three times as much service for the same amount of silver, and he was paying off old debts at one-third of their value. Nevertheless, there are limits to financing a government through inflation, and Philip had reached those limits by the end of 1303. Nobles and clergy, living on fixed rents and drawing more or less fixed salaries or wages for military service, were angry, and the king had to promise to return to "good money."[45] The return was painful, and Philip never again tried to cover a major part of his expenses by inflating the value of the

---

[41] See Strayer and Taylor, p. 21, for pressure on royal officials in 1302; A.N., JJ 36, nos. 14, 15, for efforts to borrow money in Vermandois, Amiens, and Toulouse in July 1302; B.N., ms. fr. 25993, no. 147, for a loan of 52,000 l.t. ("good money") by the Lombards in 1304.

[42] Fawtier, ed., *Comptes du Trésor*, p. lvi and nos. 267-70.

[43] Borrelli de Serres, *Recherches*, II, 445 and App. D.

[44] See below, p. 335.   [45] See below, pp. 395-96.

currency. He did try one experiment in 1311, overvaluing some small coins (the "bourgeois") by one-fourth, but this stirred up the opposition of those who feared that another great inflation was beginning and brought in relatively little profit. "Good money" was restored in 1313.[46] Philip's successors did not forget the precedents that he had established, and French currency fluctuated wildly during the rest of the century; but Philip himself profited from currency manipulation only during the crisis years of the Gascon and Flemish wars.

It had become apparent during the 1290s that the ordinary revenues of the crown might be insufficient even in times of peace and that they were utterly inadequate to meet the costs of war. Nevertheless, the country as a whole was not willing to face these facts, and Philip and his advisers may not have fully realized how great a change had taken place. They certainly were aware that it would be difficult to make permanent the new sources of revenue that had been used to pay for the great wars. The one possible exception was the tenth paid by the clergy. This was collected almost every year from 1295 to the end of the reign, but the "almost" is significant. No tenths were granted for 1302, 1303, 1305, 1306, 1309, or 1311. Each tenth had to be negotiated separately—with the French clergy down to 1304, with the pope thereafter. Each tenth was for a specific purpose, such as defense of the realm, restoring "good money," or a projected crusade. It is true that the crusade tenth, granted by Clement V in 1312, was for six years, but the income of the last year was reserved for the pope, and there was no assurance that the grant would be renewed. The tenths were a very welcome addition to the king's ordinary income; they could amount to a quarter of the receipts of one term, but they were not large enough to cover any extraordinary expense.

The general subsidies for war clearly could not be made a regular source of income. They were taken in seven of the ten years from 1295 through 1304, but they were more and more closely tied to the idea that they were a substitute for the service owed by all men for defense of the realm. As a result, the doctrine emerged that they could be collected only in time of actual warfare. If there were no war, there should be no tax. This rule was accepted by Philip in 1313, forced upon him in 1314, and con-

---

[46] Borrelli de Serres, *Les variations monétaires sous Philippe le Bel* (Chalon-sur-Saône, 1902 [extracted from *Gazette numismatique française*, 1902, pp. 246-425]), pp. 355-59.

secrated in the provincial charters of 1315.[47] Strictly interpreted, the rule would have made it difficult to prepare for a war that seemed inevitable or to mobilize an army to prevent the outbreak of a war. Even by a loose interpretation, subsidies could not be used for ordinary expenses of government or for grants to potential foreign allies and other costly diplomatic undertakings.

There were no satisfactory substitutes for general taxation. One-shot operations, such as the expulsion of the Jews or the attack on the Temple, gave only temporary relief. The expulsion of the Jews seems to have been fairly profitable, judging by the entries in the Registers, but the money came in slowly, as goods were sold piece by piece.[48] There was little immediate profit from administering the goods of the Temple, and the final settlement (only 260,000 l.t.) went to Philip's son, not to Philip.[49] The attempts to generalize the customary aids for the marriage of the king's daughter and the knighting of his son were not very successful. Some money was raised, but many areas proved that they owed no aid,[50] and of the few totals given by Mignon, only two are impressive. Hugues de la Celle, the very energetic viceroy of the west, squeezed 19,053 l.t. for the marriage aid out of Saintonge-Poitou, La Marche, Limousin, and Angoumois.[51] Champagne, which after all was Louis X's own county, gave 14,981 l.t. for his knighting, but not without some resistance.[52] At best these were, like the expulsion of the Jews and the attack on the Temple, one-shot operations.

The same remark, with some qualifications, could be made about lesser sources of income—regalia, annates, fines for amortization, amercements by royal courts and by the *enquêteurs*, and export duties. The king had the right of regalia in less than half the dioceses of the realm;[53] income from this source was sporadic, unpredictable, and could not be increased. Annates (a year's in-

[47] See below, p. 419.

[48] G. Saige, *Les juifs de Languedoc* (Paris, 1881), pp. 244 ff., lists profits from all sales of Jewish goods in the south, where Jewish wealth was concentrated. Some of the early payments were in "weak money." Adding in figures for the north, a rough guess would be that the confiscation produced about 200,000 l.t. by the end of 1310.

[49] See below, Chapter IV, note 152.

[50] See below, p. 393, and Strayer and Taylor, pp. 77-80.

[51] Mignon, no. 1575.

[52] Ibid., no. 1601.

[53] Jean Gaudemet, *La collation par le Roi de France des bénéfices vacants en régale* (Paris, 1935), pp. 63-66.

come, less expenses, from clerics appointed or promoted to new benefices) were granted only twice, for a three-year period each time (1297-1299 and 1304-1306). The entries in the Journals of the Treasury for the first grant of annates suggest that they brought in much less money than a tenth.[54] They must have been helpful in 1304-1306, when the tenth granted by Benedict XI could not yet be collected because it was tied to restoration of "good money," but annates were not a regular or predictable source of income. Fines for amortization were also unpredictable; they could be increased by careful investigation, but not to a point where they provided a steady income. Amercements could be very large, but no one could predict when a count of Foix or a town like Laon or Carcassonne would misbehave, nor could one be sure that the king would insist on collecting the full amount of the amercement. There is just a possibility that Philip, irritated by his financial problems and especially by the opposition to the marriage aid, encouraged the imposition of large fines on towns in the period 1306-1310;[55] but even if this were a royal policy, it could not be repeated. As for export duties, Pierre de Chalon worked hard to make them more productive, but to no avail.[56] The few Italians who bought licenses to export large amounts of wool found it an unprofitable operation; payments by small exporters amounted to only a few hundred pounds a year.

Thus, even after the experiments of the war years, the domain still produced the only royal revenues that were predictable and rendered at fixed intervals. For this reason, the royal financial

[54] For example, in July 1299 the figures for dioceses taken at random are: Clermont, double tenth, 7,954 l.t., annates, 997 l.t.; Le Puy, tenth, 1,484 l.t., annates, 104 l.t.; Rodez, tenth, 4,932 l.t., annates, 1,350 l.t.; Albi, tenth, 3,271 l.t., annates, 865 l.t.; Angers, tenth, 2,079 l.t., annates, 420 l.t.; Le Mans, tenth, 2,250 l.t., annates, 158 l.t. For these figures see *J.T.P.*, nos. 3008-10, 3012-13, 3015-17, 3021-23, 3041-43, 3044-45. The two largest sums for annates are 11,810 l.t. for nine dioceses in the province of Narbonne for three years (1297-1299), which works out to about 441 l.t. per diocese per year (Mignon, no. 521), and 18,196 l.t for six doceses in the province of Rouen for three years, or 1,012 l.t. per diocese per year (ibid., no. 549). Rouen was a very rich province, but at least two years (1304, 1305) of this grant were collected in a period of "weak money," which would mean that the annual charge in "good money" would have been only about 340 l.t. per diocese.

[55] See *Olim*, III: p. 183, Beauvais, 10,000 l.p., 1306; p. 197, Amiens, 20,000 l.p., 1306; p. 299, Cahors, 3,000 l.t., 1309; p. 324, Castelnaudary, 4,000 l.t., 1309; p. 362, Montbrison, 5,000 l.t., 1309; p. 366, ex-consuls of Périguex, 6,000 l.t., 1309; p. 610, Laon, 10,000 l.t., 1311.

[56] Strayer, "Pierre de Chalon," pp. 234-38.

administration continued to be organized on the basis of the domain. Only in the domain were there resident financial agents of the crown—*baillis*, seneschals, receivers, viscounts, *prévôts*, foresters, and their subordinates. Accounts of extraordinary income were arranged by *bailliages* and *sénéchaussées*, except, of course, for tenths, annates, and regalia, for which the only sensible units were ecclesiastical provinces and dioceses. Even income from the Church, however, was sometimes collected on the basis of secular administrative units, especially when payment of arrears was being demanded.

Whatever unit was used for collection of extraordinary income, a very large number of men were needed to bring in the money. There were chief collectors for each *balliage*, *sénéchaussée*, and ecclesiastical province or diocese. The chief collectors often had one or more colleagues or deputies (it is at times difficult to tell which was which). Under the chief collectors were subcollectors, going down to the village level in the case of subventions.[57] Yet this vast body of agents had no structure and no permanence; collectors were appointed ad hoc for each extraordinary levy. There was no rank of collector, as there was of receiver; there was no central office (as there was to be later) concerned exclusively with overseeing extraordinary income; there was no continuity in the process of collecting a tenth or a subvention. A tax might be imposed by one man, collected in part by two or three others, while still another man would be responsible for arrears.[58] Some men acted only once or twice as collectors, others spent much of their time in this work; but even the most active collectors had other duties.

If Biche and Mouche had remained in control of royal finance,

[57] See Mignon, no. 1289, for accounts of "collectorum villarum et locorum" of the *bailliage* of Sens; Auguste Longnon, ed., *Documents relatifs au comté de Champagne et de Brie 1172-1362*, 3 vols. (Paris, 1901-1914), III, 144-46, for village collectors in Champagne; B.N., ms. fr. 25992, nos. 8, 32, for collectors for each sergeanty in Poitou in 1302-1303 (six collectors in one sergeanty) and collection by sergeanties in Caux in 1298.

[58] In the case of a subvention in Sens that was to be collected by Pierre de Latilly and Jean de Vères (the *bailli*), they used a chief substitute and several subcollectors; two other men collected arrears (Mignon, nos. 1443-41). A subvention "imposed" in Orléans by Jean de Yenville was raised by Thibaud Bouchier (nos. 1473-74); G. de la Poterie and others instituted by him accounted for a subvention in Tours (no. 1527); P. de Mouchy and P. de Hangest "imposed" a subsidy in Rouen, which was collected by Jean de Chambly (no. 1531).

as they were in 1295, when they were receivers-general and Treasurers, they might have set up a separate office to deal with extraordinary income. Almost all of the loans to the king, much of the tenth granted by the Church, and some of the hundredth imposed on laymen was paid to Biche and Mouche or their procurators.[59] This concentration of responsibilities in their hands could have forced Biche and Mouche to make a clear distinction between the agents receiving domain income, those receiving tenths, and those handling loans and subsidies. There are some signs in Mignon's list of accounts that they were beginning to do this, but if they were, they had no chance to develop the idea. After 1295 their financial role decreased steadily. Philip trusted them as advisers to the end of their lives (notably in the attack on Boniface VIII), but he may have disliked the idea of letting foreigners control his finances. Conversely, Biche and Mouche may have found that there was little profit in acting as financial managers for the king, especially after manipulation of the currency (which they opposed) had begun.

The experiences of the war years did produce a group of men who developed certain skills in collecting extraordinary revenues, but these men did not specialize in any one kind of levy. The same collector could handle tenths, annates, loans and subventions, and often fines for amortization, or income from sales of confiscated Jewish goods as well. There was some geographical specialization; it was rare, but not unheard of, for a man who had worked in northern *bailliages* to be sent to the south, and even rarer for a southern collector to act in the north. On the other hand, most of the really active collectors worked in at least two areas—for example, Normandy and Champagne, Caen and Sens, Tours and Brittany, or, to take an outstanding man, Guillaume de Gisors, Caen, the Contentin, Orléans, Narbonne, Sens, Bourges, Paris, and Reims.[60] Guillaume clearly had unusual talents for finance; early in his career he had been a procurator of Biche and Mouche, but instead of becoming a *Maître des Comptes* or a Treasurer, as might have been expected, he wound up one of the

---

[59] Ibid., nos. 691, 703, 706 (the tenth); nos. 1113, 1114, 1117, 1161, 1162 (loans); nos. 1187, 1247, 2059, 2106 (subvention).

[60] Fawtier, ed., *Comptes du Trésor*, no. 448; Mignon, nos. 519-20, 756, 777, 789, 790, 818, 1234, 1249, 1472; *J.T.P.*, nos. 158, 184, 1581, 3422, 5292; A.N., JJ 36, fol. 71v, JJ 42A, fol. 70, no. 18; *Codex Dunensis*, ed. J.B.M.C. Kervyn de Lettenhove (Brussels, 1875), pp. 159, 168, 401. Guillaume collected subventions, loans tenths, and annates over a period of 15 years.

curators of the goods of the Temple and, with Bernard de Mès, as guardian of the regalia of the realm.[61]

Guillaume's career shows how difficult it is to generalize about the collectors. He had a wider and longer experience than most of them, but it is difficult to describe just what his responsibility was on each occasion. Thus in Caen in 1295-1296 he was an agent of Biche and Mouche; he had a colleague; he had subcollectors working for him, but he handed in and thus was responsible for their accounts. In Narbonne he had two colleagues in collecting the tenth, but apparently he was solely responsible for the annates. He "procured" the grant of a tenth by a council of the province of Bourges in 1304 but probably did not collect it (at least Mignon did not think so). He and a colleague (Guillaume de Marcilly) "imposed" a subvention on the *bailliage* of Sens in 1303; this we know was collected by another man. With Guillaume de Marcilly, he was ordered to impose and raise the subvention of 1304 in Paris, but there were subcollectors in at least one area, the lands of the countess of Montfort. Finally, he was general collector of the tenth of 1307 for the province of Reims, but in the diocese of Thérouaune, and presumably in other dioceses, he had subcollectors.

What this and similar investigations prove is that chief collectors did not have to bother with the grubby details of collecting money directly from the inhabitants of the realm. They had subcollectors and sub-subcollectors to do most of this work; they had clerks to write their accounts and to see that the money reached Paris; they could often arrange things so that the subordinate rather than the chief collector was responsible for questionable entries in the accounts and for arrears in payments. Nevertheless, the chief collectors had heavy responsibilities. As the case of Guillaume de Gisors shows, the chief collector often "imposed" the tax. Since the rate was fixed, this must have meant setting quotas for individual districts and communities. This interpretation is supported by the fact that collectors were often empowered to bargain with nobles, towns, or *vigueries* for lumpsum payments in place of the official rate or to accept other forms of assessment in place of the rates originally fixed by the king and Council. For example, in the south a *fouage* was often substi-

---

[61] Mignon, nos. 1396, 2106; A.N., K 37B, no. 39, JJ 59, fol. 16, no. 44; B.N., ms. fr. 20334, no. 59 (appointed as curator by the king in 1307 and by the pope in 1310); *H.L.*, IX, 347, Lacoste, *Histoire générale de Quercy*, II, 455 (general guardian of regalia by 1312).

tuted for a tax on property.[62] This must have involved a good
deal of travel and tedious negotiations. Even when the original
bargains were made by assemblies representing fairly large districts, such as the *sénéchaussées* of Beaucaire, Carcassonne, and
Toulouse or the nobles and towns of Normandy, individual towns
or nobles could secure still further concessions.[63] It was also possible to bypass the collector and make a deal directly with the
king's people in Paris, as the men of the bishop of Albi did in
1297.[64] This would complicate the collector's calculations even
more.

Finally, although some collectors were able to find deputies
or subcollectors who accounted directly with the Treasury, in
most cases the collector was responsible for the final account.
Since money for extraordinary revenues came in more slowly
than revenues from the domain, there were apt to be delays in
completing a final account, and even then there could be arrears.
Tenths, on the whole, were paid more promptly than subventions, but even accounts for tenths could be seriously delayed.
Thus, for the tenth of 1310, the first account for the province
of Sens was rendered in April 1312, but arrears were collected
only in 1322. The account for Bourges came in on 3 September
1319, but at that time there were still arrears of 829 l.t. Most of
the tenth of the province of Tours was paid by 15 June 1311,
but arrears were collected in 1315 and 1317.[65] The greatest delays in accounting for subventions came in 1303-1304, when the
country was nearly exhausted by the Flemish war. Thus arrears
of the tax of 1303 in the *bailliages* of Tours and of Vermandois
were accounted for in 1311 and 1313, and the accounts of the
tax of 1304 for a part of Paris and all of Vermandois were rendered only in 1312 and 1313, respectively. The account of Tours
was heard in June 1309 and that of Bourges in 1308. On the
whole, the old domain had the worst record for the subvention
of 1304.[66] The accounts for Normandy and Champagne came in
promptly, and the only serious delay in the south was in Beaucaire, where the collector reported to the Chambre des Comptes
in April 1307 (not entirely to their satisfaction, as far as his roll
of towns and hearths was concerned).[67] Arrears did not require

[62] Strayer and Taylor, pp. 50-55, 60-62, 67-69, 71-72.
[63] Ibid., pp. 52-55, 67-71.   [64] *H.L.*, x, col. 345.
[65] Mignon, nos. 816, 819-21.
[66] Ibid., nos. 1469, 1485, 1515, 1517, 1526, 1527.
[67] Ibid., no. 1554.

much additional work for the collector, since they were usually collected by someone else (often by a *bailli*), but it must have been difficult to explain an account to the *gens des comptes* nine or ten years after the work had been done.

Most of the chief collectors were king's clerks, and many of them had to be detached from their regular duties in order to supervise the work of collection. Thus southern judges were occasionally used as collectors of tenths, subsidies, and aids. The most eminent was Sicard de Lavaur, *juge-mage* of Toulouse and then of Carcassonne, who was chief collector of the double tenth of 1297 in the province of Narbonne, of the tenth of 1300 in the province of Auch, and of the subsidy of 1303 in Toulouse, Rouergue, and Agenais.[68] Yves de Loudéac, who was *juge-ordinaire* of Toulouse until some time in 1309, was given in that year (with Géraud de Sabanac) the thankless task of collecting in the *sénéchaussée* of Périgord-Quercy the aid for marrying the king's daughter.[69] This was his only adventure into financial administration; he became a specialist in diplomacy (notably the affair of the Val d'Aran) and was a member of the Council in 1312. Mathieu de Courjumelles, judge of Cahors, was one of the two men who imposed the ill-fated subsidy of 1314 in Périgord-Quercy. He eventually became a *rapporteur* in the Parlement.[70] Or, to take a clerk who was certainly working in the Parlement by 1294,[71] Clément de Savy collected fines for amortization in Caux in 1292-1293, "corrected" the levy of the fiftieth in Senlis in 1297 and 1298, and at about the same time collected some annates in Cambrai and took money for exemptions from army service in Tours.[72] His main work was clearly in judicial, not financial, administration, but he had to be used to clear up some problems in raising extraordinary revenues.

---

[68] Ibid., nos. 759, 779; *Ord.*, I, 369; A.N., JJ 36, fol. 19, no. 35.

[69] A.N., J 356, no. 7, JJ 42A, fol. 97, no. 72. See my *Gens de justice*, pp. 145, 180-81, for details on the careers of these two men; see above, p. 29, for Yves's work as a diplomat.

[70] Mignon, no. 1635; Boutaric, ed., *Actes du Parlement*, II, no. 4656; Strayer, *Gens de justice*, pp. 141-42.

[71] Clément made *enquêtes* for the Parlement in 1294 and 1295 (Ménard, *Nismes*, I, 124; Boutaric, ed., *Actes du Parlement*, I, no. 2884G); he took an *arrêt* to the *greffier* in 1296 (*Olim*, II, 411). He was paid for his services in the Parlements of 1296-1297 (121 days), 1297-1298 (131 days), and 1299-1300 (110 days) (*J.T.P.*, nos. 2377, 4469).

[72] Mignon, nos. 1175, 1274, 1837; *J.T.P.*, no. 2232; B.N., ms. Clairembault 469, p. 81.

At the other extreme were men who rose high in the government but who first achieved recognition as collectors or imposers of fines, tenths, and subventions. Two have already been mentioned, Pierre de Latilly and Simon Festu. Latilly seems to have begun his career as a collector of fines for amortization in Senlis and Gisors in 1292. He secured the grant of a tenth from the exempt clergy of the provinces of Bourges and Narbonne in 1294 and collected the hundredth in Mâcon in 1295. He was responsible for the tenth of 1297 in the diocese of Rodez and Albi and collected a subvention in Toulouse in the same year. His rather too vigorous attempt to squeeze money out of the southern consulates came in 1298. At the same time, he was acting as one of the paymasters of the army of occupation in Aquitaine. After 1300 he was less active in financial administration, though he collected a subsidy in Sens in 1303 and annates in the province of Reims in 1305. He had worked in the Parlement since 1296 and was one of Philip's principal counsellors by the early 1300s. He became Keeper of the Seals and bishop of Châlons-sur-Marne in 1313. He was involved in the reaction against Philip's ministers in 1315 and never held office again, though he retained his bishopric until his death in 1328.[73]

Simon Festu had a less spectacular, but still quite successful, career. He collected tenths and annates in various southern dioceses from 1294 to 1300 and was especially active in seeking out arrears. He also collected subventions in Poitou (the dates are not certain, except for the tax of 1300, which he helped to impose). In 1301 he collected annates in Saintonge-Poitou, and in 1303-1305 he secured loans to the king in the fairs of Champagne. He was one of the king's representatives in the Treasury while it was in the hands of the Temple (1303-1307) and was made one of the Treasurers in 1307. He became bishop of Meaux in 1308 but remained Treasurer until November 1309. He was again Treasurer in 1315 and 1316.[74] His appointments as Treasurer were rather unusual; for some reason Philip usually selected as his Treasurers men who had had experience in spending money, not in collecting it.[75]

A rather curious case is that of Guillaume d'Outremer, a king's clerk whose promising career was continued after his death by his clerk, Guillaume de la Poterie. The first Guillaume collected

[73] See above, pp. 69, 79.
[74] See the Appendix to Chapter IV below.
[75] See below, pp. 172, 175-76.

subventions, tenths, and annates in the *bailliages* of Sens and Tours and in the province of Sens and the dioceses of Troyes and Meaux from 1297 to his death late in 1301.[76] He must have worked for the king before 1297; he had a pension of 4 d.p. a day, later 6 d.p. a day, on the revenues of Paris by 1293, and he had some connection with the Parlement, since his clerk returned 18 *enquêtes* to the *greffier* after his death.[77] This clerk, Guillaume de la Poterie (probably a Norman), had assisted Guillaume d'Outremer during the 1290s and cleared his accounts after his death.[78] He also collected arrears of various tenths and subsidies imposed in the *bailliage* of Tours by Robert de Vernon, subdean of St. Martin's of Tours, who became receiver of the county of Burgundy in 1302.[79] In 1304 Guillaume collected a tenth in the province of Tours, and in 1305 he was commissioned to collect a tenth from the bishops of Brittany.[80] There was great opposition to the tenth by the clergy of Tours, and Guillaume was ordered in 1305 to show them the famous letter of Philip the Fair asserting his right to take, and their obligation to give, aid to defend the realm.[81] From 1307 to 1313 he was busy seeking out goods of the Jews and clearing up arrears in the region of Tours.[82] By 1312 he was a clerk of accounts but was specifically attached to the Treasurer of the Temple, where the records were kept.[83] He probably was working in the Temple earlier; this would explain why he was so busy as a collector of arrears, since he knew which accounts were seriously deficient. He accounted for the tenth of 1313-1317 in the province of Lyon and was still collecting annates in Rouen, a tenth in Autun, and squeezing the Jews of Normandy in 1322; but by February 1323 he was mentioned as "quondam collector."[84]

Jean de Serez, king's clerk and treasurer of Lisieux, and Jean Gaidre, king's clerk and canon of Caen, were both Normans and occasionally worked together. Jean de Serez collected tenths in Caux (1297), in the province of Sens (1310, 1312, 1313-1316;

[76] Mignon, nos. 473, 478, 724, 1180, 1289, 1367-68; *J.T.P.*, nos. 1073, 4927, 5088, 5104; *C.R.*, I, no. 2989.

[77] *C.R.*, I, nos. 99, 652; Langlois, ed., *Textes*, p. 214.

[78] Mignon, nos. 473, 478, 724, 768, 1230, 1289, 1367-68.

[79] Ibid., nos. 1379-82.

[80] Ibid., no. 792; A.N., JJ 36, no. 203.

[81] A.N., J 350, no. 5.

[82] Mignon, nos. 1481, 1484-86, 2141; *J.T.P.*, nos. 5824, 5863, 5987.

[83] Borrelli de Serres, *Recherches*, II, 182, III, 49; *C.R.*, II, no. 27665.

[84] Mignon, no. 576; *J.T.C.*, nos. 28, 101, 445, 1542, 2324.

Jean Gaidre took his place for 1317), and in the province of Rouen (1318-1320).[85] He was one of the commissioners who took over the goods of Biche and Mouche after their deaths,[86] and he was also a commissioner for the goods of the Jews.[87] He was an *enquêteur* in Vermandois in 1316 and in Paris in 1325.[88] He was a judge in the Chambre des Enquêtes by 1316 and probably kept this post until his death in 1327.[89] As in several other cases, one wonders why he ended his career in the Parlement rather than in the Treasury or the Chambre des Comptes.

Jean Gaidre was a sort of trouble-shooter for Norman financial problems; he worked on income from the domain there as well as on extraordinary revenues. He revised the assessments and collected arrears of the sales-tax and the subventions of 1295, 1296, and 1297 in the *bailliage* of Rouen; he did the same for the *fouage* of Normandy (a traditional payment for a stable currency) in 1302 and 1308; he collected a special sales-tax of 4 d. in the pound imposed on Norman ports for coast defense in 1302-1303 and accounted for the subvention of 1303 in the *bailliage* of Caux in 1303.[90] He was given a general commission (about 1305) to collect arrears from the royal domain in the *bailliage* of Gisors, arrears that went back to the beginning of the reign. At about the same time, he had a commission to farm all the king's mills and ovens in Normandy, a commission that was extended to the *prévôté* of Paris in 1310.[91] He was then moved to Bourges, where he was superintendent of the affairs of the Jews, 1311-1312,[92] and then to Sens, where he collected arrears of annates and was in effect collector of the tenth of 1313-1317. (Jean de Serez was officially collector into 1316, but Jean Gaidre did most of the work and was sole collector by 1317.)[93] Jean returned briefly to Normandy as one of the three collectors of

---

[85] Mignon, nos. 751, 816-17, 829, 839-40, 872, 2116; *J.T.P.*, no. 6009.

[86] *J.T.P.*, no. 5959; A.N., JJ 45, fol. 48, no. 61, JJ 46, fol. 67, no. 89.

[87] A.N., JJ 48, fol. 129, no. 216, JJ 49, fol. 70, no. 164, JJ 50, fol. 26v, no. 34, JJ 52, fol. 23, no. 46 (acts running from July 1311 to June 1314).

[88] Mignon, no. 2698 and p. 368.

[89] Boutaric, ed., *Actes du Parlement*, II, no. 4482A; *J.T.C.*, nos. 3684, 8485; Lehugeur, II, 50, 196; A.N., JJ 57, fols. 43v, 65.

[90] Mignon, nos. 1657 a-l, 1394, 1490-94, 1498-99.

[91] Ibid., no. 1657 g, A.N., JJ 41, fol. 41, no. 65 (both for Gisors). Mignon, no. 56 on p. 20, A.N., JJ 60, fol. 128v, no. 204 (mills and ovens).

[92] A.N., JJ 46, fol. 83v, no. 141, JJ 48, fol. 128v, no. 215.

[93] Mignon, nos. 840-42; Fawtier, ed., *Comptes du Trésor*, nos. 543, 562, 568, 582-83, 585.

the subvention of 1314 in the Cotentin, but he worked there for only three months,[94] doubtless because the tax was canceled. He was dead by 9 August 1322.[95]

This was an unusual career, and yet Jean was not lavishly rewarded for his versatility or his skill in finding lost revenues. In 1304, when he gathered together money from the subvention of 1304 in Rouen, Gisors, and Caux and sent it to the paymasters of the fleet (mainly galleys) in the Seine, he was allowed expenses of 25 s.t. a day.[96] This would have been a high salary if he had kept it all for himself, but he doubtless had a clerk, a servant, and various travel expenses. He received no preferment in the Church beyond his prebend at Caen and had no pension. It is to be hoped that he enjoyed his work, for he gained little else for his years of service.

Jean Gaidre's fate could be contrasted with that of another Norman, Bertaut Mahiel of Pont-Audemer. Unlike most of the collectors, Bertaut was a layman, not a clerk, and he was active for only a few years. He collected some sizable loans in Troyes and Meaux in 1294, a tenth in the western dioceses of Normandy in (probably) 1298, the subventions of 1295, 1296, and 1297 in the *bailliages* of Caen and the Cotentin, and assessed the same taxes in the *bailliage* of Troyes.[97] He also imposed a special subsidy on the county of Champagne for the war with the count of Bar in 1297. This was a sizable operation; Mignon said that the total assessment ran to 94,562 l.t.[98] In 1300 Bertaut accounted for arrears of tenths and annates in the dioceses of Nantes, Rennes, and St. Màlo. This is not a very impressive record, except for the subsidy for the war of Bar. Yet Bertaut was *bailli* of the Cotentin for part of 1308 and of Gisors during 1309.[99] It is true that these were brief appointments, but they gave prestige, especially to a man who was probably of bourgeois origin.

If the collectors of extraordinary revenues were a disparate and unorganized group, the men who spent those revenues were just as diverse in origin. Nevertheless, there was some attempt to centralize direction of the largest expenditures, those for war. The process was complicated by the fact that there was no standing

---

[94] Mignon, no. 1627 and p. 369.

[95] *J.T.C.*, no. 1416. He was still active in 1317 (nos. 1455, 2937-40).

[96] *C.R.*, I, no. 6635.

[97] Mignon, nos. 740, 748, 1151, 1194, 1400, 1401-3; *J.T.P.*, nos. 3078, 4195; *C.R.*, I, no. 3548.

[98] Mignon, no. 1404.　　　　　　　　　[99] *H.F.*, xxiv, *153.

army, so there could be no permanent staff for military finances. Further complications arose when army commanders ordered payments to their subordinates on their own account, as the counts of Artois and Valois did in Aquitaine in the 1290s,[100] and from the custom of having a special paymaster, the clerk of the arbalesters, for the infantry. Distant operations could not easily be paid for by men who were busy in the main theater of a war; for example, Jean Arrode had to pay troops in Saintonge while other paymasters and most of the army were further south.[101] The fleet based in Normandy also had to have its own, rather unorganized system of payments.[102] It was also true that large sums of money had to be given to local officials to buy equipment and pay troops from their region. Jean l'Archévêque, acting seneschal of Toulouse and an army commander, spent 10,176 l.t. on arms for nobles of Toulouse, 27,306 l.t. for pay of foot soldiers, and 23,477 l.t. for pay of nobles;[103] other seneschals also paid troops. Nevertheless, there was a real effort to keep overall control of payments for the war of Aquitaine in the hands of a few men. By far the most important of these was Jean de Dammartin, who first appears in royal accounts as a collector of the regalia of Tours (1290), Angers (1291), Sens (1292), and Le Mans (1291-1292).[104] He must have done this work very well to have been given the responsibilities that he had in the Gascon war. He did not handle, or even account for, all payments, but his name appears more frequently in the entries in the Journal of the Treasury dealing with the war than that of any other financial officer, and many of the accounts in Mignon prepared by others passed through his hands. He spent directly 239,842 l.t.,[105] less than did Gérard Balène, who was, after Jean, the most active of the paymasters. Gérard, as receiver of Périgord-Quercy and, for a while, receiver

---

[100] J.T.P., nos. 774, 858, 1794, 3314, 3371, 5818.

[101] Mignon, no. 2489; J.T.P., nos. 2619, 2810, 2975, 4842.

[102] Mignon, nos. 2310, 2319, 2479, 2481, 2486; C.R., II, nos. 24291, 24488, 24639, 24687.

[103] C.R., II, nos. 26044, 26364, 26567-68, 26776. Cf. J.T.P., nos. 992, 1025, 4786.

[104] Mignon, nos. 187, 318, 327, 335.

[105] Dammartin was responsible for the accounts of the army of the count of Artois in 1296-1298 (Mignon, nos. 2340, 2353-54; Joseph Petit et al., *Essai de restitution des plus anciens mémoriaux de la Chambre des Comptes de Paris* [Paris, 1899], p. 176), but he also received accounts of other commanders (Mignon, nos. 2313, 2361, 2366, 2376, 2384). Mignon, no. 2436, gives the total he spent up to the spring of 1299.

of French-occupied Gascony, spent at least 433,260 l.t.[106] Gérard's name appears frequently in the Journal, but he clearly had less responsibility and a less distinguished career than Jean de Dammartin. Jean became a *Maître des Comptes* by 1301 and held the position until his death in 1321;[107] Gérard was never more than a receiver.[108] After Gérard came Guillaume de Montmaur, clerk of the Constable Raoul de Nesle, with 169,392 l.t.,[109] a good example of the independent accounting of an army commander. No one else handled very large sums. Even Denis d'Aubigny, clerk of the arbalesters, was charged with only 20,107 l.t., and his successor, Hélie d'Orly, reported only 7,124 l.t. in the list of "fines compotorum,"[110] although the accounts of both men are frequently mentioned in the Journal of the Treasury. On the other hand, Henri d'Elise, seneschal of Carcassonne, who was also a captain of the army of Gascony, spent 54,379 l.t. (weak money); Guichard de Marzi, seneschal of Toulouse and also a captain, spent 75,348 l.t.; and Jean de Barres (Peau de Chat), who governed the formerly English areas of Périgord and Quercy, spent 45,197 l.t.[111]

Obviously, paying for the war of Aquitaine was not a completely integrated operation, although an effort was made to give a dominant role to Jean de Dammartin, with Gérard Balène, a local man, as second in authority. The finances of the Flemish war were better organized, partly because of the experience gained in Aquitaine and partly because the army was operating much closer to Paris, and therefore less reliance had to be placed on local authorities.

Both Mignon in the fourteenth century and Borrelli de Serres in our own thought that the first treasurers for war emerged during the conflict with Flanders. Mignon, writing in or soon after 1328, called Guillaume, cantor of Milly, and Thomas du Petit-

---

[106] Mignon, nos. 2370, 2447-48 (to the end of 1298). The total may well have been over 500,000 l.t.; it is difficult to tell whether nos. 2447-48 sum up all the expenses mentioned in no. 2370.

[107] He seems to be acting as a Master by Christmas 1301 (*C.R.*, II, no. 15652). See also Borrelli de Serres, *Recherches*, II, 25, 182; A.N., JJ 59, fol. 117, no. 244 (not very precise, but he may have been a Master in 1299); B.N., ms. fr. 23256, fol. 34v; Lehugeur, II, pp. 223-24; Fawtier, ed., *Comptes du Trésor*, no. 765.

[108] See above, pp. 117-18.

[109] Mignon, nos. 2337, 2438; *H.L.*, x, col. 296. Guillaume de Montmaur continued as clerk of the Constable in Flanders; see *J.T.P.*, nos. 2248, 2281, 3049.

[110] Mignon, nos. 2445-46, 2453.   [111] Ibid., nos. 2441, 2443-44.

Cellier (clerk of the arbalesters) "thesaurarii guerre" for 1304 but remarked that in 1302 Geoffroi Cocatrix was "thesaurarius unicus."[112] Borrelli de Serres more cautiously wrote that Guillaume de Montmaur, Guillaume de Milly, Geoffroi Cocatrix, and Thomas du Petit-Cellier "ont fait les fonctions de Trésorier des guerres, sans avoir le titre" in the period 1297-1304.[113] Neither writer was completely wrong; these four men did handle most of the payments in Flanders during the acute period of the war. Guillaume de Milly and Geoffroi Cocatrix were especially active, the former in paying soldiers, the latter in procuring supplies (though he often worked with Guillaume de Milly as a paymaster).[114] Guillaume de Montmaur, as clerk of the Constable, and Thomas du Petit-Cellier, as clerk of the arbalesters, also had wide responsibilities. It should be noted, however, that Guillaume de Milly or Geoffroi Cocatrix were often named as coauthors of the accounts rendered by the two clerks.[115]

The accounts of the Flemish war were already very spotty by Mignon's time, and few have been found since. On the other hand, a large number of individual documents have survived, either receipts from soldiers paid by one of the king's men or acknowledgments by those officials that wages were owed. These documents bear out the impression that one gets from Mignon's fragmentary list. Without pretending to give a complete listing (it is easy to overlook these little strips of parchment in going through large volumes of miscellaneous documents), I have found 50 receipts or acknowledgments by Guillaume de Milly, 22 by Geoffroi Cocatrix, and less than 10 by either Guillaume de Montmaur or Thomas du Petit-Cellier.[116] Guillaume de Milly was surely the chief paymaster.

Besides those four men, few others had much to do with paying

---

[112] Ibid., nos. 2583, 2585. An extract by Joursanvault lists Cocatrix and Milly as "trésoriers des guerres" in 1302, but the source is not indicated (B.N. ms. fr. 10430, p. 5).

[113] Borrelli de Serres, *Recherches*, III, 223-24.

[114] Cocatrix spent at least 182,718 l.p. in buying supplies, 1302-1304 (Mignon, nos. 2513-14). He very wisely obtained a quittance for his purchases early in the war and another quittance in 1318 (A.N., JJ 59, fol. 117, no. 244. The latter gives his total purchases as only 102,614 l.p.

[115] Mignon, nos. 2543 (Montmaur and Milly), 2550 (Montmaur), 2592 (Montmaur and Milly for 1297-1299; total 109,654 l.t.), 2593 (Montmaur), 2556 (Petit-Cellier), 2558 (Petit-Cellier), 2584 (Petit-Cellier), 2585 (Petit-Cellier and Cocatrix), 2638-40 (Petit-Cellier and Milly).

[116] B.N., ms. fr. 25992-93, ms. nouv. acq. fr. 3637, mss. Clairembault 6, 14, 35, 36, 57, 71, 113, 210.

troops. Hélie d'Orly, clerk of the arbalesters before Thomas du Petit-Cellier, naturally accounted for some wages for the early part of the war, and Jean de Dammartin ordered one payment in 1300.[117] Geoffroi du Bois, who eventually became clerk of the arbalesters, also ordered a number of payments, usually with Thomas du Petit-Cellier or Guillaume de Milly.[118] It is also true that many payments to soldiers listed in the Journal of the Treasury do not mention the account that warranted them. It is clear, however, that receivers and *baillis* (= seneschals) did not play the role in Flanders that they did in Aquitaine.

Procuring food and other supples for the army could not be arranged quite so neatly. Geoffroi Cocatrix had overall responsibility until 1304; Renaud de Roye, who had already bought supplies worth 22,378 l.t. in 1303, took over in 1304 and was chief buyer of supplies until his death in 1311.[119] But, as a glance at Mignon's entries under "Garnisiones" shows, *panetiers* and *valets le roi*, *baillis* and *prévôts* also had to find supplies.[120] Some of these men were certainly acting under the orders of Geoffroi Cocatrix and are mentioned in his accounts; the *baillis* may have been asked to assist Geoffroi, but they were not accountable to him. Robert Ausgans, *panetier le roi*, had his own account in 1303 and paid directly for supplies he took, but on other occasions he accounted through Geoffroi.[121] Probably the bulk of army supplies was collected and paid for by Geoffroi (or later, by Renaud de Roye) and his assistants, but when shortages occurred, any royal official in Paris or the northeast could be asked to help.

The plan for handling the finances of the Flemish war was a

---

[117] *J.T.P.*, nos. 1196, 2866, 2980, 3638, 3679, 4238, 4399, 4747, 5306; Mignon, nos. 2538, 2594. The payment by Dammartin is *J.T.P.*, no. 4370.

[118] Geoffroi du Bois, canon of Nevers, collected the double tenth of 1297 in the northeastern dioceses and arrears of subsidies in the *bailliage* of Amiens in 1298 (Mignon, nos. 727, 1284-85). He made payments with Milly for the army of Flanders in 1299 (ibid., no. 2545). Other mentions of him as a paymaster may be found in B.N., ms. Clairembault 7, nos. 93, 158, 160, ms. Clairembault 37, nos. 5, 122, 162, Clairembault 66, no. 199, ms. Clairembault 113, no. 164. He was clerk of the arbalesters by 1307 (B.N., ms. fr. 25993, no. 145, and ms. fr. 25697, no. 46) but resigned in 1311 (Mignon, no. 2588). The *Codex Dunensis*, p. 52, calls him receiver of the king in Flanders but gives no date.

[119] See note 114 above for Cocatrix; for Renaud de Roye see Mignon, nos. 2502, 2506.

[120] Mignon, nos. 2994-95, 2497-99, 2501, 2509; see also *J.T.P.*, nos. 79, 921, 1569, 3191.

[121] Mignon, no. 2494; *J.T.P.*, nos. 1705, 2858.

distinct improvement over that for the Gascon war; if there had been enough money, it would have worked very smoothly. Unfortunately, there were serious shortages in income. There were bitter complaints that supplies were taken without payment, and there were mutinies by unpaid soldiers.[122] The *bailli* of Amiens had to lend money to foot soldiers and crossbowmen in 1302.[123] In 1304 Thomas du Petit-Cellier could only issue slips acknowledging that money was owed for military service;[124] normally he would have paid cash and gotten a receipt. The cost of the Flemish war delayed payments for service in Aquitaine (there were still French garrisons there when the war in Flanders was at its height), so that many unfortunate men received their wages only in 1309 and later.[125] Even more indicative of financial problems is that by 1305 the Treasury was so short of money that it had to assign some of the debts it owed for wages on local and casual sources of revenue. An amusing example is the case of the man who was paid for his service by Renaud de Roye (then in charge of supplies) with two barrels of wine and a little loose change.[126] Less amusing are the orders to pay wages out of confiscated Jewish goods. Most of these orders were sent to Jean de Crépy, superintendent of Jewish affairs at Toulouse in the period 1309-1311.[127] It is also worth noting that a mere slip of parchment from a paymaster acknowledging that the king owed money for military service was not always enough to ensure payment; one had also to have a letter from the Chancery ordering a receiver, a *bailli*, or some other local official to pay. It must have taken a good deal of influence at court to obtain such letters; some of them are warranted by such great men as Marigny and Nogaret.[128]

[122] See below, Chapter V, p. 335, and Chapter VI, note 81.

[123] Mignon, nos. 2595-96.

[124] B.N., ms. fr. 25992, nos. 96, 97, ms. nouv. acq. fr. 20025, no. 63, ms. Clairembault 35, nos. 173, 190.

[125] B.N., ms. fr. 25993, nos. 146, 148, 149, 160 (paid in 1309); nos. 174, 178 (two cases), 180 (paid in 1311); nos. 188, 194, 198 (paid between 1312 and 1314).

[126] B.N., ms. Clairembault 14, nos. 144, 184, 185 (1305); ms. Clairembault 35, nos. 191-92 (payment in wine, 1305); ms. Clairembault 57, nos. 60, 61 (payment in wine, 1305); ms. Clairembault 8, no. 11 (payment in wine and a little money, 1305).

[127] B.N., ms. fr. 25697, nos. 35-38, 44, 46, 47, 49, 51, 52, 54, 61 (orders to pay wages due for service in Gascony or Flanders from Jewish goods; dates run from 1307 to 1311). See also B.N., ms. fr. 25993, nos. 148, 149, 174, 178-80, 188, 194, 198 (similar orders, 1309-1314).

[128] No. 48 in B.N., ms. fr. 25697, is warranted by Nogaret, nos. 52 and 60

In spite of these difficulties, payments for the Flemish war were made more smoothly than those for the war of Aquitaine, and, if the surviving documents are a fair example, there were fewer arrears left after the Flemish than after the Gascon war. Concentration of responsibility had proved its value. It the brief war against Lyon two men, Anseau de Morgneval and Jean de Helesmes, were in charge of payments. The Constable kept his own account but sent it in through Anseau. However, Pierre de Condé did account separately; he paid the wages of the knights and men-at-arms under the command of Louis of Navarre.[129] The Lyon war was too small a campaign to test the new system, but the demonstrations against Flanders in 1313 and 1314 showed that the process of centralizing payments for war in the hands of one or two men was continuing and that the office of Treasurer for War was emerging.

The Treasurers, of course, had always had overall responsibility for all expenditures, and in both the Gascon and Flemish wars one particular Treasurer, Pierre La Reue, had been deeply involved in payments to ground and naval forces. That he had to arrange to meet the expenses of the fleet in Norman ports is not surprising; it was far removed from the land forces, and the chief paymasters could not reach it. But there were plenty of paymasters in the south, perhaps so many that it was difficult to allot money among them. In any case, Pierre La Reue had to make trips to the south in 1298, 1299, 1300, and possibly in 1301 to pay off debts owed for the war.[130] Apparently neither Jean de Dammartin nor Gérard Balène, nor any of the other paymasters, had been able to raise enough money to meet all the expenses that had been incurred. Even Pierre was not entirely successful in clearing the accounts; some of the wages that he warranted were paid only in 1306, 1309, 1310, or 1311.[131] Nevertheless, he did remedy some of the problems caused by a multiplicity of accounts. He was a sort of emergency paymaster who could act when the regular paymasters were in trouble.[132]

---

by Marigny, no. 54 by Renaud Barbou. Nos. 46, 51, 54, and 61 include the clause "ordinacione contraria non obstante."

[129] Mignon, nos. 2606-7, 2643, 2645.

[130] Mignon, nos. 2310, 2481, 2529 (for Normandy, often with Renaud Barbou); *J.T.P.*, nos. 1581, 1588-91 (Montpellier and Sommières, 1298); B.N., ms. fr. 17658, fol. 41 (Toulouse, 1299); ms. fr. 25992, nos. 27-39 (Toulouse, 1300); *J.T.P.*, no. 4683 (1301).

[131] B.N., ms. Clairembault 210, nos. 42, 43, 54, ms. fr. 25993, nos. 146, 160.

[132] Wages owed by the account of Jean l'Archévêque were paid at Tou-

Thus it is not surprising to find Pierre acting as a general supervisor of accounts for the Flemish war. He did not pay out money directly (except for the fleet stationed in Normandy), but he did keep accounts "de pluribus receptis et misiis pro exercitu Flandrie" from early 1302 to January 1305.[133] One entry by Mignon can be misread as saying that he was treasurer for war: it runs "compotus istius magistri P. thesaurarii pro exercitu Flandrie." There should be a comma after "thesaurarii"; Pierre was a Treasurer of France at this time. Moreover, Mignon regularly says "thesaurarius guerre" or "guerrarum" (not "pro exercitu") when he means treasurers for war.[134] The real nature of Pierre's duties can best be seen in his relations with Geoffroi Cocatrix. There is no doubt that Geoffroi was responsible for obtaining supplies for the army and that he kept his own accounts. But at some date before 1305 Pierre La Reue gave the abbot of Bonneval a letter acknowledging that the abbot was owed over 267 l.t. for provisions taken by Geoffroi Cocatrix "provisor exercitus."[135] Pierre was also a member of the *curia in compotis* that approved Geoffroi's accounts in 1299.[136] In short, Pierre knew what Geoffroi was doing; he would warrant it if necessary, but he was neither collecting nor paying for provisions.

In the troubled years of 1313 and 1314 this precedent of involving one or more of the Treasurers in overseeing military expenditures was continued. The Treasurer Baudouin de Roye (1314-1316), brother of Renaud de Roye, naturally was given responsibility for supplies (he had some experience in this field while working with Renaud).[137] He accounted for supplies and payments to troops in Flanders for the years 1313-1321 and later served both Charles IV and Philip VI.[138] Gui Florent, a Treasurer since 1311, accounted for supplies to Lille and other strongholds in 1312 and to St. Omer in 1314.[139] According to Borrelli de

louse by Pierre and his clerk, Michel Aygraz, at All Saints 1299 (B.N., ms. 17658, fol. 41). Jean l'Archévêque died in 1296 (C.R., I, no. 12089); he had spent a great deal of money (see above, p. 165), and only a senior official could settle his account.

[133] Mignon, nos. 2561, 1987.

[134] Ibid., nos. 1987, 2576-77, 2583, 2604.

[135] B.N., ms. Doat 141, fol. 100.

[136] A.N., JJ 59, fol. 117, no. 244. Cf. Mignon, no. 2513, which describes one of the accounts that was approved.

[137] Borrelli de Serres, *Recherches*, II, 183; Mignon, nos. 2502, 2516.

[138] Mignon, no. 2518 (2d para.); Fawtier, ed., *Comptes du Trésor*, nos. 1167-70; Borrelli de Serres, *Recherches*, III, 66; J.T.C., col. 889n.

[139] Mignon, nos. 2503, 2574.

Serres, Guillaume du Bois, also a Treasurer (1312-1315), took some responsibility for payments to the army,[140] but I have found no evidence of this activity. In any case, the establishment of a Treasurer for War in 1315 and of a second Treasurer for War in 1317 was only the culmination of a long process. The first Treasurer for War, Renier Cocatrix,[141] was almost certainly related to Geoffroi Cocatrix, who had had many years experience in paying wages and buying supplies. The second, Thomas du Petit-Cellier,[142] did not have to rely on family experience; as a former clerk of the arbalesters he had had ample opportunities to learn about army finance. The fact that Baudouin de Roye was in charge of supplies until 1321 meant that the new Treasurers did not at first have full control over military expenditures. There had been a great improvement over the situation of the 1290s, but there was still some division of responsibility.

This long discussion of extraordinary receipts and expenditures may seem to have been a digression, but it is necessary to know something about these complicated processes of collection and disbursement in order to understand the fundamental changes in the central financial administration that took place during Philip's reign. The passive system of using the Temple as a bank that received the king's revenues and paid his debts on order did not work very well in time of war, when agents of the Treasury had to go out into the provinces to rake money together and to pay army commanders in the field. The brothers of the Temple, after all, had other clients; they could scarcely be expected to roam about France on the king's business.[143] For the same reasons, the accounting system needed strengthening. There was a great deal more money to account for, and it came in and was spent at irregular intervals and in unpredictable amounts. A few clerks, intermittently supervised by the great men of the court, could not do this work; a permanent bureau headed by men who had both financial skill and high standing in the government was needed.

The problem of the Treasury was the easier to solve, although

[140] Borrelli de Serres, *Recherches*, III, 224.

[141] Mignon, no. 2576; Fawtier, ed., *Comptes du Trésor*, nos. 829, 1139, 1178-79.

[142] Mignon, no. 2577.

[143] They were not entirely sedentary (see Borrelli de Serres, *Recherches*, I, 246), but they were certainly not as active as, for example, Pierre La Reue.

Philip was not satisfied with the obvious answer and kept making experiments until the end of his reign. The first step was to make Biche and Mouche Guidi Treasurers in 1295. This was perhaps meant only as a temporary expedient; in any case, it did not last very long. The Guidi brothers, who had been receivers for a good part of the kingdom,[144] certainly had intimate knowledge of royal finance, but they were also heads of a private bank. It was not to their interest to get into a position where their funds might be used to pay royal debts, something quite likely to happen in a period of war. Nor was it in Philip's interest to risk having his revenues used to back up speculations of the Guidi.[145] Even rumors that the brothers were profiting at the king's expense would be dangerous in a period when there was already resentment over taxation. Biche and Mouche were useful as interim Treasurers while Philip made preparations to transfer the Treasury to the Louvre, but there were no hard feelings on either side when they were replaced by three royal officials.

The new Treasurers were Henri, abbot of Jouy (a Cistercian house in Champagne), Guillaume de Hangest, who was just finishing a term as *bailli* of Amiens, and Pierre La Reue, a former notary in the Chancery who had been receiver of Navarre from 1287 to 1294.[146] Pierre was certainly the least distinguished of the three, and he was kept busy arranging for payments to troops, especially in the south.[147] Guillaume de Hangest also arranged for payments to soldiers, notably at Orléans in 1300,[148] and in 1298 and 1299 he made two trips to Flanders to discuss affairs with the Constable and one to bring 80,000 l.t. to Jacques de Saint-Pol.[149] Nevertheless, he was far less concerned with war expenditures than Pierre La Reue. As for the abbot of Jouy, he was almost completely sedentary, except for trips to the Norman Exchequer. Certainly he had more time to spend on organizing the Treasury than his colleagues, and as the highest-ranking member of the trio he had the power to do so.

The Journal of the Treasury suggests that the three Treasurers kept the king's affairs running smoothly and that they were fairly

[144] See above, p. 113.

[145] Borrelli de Serres, *Recherches*, III, 161.

[146] Langlois, "Registres perdus," p. 161; Mignon, no. 94; *H.F.*, xxiv, *267.

[147] See above, note 130.

[148] Mignon, nos. 2597-98. He was assisted by Pierre de Latilly and Jean de Lillers, a clerk of accounts.

[149] *J.T.P.*, nos. 1829, 2253, 3989.

successful in transferring money from one account to another in order to meet the expenses of war. Why, then, did Philip decide to shift the Treasury back to the Temple in 1303? He was not displeased with his Treasurers. The abbot of Jouy became abbot of Cîteaux in 1304, certainly with Philip's approval, since the king had forced the resignation of the previous abbot for supporting Boniface VIII. Guillaume de Hangest remained a member of the Council and was to be Treasurer again. Pierre La Reue was a *Maître des Comptes* in 1304. (Borrelli de Serres thinks he may have remained as a representative of the king in the Temple, but Pierre could not have held this position long; he retired in 1306 or 1307 and died before 1308.)[150] Pierre's clerk, Guillaume de Montfaucon, continued in the king's service for many years and was clerk to the Treasurers Baudouin de Roye (1314-1316) and Guérin de Senlis (1316-1320).[151] It is unlikely that he would have held these posts if the work of the first Treasurer he served had been unsatisfactory.

This conclusion, however, simply adds to the difficulty of explaining Philip's decision. Politically, 1303 was a bad year in which to make any drastic change in the structure of government. The war in Flanders was going badly, and the quarrel with Boniface VIII was reaching its crisis. One can only conclude that Philip did not think that he was making a drastic change. Reasonably satisfactory solutions for most of the problems of financial administration had been found. Receivers and a group of experienced tax collectors were bringing in money as fast as it was available. Payments for war expenses were concentrated in the hands of a few skilled men; the confusion and overlapping responsibilities that had marked the financing of the war in Aquitaine had largely been overcome. The formation of the Chambre des Comptes—certainly by 1303 and perhaps a little earlier[152]— meant that accounts were audited and corrected more carefully and more regularly than they had been before. Thus in returning the Treasury to the Temple Philip was in fact only transferring

---

[150] Borrelli de Serres, *Recherches*, III, 22, 30-31; Favier, *Marigny*, p. 231. When "good money" was restored in 1306 Brother Pierre La Reue and Brother Pierre de Condé (a former *Maître des Comptes*, but by then a Dominican) were ordered to adjust perpetual rents in Paris (*Archives anciennes de la ville de St. Quentin*, ed. Emmanuel Lemaire [St. Quentin, 1888-1910], p. 154, no. 172).

[151] *J.T.P.*, nos. 5860, 5885, 6003; Fawtier, ed., *Comptes du Trésor*, nos. 791, 1192; Borrelli de Serres, *Recherches*, III, 25, 49, 59.

[152] See below, p. 181.

its banking operations, that is, entering money received and deb-
iting various accounts for money spent. Even those operations
were supervised by representatives of the king. As Delisle pointed
out long ago, in 1304, 1305, and 1306 Philip sent orders to the
Treasurers of the Temple.[153] Since the Temple had only one
Treasurer of its own, the others must have been royal officials.
Borrelli de Serres and Jules Picquet think that these "trésoriers
adjoint" were Guillaume de Hangest and Pierre La Reue.[154] The
evidence for Hangest is fairly good, for La Reue less good; but if
the latter died soon after 1304, this is not surprising.

The arrangements of 1303 were not very neat, but they worked
fairly well until Philip's attack on the Temple in 1307. The reasons for this attack are not clear. The king may have coveted
the goods of the Temple (see Chapter IV below), but he had
no grounds to complain about its administration of the Treasury.
As Borrelli de Serres argued, the final settlement made with the
Hospital when it received the goods of the Temple (260,000 l.t.)
amounted to no more than a normal credit to the king in the
Temple bank, especially since it was reckoned as of a date (13
October) when a large part of the year's income had been received but when the pensions and other payments due at All
Saints and Christmas had not yet been made.[155] Moreover, the
extracts from the Journal of the Treasury for late 1307 and 1308
show no signs of disorder or financial embarrassment; the Treasury was operating as it had always done.

The new Treasurers were Renaud de Roye, Simon Festu, and
Guillaume de Hangest the elder. All were financial experts; Festu
had been a collector and Hangest a Treasurer and probably a
trésorier adjoint after 1303. As for Renaud de Roye, he had been
responsible for the service of supply in Flanders, and since he was
given immediate charge of the Treasury after the arrest of the
Templars, Borrelli de Serres's guess that he was already in the
Temple as trésorier adjoint seems reasonable.[156] Festu became
bishop of Meaux in 1309 and left the Treasury at the end of that
year; Renaud de Roye died early in 1312. Guillaume de Hangest,
a very senior member of the Council, apparently gave up his
treasurership in 1311. Perhaps he was already thinking of retiring

[153] Delisle, Templiers, p. 58.
[154] Borrelli de Serres, Recherches, III, 22, 27, 29-31; Jules Picquet, Des
banquiers au Moyen Age. Les Templiers (Paris, 1939), p. 187.
[155] Borrelli de Serres, Recherches, III, 35-36.
[156] Mignon, nos. 2502, 2506; Borrelli de Serres, Recherches, III, 46.

when Gui Florent was named as a fourth Treasurer in 1310. Gui
had been one of the executors of the will of Queen Jeanne and
had worked on building the College of Navarre.[157] Festu was
replaced by Geoffroi de Briançon in late 1309, and Renaud de
Roye by Guillaume du Bois in 1312.[158] These last two appointments are interesting, for they show Marigny's growing power
in the Treasury. Geoffroi de Briançon had been a clerk and devoted follower of Marigny; his career ended with the downfall
of his old master.[159] Guillaume du Bois was not as close to Marigny; in fact, Favier found no proof of a connection. But Guillaume du Bois was *bailli* of Caux from 1305 to 1311, and these
are exactly the years in which Marigny was building up a domain
around Longueville-la-Giffard in Caux.[160] The two men must
have met many times in that period. One cannot prove that
Marigny was responsible for Guillaume's promotion, but it was
unusual, though not without precedent, for a *bailli* to become
Treasurer (witness the case of Guillaume de Hangest). Guillaume
du Bois was an able man, and he regained his treasurership in
1317 on his own merits. But if Marigny did not make the appointment, he certainly tried to gain Guillaume's support. In 1312 he
warranted a charter that gave Guillaume a fief worth 100 l.t. a
year in the viscounty of Pont-Audemer.[161] After Marigny's execution Guillaume was considered one of his men and lost his liberty, his job, and his lands. He was restored to favor only in
1317.[162]

Marigny seems to have wanted connections with the Treasury
in order to increase his political power, not his fortune. He could
obtain gifts from the king as long as he enjoyed the king's favor,
but he might have lost that favor if his policies had turned out
badly. Knowing the state of the king's finances, he could find
reasonable arguments against waging an all-out war with Flanders
or sinking money in a hopeless crusade.[163] Secondhand knowledge, however, was not enough; by the end of 1313 Marigny
wanted direct knowledge and control of all operations of the

[157] Mignon, nos. 89, 2228.
[158] Borrelli de Serres, *Recherches*, III, 47-49.
[159] Favier, *Marigny*, pp. 21, 29, 218.   [160] Ibid., pp. 34-36.
[161] A.N., JJ 48, fol. 108v, no. 188. Borrelli de Serres, *Recherches*, III, 64,
thought it probable that Guillaume du Bois owed his appointment to Marigny.
[162] Fawtier, ed., *Comptes du Trésor*, p. xxiii; Borrelli de Serres, *Recherches*, III, 63-64.
[163] Favier, *Marigny*, p. 105.

Treasury. Perhaps he also had some idea of separating ordinary from extraordinary income, and even of preparing a rough budget for the kingdom. These seem to be the motives that lay behind the preparation of the ordinance of 19 January 1314, which split the Treasury into two sections and gave Marigny final power over all expenditures.

The importance of this ordinance is shown by the composition of the Council that accepted it: the king, his sons, his brothers, all the great officers (except the Constable and the Keeper of the Seals), the Treasurers, the *Maîtres des Comptes*, and three officials concerned with the finances of the Household.[164] The ordinance created two treasuries, a Treasury of the Temple under Gui Florent and Geoffroi de Briançon, and a Treasury of the Louvre under Guillaume du Bois and Renaud de Roye. The Treasury of the Temple was to pay the expenses of the Household, the chief departments of the government, gifts, and pensions, that is, roughly the ordinary expenses of government. To meet these expenses, it was assigned the revenues of Normandy (except for the *fouage*), Auvergne, and the *sénéchaussées* (except for Carcassone, Lyon, and Beaucaire) and fines and amercements over 1,000 l. Income (200,000 l.t.) and expenditure (177,500 l.t.) were roughly equal; unfortunately, as Borrelli de Serres proved, the copy of the ordinance that has survived was written at a later date, and these figures cannot be trusted.[165] The Treasury of the Louvre was to handle extraordinary expenses, the king's works (the Palace and Poissy), pay of troops in Flanders, and debts. It was to have the income of the old domain, the *fouage* of Normandy, the income from *sénéchaussées* of Carcassonne, Lyon, and Beaucaire, reliefs, fines below 1,000 l., the aid for knighting Louis of Navarre, and all extraordinary income. No figures (even erroneous ones) are given for income and expenditures of this Treasury, and probably they never existed, since no one could have estimated expenses for troops or the yield of an aid or a subsidy.

Two final and highly important articles confirmed Marigny's control of royal finances. The Treasurers were to make no payments except when ordered by the king or Marigny, and they were to swear to keep secret the amount of money they received

---

[164] The text was printed by Boutaric in *Notices et extraits*, xx, pt. 2 (1861), 209 ff. It was carefully analyzed by Borrelli de Serres, *Recherches*, III, 54-57.

[165] Borrelli de Serres, *Recherches*, II, 481-82.

unless the king asked for an accounting. Thus Marigny alone would know what funds were available, and he would determine the rate of expenditure (the king would probably warrant only gifts and pensions).[166]

Borrelli de Serres had no trouble in demonstrating that this or-dinance was unworkable and that its terms were violated almost as soon as it was put into effect. But to say that Marigny delib-erately created confusion in order to have exclusive knowledge and control of the king's finances is unfair.[167] In the first place, the ordinance may have been more logical than it seems; the existing copy was altered after Marigny's death. Second, the new system was in effect for little more than a year. Old habits could not have been broken in so short a period, and neither treasury would have had its projected annual income in hand when the first ordinary or extraordinary payments had to be made. Ma-rigny took money where he could find it in 1314; he might not have found this necessary in 1315. Third, Marigny certainly did not love confusion for its own sake, and the ordinance itself shows that he had been able to gain control of royal finance without causing confusion. He would not have improved his reputation or his standing with the king if he had made a mess of the finan-cial system, nor would his control of finances have been very effective if his subordinates did not know what they were doing. As a matter of fact, a fragment of the Journal of the Treasury of the Louvre that has survived suggests that the new rules were causing no great difficulties.[168] Most expenditures were properly warranted by the king or Marigny, and most of the income came from extraordinary sources, such as the aid for knighting Louis of Navarre and the imposts on the Lombards. The real problem was not confusion but extra work; more care had to be taken in justifying payments, and some clerk must have had to coordinate the accounts of the two treasuries so that Marigny and the *gens des comptes* could know the total sum available for the king's needs.

In favor of Marigny it should be said that many of his experi-ments were repeated sooner or later by the kings who succeeded Philip the Fair. Obviously, it was helpful to have a single man instead of a group as head of the financial administration. Miles de Noyer was "souverain establi par dessus les Trésoriers" under

166 Ibid., III, 56-58. Cf. *J.T.P.*, nos. 6003-79.
167 Borrelli de Serres, *Recherches*, III, 55-57.
168 *J.T.P.*, nos. 6003-79.

Louis X; Henri de Sully had the same position under Philip V. The ordinance that established Sully as head of the financial administration had the same clause as did the ordinance of 1314: no payment was to be made by the Treasurers except by order of the king or by the "souverain."[169] It took somewhat longer to reestablish a separate administration for extraordinary income, but the process was under way in the second half of the fourteenth century as the Cour des Aides began to take shape. The one part of Marigny's plan that did not survive was the weakest part—the separate treasuries. Borrelli de Serres has shown that there was only one Treasury after the end of 1315.[170] And while Marigny's friends, Guillaume du Bois and Geoffroi de Briançon, lost their posts as Treasurers, Gui Florent and Baudouin de Roye kept theirs. Simon Festu, bishop of Meaux, was briefly (1315–June 1316) reinstated in his old position; Frémin Coquerel, a *Maître des Comptes*, and Pierre de Rémy, who had handled the finances of Louis of Navarre before he became king, were added to the group.[171] Thus there was no sharp break in personnel after Philip's death; three of his old Treasurers remained in or were restored to office.

The Treasurers were definitely subordinate to the king and Council; few of them (Guillaume de Hangest would be an exception) were influential in making policy. They were expert, well-paid (600 l.p. a year) heads of a technical operation, but men like Latilly and Marigny (both of whom had considerable financial ability) did not want the job of Treasurer because they knew that it would give them little real power. Simon Festu, who had political ambitions, had to accept a post as Treasurer twice, probably because nothing better was offered, but he never became an important figure in the Council. On the other hand, for men like Renaud and Baudouin de Roye, the post of Treasurer increased both their income and their prestige. Both were professional financial agents, skilled in handling large sums of money for the Household and for the army; a treasurership was a logical climax to their careers.

---

[169] *Ord.*, I, 628; Fawtier, ed., *Comptes du Trésor*, no. 1138. Note Miles de Noyer's remarkably high salary—8 l.t. a day, or 2,930 l.t. a year, far above the old salary of 600 l.p. for a Treasurer, and more than twice that of Thibaud de Pouancé, one of Philip's best-paid officials, who had 3 l.p. a day.

[170] Borrelli de Serres, *Recherches*, III, 75-76.

[171] Ibid., pp. 76-79.

The Treasury was an old institution; the only problem for Philip was to decide who should run it. The Chambre des Comptes, however, had not existed before his reign; it developed during the period of maximum financial strain, when Philip had to keep an army of occupation in Aquitaine while supporting another army that was fighting in Flanders.[172] The expert accountants who were already checking the various statements of receipts and expenditures that came to the court were busier than ever; they ceased to accompany the king on his travels and settled down in the *chambre aux deniers*, the room in the palace where the accounts and money for Household expenses was kept. They were paid regular wages, 16 s.p. (20 s.t.) a day for the senior members (the salary of a *bailli*) and 6 (or 4) s.p. for their assistants.[173] The commission of the *curia* that heard accounts at the end of each term could not possibly cover in a few days all the work that had been going on for months before; the most that it could do was to settle a few difficult questions and give official approval to the statements produced by the experts. Theoretically, all who took part in the work of the commission were *magistri compotorum*, even the bishop of Dol, who was acting Keeper of the Seals.[174] But the men who worked on accounts throughout the year were naturally called *magistri compotorum* more often than those who only occasionally attended meetings, and they gradually gained a monopoly of the title. A neat distinction between the two groups was made in January 1300; the income from certain rights in the Grands Jours of Champagne was to be a perquisite of the "magistrorum habentium clericos compotorum," that is, the full-time Masters, who would be the only ones who would have clerks working regularly on the accounts. These payments were due for two years beginning in 1297. The distinction goes back even further; Nicolas Brussel cites a document of 1290 that mentions these rights.[175]

Since the full-time Masters worked in the *chambre aux deniers*, their decisions were often cited as orders of that Chamber, for example, a payment to an envoy to the king of Castile (1293) or orders to pay wages for the Gascon war (1300).[176] But this

[172] For a detailed description of the formation of the Chamber see ibid., I, 308-33.

[173] Ibid., pp. 312-13, 316.

[174] *J.T.P.*, no. 2026. See above, pp. 71-72.

[175] *J.T.P.*, no. 4204; Brussel, II, 55; Borrelli de Serres, *Recherches*, I, 305.

[176] *C.R.*, I, no. 145; B.N., ms. fr. 25697, nos. 22, 23; Borrelli de Serres,

was confusing; the work being done by the *magistri compotorum* was not the work that had been (and would in the future be done) by the Household *chambre aux deniers*. Borrelli de Serres was probably right in saying that the group of full-time Masters was not officially called the Chambre des Comptes until 1303, but the term was used unofficially several years earlier. Mignon, writing a generation later, probably slipped into the usage of his own day when he spoke of an account "factus in camera compotorum" in 1296,[177] but the Journal of the Treasury, an absolutely contemporary document, records a payment "in camera compotorum" on 12 May 1301.[178] Although some orders of Jean de Dammartin were warranted by the *chambre aux deniers*, one original, dated Tuesday after Candlemas 1300 (n.s.), is warranted "per cameram compotorum."[179] Finally, the account of Beaucaire, 1302-1303, mentions a payment to Guillaume de Plaisians (acting in his capacity of *juge-mage* of Beaucaire) that had been struck from the roll of 1302 "per magistros camere Compotorum regiorum" in that year.[180] There clearly was a need for the term; official recognition merely justified a fait accompli.

The final stage in the change in nomenclature came in or about 1303, when the new Palace (Palais de la Cité) had been partially completed and the Masters and their clerks moved from the Louvre to the new building. The office that handled Household expenses remained in the Louvre, so that there were, in effect, two *chambres aux deniers*, separated by some distance.[181] As long as the records and the funds of the two offices were in the same place, the confusion was not unbearable; any clerk in the Chamber would know to whom an inquiry should be directed and by whom an order to pay should be drafted. Now the distinction had to be made clear, and the office of the *Maîtres des Comptes* was regularly called the Chambre des Comptes after 1303. Both the move and the change in name were probably associated with the transfer of the Treasury back to the Temple in 1303. Philip

---

Recherches, I, 319-25. See Fawtier, ed., *Comptes du Trésor*, no. 425: "pro burello [a coarse cloth, hence the word "bureau"] ad computandum in camera denariorum . . . 4 l. 16 s." (account of All Saints 1296).

[177] Mignon, no. 2398.   [178] *J.T.P.*, no. 4659.

[179] B.N., ms. nouv. acq. fr. 3637, no. 25. In this case and in the next, "camera compotorum" cannot be simply the name of an accounting room, as Borrelli de Serres argued (*Recherches*, I, 326).

[180] *C.R.*, I, no. 13954.

[181] Borrelli de Serres, *Recherches*, I, 326.

wanted to keep a close watch on the operations of the Temple. He had his own men in the Temple working with the Treasurer; he also wanted an independent bureau to check accounts. The new name was more appropriate and more dignified; it gave greater prestige to the office.

Whatever its name, during the 1290s the Chamber acquired functions that made it one of the most important departments of the central government. The description given by Borrelli de Serres of its work and powers cannot be improved: under the direction of the king and Council it controlled the finances of the kingdom.[182] Thus the king might send an envoy to the pope or a foreign prince, but the envoy could not recover his expenses until his account had been approved by the Chamber; the king might make a gift, but the money would not be paid until the Chamber had registered the letter. If expenditures authorized by the monarch were subject to this scrutiny, one can imagine what happened to local officials. As early as 1294 wages of the *prévôts* of Champagne were fixed by the Masters.[183] The accounts of *baillis* and seneschals are full of items that were questioned or disallowed by the Chamber. Another, perhaps more difficult task was switching money back and forth between different accounts to meet immediate needs. (The Treasury, however, could also perform such operations.) Finally, the Chamber operated in some respects as a court;[184] it made *enquêtes* for the Parlement and decided controversies about payments owed to the king and about misdeeds of its own subordinates.

The Chamber's relations with other branches of the government were not always very clear. The old commission of the *curia* for accounts continued to exist for some years after 1303, but it met irregularly and was finally absorbed by the Chamber.[185] The Treasury was independent, but its accounts were reviewed by the Chamber, and the Treasurers often sat with and were outnumbered by the Masters.[186] There was some rivalry between Treasury and Chamber, which may be one reason why it was necessary to establish a "souverain" for finance (such as

[182] Ibid., pp. 320-25. See also H. Jassemin, *La Chambre des Comptes de Paris* (Paris, 1933), pp. xii-xvii.

[183] Petit et al., no. 205.

[184] Borrelli de Serres, *Recherches*, I, 324; Jassemin, *Chambre des Comptes*, p. xvi; *Olim*, III, 119.

[185] Borrelli de Serres, *Recherches*, I, 327-33.

[186] Ibid., III, 46-47.

Sully), who was the chief of both offices, and why Philip V in 1319 forbade the Treasurers to sit in the Chamber.[187] But, although there were difficulties, the personnel was interchangeable: Baudouin de Roye, Gui Florent, and Guillaume du Bois, Treasurers under Philip the Fair, became Masters under his sons; Frémin Coquerel, Master in 1314, was a Treasurer in 1315.[188] In the latter part of the fourteenth century the Chamber became more powerful and influential than the Treasury, but under Philip V it showed no desire to dominate its sister institution; instead, it asked to be relieved of the task of reviewing Treasury accounts.[189]

The Chamber was also in close contact with the Household, if only because it received the Treasury account of payments made for Household expenses. But there was also interlocking personnel in the three offices. Renaud de Roye paid Household and war expenses and was also a Treasurer.[190] His brother Baudouin, a *maître d'hôtel*, became a Treasurer and eventually a Master; Michel de Bourdenay, *argentier* of the king in 1305, clerk of the king's chamber, master of the *chambre aux deniers* of Louis of Navarre, was also a Master by 1310.[191] Michel owed his unusual position to his patron, Marigny, but the Roye were already high in the king's service before Marigny had much influence.

The Chamber was, of course, always subject to the orders of the Council. Here again there was overlapping; the Masters were members of the Council, and the Council often asked the advice of the Chamber on financial matters. The ordinance of 1314 establishing a double Treasury is a good example of both points; it was adopted by a Council at which all the Masters were present. But it also shows the difficulty of assigning responsibility for an act; the ordinance was the work of Marigny, not of the Masters or Treasurers. A better example of the influence of the Masters as members of the Council is the fact that they ordered acts in the king's name, either as a group (*per cameram compotorum*)

---

[187] *Ord.*, I, 656 (no. 14).

[188] *J.T.C.*, col. 889, nn. 2, 3; Fawtier, ed., *Comptes du Trésor*, no. 1200; Borrelli de Serres, *Recherches*, III, 66, 80.

[189] Jassemin, *Chambre des Comptes*, pp. xviii, xxviii. Philip refused the request.

[190] Mignon, nos. 2502, 2506; Borrelli de Serres, *Recherches*, III, 30, 46; *J.T.P.*, nos. 5821, 5822 and n.

[191] See Borrelli de Serres, *Recherches*, III, 55, 60, and *J.T.C.*, col. 889n, for Baudouin; see Borrelli de Serres, *Recherches*, III, 55, 66, Favier, *Marigny*, pp. 79-82, and *C.R.*, II, nos. 23996, 27785, for Michel de Bourdenay.

or as individuals (Dammartin, Bourdenay, Sanche de la Charmoye).[192] Most of these documents dealt with farms of the domain or transfers of rents, but some were of wider interest—
promises never to sever a community from the domain, confirmation of acts of lords freeing their men from various obligations,
and a grant of fairs.[193] These matters concerned the king's financial interests, directly or indirectly, but they also were of concern
to other branches of the government and need not have been
warranted by the Chamber.

When Philip V tried to reorganize the financial administration
he not only defined the powers of the Chamber but also fixed its
personnel. There were to be three Master Clerks (to whom he
added a fourth), three lay Masters, and eleven clerks of accounts.[194] This was roughly the same table of organization that
had existed under Philip the Fair. The three Master Clerks can
be identified in the records as early as 1285. The lay Masters
appear a little later, in 1287, and were still not full-time members
of the Chamber; Oudard de Chambly, the most active, worked
for only 91 days. By 1301, however, Oudard received wages for
the full year, and from that time on there were permanent lay
Masters.[195]

The junior clerks also appear in the 1280s. Those who were
king's clerks were paid by the king; others were only private
secretaries of the Masters. In either case, the junior clerks were
closely attached to one of the senior clerks; Sanche de la Charmoye, for example, worked with Pierre de Condé. When Sanche
himself became a Master in 1299, he took his nephew Amaury
(who had already been his private clerk) as his official clerk.[196]
This kind of relationship apparently worried the government.
The ordinance of 1319 forbade the clerks to live with any of the
Masters; each clerk was to have his own home.[197]

In the time of Philip the Fair the Masters and clerks of accounts
were the most professional and highly specialized group of royal
officials. They had long careers, but these careers were devoted
almost entirely to financial business. Most of the Master Clerks
had at one time been junior clerks; many of the Master Clerks
who served Philip's sons and Philip of Valois were related to ear-

---

[192] See the index of Fawtier et al., eds., *Registres*, under these names.
[193] Fawtier et al., ed., *Registres*, nos. 1313, 2038, 1668-71, 1875.
[194] *Ord.*, I, 703, paras. 1-6.
[195] Borrelli de Serres, *Recherches*, I, 309, 311-18, 328.
[196] Ibid., pp. 316-17.   [197] *Ord.*, I, 704, para. 5.

lier Masters. Thus Pierre de Condé, whose career began under St. Louis and who retired in 1299 was succeeded by his nephew Pierre (but only after the latter had served a long apprenticeship as chief financial officer of Louis of Navarre).[198] Jean de Saint Just, who had been *caissier* of the Household at least since 1286 and was then a Master of the Chamber (1305-1315), had his nephew Jean received as a clerk of accounts by the end of 1315. Jean de Saint Just II became a Master in 1319 and remained in office until 1346, when he was transferred to the Parlement.[199] The record for continuity was held by the Charmoye. Sanche de la Charmoye was a clerk of accounts in the 1290s, replaced Pierre de Condé as a Master in 1299, and served until his death in 1314. His nephew Amaury, who had served as his clerk, was a clerk of the Chamber at 6 s. a day by 1316 and soon became a Master (immediately after the death of Louis X, according to Lehugeur; only in 1323, according to Cazelles).[200] Lehugeur is nearer the truth, since Amaury warranted a letter in January 1317 with Pierre de Condé II and Guillaume Courteheuse, both of whom were Masters.[201] In any case, Amaury was certainly a Master under Charles IV and Philip VI until his death in 1338. He was eventually (1346) succeeded as Master by his clerk, Ligier Morand.[202] A Jean de la Charmoye, who was perhaps the son of Sanche who had served Marigny, was also a clerk of accounts in 1316 and 1322, and perhaps as late as 1350, although the Jean of 1346 and 1350 was probably a younger member of the family.[203]

The long argument between the Parlement and the Chamber of Accounts on precedence and date of foundation has no significance today, but the Chamber had many points in its favor. It

[198] For Pierre de Condé I see *H.F.*, xx, 61, and Petit et al., no. 141 (service under St. Louis); Borrelli de Serres, *Recherches*, I, 310, 312, 316-17, and *J.T.P.*, nos. 481, 2110, 2498, 3297 (as *Maître des Comptes*). For Pierre de Condé II see Mignon, no. 2607, and Fawtier, ed., *Comptes du Trésor*, no. 1129 (service under Louis of Navarre), and Lehugeur, II, 31, 52, 221, 223 (service as a Master).

[199] Borrelli de Serres, *Recherches*, II, 75, 239; Fawtier, ed., *Comptes du Trésor*, nos. 667, 776; Cazelles, pp. 69, 218, 348.

[200] Fawtier, ed., *Comptes du Trésor*, no. 772; Lehugeur, II, 223; *J.T.C.*, nos. 148, 481, 869, 1324 and n.; Cazelles, p. 68.

[201] A.N., JJ 53, fol. 2v, no. 6.   [202] Cazelles, p. 185, n. 7.

[203] Favier, *Marigny*, p. 21; Fawtier, ed., *Comptes du Trésor*, nos. 665, 774; C.R. Maillard, II, no. 13743; *Ord.*, II, 252, 335 (1346 and 1350). The Jean of these last entries is only a "parvus clericus"; it is unlikely that a man who held this rank in 1316 would not have been promoted by 1346.

had permanent, full-time members long before the Parlement; it had a system of apprenticeship and training on the job before 1300; it was showing a tendency to favor hereditary membership by 1314. It was the first of the great Companies that were to play such an important role in the Old Regime.

The Chamber did its preliminary work well and carefully, but it was not very efficient in following up on its findings. When Robert Mignon was compiling his inventory in the early years of Philip of Valois, he noted a large number of arrears or possible arrears that had not been recovered. In fact, the chief purpose of his work was to find accounts "per quos aliquid videbatur posse recuperari." There were many of these, there were also many missing accounts. The latter had probably been taken for inspection by some other member of the Chamber and never returned.[204] Probably there were so many accounts to review that there was not enough time to dun the hundreds of collectors who had not paid in full, and these collectors in turn had often moved on to other areas and were in no position to go back to the districts where they had formerly worked and dig up arrears. There was always the possibility of asking a *bailli* or some other collector to take the accounts of the first collectors and put pressure on debtors to pay, but Mignon was usually uncertain as to how much was produced by these efforts.

As was pointed out above, the largest arrears were those of the collectors of subventions, but there is no consistent pattern even in these accounts. Some collectors wound up their work owing only a few pounds, or even with a few pounds owed to them for expenses; others reported thousands of pounds "ad levandum." Thus there was still 10,283 l.p. of the fiftieth of 1297 to be collected in Vermandois after the first account of the collectors. The collectors sent in lists of names of those who had not paid, but, Mignon remarks sadly, "nec videtur quod tradite fuerint ad solvendum."[205] This was one of the largest lists of arrears; usually they ran from 2,000 to 3,000 l. For example, in Senlis there was 2,410 l.p. in arrears for the tax of 1297; this list was given to certain sergeants "ad explectandum," but Mignon, as usual, could not discover whether the money had been collected.[206] Sums such

[204] Langlois, introduction to Mignon, pp. xxix, xxxi.
[205] Mignon, no. 1176.
[206] Ibid., no. 1273. See also nos. 1272 (Paris, 2,155 l.p.), 1279 (Vermandois, 3,221 l.p.; this was collected by an ex-*bailli*), 1291 (Sens, 1,425 l.p.), 1435 (Vitry and Chaumont, 3,500 l.p.), 1448 (Cotentin, 1,177 l.t.), 1457 (Poitou,

as this (and most of those given in the footnote) are not surprising; they would be 5 to 10 percent of the total imposition, and in any tax system this is not an abnormal percentage of late or defaulted payments. But a shortage of 14,442 l.t. for Bourges in 1303 (more than half of the expected tax) is far too high, and Mignon did not know who collected it. Bourges was also far in arrears the next year (5,676 l.t.), though, since the tax rate was much higher, the deficit was only about 12 percent of the expected total.[207] The worst problems were encountered in the *bailliage* of Tours, a province where the Church was also resisting taxation.[208] Apparently the collectors there had been careless, inefficient, or too weak to overcome opposition since the first general tax of 1295. Gaullaume de la Poterie was sent there in 1309 to clear up these debts. He collected 17,110 l.t. and 8,230 l.t. These sums are given in two separate accounts, but Mignon does not state how much of this money was credited to old arrears and how much to the *fouage* of 1304.[209] He does state that the *fouage* was supposed to produce 45,895 l.t. and that only 25,017 l.t. was raised, leaving a deficit of 19,878 l.t.[210] He was not sure how or by whom these arrears were collected, but it seems likely that Guillaume could have recovered more from a recent tax than he could have from taxes that went back to 1295-1297 and that he may have wiped out much of the deficit of 1304.

Another weakness of the Chamber was its inability to compile, or lack of interest in compiling, grand totals of sums received from any one source or spent for any one purpose. Individual accounts were carefully scrutinized and the addition checked

---

2,660 l.t.), 1460 (Périgord-Quercy, ca. 3,000 l.t. to be found by the receiver), 1475 (Orléans, 5,816 l.p.—rather high), 1495 (Caen, 2,136 l.t.), 1497 (Cotentin, 1,285 l.t.), 1507 (Auvergne, 3,228 l.p. [*sic*], 1519 (Sens, 2,729 l.p. "weak money," to be collected by m^e R. de S. Benoît), 1521 (Orléans, 3,233 l.p.), 1526 (Bourges, 5,676 l.t.—rather high [see note 207 below]), 1533 (Caen, ca. 800 l.t.), 1540 (Poitou, 12,614 l.t. missing of 39,458 assessed —very high), 1542 (Saintonge, 4,992 l.t. "weak money").

[207] Ibid., nos. 1478, 1526. For 1304, *H.F.*, xxi, 564, does not agree with Mignon; this list has only 3,759 l.t. missing, or about 8 percent of an expected 43,758 (high, but not abnormal). This suggests that Mignon's records were not very complete, as he well knew.

[208] Strayer and Taylor, pp. 41-42.

[209] Mignon, nos. 1481, 1484-86.

[210] Ibid., no. 1487. This time the account in *H.F.*, xxi, 564, is very close to Mignon: the *fouage* of 1304 was supposed to produce 45,896 l.t. and only 26,017 l.t. was collected.

down to the last penny, but little was done to give the king an idea of his total income or total expenditures. The net income of a *bailliage* or *sénéchaussée* is stated in its account, but no account sums up the income of all *bailliages* or of all *sénéchaussées*. The same is true of taxes. From time to time the amount received or imposed on a district is mentioned, but there is never a total for any one tax. An unknown member of the Chamber did try to sum up the income from the great tax of 1304, but his work was woefully incomplete; he had no figures for Paris, Meaux, Troyes, Senlis, Mâcon, Carcassonne, and Rouergue, and wrong figures for Caux and Beaucaire.[211]

Expenses are just as unclear. The war in Aquitaine cost well over 1,500,000 l.t., but there is no way of obtaining a total. Some clerk of the Chamber tried to tabulate expenditures under the heading "Debite qui debentur per fines compotorum guerre Vasconie,"[212] but although he repeated some of the amounts that are recorded for individual captains and paymasters in earlier entries, he must have omitted many others. Naturally, he left out the costs of the very expensive fleet being fitted out in the lower Seine,[213] but even this does not bring his total up to a reasonable figure. Adding in everything that seems to belong under his heading, he accounts for only 1,243,529 l.t. Early in the war someone in Paris estimated that about 1,734,000 l.t. was available for the operation, and my own guess is that about 2,000,000 l.t. was spent.[214] The records of the Treasury for only three terms (Christmas 1298, St. John's and Christmas 1299) give a total of 1,337,149 l.t. for "Guerra," but much of this would have been needed in Flanders.[215] The English, who kept much better records than the French, prepared an account for Edward II that put the total cost

211 This is the document referred to in notes 207 and 210 above; it is printed in *H.F.*, xxi, 564-65. See my comments in Strayer and Taylor, pp. 73-74.

212 Mignon, nos. 2436-58.

213 Ibid., no. 2481; *C.R.*, ii, nos. 24422, 24501, 24557, 25449, 25992. To be fair, the northern fleet was meant to cut communications between England and Flanders, as well as to deter the English from sending troops and supplies to Aquitaine, so that only part of the expense could be charged to the Gascon war.

214 Funck-Brentano, "Document," pp. 326-48. See my article, "The Costs and Profits of War," in H. A. Miskimin, D. Harlihy, and A. L. Udovitch, eds., *The Medieval City* (New Haven, 1977), pp. 269-91, esp. n. 11.

215 Fawtier, ed., *Comptes du Trésor*, pp. lvi-lvii, and Borrelli de Serres, *Recherches*, ii, App. D.

of the war to them at £360,000.[216] Some items were omitted, and the total cost was probably nearer £400,000. At the official exchange rate (£1 sterling = 4 l.t.) even the lower figure would equal 1,400,000 l.t., and the English wage scale for soldiers was lower than that of the French. The French must have spent at least as much as the English, and probably more.

Thus no accurate total of the costs of the war of Aquitaine was available, and there is no indication that anyone ever tried to prepare a summary or summaries of expenses for the Flemish war. It was not the business of the Chamber to keep track of expenditures for the Household or for gifts, alms, and pensions. That was the work of the Treasury, but the Chamber possessed information that was never fed into the Treasury summaries. Many alms and pensions were assigned on the revenues of a *prévôté* or a *sénéchaussée*. These expenditures were duly recorded in the accounts of each of these districts, but although the Chamber made sure that each payment was warranted, it did not prepare totals of all alms and pensions reported to it in a given term. The same problem occurs with expenditures for "public works." The Treasury knew how much was being spent on the new Palace in Paris. It did not know how much was spent on royal buildings, castles, and fortifications or mills and market facilities in the provinces. All such expenses were listed in the accounts received by the Chamber, but again no totals were prepared. In short, the Chamber seems to have felt that its primary duty was to keep the king from being cheated, not to keep him informed about the state of his finances.

The Treasury was supposed to keep the king informed, and up to a point it did. Nevertheless, it would have been difficult to make plans for the coming year or for a sudden emergency from the information it provided in its accounts for each term. Totals were given for receipts from the *bailliages* and *prévôtés* of the old domain, from Normandy, Champagne, and the *sénéchaussées*, from loans, subventions, and tenths; but various odds and ends (debts, fines, reliefs, amortizations) were not summarized, though they were added in with receipts in Paris or Tours money.[217] Expenses were also added up under various headings—the House-

[216] Public Record Office, London, E372/160. The most important parts of this roll were published by Charles Bémont, ed., *Rôles Gascons*, 3 vols. (Paris, 1896-1906), III, cxli-cxlii, clxvii-clxviii.

[217] Fawtier, ed., *Comptes du Trésor*, p. lvi and nos. 1, 2, 60-117, 145, 155, 318.

hold, hereditary pensions, life pensions, and "alia" (mainly salaries and expenses of royal officials).[218] Even in 1296 there does not seem to have been a special account for the war, although the fragment of expenses in Tours money that has survived looks as if it had had entries concerning money that could have been used to pay the army.[219] By 1316 there was an account for the Flemish war, but only subtotals were given.[220] These weaknesses made financial predictions almost impossible. A fiftieth might bring in 116,810 l.p. for one term,[221] but only a series of additions covering several years (since there were always arrears) would show the true yield of such a tax. The fact that the Exchequer produced 70,000 l.t. in the second term of 1299 proved nothing; it produced only 52,000 l.t. in the same term of 1298 and 53,854 l.t. in 1301.[222] Additions and averaging over several years would have been needed to estimate the income that could be expected from Normandy, but this was never done. It was equally hard to keep track of expenses, not only major expenses, such as those for war, but also smaller expenses, such as pensions or grants of land. In short, the Treasury could tell the king at the end of a term that he had a surplus or a deficit in his account, but it could not tell him how much he could expect to receive during the next term.

Thus, even though financial records for the reign of Philip the Fair are relatively plentiful, it is impossible to say what his gross or net income was for any year. Borrelli de Serres labored mightily with this problem and concluded that the total income and expenditure for the kingdom for any one year could never be known with any exactness and that after the last years of the thirteenth century (when the existing fragment of the Journal of the Treasury breaks off) it was useless to try to figure out gross receipts.[223] In spite of these gloomy remarks, he did make estimates,[224] which are at least helpful in showing general trends. As was noted earlier in this chapter, he saw a sharp decrease, beginning at the end of 1291; by 1295-1296 this was compensated for by loans and taxes. He found a large surplus for the last half of 1298 and the first half of 1299, followed by a deficit in the second half of 1299, and another deficit in 1301. These results fit in well enough with my own calculations, but I have no great

[218] Ibid., nos 323 (Household), 324-57 (pensions), 359-453 (alia).
[219] Ibid., nos. 457-59.   [220] Ibid., nos. 1139-84.
[221] Ibid., no. 155.   [222] Ibid., pp. lvi, lviii.
[223] Borrelli de Serres, *Recherches*, II, 487-88.
[224] Ibid., 490-93 and App. D.

confidence in them. There were too many unpaid debts for the wars, too many unpaid loans, too many sums paid directly to soldiers and suppliers by southern receivers and not yet entered on the books of the Treasury.[225] The apparent surplus may never have existed, and the real deficit may have been greater than it appears. It is doubtful that we can be any wiser than Clement V, who said that Philip's early prosperity turned to adversity with the coming of the wars and that there was no real recovery even after the wars ended.[226] Heavy taxation barely paid for military expenses from 1294 to 1305, and there was no large general tax after the subvention of 1304. Philip improved French financial administration, but not to the point where it could meet ordinary expenses and still leave a surplus for an active foreign policy.

The Administration of Justice*

For Philip the Fair the basic sign of sovereignty was his right to act as the final and supreme judge in all cases (except those dealing with purely ecclesiastical matters) that arose in his kingdom. As a corollary, he insisted on his right to protect anyone who had invoked his intervention in order to remedy an act of injustice. But once these principles were admitted, Philip was satisfied; he had no desire to have his officials judge every case in first instance. Not only did he lack the resources for undertaking such a vast responsibility; it also would have offended his sense of the fitness of things to try to deprive the upper classes of their rights of justice. In fact, his courts spent a great deal of time in adjudicating conflicting claims of nobles, churchmen, and communes to jurisdiction over certain men or certain areas, and considerably less time in asserting the king's rights to justice. To simplify a little, the three chief tasks of the royal courts were to ensure that the right of appeal to the king was not denied or delayed, to protect those who were in the king's "guard," and to prevent conflicts among nobles, churchmen, and communes over their possessions (which of course included rights of justice).

---

[225] See above, pp. 165-66.   [226] Boutaric, *Templiers*, p. 63.

* I should here thank Dr. Elaine Robison, who prepared for me a careful and thorough analysis of the *Olim* from 1285 through 1314. Most of my statistics on the geographical distribution of suitors in the Parlement, the number of appeals, and the relative success of different social groups in proving their cases are based on her work.

None of these was an easy task. There were two major problems. First was the existence of virtual principalities in which a duke, count, or bishop had extensive powers of government. In these principalities it was difficult for subjects to appeal to the king or for the king's protection to be effective. Aquitaine and Flanders are obvious examples of such principalities, but lesser men, such as the count of Foix, were not always very willing to cooperate with royal officials, and the bishop of Mende, count of the Gévaudan, could suggest that he was the supreme ruler and judge of his county, the equivalent of a king, though he did not claim the title.[1] The duke of Burgundy was a kinsman and a loyal supporter of the king. He did not deny the king's power as supreme judge (as the bishop of Mende did), but somehow he was seldom impleaded in the royal courts, and I have found few appeals from his jurisdiction. Doubtless he gave good justice; doubtless, as a peer who often sat in the Parlement, he knew how to avoid difficulties with the king's lawyers; but Burgundy can hardly be said to be included in the royal system of justice during Philip's reign. The same could be said of the apanages, such as Anjou and Artois, but as Charles T. Wood has shown, the apanage princes were careful to follow the example of the king and often used former royal officials in their governments, so that the apanage courts were very like the royal courts.[2] Nevertheless, they were not royal courts, and there were few appeals from their judgements and little interference with their operations.

The second problem was just the opposite of the first: fragmentation rather than monopolization of rights of justice. In a sense it was easier to deal with a duke of Aquitaine, who might be recalcitrant but who at least had a well-organized government, than to carry on simple police operations in an area where one lord might have justice on one side of a street, another lord have justice on the other side, and neither one have justice over certain houses at the end of the street.[3] In spite of the later adage

[1] *Mémoire relatif au paréage*, p. 531.

[2] Charles T. Wood, *The French Apanages and the Capetian Monarchy 1224-1328* (Cambridge, Mass., 1966), pp. 92-102, 110-17. These citations come from his chapter on "Sovereignty and Jurisdiction," an excellent discussion of the meaning of the term *superioritas*.

[3] See Gustave Ducoudray, *Les origines du Parlement de Paris*, 2 vols. (Paris, 1902), II, 573-84, 600-611, for examples of this fragmentation of justice.

that "fief and justice have nothing in common," free possession of almost any piece of revenue-producing property could generate a right of justice, if only the right to seize goods for default of payment of a rent or toll. Justice itself was a valuable possession, since most offenses could be compounded for by fines— usually only a few shillings, but the shillings could add up to considerable sums in the course of a year. Thus one source of unrest, running from petty scuffles to riots to private wars, was argument about rights of justice. If these arguments were to be stopped before they had dangerous consequences, the king's courts had to intervene; this took up a good deal of time, especially if the losing party used all his rights of appeal. And even when there were not arguments among the court holders, the fragmentation of rights of justice caused problems for royal officers. Theoretically they could not arrest and punish men living in another jurisdiction. If they observed these limits, notorious malefactors could escape with little or no punishment. If they overstepped the limits, there would be complaints to the king, complaints that might be very effective if the rights of a bishop, an abbot, or a baron had been infringed. Royal sergeants were often tough and brutal men, but one can sympathize with their frustrations. Frequently they decided to act first and take their chances on future reprimands or penalties. They would arrest, maltreat, and even hang suspects; such behavior might start a lawsuit, but, meanwhile, justice, as they saw it, had been done. The central government was not very severe about such offenses. The sergeants might have to humiliate themselves by carrying a corpse or an effigy of a corpse on their shoulders to the rightful judge, or they might be amerced; but only in extreme cases did they lose their jobs.[4]

Quarrels over jurisdiction were especially acute when the Church was involved. The first difficulty was in deciding who had the privileges of clerical status. Many clerks in minor orders were married and engaged in business; they caused endless problems for the towns and for royal officials, since most of the time

---

[4] Boutaric, ed., *Actes du Parlement*, I, no. 2975B; *Olim*, II, 543 (cf. p. 545). Sergeants who executed a clerk were excused because he was a notorious criminal (*Olim*, II, 545). Fines were levied against those who tortured a clerk (III, 49-50); in a similar case, some were fined, and some lost their jobs because they could not pay the fines (III, 319-20). All those involved in another case lost their jobs, but they had mistreated a Treasurer's clerk (III, 747).

they could not be distinguished from laymen. Laymen also falsely claimed clerical status; the most amusing example is the case of two men who managed to get themselves tonsured while they were being held in the royal prison of the Châtelet.[5] Even more troublesome were the claims of abbots and bishops to territorial jurisdiction in secular cases. Churchmen had good records and good lawyers; they seldom forgot their rights, and they could keep a case open for many years. They brought more suits in the Parlement than any other group (about 40 percent of those I analyzed), and most of these suits concerned their rights of jurisdiction.

Nevertheless, the problems caused by the division of rights of justice among many lords and many communities can be exaggerated. It was criminal justice that was most thoroughly fragmented, and especially criminal low justice, that is, cognizance of minor offenses, such as insulting words, simple assault, petty larceny, and the like. High justice over what might roughly be called felonies was less widely distributed, although it is still true that there were hundreds of nonroyal courts in the country that could impose heavy fines on, or mutilate, or hang convicted criminals. The king and his officials were not greatly concerned about such matters; they tried criminals caught in their jurisdictions and, in theory at least, let bishops, abbots, barons, knights, and communes try criminals taken in theirs. There was a certain amount of poaching by minor royal officials but no concerted effort to interfere with private courts.

If, however, royal sovereignty or the king's dignity were touched, then no attention had to be paid to the rights of local lords or communities. To attack a person or a place under the king's protection was a serious offense, punishable only in the royal courts. All the king's servants, down to the most obscure sergeant, enjoyed this protection, as did a large number of religious establishments. Anyone pleading in a royal court or anyone who had appealed to a royal court was also under the king's protection. If two quarreling men (or families) had given security in a royal court not to harm each other, then breach of this promise could be judged only in a royal court, no matter where the offense occurred.[6] Even without the giving of security, private war was discouraged by the general rule against carrying arms in order to attack an enemy. In the south this offense was

---

[5] *Olim*, II, 501.
[6] E. Perrot, *Les cas royaux* (Paris, 1910), chaps. 5-7.

repeatedly declared to be punishable solely by the king.[7] Perrot doubted whether this rule was enforced throughout the kingdom in the time of Philip the Fair,[8] but since the most dangerous private wars of this period broke out in the south, it sufficed to claim exclusive jurisdiction over private war in that region.

In short, the fact that subjects controlled the administration of criminal justice in many parts of the realm did not weaken the position of the king. Subjects could not use their rights of justice to harm royal officials or to attack men and communities under his protection. The king's own rights of justice were wide enough so that he could punish anyone who interfered with the operations of his government. At the same time, he and his officials were freed, to some extent, from the burden of having to hear and determine the thousands of petty cases that make up the largest part of the work of criminal courts in any society.

On the other hand, the first and chief duty of kingship was to see that justice was done. It was common knowledge that many private courts were at best careless, and at worst corrupt and cruel, in administering justice. It was obvious that many malefactors avoided punishment because a large number of courts had such limited territorial jurisdiction and such small police forces (their sergeants) that escape was easy. Was it the king's duty to try to remedy these evils?

It was a long time before Philip and his officials began to face this question. They should not be blamed; in any federal system

---

[7] This claim was made as early as 1292: "pacis fractio, portacio armorum . . . generaliter pertinent domino rege in solidum per totum regnum Francie racione sue superioritatis, eciam in locis ubi alii domini habent merum imperium" (*Ord.*, VII, 611). See also the statement of the procurator of Carcassonne, upheld by the Parlement in 1309: "cum dicti delicti cognicio et punicio, racione delacionis armorum et fractionis pacis ad nos solum pertineret" (*Olim*, III, 301). It is repeated almost word for word in a mandate to the seneschal of Toulouse, 1310 (*Olim*, II, 514). Philip's agents claimed in 1311 that the king alone could make rules about carrying arms; cf. Pierre Chaplais, "La souveraineté du roi de France et le pouvoir legislatif en Guyenne au début du XIVe siècle," *Le Moyen Age*, LXIX (1963), 461. In a *paréage* with Silvanès the king reserved cases of carriage of arms as one of the "specialibus superioritatis casibus consuetis domino regi . . . reservatis" (P. A. Verlaguet, ed., *Cartulaire de l'abbaye de Silvanès*, Archives historiques du Rouergue, I [Rodez, 1910], p. 513).

[8] Perrot, *Cas royaux*, pp. 158-68. The count of Foix insisted, with some success, that he could judge cases of carriage of arms, and the 1316 charter for Languedoc more or less allowed concurrent jurisdiction of this offense to lords with high justice (*H.L.*, x, cols. 289-90, 407, 453, 533).

(and in many ways thirteenth-century France was a federation of lordships) it is difficult to interfere with local courts. (How long was it before the Supreme Court of the United States began to worry about the quality of criminal justice in the states?) In the last years of the reign, however, the Parlement began to intervene, both in cases of flagrant abuse of power by seigneurial judges and in cases where local officials had not moved to arrest and punish criminals. An early example of the first type of intervention came in 1306. The lord of Poix (in the *bailliage* of Amiens) had mutilated several men of the commune. He lost all rights over them and the town and had to turn over 500 librates of land to establish pensions for the injured men. He was also fined 5,000 l.t. to the king.[9] In 1310 the count of Nevers was ordered to surrender two clerks whom he had arrested and forced to pledge a fine of 1,200 l.p. for an alleged rape.[10] In 1312 the court of the archbishop of Reims freed certain people accused of homicide. Complaint was made to the Parlement that this was by collusion with the judge. An *enquête* was ordered, but while it was pending the real criminals confessed and the investigation was dropped.[11]

These and similar cases gradually led the Parlement to establish regular procedures for investigating abuses and negligence in the administration of criminal justice. A separate register for criminal cases was opened in 1313 (though some cases that seem clearly criminal were not included in the first entries). At the same time, the Parlement began to order investigations of crimes that had not been prosecuted by lower courts, royal or seigneurial. Very few criminal cases were actually tried in the Parlement, but it did rule on procedural questions that were raised during the investigations. Ducoudray exaggerated somewhat when he said that soon after Philip's death the Parlement had become the "Grand Parquet" of the kingdom, but it is true that by 1314 the Parlement was taking more responsibility for overseeing the administration of criminal justice than it ever had before.[12]

Nevertheless, the chief business of the king's courts, as with most courts in western European countries, was on the civil side —deciding questions of the ownership or possession of land, of

---

[9] The lord's land was in the king's hand by Ascension 1305 (*C.R.*, I, no. 4483); the judgement came in the next year (*Olim*, III, 176).

[10] *Olim*, III, 424.   [11] Ibid., p. 714.

[12] Ducoudray, II, 689-93. For examples of criminal investigations ordered by the Parlement see Guilhiermoz, pp. 379-81.

rights of justice and of government or of profitable monopolies such as tolls, market rights, and the like. These were matters that deeply concerned the king, for many reasons. He had to preserve his own lands and rights of government, for his income and his power were based upon them. He also had to prevent other lords from illegally extending their possessions, first of all, because a too successful lord could establish an independent center of power (as Henry II had done in the twelfth century and as the Valois dukes of Burgundy were to do in the fifteenth), and, second, because the usual way of gaining more land and power was through war and violence. It was the king's duty to do justice and to keep the peace; a king who could not do this would soon cease to be anything more than a figurehead. Private war was not always and everywhere illegal (though Philip tried to make it so, especially in periods of emergency, such as 1296, 1304, and 1314);[13] the surest way to prevent it was for the royal courts to settle disputes that might lead to war. Finally, since the king and his advisers thought of sovereignty in judicial terms—the king's *superioritas* was demonstrated by his right to make final decisions in all cases —it was important to demonstrate that even the greatest men of the realm had to accept the judgements of his Court. Only rarely was a great lord involved in a criminal case, either personally or by way of appeal from his judgement, while in civil cases lay and ecclesiastical seigneurs were frequently impleaded directly or brought to the king's Court to argue appeals from their judgements.

As in criminal cases, there was a distinction between low justice, which gave cognizance of suits for chattels, small debts, and the like, and high justice, which dealt with cases of "eritage." "Eritage" meant possession of land and of rights that produced permanent revenues, such as courts of justice, tolls and market rights, mills (and the power to compel everyone in a given district to use a mill), the right to name the priest of a parish church or to "guard" a monastery. Decisions in such cases could affect the fortune of a family for many generations; they had to be made carefully, slowly, and with great formality. The number of lay lords who could hear pleas of "eritage" was necessarily smaller than the number of lords who had rights of high justice in criminal cases, since no man could be judge in his own case. A lord who had extensive lands and rights over peasants but had

---

[13] *Olim*, II, 405; *Ord.*, I, 390, 538. See also Perrot, *Cas royaux*, p. 155, and note 7 above.

no vassals would never hear a plea of "eritage." If his rights, including his right of high justice were challenged, his suit would go to the court of a superior lord. Thus, to take a case that illustrates several other points as well, when Guillaume le Bouteiller wanted to prove that he had high justice at Lorris, he had to sue in the lay court of his lord, the bishop of Orléans. This court denied his claim, but on appeal to the Parlement his right to justice was recognized.[14]

Ecclesiastical courts, on the other hand, could come very close to deciding matters of "eritage," though they were not supposed to do so. They had exclusive jurisdiction in cases dealing with marriage and wills and concurrent jurisdiction over those contracts authenticated by the seal of the official of a diocese. (Letters sealed by a royal court, for example, the Châtelet, or by the keeper of a *bailliage* seal were judged by the king's men.) To declare a marriage invalid might disinherit a man who thought he was the rightful heir; to uphold a will that made excessively large pious donations might ruin an inheritance. The will of Philip the Fair was attacked and modified precisely for this reason.[15] Ill-considered contracts could, of course, have the same effect. In any case, most French prelates had a lay court with lay members and officials, and in such a court they could try cases of "eritage" (as the bishop of Orléans did in the case cited above) and cases of high criminal justice.

Overall, however, the number of courts that could try important civil cases was smaller than the number that could try capital crimes. Because the procedure in civil suits demanded many formalities and technical skill on the part of the judges, some lords who could have heard these cases allowed them to go directly to higher jurisdictions. This saved them time, expense, and the danger of being reversed on appeal. It was also true that the rule of "prévention" applied in many civil suits and especially in cases of novel disseisin.[16] Whichever court was first approached had jurisdiction, and any well-advised suitor would prefer a royal (or, in the great fiefs, a ducal) court staffed by experienced and often professionally trained judges to a court held by a minor

---

[14] *Olim*, III, 177 (1306).

[15] A.N., J 403, nos. 20, 20 ter, JJ 52, fol. 25, no. 47. I must thank Professor Elizabeth A. R. Brown for calling my attention to these documents.

[16] Perrot, *Cas royaux*, pp. 190-99. See Bernard Guenée, *Tribunaux et gens de justice dans le bailliage de Senlis (1380-1450)* (Paris, 1963), pp. 120-22, for the further development of this rule in the fourteenth century.

baron, which might commit reversible errors. The king himself made this distinction; his lesser judges, such as *prévôts* and viscounts, could not try cases of "eritage." The result was that, outside of the great fiefs, justice in important civil cases was more and more concentrated in the higher royal courts—in the assizes of the *baillis* and seneschals, the Exchequer of Normandy, the Grands Jours of Champagne, and, above all, in the Parlement of Paris.

Within this general tendency toward concentration there were important regional variations. In Normandy the *baillis* sent their most difficult cases to the Exchequer;[17] the Exchequer, held by a group of Masters of the Parlement, made the final rulings. There was no real appeal from the Exchequer to the Parlement (though a few cases touching the king were sent to Paris for decision),[18] and so the Parlement had little to do with Norman justice. The Grands Jours of Champagne were not in as strong a position as the Exchequer; more cases floated back and forth between the Parlement and the Jours, and by the end of Philip's reign there were regular appeals from the Jours to Paris.[19] Nevertheless, the Parlement did not spend much time on the problems of Champagne. There may have been some idea of establishing a body like the Exchequer or the Jours of Champagne for the region of written law. In 1280, 1282, 1287, and 1289-1291 a delegation from the Parlement sat in Toulouse,[20] but the experiment was abandoned, partly, perhaps, because of the coming of the war with England, but more likely because the Parlement of Toulouse had no real roots. The Exchequer was a venerable institution, the Jours went back to the days of Thibaud IV; but no similar court had ever existed in Languedoc. Nevertheless, the failure to establish a branch of the Parlement in Toulouse did not mean that many cases went from the south to Paris in the first instance. A very rough count shows that although there were hundreds of cases of this sort in the Parlement from Paris and the region

---

[17] E. Perrot, ed., *Arresta communia Scacarii* (Caen, 1910), nos. 103, 136 (in 1293 and 1294).

[18] Joseph R. Strayer, "Exchequer and Parlement under Philip the Fair," in *Droit privé et institutions régionales. Etudes historiques offertes à Jean Yver* (Rouen, 1976), pp. 655-62.

[19] John F. Benton, "Philip the Fair and the *Jours* of Troyes," *Studies in Medieval and Renaissance History*, VI (1969), 292-96.

[20] *H.L.*, IX, 72, 129, 159, X, cols. 209-19, 257, 272; Langlois, ed., *Textes*, pp. 108, 153, 155, 159; Baudouin, ed., *Lettres inédites, annexes*, nos. 3, 7, 10-13, 16, 17.

around Paris during the 29 years of Philip's reign, there were only about 45 from Languedoc. Distance doubtless had something to do with this failure to seek the High Court, but distance was not the only reason; there were only about 70 cases from the nearby *bailliages* of Orléans, Tours, and Sens, and only about 20 from Berry. Difference in the rules of law was surely more important, but again this cannot have been a controlling factor. The customs of Orléans were not very different from the customs of Paris, yet few men of Orléans went to the Parlement, while many men of Laon did, even though the custom of Laon was less like the custom of Paris. It seems possible that the men of Languedoc were reasonably well satisfied with their local judges, royal and seigneurial. Most of these judges were professionals, trained in the southern schools of law. What was to be gained by going before less expert men in Paris? True, there was, at least from 1296, a special section of the Parlement to hear the preliminary pleas of the men of the region of written law, but, as the Parlement lists of 1296 and 1307 show, this section was not staffed by southern lawyers. On the other hand, although the suitors of Languedoc had no great desire to plead in the Parlement in the first instance—and secured a grant from Louis X in 1315 to prevent such suits[21]—they were very ready to appeal from decisions of their local judges. The right of appeal was an essential part of the written law, and appeals were lodged in many apparently simple cases. Most of these appeals were purely tactical, but a number were pushed through to the end. Next to Paris itself, where appeal was very easy (especially from sentences of the Châtelet), the largest number of appeals (83) came from Languedoc. There were about 100 appeals from Paris, and about 150 from Paris and the northeastern *bailliages* combined.

The control of the king and the central government over the administration of justice by the barons and prelates of the realm was very spotty. It was practically nonexistent in the great fiefs, even by way of appeal. For example, only about 10 cases from either Burgundy or Brittany reached the Parlement during the entire reign, and most of these concerned bishops and religious communities. Philip could collect taxes in these principalities, even if he had to share them with the lord, but he did not have even a share in the administration of justice. As might be expected, there were more cases in the Parlement from Flanders and Aqui

21 *H.L.*, x, col. 540.

taine—but not many more, about 20 for the first and about 38 for the second. It should be pointed out, however, that almost all the cases concerning Flanders and Aquitaine came in the years just before the wars in these provinces. The king was using his courts to assert his supremacy and, in Flanders at least, to protect the pro-French party. For the period following the peace of Athis, I have found only one Flemish case in the *Olim*.[22] There was a small flurry of Gascon cases from 1311 to 1313; this may have been connected with the "process of Périgueux" (1311), in which the English were complaining of French encroachments in Aquitaine.[23] Yves de Loudéac, who had been an *enquêteur* in Gascony, was also one of the French commissioners at Périgueux, and most of the cases that reached the Parlement concerned his acts or those of the French seneschal of Périgord.[24] There had also been a private war between officers of the duchy, their adherents, and Amanieu d'Albret, which gave Yves an excuse for levying heavy fines. By 1313, however, the Flemish problem was becoming dangerous again, and Philip wanted to preserve his alliance with England. He forgave amercements, revoked summonses and banishments, and quashed appeals in 27 cases in which his *enquêteurs* and seneschals had moved against Edward's subjects.[25] Nevertheless, enough cases had reached the Parlement to remind Edward that he was subject to Philip's justice and that French courts could cause him a good many problems, especially in the border areas of the duchy.

This was about all that Philip wanted. It was well to impress a great baron with the supremacy of royal justice, but it was folly to push these assertions of supremacy to a point where they might lead to revolt. Royal officials might begin actions against or hear appeals from lords with high justice, but not all these cases were pushed to a conclusion. Even when a final judgement was made, it was not always enforced. As was pointed out above, Philip forgave Edward and his subjects many of the amercements imposed by the *enquêteurs*. In a similar case the count of Foix

[22] *Olim*, III, 352.

[23] George Cuttino, *English Diplomatic Administration 1259-1339*, 2d ed. (Oxford, 1971), pp. 87-100.

[24] Boutaric, ed., *Actes du Parlement*, nos. 4079, 4133-35, 4160; *Olim*, III, 624, 716, 780, 794-95, 807, 814, 905, 908.

[25] A.N., JJ 49, nos. 50-55, 82-88, 90, 95-99, 103, 105-11 (summarized in Fawtier et al., eds., *Registres*, nos. 1970-75, 2002-8, 2011, 2016-20, 2024, 2026-32). See also *Olim*, III, 814. For the Albret affair see A.N., JJ 49, fol. 49, no. 115; by Philip's arbitration, Edward was to pay 20,000 l.t.

was fined 30,000 l.t. for attacking the count of Armagnac; little by little the sum was reduced until it was canceled by the surrender of a rent of 551 l.t. (worth about 5,511 l.t. as capital values were then estimated).[26] Both Edward and the count remained loyal for the rest of the reign, which was what Philip most desired. Both kept their rights of justice almost completely unimpaired, as did other lords in similar circumstances.

It is true that in the south there were ecclesiastical lords who were sufficiently bothered by pressures from royal officials to accept *paréages*, agreements that created common courts in which the judges were appointed jointly by the king and the bishop or abbot. Very few lay lords, and none of any importance, accepted such an arrangement. Bishops, however, were often harassed by their lay vassals and were glad to get royal protection (as in the case of Mende).[27] All the *paréages* put together, however, did not greatly increase the area subject to direct royal jurisdiction.

Nevertheless, more lawsuits were going to the king's courts in the early fourteenth century than ever before. This was owing, in part, to the fact that there were more lawsuits in all courts; litigation was an increasingly popular substitute for combat. The king, however, was getting more than his share of the increase. Appeals and investigations by *enquêteurs* accounted for only a small fraction of the increase; not many cases were diverted from baronial courts by these procedures. The zeal of the newly installed procurators accounted for another, and perhaps larger percentage. These men, who often acted as prosecuting attorneys, uncovered many acts that affected the king's rights and that would not have been noticed before. However, the most important reasons for the increase in the business of the royal courts were, first, that they were staffed by more competent and more experienced men than those to be found in many baronial courts (Aquitaine and Burgundy would have to be excluded from this generalization), and, second, that they could enforce their orders more effectively. There were, of course, long delays between judgements and their implementation, but at least the king's courts did not forget their judgements or tolerate persistent refusal to obey them. Thus when there was a choice of jurisdic-

[26] *Olim*, III, 381-87; *H.L.*, x, col. 498.
[27] Joseph R. Strayer, "La noblesse du Gévaudan et le paréage de 1307," *Revue du Gévaudan*, n.s., XIII (1967), 66-71.

tions (as in the case of disseisin), there would be a tendency to go to a king's court. This is not to say that the royal courts were models of justice and equity. At the lowest level, that of the petty courts held by *prévôts* and *bayles*, there was a considerable amount of corruption, oppression, and, at times, ignorance of the law (especially when the *prévôt* or *bayle* farmed his office). The jurisdiction of these courts was limited; they could not punish nobles, judge civil suits of any importance, or impose large fines (30 s. was often the limit). The vast majority of the king's subjects, however, were not noble and not rich. Peasants could be hanged by many of these courts, and a fine of 30 s. for a man earning 6 d. a day meant the loss of two months' wages. The royal government was aware of these problems, and the *enquêteurs* spent a considerable amount of time hearing complaints against *prévôts* and their sergeants.[28] But the *enquêteurs* came infrequently, and although it was always possible to appeal from the decision of a *prévôt*'s court to the *bailli* or even to the Parlement, not many such cases are recorded. The appeals from *prévôts* that are recorded in the *Olim* came largely from the old domain, for example, from Senlis, Laon, Orléans, Montlhéry, St. Quentin, Compiègne, Pontoise, and Gonesse.[29] This is only a sample; there were many other cases, but still not enough in any one district to put a real check on the *prévôt*. The *prévôts* who had a chance of promotion, such as those of Orléans, were probably anxious to preserve a reputation for honesty. Others were somewhat restrained by the fact that men of the community sat in their courts and expressed community opinion that was not easy to override. The worst excesses were usually committed out of court—maltreating the accused at the time of arrest or in prison, or taking bribes to let them escape. The Norman viscounts had greater financial and fewer judicial responsibilities than the *prévôts*. The *bayles* of the south were less powerful in both regards; none of them would rank with a *prévôt* of Orléans or a viscount of Rouen. Thus in the movement of 1314 the *prévôt* was the royal officer most frequently accused of judicial misconduct.

Above the courts for small people and small cases were the assizes of the *baillis* and the various courts held or supervised by the seneschals. At this level the judges were more competent and

[28] Langlois, "Enquêteurs," pp. 64-65, 70-80.
[29] *Olim*, II, 264, 433, III, 92, 101, 158, 171, 465, 619, 632, 645, 851.

more honest than those of the lower courts. In the north some
of the *baillis* became real legal experts. The most famous example
is Beaumanoir, who had been *bailli* for the count of Clermont,
seneschal of Poitou, and *bailli* of Vermandois, Tours, and Senlis
while writing his great book, the *Coutumes de Beauvaisis*. Renaud
Barbou the elder and Jean de Montigny were *baillis* of long experience who became permanent and prominent members of the
Parlement.[30] The *baillis* who were not such well-regarded lawyers
were carefully supervised. In Normandy appeals from their decisions went to the Exchequer; in Champagne, to the Jours of
Troyes. Elsewhere appeals went directly to the Parlement. As
might be expected, the largest number of appeals came from the
court of the *prévôt* (in effect the *bailli*) of Paris. He had more
people in his jurisdiction than any other *bailli*; many of these
people were engaged in large-scale business operations; appeals
to the *prévôt* from the courts of the many ecclesiastical establishments of the Paris region were frequent, and the losing parties
were often dissatisfied with his decisions; finally, and obviously,
a citizen of Paris could file and prosecute an appeal without having to undertake a long and expensive journey. There were also
a large number of appeals from the *baillis* of the northeast
(Amiens, Vermandois, Senlis). Again, the journey to Paris was
relatively short, but this is not a completely satisfactory explanation. The journey from Orléans or Sens to Paris was no more
difficult than the journey from Amiens or Laon, yet there were
relatively few appeals from the *baillis* of Orléans or Sens and
(here distance was a factor) even fewer from Tours and Bourges.
The primary reason for the difference is that the northeast was
a region of communes, which zealously defended their rights of
justice and administration against royal officials, while there were
relatively few communes in the *bailliages* of Orléans, Tours, and
Bourges. In fact, Philip in 1313 ordered the *bailli* and *prévôt* of
Orléans to see to it that meetings of the citizens of Orléans did
not go beyond the very narrow limits set in his charter, since
they did not have the rights of a "corpus et communiam."[31] Nevertheless, although there were relatively few appeals from the
three *baillis* of the central part of France, they were still numerous
enough to warn these officials that their judgements could be
scrutinized and perhaps reversed by the Parlement.

[30] Langlois, ed., *Textes*, pp. 163, 179; Borrelli de Serres, *Recherches*, II,
329. See below, p. 213.
[31] *Olim*, II, 587.

In the southern provinces the seneschals had less responsibility for the administration of justice than did the *baillis* of the north. There were district judges, who, roughly speaking, did much the same work that was done by a *bailli* as he moved from town to town holding assizes. The seneschal was supposed to hold one assize a year in each district, and he certainly did sit in district courts from time to time, but this was not common.[32] Even in the city of Toulouse there was a district judge, and the *viguier* of Toulouse (unlike other *viguiers*) had a jurisdiction of his own. In every *sénéchaussée* there was a *juge-mage* who could handle most of the cases brought to the seneschal's court. In Toulouse there was even a judge of appeals (and by the 1320s an additional judge of criminal appeals). This is not to say that the seneschals never acted as judges; but when they did, they were usually careful to surround themselves with lesser judges and other men learned in the written law of the south. The result was that, although there were a considerable number of appeals from the administrative actions of the seneschals, there were relatively few from their judicial decisions.[33]

It was a basic principle of the French government that there should be only two appeals before a case went to the Parlement. This rule was adopted to keep lords with high justice from multiplying appellate courts and thus discouraging their subjects from seeking relief in royal courts. The same principle, however, was regularly applied to the courts of *bailliages* and *sénéchaussées*. It caused no particular problem in the north, where the usual sequence was *prévôt* (or agent of a lord or community with high justice) to the *bailli* to the Parlement. But in the south it meant that a seneschal might be bypassed entirely. Thus appeals could go directly from a *juge-mage* or (in Toulouse) the judge of appeals to the Parlement.[34] On the other hand, the law of the south

---

[32] The seneschal of Toulouse was required to hold assizes in each *judicatura* (A.N., J 329, no. 43); the seneschal of Beaucaire held an assize at Alès in 1302 (*H.L.*, x, col. 390); the seneschal of Rouergue held assizes at Villefranche in 1296 and at Peyrusse in 1299 (A.D. Aveyron, G 575, G 639). In most cases the seneschal could be represented by his lieutenant.

[33] On this paragraph see my *Gens de justice*.

[34] See *Olim*, III, for an appeal from the judge of appeals by the royal procurator (p. 70), an appeal from a *juge-mage* (p. 725), an appeal from a district judge to the judge of appeals to the Parlement (p. 146), and an appeal from the *viguier* of Toulouse to the judge of appeals to the Parlement (p. 348). See Boutaric, ed., *Actes du Parlement*, II, no. 4158, for an appeal from the count of Armagnac to the judge of appeals to the Parlement.

allowed the king's procurator to appeal to Parlement from the sentence of a seneschal on the grounds that it was insufficient or unfounded, so there was some danger that what a seneschal gained by making his judges responsible for appeals, he might lose through the zeal of a procurator.[35] In Philip's day, however, an appeal by a procurator was not very common, so that, on the whole, the statement made above is valid; the seneschals were less troubled by appeals to the Parlement than were the *baillis*.

In most cases the Parlement approved the decisions of the seneschals and *baillis*, and on the record as it stands, it would be difficult to prove that these judgements were wrong. There were enough reversals, however, so that one cannot say that the Parlement would uphold any act of the lower courts. A large number of cases raised problems that had never been adjudicated before, especially cases that arose from Philip's ordinances forbidding private war, the use of foreign coins, or the export of precious metals, or cases involving the readjustment of leases and contracts after "good money" had been restored in 1306. For others there were numerous precedents, but the precedents were not very clear—for example, the exact boundaries, both geographical and legal, between the king's rights of justice and those of a secular lord or a religious community. It was the duty of the *baillis* and seneschals to enforce the king's ordinances and to protect the king's rights, not to question royal orders or to abandon even a tenuous claim to lands or jurisdictions. Royal officials must have been overwhelmed at times by the number of controversies that had to be decided and by the number of people who could show some sort of right to a given piece of property. Certainly they had a tendency to favor the king in their judgements, but the king usually had about as good a case as his opponents. And it should be remembered that in many cases the king's interests were not even indirectly involved, for example, in suits between two religious houses for possession of lands or profitable rights. Some of the *baillis* and seneschals were not very expert in the law, though they usually had men skilled in the law to advise them —the regular attendants at the assizes in the north, and the *iuris-periti* (judges and procurators) who were present in all the south-

---

[35] See *Olim*, III, 47-48, 63-64, 330, 509, for appeals by a royal procurator against the judgement of a seneschal (in the first three cases the losing party also appealed). For a rare example of an appeal (unsuccessful) by a royal procurator against a *bailli* (of Sens), see ibid., p. 804.

ern courts.[36] The more common source of error, however, was not ignorance of the law but failure to obtain all the facts in the case. *Baillis* and seneschals (and the seneschals' judges) were all busy men; they might make a hurried judgement because the case seemed clear or because they had been deceived by false documents.

Deliberate perversion of justice, however, was not common. The case of Hugues de Filaines, *bailli* of Amiens, is almost unique. Hugues certainly took a bribe on one occasion and abused his power on others; he was fined and barred forever from office.[37] Guillaume de Mussy, *bailli* of Troyes, was amerced heavily for violence to a priory, and perhaps other misdeeds, but he later served as an *enquêteur*.[38] At a lower level, the southern judges did not have a spotless record. Pierre Peitavi, *juge-mage* of Carcassonne, was demoted and later fined 5,000 l.t.; a judge of Marvéjols was removed from office; and a judge of Villeneuve was fined 100 l.t. for arresting and torturing a clerk.[39] The most spectacular case was that of Pierre Roque (or Roche), judge of Limoux and then of the Minervois (1305-1310). Condemned by the *enquêteurs* in 1310, he was pardoned by Philip in 1314, and was even ennobled for his good services in 1317. His enemies did not forget him, however; in 1318 a new *enquête* was opened, and Pierre was executed. His forfeited goods were sold for the enormous sum of 11,000 l.t.;[40] such wealth certainly suggests corruption.

Doubtless there were other cases of judicial corruption that have not been preserved in the records. Doubtless also, the more subtle forms of corruption—family connections, pressure from great men, desire to curry favor with highly placed officials in Paris—would have left no trace even if the records were more abundant. It is remarkable, however, that neither in the acts of

---

[36] For Normandy see my *Administration of Normandy*, pp. 21-22, 104, and Perrot, ed., *Arresta communia Scacarii*, nos. 71, 151; for the south, my *Gens de justice*, pp. 30-31.

[37] *Olim*, III, 579, 635, 669.

[38] On this *bailli* see R. H. Bautier, "Guillaume de Mussy," *Bibliothèque de l'Ecole des Chartes*, CV (1944), 64-98; *Olim*, II, 337; *C.R.*, II, nos. 15346-47; and A.N., JJ 38, no. 134. He was certainly unscrupulous in his private affairs and probably harsh in enforcing royal rights, but the evidence does not prove that he took bribes.

[39] Strayer, *Gens de justice*, p. 26.

[40] Ibid., pp. 116, 118-19. Note that Pierre was connected by marriage with the demoted *juge-mage* Pierre Peitavi.

the *enquêteurs* nor in the protests of 1314-1315 is there much talk of miscarriage of justice. Abuse of administrative, not judicial, authority is the chief subject of complaint. Sergeants and *prévôts*, not *baillis*, seneschals, and their judges, are the royal officials most frequently attacked. A study of the hundreds of appeals from provincial courts to the Parlement leaves the same impression. Sergeants were ruthless and violent; royal procurators were overzealous in asserting the king's rights; *baillis* and seneschals were not always careful to observe the elaborate rules about proper procedure in making *enquêtes*. Hardly ever is there a suggestion in these appeals that the errors were due to corruption.

The provincial courts were reasonably honest, but somewhat impatient with legal niceties. The High Court of Parlement, the king's own court, was even more free of corruption. It seldom, if ever, gave judgements that were patently unfair, and it improved its procedures steadily throughout the reign of Philip the Fair. The integrity and skill of the Parlement is especially remarkable when one considers the shifting membership of the Court. The Parlement was still a committee of the *curia*, and the king could change the membership of this committee whenever he wished. It is easy to say who was *bailli* of Rouen or seneschal of Toulouse in any year of Philip's reign; it would be very difficult to name all the men who worked in the Parlement of any year. Official lists exist for three years—1286 (partial), 1296, 1307 or early 1308[41]—but it would be a great mistake to assume that each man on the list actually sat in the Parlement, or, even if he did, that he was present at all the meetings. The official lists of 1296 and of 1307-1308 can be compared with the Treasury records of wages paid for service in the Parlement and with the occasional entires in the *Olim* that give the names of those present at a judgement. Neither source is completely satisfactory; a great lord of the Council did not draw wages as did a simple king's knight or king's clerk, and the scribes who recorded the names of judges could easily have omitted some of the less important people. Nevertheless, the discrepancies are startling. The existing fragment of the Journal of the Treasury begins in 1298

---

41 Langlois, ed., *Textes*, pp. 129, 162-64, 178-80. Langlois was not sure of the date of the last list; my reasons for accepting 1307–early 1308 are given above, Chapter II, "Policy Makers and Technicians," note 58. He had some reservations about dating the second list in 1296, but it is so different from the 1298 list given in *Olim*, II, 422, that it must be earlier, and 1296 is the traditional date.

and records several payments for 1296-1297; one would expect a considerable similarity between the names in the list of 1296 and the names of those paid for service in the Parlement during the next four years. There is none. There is also a list of 38 men present at a judgement in 1298;[42] again there is little agreement between this list and that of 1296. More than half of the people named by Philip in 1296 do not appear in records concerning the Parlements of 1297-1301, even though the king said that they were to be "resident au Parlement continuement." Conversely, some important new names are found (for example, Guillaume de Nogaret) and also those of men who, although never prominent, worked for the Parlement for many years (for example, Master Clément de Savy, 1295-1299, 1301, 1302, and Pierre de Blanot, knight, 1299-1307).[43] The king in the early years of his reign did not expect assignments to the Parlement to be permanent. Thus in 1291 he named three persons to hear "requests" (that is, to accept cases for judgement) and four to hear cases concerning the written law of the south, but both sets of appointments were "ad presens," that is, temporary.[44] By 1307, however, there was a little more stability. The men named on the list of that year appear fairly regularly in the accounts and other documents as working in the Parlement, and this stability increases in the reigns of Philip's sons.

Even when a man is known to have served in a Parlement, it is often true that he did very little work. Here again the Treasury record of wages is instructive. In the Parlement of All Saints 1299 (extending into 1300), Pierre de Blanot, who had been very active earlier, was paid for only 9 days, while Jean le Duc and Jean de la Forêt were each paid for 128 days. Clément de Savy, with 110 days, and Pierre de Latilly, with 120, were not far behind, but Raoul de Breuilly, with only 99 days, may have missed some important cases.[45] There can be no question of trying to freeze out less capable men; these were all well-known members of the

---

[42] Langlois, ed., *Textes*, p. 169 (also in *Olim*, II, 422). This is probably a fairly complete list, as opposed to the one of 1290 (p. 150), which gives eight names and then says, "et alii de consilio regis usque ad sexaginta et plus."

[43] For Clément see *J.T.P.*, nos. 2377, 4469, *Olim*, II, 410, *C.R.*, I, nos. 1427, 1466, Boutaric, ed., *Actes du Parlement*, I, no. 2884G, and Langlois, ed., *Textes*, pp. 169, 170, 202, 216. For Pierre, a knight of the Council, see *J.T.P.*, nos. 4877, 5976, and Langlois, ed., *Textes*, p. 179.

[44] Langlois, ed., *Textes*, pp. 156-57.

[45] *J.T.P.*, nos. 4088, 4457, 4469, 4529, 4541.

Council and continued for many years in the king's service. Simply, as members of the Council they could be and were called on for many other duties. They were not confined exclusively to judicial work, any more than was a *bailli*, or a seneschal.

Fluctuations in personnel might have been expected to cause some inconsistencies in deciding cases, but there are no convincing examples of such inconsistencies. One could probably find more in the record of the United States Supreme Court over a 30-year period. One might also have expected that improvements in the organization and in the procedures of the Parlement would have been slow; instead, Philip's reign saw some important and useful changes. What factors ensured continuity in an organization that included so many part-time workers and that had no clearly defined leadership?

Philip himself may deserve some credit for this result. After all, the Parlement was *his* Court, staffed by his men. The king himself might attend the Court, though he seldom did so.[46] He might also send orders to the Court, telling it to quash a grant improvidently made or to reopen a case already decided.[47] Such direct intervention, however, was rare. The king seems to have been satisfied with the decisions made by the Parlement; he did not try to overturn rulings that reduced his income or his jurisdiction. In the same spirit, he issued ordinances that improved the structure and clarified the procedures of the Parlement, but that, at the same time, tended to make it a continuing and semiautonomous body.[48] These ordinances were logical developments of trends that had begun in the time of St. Louis and Philip III, and they were probably drafted by members of the Council who had had long experience in the Parlement. Nevertheless, nothing compelled Philip to be logical or to accept proposals made by his subordinates. If the Parlement became better organized, it was because Philip saw the need for better organization. He wanted his Court to be accepted as the supreme administrative authority in France. It was easier to attain this goal if the Parlement was consistent in its decisions, if its staff became more professional in outlook, and if its procedures could be clearly understood. The Parlement was a more effective body in 1314 than it was in 1285, and Philip had certainly encouraged this development.

Philip, however, could only give general direction to the Parle-

---

[46] Langlois, ed., *Textes*, p. 150; *Olim*, II, 301, 485, 614, III, 610.
[47] *Olim*, II, 547, 597.
[48] Langlois, ed., *Textes*, pp. 156, 161, 178, 183.

ment through his appointments and ordinance. The Court learned a great deal through experience. As the number of cases that it heard increased, its decisions became more refined. Part of this improvement may be only apparent, since cases were better reported after 1299 (when a new *greffier* took office), but better reporting was in itself a refinement. The Parlement had long been learning from experience; it had its own traditions and its own records (the *Olim*) going back to the days of St. Louis. The *greffier*, who preserved these records, was a permanent official, and each *greffier* trained his successor. Thus Jean de Montluçon (1254-1273) was followed by his assistant, Nicolas de Chartres (1273-1299), and Nicolas by his assistant, Pierre de Bourges (1299-1318).[49] There was a notable increase in the quality and quantity of the records kept by these men as time went on. Pierre de Bourges, especially, was a master of the art of summing up the facts in a case and the reasons for a judgement. The Parlement was not bound by precedents, but it tended to follow them (at least in spirit), and precedents were easily available in the *Olim*. Thus the *greffiers* supplied a strong element of continuity.

The king also appointed leading members of his Council to direct the work of the Parlement. This was necessary because the Court could hear cases concerning prelates and barons, and its decisions could have been challenged if men of their rank had not been present. At least two of these *presidents* or *souverains* (one bishop and one baron) were supposed to be present whenever a judgement was made. This rule may not have been strictly enforced, but these men sat in the Parlement often enough to prevent any wide swings in jurisprudence or in procedure.

On the other hand, the *presidents* were occupied with many other tasks and could not have paid much attention to unimportant cases or to checking details of procedure. The most complete list of *presidents* is that of 1296. It includes Gilles Aicelin, archbishop of Narbonne, Simon Matifas, bishop of Paris, Jacques de Boulogne, bishop of Thérouanne, the duke of Burgundy, the count of Saint-Pol, and the Constable (Raoul de Clermont). The last two held military commands and cannot have attended many sessions in time of war. The duke of Burgundy had to look afer the affairs of his duchy, but he was present at a reasonable number of meetings of the Parlement.[50] The prelates should have had

---

[49] On the *greffiers* see Grün's excellent account in Boutaric, ed., *Actes du Parlement*, I, lxv-lxxxii, and Ducoudray, I, 239-43.

[50] Langlois, ed., *Textes*, pp. 107 (1280), 118 (1281), 150 (1290).

a better record, but Jacques de Boulogne had been in the Parlement at least as early as 1278, and Simon Matifas had never been very active in governmental affairs. They were both old men (Jacques died in 1301 and Simon in 1304) and left little trace of their work in the records.⁵¹ Gilles Aicelin was certainly the most influential member of the group and probably the best lawyer, but precisely because he was an intimate adviser of the king, concerned with policy decisions and with diplomacy, he cannot have had much time for his work as a judge. His sense of equity may have helped to set the tone of the Parlement, but it is difficult to see how he could have attended to developing refinements in procedure or to solving difficult questions of law.

The ordinance of 1307 suggests that the *presidents* had not been very effective in providing leadership for the Parlement. In 1296 they had held the power to assign men to various tasks—to view inquests, to hear requests, to deal with cases coming from the region of written law, or to sit in the Chamber of Pleas. They were also to determine cases in which there was a division of opinion among the judges of the Chamber of Pleas.⁵² In 1307 the king, in his ordinance on the Parlement, appointed the members of each chamber, and nothing was said of the procedure to be followed if the judges did not agree. In fact, the word *president* was not used, although Gilles Aicelin, the bishop of Rennes, the count of Dreux, and the count of Boulogne were named as the prelates and barons who were to be present in the Parlement. These men, and especially Gilles Aicelin, had an honored position, but they did not control the Court.

The shift in emphasis is probably owing to two developments that will be discussed below: first, service in the Parlement was becoming more and more a full-time occupation; second, the division of the Court into three chambers, more or less an ad hoc affair in 1296, was becoming institutionalized by 1307. A continuing body, in which each man had specific duties, needed less direction from the *presidents* than the more loosely organized Court of 1296.

---

⁵¹ For Jacques see ibid., pp. 102 (1278), 123 (1285), 129 (1286), and *Olim*, II, 301 (1290), 423 (1299). Simon Matifas had done little work for the king, but he belonged to an important family of Champagne, where he was archdeacon of Reims and had served in the Jours of Troyes in 1286 and 1289; see Benton, "Philip the Fair and the *Jours* of Troyes," pp. 331, 333. As bishop of Pairs he took part in judgements of the Parlement in 1290 (Langlois, ed., *Textes*, pp. 149-50).

⁵² Langlois, ed., *Textes*, pp. 162, 164.

The real leadership of the Parlement in Philip's reign can probably be found in the level just below that of the *presidents*, among men who had had long experience in the Parlement and who were primarily, if not exclusively, judges. Renaud Barbou, *bailli* of Rouen (1275-1286), is a good example of this group. He had attended the Parlements of Philip III at least since 1278 and was even more prominent under Philip the Fair. In 1296 he was the one who pronounced the judgements of the Court. He also drew an annual salary of 600 l.p., unlike his colleagues, who were paid by the day.[53] Jean le Duc, canon of St. Quentin, had an equally long career, from 1286 to at least 1311; he is the only man who appears in every official list.[54] Jean de Montigny (another ex-*bailli*), who pronounced the judgements of the Court in the absence of Renaud Barbou, was also a permanent member of the Court from 1296 to his death in 1307.[55]

In must be said, however, that a number of very competent men with legal experience were not used as much in the Parlement as they might have been because the king needed them for other work. Pierre de Belleperche, for example, who was probably the most eminent lawyer in the Parlement, could sit there only occasionally because he was sent on many missions abroad.[56] Nogaret and Plaisians, both former *juges-mages*, were busy with the work of the Council. Denis, dean of Sens, and Jean d'Auxois, cantor of Orléans, both worked in the Parlement for many years (ca. 1298-1316, and 1296 to at least 1309), but both were kept busy in collecting adhesions to the appeal against Boniface and in acting as *enquêteurs* or negotiators. Denis had a high reputation as a lawyer, but he had little time for the Parlement.[57] A much less prominent man, but one who sat in many sessions of the Parlement from 1295 to 1302, Clément de Savy was often

[53] Ibid., pp. 97, 102, 107, 111, 112, 114, 123, 149, 163 (he is to pronounce the judgements), 220, 226; Funck-Brentano, *Philippe le Bel en Flandre*, p. 122, n. 4.

[54] *J.T.P.*, nos. 2324, 4529; Langlois, ed., *Textes*, pp. 156, 163, 178; *Olim*, II, 356, III, 610; *C.R.*, II, nos. 20509, 20578; A.N., K 36, no. 21, J 178B, no. 51; B.N., ms. lat. 17658, fol. 7.

[55] Langlois, ed., *Textes*, pp. 163, 179; *Olim*, II, 397, III, 49, 126-27; Borrelli de Serres, *Recherches*, II, 329; *C.R.*, I, no. 6612 (he bought seals for the Parlement in 1305); B.N., ms. fr. 20685, fol. 14.

[56] For his service in the Parlement see Langlois, ed., *Textes*, pp. 163, 169, and *Olim*, III, 126. His missions to England, Flanders, the pope, and Lyon are summed up in *Hist. litt.*, xxv, 357-58; see also Perrichet, p. 524.

[57] For Denis and Jean see the Appendix to Chapter IV, notes 25 and 47. *Gallia Christiana*, XIII, col. 111, praises Denis as skilled in law.

used as a collector of subsidies.[58] One source of distraction was removed when it was ruled in 1303 that *baillis* and seneschals could not be members of the Council (and hence of the Parlement) while they held their provincial offices.[59] Renaud Barbou and Jean de Montigny were the last *baillis* to play prominent roles in the Parlement, and both of them gave up their *bailliages* as their parlementary duties became heavier. Nevertheless, even with this reform, there was less concentration on parlementary duties than there should have been or than there was in later reigns.

This weakness was repaired, to some extent, by the existence of a group of *rapporteurs*, men who examined and summarized inquests for decisions by the judges.[60] They were less distracted by other duties, and they served for many years, often rising to higher positions in the Court. The career pattern is much the same for many of them—early experience as a collector of tenths and subventions (an experience that certainly demonstrated devotion to the king), then service as a *rapporteur*, and final promotion to a judgeship in the Chambre des Enquêtes. Jean de Roye, for example, collected a tenth in 1299 and a subvention in 1304. From 1306 through 1315 he was very busy as a *rapporteur*; in 1309 he reported on 15 cases. He became a canon of St. Quentin, and by 1316 he was a judge in the Chambre des Enquêtes. He held this position until 1325.[61]

Pierre de Monci moved ahead more rapidly than did Jean de Roye, partly because he had entered royal service a little earlier, partly because he seems to have been very successful as a collector of extraordinary revenues, always a sure way to the king's favor. (It was also a way of learning a great deal about local conditions in many provinces, knowledge that could be very useful in examining evidence from *enquêtes*.) In the period 1297-1299 he collected annates and a double tenth in parts of the province of Reims, in 1301 he imposed a subsidy in the *bailliage* of Bourges, and in 1304 he imposed the subsidy in the *bailliage* of Rouen. At the end of the reign he worked again on extraordinary revenues;

---

[58] For Clément's service in the Parlement see above, note 43. During that period, however, he collected subsidies and annates and was sent on a mission to England; see Mignon, nos. 1175, 1274, and *J.T.P.*, nos. 811, 2332.

[59] *Ord.*, I, 321, 360.

[60] On the *rapporteurs* see Guilhiermoz, pp. 140, 161, and below, pp. 219, 221-22.

[61] *J.T.P.*, no. 2045; A.N., JJ 36, fol. 71v; *Olim*, III, 277, 280, 285, 290, 293-94, 307, 314, 321, 324, 345, 347, 355, 375, 376; Boutaric, ed., *Actes du Parlement*, II, 143, 147; Lehugeur, II, 195-96; *J.T.C.*, nos. 231, 8466.

he was chief collector of the tenth of 1313-1317 in the province of Bordeaux and helped to impose the ill-fated subsidy of 1314 in Touraine and Saintonge-Poitou.[62] He was viewing inquests for the Parlement by 1300 and was especially busy on this work in 1306 and 1307. In the latter year he was paid for 164 days of service. Soon after this date (perhaps early in 1308) he became a judge of the Chambre des Enquêtes, a post he held until 1318.[63] He was also employed as an *enquêteur* in Rouergue in 1297 and in Vermandois in 1315 or 1316. He was a member of an embassy to England in 1301 and of a mission to Germany in 1299 and again in 1309; he was sent "ad remota" on secret business in 1305.[64] In view of all these responsibilities, it is surprising that he did not rise higher in the Church. Philip nominated him as canon of Angers in 1305, and that was all.[65]

The career of Master Raoul de Meulan barely fits into the standard pattern, since he was so busy with his duties as a collector from 1295 to 1303 that it is hard to see how he had time to learn much about the workings of the Parlement. He helped to obtain loans for the Gascon war in Senlis and Amiens in 1295; he was concerned with the subvention in Caen, the Cotentin, Reims, and Châlons; he was a collector of tenths in the province of Rouen, 1301-1302, and was also responsible for the regalia of Clermont in 1301; and he was one of the men who raised the subvention of 1303 in Paris.[66] After 1303 he was much less involved with financial affairs, though he did collect the tenth of 1307-1308 in Paris and raised money in Vitry and Chaumont for the Flemish campaign of 1315.[67] Even during his early career in the king's service, however, Raoul found some time for work in the Parlement. He was paid for 83 days' service in late 1298 and early 1299, and for 132 days of viewing *enquêtes* from Easter 1299 to All Saints 1299.[68] He may have owed this opportunity to Philippe le Convers (Philippe de Villepreux), with whom he had worked when raising the subvention of Châlons and Reims; at least Phi-

---

[62] Mignon, nos. 484, 726, 1186, 1531, and nos. 858, 1622, 1634.

[63] Langlois, ed., *Textes*, pp. 179, 203; *J.T.P.*, no. 5881; Lehugeur, II, 152, 195-96.

[64] B.N., ms. Doat 176, fol. 217v, Mignon, nos. 2698-99 (as *enquêteur*); *J.T.P.*, nos. 4103, 4863; *C.R.*, I, no. 5945. See Schwalm, "Reichsgeschichte," p. 381, for missions abroad.

[65] Petit et al., p. 149.

[66] Mignon, nos. 1119, 1193; *J.T.P.*, nos. 690, 694, 936; *C.R.*, II, nos. 20915, 20954; B.N., ms. fr. 25992, no. 54.

[67] Mignon, nos. 801, 1670; Fawtier, ed., *Comptes du Trésor*, no. 535.

[68] *J.T.P.*, no. 2618; *C.R.*, I, no. 1573.

lippe's name follows his in the accounts that mention payments for their service in the Parlement, and the two names come in a very odd place (under *opera*), as if someone with influence had had them inserted at the last minute.[69] From 1299 on, Raoul's name appears in the *Olim* from time to time, but not very frequently; the largest number of reports is four in 1306. In 1308 Raoul was paid for viewing *enquêtes* for 122 days;[70] the rest of his time may have been spent in collecting the tenth in Paris. Altogether, it is a little surprising that late in 1307 he was named first in the list of those who were to hear the "Requestes de la langue françoise."[71] Granting that he was a man of wide experience, that he had been an *enquêteur* in Sens and Senlis (and the work of an *enquêteur* also involved hearing "requests" or complaints),[72] and that he had some very capable colleagues, it is still hard to see why he should have been given the delicate task of deciding whether and how suitors should invoke the jurisdiction of the Parlement. Again there is the possibility of influence by Philippe le Convers, who was named to the Grand'Chambre at the same time, but this is a pure guess. In any case, Raoul seems to have given satisfaction; he became a canon of Paris and continued to serve both Louis X and Philip V. He was hearing the *requêtes* as late as 1319.[73]

Finally, there is the sad case of Master Guillaume Boucel, which illustrates the dangers as well as the advantages of continuity. Boucel was in royal service for at least 20 years. He began, as did most of his colleagues, as a collector of extraordinary revenues—in his case, fines for amortization in the *bailliage* of Caen in 1292. Later, in 1299, he visited the dioceses of the province of Reims to check on payments of tenths and annates, and in 1305 he was sent for the same purpose to the dioceses of Bayeaux, Coutances, and Séez.[74] But his real business from 1295 on was viewing inquests; he spent 1,080 days in this work from All Saints 1295 to St. Andrew's 1299. Moreover, his wages were suspended

---

[69] *C.R.*, II, no. 20906 (a joint account of Philippe and Raoul), I, nos. 1573-74.

[70] *Olim*, III, 69 (in 1300); Guilhiermoz, pp. 351, 353, 358 (after 1299), pp. 169, 182, 188, 189 (in 1306); *J.T.P.*, no. 5864.

[71] Langlois, ed., *Textes*, p. 179.

[72] Fawtier, ed., *Comptes du Trésor*, no. 431; Mignon, no. 2652.

[73] Fawtier, ed., *Comptes du Trésor*, no. 831 (142 days in the Parlement of 1314-1315); *J.T.C.*, no. 1382.

[74] Mignon, nos. 1841-42; *C.R.*, I, no. 7748, II, no. 14460 (amortization); *J.T.P.*, no. 3841; *C.R.*, I, nos. 3181-91, 6641-43 (for tenths and annates).

for part of this period (probably while he was working on the tenths in the province of Reims), so that he must have spent over 300 days a year in viewing inquests while he was in Paris.[75] He was not quite so busy thereafter; he was paid for only 208 days in 1301 and for 132 days from All Saints 1306 to 8 September 1308. He may have had other duties, but he was still very active as a *rapporteur* from 1306 to 1310, as a glance at the *Olim* will show. After 1310 Boucel almost disappears—one report in 1312 and one in 1313.[76] Perhaps there were already some doubts about his honesty. Early in 1314 he was accused of taking bribes for revealing the contents of inquests (and perhaps the recommendations of the reporter). Boucel confessed his misdeeds, but the Parlement acted only after consulting the king. Philip was rather lenient. Boucel was barred forever from royal office and was turned over to the official of Paris as a convicted clerk. The official had already seized Boucel's chattels; nothing is said of further punishment.[77]

This story illustrates some of the points that have been made before. Guillaume Boucel, like the other *rapporteurs*, was an expert, well acquainted with the procedures of the Parlement and the attitudes of the judges. He would not have been worth bribing if he could not have advised his clients of the probable results of the inquests that he was revealing. Boucel had served many years without receiving promotion, either in the Parlement or in the Church. Most of his companions had been promoted, though for some reason the king was rather slow to give prebends to the *rapporteurs*. Like the other royal clerks of the Parlement, Boucel was paid only 5 s.p. a day, a respectable income, but not wealth. (Laymen were paid 10 s.p. a day; the difference was supposed to be made up by ecclesiastical benefices.) By 1312 he could have had little hope of preferment, and he may have been in financial difficulties. Even in 1299 he might be suspected of padding his expense account; he collected 751 l. 13 s.p. in the province of Reims but spent 184 l. 15 s.p. for his journey. There were certainly other clerks in the Parlement who were disappointed over

[75] *J.T.P.*, no. 3949; cf. no. 2442.
[76] Ibid., nos. 5658, 5971. See *Olim*, III, 164, 167, 190, 201 (1306); 211, 220, 224 (1307); 249, 251, 253, 262 (1308); 276, 283, 285, 292, 299, 300, 323, 337, 394 (1309); 398, 413, 442, 487 (1310). See also Guilhiermoz, pp. 351-52 (five *enquêtes* given to Boucel, no dates). For 1312 and 1313 see *Olim*, III, 722, 739.
[77] *Olim*, II, 590. Boucel was called "unus de clericis reportatoribus inquestarum et processuum parlamentorum."

their failure to achieve promotion and who were short of money. If the *rapporteurs* were the most professional group in the Parlement, they were also the ones who could be most easily tempted by bribes. There are no other cases like Boucel's, but Philip was expecting a high degree of honesty for five shillings a day.

With all its weaknesses—rather low pay and slow promotion —the Parlement did become a more professional body after 1300. For many members, service in the Parlement was a full-time occupation and almost a lifetime occupation. Careers of 20 years or more were not uncommon. The gradual lengthening of the sessions, until they filled eight or nine months of the year, encouraged both of these developments. A man who was busy most of the year with the affairs of the Parlement had little time for other work, and a man who understood the procedures and the jurisprudence of the Parlement was too valuable to lose. These observations apply, of course, to the routine work of the Parlement, but this was the work that took most of its time. Deciding what cases were to be heard, arranging for inquests, digesting and summarizing the evidence obtained from inquests, charters, pleadings and other sources—all these tasks required technical skill, patience, and concentration on the job at hand. The great men of the Council could not concentrate to this extent. They could and did intervene when it was a question of high policy, the claims of a great lord, or the interpretation of a royal charter. For example, when a grant to the duke of Burgundy apparently conflicted with a royal charter the judges included Charles of Valois, the count of Saint-Pol, Gilles Aicelin, Hugues de la Celle, and Mathew de Trie—and the king himself was present.[78] But such cases were rare; the ordinary affairs of lesser men were left to the professional members of the Parlement. This was especially true when the outcome of a lawsuit depended on an inquest. The rules for making and judging inquests were very detailed and technical; the art of digesting and summarizing the evidence produced by an inquest could be learned only through long experience; and yet far more cases were determined by inquests than by judgements based on charters or oral pleadings. For this reason the *rapporteurs* and the judges of inquests were the key men in developing the procedure and the jurisprudence of the Parlement. In this sense, a man like Pierre de Monci was more important than a Pierre de Belleperche.

[78] Ibid., III, 610. See below, p. 223.

The remoteness of the Parlement from the regions in which many lawsuits originated and the strong influence of canonical procedure led it to rely almost exclusively on written arguments and evidence. This in turn brought about a division of the court into three chambers: Requêtes, Enquêtes, and Grand'Chambre, or Chamber of Pleas. The division began under Philip III, but it was fully implemented only under Philip the Fair. Even in 1296 the chambers of Requêtes and Enquêtes do not seem to be completely organized,[79] but by the end of 1307 they are clearly separate and continuing bodies.[80] The men delegated to the Requêtes heard the arguments of suitors who wanted their cases to be decided by the Parlement and ruled out the ones who could not show probable cause or whose problems seemed too trivial to take up the time of the High Court. (Note that there was a division of the Requêtes into two groups: one heard suits from the region of customary law, the other, suits from the region of written law.) When an inquest into the facts was ordered, as happened more often than not, the report of the men who made the inquest was sent to the Chambre des Enquêtes, sometimes with a broad commission to examine and judge, sometimes with an order to examine first whether it was "in statu judicandi."[81] The Chambre des Enquêtes then turned the inquest over to a *rapporteur*, who was usually an inferior member of the Court, but who, down through 1307, might be someone as important as Nogaret or Raoul Rousselet.[82] The *rapporteur* summarized the inquest and read his summary to the Chamber, which then gave a decision and ordered the *rapporteur* to prepare a final judgement (an *arrêt*). The *arrêt* was sent to the Grand'Chambre, which endorsed it and thus gave it the effect of a final judgement.

It might seem that the Grand'Chambre was merely a rubber

---

[79] Those who worked on the *enquêtes* were chosen ad hoc at each session (Guilhiermoz, pp. 158-59; Langlois, ed., *Textes*, pp. 161 ff., esp. paras. 4, 28, and 30).

[80] Langlois, ed., *Textes*, pp. 178-79, 218-19 (the latter is a document of 1343 that assumes the existence of the three chambers under Philip the Fair). In *Olim*, II, 262, there is specific mention of the masters of the "camera inquestarum," 14 January 1308. Note that the *Requêtes du palais* (of Parlement) were not *Requêtes de l'hôtel* (petitions addressed to the king). The latter were not formally organized in Philip's day; see Guillois, pp. 30-44.

[81] Guilhiermoz, pp. 121-23.

[82] Ibid., pp. 140, 161; *Olim*, III, 63, 64, 65, 164 (reports by Rousselet in 1301 and 1306), 179, 223 (reports by Nogaret in 1306).

stamp, but, in fact, it had not only the prestige of being *the* Parlement (the other chambers were merely auxiliaries) but also very real power. In the first place, it heard and decided directly all cases based on the interpretation of charters and judgements of royal courts, and all cases involving the great barons and prelates. Second, the preliminary pleadings that led to an inquest were heard by the Grand'Chambre; it tried to narrow the case down to a point where a few questions, posed to witnesses of the region where the dispute had arisen, could elicit answers that could be used to decide the issue. Third, the Grand'Chambre reviewed the inquests when they came in and decided whether they were satisfactory or whether further enquiry was necessary. The Chambre des Enquêtes could give no opinion on an inquest until it had been requested to do so by the Grand'Chambre.[83] The English analogy is suggestive, though imperfect: the Grand'Chambre, like English judges, determined the law; the Chambre des Enquêtes, like an English jury, determined the facts. The basic difference was that the Enquêtes determined the facts at second hand, on the basis of written reports of answers to questions posed by the commissioners who made the inquests. It is also obvious that in deciding the significance of the answers the members of the Enquêtes would in fact be determining points of law, but an English judge could do the same thing in interpret-ing the answer of a jury. The real difference was that an English jury could decide many cases by a simple "yes" or "no," while the witnesses in a French inquest had to answer a multiplicity of questions as to what they had seen or heard, thus leaving a mass of overlapping and often contradictory evidence for the judges to sort out. Another difference was that while in England appeals were rare, in France they often formed a large part of the work of a Parlement. Here again, the Grand'Chambre should have decided whether the appeal had been made in due form and then left to the Enquêtes the question of whether new or misinter-preted facts justified a reversal. In actual practice, the Grand'-Chambre at times asked the Enquêtes to rule on the validity of the procedure (and especially on the form of the appeal) as well as on the facts.[84]

[83] Guilhiermoz, pp. 1-9, 107-38.
[84] Ibid., 125-27. Technically, in regions of customary law new facts were not to be introduced; an appeal was based on the record. In practice, able lawyers could work in new facts while challenging testimony or arguing a point of law.

FIG. 2. The Great Seal of Philip IV. (Collection of **Joseph Strayer**)

FIG. 3. A *Gros Tournois* of Philip's Reign. This is the coin that played a key role in Philip's manipulation of the currency. Originally, it was valued at 12 pence *tournois*. At the peak of Philip's financial problems (1303-1304), it was valued at 36-40 pence (the silver content was also slightly diminished). This was "weak money." Return to "good money" in 1306 brought the value of the *gros* down to about 13 pence. (Collection of Joseph Strayer)

Fɪɢ. 4. Philip and His Family. Left to right: Charles (son); Philip (son); Isabelle (daughter), queen of England; Philip IV; Louis of Navarre (eldest son); Charles of Valois (brother). (Note the omission of Philip's half brother, Louis of Evreux.) (Ms. lat. 8504 fol. ɪv; courtesy Bibliothèque Nationale, Paris)

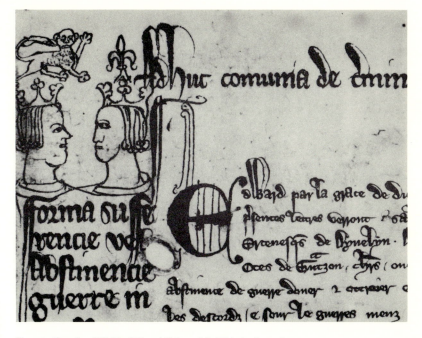

Fig. 5. Sketch of Philip IV and Edward I. This is the only contemporary picture of Philip the Fair. It was discovered by Dr. Elizabeth Kimball in the margin of a copy of the truce between Edward and Philip at Tournai, 31 January 1298 (see *English Hist. Rev.*, LIV [1936], 493). This may not be an actual portrait, but the scribe certainly caught the stern, impassive stare that Bernard Saisset mocked. Edward is much less on his dignity. (Lord Treasurer's Remembrancer [E368/69M54]; Crown Copyright; courtesy Public Record Office, London)

Fig. 6. Parchment Receipt for Army **Wages.** "Guillaume de Fraisnay of the *bailliage* of Gisors acknowledges that he has received from master Guillaume, cantor of Milly, and Geoffroi Cocatrix [army paymasters] seven and a half l.p. for wages in the army of Flanders. Arras, St. Mathew's Day [21 Sept.] 1302." A Faber de Fraisnay of the *bailliage* of Gisors served in the army of Foix in 1272 (*H.F.*, XXIII, 749). (Collection of Joseph Strayer)

FIG. 7. View of the Palais de la Cité. The Sainte-Chapelle, on the right, was built by St. Louis; almost all the other buildings are those built for Philip the Fair. Miniature for June by the Limbourg Brothers from *Les très riches Heures du duc de Berry* (1413-1416). (Courtesy Musée Condé, Chantilly)

Nevertheless, although there was some overlapping of duties, the division of the work of the Parlement among three chambers, as established in 1307, proved useful and continued, with minor modifications, throughout the century. The one weakness was that the procedure might be very slow. In the first place, it was hard to find proper persons to conduct the inquests, especially in regions that were not close to Paris. As the sessions of the Parlement lengthened, it became more and more difficult to detach men from the High Court and put them to work on presiding over inquests that might take many months to complete. The alternative was to empower *baillis* and other royal officials, or specially chosen auditors, to hold the inquests. But the *baillis* were often too busy to do the work properly, or, indeed, to do it at all, and both *baillis* and auditors were apt to make grave errors in procedure. In such cases serious delays could occur, for a defective or unfinished inquest would lead to a protest or an appeal to the Parlement or to an objection by the Parlement itself, and the whole case would have to be referred to new auditors.[85]

Even when the officials who made the inquests did their work properly, there were many opportunities to slow down lawsuits. If the parties were anxious to get a quick decision, they could waive many possible objections and speed up the procedure; but even then there were formalities that could not be omitted and purely physical problems, such as the need to put everything in writing, that were bound to cause delays. In the first place, the parties had to obtain an audience before the Grand'Chambre and prepare oral arguments. Almost always they were asked to put their pleas in writing—the main point to be proved (or disapproved) and the subsidiary articles that would support the pleader's case. If an inquest were ordered, as usually happened, each party had to search out witnesses to be questioned about the articles. The witnesses were examined on each article, and there were usually many articles; the answers were written down, and the record was sent back to the Grand'Chambre. Here there could be further delays while the judges decided whether the inquest was in a fit state to be judged. If it were accepted, it went to the Enquêtes, where the record was given to a *rapporteur*.

---

[85] In this respect the reform of 1307 did not help. In the two years preceding the reform and in the two years following, the number of defective inquests is about the same; see *Olim*, III, 199, 229, 236-38, 254, 262, 268, 280, 285, 290, 312, 313, 333, 390, 391, 396, 403, 442, 454, 467, 501.

This man had the tedious task of digesting the information, deciding what had or had not been proved by each witness, and presenting a summary to the chamber. Anyone who has ever read one of these long, repetitious, and at times inconclusive inquests can sympathize with the problems of a *rapporteur* and realize why he could not prepare his report very rapidly. When the report was complete, it was presented to the full chamber, and each member gave his opinion. The *rapporteur* spoke last; if he had done his job competently, his findings were usually accepted, at least on matters of fact. The chamber then gave its judgement, and the *rapporteur* was asked to put it in final form as an *arrêt*. The *arrêt* was checked over by the Chambre des Enquêtes and then sent to the Grand'Chambre which gave it the official sanction of the Parlement.[86]

This lengthy procedure could be shortened if the Grand'Chambre decided that no inquest was necessary, either because both parties relied entirely on the production of charters and other documents that could be judged immediately, or (a rare occurrence) because the original pleadings showed so clearly that right was on one side that no further investigation was necessary. Otherwise, there would be an inquest. Even with the best will in the world, an inquest could not be ordered, made, and judged in less than a year to two years. This was the limit set by the reform ordinance of 1303, and if the authors of the ordinance thought that a two-year limit was a reform, it is easy to guess what actual practice was. Good will, in legal controversies, is a rare article, and it was especially rare in an age that thought of a lawsuit as a barely acceptable substitute for war. Almost always one party, and sometimes both parties, had reasons for seeking delay. Delay gave an aggressor a chance to consolidate his position, to suborn, threaten, or merely outlive witnesses who might testify against him, or to confuse the issue by seeking interlocutary judgements that did not touch the basic problem but that might give him some shadow of right. On the other hand, a claimant who had right on his side but who had difficulty in proving it might seek

---

[86] Ducoudray, pp. 417-68, gives a detailed account of the various steps in the procedure, summarized in a table on pp. 464-65. For examples of lengthy *enquêtes* see Boutaric, ed., *Actes*, I, nos. 2122D, 2122E; these are fairly early and simple examples. The procedure in the local courts of the region of written law was a little less complicated, but the written inquests were just as long. Procedure in local courts in the north was quicker and gave more room for oral testimony, but nowhere was justice in a civil suit speedy.

delay in order better to prepare his case. Or, to take a fairly common situation, each party might have some justification for his claim, in which case it would be important to hold long debates about the articles on which the inquest was based, so that the questions put to the witnesses would bring out strong points and conceal weak ones and vice versa.

The result was that at every stage of the procedure, from the first debate before the Grand'Chambre to the final referral of an inquest to a *rapporteur*, there could be time-consuming arguments, appeals for rulings on procedural problems, attacks on the character and credibility of witnesses or on the competence of the auditors who held the inquest, belated demands to introduce new evidence, or complaints that the inquest was incomplete or that it had been tampered with after the hearing had closed. A suitor with a good lawyer could keep a case open for years while his objections were being answered, and even if in the end he lost his case, he might reopen it after a brief interval by finding a new basis to support an old demand. To give only one example, the question of whether the king could cede his rights of justice in the village of Couches (which Philip III had placed in his special and perpetual guard) to the duke of Burgundy was decided in the duke's favor in September 1291. Before February 1299 the Parlement had reversed this decision, and the reversal was sustained in a judgement of that year. The duke of Burgundy, however, was still not willing to concede defeat, and the case came up again on 5 June 1311. As was said above, this was one of the most impressive meetings of the reign. The king himself was present, as were Charles of Valois, the count of Saint-Pol, Gilles Aicelin, archbishop of Narbonne, Robert d'Harcourt, bishop of Coutances, Pierre de Latilly, Jean d'Auxy, Jean le Duc, Hugues de la Celle, Mathew de Trie, Guillaume de Hangest, and 12 others. The list is very like the parlementary list of 1307, reinforced by the two counts, who were needed because a peer was being judged.[87] It is easy enough to say that the duke of Burgundy was one of the greatest men in the realm, that of all the peers, he was the strongest supporter of the king, and that he would naturally be given every opportunity to prove his case. But what of the men of the little village of Couches? How did they secure a reversal of the first judgement against them, and how did they manage to defend themselves for 20 years against the duke? From

[87] Boutaric, ed., *Actes du Parlement*, I, nos. 2715C, 2975A; *Olim*, III, 608-10.

the record it seems clear that Philip wanted to give the justice of Couches to the duke in order to put an end to an irritating administrative problem. Couches lies near Autun, and the royal officers stationed in Couches could easily interfere in this important town of the duchy.[88] It may well have been these royal officers who supported the men of Couches in their long struggle. Perhaps they gave legal advice; perhaps they waived some of the usual legal fees; perhaps they suggested to their colleagues in Paris that Couches was too important an outpost of royal authority to be abandoned. But although they could assist the men of the village, they could not prevent the process from being reopened at least three times.

The case of Couches illustrates both the flaws in the procedure of the Parlement and the sense of equity that pervaded its judgements. Under the best conditions a suit in the Parlement consumed a great deal of time and required expert legal advice. The poor had neither the time nor the money to sue in the Parlement, and middle-income people must have hesitated before making such a risky investment. (This is why it seems likely that Couches was aided by local royal officials.) But if a suitor had the time and could afford to engage a good lawyer, there was a very good chance that justice would be done. On the record, as we have it, the decision in the case of Couches seems equitable. Perhaps opposing pressures canceled each other—desire to please the duke (and the king?) against distaste for surrendering any royal right. This would have made it easier to honor the promise of Philip III that Couches would always remain under royal protection. Whatever the reasons, a court that certainly had no great sympathy with the lower classes did protect a small rural community against a peer. And, as was pointed out above, the professional members of the Court that made this decision in 1311 were basically those named in 1307. Continuity of personnel was increasing, and if the Court gave an equitable judgement in one case, the chances were good that it would continue to be equitable in its other judgements.

Two segments of the population, the towns and the clergy, that might have been suspicious of the Parlement obviously felt that it gave good justice. By and large, the government of Philip the Fair had no great fondness for the towns, partly because they resisted taxation and zealously defended their privileges, partly

[88] Jean Richard, *Les ducs de Bourgogne et la formation du duché du XIe au XIVe siècle* (Paris, 1954), pp. 193-94.

because they were as prone to violence as the most disorderly nobles. The clergy were less disorderly (although their sergeants could be as oppressive as those of the king, and armed attacks by one religious house against another were not unheard of),[89] but the clergy were even more determined to protect their privileges and their lordships. A large part of the time of *baillis* and seneschals was spent in trying to make the towns and the clergy pay what they owed the king, accept the king's definition of their privileges and rights of jurisdiction, and obey the king's ordinances. Yet the clergy showed no distrust of the Parlement; they were by far the most numerous group of suitors, especially before the crisis of 1303. After 1303 the percentage of cases involving the clergy declined somewhat, but this is because other classes began to use the Parlement more often. In spite of the obvious prejudice of many local officials against clerical privileges, the Parlement seems to have dispensed evenhanded justice to churchmen; they won about 55 percent of their cases. The percentage can only be an approximation, since in some cases the clergy gained only partial victories, but there was certainly no concerted attempt to use the High Court to weaken the position of ecclesiastical communities.

The bourgeoisie was a little more suspicious of the Parlement than were the clergy, especially early in the reign. Towns and townsmen appeared in less than 25 percent of the cases before 1300, and, more often than not, only as defendants. The Parlement obviously had a problem with the townsmen because many of the suits in which they were involved concerned quarrels with bishops, cathedral chapters, and monasteries. The towns had their privileges, the clergy had theirs, and there was often an overlapping, or apparent overlapping, of rights. If the Parlement was very cautious (as it was) to avoid the appearance of being unjust to the churchmen, then it was almost forced to interpret the privileges of the bourgeoisie narrowly. After 1300 the towns were more willing to plead their cases in the Parlement; they appeared about as often as the nobility, though still less frequently than the clergy. They were also reasonably successful; they gained more

---

[89] The agents of the abbey of St. Saturnin were accused of instituting a veritable reign of terror in the abbey's lands, 1305 (A.N., J 1030, no. 28, J 1034, no. 44). Cluny used force to collect tithes claimed by the bishop and chapter of Mâcon and ignored the protests of royal sergeants; some of its agents said: "Non habemus regem." In 1300 the abbot was fined 5,000 l.t. for these acts (*Olim*, III, 53-54).

or less favorable judgements in about 52 percent of their cases. With the towns, of course, the caution expressed above is particularly applicable: their cases often involved many claims, some of which they won and some of which were denied or postponed. A nice example is the case, or, rather, a consolidation of many cases, between the commune and the abbot of St. Riquier in 1313.[90] There were 25 articles, some of which were not decided. Of those that were, my impression is that the commune gained more than it lost, but perhaps to lose anything may have seemed a defeat. On the other hand, a clear-cut decision upholding or denying the claims of the town was preferable to the bickering and uncertainty that had gone on for many years.[91]

The relative impartiality of the Parlement cannot be explained entirely on grounds of self-interest or class interest. Clerks were certainly the most numerous group in the Parlement, but the social origins of the clerks ranged all the way from Philippe le Convers, a converted Jew who owed everything to the king, to members of provincial aristocracies like Gilles Aicelin or the Maumonts. One can say that most of the clerks were primarily servants of the king and only theoretically servants of the Church, and that they paid little attention to their ecclesiastical duties. Nevertheless, most of them received, or hoped to receive, lucrative offices in the Church as canons, deans, archdeacons, and (for the most successful) bishops. There was no point in impoverishing an institution from which they derived a considerable part of their income. Even men like Pierre de Latilly or Philippe le Convers, who could be very tough about guarding the king's interests, do not seem to have been unduly harsh in dealing with French churches and monasteries.

The bourgeois members were not very numerous, unless one includes clerks of bourgeois origin, but some of them were very influential. Like the clerks, they were primarily servants of the king, but they did not lose all ties with their home towns. Thus Renaud Barbou, one of the most important members of the Grand'Chambre, was a citizen of Chartres and proud of it; he founded a hospital for the blind in his native city.[92] It will be

[90] *Olim*, II, 561-72 (1313). In a case that came up soon after, the inhabitants of Le Puy (they had no commune) complained about innovations in measuring and marketing introduced after the *paréage* with the bishop. They seem to have been treated fairly.

[91] This and the preceding paragraph are based on Strayer, "Clientèle du Parlement," pp. 166-67.

[92] Carolus-Barré, "Baillis de Philippe III," pp. 155-57. Renaud Barbou the

remembered that in 1296 Renaud was appointed to pronounce the *arrêts* and that he was paid 600 l.p. a year, one of the highest salaries in the Court. In Renaud's absence Jean de Montigny, also a bourgeois (of Senlis), was to perform his duties.[93] Pierre de Dicy was another longtime and influential lay member of the Parlement who was definitely not a noble, though he was ennobled in 1316. He may have begun his career as *prévôt* of Villeneuve-le-Roi; in any case, like Renaud Barbou and Jean de Montigny, he had served as a *bailli*.[94]

One might assume that these bourgeois members of the Court would have been inclined to curtail the privileges of the clergy (Renaud Barbou had once been excommunicated for supporting the count of Chartres against the cathedral chapter of the city). But there is nothing to indicate any particular bias on their part against churchmen. In fact, to take Renaud Barbou again as a representative of this group, one of the first duties he ever performed for the crown was to make an *enquête* in 1269 on the misdeeds of a knight who had violently attacked a convent in Chartres. His findings were entirely favorable to the convent.[95] Nor can we say that there was any visible tendency to favor the towns during the period when Barbou (and Montigny) had great influence. In fact, the towns seem to have been more suspicious of and less successful in the Parlement before 1300 than later.

As for the nobility, on solemn occasions some of the great barons, such as the count of Saint-Pol, the duke of Burgundy, or even Charles of Valois, would be present, but the working members (as was the case with the clergy and the bourgeoisie) were career civil servants—ex-seneschals, such as Alfonse de Rouvrai, Jean d'Arrablay, and Hugues de la Celle, a Master of Forests (Etienne de Bienfaite), or men who worked in the Chambre des Comptes, such as Guillaume Courteheuse and Guillaume de Marcilly. They were the king's servants just as much as were the clerks and the bourgeois members; their advancement and their income depended on giving the king good service and not in indulging any prejudices they may have felt against the clergy or the bourgeoisie or in favoring their own class.

younger, who was also to sit in the Grand'Chambre, continued his father's benefactions; see ibid., pp. 159-60, and Guillois, p. 264.

[93] See above, p. 213. For Jean de Montigny see Carolus-Barré, "Baillis de Philippe III," pp. 209-11.

[94] *H.F.*, xxiv, *32; Langlois, ed., *Textes*, p. 179; *J.T.P.*, nos. 3924, 4339.

[95] Carolus-Barré, "Baillis de Philippe III," pp. 153-54; *Olim*, i, 322.

If pleasing the king were more important than protecting class interests, then there might have been a danger that the Parlement would always rule for the king when subjects made claims against him. This danger was especially great when the Parlement had to interpret the terms of a royal charter, an area in which it had exclusive jurisdiction. Charters, especially those of the period before Louis IX, were not always very precise, and narrow interpretations could have limited the rights and diminished the income of many subjects. An opinion on this matter can only be subjective, but I see no evidence that there was a deliberate bias in favor of strict interpretations. The one area in which the court was clearly inclined to limit or regulate the rights of subjects was in disputes over jurisdiction, but, except for the communes, jurisdiction in civil and criminal cases was not necessarily based on royal charters. The most important jurisdictional problem— that of ensuring the right of appeal to royal courts—was scarcely ever a matter of charter interpretation (agreements of *paréage* would be an exception), and yet the problem of appeals caused the most serious jurisdictional disputes between the king and his subjects. Appeals to the Parlement irritated not only the king of England and the count of Flanders, who were ready to quarrel with Philip in any case, but even a pacific and friendly baron like the count (later duke) of Brittany.[96] Appeals, as a regular and frequent procedure, were relatively new in French jurisprudence, and the Parlement had to base its decisions in such cases on slender precedents and on directives from the king.[97] With this exception, one can say that the Parlement did not unduly favor the king and that, although some judgements might have gone either way, there was always some plausible reason for the final decision.

Moreover, as was said above, the king seldom interfered directly with cases that came before the Parlement. He was certainly consulted on many occasions, even on such a minor matter as the punishment of the *rapporteur* Guillaume Boucel, but he did not make the judgements of his Court. He did intervene after judgements—once to reverse a judgement completely—but usually only to lessen or forgive a penalty.[98] The right of pardon,

[96] Langlois, ed., *Textes*, pp. 168, 171.

[97] Ibid., pp. 130, 133, 142, 168, 171, 187, 189.

[98] In 1311 the Parlement had ordered that an amortization in favor of the Augustinian Hermits was invalid unless approved by the bishop and chapter of Amiens and the mayor and *jurés* of the town. It took a formal diploma

however, has always been a prerogative of the sovereign, and the reversal of a judgement was unique. It is significant that the document annulling the judgement of the Court had to take the form of a solemn diploma and that it was not entered in the *Olim*. Philip did not use his courts to justify his most arbitrary actions; he worked through his Council and used administrative procedures (ordinances, instructions to central and local officials), not judicial procedures, to ensure that he was obeyed. The most dubious decisions of the reign—the attack on Boniface VIII, the expulsion of the Jews, the accusations against the Templars—were not referred to or justified by the courts. It is true that the confrontation with Edward I was prepared by encouraging appeals to the Parlement, but Edward was willing to accept a reasonable compromise on such matters. It was Philip's deceitful diplomacy that brought on war in 1293, not the decisions of the Parlement. The same can be said of Philip's dealing with Flanders. The king did use his right to protect the groups that had appealed to him in order to put his agents into the Flemish towns, but it was the administrative decisions of those agents that stirred up revolt, not the decisions of the Parlement. It is true that in the south the local royal courts were rather aggressive in their dealings with lords who had high justice and that many of the *paréages* in that area were based on judicial as well as administrative pressure. But the Parlement did not rule on these cases. This is unfortunate; it would have been interesting to know its opinion about such controversies as the ones over Gévaudan and the Vivarais.

Thus the Parlement was not a façade behind which the king could conceal unscrupulous acts. Certainly in any case touching the king's rights there would be a tendency to rule in his favor, but there had to be some basis in the law and in the evidence to justify such decisions. Almost all of the men who sat in the Enquêtes and the Grand'Chambre had served in some capacity in the provinces; they knew the limits of royal power. Flagrantly unjust judgements could cause riots or attacks on royal officials. Even just but rigorously implemented judgements could lead to the subtraction of obedience to the king (as in the case of Aquitaine and Flanders). Moreover, these men realized, perhaps better than the king himself, that if royal sovereignty were defined as

to reverse this action (A.N., JJ 47, fol. 96, no. 134). The pardons, or reductions of penalties are in *Olim*, III, 120, 282, 290, 542-43, 549-50, 705-6, 807-9.

the right to make final judgements, then those judgements had better be just. If royal justice were superior to justice in private hands, then there would be good reason to seek royal courts, either in the first instance or on appeal. If the royal courts, and, above all, if the Parlement were obviously being used simply as instruments for increasing the king's power and revenues, then there would be every reason to shun them. There was, in any case, a sort of competition between royal and other courts for business. For example, the right to enforce contracts and constrain debtors to pay their debts could be claimed by royal, ecclesiastical, and communal courts. A reputation for biased judgements would not have been helpful in defeating competitors.

Finally, the jurisprudence of the Parlement made it difficult to be blatantly unjust. Many cases depended on proof of seisin, that is, possession of certain rights or lands. To hear cases of novel disseisin in France was not a royal monopoly, as it was in England, but it was very easy to bring cases of disseisin before the Parlement.[99] To prove absolute ownership was difficult, and judgement on these matters was equally difficult. Even an utterly impartial judge could go wrong in such cases, and a biased judge could not easily have been proved wrong. Seisin, however, was a fact that could, in most cases, be easily ascertained. Procedure by *enquête* was a good way of gettting the necessary information; the men of the neighborhood would have seen which of two claimants had hanged a thief or collected certain dues. It might not be so easy to prove seisin of a county (for example, La Marche-Angoulême), but it was done successfully in 1304.[100] Once an *enquête* on seisin had been made and accepted by the Court, there was not much opportunity to make a deliberately wrongful judgement. The "questio proprietatis" could be reserved, but, meanwhile, the claimant whose seisin had been proved by the *enquête* was almost sure to get it. In most cases this was sufficient; very few suitors tried to overturn a judgement based on proof of seisin.

A broader, but less conclusive, principle was the duty of the king to keep peace in his realm. Protection of seisin was, of course, part of the work of peacekeeping, since disseisin was apt to be

---

[99] Perrot, *Cas royaux*, pp. 188-203, argues that under Philip novel disseisin was, in most of France, a case of "prévention absolue"; that is, anyone who was disseised could seek his remedy in a royal court, and once the royal court had taken the case, all other judges were barred.

[100] *Olim*, III, 134-35.

achieved through violence. But the concept was much broader than this; it included almost any act of violence, and especially acts of violence against people and institutions under royal protection or acts of violence (such as private wars) committed after the king had forbidden them. Here again there could be little question about the facts. Violence was fairly easy to prove, and excuses for violence were usually irrelevant, especially if the violence occurred after a warning by a royal official. All that the Parlement had to do was to register the facts and assess the penalty. The one danger was that the degree of violence might be over-stated by a plantiff, and there are some scandalous cases in which this was done.[101] Generally speaking, however, there was little argument about the existence of an offense, although there might be some argument as to who had led or participated in an assault on persons and property. The real weakness of the Parlement in such cases was that it was difficult to make the punishment fit the crime. The usual penalty was a large fine to the king and to the injured party, accompanied at times by an order to establish a pension for a victim who had been maimed. A heavy fine could ruin a minor noble or a bourgeois, but it would not have as much impact on a great noble, a great monastery, or a large town. More-over, the really large fines were not easily or quickly collected. Often they had to be reduced, as in the case of the count of Foix or the city of Carcassonne.[102] And a fine does seem a light pun-ishment for such offenses as arson, blinding, mutilation, and tor-ture.[103]

The problem was that the Parlement was primarily a court for civil cases and that it had no tradition of physical punishments. Men could be imprisoned in the Châtelet (or elsewhere) in addi-tion to paying a fine, but such cases were rare, and the term of incarceration was usually short, from one month to two years.[104] There were also cases in which a culprit was imprisoned at the

[101] A fine for willful drowning that had been upheld by two *enquêteurs* and by the Parlement was finally reversed by the Parlement because it was based on a forged notarial document (*Olim*, II, 464, III, 181). An accusation of murder and breach of peace that had reached the Parlement was proved false (the "murdered" man was alive and well) (ibid., III, 381); a charge of carrying arms and threatening violence reached the Parlement on appeal and was proved false (ibid., p. 737).

[102] The amercement of the count was reduced from 30,000 l.t. to the loss of a rent of 551 l.t. (capital value about 5,500 l.t.) (*H.L.*, x, cols. 498-99).

[103] *Olim*, III, 46, 120, 222, 307, 490, 502, 505.

[104] Ibid., II, 339, III, 101, 320, 708, 819.

king's pleasure, which probably meant until he or his friends could buy his way out.[105] It was more common to imprison men to ensure that they would accomplish some act required by the Court, such as restoring money wrongfully taken or paying a fine.[106] Finally the Parlement, like other courts, imprisoned some people accused of serious crimes until they were convicted or cleared.[107] These imprisonments could last a long time; on at least one occasion it was necessary to create something like an English commission of gaol delivery. Men were sent to the Châtelet in 1311 "ad deliberacionem predictorum [two accused of poisoning] et nonnullorum aliorum in dicto Castelleto detentorum. . . ."[108] Even a one-night stay in the Châtelet could be quite unpleasant, as two servants of the Treasurer Geoffroi de Briançon discovered. Sent on an errand at night by their master, they were arrested by the watch, who took them to the Châtelet, "adeo stringendo, verberando, ledendo, et male trahendo ipsos, sicut est de latronibus et murtrariis fieri consuetum. . . ."[109] Several months of detention must have been almost unbearable, but mistreatment of prisoners was not officially ordered by the Court; it was simply accepted as being in the nature of things. If the two servants of the Treasurer had not had the backing of a great man, no notice would have been taken of their sufferings. As it was, the sergeants of the watch were punished only by dismissal from royal service, and for some of them the dismissal was to be for only one year.

Imprisonment, then, was normally a procedural matter and was only occasionally meant to be a form of punishment. The most severe penalty that could be inflicted for violence was banishment from the realm; banishment could also be imposed by lower courts, and the Parlement rarely pronounced such sentences.[110] Moreover, banishment was not necessarily perpetual; the king could always revoke the penalty.

To sum up, although the Parlement was usually correct in deciding whether or not there had been violence, it was not very successful in decreasing acts of violence. It usually heard only those cases in which men of some standing were involved; such men could find many ways of delaying a decision. When delay

[105] Ibid., III, 282, 429, 705-6, 735.   [106] Ibid., 494, 646-47, 858, 927.
[107] Ibid., II, 576, III, 678, 726.
[108] Ibid., III, 678. The two accused were freed.
[109] Ibid., 747-48.
[110] Ibid., II, 405, III, 373; Boutaric, ed., Actes du Parlement, II, nos. 4082, 4104, 4268, 4326, 4464. Cf. Ducoudray, I, 472.

became impossible, they would receive a judgement of the king's Court, but such a judgement did not persuade them to give up their rights (as they saw them) of vengeance and of private war. The penalties were almost always purely pecuniary, and they could hope, with some reason, that the full amount would never be collected. The real unfairness was in the penalties, not in the judgements. At a time when poor men were hanged for theft, when counterfeiters were quite literally boiled alive,[111] men who were guilty of arson, looting, and homicide merely had to pay fines. The communes were treated more harshly than were the nobles, a town riot was usually more expensive than a private war (though not in the case of the count of Foix);[112] but even the leaders of town riots were not punished physically. Ducoudray may exaggerate the prevalence of violence during Philip's reign,[113] but there was enough of it to be worrisome. The most that can be said is that the royal courts, and especially the Parlement, never let violence get completely out of hand. They could not stop rioting, raids, and private wars, but they could make the people who engaged in such activities uncomfortable. No part of France in Philip's reign suffered the kind of anarchy that prevailed in many regions during the Hundred Years' War.

One last problem remains: What part did the courts, and especially the Parlement, play in making, or at least in validating, laws? Unconsciously, of course, the courts were always making law through their interpretations and clarifications of existing customs, but formal lawmaking was not unknown. As Beaumanoir said, the king could always make laws for the common welfare that had to be obeyed throughout the realm, but he should act only "par grant conseil."[114] The Parlement was a committee of the Council; obviously it would be consulted on some occasions, and even if it were not, many members of the Council would be men who had sat at one time or another in the High Court. At the other extreme, the Masters of the Exchequer of Normandy were a delegation from the Parlement; they could make ordinances interpreting and modifying Norman law,[115] apparently

---

[111] C.R., I, nos. 300, 4448.

[112] See above, n. 102. The count was fined 30,000 l.t. (though this was much reduced later). For Carcassonne see H.L., x, cols. 473-75 (a fine of 60,000 l.t. reduced to 20,000 l.t.).

[113] Ducoudray, I, 337-45.   [114] Beaumanoir, paras. 1510-15.

[115] F. Soudet, ed., Ordonnances de l'Echiquier de Normandie (Rouen and Paris, 1929), pp. ix-xvi; Perrot, ed., Arresta communia Scacarii, pp. 1-2 (cf. nos. 44-50, 73).

without consulting the king. In practice, lawmaking was not a very common occurrence, and the rules about lawmaking were not very precise. The political situation, rather than strict constitutional principles, determined who should give the king advice and how many people should be consulted.

Nevertheless, there was some understanding of the difference between temporary measures that were taken to meet an immediate emergency and ordinances that made permanent changes in the law. Subsidies for war belonged in the first class. They were one-shot operations; a subsidy ordered for one year did not continue in succeeding years, and, in theory at least, it did not set a precedent. There was no expectation that subsidies could be made a regular part of the king's income, and, in fact, during more than half the reign there were no subsidies. Thus the king could ask for a subsidy without going through any elaborate legal formalities. The great subsidy of 1304 was approved by a very small Council (11 or 12), including Gilles Aicelin, Pierre de Mornay, the king's two brothers, Duke Robert of Burgundy, and the Constable. Requests for other subsidies simply mention the advice of the Council, without giving names.[116] Actual consent to subsidies was obtained through negotiations with individual nobles and towns or local assemblies, and in these negotiations the form of the tax could be substantially altered. In short, a request for a subsidy was not a law, and the courts had little to do with either the request or its implementation.

In contrast, the request for an aid to marry the king's oldest daughter (Isabella) was a matter for the courts. This was a customary aid, a permanent part of the law, and individuals and communities could claim that they were historically or by charter exempt from this particular custom. Philip was not very happy about this opposition, but he finally admitted that those who claimed exemption could send procurators to prove their case in the Parlement.[117] Judging by the relatively small sums collected, the Parlement must have accepted or compromised many of the claims to exemption.[118]

The fact that the Parlement was involved in making new law, as opposed to merely interpreting the old law, is perfectly clear in certain ordinances. For example, the ordinance specifying how the right of bourgeoisie could be acquired and maintained was made in the Parlement of 1287. In the same year the ordinance

116 *Ord.*, I, 408-9; Strayer and Taylor, pp. 48-64.
117 *Olim*, II, 502, 508.   118 See above, pp. 79-81.

ordering all lords with temporal justice to have only laymen as *baillis, prévôts,* and sergeants was "registered in the Parlement."[119] In 1291 the king ordered, in the Parlement, that all Jews fleeing from England or Gascony be expelled from the realm.[120] This was scarcely a law; the order was probably proclaimed in the Parlement to obtain maximum publicity. On the other hand, the long and detailed ordinance on amortization was quite properly made in the Parlement of 1291. It was a revision of the earlier ordinance of Philip III on this subject, and it was meant to be permanent law. It certainly had to be brought to the attention of legal experts, and it probably profited from their advice.[121] The ordinances forbidding private wars while the king was at war (1295) and the general order to aid the Inquisition (1296) were both recorded in the *Olim*,[122] but they were not in any sense acts of the Parlement, and they made no permanent change in the law. Probably the *greffier* included them for the information of the judges. On the other hand, the ordinance of 1301, which regulated the procedures to be used in taking mainmorte, or the goods of deceased bastards and foreigners, did make a permanent change in the law, even if it did not directly touch substantive issues. Yet it is enrolled in the *Olim* in the same form as the administrative orders about private wars and the Inquisition.[123]

The return to "good money" in 1306 naturally raised the question of how contracts made in the period of overvalued currency should be satisfied. Philip had to send out a large number of letters dealing with this problem; it is interesting that the only one registered in the *Olim* deals with long-term rents sold by monasteries and communes.[124] Even if this were not a permanent change in the law, at least it was a ruling that would be effective over many years, and the Parlement was charged with enforcing it. The ordinance regulating the right of prise (1309) could not, by its very nature, be permanent, since the king could always remove the limitations that he put upon his officials. Nevertheless, Philip wanted the ordinance to be more than a temporary reform, and it was made in the Parlement.[125] The ordinance of 1313, which reorganized the personnel and refined the procedure of the Châtelet, was also meant to be a lasting reform. In any case the Parlement has close connections with the Châtelet and heard many

[119] *Ord.,* I, 314, 316.
[121] *Ord.,* I, 323.
[123] Ibid., 456.
[125] *Olim,* II, 497.

[120] *Olim,* II, 311.
[122] *Olim,* II, 405, 413.
[124] *Ord.,* I, 441-52; *Olim,* II, 493.

appeals from that court; it was only sensible to consult the Parlement on such a matter. The king first spoke with his Council (presumably the inner group of advisers), but the actual ordinance was made in the Parlement.[126]

The most interesting case of all came in 1310. The occasion was not important; Yves de Loudéac and Jean Robert, collectors of fines for amortization in Périgord had apparently been over-zealous and had been taking money in cases in which the value, and potential for service, of a fief had been increased rather than decreased. A form letter, ordering them to stop these demands and return money unduly collected, was inserted in the *Olim*. Someone (probably the *greffier*) was not satisfied and added: "De hoc facte fuerunt plures littere, sed tamen visa non fuit ordinacio financiarum, unde bonum videtur esse quod videatur."[127] This is perhaps the beginning of the claim that all royal edicts should be registered in the Parlement.

To sum up, the Parlement, as such, was consulted on several occasions when basic changes in law or administrative practices were being considered. Even when ordinances and mandates were made in the Council without reference to the Parlement, there were always men in the Council who had had experience in the Parlement (for example, Gilles Aicelin). Many important decisions of king and Council were reported to the Parlement and inserted in its records. Toward the end of the reign the number of acts reported to the Parlement increased, and some people may have felt that the registering of royal edicts should be the rule, rather than an exceptional procedure. If this is true, then the first evidence for the privilege that made the Parlement the most powerful (and from the king's point of view, the most irritating) of the great Companies of royal officials may be found in the reign of Philip the Fair.

[126] Ibid., 587-89.

[127] Ibid., 505-6. Note that this letter is followed immediately in the *Olim* by a letter regulating the behavior of the collectors of debts that had been owed to the Jews. These collectors had also been too zealous, and apparently the Parlement was to be informed of restrictions put on their actions.

IV. The King and the Church

It was easy for nineteenth-century historians to see Philip as an implacable enemy of the Church and as a forerunner of the anticlericals of their own day. The bitter quarrel with Boniface VIII colored their views of the whole reign, and all disputes between royal officials and the clergy were interpreted as parts of a deliberate plan to subject the French Church to lay authority. In actual fact, Philip was on good terms with the papacy during all but 5 of the 29 years that he was king; even in the pontificate of Boniface there were periods of cooperation. As for the disputes with French prelates, most of them were part of the process of determining the nature and extent of royal authority that had begun in the twelfth century and that ended only with Louis XIV. To question the privileges of a bishop of Poitiers was no more anticlerical than to question the privileges of a count of Foix was antiaristocratic. Philip needed the Church just as he needed the aristocracy. He could not have governed France without the moral support of the clergy and without the professional skills of the bishops, archdeacons, and canons who filled his court, just as he could not have governed France without the loyalty of the nobility and the military and administrative skills of noble army commanders, councillors, and provincial governors. To retain the support and assistance of the clergy, Philip had to show some respect for their privileged status. He could argue about the definition of clerical privileges, just as the clergy could argue about the limits of royal power, but he could no more have thought of abolishing the special status of the clergy than the clergy could have thought of abolishing the monarchy. Neither the royalist pamphleteer who suggested that the kings of France had ruled their country quite successfully before there were clerics nor the bishop of Angers who invited Philip to contemplate the fate of Rehoboam expected to be taken seriously.[1] The king and the Church were bound to each other by unbreakable ties, and they knew it.

[1] "Antequam essent clerici, rex Franciae habebat custodiam regni sui et poterat statuta facere quibus ab inimicorum insidiis et nocumentis sibi et Regno praecaverat . . ." (Dupuy, *preuves*, p. 21). See *Le livre de Guillaume le Maire*, pp. 322, 369, for the references to Rehoboam.

Our final caution: the overwhelming bulk of the evidence on relations between Philip and the Church comes from lawsuits or from documents drafted by lawyers. Lawyers do not win cases by using mild language, and trivial disputes about jurisdiction could be made to sound as if royal and ecclesiastical officers were trying to annihilate each other's powers. When there was violence, as there often was, when arrests or seizure of property took place, the language became even more violent. This vehemence did not deceive the authorities in Philip's time—most of these disputes were settled at a higher level without much bad feeling on either side—but it has deceived some modern historians. No one believes the wild accusations of Flote and Nogaret against Boniface VIII or the exaggerated (though less specific) charges against the king's councillors made by Boniface VIII in the bull *Ausculta fili*.[2] There is no more reason to take at face value the statements of royal procurators in the provinces or the complaints of the lawyers who represented bishops, abbots, and cathedral chapters in the courts. A certain amount of exaggeration was necessary to secure any results, and the final settlements come closer than the opening statements to revealing the real substance of the disputes.

With these reservations, it is fair to say that Philip's policies caused problems for the clergy. The king wanted to draw on the financial and human resources of the French Church to aid in the government and defense of the realm. He wanted to limit the jurisdiction of ecclesiastical courts and to subject the temporal courts held by some prelates to the same rules about appeals and procedure as governed the courts held by lay lords. He wanted to reform what seemed to him to be abuses of the personal privileges of the clergy, especially the exception of clerks in minor orders from secular jurisdiction. He wanted to discourage, or at least to keep some control over, the transfer of land, and of rights annexed to land, to the Church.

There was nothing very new about this program, nor was it very different from that of other rulers of the late thirteenth century, such as Edward I of England. Even payments for amortization had been instituted in 1275, ten years before Philip be-

---

[2] Dupuy, *preuves*, p. 51. The king's evil councillors "devorant incolas regni tui, et non tibi sed eis mellificarent apes, . . . tua et aliorum bona diripiunt et sub obtentu iustitiae palliati subditos opprimunt, Ecclesias gravant, . . . pupille et viduae non intendunt sed impinguantur lacrymis pauperum, . . . guerras nutriunt ac pacem de regno tollere pravis operationibus non verentur."

came king. In fact, it is scarcely correct to say that there was a program. Rather, there was a general tendency that was more evident at some times than at others and that was implemented more vigorously by some officials than by others. There was fairly wide agreement among laymen (as there had been since the days of St. Louis) that the Church was trying to increase its jurisdiction and that it had to be watched carefully or it would pull more and more secular cases into its courts. There was also agreement, as there was everywhere in Europe, that many unworthy people were being protected by benefit of clergy. There was, as was said in the previous chapter, a consensus that the Church should bear some of the expense of defending the realm. Some of the lawyers, both at Court and in the provinces (one thinks of Pierre du Bois), wrote angry tracts on these subjects,[3] but, on the whole, the royal government was quite flexible in its dealings with the French Church. Many disputes were settled by negotiation and compromise, and others by decisions of the Parlement (and the Parlement almost never took an extreme position). No important case was decided by the use of brute force. Even Bernard Saisset, arrested on charges of treason, was released and eventually restored to his bishopric. In fact, although it was not uncommon for a royal official to be rebuked for excessive severity in enforcing the king's rights against the Church,[4] few, if any, were ever criticized for being too lenient. Perhaps all royal officials were so well indoctrinated that they could not have favored the clergy, but it seems more likely that there was a real desire in the higher circles of government to avoid bruising conflicts.

On the whole, the French prelates also sought to avoid head-on collisions. There was much talk of excommunication, but this ecclesiastical weapon was seldom used against high officials and not with any great frequency against lesser men, such as *prévôts* and sergeants. The French clergy preferred to complain to the king and to seek letters confirming their privileges or favorable

---

[3] Pierre Du Bois, *Summaria brevis*, ed. Hellmut Kämpf (Leipzig, 1936), is basically a lawyer's brief suggesting ways of curbing the power of ecclesiastical courts.

[4] Baudouin, ed., *Lettres inédites*, nos. 1-121, are mostly letters telling royal officials to deal more gently with the clergy of Toulouse. See especially no. 55, rebuking the seneschal of Toulouse for not obeying an earlier (1293) mandate in favor of the bishop: "Vos in hujusmodi executione mandate negligenter et tepide habuistis," so much harm has been done (21 September 1300). See *Le livre de Guillaume le Maire*, pp. 333, 334, 341, 342, 370, for similar letters for the bishop of Angers and the archbishop of Tours.

judgements in the king's courts. Over half the cases recorded in the *Olim* for the period 1285-1314 concern the clergy. Bickering at the local level had not destroyed confidence in the quality of justice rendered by the Parlement. In fact, the French clergy, or at least the secular clergy, often seem to have had more confidence in the royal government than in the papal curia. The price of papal intervention was papal interference in local affairs, which was always expensive and not always helpful. The visit of a papal legate was a serious financial burden; to have a case heard in Rome was worse. Decisions made by outsiders might be impartial; they might also be ill-informed. The pope might sacrifice the interests of a particular church in order to gain political advantages, as the bishop of Poitiers and the chapter of Chartres discovered in 1290.[5] There was much to be said in favor of relying, as far as canon law permitted, on the Parlement, where many of the judges were eminent and well-informed members of the French clergy.

The regular clergy, especially the mendicant orders and the Cistercians, were somewhat less willing to trust the royal government. The mendicants were well protected by papal privileges, and they were less vulnerable to pressure by the king's officials, since they had little property and no temporal jurisdiction. Their main problems were doctrinal, and these could be determined only by the pope. The Cistercians, like the mendicants, were less involved in wordly affairs than the older monastic orders and were more willing to support the pope in his disputes with the king. Thus it is not surprising that the Dominicans of Montpellier and the abbot of Cîteaux were the most conspicuous opponents of Philip's appeal to a council against Boniface VIII. Nevertheless, the independence of the French regular clergy should not be exaggerated. Abbots and priors served as *enquêteurs* and as envoys of the king. The Cistercian abbot of Jouy was Treasurer during the struggle with Boniface VIII and became abbot of Cîteaux when his predecessor was forced to resign because he would not adhere to the charges against the pope. The Cistercians, however unwillingly, paid their share of tenths imposed on the French clergy. Although exact statistics are lacking, it appears that the largest fines for amortization were paid by monasteries, which were unable to secure as many exemptions from these levies as the seculars did. Finally, the regular clergy accepted the jurisdiction of the Parlement just as willingly as the secular clergy

[5] See below, pp. 245-46.

did; in fact, there were sessions in which the number of cases concerning monasteries and priories greatly exceeded the number concerning bishops and chapters.

Since the secular clergy trusted the king at least as much as they trusted the pope, there was no great opposition to royal intervention in the choice of bishops, cathedral dignitaries, and canons. The chapters were losing their freedom of election in any case, and there were some advantages in letting the king rather than the pope make the nominations. The king would name members of his court, but they would be men who had ties of kinship or clientage with leaders of the French Church. The pope, down to 1305, might appoint nonresident Italians, thus reducing the number of benefices available for natives of the realm. The election of Clement V in 1305 brought no great improvement; when Clement did not accept royal nominees, he was apt to select Gascons, very often members of his own family. This was no consolation to the clergy of the rest of France, especially when it became evident that Clement's relatives were not very competent. For example, Bernard de Fargues was a disaster as archbishop of Rouen; he had to exchange sees with Gilles Aicelin, archbishop of Narbonne and one of the chief councillors of the king. This exchange meant a large increase in income for Aicelin, but most politically conscious Frenchmen would have said that he deserved it; he was an able and an upright public servant.

In short, the French Church seems to have concluded that its welfare could best be preserved by working with and through the prelates who were royal officials and friends of the king. This conclusion was not mistaken. The decisions of the Parlement in cases concerning the clergy were equitable, as far as can be determined from the record. Ordinances concerning the Church repeatedly attempted to remedy the the grievances of the clergy. The problem, of course, was to make sure that the decisions of the central government were carried out at the local level. *Prévôts* and sergeants kept up a running feud with their counterparts in ecclesiastical territories; collectors of royal revenues tried to squeeze all they could out of royal rights over the clergy (such as regalia and amortization); seneschals and *baillis*, judges and procurators sought to limit the temporal jurisdiction of prelates and chapters. There may have been some anticlericalism in this activity, especially in the lower ranks of the administration, but desire for power and prestige was probably more important. Individual rebukes, court decisions, and general legislation could not stop the harassment, but they probably helped to keep it within endurable limits. Certainly the royal government could do more to restrain local officials than could the prelates or the papacy. A royal mandate was more efficacious than an excommunication.

All these points may be illustrated by a discussion of the first great controversy with the Church in Philip's reign, in 1288-1290. The date should be stressed: the trouble began before the election of Boniface VIII, before Flote or Nogaret became royal councillors, before the financial pressures on the Church caused by the war of Aquitaine. Yet some of the demands of Nicholas IV were at least as extreme as those of Boniface VIII, and the language of the king's answer to these demands was as firm—and as sarcastic—as that in any of the documents drafted by Flote or Nogaret.[6] The result was a compromise, on the whole favorable to the king. Ironically enough, one of the chief architects of the compromise was Cardinal Benedict Gaëtani, the future Boniface VIII.

The basic problem was that of royal jurisdiction; it arose in two dioceses where the king's rights were not firmly established. The first was Chartres. The king had acquired the county by purchase only in July 1286, and he had inherited a quarrel between the *prévôt* of the countess of Chartres and the cathedral chapter over the arrest by the *prévôt* of a man of the chapter. The king continued to support the action of his predecessor, and an interdict that had been imposed on Chartres in the time of the countess was renewed.[7] The second conflict was with the bishop of Poitiers. Poitou also had reverted to the crown recently, after the death of Alfonse de Poitiers in 1270. Here the bishop claimed that, because the king did not have the right of regalia in Poitiers, he held nothing of the king, and therefore appeals from the bishop's temporal courts ran to the archbishop of Bordeaux and not to the Parlement. He refused in 1288 to appear before the High Court to answer a complaint that he was unjustly refusing inves-

---

[6] In answering charges of the chapter of Chartres, Philip said: "Inde ergo nostrum gaudium est sumendum quod sola suspicio et auditus ipsum sanctissimum patrem citius et magis sollicite ad nostram quam ad aliorum principum correctionem . . . reddit sollicitum et attentum, quam quidem processum nemo forsitan dubitat procedere ex zelo specialis et inthime charitatis" (Digard, II, 247-48).

[7] Ibid., p. 250; see also I, 87.

titure to the acquirer of one of his fiefs; judgement went against him by default, and the royal seneschal of Poitou (the famous Philippe de Beaumanoir) was ordered to enforce the decision of the king's court.[8]

The chapter of Chartres had already complained to the pope, and the bishop of Poitiers joined them in requesting support. In March 1289 Nicholas IV ordered a double investigation, by the archbishop of Sens and the bishop of Auxerre for Chartres, and by the bishops of Evreux and Senlis for Poitiers. These prelates were not hostile to Philip the Fair; Gautier of Senlis had sat in the Parlement of 1285, and Guillaume of Auxerre was sent as an envoy to the pope in 1289.[9] They were, however, given very wide powers to use spiritual weapons against royal officials. So were the bishop of Poitiers and the chapter of Chartres, a tactic that made the king especially angry,[10] since he felt that this gave an unfair advantage to his opponents.

Philip and his councillors responded by sending a long and bitter letter to the archbishop of Sens and the bishop of Auxerre (probably early in the fall of 1289).[11] This is the letter that has been mentioned before, in which the king sarcastically thanked the pope for his solicitude, and then continued with a long string of legal arguments justifying the actions of his officials in Chartres. The tone is not unlike that of the attacks on Boniface VIII, but the style lacks the biting simplicity of the work of Flote or Nogaret, and the train of thought is not always easy to follow. The king was already using the knowledge of the lawyers (the Code was cited three times, for example) but not as skillfully as he did later. Nevertheless, the basic point was stated clearly: no territory in the realm is exempt from the king's jurisdiction; all those in the realm who have rights of justice hold them from the king, directly or indirectly.

After making this essential point, the letter wanders off into a rather vague and rhetorical attack on the abuses in the Church.

[8] Ibid., I, 88-89; *Olim*, II, 167, 265.

[9] Langlois, ed., *Textes*, p. 129. For the bishop of Auxerre see Digard, I, 93.

[10] Philip claimed that his adversaries wanted him to admit that "eos super nos judices faciamus et suum judicem expectemus," and he protested that the letters authorizing excommunication and interdict were "generales," specified no injury, and subjected the king to the power of his enemies (Digard, II, 249, 256-57). See also note 14 below.

[11] Published in Digard, II, 247-55.

Merchants and usurers are tonsured and claim clerical privilege; soon half the inhabitants of the realm will be exempt from secular justice. Ecclesiastical judges try cases of inheritance that should go to temporal courts. Excommunication is abused, to the point where the king's councillors are afraid to defend his rights. The greed of the clergy is destroying the devotion of the French people. If this continues, the king will be less than a count and the kingdom will cease to exist.[12]

The next step was to send the bishop of Auxerre and Philippe de Beaumanoir to Rome. They were given a long, rambling memorandum that repeated many of the points and some of the language of the letter to the two bishops.[13] The legal arguments were longer and more specific, but the basic propositions were the same. The most important additions were an indignant protest against allowing the bishop of Poitiers to impose an interdict before the king's arguments had been heard[14] and an appeal to God and the Church Triumphant against the false judgements of men.[15]

This was a "talking paper" (as modern diplomats would say), and it is doubtful that it was ever presented to the pope in full. But even if the envoys quoted or paraphrased only a few sections, there could be no doubt that the king was furious. Nicholas IV was deeply involved in trying to settle all the problems that had been created by the Aragonese conquest of Sicily and the subsequent Crusade against Aragon. No solution to these problems was possible if France were hostile. This conclusion was reinforced by the arrival of a new embassy in Rome, headed by Jean d'Acre, Butler of France, and Gérard de Maumont, one of the king's councillors. They brought with them the news that Philip was not going to give much help in recovering Sicily from the Ara-

---

[12] Ibid., p. 255: "rex Francorum ad minus quam ad comitem redigatur." Let the Church be careful lest our kingdom, "per talium avaritiam . . . et manifestum rapinam non desinat esse regnum." As a poor beggar said: "non cessabit exactio clericum quousque minuatur devotio Gallicarum."

[13] Published in ibid., pp. 256-75. As examples of repetition, the complaint against giving the tonsure to merchants and usurers (p. 253) is repeated (p. 272), and so is the remark about taking advantage of the king's youth (p. 271).

[14] Ibid., p. 258: "ad simplicem requisitionem nostri adversarii episcopi Pietavensis . . . ab ipse matre nostra optinuit potestate, ut contra nos judex esset, et nostram terram subiceret interdicto . . ."

[15] Ibid., p. 274: "nos et regnum nostrum supponimus curie Ecclesie triumfantis, cujus judicium nec fallit nec fallitur . . ."

gonese, and also a new set of grievances against the French clergy. They claimed that they spoke not only for the king but also for the "counts, barons, and communities of the realm." Whether Philip had held an assembly of notables or had secured individual assurances of support is uncertain,[16] but the phrase suggests that someone was thinking of the techniques that were actually used in 1303. Nicholas IV understood the message: it was time to cut short the dispute with France. He therefore decided to send two cardinals, Gerard Bianchi of Parma and Benedict Gaëtani, to negotiate with Philip.

A settlement was reached in 1290. The first step was to revoke all actions taken against royal officials and inhabitants of the royal domain by the bishop of Poitiers and the chapter of Chartres. Then a council of French prelates was assembled at Sainte-Geneviève in November 1290 to discuss matters in dispute between them and the king. Finally, Philip, "at the request of the prelates," issued an ordinance that defined both his rights and the privileges of the clergy.[17] The legates doubtless had some influence on the wording of the ordinance, but it is significant that the dispute was ended by royal decree, not by an act of the Roman curia, and that the privileges of the clergy were guaranteed by the king, not by the pope.

On the basic question of jurisdiction, the king gained a substantial victory. All prelates could be judged by the Parlement, and appeals from their temporal courts were to go to the Parlement whether or not they held their lands from the king. Their goods could be seized, by order of the king, to compel obedience; in fact, if delay caused danger, goods could be seized by royal officials acting on their own initiative. The claim that there were enclaves in the realm that were exempt from ordinary secular justice had been disallowed.

On the other hand, the king, by special grace, waived his right to take fines for amortization for recent acquisitions by the Church. He also recognized the exemption of all clerks from tallage (unless they were merchants or artisans) and the jurisdiction of prelates in cases concerning tithes, wills, and marriage

[16] Ibid., I, 101, II, 278. Boutaric, *La France sous Philippe le Bel*, p. 22, n. 1, quotes a letter of Nicholas IV to Philip saying that Jean and Gérard were "tuos et alios comitum, baronum ac universitatum seu communitatum regni predicti nuntios."

[17] These negotiations are fully discussed by Digard, I, 110-15. The ordinance is printed in *Ord.*, I, 318-19.

settlements (as long as property held by feudal tenure was not involved). Some provision was made to prevent abuses when the goods of the clergy were legitimately seized by secular authorities. Minor royal officials were forbidden to hold courts or to accomplish official acts within the lands of prelates (unless they could show that this was allowed by ancient custom). The jurisdiction of prelates was not to be lessened because a community had been placed under royal guard.

Even Digard, who thought that this ordinance was in general helpful to the Church, was troubled by the vagueness of some of the clauses, by the fact that many of the definitions of Church privileges included phrases that allowed the king to override those privileges in certain situations, and by the lack of any sanctions against royal officials who violated the privileges.[18] If this was the opinion of a scholar who admired the work of Benedict Gaëtani, one can imagine the relief in Philip's court at the end of the year 1290. In a direct confrontation with the clergy of two important dioceses, who had been strongly supported by the pope, the king had prevailed. The sanctions of the Church had been withdrawn, and the king's rights as sovereign of all France—at least in judicial affairs—had been recognized. This success had been achieved by taking the offensive, by asserting the king's authority over all inhabitants of the realm in unqualified terms, by attacking the arguments of the clergy and the actions of the pope in strong, even abusive language, and by exaggerating evils that existed in the Church. The king and his Council had acted in the belief that the papacy could not carry out its policies without French co-operation, that France was "the principal pillar supporting the Roman Church" (as Nogaret was to say later),[19] and events had proved them right.

This was the real significance of an otherwise minor conflict. Very early in his reign Philip had worked out the principles and the tactics that he was to use in the much more serious struggles with Boniface VIII. He was determined to preserve his sovereign power as he defined it, and he was not going to let the Church interfere with his use of that power. If he was threatened with ecclesiastical censures, he would counterattack, using every available weapon—legal arguments, political pressure, invective against the policies and behavior of the clergy, including the pope—and preparing propaganda that would appeal to the laymen of his realm.

[18] Digard, I, 14.   [19] Dupuy, pp. 241, 309, 325.

The lesson was not forgotten by the French clergy. There were numerous disputes between the king and the prelates and religious communities of France after 1290, but in no case did any of the clergy go as far in resisting Philip as the bishop of Poitiers and the chapter of Chartres had gone in the 1280s. The pope might excommunicate the king's men; the bishops did not, and interdicts were almost unheard of after 1290.

During the remaining years of Philip's reign the basic principles of the settlement of 1290 were followed by both the king and the clergy, although there were naturally arguments about their applicability to specific cases. The king's position as final and supreme judge in all temporal affairs in the realm was not challenged. Appeals from the secular courts of the bishops went regularly to Parlement. Seizure of the temporalities of the clergy to compel obedience was not infrequent, but there was a real attempt to stop the abuses associated with such seizures.[20] The king kept his share of the bargain by issuing ordinances that repeated many of the provisions of the ordinance of 1290—forbidding interference with ecclesiastical jurisdiction, exempting from tallage those clerks living clerically, allowing prelates to buy up tithes that had been alienated, forbidding royal officials to live and hold court in lands of the Church, and so on.[21] Two observations, however, should be made about these ordinances. First, the fact that there were so many of them shows that it was difficult to make royal officials respect the privileges of the clergy, in spite of the king's promises. Collections of royal mandates to local officials (such as the one of Baudouin for Toulouse) make this fact even more clear. From 1290 to 1296 there are at least 27 letters from Philip to the seneschal, the judges, the consuls, and other officials in Toulouse, ordering them to respect the rights of the clergy.[22] Second, there were almost no ordinances in favor of the Church and relatively few mandates after 1304. The peak came in the

[20] See *Le livre de Guillaume le Maire*, pp. 331 (1294), 370 (1299), for Angers and Tours, and Baudouin, ed., *Lettres* inédites, nos. 5 (1290), 17 (1293), 54 (1300), for Toulouse. "Comestores" (sergeants who used up supplies in occupied buildings) are mentioned as a special grievance.

[21] *Ord.*, I, 329 (ca. 1297), 334 (1300, for Rouen), 340 (1302, for Narbonne), 357 (1303, for the reform of the realm; repeats much of the ordinance for the Church of 1303), XI, 390 (1300, for Mende), XII, 338 (1300, for Narbonne). See also the large number of privileges issued in 1304 for individual churches, discussed in Strayer and Taylor, pp. 39-41. They include many of the provisions of 1290.

[22] Baudouin, ed., *Lettres* inédites, nos. 4-8, 11-13, 16-26, 32-39.

period 1299-1304, and the strongest and most inclusive statement of the rights of the Church was the great privilege of 1304, which was granted individually to each bishop and exempt abbot and, in abbreviated form, to other abbots.[23] This is understandable. The struggle with Boniface VIII and the war with Flanders both reached a climax in 1302-1303; the king needed the moral and material support of his clergy, and he paid for that support with privileges. But even when he was on the defensive, he granted nothing that he had not granted in 1290. Thus in 1304 there was again a suspension of fines for recent amortizations, but no abandonment of the right to take the fines. The jurisdiction of the ecclesiastical and temporal courts of the Church was defined more exactly,[24] but it was not increased in any substantial way. A promise to restore "good money" was made, but this was not a purely ecclesiastical grievance, and Philip did not accept the suggestion of the prelates that future changes in the currency should be made only if the Council declared a state of emergency and the greater barons and prelates gave their consent.[25]

If this was the most that the Church could gain in a period of crisis, it is understandable that in time of peace and with the election of a weak pope the French clergy could obtain no new concessions from the king. It is of course true that most of the problems of interpreting the terms of the compromise of 1290 had been worked out in the period before 1305 and that there was less need for ordinances and letters defining the limits of the two jurisdictions than there had been before. Nevertheless, friction at the local level continued, and most of the grievances of the 1290s were repeated at the Council of Vienne in 1312. It is not surprising that some prelates grew weary of defending their temporal jurisdiction against royal officials (and often against neighboring barons as well). It was easier to make a *paréage*, that is, to associate the king as a partner in the government of lands held by the Church by establishing a common court with officers chosen jointly by king and bishop. A *paréage* removed most of the causes of conflict with royal officials; it also gave some protection against aggression of local nobles. In one year alone (1307) the bishops of Cahors, Le Puy, Limoges, Mende, and Viviers took this step. (This was the same year in which Lyon became irrevocably attached to the realm; the basic problem in Lyon, however, was not a conflict between ecclesiastical and secular jurisdictions but

---

[23] Strayer and Taylor, pp. 39-41.   [24] Ibid., pp. 39-40; *Ord.*, I, 403.
[25] Strayer and Taylor, pp. 35, 40, 98-103.

the question of whether the city lay within the boundaries of the realm.)

Prelates and communities that did not chose to accept a *paréage* could always defend themselves against local pressures by taking their cases to the Parlement. They did so with increasing frequency—and were often successful in obtaining favorable rulings. But it was expensive to sue in the Parlement, and it was also nearly impossible to speed up the deliberations of the Court. Moreover, many administrative acts that injured the Church were scarcely matters that fell within the jurisdiction of the Parlement. They could be remedied only by mandates from the king, and much harm could be done before a mandate could be received and applied. For example, in certain cases the lands of a churchman could be occupied by royal sergeants to enforce obedience to a court order. If there were too many sergeants, they might consume provisions or damage utensils and buildings before a royal mandate could arrive. Or a clerk who had been wrongfully arrested might endure a good deal of suffering in a royal jail before he was freed.[26] Besides these administrative cases, there were areas where rights overlapped and where the king alone could determine the course to follow. Usury was doubtless a sin, but the king reserved to himself the right to punish "enormous usurers."[27] Wills and marriage settlements were the business of the Church, unless they concerned fiefs;[28] but when they did concern fiefs, how were the two authorities to cooperate? In short, the French clergy had to be vigilant politicians and skilled in the law if they were to protect their jurisdictions. They were barely holding their own in the last part of the reign. The fears of Pierre du Bois and of the authors of the memorandum of 1289 that the Church was going to increase greatly its jurisdiction over laymen had proved groundless.

Disputes with the Church over the king's demands for financial support began later than conflicts over jurisdiction and, as far as the French clergy were concerned, caused less irritation. Here again, the increased power of the papacy had the curious result

[26] See examples of these problems in Baudouin, ed., *Lettres inédites*, nos. 5, 12, 17, 18, 23, 33, 54; *Le livre de Guillaume le Maire*, pp. 349, 359, 370; Guillaume Bessin, *Concilia Rotomagensis Provinciae*, 2 vols. (Rouen, 1727), I, 163-64, 168, II, 88.

[27] *Le livre de Guillaume le Maire*, p. 505. This phrase appears in the privilege for the church of Angers, December 1315, as a quotation from an act of Philip the Fair.

[28] *Ord.*, I, 318, art. 8.

of reducing opposition to the demands of the king. Since Innocent III had established the principle that all beneficed clerics could be taxed for the support of papal policies, the clergy had become accustomed to paying a tenth or a twentieth of their revenues when the pope required the grant. The money was supposed to be spent on crusades, but crusades were more and more becoming purely political operations. A crusade to conquer the kingdom of Sicily or the kingdom of Aragon for a French prince cannot have seemed to most French clerics to be very different from a war to establish the authority of the French king in Aquitaine. The great canonist Hostiensis was aware of the unpopularity of political crusades and did his best to explain that disobedience to the pope was worse than the errors of the Saracens, but he admitted that the "ignorant" (that is, most of the people of Europe) did not understand why the Church had to wage war in Europe.[29] Whether "ignorant" or not, the French clergy certainly knew that tenths collected by order of the pope had been given to French kings—to St. Louis for his crusades overseas, to Philip III and Philip the Fair for the Crusade against Aragon. If they had to contribute to the military expenses of their rulers, there was much to be said for making direct grants instead of paying through the papal curia. There was no possibility of arguing against a papal order; there was every possibility of receiving some favors from the king in return for the grant of a tenth. Moreover, most of the French prelates had some sense of loyalty to their king; they were more inclined to help him than to help the pope. In short, since they would have to pay tenths anyway, paying tenths directly to the king could give the French clergy more control over the terms of the grant and the use made of the grant.

For a brief period, from 1294 to 1304, this was the policy followed by the French Church. The tenths that the popes had ordered for the Aragon war had expired and were not renewed. The war of Aquitaine (1294-1303) was not bloody, but for that very reason it was terribly expensive. Large bodies of troops had to be supported in the field or in garrisons for many years, and since they did little fighting, their numbers did not diminish. Philip needed the help of the Church, and in 1294 a series of provincial councils granted him a tenth for two years. The coun-

---

[29] Hostiensis, *Summa aurea* (Venice, 1586), III, 34 (de voto), par. 19 (in quo casu).

cils imposed some conditions on their grants. None was of much importance except the statement of the principle of *cessante causa*: if peace or truce were made, collection of the tenth was to cease.[30] On the other hand, although the Council of Tours imposed no more conditions than did other councils, Bishop Guillaume le Maire of Angers took advantage of the occasion to send in a long and angry letter complaining about the behavior of royal officials. He received an immediate and full response. Philip sent back a series of mandates forbidding the acts that had caused the bishop's protest.[31]

Philip again requested a grant of tenths in 1296, and this time the clergy (or at least the clergy of the province of Narbonne) asked for much more extensive privileges.[32] Before negotiations could begin, Boniface VIII issued the bull *Clericis laicos*, forbidding all contributions by the clergy to lay governments. The bull was not directed specifically against the king of France (it caused just as much trouble to the king of England, who had also been taxing his clergy to pay for the war), but it put an end to negotiations that might have been very profitable for the French Church. It also started a bitter quarrel between Boniface VIII and Philip the Fair.

On 17 August 1296 the king issued an ordinance forbidding the export of arms, horses, and other war equipment, and also the export of money.[33] Such embargoes were common in time of war,[34] and Philip, who was just beginning to tinker with the currency, had good reason to fear that there would be a heavy outflow of precious metals from France.[35] If the ordinance was a direct response to *Clericis laicos*, the reaction was somewhat delayed, since it came almost four months after Boniface had ordered publication of the bull (21 April).[36] Nevertheless, forbid-

---

[30] Strayer and Taylor, pp. 25-28.
[31] *Le livre de Guillaume le Maire*, pp. 322-34.
[32] Strayer and Taylor, p. 29.   [33] Dupuy, *preuves*, p. 13.
[34] Joseph R. Strayer, "Notes on the Origin of English and French Export Taxes," *Studie Gratiana [Post Scripta]*, xv (1972), 417-18. Philip had forbidden export of precious metals before *Clericis laicos*; he also forbade such exports after the death of Boniface.
[35] *Ord.*, I, 334. In 1295, when he was first considering changing the currency, Philip forbade the export of gold and silver.
[36] The bull was dated 24 February; the pope ordered it published in France and England on 21 April. See J. Marrone and C. Zuckerman, "Cardinal Simon of Beaulieu," *Traditio*, xxxi (1975), 212-17. These authors think that there was a delay in publication, since Boniface was not sure

ding the export of money did interfere with the operations of the papacy, notably by making it impossible to transfer 15,000 l.t. to the king of Aragon and thus delaying a proposed alliance between Aragon and Rome.[37] Philip and his councillors cannot have ignored the possibility of such embarrassments, and even if the ordinance was not directed specifically against the pope, it doubtless caused no grief in the French court when Boniface found himself in difficulties.

The pope chose to interpret the ordinance as an attack on the liberties of the Church and the principles of *Clericis laicos*. In the bull *Ineffabilis amor* he claimed, in rather vague terms, "dominion" over all the faithful.[38] Then he denounced Philip's behavior, criticized his financial exactions, and threatened to join the kings of England and Germany, who were justly complaining of French aggression.[39]

This unyielding attitude stirred up a campaign against Boniface in France. Scurrilous stories about the morals and faith of the pope were circulated in Paris. They had been inspired by the Colonna and other cardinals who disliked Boniface,[40] and they had no great impact in 1296-1297, but they were remembered and used in the next crisis. At a higher level, two remarkable treatises appeared supporting the king: the *Disputatio inter clericum et*

---

in August that the bull had been published. Digard, I, 262, 269, points out that the king's itinerary would indicate publication in April and that the clergy of France were concerned by 20 May about the situation caused by the bull. Formal publication in England was certainly much later than in France.

[37] Digard, II, 302 (letter of James of Aragon to the pope, 29 September 1296).

[38] Dupuy, *preuves*, p. 15. Christ gave the Church liberty and many graces. "Voluit enim peramabilem sponsam eius libero fidelibus populis praeesse dominio," so that she could have "potestatem" over everyone and be honored by all as "universalem matrem et dominam."

[39] Ibid., p. 17, and especially p. 19. "Quid ergo tibi accideret si, quod absit, sedem ipsam offenderes graviter, eamque hostium tuorum constituere adiutricem, quin potius contra te faceres principalem." Boniface also warned Philip that he was losing the support of his subjects (ibid., p. 16).

[40] Digard, I, 248, 286-89. Finke, "Zur Charakteristik Philipps des Schönen," p. 211, thinks that the cumulative effect of this propaganda was great. Most of the stories about Boniface may be found in Dupuy, pp. 523-75, and in the *Processus super zelo* (on the good faith of Philip the Fair), edited by C. Höfler, in "Rückblick auf P. Bonifacius VIII," in *Abhandlungen der historische Klasse der Königlich Bayerischen Akademie der Wissenschaften*, III (Munich, 1843).

militem and the *Antequam essent clerici*.[41] The first tract certainly did not represent the official position of the government, though it would not have displeased many members of the Council. It denied all power to the pope in temporal affairs, even "ratione peccati," and insisted that all church property could be used to defend the country against its enemies. The author ended with an emphatic assertion of the king's legislative power: he can change laws and customs as he wills after consulting the magnates.

Antequam essent clerici is closer to the statements of royal officials and may have been written by one of them; at least it was preserved in a register of the Trésor des Chartes. It is just as firm on the essential points. The king may take any steps necessary to defend the realm, including an embargo on the export of money. He may also ask the clergy to contribute to the cost of defense; to forbid them to do so is against natural law. But although the author insists on these rights, he does not argue that royal power is practically unlimited; nor does he deny that the Church has some reason to be concerned about temporal affairs. The trouble, he says, is that the Church is following the wrong policy; it should be helping, not threatening, the king.

Gossip and propaganda doubtless had some effect, but the most direct way of putting pressure on the pope was to work through the French clergy. Even before *Ineffabilis amor* Pierre Flote had warned the northern archbishops (Sens, Reims, and Rouen) that refusal to aid the king was endangering the French Church, and the papal legate had agreed. During June 1296 a large number of bishops and abbots met at Paris to discuss the danger. The assembly sent two bishops to the pope with letters explaining the plight of the French clergy; if the pope would not arrange a compromise, the Church of France would be ruined.[42]

Boniface did not heed this warning, but he soon discovered, as Nicholas IV had in 1290, that he could not carry out his European policies, and especially his Italian policies, without French

---

[41] For the *Disputatio* see Melchior Goldast, *Monarchia* (Munich, 1612), I, 13-18. There is a new critical edition, with translation by Norma N. Erickson, in *Proceedings of the American Philosophical Society*, CXI (1967), 288-309. For *Antequam essent clerici* see Dupuy, *preuves*, pp. 21-23.

[42] Digard, I, 268-69. The documents may be found in Martène, *Thesaurus novus anecdotorum*, 5 vols. (Paris, 1717), IV, cols. 219-23, and Dupuy, *preuves*, p. 26. The latter document, a letter from the archbishop of Reims, speaks of the persecution of the clergy by laymen and the danger of the "final ruin" of the Gallican Church.

support. He was determined to drive Frederick of Aragon out of Sicily; he dreamed of a universal peace in western Europe that would allow a new crusade to be proclaimed. Neither project had any chance of success if France were hostile. To make matters worse, in 1297 the great Roman family of the Colonna openly broke with the pope and declared the abdication of Celestine V illegal. If this were true, then the election of Boniface VIII as Celestine's successor would be void. The real issue was a power struggle in central Italy in which neither side was guiltless. Boniface had been trying to build up his family's possessions at the expense of the Colonna, and the Colonna had responded by hijacking some money being sent to Rome to enable the pope to acquire new lands. These details of petty Italian politics were not known north of the Alps, although the Colonna accusations made a considerable impression in France as well as in Italy. Boniface could depose the two Colonna cardinals and seize many of their possessions, but he still had a very messy local war on his hands and the time bomb of the accusations ticking away. The Colonna were given some secret assurances of support by French officials (according to their story, by Pierre Flote).[43] It was obviously time for a change of course.

In January 1297 the archbishops of Reims, Sens, Rouen (and probably Narbonne) again asked permission to aid the king.[44] This time Boniface authorized the grant (28 February 1297), but only for evident necessity and for this one occasion.[45] By summer, however, the dangers in Italy were greater, for the Colonna were openly attacking the legitimacy of the pope. On 31 July Boniface, in the bull *Etsi de statu*, authorized the king to demand subsidies from the clergy, without consulting the pope, whenever it seemed necessary for defense.[46] A few days later (11 August) the canonization of Louis IX, long requested by the king, was proclaimed. The complete dependence of the papacy on French support had never been made more clearly manifest. It must have been a galling experience for Boniface VIII, and it explains some

[43] Digard, I, 338-40.   [44] Ibid., pp. 305-6.
[45] *Les Registres de Boniface VIII*, ed. Georges Digard, M. Faucon, Antoine Thomas (Paris, 1907-1939), no. 2333.
[46] Dupuy, *preuves*, p. 39. Here and elsewhere I have preferred to use Dupuy's transcriptions, even though they are at times faulty, in preference to those of the *Register*, because Dupuy gives the versions preserved in French archives and therefore the ones on which French polemicists relied.

of the angry remarks about French arrogance that he is supposed to have made at this time.

Even before *Etsi de statu*, the French clergy had taken advantage of the limited concession of February 1297, and a council held at Paris in March gave the king a double tenth. The only important reservation was that collection was to cease if the war ended. *Etsi de statu* discouraged the French Church so completely that it renewed the grant of a double tenth in 1298 without receiving any concessions from the king.[47] Thus the French clergy paid four tenths in two years—which was exactly what Philip had requested in 1296. As in 1290, papal intervention had weakened, not strengthened, the position of the French Church. Its interests had been sacrificed to the exigencies of papal policy. Direct negotiation with the king must have seemed to many prelates to be preferable to reliance on the pope.

Meanwhile, Philip acted as if tenths were now a regular part of his income. When the double tenth of 1298 had been collected, he immediately asked for a new grant. It is not quite clear how the negotiations were conducted; probably there were discussions in provincial councils, as there had been in 1294. Philip took a very firm position at a meeting in Paris, according to one report, and threatened to use force if a grant were not made, but the story comes from an unfriendly source, the Cistercian abbey of Dunes.[48] It seems more likely that the councils conceded a tenth for two years without much hesitation but requested confirmation of clerical privileges in return. In March 1300 the provinces of Rouen, Narbonne, and Bordeaux and the diocese of Mende received letters restating many of the articles of the 1290 ordinance for the Church.[49] The documents are not identical, which suggests that there had been separate meetings for each province,

---

[47] Martène, *Thesaurus*, I, col. 1277. See also Mignon, no. 712: "Decime duplex . . . concesse fuit regi Philippo Pulero a papa Bonifacio VIII ad requisitionem prelatorum." The renewal of the grant in 1298, according to Mignon, was "imposita per regem virtute privilegii obtenti a dicta papa." The abbot of Cîteaux spoke of a council but agreed that the clergy were "coactus" by the pope's letter; see *Codex Dunensis*, p. 275.

[48] The king is supposed to have said, "posset si vellet, virtute regia et privilegialiter fecisse quod forte nobis fuisset intolerabile et dampnosum" (*Codex Dunensis*, p. 524). Mignon, no. 766, mentions a council at Lyon, and there may have been others.

[49] *Ord.*, I, 334 (Rouen), XI, 309 (Mende), XII, 338 (Narbonne); *Gallia Christiana*, II, *Instrumenta*, col. 395 (Bordeaux).

but all four have many points in common. If the letters of March 1300 were issued in return for the grant of the tenth, then the French Church gained more for its money in that year than it ever had before.

The fairly amicable arrangements of 1299 were upset by the quarrel between Philip and Boniface VIII over Bishop Bernard Saisset. Late in 1301 the pope forbade the clergy to pay any more money to the king. A few dioceses paid one and a half years of the two-year tenth; most paid only one year.[50]

During the first phase of the struggle with Boniface VIII the king, quite sensibly, made no further demands on the French Church, but by the early summer of 1303 he could no longer hold his hand. The disastrous defeat of the French army at Courtrai had to be avenged, and the king was in desperate need of money. The French clergy could ask a high price for their aid, and they knew it. They drew up a long document criticizing the royal administration and requesting important concessions in return for their grant. The two most significant demands were for free amortization of recent acquisitions by the Church and for a reform of the currency. Even more, they asked that the currency should never again be debased, "sine magna et inevitabile necessitate," and that the existence of such a necessity would have to be certified by a meeting of great barons and prelates.[51]

This was an intelligent and far-reaching program. If it had been fully accepted by the king, the French Church might have obtained a veto power over some elements of royal policy, and its example might have been followed by the other privileged classes. But Philip and his ministers were experts in the game of making wide concessions that did not touch basic principles. After prolonged negotiations with provincial councils they received the grant of a double tenth from the bishops and exempt abbots and a single tenth from the rest of the clergy. Individual charters were issued in 1304 to each prelate and community—not, be it noted, to the French Church as a collective group.[52] The king promised to reform the currency within a year. All recent acquisitions of the churches and all future acquisitions of land for cemeteries and church buildings were to be amortized freely

[50] Mignon, nos. 766-79. Collection ceased "propter inhibitionem papae."
[51] Strayer and Taylor, pp. 34-37, 98-103.
[52] Ibid., pp. 38-39 (an incomplete list of the individual charters appears in nn. 126 and 127).

(this concession seemed to one royal official to be the key to the grant). The rules safeguarding the temporal jurisdiction of churchmen as laid down by earlier ordinances were restated. Serfs of the Church were exempt from the current lay subsidy. Collection of the tenths was to cease if peace or truce were made. Special auditors were to be appointed to hear the grievances of the clergy.[53]

These concessions were somewhat less than the clergy had asked, and some of them were only temporary (for example, the suspension of payments for amortization of revenue-producing land). There were protests in some dioceses, notably in Tours, where the king had to seize the temporalities of the archbishop.[54] But if the clergy were unhappy, the king himself was not wholly pleased. He apparently reached the same conclusion that the clergy had: the pope would give more and worry less about protecting the interests of the French Church. With the advent of a neutral and then of a friendly pope (Benedict XI and Clement V), Philip stopped asking his clergy to make their own grants of tenths. Benedict granted a two-year tenth in 1304 to restore good money (collected only in 1307 and 1308); Clement V granted a tenth in 1310 and 1312, and a six-year tenth (nominally for a crusade) in 1313.[55] The French clergy gained no new privileges on any of these occasions.

Other payments made by the French Church were fines for amortization and annates. The fines have been discussed above;[56] they were an annoyance, but not nearly as expensive as the tenths, especially since there was always a chance of having them forgiven. Annates were granted only twice, in 1297 and in 1301; they brought in very little money in comparison with the tenths.[57]

---

[53] Ibid., pp. 40-41. The collector for Sens thought that the waiver of payments for amortization was the chief reason for the grant: "Decime duplex a prelatis et personis provincie Senoneusis pro admortisationibus suorum acquestuum concesse . . ." (Mignon, no. 794).

[54] A.N., J 350, nos. 5, 6, 7. In no. 5 Philip insisted that "tanquam rex et princeps auctoritate sue potest facere impositiones super quascumque personas regni sui et eas capere et levare, specialiter in casu necessitatis." The king apparently was willing to lose money to establish this principle, for his collectors told him that there was more profit in a single tenth paid freely than in a double tenth taken by force.

[55] Mignon, nos. 796, 815, 828, 838-62. The income of one year of the six-year tenth was reserved for the pope.

[56] See p. 256.

[57] Mignon, nos. 469-528 (grant of annates for three years, 1297-1300, and

A tenth was worth about 260,000 l.t.,[58] a sum equal to about half of the king's regular revenue from other sources.[59] It was the only financial burden that affected the clergy as a whole, although amortization fines hit individual communities hard in certain years. But the tenth was not an impossible burden; it was assessed at conventional figures, and after 1304 it caused little controversy. In fact, even before 1304 the basic problems of the relationship between the king and the French Church had been decided, and the conflict with Boniface VIII in 1301-1303 did not greatly change the terms of the settlement. The ordinance of 1290 (with its reenactment and interpretations) had provided rules to determine conflicts of jurisdiction. *Etsi de statu* had given a reasonable solution to the question of the taxation of the clergy. Although there was a good deal of scolding in 1301 and 1302 about appointments to benefices, this does not seem to have been a major issue at other times. Doubtless Philip was not entirely pleased with some of Boniface's nominees; at Laon, for example, 22 of the 51 men named to prebends between 1294 and 1303 were Italians.[60]

---

notes on collector's accounts), 535-60 (grant of annates for three years, 1304-1307, and notes on the accounts). Mignon gives no complete totals, but arrears in the province of Narbonne for 1297-1300 were at least 12,000 l.t. (no. 520), which works out to 400 l.t. per diocese per year. Since arrears were high everywhere, this may be close to actual payments. The arrears for Rouen (a much wealthier province) for 1304-1307 were 18,200 l.t. (in round figures), or about 867 l.t. per diocese per year (ibid., no. 549). Payments for annates in 1297-1300 were regularly much smaller than those for tenths; for example, on 11 July 1299 the collector for Clermont turned in 7,954 l.t. from a double tenth and 996 l.t. from annates (*J.T.P.*, nos. 3008-10). Other examples include: 1,484 l.t. from the double tenth and 104 l.t. from annates of Le Puy (ibid., nos. 3012-13); 4,932 l.t. from the tenth and 1,350 l.t. from annates of Rodez (nos. 3015-17); in Mende, 1,316 l.t. from the tenth and 410 l.t. from annates (nos. 3018-19); for the province of Narbonne, without Carcassonne, 4,853 l.t. from the tenth, and 2,336 l.t. for annates *including* Carcassonne (nos. 3029-30); in Angers, 2,079 l.t. from the tenth and 420 l.t. from annates (nos. 3041-43); in Le Mans, 2,250 l.t. from the tenth and 148 l.t. from annates (nos. 3044-45).

[58] *H.F.*, xxi, 545, 560; Borrelli de Serres, *Recherches*, ii, 465 ff.

[59] Borrelli de Serres (*Recherches*, ii, 489 and App. A, table 2) estimates annual revenue in the period 1286-1292, including tenths, at about 650,000 l.p., or 812,500 l.t.; subtracting 260,000 l.t. for the tenth, ordinary revenue would be about 550,000 l.t. Elizabeth A. R. Brown, "Royal Salvation," p. 375, estimates annual revenue in the last years of the reign at 600,000 l.t.

[60] I take these figures from the unpublished work of Fr. Fernando Pico, S.J., "The Cathedral Chapter of Laon, 1155-1318," which he kindly allowed me to consult. Some of the dates of appointment are not entirely certain,

On the other hand, the king had had little difficulty in securing bishoprics for his senior officials and benefices for his younger men. There had been some bickering about what was later called "spiritual regalia," that is, the right of the king to fill benefices that became vacant while he held the temporal regalia of a see, but these quarrels affected only a few men and were limited to a few dioceses.[61] Arguing about appointments to benefices was a symbol rather than a cause of the final conflict. To Philip, the right to name his own men demonstrated his exceptional position in the Church; to Boniface, absolute control of appointments was a sign of the plenitude of papal power.

Even this latent quarrel was almost buried at the end of 1297. Boniface gave Philip the right to fill one benefice on every cathedral or collegiate church in the kingdom; this grace would have provided for all of Philip's unbeneficed clerks.[62] In addition, Boniface had granted annates from all new appointments for three years. The final favor—the canonization of Louis IX—should have marked the beginning of a new era of cooperation between king and pope. Instead, the reconciliation was only temporary, perhaps because it had been forced on the pope by rather unscrupulous means, such as the threat to support the Colonna, but even more because both Philip and Boniface were a little too conscious of their dignity. They were both aware that they embodied ancient traditions that must be passed on, untarnished, to their successors, and they were therefore too ready to take offense. In addition, Boniface was vulnerable because, even according to his most sympathetic biographers, he could not control his temper. Philip doubtless felt human anger at times, but it is very difficult to find a statement of his that expresses such anger. Here he reaped one of the advantages of always allowing his ministers to speak for him. They could make outrageous charges while Philip preserved an attitude of cool reasonableness. It is significant that all the striking anecdotes about the controversy

but Boniface was surely responsible for most of these Italians, and Laon was one of the oldest royal bishoprics.

[61] Philip finally established his right to spiritual regalia in Sens, Paris, Chartres, Orléans, Meaux, Reims, Thérouanne, Tournai, Beauvais, Laon, Noyon, all the Norman dioceses except Séez, and Tours (Gaudemet, pp. 63-66).

[62] *Registres de Boniface VIII*, no. 2356. The number of benefices is not given, but when Clement V in 1306 gave a similar grace, 186 prebends were awarded; see Petit et al., pp. 148-54.

refer to Boniface. He may never have said that he "would humble
the pride of the French," that he "would rather be a dog than a
Frenchman"; the point is that people believed that he could say
such things.[63] Even before he became pope he had had a tendency
to use violent language. The French clergy remembered that as
a papal legate in 1290 Boniface had called the masters of the University of Paris fools and pedants for daring to question the privileges of the mendicant orders.[64] This memory made them more
willing to believe stories about threats made to French ambassadors. The councillors of Philip the Fair, who were condemned
rather indiscriminately in the bull *Ausculta fili*,[65] were also not
inclined to trust the soundness of the pope's judgement. It had
not been difficult to start a propaganda war against Boniface in
1296; it was even easier in 1302 because of the increasing number
of reports about the pope's bad temper.

The events that caused the final break between Philip and
Boniface occurred in Languedoc, a region where the authority
of both pope and king had been challenged throughout the thirteenth century. The Cathari (the Albigensian heretics) had been
driven underground, but they still survived in relatively large
numbers. The Inquisition was still busy—too busy, in the opinion
of many southerners. The Spiritual (radical) Franciscans, uphold-
ers of the rule of absolute poverty, usually mingled this dangerous
idea with the doctrines of Joachim of Fiore about the end of one
age of the Church and the beginning of a new and different order.
They had strong support in Languedoc. They may have only
skirted the edge of heresy, but their doctrines certainly threw

---

[63] Boniface is supposed to have told Philip's envoy in 1296 that he would
humble the pride of the French (Digard, 1, 289). He almost certainly did
say, in recognizing Albert of Habsburg as emperor-elect, that the emperor
was monarch of all kings and princes, and he added: "nec insurgat hic
superbia Gallicana quae dicit quod non recognoscit superiorem. Mentiuntur,
quia de jure sunt et esse debent sub Rege Romanorum et Imperatore." This
account comes from a note by Baluze on chapter 3, book 2 of Peter de
Marca, *De Concordia sacerdotii et imperii* (Frankfurt, 1708), p. 105. The
story about preferring to be a dog rather than a Frenchman comes from
Plaisians (Dupuy, *preuves*, p. 102), not a good source. But Boniface did say
that he could depose the king as if he were getting rid of a petty servant
("sicut unum garcionem"), and in the same speech he implied that the
king was a fool (Dupuy, *preuves*, pp. 78-79). There are many other examples of the pope's intemperate language.

[64] Heinrich Finke, *Aus den Tagen Bonifaze VIII. Funde und Forschungen*
(Münster, 1902), *Quellen*, pp. vi-vii.

[65] See above, note 2.

some doubts on papal power. One of their most venerated, if most cautious, leaders, Pierre Jean d'Olive, lived in the Franciscan convent of Narbonne. Being persecuted themselves, the Spiritual Franciscans felt some sympathy for other victims of persecution. Bernard Délicieux, a Franciscan of Carcassonne, led the movement against the Inquisition of Languedoc in the early 1300s. Finally, the Colonna, whose feud with Boniface VIII had reached the level of civil war politically and of schism ecclesiastically, had married into the leading families of Languedoc. They could live there securely, and they had the support of a large part of the population.[66] Since the Colonna had denied the validity of the abdication of Celestine V—and thus the legitimacy of the election of Boniface VIII—and since Boniface had preached a crusade against them, supporting the Colonna was about as bad as embracing the open heresy of the Cathari or the borderline heresy of the Spirituals. Boniface simply could not risk any further weakening of his authority in Languedoc.

Philip the Fair was in much the same situation. He never felt entirely happy about Languedoc. It was full of almost independent bishops, cities with a strong tradition of self-government, and nobles who had only a tenuous connection with the government in Paris. The border with Aquitaine was uncertain; the border with Aragon was still not fixed at an essential point (the Val d'Aran). The people of Languedoc were not French in language or in spirit. They had not rebelled since 1242, but the idea of rebellion was not dead. In 1300 they were ready to rebel against the Inquisition, and Philip, though he sympathized with their grievances, decided in the end (probably rightly) that rebellion against the Inquisition might lead to a rebellion against French domination.[67] Therefore, he kept a careful eye on Languedoc through frequent visits of *enquêteurs*[68] and through extensive

[66] E. Martin-Chabot, "Contribution à l'histoire de la famille Colonna," *Annuaire-Bulletin de la Société de l'Histoire de France*, LVII (1920), 137 ff. Gaucerande de l'Isle-Jourdain, daughter of one of the most powerful barons of Languedoc, married Stefano Colonna, nephew of cardinal Giacomo Colonna in 1285, and her sister married the viscount of Narbonne (ibid., pp. 140, 145-47). When Boniface attacked the Colonna in 1297, Stefano took refuge in the region of Narbonne. The pope asked Philip to expel him, but Philip did not act, nor did Gilles Aicelin, archbishop of Narbonne.

[67] See above, p. 14.

[68] For the basic list of *enquêteurs* see Glénisson, II, 260-74. See also B.N., ms. Doat 156, fols. 1, 39, ms. Doat 176, fols. 143, 217v; *Olim*, II, 464, III, 336-72; *H.L.*, X, cols. 257, 414; B.N., ms. nouv. acq. fr. 7430, fol. 295; A.M.,

correspondence with his seneschals. Like Boniface, Philip felt that he could not risk any weakening of his authority in the region.

Thus both king and pope were ready to exaggerate the importance of a rather trivial incident that occurred in 1301. Bernard Saisset, bishop of Pamiers, was a quarrelsome and somewhat too talkative man. He was something of a protégé of the pope, but he was on bad terms with his immediate neighbors—with the bishop of Toulouse because the diocese of Pamiers had been carved out of the (admittedly too large) diocese of Toulouse, with the count of Foix, who had claims to the town of Pamiers, and with the consuls of Pamiers, who wanted greater rights of self-government.[69] He had been involved in long and undoubtedly costly lawsuits—and the diocese was not rich. One can imagine the irritable old bishop, sitting by his fireplace after a few drinks (*post potum*, said one witness), grumbling about the stupid king and his foolish policies and about how much better it would be if they could get rid of the damn French.

That he said something like this seems to be certain. There was no reason to invent the original charges against Bernard Saisset; he simply was not that important. He had, as far as can be seen, done little to annoy local or central royal authorities. If he had been slow about obeying court orders, so had everyone else. Moreover, most of the conversation rings true; this is just what a good Occitanian would say about the French whom he feared, obeyed, and detested.[70] To complain about the king's monetary policy was not unusual; most other French bishops did the same. To compare the king with an owl, the handsome bird who simply stares and can say nothing, was an insult that deeply annoyed the king,[71] and it seems very likely that Saisset invented the phrase. There is no exact parallel in other criticisms of Philip, though the idea, of course, was a commonplace; everyone had noticed that Philip let his ministers speak for him on important occasions. It is also quite possible that the bishop repeated prophecies about

Périguex, FF 6. Between 1301 and 1304 the *enquêteurs* were almost in permanent residence in the south; they were especially active in Toulouse and Carcasonne.

[69] Baudouin, ed., *Lettres inédites*, nos. 54n, 129, 131-32, 134.

[70] See below, p. 388.

[71] See Dupuy, *preuves*, pp. 632-57, for the accusations. The owl simile appears on pp. 643, 656. Professor Charles Wood suggests that it stung because the unblinking pose was that of majesty, and the bishop was ridiculing it.

the approaching downfall of the Capetian dynasty; stories of this sort circulated everywhere in Europe about all prominent families. Insults and criticism of the king were annoying, but they could hardly be called treason. There was some evidence about treason, but it was vague and unconvincing; it sounds like more of Saisset's after-dinner ramblings. He may have told the count of Foix that he should join the count of Comminges, seek Aragonese support, and establish an independent principality in western Languedoc,[72] but no witness suggested that he raised a finger to implement such a plan. The count reported this conversation to the bishop of Toulouse, not to a royal official, and the bishop was so unimpressed that he did not mention the matter to anyone until a year had passed.[73] The fact that Bernard Saisset was allowed to return peacefully to his diocese after the storm was over shows that no one felt that he was guilty of any serious crime. He did have to surrender some land and a considerable amount of money,[74] probably just because he had made a lot of trouble.

It is still difficult to understand why the grumblings of an obscure bishop should have caused one of the great crises in the history of the medieval Church. After all, Guichard, bishop of Troyes (a much more important diocese), who was accused only a few months earlier of allowing the escape of a man who had embezzled some of the income of the county of Champagne, was ruined both politically and financially by Philip. Yet the pope never lifted a finger to protect Guichard, even though the accusations against the bishop were probably completely false instead of merely exaggerated, as in the case of Bernard Saisset.[75] It is true that Philip observed the forms of due process more closely in the case of Guichard than in that of Bernard; but even in Bernard's case he eventually acted correctly. One can only say that the explosive situation in Languedoc in 1301 made both Philip and Boniface ready for a confrontation. The war of Aquitaine was suspended, but not officially ended; Bordeaux was to rebel

[72] Ibid., pp. 633-34, 645, 648-50.   [73] Ibid., pp. 634, 641.

[74] Bernard Saisset was restored to favor in 1308 (*H.L.*, x, cols. 478-79, 481). He made what Clement V considered a disadvantageous exchange of property with the king at this time. According to A.D. Aude, H 325 (published in part in the Inventory of series G and H), 40,000 l.t. was taken from the bishop when he was arrested and deposited, "with his consent," in a monastery. It is not clear whether Saisset ever recovered the money. At least 15,000 l.t. of the deposit was used in suppressing the rebellion in Bordeaux (see note 76 below).

[75] See the Appendix to this chapter.

against French occupation only a year later.[76] The count of Foix was loyal to Philip—at a price. He had to be grossly overpaid for his military assistance, and Edward of England had come close to getting his support.[77] Opposition to the Inquisition had reached alarming proportions in Albi and Carcasonne, and the king was trying to appease the laymen of western Languedoc by curbing the powers of the inquisitors.[78] This intervention in turn annoyed the bishops, who had not been entirely placated by the confirmation of their privileges in 1300.[79] The teams of enquêteurs whom Philip kept in Languedoc during this period had an almost impossible task. If they took steps to satisfy the lay (and especially the urban) population, they ran the risk of ecclesiastical censures. It would not be surprising if the chief enquêteurs, Richard Leneveu and Jean de Picquigny, had decided to counter charges that they were betraying the Church by reporting charges that a bishop was betraying the king.[80] Bernard Saisset was a good target. His complaints were widely known and scurrilous enough to give some excuse for action. He was important enough to show that no one could attack the king with impunity, unimportant enough so that there would be no demonstrations in his favor. Digard thought that Flote concocted this plan.[81] Perhaps he did, but Flote must have received his essential information about Saisset from the enquêteurs, and they were both tough enough and experienced enough to have recommended the action on their own account. Richard Leneveu, archdeacon of Auge, was a friend of Pierre du Bois, well acquainted with the south, and ready to back Philip in any enterprise.[82] He served as administrator of the diocese of

[76] This was a serious affair; it cost at least 124,000 l.t. to regain control of Bordeaux (Mignon, nos. 2430-35).

[77] The count was owed 48,000 l.t. for his services in Gascony, but he did little (H.L., IX, 183, 199, 200, X, cols. 338-39). See Bémont, III, no. 2936, and H.L., IX, 184, for Edward's overtures.

[78] H.L., X, cols. 273, 379, 382-85.   [79] Ord., XII, 338.

[80] See H.L., X, col. 415, and Hist. litt., XXVII, 427, for attacks on the two enquêteurs. Picquigny was eventually excommunicated for attacking the Inquisition, see H.L., IX, 258, and Hist. litt., XXI, 417, XXXIV, 105.

[81] Digard, II, 55. The orders to investigate the bishop came from Paris, but only because trustworthy persons had reported his offenses (Dupuy, preuves, 627-28).

[82] Pierre sent one of his briefs to Richard Leneveu in 1302 (du Bois, De recuperatione, p. ix). Richard was already working in the south early in 1298 (J.T.P., nos. 3029, 3057); he helped make an inquest on dues levied at Aigues-Mortes in January 1299 (A.N., J 892, no. 9, fol. 1).

Nîmes when the bishop was driven out for supporting Boniface[83] and, as a crowning irony, ended his life as bishop of Béziers. Jean de Picquigny, vidame of Amiens, was especially hostile to the Inquisition and died excommunicate because he had offended an inquisitor.[84] They certainly collected the testimony against Bernard Saisset and used torture on some witnesses, though even then no really damning evidence was recorded.[85] Pierre Flote had to add a few embellishments of his own about heresy in order to make a plausible case against the bishop.[86] This is another reason for believing that it was the *enquêteurs* who initiated the action. Pierre Flote had usually prepared a complete story before he acted.

In any case, Richard Leneveu and the vidame could claim that they acted "de mandato domini regis."[87] Either they, or someone at Paris, had persuaded the king to make an example of Bernard Saisset. The rather unimpressive testimony against him was collected in May and July 1301, and the *enquêteurs* must have wondered whether they could do much with it. Fortunately for them, the bishop became alarmed and announced that he was leaving for Rome. This attempt to flee was obviously a sign of guilt. On 12 August Bernard's subordinates were arrested and questioned; his palace was searched, and he was ordered to appear in person before the king. After some delay, he was conducted under armed guard to the north and on 24 October appeared before the king at Senlis.[88] There were several stormy meetings of the Council. Obviously, laymen could not judge a bishop, or even keep him

---

[83] *Hist. litt.*, xxvi, 549-50; *H.L.*, ix, 239.

[84] The prior of the Dominicans of Toulouse said that Jean encouraged the enemies of the Inquisition to a point where no Dominican was safe in the region (*Hist. litt.*, xxvii, 427). For the excommunication see above, note 80.

[85] See Dupuy, *preuves*, p. 652, for Saisset's complaints about torture of some of his followers. There is a more accurate version of this complaint in Digard, ii, 59, n. 4. The testimony of the witnesses is in Dupuy, pp. 633-51.

[86] Dupuy, *preuves*, pp. 628-29. The charges of heresy are clearly an addition to the original accusation, as Digard, ii, 81-82, points out.

[87] Dupuy, *preuves*, p. 633.

[88] Most of this information comes from the protest of Saisset to the king (ibid., *preuves*, pp. 651-53). The expense account of Jean de Burlas, master of the arbalesters, for arresting Saisset and bringing him before the king is in *J.T.P.*, no. 5562. The journey cost almost 500 l.t., which suggests that the escort was fairly large.

in custody, and, just as obviously, Philip was too irritated with Saisset to set him free. Gilles Aicelin, archbishop of Narbonne and thus Saisset's metropolitan, did his best to preserve the basic privilege of clergy; he insisted that Saisset should be sent back to Narbonne to be guarded there by his ecclesiastical superior. The most that Gilles could obtain was a compromise by which he was given "territory" in Senlis (that is, a house there was temporarily annexed to his diocese) and responsibility for guarding his suffragan. The date is uncertain, probably near the end of November 1301.[89]

This decision ended the case as far as Bernard Saisset the man was concerned. His confinement at Senlis did not last long; Philip sent him to Rome sometime in February 1302,[90] where he dropped out of sight until the crisis was over. But Bernard Saisset the symbol became the center of a violent controversy. Philip had certainly broken his own rules, as laid down in the ordinances for the Church. He had seized Saisset's lands without need and had filled them with *comestores*. He had not allowed the bishop to plead his case through a procurator. He had, at the very least, considered judging Saisset before a lay tribunal for a personal offense.[91] Although there had been some attempt to preserve appearances, a bishop had in fact been arrested and held as a prisoner by laymen. If this was the case against Philip, even under French law, it is easy to imagine how much worse it looked to the pope. Boniface was furious and showed his anger immediately.

Philip would have been glad to hush up the whole matter. He must have realized by November that Saisset, though an irritating person, was no danger to the realm. Some of the lay members of

[89] Dupuy, *preuves*, pp. 629-30 (the king's version of these events); Martène, *Thesaurus*, I, 1325-30 (Gilles Aicelin's version). See also *Gallia Christiana*, XIII, cols. 107-15.

[90] Digard, I, 95-96.

[91] On the ordinances in favor of the Church see above, pp. 245-48. In his protest (see note 88 above), Saisset quotes these ordinances fairly accurately. As for threats to judge the bishop in the king's court, see Dupuy, *preuves*, p. 630: "quod licet dominus rex de magnorum consilio conveniret quod tantum et talem proditorem suum coram se convictum posset et debet statim supplicio ipsum tradendo de medio tollere regni sui. . . ." Digard, I, 343, points out that the bull *Nuper ad audientiam* (27 July 1297) allowed royal officers to arrest clerks guilty of treasonous acts, provided that they were then turned over to designated prelates. It is curious that neither Philip nor Boniface mentioned this bull during the controversy over Saisset, perhaps because Gilles Aicelin was not one of the designated prelates.

the Council were less forbearing and expressed their anger in violent terms, but the experienced administrators were calmer, and they helped to work out the face-saving compromise by which Saisset was turned over to Gilles Aicelin.[92] The complete release of the prisoner soon followed, and Philip and his closest advisers may have hoped that these tactics would end the problem.

Unfortunately, the timing was bad. The seizure of Saisset's possessions and the arrest of members of his household had coincided almost exactly with a renewal of the agitation against the Inquisition, an agitation supported by the same *enquêteurs* who were collecting charges against the bishop. The proceedings against Saisset at Senlis coincided with efforts to force the Inquisitor of Toulouse out of office.[93] Boniface could easily have felt that there was a concerted effort to destroy his authority in Languedoc. And although the release of Saisset to the custody of the archbishop of Narbonne removed some of the worst breaches of privilege, Boniface must have decided to attack Philip before he knew of this decision. Bulls such as those of 5 December are not prepared in a single day, and even if couriers had traveled with extraordinary speed, the pope could not have had a report of the proceedings at Senlis until after the final drafts of *Ausculta fili* and its companions had been written.[94] If Philip had acted more rapidly— say, at the end of October rather than in late November—Boniface might have been less severe, but even then he would have been indignant about the events of the summer.

As it was, the pope went as far as he could without actually excommunicating or deposing the king. All privileges granted to Philip, including the right to take tenths from the clergy without seeking papal consent, were suspended.[95] All French bishops were summoned to a council to discuss the injustices of the king and his officers, not only to the clergy, but also to the laity of the realm.[96] Finally, in a long and angry letter to Philip (*Ausculta*

[92] *Gallia Christiana*, XIII, cols. 110-13. The councillors who recommended the final solution included Gilles Lambert, Guillaume Bonnet, Pierre de Belleperche, and Pierre de Mornay—all men with legal experience who were more moderate than Flote or Nogaret.

[93] *H.L.*, IX, 228, 239, 257, X, cols. 379-83; Digard, II, 79-81.

[94] Digard, II, 85, doubts that in drafting his bulls Boniface could have known about a statement in favor of Saisset made by the archbishop of Reims on 23 November.

[95] Dupuy, *preuves*, pp. 42-43.

[96] Ibid., *preuves*, pp. 53-54. Boniface included in his summons French doctors of theology, teachers of canon and civil law, and procurators of

fili) he listed the king's misdeeds, one by one, and declared that it was the pope's duty to correct them.[97]

Both the general tone and the specific details of the letter seemed deliberately planned to enrage the king. Boniface began with the flat statement that the king, who claimed to have no superior, did in fact have a superior: the Head of the Church. This was harmless enough, if Boniface had added "in spiritual affairs"; but he left out this phrase, and all the rest of the letter suggests that he did so deliberately. He criticized Philip's monetary policy, his embargo on exports, his choice of councillors, the administration of justice, and the financial system of the country.[98] He announced that the council of the French clergy would discuss measures to assure the good government of France,[99] again with no restriction to Church-state relationships. Philip was told that he or his envoys could attend the council if they wished, but that (in accordance with canon law) it would proceed whether or not he was represented. There were ambiguities and reservations in some phrases, but it is hard to see how any layman could have read the document without interpreting it as an assertion of papal sovereignty in temporal as well as in spiritual matters.

Even on the purely ecclesiastical side, there were items that were bound to annoy anyone who could remember the history of the last 15 years. In some passages Boniface seemed to be repudiating the compromise that he had helped to work out as papal legate in 1290. Thus he complained that Philip cited prelates to his Court who did not hold fiefs of him and that he seized church possessions to compel obedience to his orders.[100] Boniface de-

---

cathedral chapters. They were to consider the "conservationem Ecclesiastice libertatis, et reformationem regni, et regis correctionem preteritorum excessuum, et bonum regimen regni. . . ."

[97] Ibid., *preuves*, pp. 48-52.

[98] Ibid., *preuves*, p. 50: "bona propria mobilia de regno nequaquam extrahere permittuntur"; "de mutatione monetae aliisque gravaminibus . . . per te ac tuos magnis et parvis regni incolis irrogatis et habitis contra eos . . . taceamus ad presens. . . . ." The passage on evil councillors, injustice, and oppressive financial practices (ibid., *preuves*, p. 51) is quoted in note 2 above.

[99] The council was to advise on measures concerning "directionem, quietem atque salutem, ac bonum et prosperum regimen ipsius regni . . ." (ibid., *preuves*, p. 51).

[100] Ibid., *preuves*, p. 49: "Prelates . . . super personalibus actionibus, iuribus et immobilibus que a te non tenentur in feudum ad tuum iudicium pertrahis . . ."; "ad saisienda et occupanda ecclesiastica bona et iura . . . manus extendis in casibus tibi non concessis ab homine vel a iure."

nounced Philip's attempts to name his clerks to vacant benefices, although this had long been a matter of negotiation between king and pope.[101] He complained about the abuse of the right of regalia,[102] again a problem that was being worked out in individual negotiations. Boniface was on firmer ground when he protested against the attempts to bring Lyon within the boundaries of the kingdom, although Philip was not the first French king to follow this policy, and Boniface had given him some encouragement to do so in 1297.[103] On the whole, the detailed charges were weak because they were not specific. Boniface would have made a better case if he had concentrated on the abusive treatment of Bernard Saisset and the attacks on the Inquisition.

This weakness of *Ausculta fili* was immediately seized upon by Philip and his court. Since there were no demands for specific redress of grievances, it was easy and profitable to concentrate on the general theory laid down in the bull. That theory could be summarized, by hostile readers, as a claim to temporal sovereignty over France (and, by implication, over other countries as well).[104] With only a little more distortion, it could be argued

[101] Ibid., *preuves*, p. 49: "ad te tamen huiusmodi ecclesiarum, dignitatum, personatuum et beneficiorum collatio non potest quemodolibet pertinere. . . ." On the problem of choosing bishops, canons, and other church officials see B. A. Pocquet du Haut-Jussé, "Le second différend entre Boniface VIII et Philippe le Bel," in *Mélanges Albert Dufourg* (Paris, 1932), pp. 75-108. The author thinks that this was a major cause of friction between Philip and Boniface. Certainly the threat to deny the king's right to appoint clerks to benefices was irritating, but in practice Philip had been able to find prebends for his men without trouble until the quarrel with the pope, and there had been no major controversies over the choice of bishops.

[102] Dupuy, *preuves*, pp. 49-50: "Vacantium regni tui ecclesiarum cathedralium redditus, . . . quos tui et tu appellas regalia per abusum, tu et ipsi non moderate percipitis, sed immoderate consumitis. . . ." It might be noted here that Philip did not have the right of regalia in most of the dioceses outside the old royal domain (for example, in Burgundy, Brittany, Aquitaine, or Languedoc).

[103] Ibid., *preuves*, p. 49: "Lugdunensem ecclesiam . . . tu et tui iniuriosis gravaminibus et excessibus ad tantum inopiam . . . deduxistis quod vix adiicere poterit ut resurgat, quam constat non esse infra limites regni tui. . . ." In 1297 Boniface ordered the archbishop and chapter to cause no prejudice to the king and not to harbor his enemies (Digard, I, 344). Moreover, he named Pierre de Mornay and the duke of Burgundy (both members of Philip's Council) as guardians of the city.

[104] In a letter (not dated, but written in 1302) Philip wrote to the king of Aragon that "papa qui contra regem et regnum regis et regni honoram adeo motus est quemadmodum facta sua notorie manifestant, qui inter cetera nititur regem ipsum et regnum in temporalibus sibi subicere. . . ."

that the pope was acting as if France were a fief of the Church. After all, if he and his council could review and correct acts of the French government, did this differ greatly from Philip and his Council reviewing and correcting the acts of the officials of the duke of Aquitaine? There was, of course, a considerable difference, as Boniface remembered to point out later.[105] He was concerned mainly with the grievances of the clergy; he was acting *ratione peccati*, and he had never been foolish enough to claim that France was a fief of the Church. These statements were true enough, but not entirely relevant. As Philip spent his whole reign demonstrating, one did not have to hold a fief of the king to be subject to his courts; anyone who was *in regno* and *de regno* had to accept the king as final and supreme judge. Boniface said exactly the same thing: anyone who was a member of the Church had to accept the jurisdiction of the pope.[106]

Political theory, however, was less important than practical politics. It is easy to imagine the wrath of Philip the Fair, the high priest of the religion of monarchy, when he was told that a council of his subordinates was to discuss the wisdom and justice of his policies. Philip can have had little hesitation in giving Pierre Flote, his chief minister, full authority to refute this heresy by any possible means.

Flote's first step was to suppress the bull *Ausculta fili*. There are stories that he, or the count of Artois, burned the bull. None of them can be proved to be true, and the act seems unnecessary. The bull could have been suppressed in various ways; it is clear that only the king and a handful of his closest advisers knew its contents.[107] Instead, Pierre Flote concocted a summary, which had

---

Philip later added the warning, "aliquo casu posset contingere quod . . . contra vos et alios principes temporales vellet similia atemptare et maxime si regem Francorum sibi in temporalibus quomodolibet subjugasset . . ." (Digard, II, 316).

[105] The cardinal-bishop of Porto, speaking for the pope in a consistory, 24 June 1302, said that the pope had never asked Philip to recognize "se tenere regnum suum ab aliquo"; in the same consistory Boniface angrily denied the charge "quod nos mandaveramus Regi quod recognosceret regnum a nobis" (Dupuy, *preuves*, pp. 73, 77). This, as the pope said, was folly, but he added that the king, like any other Christian, was "nobis subiectus ratione peccati."

[106] This, of course, is the theme of the famous bull *Unam sanctam* (18 November 1302): "Porro subesse Romano pontifici omnem humanam creaturam declaramus, dicimus, diffinimus et pronuntiamus omnino esse de necessitate salutis."

[107] Boniface was at first not sure of what had happened to the bull; he

as its punch line: "Know that you are subject to us in temporal as well as in spiritual affairs."[108] Unfair, perhaps, but not entirely so; in spite of all the verbiage with which it was surrounded, this was the basic message of *Ausculta fili*. At the same time, the prelates, the barons, and representatives of the towns of France were called to Paris to deliberate on matters that touched everyone in the kingdom.[109]

That meeting, on 10 April 1302, proceeded about as might have been expected. One of the king's men (almost certainly Pierre Flote)[110] went through the inevitable argument: Boniface says that the king is subject to him in temporal matters; he considers the king his vassal, as is proved by his summons of the French clergy to Rome to reform the kingdom. The king will redress legitimate grievances when and as he wishes; meanwhile, he asks your support.[111] The barons and the representatives of the towns supported this statement wholeheartedly and wrote to the cardinals, complaining of the enmity and misdeeds of the pope. It is significant that they wrote to the cardinals and not to Boniface, and equally significant that the pope was never given his proper title but was described as "he who now presides over the government of the Church."[112] One can already sense the threat to depose the pope.

The clergy, caught between two masters, could only equivo-

---

simply said, "litere predicte fuerunt celate baronibus et prelatis" (Dupuy, *preuves*, p. 77). The letter of the French clergy to Boniface, 10 April 1302, said the bull was shown to "quibusdam, licet paucis, baronibus suis" (ibid., p. 68). For the story of the burning of the bull see Digard's judicious remarks, II, 95, n. 2.

[108] "Scire te volumus quod in spiritualibus et temporalibus nobis subes" (Dupuy, *preuves*, p. 44). Boniface knew of this piece of propaganda; he said that Flote "false de ea [his bull] confixit" (ibid., p. 77).

[109] Picot, pp. 1-5.

[110] The cardinals said that Flote spoke in a large assembly (Dupuy, *preuves*, p. 63); the chronicler Geoffroi de Paris said that Flote spoke (*H.F.*, XXII, 97).

[111] The clergy quoted this speech in their letter to the pope, and the nobles quoted part of it in their letter to the cardinals (Dupuy, *preuves*, pp. 68-69, 60-61).

[112] Ibid., *preuves*, p. 61 (letter of the barons): "cil qui à présent siet ou siege du gouvernement de l'Eglise." The letter of the town representatives is lost, but judging by the reply of the cardinals (ibid., p. 71), they must have used the same phrase, for they are rebuked for speaking of the pope only in "quibusdam verborum circumlocutionibus." (Note that the best edition of the letters of the clergy, the barons, and the cardinals is in Picot, pp. 5-22.)

cate. They wrote directly and respectfully to Boniface, pointing out the dangerous temper of French laymen and the hostility that was being shown to the clergy. To avoid these dangers, they begged the pope to revoke the summons to the council.[113] All the proper forms had been observed, but they had come much closer to supporting the position of the king than that of the pope.

The arguments of the nobles and towns had little effect on the cardinals, and the cautious letter of the clergy simply infuriated the pope. He denounced their cowardice and condemned those who had spoken against him at Paris, especially Pierre Flote—"half-blind in body and completely blind in spirit." He prayed that this new Achitophel would be punished as was the first one, and he promised to depose prelates who disobeyed his summons.[114]

Boniface's curse was fulfilled rather speedily and more precisely than is usually the case. In May 1302 the Flemings rebelled against the French army of occupation and drove out the garrison of Bruges. On 11 July they crushed a French army at Courtrai. Pierre Flote was killed; so were the counts of Artois and Saint-Pol, two of the councillors who had threatened Bernard Saisset, and Jean de Burlas, who had brought the bishop under armed guard to Senlis. The judgement of God had apparently vindicated Boniface VIII.

This is one of the occasions when Philip the Fair clearly had to make the crucial decisions. Nogaret was not yet fully tested; Gilles Aicelin had never been happy about the Saisset affair; Pierre de Mornay was an excellent operator in foreign policy but not a forceful policy maker. Philip stood firm, even though his first attempts to avenge the disaster of Courtrai were utter failures. He did allow the duke of Burgundy to negotiate, unofficially, with the pope, and he did send Pierre de Mornay on a mission to Rome. But he did not yield the essential point: all persons, including prelates, were forbidden to leave the realm. The clergy

[113] Dupuy, *preuves*, pp. 67-71; also Picot, pp. 5-11. Anyone disagreeing with the king "pro inimico regis et regni notorie habebatur," "obedientia omnimodo laicorum et totius populi . . . tollebatur," the laity "prorsus effugiant consortia clericorum"; so they argue that "revocando vestre vocationis edictum ac predictis periculis et scandalis obvietur . . . ," and then harmony can be restored.

[114] Pierre Flote is a new Achitophel "quem Deus iam in parte punivit caecutiens corpore, caecus mente," "et volumus quod hic Achitophel puniatur temporaliter et spiritualiter, sed rogamus Deum quod reservet nobis eum puniendum sicut iustum est" (Dupuy, *preuves*, p. 77). Ibid., p. 79: "qui non veniant, nos deponemus. . . ."

were allowed to send three representatives to explain why others could not come, but the king did not relax his general order.[115]

The French bishops soon made it apparent that they feared the king more than the pope. Of the 79 bishops summoned, only 33 appeared, not including 6 who were already in Rome for other reasons.[116] (The 6 were Bernard Saisset, expelled from the kingdom, Pierre de Mornay, ambassador of the king, the 3 envoys of the French clergy who had been sent expressly to ask forgiveness for those who failed to attend the council, and the bishop of Toulouse, who was at Rome to deal with his quarrel with the bishop of Parmiers.) Even more important, there were almost no bishops from the old royal domain. Bishops of Aquitaine, Languedoc, Brittany, and Burgundy could not speak for the heartland of the kingdom, and both they and the pope knew it. Digard was probably right when he said that Philip had permitted this representation simply to confuse the issue. Boniface could not say that Philip had stopped all travel by the clergy; he could simply note that the most influential prelates of France had not been able to appear.

It was obvious that such a council could do nothing. Boniface, in passing, issued a bull condemning anyone who interfered with relations between the clergy and the Roman curia. But the real answer to the check that he had received was the bull *Unam sanctam* (18 November 1302), a much more carefully worded version of the claims made in *Ausculta fili*. While not using the phrase, it came closer to basing jurisdiction over laymen on the principle of the pope's right to rebuke sin. But there was also a

---

[115] For the duke's attempt to calm the dispute see the letter of Cardinal Matteo Orsini (ibid., *preuves*, p. 50). The three bishops sent to excuse the absence of the others were Pierre de Ferrières of Noyon, Robert d'Harcourt of Coutances, and Bérenger Frédol of Béziers (ibid., p. 183). The letter accrediting Pierre de Mornay and Mouche (7 October 1300) was published by Digard, II, 317. The mandate forbidding the clergy to leave the realm is mentioned in June 1305, when the king ordered the *prévôt* of Paris to seize the goods of all the clergy who had departed (Dupuy, *preuves*, p. 83). This letter may refer to the general order of 1302, which forbade all persons to leave the realm or to take out money or horses (ibid., p. 86). See Digard, II, 122, for a discussion of the date.

[116] Dupuy, *preuves*, p. 86, lists 39 names, including the 6 bishops who were in Rome for other reasons. See Digard's discussion, II, 132. It is interesting to note that of the dioceses where the king had regalia, only four were represented, two (Noyon and Coutances) by envoys of the clergy and two (Tours and Angers) by prelates who were under Charles of Valois. Also, although most of the suffragans of his province appeared, Gilles Aicelin, archbishop of Narbonne, did not.

studied vagueness that confused contemporaries and has confused commentators ever since. All Christians are subject to the one Church and its Head. The temporal power is under the spiritual power, and temporal power should be used only as the pope permits. The temporal power should be judged by the spiritual power if it does wrong. And, finally, the great, resounding conclusion: "We declare, pronounce, and define that it is absolutely necessary for every human being to be subject to the Roman pontiff to attain salvation."[117]

The bull can be and has been interpreted as merely a restatement of well-known and fully accepted principles of canon law. As Head of the Church the pope can judge any sinner. It can also be interpreted as a claim that the Roman curia had final appellate jurisdiction in temporal affairs, and Boniface's behavior after the issuance of *Unam sanctam* suggests that he was leaning toward this interpretation. He sent Cardinal Lemoine to the French court with what even Digard could only call an ultimatum.[118] The instructions given to the cardinal repeated most of the complaints made in *Ausculta fili*, but they began with an order that all measures taken by Philip to prevent his prelates from going to Rome must be revoked, and they ended with the threat that, if the king did not satisfy the pope on all these points, the Roman curia would proceed in both spiritual and temporal matters as it saw fit. It should be remembered that *Ausculta fili* had definitely criticized royal policy in purely secular affairs (the jurisdiction of the king's courts, control of the currency, behavior of royal officials); Boniface was insisting again on his right to judge these offenses.

In short, the frustrations of the council had not discouraged Boniface VIII any more than the defeat at Courtrai had broken the will of Philip the Fair. But the attempt to call a council was about to rebound; if a council could be called to rebuke the king, why not a council to depose the pope? Spiritual Franciscans were

---

[117] See *Registres de Boniface VIII*, no. 5039, for the bull condemning those who interfered with relations with Rome. *Unam sanctam* has been published and discussed many times; see the bibliographical note of Digard, II, 133-34.

[118] Digard, II, 138. The instructions are in Dupuy, *preuves*, pp. 90-92. The one entirely new clause was a demand that the king prove that he had not burned a papal bull (*Ausculta fili?*). The final threat was that if Philip "predicte non correxerit et emendaverit . . . nos et sedes eadem super premissis providebimus, statuendo, declarande et procedendo spiritualiter et temporaliter prout et quando videbimus expedire."

ready to denounce Boniface; the Colonna had already challenged the legitimacy of the resignation of Celestine V; Italy was full of men who had been injured by the pope's political maneuvers and by the greed of the members of his family. It is impossible to say who first picked up the idea at the court of France, but the actual challenge was voiced by Nogaret. At a small assembly at the Louvre on 12 March 1303 (Aicelin, Mornay, three other bishops, the king's brother, the duke of Burgundy, and other magnates were present), Nogaret accused the pope of having been wrongfully elected and of being guilty of heresy, simony, and other (as yet unspecified) crimes. He called for a council to judge the unworthy occupant of Peter's throne and suggested that Boniface must be arrested in order to make it possible to hold such a council.[119] Nogaret and Mouche already had letters from the king that gave them full power to act in his name and unlimited rights to draw on the royal treasury.[120] The king's advisers obviously approved the plan to demand a council. Nogaret left Paris almost immediately to join Mouche in Tuscany.

Meanwhile, Boniface realized that his ultimatum had failed. The king had not yielded on any point, least of all on the question of allowing the clergy to attend the council at Rome. He had therefore incurred the penalty of excommunication. If Philip did not repent, this sentence was to be promulgated throughout the country.[121] A little later (30 April), while recognizing Albert of Habsburg as emperor-elect, Boniface denounced the pride of the French, who claimed to have no temporal superior; legally, of course, they were under the emperor.[122] This was empty rhetoric; nor was there much more significance to his proclamation freeing all inhabitants of the western borderlands of the Empire from any oaths of allegiance that they had made to the king of France.[123] All these actions simply showed that Boniface was still convinced that he could force Philip to yield by multiplying threats.

Philip had accepted in March the idea of calling a council to depose Boniface, but he took no overt action until June, when the papal envoy bearing the letters of excommunication was arrested at Troyes. On 13 June the king called a great assembly of barons and prelates at the Louvre. This time Guillaume de Plai-

[119] Dupuy, *preuves*, pp. 56-59.

[120] Ibid., *preuves*, p. 175. The letters were dated 7 March 1303.

[121] Ibid., *preuves*, p. 98 (13 April).   [122] See above, note 63.

[123] Published by Boutaric in "Documents inédits," p. 147, no. 17. The date is 31 May 1303.

sians was the speaker; he read a formal, but rather brief, set of accusations against the pope. On the next day he rehearsed all the reasons for doubting that Boniface was a legitimate pope (and here there were some plausible arguments) and then moved on to a long list of charges of heresy, sexual perversion, and crime. One example is enough to illustrate the quality of the accusations. Boniface had said that he would rather be a dog than a Frenchman, and a dog has no soul, while even the most miserable Frenchman has one. Therefore Boniface did not believe in the immortality of the soul and was a self-avowed heretic.[124]

The truth or even the reasonableness of the charges was of little importance to the assembly; the essential fact was that they were serious enough to justify an appeal to a general council. The laymen present agreed at the final meeting to support the demand for a council; the clergy hesitated, but gave in the next day and agreed that a council was necessary "in order to allow the pope to manifest his innocence." The bishop of Autun refused to adhere to this action but was not molested; the abbot of Cîteaux, who also refused, was arrested and, eventually, deposed.[125] However, the vast majority of the French clergy supported the appeal for a council. The prelates of France had learned during the last 15 years that the king could help them more and hurt them more than could the pope. Papal intervention had not saved them in 1290 or 1297; accommodation with the king had preserved and even increased some of their privileges. The mendicants, dependent on the pope for their very existence, might grumble a little;

[124] Dupuy, *preuves*, pp. 102-6, gives the charges against the pope. They are also in Picot, pp. 36-45. Digard, ii, 166, is perhaps right in saying that the arguments against the validity of the abdication of Celestine V (and hence against the validity of the election of Boniface) and for the need to call a council to rectify this evil come from manifestoes of the Colonna. But see Scholz, pp. 198-207, who shows that the Colonna were rather suspicious of councils (though of course they had to find some way of denying the legitimacy of Boniface's election).

[125] See Dupuy, *preuves*, p. 102, for the support of the laymen; the prelates "quadam quasi necessitate compulsi" agreed that a council was needed "ut ipsius domini Bonifacii innocentia claret" (ibid., p. 108). For the treatment of the bishop of Autun and the abbot of Cîteaux see Digard, ii, 170, and *Gallia Christiana*, iv, cols. 998-99. The arrest of the abbot is one of the grievances mentioned in Boniface's proposed excommunication of the king (*Super Petrisolio*), never issued because of the attack at Anagni (Dupuy, *preuves*, p. 184). Three Cistercian abbeys in the diocese of Bourges refused to adhere to the appeal to the council, but their resistance was not followed by other houses of the order; see Picot, pp. 330, 333, 334.

otherwise there was no opposition. It was better to serve the most Christian king than a pope whose title could be contested and whose policies were of doubtful value to the French Church.

Philip nailed down his victory through a series of regional meetings where adhesions to the demand for a council were received from individual clerics, barons, and communities. Propaganda and threats of the king's displeasure certainly played a role in securing these adhesions, but, as was said above, they expressed the basic sentiments of the politically conscious people of France. There were riots about taxation, about manipulation of the currency, about conflicts of jurisdiction, but there were no riots in favor of Boniface VIII.

It would have been well for the pope if he had realized how little support he had. But he continued to denounce Philip, and, indeed, after the meetings at the Louvre and the adhesions to the appeal to a council, it is hard to see what other course he could have followed. A series of minor acts prepared the way for drafting the bull *Super Petri solio,* in which he stated that Philip had been automatically excommunicated for having prevented the French prelates from going to Rome (and for having given refuge to Stefano Colonna) and that, in consequence, he had lost all public authority and all claim to the fidelity of his subjects.[126]

It is probable, as Nogaret himself said, that the danger that this bull would soon be published (on 8 September) forced him to act against the pope before his plans were entirely ready. He had been in Italy for several months and was in touch with most of Boniface's enemies, but the decision to force his way into Boniface's palace at Anagni seems to have been a hasty improvisation. Fawtier was probably right in saying that Nogaret's basic mission was to summon the pope before a council,[127] but the plans for a council were still nebulous. A summons that could not name a

---

[126] Dupuy, pp. 182-86. The key phrases are on p. 185: "eundem regem manifestis excommunicationibus esse ligatum, per consequens . . . imperium sive iurisdictione aliqua per se, vel alios, aut communes actus seu legitimos exercere et collationem et exercitium ipsa nullius existere firmitatis, ac fideles et vassallos ipsius esse a fidelitate et enim iuramento quibus astringuntur eidem homini debito et totius obsequii auctoritate canonum absolutos."

[127] Robert Fawtier, "L'attentat d'Anagni," *Mélanges d'Archéologie et d'Histoire, Ecole Française de Rome* (1948), pp. 169-71. Holtzmann, pp. 215-27, agrees that the purpose of the mission was to summon Boniface to appear before a council, but he is sure that from the beginning it was understood that the pope would come only as a prisoner.

time and place would not have been very effective. Even though a citation to answer a charge of heresy ended the authority of the person cited, it had to be more precise than anything Nogaret could have produced. Thus the summons could have been postponed; preventing publication of the bull could not. It is clear that the force that attacked Anagni was not well organized. Nogaret had some control over Rinaldo da Supino, captain of the people of Ferentino, and over Adinolfo di Papa. The latter showed the respect for legal forms that would have been part of Nogaret's basic plan by having himself elected captain of the people (of Anagni) as soon as he entered the town. But Nogaret had no control over the faction led by Sciarra Colonna (brother of Pietro and nephew of Giovanni, the two deprived Colonna cardinals).[128] It was Sciarra (who had good reason to hate the pope) who began the attack on the palaces of the pope and his relatives, and it was Sciarra who abused the pope verbally (he almost certainly did not strike him, as an old legend has it). It was probably Sciarra who encouraged the plundering of the papal treasure, an act that weakened Nogaret's attempt to follow legal forms. This was also the one act that Boniface's successor found impossible to forgive.

The result of this discord and uncertainty was that for two days no decision could be taken. Sciarra may have proposed killing the pope or sending him to France,[129] but Nogaret and his group did not want to make a martyr. Nogaret must also have realized that his band of Italian adventurers had neither the will nor the capacity to take a captive pope half the length of the peninsula and through the mountains to France.

In fact, it soon proved impossible to keep the pope a prisoner at all. The people of Anagni had their grievances against Boniface and his family, and they had at first collaborated with Nogaret. But they had no reason to run risks for the Colonna, especially not the risk of being associated with the murder of a pope. On 9 September they drove Nogaret, Sciarra Colonna, and their followers out of town and promised to protect Boniface against his enemies. They even restored much of the loot they had taken.

---

[128] The best account of the events at Anagni is by William of Hundleby, procurator of the bishop of Lincoln at the curia. See also Fawtier, "L'attendant d'Anagni," pp. 157-58. William distinguishes clearly between the troops controlled by the king of France and those of the Colonna; Fawtier agrees, pp. 173-75.

[129] Fawtier, "L'attendant d'Anagni," p. 162; Holtzmann, p. 217.

On 13 September an escort arrived from Rome and conducted the pope safely to the Lateran.

The Boniface of old would have marked his return to Rome with a spate of bulls directed against his enemies. The Boniface who returned to Rome was a broken man. Age, anxiety, and humiliation had put him in a state of shock; he had lost all hope and all energy. He did nothing during the remaining three weeks of his life and died at the Vatican on 11 October.

The cardinals were equally discouraged. The Church needed peace above all else—peace with France and peace with the Colonna, who were still threatening the security of the Papal States. It was no time for political games. On the first ballot of the conclave (22 October) they elected Nicolas Boccasini, cardinal-bishop of Ostia, who took the name of Benedict XI. Benedict had two great merits: he came from a poor family that had no connection with the quarreling nobles of Rome, and he had been absent from the curia (as legate to Hungary) during all but the last three months of the quarrel over Bernard Saisset. It was easier for him than for any of his colleagues to be a peacemaker.

The problem of the Colonna was fairly easy to solve, at least for the moment. They asked forgiveness and received most of their confiscated goods in return, though the two cardinals were not yet restored to their dignity (this was to be the work of Clement V).[130] Peace with France was more difficult to arrange. Nogaret was continuing his attacks on the legitimacy and orthodoxy of Boniface VIII, and opposition to the Inquisition was still intense in Languedoc. It was dangerous to irritate Philip again; yet Benedict could not entirely repudiate the acts of his predecessor. Finally, a face-saving formula was worked out by which the king authorized his envoys to receive absolution and the pope absolved the king from any excommunication that he "might have incurred" and stated in an accompanying letter that the king had not asked for this absolution (thus inferring that Philip had never considered himself excommunicate).[131] Benedict also forgave all acts that had interfered with the convening of the council of the French clergy, dismissed all blame for the attack at Anagni, restored all graces and privileges revoked by Boniface VIII, and capped this mound of concessions by the grant of a two-year

---

[130] *Registre de Benoît XI*, ed. Ch. Grandjean (Paris, 1905), no. 289. See Digard, II, 194-95.

[131] Dupuy, pp. 224-25; *Registre de Benoît XI*, nos. 1311-12.

tenth and a grant of annates for three years.[132] These acts showed clearly the papacy's desperate need for the friendship of France, and the cardinals were to remember this demonstration a year later.

The only men whom Benedict could not forgive were Nogaret, Sciarra Colonna, and 15 of their followers. They were cited to Rome for sentencing on 29 June 1304,[133] but Benedict died before official action could be taken. Nevertheless, Nogaret was considered excommunicate, and he spent the next seven years of his life demanding (and finally receiving) absolution. His career was not injured; he remained one of Philip's most influential councillors and became Keeper of the Seals in 1307, but his pride and perhaps his conscience were hurt. After all, the Colonna who had first raised the question of the legitimacy of Boniface's election had been pardoned; the memory of Pierre Flote had been cleared; the officials who had arrested French prelates had been absolved. Why pick on him? And if, as a curious letter published by Langlois indicates,[134] Nogaret was in his way as good a Catholic as Philip the Fair was in his, then the excommunication would have made him worry about his spiritual welfare. In any case, the fact that Nogaret was one of the very few men not pardoned by Benedict in 1304 suggests that he was more responsible for the violence at Anagni than Fawtier believed.[135] On the other hand, Benedict XI must have been puzzled, as historians have been ever

[132] Dupuy, p. 229 (forgiveness of the clergy). Philip had already revoked his edicts forbidding exit from the realm (Digard, II, 319-20), but this cost him nothing. The forgiveness and restoration of privileges are in Dupuy, *preuves*, p. 230; see also *Registre de Benoît XI*, nos. 1253-54. Flote's memory was cleared, but Nogaret was not included in the amnesty. For the grants of a tenth and annates see ibid., nos. 1261, 901, and Mignon, nos. 796, 535. The tenth and the annates were to help restore "good money."

[133] Dupuy, pp. 232-34.

[134] On his way to Italy in 1303 Nogaret wrote to Etienne de Suisy, Keeper of the Seals (later a cardinal): "Domine mi, orate ad Dominum ut si via mea Deo placeat, me in ea diriguat, alias me per mortem velut sibi placet impediat" (Charles-Victor Langlois, "Autographes nouveaux de Guillaume de Nogaret," *Journal des Savants* [1917], p. 323). Nogaret could scarcely have played the hypocrite with a fellow councillor who knew him well.

[135] See Fawtier, "L'attendant d'Anagni," pp. 170-72, and p. 174, where he speaks of "l'appareil légal organisé par Nogaret." Note that Nogaret had found it necessary to enter the city with an armed band of soldiers and that two leaders of this band, Rinaldo da Supino and Adinolfo di Papa, were also condemned by Benedict. They were undoubtedly under Nogaret's command; see above, note 128.

since, by the lack of interest throughout Europe in the attack on Boniface VIII. As Fawtier has pointed out, there are no official reports from Rome to the courts of Europe about Anagni,[136] and, as Teofilo Ruiz has shown, the chroniclers display no great concern about the attack.[137] To single out Nogaret, a principal councillor of the king of France, for punishment would certainly bring attention to the incident. It did, but perhaps not in the way that Benedict had expected; the chief result was that Nogaret kept pressing the case against Boniface until he was absolved.

Benedict XI had secured enough tranquility so that after his death (7 July 1304) the cardinals could afford to go back to their favorite sport of holding a long and sharply divided conclave. To be entirely fair to them, a decision was not easy. Central Italy was still in a turmoil, and it was hard to find a cardinal acceptable to all the warring factions. Boniface had offended many of the cardinals (especially those chosen by his predecessors) by his dictatorial behavior. To elect a supporter of Boniface was to endorse his policies and to annoy still further a powerful faction in the College; to elect an opponent would just as certainly envenom the split. Moreover, to be anti-Boniface was almost equivalent to being pro-French, and here again there was no easy solution. It had been made very clear that French support was essential for the well-being of the Church, but to elect an openly pro-French cardinal was to suggest that French charges against Boniface were justified. It is not surprising that the conclave, which was held in Perugia, lasted for 11 months.

There is no authentic record of the deliberations of the cardinals; the best reports came from the agents of the king of Aragon,[138] as was often the case in this period. It is clear that at the beginning the cardinals were evenly divided between pro-Boniface and anti-Boniface factions—nine in each group. The numbers shifted slightly as death or illness caused withdrawals from the conclave, but neither faction ever came close to the necessary two-thirds majority. It might have been possible to compromise on a non-Italian, but there were only three cardinals in this category, and none of them had enough prestige to attract support

---

[136] Fawtier, "L'Attendant d'Anagni," pp. 155-56.

[137] Teofilo Ruiz, "Reaction to Anagni," *Catholic Historical Review*, LXV (1979), 385-401.

[138] See Finke, *Bonifaz VIII*, pp. 279-90 (an excellent account of the conclave), and pp. lviii-lxvi (the Aragonese documents on which this account is based).

from both sides. In short, by the end of 1304 it was evident that no member of the College had a chance of being elected.

If the new pope could not be a cardinal, then he could not be an Italian. Any Italian prelate would have been suspected, probably with reason, of being allied with one of the two factions. A French bishop, on the other hand, would be less involved in the politics of central Italy and of the curia. France was the largest, richest, and most powerful Catholic country. The French popes of the thirteenth century (Clement IV, for example) had been capable men; they had not unduly favored their native country, and they had not caused feuds by trying to build up family principalities in Italy (as Boniface had done). But in view of the recent unpleasantness, the French pope could not be too French; he could not, for example, be a former royal official, as Clement IV had been.

Ideas such as these must have begun to circulate among the cardinals as the deadlock in the conclave continued into 1305. It is impossible to be sure who first suggested the name of Bertrand de Got, archbishop of Bordeaux, or how support for him was built up. The Aragonese envoy was probably right in suggesting that cardinals of the pro-Boniface group were becoming suspicious of their leader (Matteo Rossi), though the account of the intrigues mounted to discredit him may be invented.[139] It is also possible that a list of three names was presented to the Rossi faction with a promise to support whichever of them was acceptable. It would not have been hard to rig the list so that Bertrand de Got was the only reasonable choice.[140] In any case, the cardinals must have been growing very weary of the conclave, and some of them were ready for any compromise that did not look like complete surrender. In the end, three of the pro-Boniface faction joined their opponents in supporting Bertrand. This provided the necessary two-thirds majority; the remaining holdouts then made the election unanimous. On 5 June 1305 Bertrand de Got was elected pope and soon after (there was some delay in notifying him) took the name of Clement V.

Bertrand must have seemed an ideal candidate to many of the cardinals. He came from a good family, and his brother, Bérard de Got, had been archbishop of Lyon and later a cardinal. Bertrand was well educated; he had studied civil law at Orléans and was something of an expert on canon law (the seventh book of

[139] Ibid., pp. 286-87, lxiii-lxiv.   [140] Ibid., pp. lxiv-lxv.

the Corpus of Canon Law, the *Clementines*, which was compiled at the end of his reign, shows his continuing interest in this field). He had been an acceptable, if not brilliant, administrator, first as bishop of Comminges and then as archbishop of Bordeaux. Best of all, though he was French, he could scarcely be considered a supporter of Philip the Fair or an opponent of Boniface VIII. Both Bertrand and his brother had served Edward I of England, Bertrand as his attorney in the Parlement, Bérard as chaplain. Bérard, as archbishop, had stoutly defended the independence of Lyon against Philip. Bertrand had not been involved in so spectacular a controversy, but, like most of the southern bishops, he had protested encroachments of royal officials on his jurisdiction.[141] He had reason to remember Boniface with gratitude, since it was Boniface who had made him a bishop and then an archbishop, and the pro-Boniface cardinals could have believed that Bertrand was on their side.[142] He had annoyed neither Philip nor Boniface during the final crisis: if he went to Paris to hear the charges against the pope, he also went to Rome to hear the charges against the king. In short, he seemed a moderate, reasonable man who could get on with anyone. If he also seemed a little weak, this would not have displeased the cardinals, who had had their fill of a domineering pontiff.

The choice of Clement V is thus understandable without the hypothesis of pressure by the French government. But ever since the fourteenth century there have been stories that Philip and his advisers did intervene in the election. In their crudest form, these stories are demonstrably false; there were no secret meetings and no secret exchange of messages between Philip and Bertrand de Got before the election. There was some pressure on the conclave; Charles II of Sicily visited Perugia at a critical period in 1305, and French envoys were also present.[143] But nothing in the Aragonese reports suggests that either Philip's cousin or his en-

[141] Lizerand, *Clément V*, pp. 29-33.

[142] The Aragonese envoy reported that Bertrand was first suggested as a candidate for the papacy by Cardinal Matteo Rossi (leader of the pro-Boniface group) "cum iste papa fuisset factura domini Bonifacii, quia promotus extitit per eundem . . ." (Finke, *Bonifaz VIII*, p. lxii).

[143] Ibid., p. lxi. The citizens of Perugia feared that the French ambassadors were going to bring charges against Boniface and the cardinals named by him, but they were assured that this was not the case, 14 April 1304 (Dupuy, *preuves*, p. 277). The instructions given to one of these envoys, Geoffroi du Plessis, were "top secret," and Geoffroi was reluctant to reveal them years later; see above, Chapter I, note 93.

voys had any influence on the cardinals. On the contrary, it seems
to have been the anti-Boniface faction that raised the question
of Bertrand de Got's attitude toward France. When his name was
first suggested they sent secret messengers to ask whether he
favored the party of the king of France.[144] (One may wonder
with Finke why the other side did not take similar precautions.)
Thus Clement had probably declared himself to be pro-French
before his election, and if Philip was as well informed as the
king of Aragon, he may have known it.

In any case, Philip had many means of putting pressure on the
pope after the election, even if Clement had not committed himself before. Clement's obvious reluctance to leave France put him
in a weak position, and the longer he hesitated, the more difficult
it became to deny the king's requests. Philip was not responsible
for the turmoil in Italy that made Clement reluctant to go to
Rome, but he could certainly profit from the situation. It was
easy to arrange secret meetings with the pope,[145] to exchange messages quickly, to repeat requests over and over. Clement was not
a strong man, either in body or in character; he found it difficult
to deny such importunities. Another form of pressure was to
keep the charges against Boniface alive. This was easy to do,
since accusations of heresy were not extinguished by death (as
the Inquisition had always insisted) and since Nogaret, still one
of the king's principal ministers, had personal as well as political
reasons for continuing the prosecution. To quash the charges
would annoy both Philip and some of the cardinals; to allow
an open investigation would produce a mass of scandalous stories
(as the partial investigation of 1310 proved). But every time
Clement showed some signs of independence, he was apt to receive
a strident request to examine the charges against his predecessor.
Clement did not always give in, and he often was able to delay
his decisions; but Finke was right in saying that no pope of the
later Middle Ages was more subservient to a king.[146]

[144] Finke, *Bonifaz VIII*, pp. 286, lxiii: "pars domini Neapuleonis [the
anti-Boniface group] . . . misit nuncios suos ad inquirendum latenter de
voluntate et intencione istius pape, scilicet, utrum faveret partem regis
Francie. . . ." Bertrand is called pope here and in the phrase quoted in note
142 because the letter was written after the election.

[145] For example, at Lyon in November 1305 (*H.F.*, xxi, 446).

[146] Finke, *Bonifaz VIII*, p. 289, speaks of the pope's "schmäliche Abhängigkeit vom französischen König . . . dieser Abhängigkeit, wie sie wohl
kein Papst des späteren Mittelalters einem Monarchan gegenüber gezeight.
. . ." Finke drew this conclusion from reports of Aragonese living in France;

Clement must have decided very early that he would have to work closely with Philip. At the very beginning of his pontificate, before he knew that he would never go to Italy, before he knew that the charges against Boniface would be repeated year after year, he made an extraordinary series of concessions to the king. He had picked Vienne as the site of his coronation; at Philip's request he shifted it to Lyon—a city already in the French sphere of influence and soon to be incorporated into the kingdom. He reinstated the two Colonna cardinals, an act that pleased his supporters in the College, but also an act that pleased the king. He shifted the balance in the College against the Italians by naming 12 new cardinals. Nine of them were French, and 3 were closely bound to the king, especially Etienne de Suisy, the Keeper of the Seals. He completed the work, begun by Benedict XI, of revoking all acts of Boniface VIII that might have annoyed Philip, including *Clericis laicos*, and he interpreted *Unam sanctam* as causing no prejudice to the king and his realm.

These concessions announced a policy: Clement was going to rely on the support of the French king and kingdom. This was politically necessary; it was also a sound judgement about the balance of power in western Europe at the time. England was bogged down in Scotland, while Germany and Italy were divided into small, quarreling principalities or city-states. France was indeed "the principal column of the Church," as recent events had proved. Moreover, Clement must have been impressed by the strength and efficiency of the French government. In contrast to the quarreling cardinals, the king's Council spoke with one voice; in contrast to the endless disputes over enforcement of papal decrees, the king's orders were executed fairly promptly; in contrast to the recent failures of papal propaganda, the French had been able to mobilize public opinion in support of their king. All this was relative, of course. France certainly did not have a model government; but it had a government that was more effective than that of the Church. Clement had dealt with the French government for many years and was far more aware of its strength than Boniface had been; he simply did not want to have it as an opponent.

These speculations receive some support from an examination of the affair of the Templars. It is perfectly apparent in this case

---

see his *Papsttum*, II, 111, 222, and especially p. 123: "el [Philip] fa tot ço ques vol del papa et de la esglea."

that Philip wanted the Templars and the Order condemned, that Clement had serious doubts about the guilt of individual brothers and the wisdom of suppressing the Order, that he tried to avoid committing himself, and that in the end Philip gained most of what he had wanted. All the factors mentioned above came into play. The efficiency of the royal government was demonstrated by the simultaneous arrest of almost all the Templars of France on 13 October 1307. This was a remarkable operation; the orders for arrest were kept secret until the proper time; they were then executed without any embarrassing delays; very few members of the Order escaped. No modern dictatorship could have done a better job. Clement's hesitations were overcome by pressure from the king, by arguments of royal councillors (especially Plaisians) that verged on insolence, by appeals to public opinion, including an assembly of nobles, clergy, and town representatives at Tours in 1308, by reminders from Nogaret that the accusations against Boniface ought to be investigated, and by the open support of most French prelates. Clement won a few delays and a few face-saving concessions. For example, the Order was suppressed, not condemned, at the Council of Vienne in 1312. Its property went to the Hospital, not to a new order, although Philip had suggested the latter solution.[147] This was an unimportant setback; Philip had gained his chief objective and had shown that he was master of the Church in his own kingdom. The arrest of the Templars by royal order was just as much a breach of clerical privilege as the arrest of Bernard Saisset, and Clement denounced the action vehemently.[148] The Temple property seized by royal agents was far more valuable than all the temporalities seized in all of Philip's earlier disputes with French prelates. But

[147] Favier, *Marigny*, pp. 145-47; Lizerand, *Clément V*, pp. 268-70. Favier thinks that Philip was satisfied with the final solution; Lizerand is more doubtful. Philip certainly had urged that a new order be established. The Aragonese envoys were sure that Philip wanted a new order, to be headed by himself or one of his family (Finke, *Papsttum*, II, 51, 116, 118).

[148] "Tu vero, fili karissime, quod dolentes referimus . . . manum tuam in persones Temploriorum et bona, et non qualitercumque, sed usque ad inclusionem carceris extendisti. . . . In quo quidem tuo sic repentino processu nostrum et ecclesie Romane vituperosum contemptium communiter omnes, et non absque rationabili causa notant . . ." (Boutaric, *Templiers*, pp. 34-35). He ends by asking that the persons and goods of the Temple be placed in his hand. Note that Clement was not impressed by the claim that Philip acted at the request of the Inquisitor of France, who was the king's confessor. See the Appendix to this chapter for similar problems concerning Bishop Guichard of Troyes.

Clement, though he scolded Philip, did nothing to save the Templars and their properties. He was satisfied with face-saving devices. Thus the prisoners, after harsh treatment and forced confessions, were released to the pope, who promptly asked the king to guard them. Churchmen were theoretically associated with royal appointees in administering Temple properties; in practice, the king's men collected the revenues and rendered the accounts.[149] Philip had been willing to make similar arrangements in the case of Bernard Saisset; in fact, the release of Saisset to the custody of his archbishop proved to be much more meaningful than the release of the Templars to the pope. Boniface VIII could not be placated by such devices, but Clement V was eager to avoid conflict. As a result, Philip was able to do what no other medieval king had done; he destroyed a large, wealthy, and influential religious order.

Why did Philip attack the Temple? The most obvious, and partially true, answer is that he was short of money.[150] His last large tax was levied in 1304; his income from manipulating the currency was cut off with the restoration of "good money" in 1306; the tenths granted by Benedict XI were yet to be collected. The wars had ceased, but ordinary expenses of government had grown, notably pensions paid to royal officials and to neighboring princes. New sources of revenue were needed. The Jews were expelled and their property seized in 1306; a vigorous attempt was made to force all subjects to pay the aid for marrying the king's daughter in 1308; the Lombards were squeezed in 1309-

---

[149] Boutaric, *Templiers*, pp. 49-50, 53-54. Accounts of Temple goods in Champagne, 1307-1309, are in the form of other royal accounts (B.N., ms. Clairembault 469, pp. 209-41); the receiver of the goods of the Temple in the *bailliage* of Senlis reported expenses to the royal *prévôt* of Senlis and took orders from Guillaume de Gisors, king's clerk and Guillaume Pizdoue, *prévôt* of the merchants of Paris, 1310-1311 (ms. fr. 10430, pp. 63-65); see ms. fr. 20334, nos. 6, 9, 10, 15, 16, 39, 54, 58, for similar entries for the same region, 1311-1312. In 1315 G. de Gisors, G. Pizdoue, and Renier Bourdon (all king's men) were checking accounts of administrators of Temple goods in the *bailliage* of Chaumont (A.N., JJ 59, fol. 16, no. 44).

[150] According to a report of French envoys who were sent to the pope in December 1309, Clement was quite aware that Philip was short of money. He said that Philip had once been rich, that war had then impoverished him, and that now, while he had peace, "regnum vestrum esset vacuatum pecuniis . . ." (Boutaric, *Templiers*, p. 63). The Aragonese envoy reported that Philip seized the Templars in order to gain their wealth; Plaisians found it necessary to deny this charge vehemently at Poitiers in 1308 (Finke, *Papsttum*, II, 51, 142).

1310. The seizure of Temple property in 1307 fits neatly into this pattern. Moreover, the king did not like to be dependent on bankers, especially bankers whom he did not control.[151] If he could repeatedly squeeze the Lombards and expel the Jews, why should the Temple escape?

It is no answer to this argument to say that Philip made very little out of the seizure of Temple holdings. In the first place, the accounts are too fragmentary to show just how much the king did make or how many of the expenses charged against Temple estates were legitimate. In the second place, Philip may have overestimated the wealth of the Temple and the sums that he could claim were owed him by the Temple. Finally, while it must have been obvious that the confiscated property would have to be devoted to pious purposes, preferably a crusade, it was not obvious that most of it would go to the Hospital. Philip certainly hoped that it would go to a new order controlled by his family, and his crusade vow of 1312 would have given him an excuse to draw on this fund. In short, he may have had reasons to hope that he would get more from the Temple than he did. In the end the crown did make some profit from its administration of Temple possessions, but Philip did not live to enjoy it.[152]

The second obvious answer, which does not contradict the first, is that Philip believed that the Templars were guilty of heresy. As a thoroughly pious man, Philip took accusations of heresy seriously. Rumors about the errors and evil practices of the Templars had been circulating since 1305. Philip discussed these rumors with Clement V at Lyon after the pope's election; he also asked Nogaret to investigate them.[153] Nogaret was fairly

[151] See my article, "Italian Bankers and Philip the Fair," pp. 239-47.

[152] The accounts cited in note 149 above suggest that Temple goods were carefully administered and that expenses (especially of imprisoned Templars) about equaled income, so that the king at first made little profit from his guardianship. The Hospital promised to pay 200,000 l.t. within three years to satisfy debts owed by the Temple to the king; this sum was increased to 260,000 l.t. by an agreement between the Hospital and Louis X in February 1316 (Delisle, *Opérations financières des Templiers*, pp. 228-33; see also pp. 234-38).

[153] See Boutaric, *Templiers*, pp. 13, 25, for the discussions at Lyon. The chronicle of Jean de S. Victor says that Nogaret began his investigation "diu ante" the arrest, which could be any time in 1306 or early 1307 (*H.F.*, XXI, 649). The otherwise unknown Esquinus de Floyran wrote to James of Aragon in January 1308, saying that he had told James of the evils in the Order. James would not believe him, so he went to Philip (Finke, *Papsttum*, II, 83). Plaisians in 1308 said that "homo parve conditionis" revealed the

sure to find evidence of heresy, whether or not it really existed, as the accusations against Boniface VIII demonstrate. Apparently he found enough so that the pope was troubled, but not convinced, and the Grand Master of the Order, Jacques de Molay, was concerned enough to ask that an enquiry be made to clear the reputation of the Order.[154] It looked as if this would be a desultory investigation that could drag on for years, and Jacques de Molay was not terribly worried. He refused to consider a fusion of the military orders, though he knew that this was a project that Philip strongly favored;[155] he did not leave France, though his headquarters were in Cyprus; he even appeared at the funeral of the wife of Charles of Valois the day before he and all the other Templars were arrested. This sudden and drastic action could have been ordered only by the king himself, and it would not have been ordered if Philip had not been concerned over the guilt of the Order. Some members of the Council were not so sure. It is significant that Philip found it necessary to replace Pierre de Belleperche, interim Keeper of the Seals, with Nogaret immediately after the arrest. Pierre was a good lawyer and a capable administrator; he could have conducted the case against the Temple himself or used Nogaret as a special prosecutor. He may have been ill at the time of the arrest (he died in January 1308), but other men, including Nogaret himself, stayed in office until their death. It looks as if Pierre did not want to be involved in the case. There is also some evidence that there had been long discussions about the Templars in the Council during the summer[156] and that it had not been easy to reach a decision. Philip, obviously, was the only person who could have

sins of the Temple to Philip and that Philip had discussed the charges with the pope at Lyon in 1305 (ibid., p. 141). Esquinus was a king's valet by 1308.

[154] Boutaric, *Templiers*, p. 25: "licet ad credendum que tunc dicebantur [concerning the Temple], cum quasi incredebilia et impossibilia viderentur, nostrum animum vix poteruimus applicare . . . quia vero magister milicie Templi ac multi preceptores . . . cum magna instancie petierunt quod nos super illis eis falso impositis, ut dicebent, vellemus inquirere veritatem . . ." (letter of 24 August 1307).

[155] Georges Lizerand, *Le dossier de l'affaire des templiers* (Paris, 1923), pp. 2-14.

[156] Lizerand, *Clément V*, pp. 93-94. Romeus de Brugaria, a professor at Paris, wrote to James of Aragon on 27 October 1307 that "a sex mensibus citra in diversis consiliis fui in quibus erat consultatio de predictis" (the charges against the Temple) (Finke, *Papsttum*, II, 49).

ended the debate, and he would not have done so if he had not thought that he could prove his case.

Finally, some benefit was gained by portraying the king as a champion of orthodoxy, quicker than the pope to detect the heresy and far more zealous in suppressing it. Bishop Guillaume le Maire, who had once compared Philip with Rehoboam, gave him full support in his attack on the Temple.[157] Even more striking is the case of the author of the *Roman de Fauvel*, Gervais du Bus. Gervais was a cynical, embittered minor functionary who served first Marigny and then the king. Page after page of his poem is filled with denunciations of the royal government and complaints about its treatment of the Church. But when Gervais comes to the affair of the Temple, he bursts into a paean of praise for Philip. The king did God's work as a true descendant of St. Louis; he labored mightily to make the pope see the truth; he performed his duty as a *prud'homme*.[158] Such praise for a king who had been on the verge of excommunication and who had still not been entirely cleared of making unjustified charges against Boniface VIII was helpful, especially if it were widely spread in clerical circles. Even if this passage is in part an interpolation, as some scholars have argued, there is little doubt that Gervais be-

---

[157] *Le livre de Guillaume le Maire*, p. 472.

[158] Gervais du Bus, *Le roman de Fauvel*, published by Arthur Langfors (Paris 1914-1919). The king rules the Church, he has made it tributary, he names prelates who work for him and not for the Church (ll. 472-75, 577-78, 637-54). Nevertheless, Gervais accepts all the accusations against the Temple and praises Philip (ll. 936-1019).

> Mais cestui neveu saint Loys
> Doit estre liez et esjois
> Car il en a ataint le voir
> Moult a mis et labour et painne
> A faire le chose certainne.
> Tres bien en a fait son devoir
> Diligaument, comme preudomme
> Devant l'apoustolle de Romme
> A poursui ceste besoinge
> (ll. 1005-13)

On Gervais see Favier, *Marigny*, p. 67, and *Hist. litt.*, xxxiv, 104. The indignation expressed in this passage makes one think that the "Remonstrance du peuple de France" (Lizerand, *Le dossier*, pp. 84-95) is not just a piece of propaganda. It was almost certainly drafted by Pierre du Bois, but Pierre often expressed opinions generally held, and in this case he criticizes Clement's reluctance to condemn the Temple and denounces his nepotism much as Gervais or his interpolator did.

lieved in the guilt of the Templars. And it seems curious for an interpolator to use this particular poem to praise the king.

Were the Templars really heretics? Fawtier was fairly sure that they were;[159] others have not been so certain. Clement V himself hesitated for a long time, and at one point he revoked the powers of the inquisitors and thought of trying the case himself.[160] He finally let himself be persuaded. But even at the end he did not condemn the Order as a whole; he merely suppressed it because it had caused scandal and had ceased to be useful. It is also striking that only in France did hundreds of individual Templars confess their crimes and that only in France were they severely punished. Less important is the fact that the French confessions were obtained through torture and threats of burning at the stake. Men may tell truth as well as lies under torture, and there probably was some truth in what the French Templars said. However, the stories they told do not add up to a consistent description of a heresy.

That the Templars were unchaste and that they often engaged in homosexual practices goes without saying. It was hard enough for professed monks, more or less secluded from the world, to keep their vows; it was nearly impossible for men deeply involved in politics, finance, and, occasionally, military campaigns to do so. Homosexuality among members of close-knit military-political groups has not been unknown in our own time. It is also possible that some commanders recommended such practices to avoid the scandal of open association with prostitutes. That there were barracks-room obscenities and blasphemies in the houses of the Templars is again what might be expected of such a group, especially when new members were being initiated. That there was any body of heretical doctrine taught or believed by the Templars is not demonstrated by the evidence. As was pointed out long

[159] Fawtier, *L'Europe occidentale*, pp. 416, 423-24. See especially p. 416: "nous refusons généralement à admettre ce qui est peut-être l'explication la plus simple, à savoir qu'ils [the Templars] ont été condemnés parcequ'on les a cru coupables." He said some years later in a private conversation that "they were dirty men."

[160] Boutaric, *Templiers*, pp. 36, 50. Clement was reluctant to restore the powers of the inquisitors, as Plaisians reported in 1308. "Item, de restitutione inquisitorum, quia rex tantum habet cordi, faciat summus pontifex, licet videatur contra honorem suum facers posse secum, cum collegio quod patienter tollentur quod una cum ordinariis associandis procedent contra singulas personas ordinis Templi."

ago by Langlois,[161] every other heresy of the period had leaders who formulated their doctrines clearly and who defended them to the end. They had their authoritative texts and generally accepted rituals. None of this comes out in the confessions of the Templars, only a mish-mash of incoherent stories. The most common are avowals of spitting on the Cross and renouncing Christ, but little is said of what was to take the place of the religion they denied. Blasphemy has no point if one does not believe in the sacredness of that which is being blasphemed, and most of the confessions show that the Templars did believe—they were shocked (according to their stories) by what they were forced to do. Men who were intelligent enough to handle the complicated administrative work of the Temple, men who could run a banking business more extensive than that of any Italian firm should have been able to produce a more coherent and appealing counter-religion, if they were foolish enough to try. There was no reason to try. Worldly, arrogant men, living a soft life on income that should have been used for redemption of the Holy Land (to take the stereotype of the Templar accepted by many Europeans of the thirteenth century) do not found religious movements that might upset the established order of things. It is also significant that those Templars who were burned at the stake were executed because they had repudiated their confessions, not because they wanted to defend their beliefs. This is a long way from the Cathars of the early thirteenth century, who threw themselves into the fire to prove their devotion to their faith.

Clement was not a strong man, but his reasons for suppressing the Order at the Council of Vienne in 1312 were reasonably honest. The Templars were no longer very useful; they had caused scandal and had offended many people, especially the king of France; any further delay would mean that Temple property would be eaten up by quiet usurpations and administrative costs. Therefore, the Order was suppressed, and its property went to the Hospital or (in Spain) to the military orders who were to fight the Moors. This was not quite what Philip had wanted. He had thought of using Temple goods as part of the endowment of a new order that could be controlled by France, and he gained less financially than he may have hoped. But from the point of view of propaganda, the king had scored heavily. The highest

---

[161] Langlois, *Saint Louis*, pp. 195-96.

officials of the Temple had been convicted of heresy and burned at the stake, and the Order had been abolished. Thus Philip's charges against the Temple were fully justified, and his zeal for the faith was manifest. The king had followed a consistent line and the pope had not; Philip's determination had prevailed over Clement's hesitations.

The attack on the Temple led to an estrangement between Philip and Clement. The king and his ministers had put tremendous pressure on the pope; they had protested and made difficulties every time that Clement had tried to give the Templars some chance to defend themselves. Philip had insisted that Philippe de Marigny (brother of Enguerran) be translated from Cambrai to Sens to make sure that the home province (so to speak) of the Capetians would be in safe hands. He had scolded the pope for his hesitations and lack of energy in pursuing heresy.[162] It is not surprising that in 1308 Clement decided to leave France and set up the papal court in a town that was not directly in the king's hand. As usual, he took no great risks. He moved to Avignon in 1309, just across the Rhône from France. He had already called a council to discuss the problem of the Temple and other affairs at Vienne, a place a little more remote from the royal domain than Avignon but still well within the French sphere of influence. Since the College of Cardinals was becoming more and more dominated by French (and Gascon) prelates, Clement's gesture of independence did not give him much more liberty of action. He could annoy Philip by confirming the choice of Henry of Luxembourg as emperor-elect rather more quickly than the king desired (Philip had pushed the candidacy of his brother Charles and wanted delay to show his displeasure and to gain some concessions); he could hesitate about authorizing ecclesiastical sanctions against the Flemings if they broke their promises to the

---

[162] See Lizerand, *Le dossier*, pp. 124-37, for a speech before the pope, at Poitiers in May or June 1308, delivered by Plaisians (though he certainly borrowed some ideas and phrases from Pierre du Bois). The pope's indecision is causing a scandal, some suspect him of favoring the Templars (p. 128); if he will not act, temporal authorities will (p. 132); delay proves that the pope favors heretics, for negligence seems to approve their errors (p. 134); let the pope fear the judgement of God (p. 136). In reporting the speech, the Aragonese envoy dates it 29 May and says definitely that it was delivered by Plaisians in the name of the king, prelates, barons, and people of France (Finke, *Papsttum*, II, 141-47). See also a long, plaintive letter of Clement (6 May 1309), denying Philip's charges that he is delaying the process (ibid., pp. 189-201).

king; he could refuse to act on the charges against Boniface VIII.[163] These actions may have restored Clement's self-respect and given him a little more room for negotiation, but he could not risk an open break with Philip. In 1311 and 1312 a series of compromises restored good relations, but they were compromises far more favorable to the king than to the pope.

In the first place, the charges against Boniface VIII were dropped. Favier thinks that this decision shows the rising influence of the pragmatic Marigny over the doctrinaire Nogaret.[164] Certainly Marigny was gaining power, but it is doubtful that Nogaret felt that the condemnation of Boniface was his chief aim in life. He had kept the charges alive, first, as a means of putting pressure on Clement (but there was not much more to be gained from that tactic), second, to establish Philip's position as the most powerful ruler in the West, and third, to protect himself and to put an end to his excommunication. All these goals were achieved in the settlement. An official investigation found enough evidence to permit the conclusion that Philip had acted with "just and laudable zeal," in other words, that there had been enough substance to the charges against Boniface so that the appeal to a council was reasonable.[165] The acts of Boniface VIII and of Benedict XI that might injure or offend the king were to be expunged from the papal registers (the erasures can still be seen). Nogaret was absolved on condition that he make a number of pilgrimages (which he never did) and go on the next crusade (which he had some reason to know would not take place).[166]

---

[163] Boutaric, *Templiers*, pp. 61-77 (a long report of French envoys to Clement in December 1309). All these subjects were discussed at several meetings. Nogaret was in Avignon but was not received by the pope; the official head of the French mission was Guillaume Bonnet, bishop of Bayeux.

[164] Favier, *Marigny*, pp. 129-30, 134-35.

[165] Höfler, "Rückblick auf P. Bonifacius VIII," pp. 45-84; Dupuy, *preuves*, pp. 522-75. The depositions confirm the statement made above (pp. 259-66) that Boniface was irritable and hasty in his speech; they do not prove (as Clement V saw) the charge of heresy.

[166] All these provisions are in the bull *Rex glorie* of 27 April 1311 (*Regestum Clementis Papae V* [Rome, 1885-1892], ann. VI, no. 7501; Dupuy, *preuves*, pp. 592-602). As before, I quote Dupuy's version, since this is the one in the French archives. The king acted with "bono, sincero et iusto zelo ex fervore Catholice fidei" (p. 596). The order to erase the bulls is at p. 600, and the long list of documents to be erased is at pp. 606-8. Nogaret's absolution and penances are at pp. 601-2. Clement had drafted a bull on 1 July 1307, making most of these concessions (though Nogaret's penance was harsher: he was to stay in the Holy Land until recalled by

Considering the fact that the pope conferred various favors on Nogaret during the next year, including the right to hear mass in a place under interdict and to have a portable altar,[167] it is difficult to believe that Clement expected the penances to be taken very seriously. The whole settlement in the bull *Rex glorie* was capped by a sentence in which Clement declared that "like the people of Israel . . . the kingdom of France, as a peculiar people chosen by God to carry out divine mandates, is distinguished by marks of special honor and grace."[168] This was almost a flat reversal of Boniface's positon. Instead of the pope having a right to intervene in secular affairs to preserve justice and peace, the king of France was praised for intervening in ecclesiastical affairs to preserve the faith. Nothing could have marked more clearly the rise of the state and the decline of the leadership of the Church.

Friction over the fate of the Temple was ended by Clement's decision, at the Council of Vienne, to suppress the Order. As we have seen, this decision did not satisfy all of Philip's wishes, and it saved Clement the task of forcing a condemnation through a group that was not entirely convinced of the guilt of the Order. But the compromise (perhaps arranged by Marigny)[169] was advantageous to Philip, if only because it proved that the enmity of the king could prevail over the interventions of the pope.

With the problems of Boniface and the Temple settled, there were no serious issues between Philip and the Church for the remainder of the reign. The Council of Vienne was supposed to deal with the reform of the Church and, as part of that reform, to check lay interference with ecclesiastical jurisdiction and properties. Grievances from all French prelates were collected. Since they were the same that had been voiced in the 1290s, they need not be repeated, but it is interesting to see how widespread they

---

the pope), but the bull was never issued (Finke, *Papsttum*, 1, 136-39, 388). Finke thinks it was held back because Nogaret would not drop the charges against Boniface. This is certainly one reason, but Clement may also have been worrying about the affair of the Temple, which had been brought up, but not thoroughly discussed, just at this time. Finke doubts that the Temple question had anything to do with the suppression of the bull.

[167] Lizerand, *Clément V*, p. 260.

[168] Dupuy, *preuves*, p. 592: "sicut iraeliticus populus . . . regnum Francie in peculiarem populum electus a Deo in executione mandatorum celestium specialis honoris et gratie titulis insignitur."

[169] Favier, *Marigny*, pp. 146-47.

were and to note that even bishops who were prominent members of the Council, such as Gilles Aicelin of Rouen, felt that lay authorities were abusing their power.[170] Obviously, the reforming ordinances of 1290 and 1304 were not being fully observed; just as obviously, the lawyers on both sides of the conflict were inclined to turn disputes over purely technical interpretations of privilege into matters of principle. In the end, nothing of any importance was done about these complaints by the council, and the king felt no need to issue another reforming ordinance. The French Church was free to complain, free to petition the king for grace or justice, but it did not receive new privileges. Nor did it seem especially disturbed by its failure to obtain remedies for its grievances. As will be shown later, the clergy played only a minor role in the protests of 1314. The lawyers of the king and of the prelates continued their endless arguments in the courts, but there were no massive protests by the clergy and no significant interventions by the pope.

Two other problems, the crusade and the Inquisition, were discussed at Council of Vienne and continued to be the subjects of negotiations for the next two years. Both Clement and Philip had always proclaimed the necessity of a crusade. They could hardly do otherwise, and there is no reason to think that they were insincere. But the crusade did not have a very high priority in their plans; there were so many other matters to clear up first, and the rising costs of war made an expedition to the Holy Land difficult to finance. There had been desultory talk of a crusade during all of Clement's pontificate, but at Vienne a real effort was made to obtain advice about the organization and financing of the expedition so that definite plans could be made. The results were not very impressive. Philip promised to take the cross, and a tenth was imposed on the clergy, but it was agreed that the expedition could not be ready in less than six years. There was some talk of a token operation in 1313 (the year in which Philip actually took the cross), but Marigny persuaded Philip that it would be a waste of money.[171] He was probably right, and, in

---

[170] Lizerand, *Clément V*, pp. 309-20, sums up the complaints very well. The old bishop of Angers, unlike some of his colleagues, denounced the behavior of the clergy as well as that of the laity—excessive use of excommunication, lax observance of monastic rules, pluralities and nonresidence, corruption of ecclesiastical judges (*Le livre de Guillaume le Maire*, pp. 478-86).

[171] Schwalm, "Reichsgeschichte," pp. 564, 566.

any case, the threatening situation in Flanders demanded all the king's attention. This episode marked the end of plans for a crusade as far as Philip and Clement were concerned. Both men died in 1314; both left money in their wills for a crusade.[172] Nothing was ever done to carry out their wishes.

As for the Inquisition, Philip had been concerned in the earlier part of his reign by the unrest that it was causing in Languedoc. This concern reached its peak during the war with Flanders and the final struggle with Boniface VIII. Philip had no desire to have a rebellion in the south while he was tied down by the Flemish problem, and the Spiritual Franciscans, who on the whole were against the Inquisition, were useful, if difficult, allies in the quarrel with the pope. Even in this period Philip had his doubts about interfering too much with the Inquisition, and he did very little to curb its powers. He did order an investigation by Richard Leneveu and Jean de Picquigny. As a result, a few reforms were made in the treatment of prisoners, an especially obnoxious inquisitor was driven from office, and there was some slowing down of arrests based on insufficient evidence. This was much less than the opponents of the Inquisition had hoped for, and in their disappointment they strengthened Philip's doubts by using extravagant language and even forming a half-baked conspiracy to end French rule in Languedoc.[173]

Once the years of crisis were over, Philip reverted to his usual conservative and orthodox position: the faith must be defended at all costs. His confessor became Inquisitor of France; if Philip had any worries about the conduct of local inquisitors (which is doubtful), he could settle them in private discussions. It was this close connection between the Inquisition and the king that made possible the coup against the Templars in 1307 and then thwarted all of Clement's efforts to give them some semblance of a fair hearing. Philip, in the last years of his reign, was naturally not interested in reforming an institution that had served him so well.

Clement felt rather differently. He had been deeply offended by the pressure put on him during the affair of the Temple, and

[172] Lizerand, *Clément V*, p. 391; Finke, *Papsttum*, I, 104; Boutaric, "Documents inédits," pp. 233-34.

[173] See above, p. 14. In early 1303 Philip told the men of Albi that he was deeply concerned and would correct the excesses of the Inquisition; see E. A. Rossignol, *Monographies communales du département du Tarn* (Toulose, 1864-1866), III, 162.

part of that pressure resulted from acts of the Inquisition. Aside from this personal feeling, he was well enough informed to know that the inquisitors were not always entirely fair and a good enough lawyer to realize that zealous prosecutors need to be checked by impartial judges. With all his faults, Clement was basically a decent man, and it is clear that he was worried about the Inquisition. Early in his reign he ordered an investigation of the Inquisition in Carcassonne and in Albi.[174] As usual, he did nothing very decisive, but some improvements were made in the prisons of the Inquisition, and the bishop of Albi, who had been overzealous in pursuing heretics, was translated to Le Puy, where there were fewer potential victims. The vidame of Amiens, Jean de Picquigny, who had died at the court of Rome while appealing an excommunication placed on him by the Inquisition for transferring convicted heretics from one of its prisons to a royal jail, received a posthumous rehabilitation. This was helpful to his family, but it also conveyed a subtle message to the king. Philip could hardly complain about the judgement in favor of the vidame, who had been one of his most loyal and useful servants, but he could not have forgotten that the vidame had been condemned for carrying out royal orders to curb the excesses of the Inquisition. Clement left no room for doubt; he denounced the process through which the vidame had been excommunicated, thus reminding the king that in the past he had been somewhat less favorable to the Inquisition than he was in 1308.[175]

The final sign of Clement's worries about the Inquisition was a series of acts of the Council of Vienne that were inserted in the *Clementines.* The basic principal was that the bishop should have equal power with the inquisitor in trying, sentencing, and overseeing the imprisonment of heretics.[176] Like all of Clement's policies, this was a weak and almost useless attempt at reform. The inquisitor had only one job; the bishop had many. The bishop simply did not have the time to act as an effective check on the inquisitor, even if he desired to do so, which was by no

---

[174] Lizerand, *Clément V*, pp. 413-15. See A. Compayré, *Etudes historiques et documents inédits sur l'Albigeois* (Albi, 1841), pp. 240, 247, on Clement's worries about the bishop of Albi. The investigation, by bishop Bérenger Frédol of Béziers and Cardinal Pierre de la Chapelle Taillefer, began in 1306 (*Hist. litt.*, XXXIV, 104).

[175] Lizerand, *Clément V*, p. 415. Cardinal Etienne de Suisy, the former Keeper, was largely responsible for this act, but Bérenger Frédol also helped (*Hist. litt.*, XXXIV, 105).

[176] *Clementines*, Book V, Title III, chaps. 1, 2.

means always the case. These reforms of Clement V had very little effect on the medieval Inquisition. It flourished under his successor; it died not because of any papal act but because it ran out of victims.

The case of the Inquisition is one more example of the lack of any anticlerical policy in Philip's reign. The king simply wanted to keep control of his country. When the harshness of the inquisitors threatened that control, he moved to moderate it. When he could use the Inquisition to increase his control, he did. But he never thought for a moment that heretics should not be punished; at the most, he only wanted to be sure that those who were punished were heretics and that the punishments were not excessive.

The scholars of the Old Regime who considered Philip a founder of the Gallican liberties were closer to the truth. Philip did not think in terms of Gallican liberties, but he did a good deal to create the conditions out of which the idea of Gallican liberties could grow.[177] He secured official acknowledgment of the preeminent position of France and the French Church in the Catholic world. He strengthened the old ties between the monarchy and the French Church by making the welfare of the French Church depend on the good will and administrative support of the king. It became perfectly apparent during his reign that the pope could do very little to protect the rights and possessions of the French clergy, whereas the king could do a great deal. Judgements of the king's Court were more speedy and more efficacious than judgements of the court of Rome. As Fredric Cheyette has shown, this tendency for the French clergy to rely on the Parlement to protect its rights grew with extraordinary rapidity during the fourteenth century. By expanding the principle of seisin, the Parlement found a technique that enabled it to intervene in purely spiritual affairs, such as the possession of a benefice.[178] This extension of the jurisdiction of the Parlement was not forced on

[177] Guillaume le Maire sent a protest to the Council of Vienne in 1312 against any act that might infringe on the liberties of the Gallican Church (*Le livre de Guillaume le Maire*, p. 488). The phrase was already in the air. Scholz, *Die Publizistik*, pp. 373-74, sees Philip's policy as an early formulation of Gallicanism. Nogaret used the phrase; see Dupuy, *preuves*, p. 585: the king and kingdom of France form a church, which may be called "ecclesia Gallicana, sicut ecclesiam orientalem et occidentalem sancti patres appellant."

[178] Fredric Cheyette, "La justice et le pouvoir à la fin du Moyen Age Français," *Revue historique de droit français et étranger* (1962), pp. 373-94.

the clergy; on the contrary, they sought excuses to invoke it. Protection of seisin simply made it easier to do what the clergy had wanted to do since the last years of the thirteenth century. It was out of the unique relationship between the French Church and the royal government that the concept of the Gallican liberties developed. And it was in the reign of Philip the Fair that this unique relationship, already evident in the policies of earlier kings, began to be expressed in the legal and institutional forms that were to be invoked in later centuries.

APPENDIX

The Case of Bishop Guichard of Troyes

In a less troubled period the case of Bishop Guichard of Troyes might have touched off a great debate over relations between the king and the Church. The bishop was accused of crimes far more serious than those imputed to Bishop Bernard Saisset—sorcery, a compact with the devil, and causing the death of the queen. Philip treated him much more harshly than he did Saisset; Guichard was imprisoned in the Louvre for about three years (the exact date of his release is uncertain) and was never allowed to return to his diocese. There was some attempt to preserve legal forms, but the king could have been accused of violating clerical privileges if the pope had wished to raise the issue. In actual fact, however, neither king nor pope wanted to make a test case out of Guichard's treatment. The bishop's first difficulties with the royal family began just as the final quarrel with Boniface was getting under way; the second and more serious accusations came at a crucial period in the argument over the prosecution of the Templars. Guichard was not a symbol of provincial separatism, as Saisset may have been, nor could he be accused of participating in a vast network of heresy, as the Templars were. He stood alone, a disagreeable man, perhaps, but no real danger to the king and no real burden on the conscience of the pope.[1]

Because the affair of Guichard remained at a personal, not a symbolical, level, because it was always being shoved out of the

---

[1] The fundamental work on Guichard is Abel Rigault, *Le Procès de Guichard, evêque de Troyes* (Paris, 1896). Rigault published or summarized all the basic documents on the case; nothing of any great importance has been discovered since his time. It is possible to differ with him on some points, but his work is reliable, his interpretations of the facts are reasonable, and this appendix is largely a summary of his book.

way by more important matters, it is impossible to fit it into a general discussion of relations between the king and the Church. Nevertheless, it deserves attention precisely because it was so personal. It reveals a good deal about the characters of Philip, of his queen, and of Clement V. It is one of the few cases in which we can follow in some detail the intrigues that went on in the royal court. Finally, it illustrates one of the unlovely aspects of Philip's reign: the technique of building up support for false accusations.

Guichard had risen rapidly in the Church—prior of Saint-Ayoul of Provins by 1273, when he was still a young man, abbot of Montier-la-Celle in 1284, bishop of Troyes in 1298—and it seems fairly certain that he owed these promotions to Blanche of Artois, dowager queen of Navarre and countess of Champagne, and to her daughter Jeanne, who married Philip the Fair in 1284. He was present at the christening of Charles, Jeanne's third son, in 1294 and may have been one of the child's godfathers.[2] The depositions collected during the investigation of the charges against him stress his close ties with the two queens and the favor that they showed him. But Guichard was not just a courtier; in fact, in his later years he was anything but courtly. He was a first-rate businessman; he enriched his monastery[3] and, probably, himself during the years of his abbacy. He certainly had an important voice in the administration of Champagne during the years of transition to royal control that followed Jeanne's marriage, and he also gained the confidence of Philip the Fair. Rigault may have exaggerated a little in calling him the king's delegate in Champagne,[4] but Guichard certainly fulfilled this function when he acted as one of the two collectors of the subsidy of 1300 in Champagne.[5] The other collector was Guillaume de la Chapelle, a not very important king's clerk; Guichard was clearly the senior member of the team. The appointment is another indication of Guichard's reputation for financial expertise. Guichard also sat in the Grands Jours of Troyes from 1296 to 1299 and, less frequently, in the Parlement. He was one of those allowed to enter the Chamber of Pleas when he wished, which would suggest that

---

[2] Rigault, pp. 11, 14.   [3] Ibid., p. 9.

[4] Ibid., p. 10. The evidence comes from witnesses who were questioned much later (1309 or 1310), when he was on trial. They said he was "mestres en Champagne," "sire en Champagne pour le roi." They had some reason to exaggerate; the more he had been trusted, the blacker his crimes.

[5] Mignon, no. 1325; *J.T.P.*, no. 5290.

he had high standing in the court but was present only from time to time. On one occasion he took part in a case that involved a rent on the fairs of Troyes.[6] He would have known more about this problem than most of his colleagues.

By 1300 Guichard was a fairly important man, not yet one of the inner circle of royal officials, but with some prospect of reaching that level. His career was ruined by the very thing that had brought him to the attention of Jeanne and Philip: his involvement in the financial administration of Champagne. Blanche, the dowager queen of Navarre, was very careful to protect her financial interests. She became suspicious of Jean de Calais, canon of Troyes, who had been treasurer for her second husband, Edmund of Lancaster, and then administrator of her dower lands. Rightly or wrongly, Blanche believed that Jean had cheated her; she had him arrested and asked Guichard to guard him in the episcopal prison at Troyes. Jean escaped and fled to Italy; Guichard was accused of taking an enormous bribe to let Jean go.[7] The accusation was not completely implausible. Guichard could not have carried out his administrative duties in Champagne without knowing Jean, and his own concessions to his cathedral chapter in 1304 show that he had been rather unscrupulous in building up his income.[8] On the other hand, no direct evidence against Guichard has survived;[9] he was never convicted of the offense, and it seems unlikely that a man who knew Blanche so well would have risked an act that he knew would infuriate her. The two chief accusers of the bishop were Jean de Calais himself and a certain Noffo Dei (Arnoldo Deghi), a Lombard whose firm had had some dealings with the treasurers of Champagne.[10] Neither man had a very good character; in fact, some writers later confused or connected Noffo with Esquinus de Floyrano who denounced the Templars to James of Aragon and to Philip the

---

[6] Benton, pp. 334-35. He was on the Parlement list of 1296 as abbot of Montier-la-Celle. The date can be confirmed by the presence on the list of Renaud Barbou, who died early in 1298, and by Guichard's own elevation to bishop in 1298. See Langlois, ed., *Textes*, pp. 161, 164, and *Olim*, II, 423.

[7] Rigault, pp. 21-22. Rigault says (p. 25) that Blanche was "non sans apreté, soucieuse de ses intérêts."

[8] Ibid., pp. 261-65 (*pièce justificative*, no. 7).

[9] Again, almost all the stories about this affair come long after the event, in the investigation of 1309-1310.

[10] Rigault, pp. 23-24. Noffo was at one time connected with Cepperello Diotaiuti, who had collected revenues in Champagne in 1295.

Fair.[11] Both Noffo and Jean retracted their accusations, Jean on his deathbed, in letters that seem sincere. Rigault suggested that both Jean and Noffo (who was also in prison at the time) were allowed to flee France in return for incriminating Guichard.[12]

This explanation solves some problems but raises others: who hated Guichard so much that they were willing to procure false testimony and spend several years in seeking his condemnation? The most likely answer is a group clustered around Simon Festu, archdeacon of Vendôme. Simon, like Guichard, was a financial expert, a collector of tenths and annates in the province of Bordeaux and in parts of the provinces of Toulouse at various times from 1291 to 1299, and a collector of subsidies in Poitou and Limousin, 1299-1300.[13] He may have been jealous of Guichard, who had gained his reputation while staying quietly at home; Simon, a native of Fontainebleau, had had to spend years roaming the southwest. He may have been annoyed by the fact that Guichard was already a bishop; Simon had to wait until 1308 before becoming bishop of Meaux. He may have seen Guichard as a rival for high office; Simon became Treasurer in 1307, a post that Guichard might well have hoped to fill. It also seems very likely that the two men were competing for the favor of Queen Jeanne; one witness later called Simon a clerk of the queen, and he was one of her executors when she died in 1305.[14] If there was such competition, Simon had already won the contest by 1300; in spite of all his efforts, Guichard never regained the confidence of the queen.

The greatest men of the Council did not become involved in the process against Guichard; they had Boniface and the Flemings on their minds. But the commission that was eventually appointed to investigate the charges included some of the ablest servants of the king. Four of them later became bishops: Raoul Grosparmi (Orléans, 1308), Robert de Fouilloy (Amiens, 1308), Richard Leneveu (Béziers, 1305), and Pierre de Grez (Auxerre, 1308; also Chancellor of the young Louis of Navarre). The others were Guillaume de Plaisians (not very active), André Porcheron, and Hélie de Maumont—all legal experts.[15] There must have been

---

[11] Villani began this confusion; see Finke, *Papsttum*, I, 113-14.
[12] Rigault, pp. 41-42.
[13] *J.T.P.*, nos. 3384, 4224; Mignon, nos. 524, 752, 754, 1206, 1331.
[14] Rigault, pp. 23, 38; *Gallia Christiana*, VIII, col. 1633.
[15] Rigault, pp. 16, 161. Rigault became a little confused as to which commissioners were named by the archbishop of Sens and which by the king,

considerable pressure on the king to name such a distinguished group. Probably the pressure came from the queen, but it is not impossible that some of these men were friends of Simon Festu or, at least, that they shared his dislike of Guichard.

The death of the dowager queen in 1302 did not help Guichard; it simply started a new rumor that he had poisoned her. This report was not taken too seriously at the time, but it was revived later. Meanwhile, Queen Jeanne proved just as hostile to Guichard as her mother had been. Guichard made a great effort to clear himself in 1303, but he had little support at court. Jean de Montrolles, bishop of Meaux, gave him some help, but although Jean had had a respectable career in the Parlement,[16] he was not a very influential member of the government. In any case, he was fright-

---

but, as the text printed on p. 161 shows, although André Porcheron and Pierre de Grez were technically the archbishop's men, they were all appointed "de mandato regis." For Pierre de Grez and Richard Leneveu see above, pp. 94, 96. André Porcheron, king's clerk, canon of Paris and of Arras, acted as a *rapporteur* in the Parlement of 1295 (*Olim*, II, 370), was a judge in the Parlement of 1301 (ibid., III, 49), was on the Parlement list of 1307 (Langlois, ed., *Textes*, p. 178), investigated for the Parlement, with Guillaume de Marcilly, the dispute between the abbot and commune of Corbie, 1306 (B.N., ms. Moreau 218, fol. 269; cf. A.N., J 231, no. 6), and was still working for the Parlement in 1313 and 1314 (A.N., K 38, no. 9², and JJ 50, no. 52). Hélie de Maumont, king's clerk, was connected with a powerful family of the Limousin. His uncle, Gérard de Maumont, was prominent in the king's service. Both uncle and nephew served in the Parlement of 1299 (*J.T.P.*, no. 2434). Hélie was an *enquêteur* in the *bailliage* of Caux about 1302 (Mignon, no. 2666). Raoul Grosparmi was a king's clerk and well versed in both laws (*Gallia Christiana*, VIII, col. 1471). Robert de Fouilloy, king's clerk, was very active in the Parlement from 1302 until his death in 1321 (Langlois, ed., *Textes*, pp. 205, 178; *Olim*, III, 157; B.N., ms. lat. 4763, fol. 65, ms. Moreau 218, fol. 253; A.N., JJ 40, fol. 79, no. 156; *Gallia Christiana*, X, cols. 1190-91). As a member of the Council he was one of the delegates to the conference of Périgueux on English rights in Aquitaine, 1311 (J. M. Maubourguet, *Le Périgord Méridional* [Cahors, 1926], p. 196), and helped to arrange the marriage of Catherine of Valois in 1313 (Fawtier et al., eds., *Registres*, nos. 2164-71, 2175, 2177-78, 2180-85).

[16] Jean de Montrolles (the name is spelled in many ways) had been in the Parlements of 1290, 1291, 1296 (as resident in the Chamber of Pleas), and 1298 (L. Tanon, *Justices des églises de Paris* [Paris, 1883], p. 351; Langlois, ed., *Textes*, pp. 157, 163; *Olim*, II, 423). He was a Master at the Jours of Troyes, 1296-1298, where he worked with Guichard, and was a minor member of an embassy sent to the pope in 1298 (Benton, pp. 334-35; *C.R.*, I, nos. 436, 437). He had enough standing to be a member of the Council that imposed a new subsidy in October 1303 (*Ord.*, I, 408), but this must have been his last service to the king; he died soon thereafter.

ened off, and Guichard's agents were accused of procuring false testimony.[17] Usually Jeanne was not so vindictive, but this case touched her personally. Her mother had been wronged; her income from her own county of Champagne had been reduced by fraud; one of her own protégés had betrayed her. It clearly was not wise to give Guichard any assistance.

Nevertheless, it was hard to proceed with the case after the deathbed letters of Jean de Calais (17 April 1304), in which he denied that Guichard had helped him to escape.[18] Jeanne had to be satisfied with regaining her losses at the expense of the bishop. She had already taken over his temporalities, and, according to Guichard, had deprived him of 40,000 l.t. of income.[19] Even allowing for the fact that she had cut down his timber trees (a very profitable operation), the sum seems exaggerated, but it could not have been completely false. Guichard had obviously been a very wealthy man. Now the queen demanded that the bishop promise to pay her 40,000 l.t.[20] This was a huge sum; even in the inflated currency of 1304 it was worth over 12,000 l.t. of "good money." It was as large as the amounts collected from the *bailliages* of Bourges, Tours, and the *sénéschaussée* of Poitou for the very heavy tax of 1304,[21] also paid in inflated money. When, how, and if Guichard raised the money is unknown. Perhaps the sums already taken by the queen were credited against the debt.

After Jeanne died in 1305, Guichard had a brief respite from his troubles. He had not been officially acquitted, but nothing more was done about the accusations of Jean de Calais, and Clement V clearly believed that the bishop had been the victim of

---

[17] Rigault, pp. 30-33.

[18] Ibid., pp. 37-39 (with facsimile). Guichard's enemies, of course, said that the letters were forgeries; but if they were, it is hard to see why the case was dropped. Moreover, Noffo Dei, when he thought that he was dying in August 1306, also admitted that he had falsely accused Guichard (ibid., p. 41).

[19] Ibid., pp. 28-29; Favier, p. 58. Enguerran de Marigny, as chamberlain of the queen, is said to have made an inventory of Guichard's goods in 1303. If he found 40,000 l.t. for her, this might explain his rapid rise to power in the following years.

[20] Guichard promised his chapter on 15 May 1304 that they would not be held liable for the "obligatione quadraginta millium librarum turonensium et earum solutione quas fecimus in manu domine reginé" (Rigault, p. 263 [*pièce justificative*, no. 7]).

[21] Mignon, nos. 1478 (Bourges, 35,095 l.t., not all paid), 1487 (Tours, 45,895 l.t., not all paid), 1540 (Poitou, 39,458 l.t., not all paid).

jealous rivals.[22] It was obvious that Guichard would never regain his position in the royal government, but he could have expected a peaceful and fairly comfortable existence as bishop of Troyes.

All these hopes were blasted by a new set of accusations that were made in 1308. Guichard was charged with killing Queen Jeanne by sorcery (the old story of the waxed image pierced by a pin) and of trying to poison Charles of Valois and Louis of Navarre. This accusation was taken seriously by Guillaume de Hangest the younger, *bailli* of Sens, who reported it to the king early in 1308.[23] The problem of the Templars caused some delay, but Philip eventually asked the pope to investigate the charges and threatened to judge the bishop himself if the pope did not act. On 9 August 1308 Clement V ordered the archbishop of Sens, the bishop of Orléans (Raoul Grosparmi), and the bishop-elect of Auxerre (Pierre de Grez) to begin an inquiry.[24] Both Raoul and Pierre had been members of the earlier commission of investigation in 1302-1303. They certainly were not favorable to Guichard, and the illness and then the death of the archbishop of Sens gave them full control of the proceedings.

Guichard was arrested and placed in the prison of the archbishop of Sens, but was soon transferred to the Louvre. Although this was clearly a breach of clerical privilege, Clement did not protest, and appearances were saved to some degree by establishing Denis, dean of Sens, as guard of the prisoner. Denis was a respectable ecclesiastic, a career civil servant, and a frequent attendant at the Parlement.[25] The imprisonment was not very harsh.

[22] Rigault, p. 268. Guichard had been cited to Rome by Benedict XI. Clement excused him, saying that "quedam sinistra de te per nonullos emulos tuos false fuerint insinuatione suggesta," but that some cardinals spoke for him and wanted the truth to shine again through the clouds of calumny (3 June 1307).

[23] Ibid., pp. 55-57, 60-65.

[24] Ibid., pp. 57-59 and *pièces justificatives*, nos. 12, 13.

[25] Ibid., pp. 60, 103 (n. 1); for Denis de Sens see p. 215. Denis was one of the most regular attendants at the Parlement from 1299 to 1316, when he sat in the Grand'Chambre (*J.T.P.*, no. 2530, 5998; *Olim*, III, 72, 89, 97; Langlois, ed., *Textes*, p. 178; A.N., JJ 57, fol. 64v). He collected subsidies in 1300 and 1303 (Mignon, nos. 1296, 1429). He was used to collect adhesions to the appeal against Boniface VIII throughout the south (Picot, pp. 101, 261, 265, 269, 279, 287, 321, 323, 482, 483), and he was especially harsh to the Dominicans of Montpellier (ibid., pp. xxv-xxx). He took declarations of fidelity from the citizens of Lyon in 1311 (Bonnassieux,

Guichard continued to issue letters as bishop of Troyes,[26] for although his temporals had been seized, he had not been suspended from his ecclesiastical functions. He also seems to have been able to speak freely with his lawyers.[27]

The first set of charges was soon supplemented by another group that revived all the old stories about cheating the king and the queens, conniving in the escape of Jean de Calais, and causing the death of Blanche of Champagne, and added some details about Guichard's abuse of power. The first drafts of these accusations were prepared by Noffo Dei (who had not died when he thought he was mortally ill) and submitted to Nogaret.[28] It is doubtful that Nogaret did more than glance at them and touch them up a little. The second version of these accusations has an addition that is typical of Nogaret: the bishop was a heretic and only pretended to take Communion. But Nogaret was a busy man, occupied with the affair of the Temple and the process against Boniface. He seems to have lost interest at this point; the new charges, as submitted to the bishops of Orléans and Auxerre,[29] do not read like a work of Nogaret's. They add many details about Guichard's relations with imps and devils and about his violent and oppressive behavior as abbot and bishop, but they have few of the picturesque and stinging phrases that can be found in Nogaret's attacks on Boniface. Moreover, Nogaret had no reason to attack Guichard. The two men had never been rivals; they had worked in quite different fields (Nogaret was no financier), and a man who had just been made Keeper of the Seals did not have to worry about a bishop who had lost all influence in the government. It was obviously sensible for Guichard's enemies to keep Nogaret informed about the case, since he was one of the leading members of the Council and the Parlement. They may have asked his advice about the second set of charges, since he was an expert in drawing up criminal accusations. He may also have helped to organize a public meeting on

---

p. 135). He was an executor of the will of Philip the Fair (*Gallia Christiana*, xii, col. 111).

[26] Rigault, *pièce justificative*, no. 19, and pp. 215-16. He was allowed to use his seal.

[27] Ibid., pp. 104-9.

[28] Ibid., pp. 95-99 (the first draft), 100-101 (the draft after Nogaret had been consulted).

[29] Ibid., pp. 110-15.

the Ile de la Cité, where the charges against Guichard were explained to the people; this technique, used against Boniface and the Templars, was also a specialty of Nogaret's.[30]

If not Nogaret, then who was responsible for the renewed attack on Guichard? Rigault's answer is basically that it was the old gang—Simon Festu and his friends.[31] But Simon and his friends are scarcely mentioned in the accusations; nor were they of any importance as witnesses. Doubtless Simon had been annoyed by the fact that the first investigation of Guichard's conduct had not resulted in a conviction, but he had gained his chief objectives. Guichard had been driven from court; Simon was now Treasurer and about to become bishop of Meaux. What good could it do him to start a new process that probably would (and did) last for several years and distract him from his official duties?

It is possible, of course, that there was such deep personal resentment between the two men that Simon could not rest until Guichard had been utterly ruined. The best evidence to support this view is that Simon had probably been associated with Noffo Dei at the time of the first accusations and that Noffo appeared again as an accuser in 1308. But Noffo came into the case only after the bishop had already been accused of sorcery and poisoning; he added some useful details, but the charges were already grave enough to have convinced both Philip and Clement that an investigation was necessary. The first official accusation was made by Guillaume de Hangest the younger on the basis of a story told by a poor hermit;[32] Noffo had nothing to do with this. Noffo probably had his own reasons for disliking Guichard; as a "Lombard" he or his associates must have had dealings with the bishop during the period when Guichard helped to manage the finances of Champagne.[33] The Lombards could always be accused of usury and were frequently forced to pay large sums to the king.[34]

[30] Ibid., p. 65. The meeting was held the day before the bishops opened their inquest, obviously to put pressure on them.

[31] Ibid., pp. 101-2: "C'étaient donc les vieux ennemis de Guichard . . . qui dirigeaient encore ce nouveau procès . . . c'étaient les vielles haines . . . qui se ranimaient contre l'éveque."

[32] Ibid., pp. 60-65.   [33] Ibid., pp. 23-24.

[34] Strayer and Taylor, p. 17. The Lombards paid a large sum (at least 152,000 l.t. and perhaps, or in addition, 221,000 l.t) in 1293, when Guichard had a prominent role in the finances of Champagne (Mignon, nos. 2073, 2076).

Guichard may have squeezed them too, for his own advantage or that of Blanche and Jeanne, and Noffo may have been one of those who suffered. In any case, Noffo Dei was not a very reliable accomplice; he failed to pay his creditors at the fairs of Champagne and was hanged in Paris in 1313 for this or for some other crime.[35] If Simon Festu wanted to destroy Guichard, more credible witnesses were available; but no connection has yet been established between Simon and those who gave the most damaging testimony.

A case could be made that there was collusion between Simon Festu and the younger Guillaume de Hangest. Why did the *bailli* take the hermit's story so seriously? Such rumors were common whenever a great person died, for example, at the time of the death of Philip the Fair's elder brother. Simon Festu must have known the Hangest family well; the elder Guillaume was a fellow Treasurer, and the two men had had dealings with each other in the 1290s, when Guillaume was already a Treasurer and Simon was a very active collector of tenths and subsidies. But there was no very good reason for a Hangest to oblige a Festu. Guillaume the elder was far more influential at court than Simon; he had reached high position much earlier; he had already established his son in a successful administrative career. There was nothing to be gained and much to be lost by becoming involved in an intrigue against an unimportant bishop.

Nogaret, Festu, Noffo Dei, and Guillaume de Hangest all played some role in the process against Guichard, but none of them was the chief promoter of the case. This leaves only one possible candidate—the king himself. We do not know how Philip felt about his mother-in-law; we do know that he was deeply attached to Jeanne. The mere suspicion, never proved, that Guichard had cheated the queen had been enough to make him drive the bishop from his court and to establish a very powerful commission to investigate the charges. Jeanne's untimely death shocked him; he remained faithful to her memory for the rest of his life. The worst possible crime, in his eyes, would have been to encompass the death of the queen. Anyone who tried to hush up such a crime, even if the evidence was flimsy, would have incurred Philip's wrath. If the hermit's story had reached Philip's ears before Guillaume de Hangest had reported it, the Hangest family would have been ruined. Therefore the *bailli* acted

---

[35] Rigault, p. 219.

promptly to start the investigation; therefore Nogaret helped to strengthen the case by endorsing the dubious evidence of Noffo Dei and perhaps by arranging a public meeting to hear the charges; therefore Raoul Grosparmi and Pierre de Grez made a tremendous effort to find witnesses who would support the accusations. Even when Guichard had in effect been cleared, Philip would not let him return to dis diocese; he could not believe that the bishop was completely innocent.

This explanation is consistent with all that we know of Philip's character. His narrow piety, his high standard of morality in his private life made him very credulous in cases involving heresy and immorality. He certainly believed the charges of adultery against his daughters-in-law, though to believe them went against his interests. He almost certainly believed the charges against the Temple and against Boniface VIII; he profited from both actions, but profit was not his only motive. There is no reason why he should not have believed the charges against Guichard; in this case the profit was psychic, not financial or political. An explanation of Jeanne's premature death would help to assuage his grief; vengeance on her murderer would be the last and most fitting tribute he could pay to her memory.

Other people were not so credulous. The depositions of the witnesses against Guichard are not very convincing.[36] Curiously enough, the stories about the construction and the piercing of the wax doll and the preparations of the poison for Valois and the king's sons are full of lifelike detail, while the evidence about Guichard's dishonesty and oppressive behavior as an abbot and as a bishop is thin and perfunctory. Yet Guichard probably did take advantage of his office to build a fortune, and in his compromise with his chapter he admitted that he had abused his power,[37] while he certainly did not attempt the poisoning and almost certainly did not practice sorcery. The two bishops, Raoul Grosparmi and Pierre de Grez, must have known Guichard very well by the time they had completed their investigation; after all, they had spent at least a year on the affair of Jean de Calais and two years on the charges of sorcery and poisoning. They clearly did not think that they had a good case. Perhaps they were too

---

[36] Ibid., pp. 209-12. Rigault points out that although more than 200 witnesses were produced, most of them knew little about the case, and that those who gave the most damaging testimony were suspect for various reasons.

[37] Ibid., *pièces justificatives*, nos. 6 and 7.

sophisticated to believe in the wax-doll technique and too knowledgeable to believe that Guichard had found scorpions (one ingredient of the poison)[38] in Champagne. In any event, they came to no conclusion and did not protest when Guichard continued to exercise his episcopal functions. If they had been convinced of Guichard's guilt, they would have asked the pope to suspend him, and they could easily have cut his communications with his diocese.

The two bishops, in fact, were in an unenviable position. On the one hand, Philip was pressing for an unfavorable report; on the other hand, the pope was asking impatiently for the results of their investigation.[39] They stalled as long as they could, but finally sent in all the pieces of the process on 1 April 1311. It is probable that Guichard was released from the Louvre and sent to Avignon at the same time; he was certainly in Avignon early in 1313.[40]

Clement had reserved judgement to himself and hoped to settle the affair at the Council of Vienne, but the case never came up. It is doubtful that Clement had ever been convinced of Guichard's guilt, and he became even more sceptical after the bishop reached the papal court.[41] The final blow to the accusation came, fittingly enough, from Noffo Dei. As he was about to be hanged "pro suo crimine" at Paris in 1313 he confessed that Guichard was innocent.[42] The prosecution was dropped.

Contemporary chroniclers and later fourteenth-century writers were convinced that Guichard was innocent.[43] Philip the Fair was not. He had driven Guichard from court in 1300; he now wanted to drive him from France. Guichard could not return to his diocese; he remained in Avignon. Finally, in 1314, Marigny found a solution that was much more pleasing to Philip than to Guichard. Clement V translated the bishop to the see of Diakovar (or Djakovo), which was almost in partibus infidelium. The bishop of Diakovar was titular bishop of Bosnia, but there were few

[38] Ibid., p. 82.
[39] Clement asked for a report on 18 June 1310 and repeated his demand on 9 February 1311 (ibid., pp. 216-17).
[40] The records of the investigation were sent to Clement on 1 April 1311 (ibid., p. 218). Guichard was at Avignon by 19 April 1313 (ibid., pp. 219-20).
[41] Ibid., pp. 219, 233-34.
[42] Ibid., p. 219, citing Guillaume de Nangis (H.F., xx, 608).
[43] Ibid., p. 219 and pp. 227-36 (the section on "Le procès de Guichard de Troyes et l'opinion").

Catholics in Bosnia and many heretics and schismatics. Diakovar was not even in Bosnia (it would now be considered in Croatia); it had become the seat of the bishop early in 1252 or 1253, when it became impossible for him to remain in his diocese. Diakovar was poorly endowed[44] and on an endangered frontier of the Roman Church; it must must have been one of the least desirable bishoprics that the pope had at his disposal.

Rigault thought that this appointment showed that Marigny had long been hostile to Guichard, but Favier has shown that there is no real evidence to support this theory.[45] Marigny was simply doing his usual job of smoothing out difficulties between king and pope, and Clement, as usual, was willing to go more than halfway to satisfy the king. Jean d'Auxy, one of Philip's most reliable clerks and long active as a collector of revenues, as an *enquêteur*, and as a member of the Parlement,[46] was named to Guichard's old see. At last the king had a bishop of Troyes whom he could trust.

As for Guichard, it is doubtful that he ever went to Bosnia. In any case, he resigned early in the pontificate of John XXII and died soon after, in January 1317.[47] He left a rent to the church of Troyes, and his executors gave an additional 100 l.t. The fact that

[44] Throughout the fourteenth century Diakovar paid only 200 florins; Troyes paid 600 florins in 1314 and 2,500 florins thereafter (H. Haberg, *Taxae pro Communibus Servitiis* [Vatican: *Studi e Testi* 144], pp. 23, 122).

[45] Rigault, pp. 223-24; Favier, *Marigny*, pp. 132-33. Both Rigault and Favier thought that it was impossible for Guichard to return to Troyes, but Saisset, accused of treason, heresy, and defaming the king, was allowed to return to Pamiers. The evidence against Saisset was rather better than the evidence against Guichard; Saisset had probably made some indiscreet remarks about Philip. Once more, it seems that the king was personally involved in the Guichard affair; he would not let the bishop go unpunished.

[46] Jean d'Auxy, king's clerk, was in the Parlements of 1296, 1299, 1300, 1302, 1307, and 1309 (Langlois, ed., *Textes*, pp. 161-67; *Olim*, II, 436, III, 76, 307, 309, 312; *J.T.P.*, nos. 4762, 5888); he was a collector of subventions in 1300 (Mignon, no. 1343); he was in charge of payments from the Jews in 1301 (*J.T.P.*, no. 5659); he secured adhesions to the appeal to the council against Boniface VIII in the central provinces in 1303 (Picot, pp. xxi, 334, 355, 370, 392, 450, 459); he summoned southern lords to the army in 1304 (A.N., JJ 36, fol. 73v, nos. 172-73); he was sent to the south with sweeping powers as an *enquêteur* in 1305-1306 (*H.L.*, IX, 282-83, 290, X, 436, 447; see also entries under his name in Fawtier et al., eds., *Registres*); he was an *enquêteur* again in 1311 and in 1313 (*Olim*, III, 520; Langlois, "Enquêteurs," p. 54).

[47] Rigault, pp. 225-26. John was elected on 7 August 1316; Guichard must have resigned soon after this date.

he is mentioned in the necrology and in the memorials of the cathedral suggests that the report that he was buried there is true.[48] Philip the Fair was dead; Guichard could at last rest in peace in his old home.

[48] Ibid., pp. 226-34. Ironically enough, Jean d'Auxy, Guichard's successor, died in the same month of 1317, perhaps in the same week.

V. The King and His Neighbors

When Edgard Boutaric, *writing on Philip the Fair over a century ago, came to the topics that I discuss in this chapter, he put them in a section of his book entitled "Politique étrangère."*[1] This was natural enough for a nineteenth-century historian, but it was a twofold mistake. In the first place, it was very difficult around the year 1300 to say what was "foreign," especially in districts that had been part of the old Middle Kingdom. Second, the sort of activities that are normally associated with foreign policy—diplomacy and war—were in Philip's reign concentrated on areas that were indubitably part of the kingdom of France. Philip's two great wars were the war of Aquitaine and the war with Flanders, and each war was preceded and followed by years of complicated negotiations. These negotiations involved not only the count of Flanders and the king of England, but also the papacy, which was trying to make or keep peace in the two provinces, and a large number of west German princes, who were being sought as allies or who were being discouraged from supporting England and Flanders. In short, almost all of Philip's military activity and much of his diplomatic activity were concentrated on internal, not external, affairs.

Unlike his father and his grandfather, Philip refused to be distracted by what were really "foreign affairs"—Germany, Italy, the Spanish kingdoms, and the Holy Land. He kept himself informed about these matters, he dabbled a little in Italian politics and somewhat more in the affairs of the Empire; but he never committed himself to expensive and continuing interventions. His chief duty, as he saw it, was to establish his authority over all inhabitants of the kingdom of France. He would tax his people to the limit of their endurance in order to secure recognition of his sovereignty in Aquitaine and in Flanders, but he would spend only a few thousand pounds to support the candidacy of his brother Charles for the throne of the Empire.

Even in concentrating on France, Philip had two problems. The first was purely military. Philip did not have the strength to do

---

[1] Boutaric, *La France sous Philippe le Bel*, pp. 379-414.

everything that he wanted to do, and he certainly did not have the strength to conduct two major operations at the same time. It was difficult to raise money for an army, difficult to bring an army together in any reasonable length of time, and difficult to keep it together once it had been assembled. Victory was almost as bad as defeat, for victory meant that the army had to be broken up into small units for garrison duty in occupied territory, and also that many soldiers would feel that their duty had been done and would simply go home. The records of payment for army service show that many men, even among the nobles, thought that participation in one campaign, or even for a few weeks during one campaign, was enough to prove their loyalty. It was very nearly impossible to keep a large army in the field and at the same time to have adequate garrisons for towns and castles that had to be defended against raids or uprisings. A two-front war would have been a disaster for Philip; he had to relax his grip on Aquitaine when he wanted to occupy Flanders. Even a one-front war would be difficult if it became prolonged. Philip was fortunate if he could concentrate as many as 30,000 men for one short campaign. He could win a battle with such an army, but he could not keep such an army together for any length of time. Therefore, he could not gain as much from his victories as he may have hoped. He could force the Flemings to accept an onerous treaty of peace, but he could not make them fulfill all the terms of the treaty because he could not keep occupation troops in the county indefinitely; nor could he send in a punitive expedition every time the Flemings made difficulties. Philip had to keep these military realities in mind in making policy decisions.[2]

Philip's second problem was to decide what the boundaries of France were. This was no easy task. Even on the fairly clearly defined frontier with Aragon there was the perplexing case of the Val d'Aran, and the eastern boundary with the Empire was neither clear nor reasonable. The western part of the county of Bar ran deep into Champagne; the Vivarais cut into northeastern Languedoc; the county of Burgundy, which was in the Empire, was inextricably involved in the affairs of the duchy of Burgundy, which was French; the mercantile part of Lyon, which controlled the main trade route to the Mediterranean, was in the

[2] On the size and composition of French armies, see the Appendix to this chapter.

Empire, but the cathedral of Lyon was in France. Behind these districts where French intervention was clearly desirable and almost inevitable lay a French-speaking, French-oriented zone where the nobles were quite willing to accept money-fiefs or pensions from Philip and where the towns (especially Metz, Toul, and Verdun) often sought French protection.

Philip obviously could not neglect the eastern borderlands, but he was careful not to commit too many of his resources to expansion in this area.[3] Though some of his advisers reminded him that the old boundary of Gaul was the Rhine,[4] he knew that he had neither the power nor any reasonable justification for annexing large blocks of imperial territory. He had an intelligent set of priorities: first, to wipe out the salients that intruded into his territories; second, to annex Lyon and the county of Burgundy (thus gaining control of the Rhône-Saône trade route); third, to establish himself as the protector of the key cities of Metz, Toul, and Verdun. He carried out this program patiently, skillfully, and at very little expense. There was one small war with the count of Bar and one military demonstration against Lyon. It cost 100,00 l.t. to persuade Otto, the count of Burgundy, to relinquish his county,[5] and there was some skirmishing with a league of Burgundian nobles who were not pleased with their new ruler. But even in this case Philip acquired a sizable territory very cheaply. The war with Flanders cost millions of pounds, and even though Philip gained Lille and Douai, he never ended Flemish hostility to French intervention. Except for these military operations and the payment to the count of Burgundy, Philip gained most of his objectives in the east by administrative pressures (as in the case of the bishop of Viviers) and patient diplomacy. It was tedious work, but it did not occupy much of the time of the king and his Council.

---

[3] Kern, *Anfänge*, chap. 2, thinks that Philip was determined to expand to the east.

[4] Ibid., pp. 19-23, 27. A French chronicler reported that at the interview between Philip and Albert of Habsburg at Quatre Vaux in December 1299, Albert recognized the Rhine as the French frontier (*H.F.*, xxi, 17). On the broad question of what Philip believed was included in the *regnum* see M. Lugge, *Gallia und Frankreich im Mittelalter* (Bonn, 1960), pp. 175-76, and Charles T. Wood, "*Regnum Francie*, a Problem in Capetian Administrative Usage," *Traditio*, xxiii (1967), 117-47, esp. 138-41.

[5] Frantz Funck-Brentano, "Philippe le Bel et la noblesse Franc-Comtoise," *Bibliothèque de l'Ecole des Chartes*, xlix (1888), 16-17. Philip also promised Otto a life-rent of 10,000 l.t., March 1295.

AQUITAINE

We turn, then, to the two great military-diplomatic problems of the reign, Aquitaine and Flanders. No one has ever satisfactorily explained why Philip drifted into a war with Edward I of England in 1294. The Treaty of Paris of 1259 had made the king of England, in his capacity of duke of Aquitaine, a vassal of the king of France, but it had not stated expressly what the obligations of the duke were, nor had it defined the boundaries of the duchy. In fact, the matter of boundaries was left for later negotiations, negotiations that dragged on for decades.[6] Even the apparently clear-cut admission of vassalage had its ambiguities, especially in the administration of justice. The king-duke had an elaborate system of courts in Aquitaine. At what point in proceedings in these courts were appeals to the Parlement of Paris justified? How far could French officials intervene in the ordinary administrative processes of the duchy when people with grievances against English officials asked the protection of the king of France? What punishments could be inflicted on officials and inhabitants of Aquitaine who disobeyed orders of the suzerain? Added to these territorial and legal problems was the hostility between the seamen of the duchy and those of France. The line between peaceful trade and piracy was not very clearly drawn anywhere in European waters, and it was especially unclear in the Bay of Biscay and in the Channel, where ships from the Cinque Ports and Bayonne were apt to tangle with ships from Normandy. In fact, a raid by sailors of Bayonne was the ostensible cause of the war that began in 1294.[7]

These causes of friction are obvious; what is not obvious is that the friction was any more unbearable in 1293 than it had been earlier. There was nothing new in Philip's complaints against Edward I; conflicts between mariners of the two countries had been going on for decades, and officials of the king of England in Aquitaine had never been very eager to obey orders of French courts. Moreover, Edward was anxious to avoid war with France at almost any cost. His objectives were not unlike Philip's; he

[6] The treasy is published in Alexandre Teulet et al., eds., *Layettes du Trésor des chartes*, 5 vols. (Paris, 1863-1909), III, no. 4554. On later negotiations see Cuttino, *English Diplomatic Administration*, pp. 7-9.

[7] *Olim*, II, 3-4. It was this case, which begins "Olim homines de Baiona" and stands at the head of a list of *arrêts*, that gave its name (*Olim*) to the first registers of the Parlement.

wanted above everything else to be recognized as sovereign throughout the island of Great Britain. Wales was his Aquitaine, Scotland was his Flanders, and he was having serious troubles with both of them. The last thing in the world that he wanted was a war on the continent.

Edward therefore sent his brother, Edmund of Lancaster, to calm down Philip. Edmund had recently married the countess of Champagne and was thus the stepfather of Philip's wife, Queen Jeanne. He should have had some influence in the French court, but the terms he received were harsh, though not unbearable. Edward was to surrender 20 of his Aquitainian officials who had disobeyed orders of the king of France and was to permit a token occupation of the duchy. In addition, he was to marry Philip's sister and agree that any child of this marriage should receive Aquitaine as a hereditary possession.[8]

In accepting these terms, Edward had demonstrated that he did not want a war. Philip should then have realized that he did not need a war. Edward had clearly recognized the sovereignty of the king of France, and the token occupation force, "one or two men in each fortified place," could have acted as a tripwire to prevent any attempt to weaken that sovereignty. Instead, Philip sent in a large army, made it impossible for Edward to defend himself in the Parlement by refusing him a safe-conduct, and thus forced Edward to renounce his allegiance—which was, in effect, a declaration of war.

One can agree with Langlois that Edmund of Lancaster was "outrageously deceived,"[9] but why was it necessary to deceive him? Fawtier admitted that he could find no good reason for the war,[10] though he suggested hesitantly that Charles of Valois might have had some influence on Philip. But it is difficult to see what Charles had to gain from a war, and he was not one of Philip's most influential councillors. Among those who were, the bankers Biche and Mouche seem unlikely to have recommended an operation that involved them in serious financial problems; Gilles Aicelin and Pierre de Mornay were men who preferred negotiation to conflict; Pierre Flote had just entered royal service

---

[8] *Foedera, conventiones, literae* . . . , ed. Thomas Rymer, new ed. by A. Clarke et al., 4 vols. (London, 1816-1869), I, pt. 2, 794-95, gives Edmund's report and the terms of the proposed settlement.

[9] Langlois, *St. Louis*, p. 297: "Edmond se fit outrageusement duper. . . ."

[10] Fawtier, *L'Europe occidentale*, p. 318: "nous avuons ne pas comprendre."

and in 1293-1294 certainly could not have pushed through a decision of this magnitude. It looks as if this is one of the cases in which Philip made his own policy, without much encouragement from his Council. He was a young man, still in his twenties; he had been humiliated by the war with Aragon and the failure of subsequent negotiations to regain Sicily for his Angevin relatives; he may have been somewhat annoyed by the respect paid to Edward I in these negotiations, as a sort of senior statesman and universal peacemaker; he may have felt that if he could make an example of his greatest vassal, everyone else would fall in line; he may have been caught up in one of those flashes of bad temper that afflicted him to the end of his life. Whatever the reasons, it seems clear that Philip wanted a war—and he got it.

The war of Aquitaine (or the Gascon war) was one of the most peculiar conflicts of the Middle Ages.[11] It was not a bloody war; there were no major battles and relatively few skirmishes. But it was a terribly expensive war precisely because it was not bloody. The French had to maintain a large army of occupation in the duchy for almost ten years, an army that was not whittled down by death and desertion and that was far better fed than would ordinarily have been the case because there were no serious interruptions of supply routes. The English, who hung on to Bayonne, Bourg, and Blaye and who made some tentative efforts to regain other parts of the duchy, also had to maintain a large army and supply it from overseas. Although there were no naval battles, the French spent large sums of money on preparing an invasion fleet, and Edward spent considerable, though lesser, amounts in building galleys to repel invasion. Michael Prestwich thought that the Gascon war was the most expensive of all of Edward's wars.[12] For France, the Flemish war was probably more expensive, but the war of Aquitaine was not cheap, as can be seen from the accounts of army commanders and the repeated taxes that had to be levied in the 1290s.

The military operations can be described in a few lines. The Constable of France, Raoul de Nesles, took over the duchy without much trouble in 1294. Edward, tied down by an uprising in Wales, could send only a small army to counterattack. It had some success, but it could not regain the key city of Bordeaux.

---

[11] See my article, "The Costs and Profits of War."

[12] Michael Prestwich, *War, Politics and Finance under Edward I* (Totowa, N.J., 1972), pp. 171-72.

Charles of Valois in 1295 and Robert of Artois in 1296 pushed the English back to their key positions around Bayonne, Bourg, and Blaye. The truce of Vyve-Saint-Bavon in 1297 ended the fighting in Aquitaine, except for the uprising in Bordeaux in 1302.[13] But garrisons had to be maintained in the occupied regions, and they were not cheap. Thus the sum allotted for the garrison of Bordeaux for the period 10 September 1298-9 April 1299 was 20,549 l.t.,[14] which would mean a yearly cost of over 40,000 l.t., since the size of armies usually increased during the good fighting weather of the summer months.

If it is easy to describe the war, it is difficult to discuss the diplomatic activities associated with the war without getting bogged down in incomprehensible and often meaningless detail. To simplify the problem a little, there were two main currents of negotiation: one, an effort to gain allies in waging the war, the other, a search for peace. Both Philip and Edward spent large sums of money in trying to gain the support of princes of the Empire. Philip, for example, granted money-fiefs of 500 l.t. a year to the count of Luxemburg and the dauphin of Vienne (1294), 2,000 l.t. to the bishop of Metz (1296), 4,000 l.t. to the count of Holland (1296), and 6,000 l.t. to the count of Hainaut (1297).[15] Edward tried to play on German resentment against French encroachments into the lands of the Empire by forming an alliance with King Adolf of Nassau and his chief supporters (1294).[16] There was some talk of an attack on France by Adolf and some of the German princes, but nothing came of it. Only the count of Bar, who had his own grievances against Philip the Fair, actually sent his forces into action with a raid on Champagne. He was soundly beaten. His county was pillaged, and in the end he had to acknowledge that the part of Bar west of the Meuse was in France and was to be held as a fief from the French king.[17]

The only other ally of Edward I who eventually became involved in the conflict was Count Guy of Flanders, but he was a reluctant participant. In 1294 he agreed to marry his daughter Philippine to Edward's son and heir, but he was summoned to Paris and forced to leave the girl in the custody of the king of

---

[13] Mignon, nos. 2430-35.   [14] *C.R.*, II, no. 25488.

[15] Lyon, *From Fief to Indenture*, pp. 213-14.

[16] Ibid., pp. 211-13; Prestwich, *War, Politics and Finance*, pp. 172-73.

[17] Mignon, no. 2634. For the homage for lands west of the Meuse see Kern, ed., *Acta Imperii*, no. 144 (4 June 1301).

France. Philip the Fair left Guy alone during the next two years, while his armies were completing the occupation of the larger part of Aquitaine, but in 1297 he began to put pressure on the count. The burghers of the great Flemish towns were encouraged to resist their lord; French support was given to Guy's enemies, the counts of Holland and of Hainaut, and finally, the Parlement ordered Guy to put Ghent, Bruges, Ypres, Lille, and Douai in the hands of the king.[18] At this point Guy decided that he might as well fight as be nibbled to death. He made a military alliance with Edward, who saw some hope of strengthening his position in Aquitaine by opening a new front in the northeast of France.[19] But 1297 was a bad year for Edward. Wallace was leading a revolt against English rule in Scotland, and the English barons were objecting to taxation and refusing to serve overseas. Edward managed to bring over a few troops but gave no real assistance to Guy. A French army led by Charles of Valois overran most of the western part of the county. Robert of Artois, coming up from the south, decisively defeated the Flemings at Furnes. The count kept some of the major cities (Ghent, Ypres, and Douai), but he could not stage a counteroffensive, and Edward's army was too small to turn the balance. Edward was glad to arrange a truce in October 1297 and to withdraw from Flanders.[20]

The English alliance had been a complete disaster for Count Guy and had apparently done nothing to help Edward's case. Nevertheless, in the long run, Edward profited from his intervention in Flanders. When the truce of 1297 finally expired, the French occupied the rest of the county. This occupation led to the revolt of 1302 and the bloody and costly Flemish war of 1302-1305. It was during that war, in 1303, that the final treaty of peace between England and France was arranged. The treaty was on the whole favorable to Edward, far more favorable than the terms that he was willing to accept in 1293.[21] But one may wonder whether the terms would have been so favorable if Philip had not been shaken by the Flemish victory at Courtrai in 1302 and by his inability to avenge that defeat in 1303. The war with Flanders strained French resources to their limits just as the quar-

[18] Funck-Brentano, *Philippe le Bel en Flandre*, pp. 139-51, 172-79, 181-86.
[19] Ibid., pp. 198-204.
[20] Ibid., pp. 237-45, 250-64; for the truce of Vyve-Saint-Bavon, see pp. 267-72, 276.
[21] Fawtier, *L'Europe occidentale*, pp. 318, 324. See below, p. 323.

rel with Boniface VIII was reaching a peak. It was only sensible to make sure that England would not take advantage of the situation to make a new attack in Aquitaine.

The French were no more successful than the English in gaining military assistance from their allies, but they needed it less. Their objective was to dislocate the English alliance system, and they were fairly successful in this endeavor. Thus pensions to to the counts of Holland and of Hainaut helped to isolate Count Guy of Flanders, just as a pension to the count of Luxembourg isolated the count of Bar. The greatest success, if the story is true, would have been Mouche's securing the neutrality of King Adolf of Nassau through a generous gift; but, although Adolf was usually glad to take money from any source, it seems clear that he had already decided to stay out of the conflict.[22] On the other hand, it was not necessary to bribe John Balliol to oppose the English,[23] though it is doubtful that he had much to do with the uprising in Scotland that upset Edward's plans in 1297. Overall, French diplomacy seems to have been very successful. If Philip the Fair ever feared that he might have to face a Flemish-German coalition, such as the one that had threatened his great-great-grandfather at Bouvines, these fears must have been dissipated by 1297. The death of Adolf in battle and the election of Albert of Austria as king in 1298 gave him even greater security on his eastern frontier.

Although no one could have been sure at the time, the truce of 1297 marked the end of the war between France and England. Edward had never wanted the war, and he wanted it even less

[22] Funck-Brentano published a document in the *Revue historique*, xxxix (1889), pp. 328-34, that gives a list of sums paid to princes of the Empire and goes on to tell of buying off King Adolf for 80,000 l.t. There has been a long controversy over the authenticity of this document, summed up by V. Samenek, "Neue Beiträge zu den Regesten König Adolfs," *Akademie der Wissenschaften in Wien, Philologische-Historische Klasse, Sitzungsberichte* ccxiv, Bd. 2, who thinks that Boniface put pressure on Adolf and that Edward gave Adolf too little, and by G. Barraclough "Edward I and Adolf of Nassau," *Cambridge Historical Journal*, vi (1940), pp. 227-30. The story was believed at the time; see an anonymous report published by Boutaric in "Documents inédits," p. 126: Mouche went to see Adolf "si bien fondé et garni qu'il ot bon odience."

[23] *Foedera*, i, pt. 2, 822, 830. Philip did feel some responsibility for Balliol. He insisted that Balliol be released from captivity, even though he had not been included in the truce. He was handed over to a representative of the pope in 1299 (Digard, i, 388-89).

after the risings in Scotland had begun to absorb all his resources. Philip had occupied the duchy of Aquitaine, but he did not know what to do with it. Technically, he had the right to confiscate the lands of a rebellious vassal, but it went against all his ideas of proper behavior to do so, just as he later refrained from confiscating Flanders. He wanted obedience from his vassals, not their lands. If he would not confiscate Aquitaine, there was nothing to be gained by continuing to occupy it. His garrisons cost more than any possible revenue he could extract from the duchy. It also seems likely that by 1297 Philip was much more concerned about Flanders than about Aquitaine, but he could not intervene in Flanders until he had peace with England. So the truce of 1297 was prolonged while peace negotiations went on. In 1298 Boniface VIII persuaded Philip and Edward to let him arbitrate the quarrel as a private person, not as pope. (This reservation was probably made because Flemish envoys, trying to protect the interests of their master, insisted that Boniface could impose a settlement because he had supreme authority in temporal as well as in spiritual affairs.)[24] But Boniface achieved little except to prolong the truce and to arrange for marriages between Edward and Philip's sister and between the future Edward II and Philip's daughter Isabella. The pope deliberately excluded the Flemings from his settlement. This made possible a conference at Montreuil-sur-Mer in 1299, which achieved a preliminary peace between France and England by ratifying the marriage agreements[25] but left undecided the fate of Aquitaine. A final peace settlement was not reached until 1303 at Paris. Philip at that time was fully occupied with the Flemish war; he returned Aquitaine to Edward and accepted the homage of Edward's son and heir.[26] Even then, all the difficult questions were postponed. Injuries inflicted on each other by mariners of both countries were to be discussed at one conference, and the exact boundaries of Aquitaine were

[24] Thierry de Limburg-Stirum, *Codex diplomaticus Flandriae* (Bruges, 1879-1889), I, 286. The Flemish envoys said that the pope had deposed a king of France before and had jurisdiction *ratione peccati*. This was said in 1299, but in June 1298 the envoys had already said that the pope was sovereign over the king of France in both temporal and spiritual affairs (Funck-Brentano, *Philippe le Bel en Flandre*, p. 288). For Boniface's arbitration see ibid., pp. 280-95, and Digard, I, 360-67. As Funck-Brentano points out, the Flemings were shamefully treated, abandoned by the English and scorned by the pope.

[25] *Foedera*, II, pt. 2, 906-7.   [26] Ibid., I, pt. 2, 952-54.

to be settled at another. The conferences were duly convened, but neither accomplished anything.[27] The war, however, was over, and Philip, in return for restoring Aquitaine, had gained an alliance strong enough to persuade Edward to help him in his struggles with Flanders. The alliance did not last much beyond his own lifetime. All the old problems reemerged in the 1320s and 1330s, but at least Philip did not have to worry about England after 1303.

This left him free to deal with the Flemish problem, a dispute just as old and even more intractable than the quarrel over Aquitaine. During the long negotiations with England it had been tacitly agreed that England would not support Flanders and that France would not help Scotland. The threat of intervention from the Empire had also been removed by 1299, when Albert of Austria agreed to a marriage between his son Rudolf and Philip's sister Blanche. There were rumors that Albert went even further and, at a meeting at Quatre Vaux, agreed that Philip could take over lands of the Empire west of the Rhine.[28] These stories are certainly false, but it is true that Albert showed very little interest in the Low Countries and in other parts of the old Middle Kingdom during the remaining years of his reign. From 1299, the date of the preliminary peace with England and the agreement with Albert, Philip could concentrate his military and diplomatic activities on Flanders.

FLANDERS

The Flemish problem was basically the same as the problem of Aquitaine: how could the king assert his rights as sovereign in a great fief? (A small part of Flanders—"imperial Flanders"—was not held of the king of France, but the wealth and population of the county were concentrated in the areas that were indubitably part of the French realm.) Could the count of Flanders be summoned before the Parlement or only before the peers of France? When subjects of the count appealed from his court to the court of the king, how far could the king and his officials go in protecting them? How were decisions of the French courts

---

[27] These conferences are discussed at length in Cuttino, *English Diplomatic Administration*, pp. 62-100.

[28] See Kern, *Anfänge*, pp. 198-210, for the reasons for and the evidence about the meeting. See p. 205 for the talk about the Rhine frontier, and *H.F.*, xxi, 17, for a contemporary report on the subject.

to be enforced in Flanders? Could the king issue orders directly to subjects of the count or change the structure of government of a Flemish city? Could the king collect money (taxes or amercements) directly from the people of Flanders? In short, how could Philip's conception of his rights and duties as king be reconciled with the existence of a highly organized and semi-independent system of local government?

The same questions had been posed in Aquitaine, but it was easier to answer them, or (as in the peace of 1303) to avoid answering them, in Aquitaine than in Flanders. Aquitaine, after all, was a largely rural area in which most of the population had no particular reason to appeal to the king of France or to be troubled by orders of the king of France. For example, royal ordinances regulating exports or the currency caused relatively little controversy in the duchy. The system of local government was very like that of neighboring provinces; it did not require modification to protect the interests of the French king. Aquitaine was not particularly wealthy and not very conscious of its identity; it could not defend itself through its own resources. If England had not poured in money and soldiers, there would have been no war of any sort in 1294-1297, and the war that did ensue posed no danger to France and aroused little animosity. Most important of all, the social structure of Aquitaine was completely different from that of Flanders. There was only one large city, Bordeaux, and it had little influence on the rest of the duchy. The class conflicts that invited French intervention in Flanders were much less acute in Aquitaine. If Philip's advisers had been sociologists rather than lawyers, they might have been worried by the fact that the immediate cause of the war was the aggressiveness of the men of Bayonne and that the final episode of the war was the rebellion of the citizens of Bordeaux, but they did not draw the obvious conclusion that townsmen could be more dangerous than barons and knights. The occupation of Aquitaine had been a simple and easy military operation, and they saw no reason to suppose that the occupation of Flanders would be any more difficult. This was not an entirely mistaken judgement. Both in 1297 and in 1300 the French army overran Flanders without much trouble. The count surrendered himself as prisoner. The nobles offered little resistance; in fact, many of them went over to the French side.[29] According to all the rules of the game, Philip should have had a

[29] Funck-Brentano, *Philippe le Bel en Flandre*, pp. 216-17, 219-22, 305-6.

free hand to settle the Flemish problem as he saw fit. What he and his advisers did not foresee was that the peculiar nature of Flemish society could produce an effective resistance movement without the count and without much help from the nobility.

Unlike Aquitaine, Flanders was thoroughly urbanized. The great towns of Bruges, Ghent, Ypres, Douai, and Lille included or dominated the larger part of the population of the county. The towns quarreled among themselves, and they were torn by class struggles, but these quarrels and struggles proved that they had strong political convictions and willingness to fight for them. In France the inhabitants of French towns were not entirely passive; they staged bloody riots from time to time, but, even in the south, they could not dream of waging open war against their king. The people of the Flemish towns had no such inhibitions. There was a thin crust of wealthy francophiles at the top, but in Ghent, Bruges, and Ypres the majority of the population spoke Flemish, not French, and felt no loyalty to France or to the king. Moreover, French attempts to regulate foreign trade or to take large sums of money out of the county could be disastrous to rich and poor alike. The Flemish economy depended on the import of wool and the export of cloth, and this trade in turn required large amounts of capital. Any interference with exports and imports and any tax or indemnity that drew out liquid capital could bankrupt members of the upper classes and cause massive unemployment among the workers. In short, Flanders had both emotional and economic reasons for fearing French domination. It also had the manpower, the resources, and the willingness to resist that domination. Unlike Aquitaine, it did not need English money and English soldiers to wage a war.

The quasi independence of Flanders had annoyed French kings throughout the thirteenth century. Philip the Fair was not the first of his family to intervene in Flanders, but he did so on a larger scale and for a longer period than any of his predecessors. And, as in the case of many of his other policies, he began to put pressure on Flanders very early in his reign. By 1289 he had intervened in disputes between the Church and the *échevins* of Ghent and Ypres over the taxation of clerks engaged in trade, and he had sent his agents to Ghent to protect the town against the demands of the count.[30] These actions were taken long before

---

[30] Ibid., pp. 101-4, 113-14. This, perhaps, is the place to say that I shall cite Funck-Brentano almost exclusively in discussing Flemish affairs. He

the new councillors, such as Gilles Aicelin and Pierre Flote, had any influence. Philip, to be sure, was only continuing his father's policy of demonstrating to the inhabitants of the Flemish towns that he, and not the count, had final authority in all disputes that arose in the county, but, as Funck-Brentano said, he was more forceful in asserting his rights.[31]

Philip's first interventions in Flanders were based on his own appreciation of the situation. Unfortunately for him, he did not fully understand the complicated politics of the county. Like his predecessors, he thought that his main objective should be to weaken the count by playing off, and often by favoring, the towns against their immediate lord. However, by 1285 Count Guy de Dampierre was already in a very weak position, and the towns were gaining strength and self-confidence. They were quite willing to use the king to keep Guy from interfering in their affairs, but they were no more willing to obey the king than they were to obey the count. Philip's original misconception continued to distort his Flemish policy for the rest of his reign. Through negotiation, or through war, he could get quite satisfactory agreements with the count, and he could not understand why the count could not force the Flemings to implement fully these agreements. The problem was still unsolved at Philip's death, and his sons were no more successful than their father in dealing with it.

In the first half of the reign, however, Philip's policy in Flanders seemed quite successful. He protected the governing group in Ghent against the count and, at the same time, made sure that they recognized the authority of the Parlement and of the royal agents sent to the town.[32] He was not embarrassed when in 1294 the mass of the population asked permission to name a procurator to sue the town council (the Thirty-Nine) in the Parlement; he forced this through in spite of the opposition of the count and his *bailli*.[33] Royal policy was still concentrating on weakening the count by any means possible; no one realized the danger of weakening the town oligarchy (where most of the French-oriented bourgeois could be found) and of encouraging independent ac-

---

published many original documents in his book, and he cited most of the other collections of documents. I have checked these citations and found them accurate; there is no point in repeating them in my footnotes when they are so easily available in his work.

[31] Ibid., p. 112.   [32] Ibid., pp. 118-23.
[33] Ibid., pp. 124-26.

tion by the lower classes (who were to prove themselves violently anti-French).

Guy de Dampierre had fulfilled his obligations as a vassal with absolute correctness and had accepted Philip's interventions in Flanders without making any serious protest, but by the 1290s he was becoming irritated. Good behavior was doing nothing to stop the steady erosion of his power in Flanders, and resistance seemed hopeless without outside support. An alliance with England seemed to be a logical solution to his problems. Even without the presure from the king of France, there were good reasons for such an alliance. Flanders depended on English wool for its cloth industry; England depended on Flanders as a market for its wool. In spite of this obvious community of interests, Anglo-Flemish relations had been bad for the last two decades. Exports of English wool to Flanders had been forbidden for several years, and there had been repeated conflicts between English and Flemish mariners. It was only sensible to try to settle these disputes, and in the process of settling them it was natural for Edward of England and Guy of Flanders to realize that they had common grievances against Philip the Fair. Philip's policy in Aquitaine was very like his policy in Flanders, and conciliatory behavior had done Edward no more good than it had Guy. Thus a conference in 1292 to end the guerrilla warfare between English and Flemish sailors led to the treaty of 1294, by which Edward's son and heir was to marry Guy's daughter Philippine.[34]

This was a dangerous move, both legally and politically, for the count. Legally, a vassal was supposed to ask the lord's consent to the marriage of his children—above all, when the marriage was to an open enemy of the lord. Politically, Edward, deeply involved in the war of Aquitaine, was in no position to help Guy of Flanders. In the short run, however, Guy profited from his apparently rash act. He himself informed the king of the alliance when he was summoned to court on another occasion.[35] He was ordered to put Philippine in the king's custody and was detained in Paris for a few months, but he was not punished in any other way. All this was so predictable that one wonders whether Guy had ever really expected the marriage to take place. Most such agreements were never fulfilled; they were simply moves in the

---

[34] *Foedera*, I, pt. 2, 803, 827; Funck-Brentano, *Philippe le Bel en Flandre*, pp. 129-30, 140-41.

[35] Funck-Brentano, *Philippe le Bel en Flandre*, pp. 144-45.

diplomatic game. Guy's move was a warning that, if pushed too hard, he would seek outside help. Philip's answer was to let the count go back to Flanders (after his sons had guaranteed his loyalty) and to treat him much more favorably than he had in the past, especially in the never-ending disputes with the towns. A minor, but not inconsiderable, advantage for Guy, who had a very large family, was that one child would be educated, supported, and eventually, if she lived, married off by the king.

Whatever Guy's plans had been in 1294, he regained some of his lost authority in 1295 and early 1296. The powers of royal officials in Flanders were sharply curtailed; Philip's agents in Ghent were withdrawn; the king washed his hands of the dispute between the oligarchy and the people of Ghent and gave the count full control of the town.[36] The one thing that Philip could not do was to end the economic difficulties caused by the wartime suspension of trade with England, but he did permit some indirect trade through Brabant.[37] In any case, there was an English embargo as well as a French embargo, and Philip could do nothing about the former. Edward I tried to keep English wool from going to Flanders, partly to hurt the French economy as a whole, partly to remind the count and his subjects of the advantages of an English alliance. He must have known, however, that some of the wool sent to Brabant would filter into Flanders.

Economic problems were an indirect cause of a renewal of the quarrel between king and count after a brief respite. Philip needed money for the war (or, rather, for the occupation) of Aquitaine; Guy was at war with the counts of Holland and of Hainaut. Both king and count were short of money. When Philip ordered the levy of a fiftieth in his realm but promised to let Guy collect it in Flanders and keep half the proceeds, both men may have thought they were making a good bargain. Guy threw himself into the task of raising the subsidy with zeal—far too much zeal, according to the complaints of his subjects. Four of the great towns (Lille, Bruges, Douai, and Ypres) offered the king lump sums of money, ranging from 15,000 l.t. (Bruges) to 7,000 l.t. (Douai), in order to be free from the exactions of the count's

---

[36] Ibid., pp. 159, 163-64.

[37] J. de Sturler, Les relations politiques et les échanges commerciaux entre Brabant et l'Angleterre (Paris, 1936), p. 185. As Funck-Brentano points out (Philippe le Bel en Flandre, p. 158), by prohibiting importation of foreign cloth, Philip gave Flanders a virtual monopoly of the cloth trade in France —if it could get the wool.

collectors. The royal government knew that a quick and voluntary payment was worth more to the king than a slow, begrudged one, if only because it cut down administrative expenses. The count was sure that he could have made more by keeping up pressure on individual taxpayers and was reluctant to give up the money that he had already collected.[38] The four towns complained that Guy was opposing them and ignoring their privileges. They appealed to the Parlement and, as was usual in such cases, the king took them in his guard and sent royal officers to protect them.[39] Ghent, which in early 1296 was fully controlled by the count, could not bargain on taxes, but it could protest against Guy's arbitrary and, as it felt, oppressive policies. Philip reversed himself, reestablished the old communal government, and took Ghent under his protection. All these acts were confirmed by judgements of the Parlement in August.[40] Thus by the end of 1296 Philip was again using the towns to weaken the count, and royal officials were established in all the great towns of Flanders. Guy was worse off than he had been in 1294.

Almost inevitably, he reverted to the policy of an English alliance, but this time he committed himself far more deeply than he had before. He renounced his allegiance to Philip, renewed the project of a marriage between the younger Edward and one of his daughters, spoke of a perpetual alliance of England and Flanders against France, and made efforts to draw neighboring princes into an anti-French coalition.[41] He tried to gain the support of the working classes in the towns by removing all obstacles to trade with England and by weakening the authority of the oligarchical urban governments. This antipatrician policy proved useful in the long run, but Guy de Dampierre had not been very friendly to popular movements in the past, and neither the upper nor the lower classes of the towns showed any great enthusiasm for his cause in 1297.[42] In fact, Guy was unable to gain solid support from any group of his subjects; his only hope was a large and speedy influx of English troops and English money.

[38] Funck-Brentano, *Philippe le Bel en Flandre*, pp. 165-69.

[39] Ibid., pp. 172-79, 182-86.

[40] *Olim*, ii, 394-95. But see Funck-Brentano's discussion of the date (*Philippe le Bel en Flandre*, p. 182). He shows that it was in August 1296, not in 1295, as the printed edition has it.

[41] Funck-Brentano, *Philippe le Bel en Flandre*, pp. 190-92, 195-204; *Foedera*, i, pt. 2, 850-51. The final treaty was sealed on 7 January 1297.

[42] Funck-Brentano, *Philippe le Bel en Flandre*, pp. 192-94, 224-30.

Edward promised both military and financial aid, but rebellion in Scotland and a near-rebellion of the baronage of England made it impossible for him to keep his promises. He arrived in Flanders only late in August 1297, with an army that was too small to hold back Philip's invading forces but large enough to irritate the people of Ghent (as allied armies are apt to do). By that time the French had occupied most of the county, although Guy still held Ghent, Ypres, and Douai. Edward could do nothing to help his ally, though he did manage to have him included in the truce of Vyve-Saint-Bavon (9 October 1297), which allowed each side to retain the territories it held when the truce went into effect.[43]

Worse was to follow. Boniface VIII wanted to gain a reputation as a peacemaker. Edward wanted to be free of French wars so that he could concentrate on his problems in the British Isles. Philip the Fair apparently decided that it was more advantageous to gain full control of Flanders than to divide his forces between Flanders and Aquitaine, with the danger of losing both provinces. In the complicated negotiations that finally led to peace between France and England, the Flemings were deliberately and cold-bloodedly excluded.[44] Powicke remarked that Edward's behavior to Guy of Flanders was not a "glorious story," and Funck-Brentano, who had little sympathy for the Flemings, was nevertheless shocked by the way in which Boniface first encouraged and then abandoned them.[45] On the other hand, from the French point of view, the operation was one of the great diplomatic successes of Philip's reign. It is true that he had to abandon the Scots in return for Edward's desertion of Guy,[46] but the weights were not even. Philip, with the best will in the world, could have done very little to help the Scots; Edward could have made a good deal of trouble in Flanders if he had wanted to concentrate his efforts there. As it was, Guy was left to his own devices. When the truces finally expired in January 1300, a new French army, commanded by

[43] Ibid., pp. 267-70.

[44] Digard, I, 358-64; Funck-Brentano, *Philippe le Bel en Flandre*, pp. 292-304.

[45] F. M. Powicke, *The Thirteenth Century, 1216-1307* (Oxford, 1953), p. 669; Funck-Brentano, *Philippe le Bel en Flandre*, pp. 286, 289, 293-94, 303-4.

[46] In the marriage treaty of 1299 (Montreuil-sur-Mer), Philip simply asked that "monsieur Johan de Baylluel" (note that he is not called king of Scotland) be handed over to a representative of the pope (*Foedera*, I, pt. 2, 907). See above, note 23.

Charles of Valois, rapidly overran the part of the county that had remained under Guy's control. The old count and his eldest son, Robert de Béthune, surrendered themselves to the king and were placed in honorable captivity in royal castles. Philip the Fair had apparently scored a complete success; Flanders was occupied by his troops and governed by his officers.

There are some indications that the king wanted the occupation to last long enough to make permanent changes in the social and political structure of the county, as opposed to the occupation of Aquitaine, which had relatively little impact on the institutions of the duchy. Thus Jacques de Châtallon was "garde de par nostre sire le roi de *sa* terre de Flanders."[47] An effort was made to build up a party favorable to the king through widespread confiscation and redistribution of property.[48] Most significant of all, Philip made a triumphal tour through Flanders in 1301 and was received as the ruler of the county. He showed that this was not mere form by changing the structure of government of Ghent and Ypres, depriving the patriciate of much of its power, and giving the gilds a chance to influence the choice of members of the town councils.[49] This was an intelligent act, but it did not put an end to the struggle between rich and poor, and it did not gain for Philip the support of the gilds.

In fact, Philip's journey through Flanders may have done more harm than good. In the first place, he had to be entertained magnificently, and, although the rich did the entertaining, the taxes imposed to meet these expenses fell heavily on the poor.[50] Second, Philip imposed heavy fines on communities that had resisted his armies (notably, 120,000 l.t. on Ypres) and, at the same time, exempted those who had supported the French cause from contributing to these fines.[51] Since the rich were more apt to be pro-French than the poor, the lower classes again bore more than their share of the burden. Finally, by retaining Jacques de Châtillon as governor of Flanders, Philip again seemed to be tilting the balance against the common people. Jacques de Châtillon, uncle of the queen and brother of the count of Saint-Pol, be-

---

[47] Funck-Brentano, *Philippe le Bel en Flandre*, p. 356, n. 1. Ed. Coussemaker, *Documents historiques sur la Flandre Maritime*, in *Bulletin du Comité Flamend de France*, Vols. v and vi, *tirage à part* (Lille, 1870), 3d fasc. pp. 59 ff.

[48] Funck-Brentano, *Philippe le Bel en Flandre*, pp. 353-54.

[49] Ibid., pp. 358, 362, 364-69.   [50] Ibid., pp. 358-59.

[51] Ibid., pp. 363 (Ypres), 364 (Furnes, 6,000 l.t.; Pamele, 800 l.t.).

longed to the highest aristocracy of France. He had already shown that he had little sympathy with the grievances of the artisans of the Flemish towns, and he relied heavily on the support of the nobles and patricians of the county. As the events of the next two years were to show, he was betting on the wrong horse.

The workers of Bruges, disgruntled by the taxes imposed by the patrician government of the town, found a leader, a weaver called Peter die Coninc (king). Peter was an eloquent orator (or rabble-rouser, if his enemies' evaluation is to be accepted); he also had considerable ability as an organizer. He began agitation against the ruling oligarchy in Bruges in 1301, and the movement soon spread to Ghent. Some of the patricians were beaten or killed; their houses were plundered; a castle where they had stored their goods under royal safeguard was sacked and the garrison massacred. Jacques de Châtillon assembled an army that brought Ghent under control. In 1302 he marched on Bruges but, wisely, decided that an assault on the town and fighting in the streets was too dangerous. The moderate party in the town was just as anxious as he to avoid the risks of a battle, and an agreement was reached by which all those who feared the king's vengeance could leave peacefully and Jacques de Châtillon could enter Bruges with some of his troops. Several thousand of the rioters departed, and Châtillon marched in with his men-at-arms. He apparently thought that there was no further danger. Instead of keeping his forces together, he allowed them to seek lodging in houses scattered through the town, and he posted only a few men at the gates. The refugees, however, had not fled in terror; instead, they kept together, collected reinforcements from neighboring towns and villages, and, during the night of 18 May 1302, reentered Bruges and began to attack the divided French forces. Many of Châtillon's men were killed in their beds; others were cut down while fleeing or were taken prisoner. Nevertheless, the total loss in killed and captured was probably under 300.[52] Châtillon, Pierre Flote (who had probably come along to reorganize the town government), and many of the men-at-arms escaped unharmed. The famous Matins of Bruges were not a great military victory; they were a proof of the deep resentment of the artisans against French and patrician domination.

[52] Ibid., pp. 360-63 (on Coninc), 370-77 (risings in Bruges and in Ghent), 388-94 (the Matins of Bruges). Funck-Brentano thought that the estimate of 120 dead, given by a chronicler of Artois, was close to the truth.

As news of the Matins spread, most of the county rose in revolt. Ghent hesitated, but came in just in time to take part in the battle of Courtrai. Gui de Namur and Guillaume de Juliers, son and grandson of Count Guy, joined the movement promptly. Both were experienced commanders and helped to organize attacks on the fortified places that were still holding out for the king of France. Still, they must have had some worries about the army that they were gradually assembling in the Flemish plain —very little cavalry, few bowmen, and, since it was composed of contingents that had never fought together before, not very maneuverable.

Fortunately for the Flemings, the decisive battle took place in circumstances where none of their weaknesses could hurt them. They were trying to take the castle of Courtrai in early July when a French army, commanded by Count Robert of Artois, came up with them. It says a good deal for the efficiency of the French administration that a formidable and well-balanced striking force could have been assembled only a few weeks after the Matins of Bruges. The only fault was the choice of the commander, and that was Philip's responsibility, not his councillors'. One hesitates to speak of hereditary characteristics, but for generation after generation the Artois branch of the royal family was distinguished for reckless bravery and utter lack of prudence. At Courtrai, Robert had the Flemish army pinned down in a marshy plain; they could not attack, and retreat would have been difficult. On 11 July he began the battle. His crossbowmen (mostly Italians) began to cut down the Flemings, who could not retaliate, and his infantry advanced slowly. This methodical and time-consuming tactic did not suit Robert's idea of knightly warfare. He wanted a quick and glorious victory, and he ordered his cavalry to charge. The terrain was bad enough for horses as it was; the Flemings had made it worse by deepening and digging ditches. The charge piled up in a confused mass of mired and crippled horses; the Flemings came out and finished off the riders at their leisure. Robert of Artois, Pierre Flote, Jacques de Châtillon, Raoul de Clermont, the Constable, two Marshals, and Jean de Burlas, master of the arbalesters—in fact, all the leaders of the French army—were killed. Only the rear guard escaped, spreading panic as they fled.[53]

[53] See Frantz Funck-Brentano, ed., *Annales Gandenses* (Paris, 1896), pp. 30-34 (with the long extract from the *Chronique artésienne*, p. 32, n. 3), for the best contemporary accounts of the battle.

Courtrai was the great crisis of Philip's reign. He was short of money, without a field army, involved in a desperate struggle with the pope, and hated by many of his subjects because of his heavy taxes and manipulation of the currency. A weaker man might have given in and cut his losses by allowing the Flemings virtual independence. Philip did not yield on any front. He showed some willingness to negotiate with Boniface VIII, but he made no substantial concessions. He levied new taxes and further weakened his currency, and he continued the war with Flanders. He was unable to make any headway. His troops, underfed and often unpaid, were at times on the verge of mutiny,[54] but he would not make peace. At most, he allowed the old count, Guy de Dampierre, to leave his prison and try to start negotiations with the Flemish leaders, but Guy had long ago lost all influence in Flanders. He could not persuade his sons and grandson to yield on any important point, and, as he had promised, he returned to captivity. Perhaps he did so with some relief; like Philip the Fair, he found the new political situation in Flanders a little beyond him.[55]

The failure of Guy's mission left Philip free to make a supreme effort in 1304. He no longer had to worry about the papacy; the death of Boniface and the advent of Benedict XI had freed him from the danger of excommunication. Internal discontent had been softened by the reform ordinances of 1303 and with a promise of "good money."[56] These reforms, in turn, made it possible to impose the great tax of 1304, the most productive of the reign. The money came in more slowly than the king wanted, but Philip could at last raise a really effective army.[57] At the hard-fought battle of Mons-en-Pévèle (18 August 1304) Philip won a victory over the Flemings, but he did not destroy their army. It was now time for negotiations.[58]

---

[54] See Frantz Funck-Brentano, ed., *Chronique artésienne* (Paris, 1899), p. 72, for a near-mutiny in 1303 over lack of pay and food. Petit, *Charles de Valois*, pp. 93-94, gives a good account of the troubles. See also A.N., JJ 36, fol. 66v, no. 151 (unpaid soldiers were pillaging on their way home, November 1303).

[55] Funck-Brentano, ed., *Annales Gandenses*, pp. 54-55, 57-58.

[56] *Ord.*, I, 357 ff. The promise of "good money" came in the request for a new subsidy, October 1303 (*Ord.*, I, 383).

[57] See A.N., JJ 36, fols. 38, 41, 69v, 71, 71v, 77, nos. 97, 105, 163, 164, 166, 177, 184, for a series of almost frantic letters to local officials, asking for speedy collection of the subsidy and the tenth, late 1303 and early 1304.

[58] For Mons-en-Pévèle see Funck-Brentano, ed., *Chronique artésienne*,

Philip must have known that a continuation of the war was almost impossible. A new tax, following the heavy subsidy of 1304, would have brought in little money and might have caused serious disorders. The king had promised to restore "good money," so that manipulation of the currency, which had covered a large part of his expenses during the last seven or eight years, was no longer possible. The Flemings were equally unable to continue the contest. Guillaume de Juliers, one of the ablest, and certainly the most popular of their leaders, had been killed at Mons-en-Pévèle. The other leader of the rising of 1302, Guy de Namur, had been taken prisoner at the naval battle of Zierikzee, fought just before Mons-en-Pévèle.[59] No help could be expected from England; in fact, Edward I had ordered the Cinque Ports to send 20 ships to aid Philip on 9 April 1304.[60] Commerce and industry were stagnating. There was bitter rivalry among the towns, especially between Ghent, which had been lukewarm in its support of the conflict, and Bruges, which had been the leader. The nobles and town oligarchies were frightened by the growing power of the artisans; they needed peace to reestablish their position. Thus, when Philip let it be known that he would restore Flanders to the count and preserve local privileges and customs,[61] serious negotiations could begin.

The basic terms of the treaty of peace were worked out early in 1305, probably by Gilles Aicelin and Pierre de Mornay. (The official heads of the French mission were Louis of Evreux, the duke of Burgundy, and the counts of Dreux and Savoy, but it is doubtful that they contributed much to the negotiations except their prestige.) The count of Flanders was to establish a rent for the king of 20,000 l.t. a year on the county of Rethel (a small district, not far from Reims, that was not part of Flanders). Until this was done (and it is doubtful that Rethel was ever worth 20,000 l.t. a year), Philip was to hold Lille, Douai, and Béthune —towns that he had already seized and that were largely French-speaking. The people of Flanders were to pay an indemnity of 400,000 l.t. in four years (another clause that was nearly a finan-

p. 85, and *Annales Gandenses*, pp. 69-77. The naval battle of Zierikzee (10-11 August), won by Philip's fleet assisted by ships of the count of Hainaut, cut off supplies from Zeeland to Bruges but came too late to have had much effect on the forces available to the Flemings at Mons-en-Pévèle.

[59] Funck-Brentano, *Philippe le Bel en Flandre*, pp. 469-71.

[60] *Foedera*, I, pt. 2, 961-62.

[61] Funck-Brentano, *Philippe le Bel en Flandre*, p. 481.

cial impossibility). Three thousand inhabitants of Bruges were to go on pilgrimages (1,000 to the Holy Land) to expiate the Matins. The fortifications of the Flemish towns were to be destroyed. The count, the Flemish nobles, and the town governments were to swear to observe these terms.[62]

The treaty was promulgated at Athis-sur-Orge in June 1305. This marked the end of serious hostilities in Flanders; but it was one thing to make a treaty and another to enforce it. Robert de Béthune, who had succeeded his father, Guy de Dampierre, as count in March 1305, was at first ready to do everything he could to carry out the terms. He wanted peaceful possession of Flanders, and he was not displeased by the fact that the burdens of the treaty would fall mainly on the towns. The towns, naturally, took a different point of view, especially when they discovered that Flemings who had sided with the king would be exempt from paying their share of the indemnity.[63] Philip was fully aware that the towns were going to make difficulties. Even before the treaty was promulgated, he had sent Hugues de la Celle (one of his most trusted councillors) and Jacques de Saint-Aubert (a collector of tenths and subsidies and frequent attendant at the Parlement) to obtain the oaths of the people and the officials of the towns to observe the terms agreed upon by the negotiators. How much was known about the exact language of the treaty at that time (March-May 1305) is uncertain, but Bruges and Ypres required a good deal of persuasion before they empowered their representatives to take the oath.[64] Once the treaty was officially published, the grumbling became worse. This time Philip summoned the procurators of the towns before the pope at Poitiers (May 1307), where they renewed their oaths. (So did Robert and the nobles, but at this moment their loyalty was not in question.)

---

[62] Ibid., pp. 492-94.   [63] Ibid., p. 503.

[64] Ibid., pp. 494-97. For Hugues de la Celle see above, pp. 86, 154. Jacques de Saint-Aubert, canon of Tournai and king's clerk, collected fines for amortization in Champagne, 1292-1297 (Mignon, nos. 1409, 1857), helped to arrange for the royal guard of Toul, December 1300 (Kern, ed., *Acta Imperii*, no. 140), collected the tenth of 1297 in the dioceses of Tours, Angers, and Le Mans (Mignon, no. 738), collected the subvention of 1302 in Champagne (Mignon, nos. 1435, 1454), was an *enquêteur* in Champagne in 1303 (A.N., JJ 38, no. 135), was a *rapporteur* in the Parlement, 1302-1308 (*Olim*, III, 78, 79, 184, 197, 214, 235, 244, 259, 261), and was a member of the Chambre des Enquêtes in 1307 (Langlois, ed., *Textes*, p. 179). He does not appear after 1308. He was obviously an expert on the Champagne border area.

Clement V pronounced excommunication and interdict on individuals and communities that broke their promises and added—an act that was to cause him trouble later—that those excommunicated could be absolved only at the request of the king.[65] As a final precaution, Philip sent Jacques de Saint-Aubert, Pierre le Jumeau (the *bailli* of Vermandois), and Ami d'Orléans (a king's clerk and notary, later a *maître des requêtes*) to obtain the oaths of the Flemish towns. They met resistance only at Bruges, where the people insisted that the pilgrimages be commuted to an amercement of 300,000 l.t.[66] Philip had done all that he could to neutralize the opposition of the towns.

Nevertheless, the opposition continued, especially in Bruges. The artisans felt, not without reason, that the king, the count, and the patricians were combining against them, trying to keep them out of town governments and making them carry an unfair share of the financial burdens imposed by the peace treaty. Philip was exasperated by this opposition. He was also irritated by the fact that payments for the indemnity were far in arrears. He put heavy pressure on Clement V in 1309 to order the excommunication of all who were obstructing the fulfillment of the terms of the treaty.[67] Clement, already annoyed by Philip's demands for the prosecution of the Templars, hesitated for over a year, but, finally, in June 1310 he authorized excommunication of the treaty breakers (though he soon modified his position).[68] Meanwhile, Philip had sent Guillaume de Plaisians to force the towns once more to swear to observe the requirements of the treaty. The oaths were obtained—even Bruges finally conformed in July 1309[69]—but they had no more effect than the earlier promises.

It was at about this time that Enguerran de Marigny began to act as the principal adviser on Flemish policy. He had already (in 1308) helped to draft a letter urging excommunication of

[65] Funck-Brentano, *Philippe le Bel en Flandre*, pp. 511-12; Lizerand, *Clément V*, pp. 70-71. The pope's letter was dated 2 June 1307.

[66] Funck-Brentano, *Philippe le Bel en Flandre*, pp. 513-15. Ami d'Orléans, who became archdeacon of Orléans and then dean of Paris, was a royal notary (1301-1318), *clerc du secret* (1318), and *maître des requêtes* (1318); he was active until 1325. On him see Guillois, p. 239; Perrichet, p. 545; *Gallia Christiana*, VII, cols. 208-9.

[67] A.N., JJ 42A, fols. 77v-79, no. 37 (published by Funck-Brentano in *Bibliothèque de l'Ecole des Chartes*, LVII [1896], 533-36). The date is 19 January 1309.

[68] Funck-Brentano, *Philippe le Bel en Flandre*, p. 559.

[69] Ibid., p. 556.

opponents of the treaty of Athis. In 1310 the subject came up again while he was discussing with Clement V the question of continuing the process against the memory of Boniface VIII. Clement certainly, and Marigny probably, wanted to wind up this miserable affair, and in the bull (23 August 1310) explaining his position on Boniface, Clement added a rather embarrassed paragraph stating that his earlier promise not to withdraw excommunication of the Flemings without the king's consent had been made thoughtlessly and was contrary to canon law.[70] Marigny made no protest, and in 1311 Philip accepted the pope's renunciation of the clause.[71]

These acts seem to mark the beginning of Marigny's later policy toward Flanders. He was willing to give up theoretical claims that could never be enforced in return for material advantages. The excommunication clause was clearly unenforceable. No one, as Clement pointed out, could keep a pope from absolving repentent sinners. (One wonders whether he thought of Gregory VII's absolution of Henry IV at Canossa, in spite of the papal promises to the German princes.) On the other hand, it was essential to have Clement's cooperation in settling the Boniface process and the affair of the Templars. The pope was already irritated by the pressure put upon him in these cases; it was senseless to annoy him further by trying to make him keep a promise that he never should have made.

Marigny soon had more serious problems to deal with in Flanders. Agitation in the towns against rule by the upper classes and over the payment of the indemnity and the fine imposed on Bruges was growing. Royal intervention in the affairs of the county was increasing. The count could scarcely take any action without running the risk of an appeal to the king, followed by an order to redress the grievance or a summons to appear before the Parlement.[72] Robert de Béthune was being whipsawed be-

[70] See Favier, *Marigny*, pp. 134, 154, for the letter of 1308 and the pope's change of mind in 1310; see also Funck-Brentano, *Philippe le Bel en Flandre*, pp. 543-45. Clement's explanation is printed in Dupuy, *preuves*, pp. 294-95. The key sentence is "nam iure divino vel humano illa clausula non fulcitur; quilibet excommunicatus sufficienti satisfactione premissa debet absolvi, etiam si adversarius contradicat, nec nos potestatem absolvendi a nobis abdicare possumus. . . ." He will, however, try to keep this decision secret.

[71] Favier, *Marigny*, p. 135.

[72] See Funck-Brentano, *Philippe le Bel en Flandre*, pp. 570-76, on slow payment of the indemnity, on arguments as to who should pay, and for examples of intervention by royal officials.

tween the demands of the artisans and the pressures from Paris. If he satisfied the lower classes, the payment of the indemnity, already in arrears, would be impossible, and the king would have new reasons for intervening in Flanders. If he satisfied the king, he risked riots in the towns and a steady erosion of his authority. There was no tenable middle ground; by 1311 Robert had angered a large part of the urban population without appeasing the king. In August Philip sent an embassy headed by Marigny to Flanders, partly to make peace between the count of Flanders and the count of Hainaut (the latter, as an ally of the king, had been included in the treaty of Athis), but also to manifest Philip's firm determination to enforce the terms of the treaty.[73]

Marigny's first idea seems to have been to solve the Flemish problem by persuading Louis of Nevers, the eldest son of Robert de Béthune, to sell his rights to the county, or at least to arrange a marriage between one of his children and a member of the royal family, which might bring Flanders into the possession of Philip's descendants.[74] This proposition was not quite as unrealistic as it seems. Louis was on bad terms with his father, and his counties of Nevers (inherited from his mother) and Rethel lay in France and could be easily seized by the king. An assured position as a great French lord might seem preferable to the troubled rulership of Flanders. Louis, however, refused all of Marigny's offers.

Marigny then called a conference at Tournai (September 1311) to end the Flanders-Hainaut dispute, but this discussion soon turned into a lively argument about the fairness of the peace of Athis. Marigny became very angry with Louis of Nevers and others who said the peace was harsh; he declared haughtily that the king had been unnecessarily merciful in giving back Flanders to the count—a manifest traitor—on any terms.[75] Nothing was decided, and the king put more pressure on the count and his son by seizing Nevers and Rethel and by summoning Robert and Louis to appear before him at Tournai on 14 October. Meanwhile, Marigny and his fellow envoys tried to conciliate the French-

---

[73] Ibid., pp. 593-99; Favier, *Marigny*, pp. 155-61. Marigny's colleagues were Jean de Grez, Marshal of France, Pierre de Galard, master of the arbalesters, Harpin d'Erquery, and Gérard de Courtonne. The inclusion of two army commanders was a definite warning.

[74] Funck-Brentano, *Philippe le Bel en Flandre*, pp. 587-88; Favier, *Marigny*, p. 156 (p. 233, for an account of Marigny's proposal).

[75] Funck-Brentano, *Philippe le Bel en Flandre*, pp. 594-99; Favier, *Marigny*, pp. 158-60.

speaking inhabitants of western Flanders, notably the people of Douai. They drew up a new constitution for the town that divided power fairly evenly among opposing factions and greatly improved the administration of the town's finances.[76]

Neither the count nor his son appeared at Tournai on the appointed date, but delegates of the towns were there. Someone speaking for the king (almost certainly Marigny, as both Favier and Funck-Brentano believed), delivered an oration that sums up, as well as any document of the reign, the political creed of Philip the Fair.[77] The king is sovereign lord in Flanders, and all inhabitants should recognize "la souvrain et la droituriere signourie" of the king. This is to their advantage "car il n'a si povre home en Flandres, se li quens li voloit faire tort et il s'en plainsist au roy, que le roy ne soumesist le conte a justice et a droiture, et, se il ne voloit obéir, que le roy et tout son royaume ne le contrainsist par forche d'armes, se mestiers estoit." Let the people remember the fate of the duke of Normandy and the count of Toulouse, greater men than the count of Flanders, who lost their lands because they defied the king. And, once more, when the counts of Flanders and Nevers appear before the king's Court, all grievances against them will be heard and redressed.

The words may be Marigny's, but the basic ideas go back to the early years of the reign, long before Marigny had come to court. The king is sovereign in his realm, and the essence of sovereignty is the right to judge, in the last instance, all men and all cases. This had been the doctrine asserted in the controversies with the churches of Chartres and Poitiers in 1290, in the disputes with Edward I, in the first quarrels with Guy de Dampierre. Marigny may have stated it more bluntly than his predecessors, but he did not invent it.

The immediate results of the conferences of 1311 were not very great. Louis of Nevers was briefly imprisoned, but he escaped with so little difficulty that one wonders whether this was anything more than a warning. The date for Robert de Béthune's appearance in the Parlement was repeatedly postponed. Meanwhile, Philip and his Council must have been wondering how they could squeeze anything more out of Flanders without another war. War was undesirable for many reasons: the Council of Vienne was about to meet; the affair of the Templars was not yet

---

[76] Favier, *Marigny*, pp. 163-64.

[77] Ibid., pp. 162-63; Funck-Brentano, *Philippe le Bel en Flandre*, pp. 602-4.

settled; royal finances were still in bad shape (Marigny would have stressed this last point). Fortunately for Philip, war was equally undesirable for his opponent. Robert of Béthune's financial problems were even greater than the king's, and his only hope of defending Flanders would have been to throw himself into the arms of the radical leaders of the lower classes, a group that had rather less respect for his prerogatives than did the king. Both sides had reason to compromise, and an agreement was slowly worked out during the early months of 1312. It had long been apparent that the 20,000 l.t. rent promised the king by the peace of Athis could not be provided from the revenues of the county of Rethel. In theory, the obligation had been reduced to 10,000 l.t. by the promise of a lump-sum payment of 600,000 l.t. ("weak money"),[78] but this was an even more impossible condition. Robert could not even meet the annual payments due for the indemnity of 400,000 l.t. How could he raise 600,000 l.t. (200,000 l.t. in the reformed currency), a sum far greater than his yearly income? On the other hand, Philip already held Lille, Douai, and Béthune as pledges for payment, and the chances of regaining them seemed slim. The obvious solution, worked out by Marigny,[79] was to cede Lille, Douai, and Béthune to Philip in return for cancellation of the rent owed by the count. The agreement was sealed at Pontoise on 11 June 1312.

If the agreement of Pontoise had been the end of the Flemish problem, one could say that Philip had scored a brilliant success. He had acquired two great Flemish towns and most of the French-speaking part of Flanders. But neither Philip nor Robert of Béthune nor their successors were really satisfied with the settlement of 1312. Philip continued to interfere in Flemish affairs and to insist on the fulfillment of some of the more unenforceable terms of the peace of Athis, such as the destruction of town fortifications. Robert could not satisfy Philip's demands, even when they were legitimate, and neither he nor his people would accept the loss of Lille and Douai. The heirs of Philip and of Robert continued the quarrel. For centuries there was war on the Flemish frontier. The boundary line swung back and forth—against France in the period of Burgundian and early Habsburg domination of Flanders, in favor of France under Louis XIV. In the end, the boundary between France and Belgium was drawn very close

---

[78] Funck-Brentano, *Philippe le Bel en Flandre*, pp. 549, 622.
[79] Favier, *Marigny*, pp. 169-70.

to the line of 1312, a belated tribute to the wisdom of the treaty of Pontoise.

There was a temporary détente in the months following the treaty, but the old grievances about fortifications, slow payment of the indemnity, and exemption of French adherents from paying were soon revived. New arguments about the exact boundaries of the districts ceded to the king added to the bad feeling. Louis of Nevers drew up solemn protests against the peace. The situation became so serious that a conference was called at Arras for 22 July 1313, and Philip at the same time took the precaution of summoning his army.[80] He could at last afford to threaten a military demonstration; he was receiving some money (not as much as he would have liked) from the aid for knighting his eldest son, and during the summer a general subsidy for defense was imposed.[81] However, the money came in slowly, and the pope sent his legate to help prevent a war that would have threatened his plans for a crusade. Philip had to content himself with receiving new promises from the towns to observe the treaty of Athis. Robert de Béthune was warned by Philip's envoys to have nothing to do with troublemakers and to appoint only supporters of the peace to office,[82] advice that was useful only if the count sincerely wanted to uphold the agreements of Athis and Pontoise.

It was on this occasion that Philip not only stopped the collection of the subsidy (*cessante causa*) but almost certainly returned the small sums of money that had been collected.[83] He has received a considerable amount of praise for this action, and it is true that his finances were in bad enough shape so that losing any income must have been painful. On the other hand, if Philip lost income, he had not incurred any great additional expense. The army had been summoned for 5 August, but all the essential agreements had been reached by the end of July. Response to military summonses was always slow; it would have been surprising if very many men had found their way to Arras before the crisis was over. Thus Philip owed no money for army wages, and not much can have been spent on supplies. The situation was very different in 1314, when an army was actually assembled and

<hr>

[80] Funck-Brentano, *Philippe le Bel en Flandre*, pp. 633-34.

[81] Strayer and Taylor, pp. 81-82.

[82] Funck-Brentano, *Philippe le Bel en Flandre*, pp. 634-38; Favier, *Marigny*, pp. 173-74.

[83] Strayer and Taylor, pp. 81-82.

marched into Flanders. To forgive the tax of 1313 cost very little; to halt collection of the tax of 1314 was a real sacrifice. Philip reluctantly made this sacrifice, but he could not afford to repeat the gesture of returning the money already received.

It became evident soon after the conference of Arras that the count of Flanders was still bitter over the loss of western Flanders. Philip, perhaps on Marigny's advice, tried to gain the support of the artisans in the towns. Bruges, which had agreed to pay a lump sum to buy off the pilgrimages imposed by the peace of Athis, was given a chance to demand help from the other towns, and the artisans of Ghent were given royal protection against the patricians.[84] These acts caused some dissension in and among the towns, but they did not swing the people of the county over to the king's side. When Robert de Béthune denounced Philip for refusing to return the lost territories (26 July 1314), he had no trouble in raising a large army.[85] He attacked Tournai and then besieged Lille. Philip immediately summoned his troops and by August was invading Flanders.

Neither side, however, was very happy about the prospect of an all-out war. If the count had won a quick success at Lille, he might have hoped for a French collapse like that of 1302, but Lille held out. Philip, on the other hand, may already have been aware of the discontent in France that was soon to be expressed in the provincial leagues of nobles. He certainly knew that the new subsidy, which he had to impose to pay his troops, was unpopular. Marigny, his chief adviser, saw no use in fighting; he wanted to consolidate the gains of 1312 rather than run the risk of a protracted war. He had no doubt that the French could win, but he knew that the cost would be great and the eventual profit dubious.[86] Finally, Clement V had died in April 1314, and both Philip and Marigny wanted to keep pressure on the conclave to elect cardinal Nicolas de Fréauville (who happened to be Marigny's cousin).

Thus, before there was any serious fighting, Marigny negotiated the conventions of Marquette (3 September 1314). They amounted to a confirmation of the *status quo ante*. Robert de

---

[84] Funck-Brentano, *Philippe le Bel en Flandre*, pp. 648-49; Favier, *Marigny*, p. 177.

[85] Funck-Brentano, *Philippe le Bel en Flandre*, pp. 655-58.

[86] Ibid., pp. 656-58. See Favier, *Marigny*, p. 178, for a letter of Marigny's mocking Flemish hopes of a victory. The French are eager for war; mere words will not tear apart the kingdom of France.

Béthune and Louis of Nevers were to ask (and to receive) the king's pardon. The "transport of Flanders"—the cession of Lille, Douai, and Béthune—was again ratified. Louis of Nevers was to regain possession of his counties of Nevers and Rethel. An indemnity of 20,000 l.t. was to be paid to adherents of the king whose property had been lost or damaged during the rising.[87]

This was a reasonable settlement if—as was always the case with agreements with the Flemings—it could be enforced. Marigny—and Philip— were certainly right in thinking that two birds in the hand (Lille and Douai) were worth more than a bird in the very prickly bush of Flemish-speaking Flanders. Moreover, Philip honestly disliked dispossessing a great baron, whether it was the duke of Aquitaine, the count of Foix, or the count of Flanders. A king without barons to give dignity and authority to his court would scarcely be a king. Marigny probably had less confidence in the great barons, but he knew, better than anyone else, that the kingdom could not stand the expense of a protracted war. The promises made at Marquette might soon be broken, but at least they gave a little more time to consolidate the king's control over the annexed territories.

As might have been expected, the conventions of Marquette were greeted with a storm of disapproval. Charles of Valois and Louis of Navarre had opposed the negotiations from the start (though Charles confirmed the agreement after it was made), and many of the nobles in the army were disgusted when the results became known.[88] The chroniclers reflected a general feeling of humiliation that the royal army had withdrawn without striking a blow, and they reported rumors that Marigny had been bought off by the Flemings. As Favier has shown, Marigny made some profit out of the reopening of trade with Flanders; large quantities of Flemish cloth were sold at his fair of Ecouis.[89] But this a was small part of his income, and, if Philip the Fair had lived, Marigny could have expected to gain much more in gifts from the king. There was no reason for Marigny to have made the agreement at Marquette unless he believed that it was the best solution to an annoying problem.

[87] Funck-Brentano, *Philippe le Bel en Flandre*, pp. 660-62 (he published the basic documents in *Bibliothèque de l'Ecole des Chartes*, LVII [1896], pp. 560-64); Favier, *Marigny*, p. 180.

[88] Favier, *Marigny*, pp. 180-81. Louis of Evreux supported Marigny, but, as usual, his opinion carried little weight.

[89] Ibid., pp. 180-82; Funck-Brentano, *Philippe le Bel en Flandre*, p. 663.

Nevertheless, the conventions of Marquette were one of the principal reasons for Marigny's downfall and execution after the death of Philip the Fair. Valois had probably been jealous of Marigny for some time, and the fact that his advice was ignored in 1314 would have strengthened his dislike. The leagues of 1314 were inspired largely by resistance to the subsidy imposed that year; they would have had a weaker case if the tax had made possible an imposing victory over the Flemings. A scapegoat was needed, and Marigny's unquestioned influence in formulating policy toward Flanders made him the logical choice.

The settlement of Marquette can be criticized, not because it was treasonous, but because it did not achieve all its objectives. It did not end the need for military pressure; by 1315 Louis X was again assembling an army against Flanders, and Philip V and Charles IV had to do the same in 1319 and 1325. It did not secure the permanent acquiescence of the Flemish counts to the "transport of Flanders"; they continued to nurse their grievance until they could use it as an excuse to join England in the Hundred Years' War. The most that can be said was that the settlement prolonged the precarious peace arranged in 1305 to the end of Philip's reign. Considering the cost, in men and money, of the Flemish wars, even one year more of peace was worth having.

THE EMPIRE*

Philip was not greatly concerned with the Empire as such; he knew well enough that it was a loose confederation of practically independent principalities that could never act as a unit. The King of the Romans (Henry VII was the only emperor-elect in this period who actually received the imperial crown) had very little power; he could, at most, organize temporary coalitions of princes that seldom held together long enough to accomplish anything. A hostile king, like Adolf of Nassau (1292-1298), could be a nuisance to Philip, since it required a certain amount of diplomatic activity and fairly generous grants of money-fiefs to make sure that Adolf's plans to aid Guy of Flanders would come to nothing.[90] A friendly king, as Albert of Habsburg (1298-1308)

---

* Here I should give special thanks to Professor John Benton of the California Institute of Technology, who, some years ago, prepared a remarkable research paper for me on Philip the Fair and the Empire. His thorough investigation of this very complicated problem has been of great assistance.

[90] See above, note 15; Kern, *Anfänge*, pp. 61-70; Lyon, *From Fief to Indenture*, pp. 213-14.

was in the early part of his reign, could be moderately helpful, for example, by recognizing that the French boundary ran to, and even in places beyond, the Meuse. But friendship was not much cheaper than enmity; money still had to be paid to German princes and members of Albert's court.[91] Even when Albert became hostile and joined Boniface VIII in the quarrel with Philip, his opposition did little harm. The papal bull releasing all inhabitants of the former kingdom of Arles (technically part of the Empire) from any obligations that they had taken to the king of France had no effect of any kind.[92] Albert's hostility did nothing to prevent the defeat of the count of Flanders. The King of the Romans had little influence on French policy. The most he could do was to force Philip to spend money on grants to princes of the Empire and on diplomatic missions.

Perhaps for this reason, Philip did not exert himself greatly whenever a new King of the Romans was to be elected. He did nothing after the death of Rudolf of Habsburg.[93] He could hardly oppose the election of Albert of Habsburg in 1298; Albert had disposed of Adolf of Nassau, who had led an anti-French coalition. Philip did make some effort to obtain the German crown for his brother Charles when Albert died in 1308, but he worked largely through underfinanced diplomatic missions. It would have taken large sums of money to secure Charles's election, and Philip gave very little.[94] He may have hoped that Clement V would

[91] These boundary agreements were made in 1299 and ratified at the interview of Quatre Vaux; see Kern, *Anfänge*, pp. 201-11. For gifts to influential Germans see *J.T.P.*, nos. 3305-6 (6,000 l.t. to the bishop of Constance and his brother, envoys of Albert, and 1,500 l.t. to lesser officials), and nos. 4205-6 (1,000 l.t. to the bishop and 300 l.t. to King Albert's secretary). See Kern, ed., *Acta Imperii*, no. 279, for a list of prominent German princes who were to receive gifts, including the dukes of Bavaria and Carinthia, and the archbishop of Mainz.

[92] Boutaric published this bull in "Documents inédits," p. 147.

[93] Perhaps he knew that he had no chance. Fournier, pp. 285-86, thought that the electors believed that Rudolf of Habsburg had been too conciliatory and were determined to choose an anti-French candidate. Digard, I, 134, agrees.

[94] Philip advanced 10,500 l.t. to Charles, but this was barely enough to cover travel expenses of his envoys (Boutaric, "Documents inédits," p. 190). According to E. E. Stengel, *Avignon und Rhens* (Weimar, 1930), p. 5, Boutaric misread the figure, which should have been 1,500 l.t., but Philip added enough later to bring the total to 10,300 l.t. Kern, *Anfänge*, p. 302, was sure that Philip promised large sums to the electors and other influential Germans; if he did, there is no record that payments were ever made.

put pressure on the electors, but although Clement officially favored Charles, his support was lukewarm, to say the least. He wrote rather vague letters to the electors and sent a personal representative to the archbishop of Cologne, but he did nothing more to help Charles.[95] Perhaps, as Petit thought, he was secretly working for Henry of Luxemburg.[96] Certainly he had no reason to exert himself for Philip at a time when he was being browbeaten over the affair of the Templars. In any case, Henry was elected without much difficulty. Philip complained a little about Clement's speedy confirmation of the election,[97] but it was his pride that was hurt, not his policies. He and Henry were on friendly terms during the first year of Henry's reign, and, even when relations cooled, it was clear that the Luxemburger was no threat to France. Henry was thoroughly French in language and in culture; he had accepted a money-fief from Philip in 1294,[98] and as emperor he was much more concerned with Italy than with the western borderlands of the Empire. This may have disappointed some of his electors, if, as most German scholars agree, Henry had been chosen because they thought he would stop French advances into the old Middle Kingdom. Henry did show some annoyance over the French occupation of Lyon, and he annoyed Philip in turn by talking of reviving the old kingdom of Arles, but it was soon clear that he could do little to hurt or to help France. The obvious weakness of the emperor may explain why, in 1313, Philip merely went through the motions of proposing a French candidate to succeed Henry. The matter was discussed in the Council, and Philip then sent a message to the pope nominating his son, Philip of Poitiers.[99] Nothing more was done, and it is doubtful that Philip the Fair expected any result from his suggestion.

[95] Petit, *Charles de Valois*, pp. 117-19. Lizerand, *Clément V*, pp. 173-79, Kern, *Anfänge*, pp. 302-9, and Stengel, *Avignon*, pp. 33-34, agree that Clement merely went through the motions of supporting Charles and that he really was opposed to the candidacy. Karl Wenck, "Französische Werbungen um die deutsche Königskrone," *Historische Zeitschrift*, LXXXVI (1901), 256, thinks that Clement did nothing for Charles.

[96] Petit, *Charles de Valois*, p. 118.

[97] Lizerand, *Clément V*, pp. 183-84; Karl Wenck, *Clemens V und Heinrich VII* (Halle, 1882), pp. 136-37, 178. Clement in 1310 was still arguing to Philip's envoys that he had not acted hastily. See also Jakob Schwalm, "Reise nach Frankreich," *Neues Archiv*, XXIX (1904), 609, 619, 622.

[98] Kern, ed., *Acta Imperii*, nos. 90, 91.

[99] Schwalm, "Reichsgeschichte," pp. 565-66. Cf. Wenck, "Französische Werbungen," pp. 258-63.

The German and Italian parts of the Empire were of no great interest to Philip, but the French or partly French-speaking areas of the old Middle Kingdom were. In the north, he wanted to be sure that the neighbors of the count of Flanders would not assist him in time of war. He granted money-fiefs to most of the princes in the region,[100] and he was especially concerned with keeping the count of Hainaut and the duke of Brabant on his side. This was not an entirely easy operation. Although both rulers had their own quarrels with Flanders, both also had ties with England, and the count of Hainaut was annoyed by Philip's claim to suzerainty over the Ostrevant, the part of the county lying west of the Scheldt. He finally admitted that he owed homage for the Ostrevant, but to keep him happy, Philip had to give up most of his claims to intervene directly in the affairs of the district, notably to control the town of Valenciennes.[101] This concession, plus substantial subsidies,[102] made the count of Hainaut a faithful and helpful ally. As for the duke of Brabant, he was at first allied with England, but switched sides when he saw that Philip was winning. His neutrality was assured in 1304, when Philip gave him a life-rent of 2,500 l.t.,[103] and without him there could be no anti-French coalition to help the count of Flanders. In short, in the Low Countries Philip's opportunities were limited by the Flemish wars. To isolate Flanders, he had to avoid antagonizing other lords. In the end, he gained Lille and Douai and the nominal suzerainty of the Ostrevant, but nothing more.

Further south, the situation was less complicated. There was less danger that the barons of the badly fragmented duchy of Lorraine would come to the aid of the Flemings. The only one who did so was the count of Bar; he was easily defeated and

[100] See above, note 15.

[101] On the Ostrevant see E. Delcambre, "Recueil de documents inédits relatifs aux relations du Hainaut et de la France de 1280 à 1297," Académie Royale de Belgique, *Bulletin de la Commission Royale d'Histoire*, XCII (1928), 1-163, esp. nos. 5, 9, 30. See also his excellent monograph, *Les relations de la France avec le Hainaut* (Mons, 1930), pp. 66-91, 117-28.

[102] Philip paid all the expenses of troops sent by Hainaut for the campaign of 1297 and promised the count 6,000 l.t. annual rent (4,000 l.t. to come from conquered lands in Flanders) (Delcambre, *Relations*, pp. 195-98, 204). The count (or his assignees) were paid the 2,000 l.t. a year regularly (*J.T.P.*, nos. 150, 1788, 2526, 3456, 5087, 5630). The count's brother Guy, archdeacon of Liège and eventually bishop of Utrecht, had a pension of 500 l.t. (ibid., no. 590).

[103] See Kern, ed., *Acta Imperii*, no. 152, for the rent, and *Anfänge*, pp. 179-80, for the circumstances.

forced to accept French suzerainty of his lands west of the
Meuse.[104] The duke of Lorraine caused no problems; he had already accepted a money-fief of 300 l.t. from Philip III, and
Philip the Fair added 200 l.t. a year to this pension.[105] The bishoprics of Toul, Metz, and Verdun were not strong states and at
times sought French protection. Toul was the most deeply involved, first, because some of its lands lay west of the Meuse and
could be considered part of the French kingdom, and, second,
because the citizens were eager for Philip to guard the city and
not just the western lands of the bishopric. In 1300 they promised
to pay 2 s.t. per hearth for royal guard and swore that this guard
should be perpetual.[106] There was a personal tie between Philip
and Bishop Burchard of Metz (of the family of the counts of
Hainaut); Burchard received a money-fief of 2,000 l.t. in 1296
but died soon thereafter. Probably some such arrangement continued under Burchard's successor, Gerard de Relanges; we know
that Philip worked for his promotion, and in 1297 the king addressed him as "dilectus et fidelis," which suggests that he held
a money-fief.[107] As for Verdun, Philip in 1305 made a treaty of
mutual defense with the bishop, but Kern is probably right in
thinking that the treaty was abrogated at the end of the year,
when a new bishop took office.[108]

South of Lorraine, Philip had more definite objectives. He had
no interest in the lands of the count of Savoy or the dauphin of
Viennois, though he was concerned about Savoyard attempts to
gain influence in Lyon. The county of Provence was held by his
kinsmen, the kings of Naples, and Philip scrupulously observed
the Rhône boundary in this area. But Philip did want full control
of the west bank of the Rhône and of both banks of the Saône.
He therefore concentrated his efforts on the Vivarais (west of the

---

[104] See above, p. 320.

[105] Kern, ed., *Acta Imperii*, no. 303 (in the year 1287).

[106] Ibid., nos. 62 (1289), 73, 74, 75 (1291), 313 (1300).

[107] Ibid., no. 155. Bishop Guillaume of Amiens was sent to Cambrai, long
before February 1299, "pro electione magistri Girardi de Relenges" (*J.T.P.*,
no. 318). This could refer to the see of Cambrai, also vacant in 1296, but
Gerard was archdeacon of Cambrai, and it would have been logical to visit
him there to discuss the situation at Metz. In any case, Philip wanted
Gerard to become a bishop. See B.N., ms. lat. 10021, fol. 209, for the
king's letter.

[108] Kern, ed., *Acta Imperii*, no. 155 (February 6, 1305). But by December
the new bishop was to swear allegiance to Albert of Habsburg without
mentioning Philip (ibid., no. 161). Kern, *Anfänge*, p. 290, is probably right
in saying that the treaty was not renewed until the time of Louis X.

Rhône) and on the city of Lyon and the Free County of Burgundy.

This is the one area in which one might argue that Philip was clearly trying to enlarge his kingdom. Elsewhere he was, by his lights, simply asserting his authority over rebellious vassals (such as the count of Flanders) or clearing up confused border situations (such as the Ostrevant). He was doubtless flattered when towns or churches of the Empire sought his protection, but he did not take undue advantage of these opportunities; Metz, Toul, and Verdun were not annexed to France until centuries later. On the other hand, Philip did spend most of his reign in making sure that his authority was recognized in the Rhône-Saône area.

Even in this area, however, there were differences in his policies. The Vivarais, west of the Rhône, was, by his rules, clearly in the kingdom. Once this was acknowledged in 1307, he was willing to give the bishop a good deal of autonomy. The county of Burgundy was just as clearly outside the kingdom. Philip had wanted it for his eldest son, in which case it might have become part of the royal domain, but in the end he arranged for it to go to his second son and admitted that it was a fief of the Empire. Lyon was a more complicated problem; it took careful, long-range planning to bring it into the kingdom. Much of the preliminary work had been done by Philip III, but it was Philip the Fair who made it, irrevocably, a part of France.

Philip did have a stronger desire than any of his predecessors to establish fixed and definite boundaries with the Empire, and perhaps a clearer idea of what a boundary was. If he was to be supreme and final judge of all people who were "in regno et de regno" then it was important to know what the *regnum* was. (The same desire for precise limits can be seen within the realm as well. How could an administrator work efficiently if he did not know the boundary between his district and that of a colleague? Hence there were inquiries like the one of 1302, which drew the line between the *sénéchaussées* of Carcassonne and Beaucaire.)[109] During the reign there was a deliberate attempt to work out a theory of the proper boundaries of France. It was a theory based on geography, history, and law, and it was a direct precursor of the expansionist policy of Louis XIV. One example

---

[109] *C.R.*, I, no. 13906 (accounts of 1302-1303). This was a very formal affair; Beaucaire was represented by its seneschal, its *juge-mage*, two other judges, and the royal advocate. See *H.L.*, IX, 264 (settlement of boundaries of Beaucaire and Auvergne in 1306).

has already been mentioned: the arguments of the French negotiators of 1308 on the question of the Val d'Aran.[110] The Val is French geographically because the Pyrenees form the boundary between France and the Spanish kingdoms, and the Val is clearly on the French side; it contains the headwaters of the Garonne. It is French historically because it was conquered by Charles Martel and given by later kings to the bishop of Comminges, whose diocese was certainly in France. The Val was also held by the count of Comminges as a fief of the duchy of Narbonne and the county of Toulouse, which were notoriously French. Even if in the marriage treaty of Philip III and Isabelle of Aragon it was agreed that the king of Aragon should hold the Val, this was not binding. The king of France, who has "ius imperii" in his realm, cannot diminish the realm any more than a pope can give up a diocese or the emperor a county. No prescription can run against the king "cum limites provinciarum et regnorum . . . prescribi non possint."

In his dealings with the Empire, Philip tended to stress the geographical argument. The French argued—and some of the princes of the Empire agreed—that the eastern boundary of France was formed by four rivers: the Rhône, the Saône, the Meuse, and the Scheldt.[111] There were gaps in this argument, first, the actual physical gaps between the rivers, and, second, the obvious fact that in some places—the Vivarais, for example— lands that had long been recognized as imperial were on the west side of a boundary river. Nevertheless, the four-river line seemed logical (it was hard to find any other simple description of the boundary) and roughly in accord with the facts. Philip used the formula successfully throughout his reign. The Ostrevant was in his realm because it was on the west bank of the Scheldt, and the count of Hainaut finally accepted the argument.[112] There is no authentic record of the conference between Philip and Albert of Austria at Quatre Vaux in December 1299, but it seems likely that Albert accepted the Meuse as a boundary at that time.[113] This, at least, had been the solution adopted to put an official end to Philip's war with the count of Bar; the part of the county west of the Meuse was to be held as a fief of the king.[114]

[110] See above, Chapter I, note 72.

[111] Kern, *Anfänge*, pp. 15-18, 320-22.   [112] See above, p. 349.

[113] See above, p. 324, and Kern, "Die Abtreten des linken Maasufers an Frankreich durch Albrecht I," *Mitteilungen des Instituts für Osterreichische Geschichtsforschung*, xxxi (1910), 558-81.

[114] See above, note 17.

It was also clearly accepted in the case of Toul. Philip's influence on the bishop and city might wax or wane, but there was no doubt that the lands of the bishopric west of the Meuse were in the kingdom of France.[115]

This was well and good, but there were still some awkward questions. What about towns like Tournai and Valenciennes, or the strategically important lordship of Mortagne, which straddled a boundary river?[116] What about Cambrai, east of the Scheldt but west of a tributary of the Meuse? Cambrai was certainly an imperial city, but Philip gained a good deal of influence there, especially while he held Flanders.[117] What, above all, could justify Philip's approaches to Metz and the eastern parts of Toul, which were on the Moselle, not the Meuse?

Nevertheless, the river boundaries worked well enough in the north to satisfy the king. They were not so helpful in the south. They could be used as a justification for forcing the bishop of Viviers into a *paréage*; the Vivarais, although it had long been considered part of the Empire, lay on the west bank of the Rhône. Philip III had found it easy to harass the bishop, who had little support from the nobles of the district and none from the kings or princes of the Empire. Philip the Fair continued to put pressure on the bishop and finally forced him to acknowledge that the Vivarais was part of the kingdom of France. This was all that the king wanted; the bishop was left with extensive rights of government in his district.[118]

---

[115] Kern, ed., *Acta Imperii*, nos. 62, 68.

[116] For Philip's interventions in Tournai and Valenciennes see Delcambre, *Relations*, pp. 54-58, 63-80, 87-91. For Mortagne, acquired by Philip in 1314, see A.N., J 529, nos. 50-53, and A. d'Herbomez, "L'annexation de la Mortagne à la France," *Revue des questions historiques*, LIII (1893), 27-55.

[117] For Cambrai see H. Dubrulle, *Cambrai à la fin du moyen âge* (Lille, 1903), pp. 253-54, 256-59. In collecting tenths and annates, Philip recognized that only part of the diocese lay in the kingdom (Mignon, nos. 540, 680, 727), except in 1304, when he was theoretically ruling all of Flanders. Two supporters of Philip held the see of Cambrai in succession, Philippe de Marigny (1306-1309) and Pierre de Lévis-Mirepoix (1309-1323). Philippe never did homage to Henry VII, and Pierre delayed his (*M.G.H., Constitutiones et acta publica imperatorum*, IV, pt. 1, nos. 267-69, 337, 340). Henry was displeased enough with these delays to name, in 1309, the count of Namur to govern the county of Cambrai (ibid., nos. 290-92) and only withdrew this commission on 10 March 1310 (no. 339). Certainly he wanted to remind the bishop where his primary allegiance lay.

[118] See J. Regné, *Histoire du Vivarais*, 2 vols. (Largentière, 1914-1921), II, 103-11. The basic documents are in *Gallia Christiana*, XVI, *Instrumenta*, cols. 267-68, 277-82 (the final agreement of 1306), and *Ord.*, VII, 7.

Although the river-boundary doctrine worked to Philip's advantage in the case of the Vivarais, it worked against two much more important projects—the acquisition of the county of Burgundy and the annexation of Lyon. All of the county, and much of Lyon, lay on the eastern side of the Saône; new arguments had to be found to justify bringing these areas under French control.

It was easier to solve the problem of the county of Burgundy, since it was not necessary to argue that it was part of the kingdom. Philip wanted to acquire the county for one of his sons, not to add it to the royal domain. Thus he could admit that it was a fief of the Empire, and although he would have preferred that homage be waived, he did not insist on this concession. In the treaty of Evreux, 1294, in which the count and countess of Burgundy agreed to make their daughter heiress of the county and to marry her to one of the king's sons, it was also agreed that the count or countess would try to secure a waiver of homage but that this was not a necessary condition for the marriage.[119] A French prince, and especially a second son, could hold a fief from the Empire without impairing the royal dignity, while the king could not.

The count of Burgundy, who had no great interest in politics and who may have been heavily indebted, was willing by 1295 to turn over the county to the king without waiting for the marriage, in return for 100,000 l.t. and a life-rent of 10,000 l.t.[120] King Adolf, who earlier had had difficulties with the count, was not pleased and pronounced the forfeiture of the county,[121] but he was busy organizing an anti-French coalition in the north and did little to stop the French takeover. The only real resistance to the transfer of Burgundy to French control came from a league of local nobles headed by the count's uncle, Jean de Chalon-Arlay. They hoped for support from Adolf of Nassau and from Edward I, but, as in the north, Adolf and Edward promised more than they could give, and the league collapsed in 1301.[122]

A less violent, but more effective, protest was made by Robert,

[119] Kern, ed., *Acta Imperii*, nos. 70-71.

[120] Ibid., nos. 95, 109; Funck-Brentano, "Noblesse," pp. 16-17. See, however, J. P. Redoutey, "Le comté de Bourgogne de 1295 à 1314," *Mémoires de la Société pour l'histoire de droit et des institutions des anciens pays bourguignons* . . . , fasc. 33 (1975-1978), pp. 7-35, esp. pp. 3, 14, who argues that the count's debts were not excessive. See his article, "Philippe le Bel et la Franche-Comté," *Cahiers de l'association interuniversitaire de l'Est*, no. 19 (1979).

[121] *M.G.H., Constitutiones*, III, no. 557 (June 1296).

[122] Funck-Brentano, "Noblesse," pp. 19-20, 27-34.

duke of Burgundy. He and his father had acquired a considerable number of fiefs in the county; they had hoped to take over the whole principality through marriage treaties. Now this hope was blocked, and, if Philip's son became king after marrying the heiress, the ducal fiefs would lose their value because the king could not do homage. It seems probable that Robert insisted that Jeanne of (the county of) Burgundy marry Philip (of Poitiers) rather than the king's eldest son, Louis of Navarre. Robert's wishes could not lightly be ignored; he was a Capetian, the only great baron who had always been loyal to the king, and an accomplished diplomat. His advice about the marriage was heeded, and he was guaranteed possession of his fiefs in the county.[123] Later he obtained a further guarantee by marrying his daughter Marguerite to Louis of Navarre. The marriage turned out badly, but that could scarcely have been anticipated. Robert had done all that he could to ensure that the county would not become part of the royal domain. He could not have foreseen that, because Philip of Poitiers had only a female heir, the county would eventually be united by marriage with the duchy, but at least he left this possibility open. It was a good job for the house of Burgundy, but not so good for the people of France; it took a series of bloody wars in the sixteenth and seventeenth centuries to bring the county back under the control of the king of France.

Meanwhile, Robert was quite ready to assist Philip in taking over and administering the county. There were no serious troubles after the local nobles made their peace with Philip; the royal receivers rendered their accounts regularly from 1300 on, while in 1296, 1297, and 1298 Duke Robert had had to take responsibility for collecting the revenues.[124] The only remaining problems were the dower rights of Countess Mahaut of Artois, widow of the former count, and the homage that the younger Philip was bound to render to Henry VII. The first problem was solved by a division of lands in the county between Mahaut and the king (1309), followed by Mahaut's renunciation of this grant in 1311.[125] The homage owed by Philip of Poitiers was repeatedly postponed.[126] I have found no evidence that it was actually given,

[123] Richard, pp. 224-26; Kern, Anfänge, pp. 223-26.

[124] Mignon, no. 110; B.M. Dijon, ms. 1105. I must thank M. Redoutey for this last reference; he very kindly sent me photostats of the accounting between the duke and the king.

[125] Kern, ed., Acta Imperii, nos. 174, 183, 222.

[126] M.G.H., Constitutiones, IV, pt. 1, nos. 281 (1309), 588 (1311), 616 (1311).

but both king and emperor agreed that it should be given at an approved time.

The acquisition of the county of Burgundy was a family affair, and Philip the Fair made no great effort to incorporate the county into the kingdom. It was listed in Mignon's inventory as a "terra foranea."[127] Lyon was another matter. Philip (like his father) felt that it was absolutely essential that Lyon become an integral part of the realm and of the domain. As soon as it was certain that all opposition had been overcome, Lyon was made the center of a *sénéchaussée*, with exactly the same status as Beaucaire or Carcassonne, and it never left the royal domain. The annexation of Lyon shows Philip's government at its best and worst—on the one hand, patient, persevering, skillful in exploiting every opportunity, keeping the use of force to a minimum, and, on the other, unscrupulous in its arguments and untrustworthy in its promises.

Like many other ecclesiastical principalities, Lyon was so torn by internal dissension that it practically invited intervention by a powerful neighbor.[128] The archbishop and chapter were at odds with each other over possession of rights of justice. The citizens wanted to have some protection against their ecclesiastical superiors. Neighboring lords, especially the count of Savoy, were eager to gain a foothold in the city by intervening in these quarrels.[129] But the strongest neighbor of Lyon was the king of France, and it was to the king that the weaker faction in Lyon (usually the citizens) was apt to turn for help. From the last year of the reign of St. Louis (1269) all through the reign of Philip III, royal officials, especially the *bailli* of Mâcon, had intervened frequently in the affairs of the city.[130] In May 1292 Philip took Lyon under his special protection, and the chapter excommunicated the citizens. The citizens appealed to the pope and to the king, asserting that they and the city "sunt de resorto domini

---

[127] Mignon, no. 109.

[128] Bonnassieux, *De la réunion de la Lyon à la France*, is a good summary of Philip's policies in Lyon; see Chapter I above for a discussion of the internal problems of the church of Lyon. A more recent, but briefer, survey appears in A. Kleinclausz, *Histoire de Lyon* (Lyon, 1939), I, 173 ff. Many of the basic documents were published by Father Ménestrier, *Histoire de la ville de Lyon* (Lyon, 1696).

[129] The count of Savoy promised on 7 May 1286 to protect the citizens of Lyon for three years, and in 1291 he was trying to build a party in the city that would support him (Kern, ed., *Acta Imperii*, nos. 55, 67).

[130] Bonnassieux, pp. 55-64.

regis Francie."[131] It was probably at this time, and certainly by June 1293, that Philip established a *gardiator* in Lyon, a permanent royal official charged with preserving the king's rights in and protecting the citizens of Lyon. His jurisdiction was limited to cases of treason, homicide, and robbery, and he was ordered not to hear appeals without a special commission, but he was clearly the final authority in the city in all secular affairs. The citizens were also allowed to tax themselves in order to repair their fortifications, and in 1297 the *bailli* of Mâcon was ordered to give them military assistance if necessary. In short, from 1292 to 1302 Philip was in effect ruling Lyon through his warden and with the support of the citizens.[132]

It was during this period that treatises justifying the king's claims were written. The first was produced by Thomas de Pouilly, royal procurator in the *bailliage* of Mâcon, at some date before 1296, and very likely soon after the protest of the chapter and clergy of Lyon (the archbishop was absent) against the acts of the royal warden (1 April 1294).[133] His arguments were repeated in official memoranda written a little later and were also used in the king's justification of the treaty of 1307, which gave him effective control of the city.[134]

Historically, the French case rested on events since 1269, when Louis IX had intervened to protect the citizens. There was no difficulty in proving that after 1269 there had been almost constant intervention by royal officials in the affairs of the city and that they had judged citizens of Lyon. But these cases could be considered pure usurpation, and they certainly did not go back far enough to constitute prescription (if, indeed, such rights could be prescribed). There was some vague talk of early docu-

---

[131] Ibid., pp. 69-70; Ménestrier, *preuves*, pp. 99, xli-xlii.

[132] Ménestrier, *preuves*, pp. 89, 90, 100, 102; Bonnassieux, pp. 69-78.

[133] Kern, ed., *Acta Imperii*, no. 84; cf. no. 265. Boniface VIII tried to end the controversy on 18 August 1297 by appointing Pierre de Mornay and Robert of Burgundy to guard the city, but this had no effect (ibid., no. 121). In fact, though Boniface may have hoped to appease Philip by naming two of his most trusted councillors, the king's reply seems to have been the order to the *bailli* of Mâcon, on 12 November 1297, to protect the citizens by force of arms (Bonnassieux, p. 76).

[134] Kern, ed., *Acta Imperii*, nos. 270 (Kern dates this as before 4 February 1296), 271 (probably 1296 or 1297), 274 (before August 1297), and 285 (1307). Some of the arguments were also repeated in a memorandum attacking the memory of Boniface VIII, sent to Clement V by Nogaret and Plaisians soon after the war of 1310 (Dupuy, *preuves*, pp. 319-21).

ments and saints' lives that proved that Lyon was the first see of
Gaul, that the kings of the Franks had founded and endowed the
church and named the first archbishops.[135] (The identification of
Gaul with France was always helpful in dealing with problems on
the eastern borders of the realm.) Another legendary story had
a king of France driving back a Vandal army from a threatened
attack on Lyon at the request of the citizens.[136] There was also a
confused reference to the treaty of Verdun,[137] though this was
not entirely helpful, because the writer believed that the treaty
established the four-river boundary and thus had trouble proving
French jurisdiction beyond the Saône. Finally, there were nega-
tive arguments: kingdoms (including France) existed before the
Empire; the emperor had never had control of Lyon; the Church
had never considered Lyon an imperial see. [138]

The geographical arguments were more factual, but just for
this reason they were also somewhat embarrassing. It could not
be denied that, as a rule, the Saône and the Rhône formed the
boundary between France and the Empire and that most of the
citizens of Lyon lived on the east bank of the Saône. On the other
hand, the cathedral, the residences of the archbishop and chapter,
and the courts held by these dignitaries were all on the west bank.
This area, then, was the "head" of the archbishopric, and the
members should follow the head. Moreover, the greater part of
the church's temporalities, the Lyonnais, not only lay in the west
bank, but also had been given to the church of Lyon by the count
of Forez, who held fiefs of the king of France.[139] All this was true

---

[135] Kern, ed., *Acta Imperii*, pp. 199, 201, 226, 227-28; Dupuy, p. 319.

[136] Ibid., p. 204: "Wandali venerunt Lugdunam, volentes ipsam civitatem
destruere. . . . Cives Lugdunenses significaverunt hoc domino regi tanquam
superiori, mandantes ei quod suam civitatem et suos cives veniret deffen-
surus. Quod et facit et Wandalos in bello devicit. . . ." Cf. Dupuy, p. 319.

[137] Kern, ed., *Acta Imperii*, p. 205: "olim quidam rex Francie habuit duos
filios, quorum unus fuit rex Francie et alter imperator, et quod magna
briga fuit intereos orta super finibus regni et imperii. . . ." They finally
agreed "quod quatuor flumina, Scalcus, Moza, Rodanus et Sagona essent
pro finibus de cetero regni et imperii," but if there were towns or fiefs
"quorum capud esset in regno et haberent aliqua accessoria in imperio, quod
totum esset de regno, et e converso. . . ."

[138] Ibid., p. 200: "nam regnum Francie et alia regna mundi ante fuerunt
quam fuerit imperium." See ibid., pp. 199, 203: no other prince has jurisdiction in Lyon; the Roman curia lists Lyon as a French see. Cf. ibid., p.
228, and Dupuy, p. 320.

[139] Kern, ed., *Acta Imperii*, pp. 200, 202, 204-5. For further discussion of
the Forez grant see below, p. 360.

enough, but it proved a little too much. Both the count of Hainaut and the count of Bar could have demonstrated that the "heads" of their principalities lay east of the Scheldt and the Meuse; therefore the Ostrevant and western Bar should have had the same status as the admittedly imperial parts of their lands. Perhaps because of this weakness in the argument the king's advisers had to modify the river-boundary theory, first, by admitting that both France and the Empire could possess enclaves ("feuda inclavata," "locus inclavatus") in regions that were on the wrong side of a river,[140] and, second, by denying (in 1307) that the rivers were definite and unchangeable boundaries. Boundaries, they said, are not always determined by rivers such as the Saône, but by the origin of the people of the country and by the fact that certain lands were subject to a kingdom from its beginning.[141] This sweeping assertion could also have been used to justify moves across the lower Rhône as well as the Saône, but it was simply a rhetorical flourish that justified a fait accompli; it had no consequences in Philip's reign.

The legal argument was perhaps the strongest. Lyon may have been in the Empire, but it was not subject to the Empire. It was a church state; one could almost say that it was a state of the Church. When Innocent IV wanted to depose Frederick II, he had taken refuge in Lyon and it was there that the council met that condemned the emperor. It would have been difficult, if not impossible, to find any act that asserted imperial authority in the city after the reign of Frederick Barbarossa, who gave all his rights in Lyon to the archbishop.[142] On the other hand, as a result of a curious arrangement between the churches of Autun and Lyon, the archbishop did take an oath of fidelity to the French king. To avoid any lay claim to regalia, it had long been agreed that the bishop of Autun would administer the regalia of Lyon when the see was vacant and that the archbishop would administer the regalia of Autun during a vacancy there.[143] Autun was certainly in the kingdom of France (so, for that matter, were

---

[140] Ibid., p. 205.

[141] Ibid., p. 229: "Flumen enim Sagone vel aliud non sunt usquequaque termini finium regni nostri, nec enim fines regnorum semper per talia fluvia distinguuntur, sed per nationes patrie atque terras prout cuilibet regno ab initio fuerint subiecte."

[142] Ménestrier, *preuves*, pp. 33-35; Bonnassieux, pp. 13-15.

[143] Kern, ed., *Acta Imperii*, pp. 202, 204, 226. For the beginnings of this system see Kern, *Anfänge*, p. 96; it went back at least to 1140.

all the other dioceses of the province of Lyon—Mâcon, Chalons-sur-Saône, and Langres), and the bishop of Autun owed fidelity to the king. Therefore, when the archbishop administered the regalia of Autun, he owed, and took, the oath of fidelity. He rendered this oath to no other ruler; if he had a superior, it must be the king of France. This was fairly plausible, but many princes of the Empire, especially the counts of Bar and Hainaut, took the oath of homage to the king without subjecting their lands in the Empire to royal authority. They did, of course, have another lord, the emperor, and the archbishop did not—a fact that weakened him politically but that should have had no legal consequences.

Another, less plausible argument drawn from the exchange of regalia was that when the bishop of Autun administered the temporalities of Lyon, Lyon became part of the kingdom because the bishop was a subject of the king. If it was at such times a part of the kingdom, how could it cease to be in the kingdom when a new archbishop was chosen?[144] The fallacy is obvious; when Charles of Valois became vicar of the pope in the Papal States, did the Papal States then become part of the kingdom of France? The argument was a debater's point and was not pushed very hard; it does not appear in the statement of 1307.

A weaker legal argument went back to the twelfth-century war between the archbishop of Lyon and the count of Forez. When peace was finally made in 1167 (and confirmed in 1173), the count ceded lands on the Rhône and Saône and whatever rights he had in Lyon to the archbishop and received in return lands held by the archbishop beyond the Loire.[145] Now there was no doubt that the count was a vassal of the king of France,[146] though whether for these lands is another matter. Still, it could be argued that, since a good part of the Lyonnais had once been held by a French vassal, these lands did not cease to be part of the kingdom when ceded to the archbishop; no treaty by a subject could impair the right of the king.[147] On the other hand, a vassal could easily have holdings in both the kingdom and the

[144] Kern, ed., *Acta Imperii*, p. 202.

[145] Bonnassieux, p. 21; Ménestrier, *preuves*, pp. 36-38.

[146] G. Duby, *La société aux XIe et XIIe siècles dans la région mâconnaise* (Paris, 1953), pp. 538, 541; A. Luchaire, *Études sur les actes de Louis VII* (Paris, 1885), no. 537. The count did homage to Louis in 1167 for his castles in Forez.

[147] Kern, ed., *Acta Imperii*, pp. 202-3, 226; Dupuy, *preuves*, p. 320.

Empire, and whatever the count possessed in and near Lyon would certainly have been in the Empire in the twelfth century. Perhaps for this reason royal propagandists (with the exception of Nogaret) did not put very much stress on the significance of the cession by the count of Forez.

It was necessary to give a color of right to the French annexation of Lyon, but the city was acquired not through scoring legal points but by careful political manipulation. Philip was playing the same game in Lyon that he was in Flanders—trying to profit from the dissension between townsmen and their rulers—but he played it more successfully in Lyon. He was aided by the fact that the archbishop and the chapter did not work well together and also by the lack of support by the nobles of the Lyonnais for the archbishop. Up to 1302 Philip had been protecting the citizens and curbing the power of the archbishop. For example, when the archbishop and chapter imposed an interdict on the city, Philip threatened to seize the church's temporalities.[148] The defeat at Courtrai forced Philip to change his position. He needed money desperately, and the clergy of Lyon joined in the grant of a double tenth made by the other French provinces in 1304.[149] They apparently turned in their contribution very rapidly and, as a result, received not only the general privilege given to all cathedral churches[150] but also mandates from the king ordering his officers not to interfere with ecclesiastical jurisdiction in the city and not to hold assizes in a town held by the archbishop and chapter.[151] This paved the way to a reconciliation between the king and the clergy, a reconciliation that was, to some extent, achieved at the expense of the citizens. The interdict was lifted on 30 December 1304, but the people of Lyon were a little suspicious of this sudden change. Their spokesman, Mathieu de la Mure (who had the title of *pannetier le roi*), promised to honor the ancient rights of the archbishop "servando et retinendo semper in omnibus . . . jus et honorem domini regis Francorum."[152]

The suspicion of the citizens was justified. Negotiations for a treaty between the king and the archbishop and chapter began in 1306, but the final draft was not ready until September 1307. Pierre de Belleperche represented the king, Thibaud de Vassalieu, archdeacon of Lyon, the archbishop and chapter. Thibaud was

---

[148] Bonnassieux, pp. 69-70, 72.　　[149] Mignon, no. 787.
[150] Strayer and Taylor, pp. 38-39; *Ord.*, XII, 358.
[151] Bonnassieux, pp. 78-79.　　[152] Ibid., p. 80.

later to prove himself a loyal supporter of royal rights, but in these negotiations he seems to have saved as much as he could for the church. In effect, in return for recognizing the king's suzerainty and position as judge of last resort, the church gained full jurisdiction over the citizens. The position of royal warden was made official. His salary was to be paid by the citizens, but he could hear only cases touching the king's rights. First appeals went to the archbishop's judge. Only in the last instance could they be heard by the Parlement.[153] Subsidiary acts revoked all privileges gained by the citizens during the struggle with the archbishop and forbade them to hold public meetings or to form "conspiracies" (that is, to have a commune).[154] It is not surprising that there was difficulty in persuading the inhabitants of Lyon to accept the treaty.

The king had suspected that the agreement might not be entirely pleasing to the people of Lyon and the Lyonnais, and he refused to publish the documents until he had proof that the laity of the archdiocese had given their consent.[155] There was no trouble in securing the adhesion of the nobles and peasants of the country districts. A notary was sent from village to village in December 1307 to assemble the people, read the treaty, and ask for approval. There was no opposition; everyone, including the nobles, expressed their joy in the settlement of a dispute that had long troubled the countryside.[156]

The city of Lyon had a rather different reaction. At a meeting called on 20 January 1308 by Thibaud de Vassalieu and Pierre de Chalon (royal procurator in Mâcon) the citizens made a formal protest against the terms of the treaty and refused to accept it.[157] Philip the Fair tried to overcome the opposition by making a few concessions—notably by preventing the archbishop and chapter from having separate secular courts[158]—but complaints continued into 1309.[159] Meanwhile, a new archbishop, Pierre of

---

[153] Ibid., pp. 92-93.　　　　　　　[154] Ibid., p. 95.

[155] Ibid., pp. 96-97.

[156] Ibid., pp. 99-102. See especially p. 101: "Nec mirandum si gaudeant rationabiliter senes cum junioribus, vidue cum pupillis. . . . O quanti meriti sunt persone que compositioni prefate opem et operam prestitere fideles!" These lovely phrases were doubtless drafted by a royal clerk, but the rural population lost nothing by the treaty and gained greater security.

[157] Ibid., pp. 105-7.　　　　　　　[158] Ibid., pp. 107-8.

[159] Philip told the citizens that the treaty could always be revised and invited the citizens to send representatives to discuss their grievances (A.N., JJ 42A, fol. 81v, no. 45 [23 March 1309]).

Savoy, was becoming more and more hostile to the terms of the treaty of 1307, so that the king had annoyed his most loyal supporters, the citizens, without gaining the full cooperation of the church.

Pierre had confirmed the treaty of 1307 at the time of his election (20 August 1308), but he soon began to have second thoughts. He did not take the oath of fidelity, and Philip began to grow impatient after the ceremony had been delayed for over a year. When Pierre was in Paris in January 1310 he was besieged, verbally, by Nogaret. It must have been a trying experience. Nogaret had an answer to every objection, and he was ready to accept any formula as long as the archbishop took the oath.[160] Pierre refused to yield to pressure; he said he would do nothing until he returned home and took counsel with his friends. The counsel must have been bad; he raised an army, arranged alliances with his neighbors, and drove royal officials from the key castle of St. Just.

The "war of Lyon" that followed was a military promenade. Young Louis of Navarre was in nominal command of the French army, but it took no great skill to drive into the city of Lyon and to capture the archbishop in his castle of Pierre-Scise (22 July 1310).[161] Béraud de Mercoeur was named governor of the conquered province, but his garrison consisted of only one banneret, eight knights, and 18 squires (doubtless some foot soldiers accompanied each of these mounted men).[162] Philip could now arrange affairs in Lyon as he wished. Clement V was not very happy, but his feeble protests had little influence.[163] Henry VII was also annoyed, but, like the pope, he could take no effective action. He did refuse to put into effect a treaty of friendship with Philip,[164] and his relations with France cooled after 1310, but his sulking could not help the church of Lyon.

[160] Bonnassieux, pp. 113-15; Ménestrier, *preuves*, pp. 48-50. Note that Pierre de Chalon, royal procurator of Mâcon, and the archdeacon Thibaud de Vassalieu were present at these discussions.

[161] Bonnassieux, pp. 115-18. Mignon, nos. 2606-11, 2613-14, accounts for the war of Lyon. It was not a very expensive operation.

[162] A.N., JJ 42A, fol. 118v, no. 129. The cost per year was 10,822 l.t., unless reinforcements were required.

[163] Bonnassieux, pp. 129-30; Ménestrier, *preuves*, p. xiv. The pope's letter of protest was sent on 24 June 1310; it was answered, along with many other things, in a document drafted by Nogaret and Plaisians toward the end of the year (Dupuy, *preuves*, pp. 319-21).

[164] See *M.G.H.*, *Constitutiones*, IV, pt. 1, no. 353, for the draft of the

By April 1312 both the archbishop and the chapter were ready to do anything that would end the quarrel that had gone on for two generations. They ceded their jurisdiction in Lyon in return for lands and income elsewhere.[165] The citizens of Lyon gained some satisfaction by the revocation of the treaty of 1307, although their rights of self-government were still severely limited.[166] The final step in the takeover was to establish a new *sénéchaussée* of Lyon.[167] The heart of this administrative district was Lyon, but it also included Forez (from the *bailliage* of Mâcon) and Le Puy and Velay (from the *sénéchaussée* of Beaucaire). The autonomous ecclesiastical principality of Lyon had become another French province, like Toulouse or Carcassonne.

The exact terms of the settlement of 1312 did not long survive Philip the Fair. There was a very real reluctance in the Middle Ages to extinguish ancient rights, no matter what grievances had caused their temporary sequestration. Louis X returned high justice to the archbishop in 1315, and Philip V gave him all jurisdiction in the city in 1320 (although first appeals went to a royal judge).[168] These acts gave some profit and more prestige to the church of Lyon. They did not change the basic situation in the city. It was now part of France, never to be separated from the crown.[169]

There were two other problems in relations between France and the Empire that caused friction. The first was the grants of tenths to Philip and his predecessors from dioceses in the old Middle Kingdom; the second was Henry VII's dream of reestablishing the kingdom of Arles. St. Louis had received grants from

---

treaty (26 June 1310). It had several advantages for France, notably recognizing Philip of Poitiers as count of Burgundy but postponing his homage. But the treaty was to have been crowned by an interview between the two kings, and by 30 August Clement V was grieving over the fact that the interview, planned for 22 August, had been canceled (ibid., no. 394). The war of Lyon began on 24 June, and the archbishop surrendered on 22 July. Professor Benton, in the unpublished study mentioned above argues (I think rightly) that Henry canceled the interview and refused to implement the treaty because he was angered by the attack on Lyon.

[165] Bonnassieux, pp. 153-55; Ménestrier, *preuves*, pp. 51-52.

[166] Bonnassieux, pp. 167 (n. 2), 169-70, 172.

[167] Ibid., p. 179; Ménestrier, *preuves*, pp. 87-88. Lyon was briefly united with Mâcon under Philip V but soon became a separate unit again.

[168] Bonnassieux, pp. 182, 196-97; Ménestrier, *preuves*, pp. liv-lvi, 68-69, 65-67; *Ord.*, xi, 437.

[169] Bonnassieux, p. 182.

the Middle Kingdom for his crusades, but since his expedition conformed to the old ideal of a holy war of Christendom against the infidel, there could be little objection to his taking tenths from non-French districts. It was rather different when Charles of Anjou received tenths from the provinces of Besançon, Vienne, Embrun, and Tarentaise for his purely political Crusade against Manfred. It was even worse when Philip III was given tenths from the same provinces, plus Liège, Metz, Toul, and Verdun, for the Crusade against Aragon in 1285. King Rudolf protested this grant, but he obtained no satisfaction. When the grant was renewed in 1289—theoretically to continue the war with Aragon, actually to pay off debts from the campaign of 1285—rich Cambrai was substituted for poor Embrun and Tarantaise; otherwise the list remained the same.[170]

As Kern pointed out, however, this policy of demanding tenths from imperial dioceses was abandoned by Philip the Fair after 1289,[171] and it was not revived in his reign or in those of his sons. The probable reason for the change is that from 1295 through 1304 all tenths were granted by councils of the French Church, which of course could not impose their wishes on imperial dioceses. The next tenth, collected only in 1307, had been imposed by Benedict XI to restore "good money" in France;[172] it would have been hard to justify extending this levy to churches outside the realm. More than 20 years elapsed between the grant of 1289 and the next unrestricted grant, by Clement V in 1310. By that time it was a little late to invoke earlier precedents, even though royal accountants left blank spaces in their records for the provinces of Vienne and Besançon.[173] It may also be true that there was little profit in tenths from imperial dioceses and that French policy could be better served by conciliating the clergy of places such as Toul, Verdun, and Besançon. The one exception was the diocese of Cambrai, which was in the province of Reims and part of whose lands lay within the kingdom. Cambrai paid a tenth in 1304, with no territorial limits specified.[174] It had al-

---

[170] Kern, *Anfänge*, pp. 83-85, 157; Lizerand, "Philippe le Bel et l'empire au temps de Rodolphe de Habsbourg," *Revue historique*, CXLII (1923), 189-92; *M.G.H., Constitutiones*, III, no. 452; *Les registres de Nicolas IV*, ed. Ernest Langlois (Paris, 1886-1891), nos. 2741-42, 1005. Honorius IV had already rejected similar complaints in August 1285 (*Les registres d'Honorius IV*, ed. Maurice Prou [Paris, 1888], no. 476).

[171] Kern, *Anfänge*, p. 157. [172] Mignon, no. 796.

[173] Ibid., nos. 826-27 (for 1310), 836-37 (for 1312).

[174] Kern, ed., *Acta Imperii*, no. 150. Mignon, no. 782, omits Cambrai,

ready paid a tenth in 1297 on the part of the diocese in France.[175] Lyon is only an apparent exception. Except for the city itself, the entire ecclesiastical province lay within the kingdom and would have been bound either by papal grants or by acts of the French clergy. Lyon paid tenths regularly with no protest.[176] In short, after 1291 the collection of tenths caused no problems in Philip's relations with the Empire.

Philip's policy concerning the phantom kingdom of Arles is one of the most curious aspects of his reign. He had no territorial ambitions there, and the two strongest principalities were held by the dauphin of Viennois, who usually supported French interests, and by the count of Provence, king of Naples, who was a friend and a kinsman. Yet Philip was always sensitive about possible threats to Languedoc, and, although there was no immediate danger, he worried about the security of the Rhône frontier. Perhaps for this reason he was also unhappy about plans to revive the kingdom of Arles, even if the king was to be one of his Angevin relatives. He insisted that the French frontier extended to the east bank of the Rhône, so that all the islands in the river were in the kingdom.[177] Moreover, when Charles II of Naples acquired rights over Avignon in 1291, Philip promptly made a *paréage* with the abbot of St. André, which gave him control of the western end of the bridge of Avignon. He built a strong tower there in 1292 to prevent hostile forces from crossing the bridge, and in 1307 he strengthened the garrison because the men of Avignon had been raiding the west bank.[178] If Philip felt this way about the distant and relatively ineffectual lordship of the king of Naples over Avignon, one can understand why he was not desirous of having an Angevin prince become king of Arles and thus create a new power center on the lower Rhône. The idea of ending the old quarrel between the Guelfs and the Ghibel-

---

"propter combustionem guerrarum Flandrie," but I have verified Kern's reference (A.N., JJ 36, fol. 71v, no. 166), and Philip certainly expected Cambrai to pay. See above, note 117.

[175] Mignon, no. 727.

[176] Mignon, nos. 687, 704, 761, 778, 787, 811, 835.

[177] *H.L.*, IX, 289. This ruling (ca. 1305-1306) went against the count of Provence.

[178] *Ord.*, VII, 611 (for the agreement); Mignon, nos. 2615, 2612, *C.R.*, I, 13917[2] (for garrisons). On the Rhône border in general see J. de Komefort; "Le Rhône . . . frontière des Capétiens au XIIIᵉ siècle," *Revue historique*, CLXXXI (1929), 74-89.

lines in Italy by a marriage treaty that would unite an Angevin prince (Guelf) with the daughter of a German king (presumably Ghibelline) had been suggested by Nicholas III in 1279. Nicholas had also had the idea that the dowry should be the kingdom of Arles, part of which (Provence) was already Angevin.[179] Nothing came of this proposal, but it was revived in 1309, when it became evident that Henry VII was planning to reassert imperial rights in Italy. Civil war, at least on a local scale, was sure to follow Henry's descent into Italy unless an agreement could be reached between the Angevins and the Germans. The obvious solution, as before, was a marriage treaty, with the kingdom of Arles as dowry for the bride. Clement V probably did not originate the plan, but he certainly supported it, and for a time it seemed as if it might be put into effect.[180]

Philip, just as certainly, was opposed to the scheme. This is evident, first, from a clause in the proposed treaty between Philip and Henry in which Henry promised not to name a king "es frontieres dou royaume de France" who would not swear to be friendly and helpful.[181] Much more important, in December 1310, when the break between Henry and Philip had already occurred, Philip sent an embassy to Clement V that complained bitterly about the pope's support of the marriage treaty.[182] Philip's opposition probably helped to end plans for the marriage, though money problems and the difficulty of reconciling Guelf and Ghibelline interests also made the alliance impossible. But Philip wanted to be sure that the project was dead; he persuaded Clement to promise that he would never allow the kingdom of Arles to be transferred, except to the Roman or another church.[183] By 1 May 1311 (the date of this letter) such a promise was hardly necessary. The fact that Philip demanded it shows how strongly he opposed the idea of reviving the kingdom of Arles.

[179] Fournier, pp. 232-35.

[180] Ibid., pp. 354-58. Clement later disclaimed any responsibility, but he was then trying to placate Philip the Fair; see the documents listed in note 182 below.

[181] *M.G.H.*, *Constitutiones*, IV, pt. 1, no. 353, para. 6.

[182] Ibid., no. 514, paras. 12-15; cf. no. 467, para. 7. Note that Nogaret, who could not be received by the pope because he was still excommunicate, was nevertheless the leader of the mission.

[183] Ibid., no. 612. Clement said that he was not encouraging the plan to revive the kingdom of Arles (Schwalm, "Reise nach Frankreich," pp. 611, 619, 629).

ITALY AND SPAIN

Philip had no ambitions in Italy and Spain, only problems—some inherited from his father's reign, some created by his brother, Charles of Valois. The most difficult problem was to wind up the war with Aragon, which had been caused by the Aragonese occupation of Sicily in 1282. Philip's cousins, the Angevin family of Sicily-Naples, had lost half their kingdom; Charles of Valois, who had been promised Aragon by the pope, wanted compensation for his unattainable crown; the popes kept urging a renewal of the war. Philip saw no profit in a new attack on Aragon; in fact, for the first two or three years of the reign he was more concerned about defending his southern border and the lands of his ally, the king of Majorca, against Aragonese raids.[184] He was quite ready to make peace if some compensation were given to his brother Charles, nominal king of Aragon, and if the pope were willing to accept the settlement. On the other hand, the kings of Aragon began to lose interest in Sicily after the death of Pedro III in 1285. The nobles of Aragon (the old, landlocked kingdom), as opposed to the seafaring Catalans, saw no profit in the occupation of a distant island, and in his will Pedro had separated Sicily from his own kingdom by leaving it to his second son, Jaime. Alfonso III of Aragon, like Philip the Fair, was not inclined to wage an expensive war on behalf of a younger brother. Thus it was not difficult for Edward I, who had been accepted as arbiter by the opposing parties, to work out the principles of a settlement. The Angevin king of Naples-Sicily, Charles II, was to be released from captivity (he had been taken prisoner, while still only heir-apparent, during the war of the Sicilian Vespers). Charles of Valois was to give up his claim to the throne of Aragon. Charles of Sicily would allow Jaime to keep the island of Sicily.[185]

Philip the Fair took no part in these negotiations, and he may have been a little annoyed by the way in which Edward I was acting as arbiter among the kings of the West. Pope Nicholas IV was considerably more annoyed. After all, Sicily was a fief of the Church. He freed Charles II from his promises and tried to clear the way for direct negotiations between Aragon and Sicily-Naples. Charles of Valois was to renounce his claim to Aragon,

[184] Petit, *Charles de Valois*, pp. 13-15; Digard, I, 47, 52.
[185] *Foedera*, I, pt. 2, 677; Digard, I, 43-44, 63-64.

marry the daughter of Charles II, and receive with her the ancient possessions of the founder of the Angevin house of Sicily, the counties of Anjou and Maine.[186] Philip the Fair could only applaud this decision. His obligations to his brother were now satisfied, and he had no further reason to concern himself about a renewal of the war with Aragon. The marriage took place on 16 August 1290, and, except for the dispute over the Val d'Aran, there were no further problems on the frontiers between France and the Spanish kingdoms.

The Sicilian question was far from settled, but Philip took no interest in it. When Jaime of Sicily succeeded his brother Alfonso III as king of Aragon in 1291, he left a younger brother, Fadrique (Frederick III), there as regent. Like Alfonso, Jaime was ready to give up his hold on the island in return for papal reconciliation with the Church and (a new twist) the right to acquire Sardinia and Corsica.[187] But Fadrique did not want to give up his hopes of having Sicily for himself, and the people of Sicily would not accept Charles II as their king, in spite of his renewed attempts to reconquer the island. So Fadrique became king as a champion of Sicilian independence.[188] Charles II naturally sought French help—and gained it in the person of Charles of Valois.

Valois had been addressed as a king when he was still in his teens and had never quite recovered from the experience. He wanted a crown for himself, or, if he could not be a king, at least to be a kingmaker. He had no great qualifications for either role; his princely qualities were largely on the surface—a spirit of adventure, courtliness, magnificence, and generosity (when he had the money). He was neither very intelligent nor a good organizer, and he lacked the toughness and tenacity to carry through difficult projects. In 1300, when French relations with Boniface VIII were still good, the pope invited Charles to Italy to pacify the States of the Church and to drive Fadrique from Sicily. This was part of a complicated project by which Charles was to marry Catherine of Courtenay, heiress of the last Latin emperor of Constantinople, and bring the Byzantines once more into the western Church.[189] (Charles' first wife, Marguerite of Sicily, had died in 1299. She was the real kingmaker in the family; her son was to

[186] Digard, I, 76-79, 100-101; Petit, Charles de Valois, pp. 17-19, 22. Charles did not officially renounce his title until 1295 (Digard, I, 233).

[187] Digard, I, 223-24, 290-93.   [188] Ibid., I, 258-59.

[189] Petit, Charles de Valois, pp. 52-53, 55-56; Digard, II, 21-22.

become Philip VI of France in 1328.) It is doubtful that Boniface really expected to regain Constantinople, but it was a useful bait in luring Charles to Sicily.

Philip the Fair had no illusions. He gave Charles 40,000 l.t. "pro subsidio vie Constantinopolitane,"[190] but this was inadequate to meet even the preliminary costs of the expedition to Italy. Philip had also promised to give Boniface VIII 100,000 l.t. for the reconquest of Sicily, but this money, which Boniface was to turn over to Charles, had not been received by the pope's bankers by 8 May 1301, and Boniface had some doubts that it would be available.[191] Charles was also promised a tenth from the French clergy,[192] but it is doubtful that this was ever paid, since Philip's own attempt to collect a tenth at the same time was blocked by the pope. Charles was in debt before he left France,[193] and he was short of money all the time he was in Italy.

This is probably the reason why he behaved more like one of the less reputable condottieri than a future emperor. He took money and presents from anyone who would offer them, and gave very little in return. He "pacified" Florence in November 1301 by allowing the Blacks to drive out the Whites—after having taken presents from both sides.[194] Dante, one of the exiles, conferred a dubious immortality on Charles by denouncing his treachery in the *Divine Comedy*.[195] Boniface VIII, who should have been grateful (the Blacks were his supporters), did not allow gratitude to dissuade him from pursuing his quarrel with Philip the Fair.

From Florence Charles went to Naples and took over command of an army that was to invade Sicily in May 1302. It was a nasty war; Charles wasted his time in useless sieges, while the countryside remained largely in the hands of Sicilian guerrillas. Charles had neither the temperament, the time, nor the money to conduct a long and tedious pacification program. It was clear that the Sicilians would not accept mainland domination unless they were utterly crushed, and Charles was needed in France,

[190] *J.T.P.*, no. 4612 (5 May 1301).

[191] Petit, *Charles de Valois, pièces justificatives*, no. 3.

[192] Ibid., p. 57; Digard, II, 41.

[193] Charles borrowed 24,000 l.t. from bankers of Pistoia in May 1301 (*J.T.P.*, nos. 4623, 4761).

[194] Petit, *Charles de Valois*, pp. 67-75.

[195] Charles will strike Florence with the lance of Judas; he will gain nothing but sin and shame (*Purgatory*, 20).

where the battle of Courtrai had wiped out a French army and where the conflict with Boniface VIII was reaching a peak. Philip the Fair had never been greatly interested in Sicily, and the pope could not give much attention to the island while he was trying to humble the king of France. Charles was probably wise to make peace with Fadrique of Sicily (as he had been empowered to do by Charles II of Naples) on 31 August 1302. The terms of the treaty of Caltabellota allowed Fadrique to keep Sicily for the rest of his life, without the title of king. These limitations were soon forgotten; Fadrique became king of Sicily (or Trinacria, to distinguish him from the king of Naples, who also called himself king of Sicily), and his son inherited his throne.[196] Philip the Fair showed no concern over these developments.

One final example demonstrates Philip's lack of interest in the problems of the southern kingdoms. There had been a dispute over the succession to the throne of Castile ever since 1276. The eldest son of Alfonso X, Ferdinand de la Cerda, had married Blanche of France, daughter of St. Louis, and had had two sons by her. He died before his father, however, and Alfonso and the Cortes of Castile recognized Sancho, Alfonso's second son, as heir, rather than the children of Ferdinand. This was contrary to Castilian (and French) law and to the terms of the marriage treaty between Ferdinand and Blanche. Philippe III of France threatened war (1276) but could not get his army across the frontier.[197] Alfonso X disinherited Sancho on his deathbed (1284) and named his oldest grandson, Alfonso de la Cerda, as his heir, but Sancho ignored these provisions and was recognized as king.

The la Cerda children had taken refuge in Aragon, while their mother returned to France. During the troubled reign of Sancho IV (1284-1295) and the equally troubled minority of Ferdinand IV (1295-1301) the kings of Aragon tried to use the la Cerdas to stir up civil war in Castile and to split their large and powerful neighbor into several smaller kingdoms. There were times when it seemed possible that Alfonso de la Cerda would receive Murcia as a realm of his own, but all these schemes collapsed. Early in his reign (1288) Philip the Fair favored such an arrangement,[198] but he did nothing to implement the agreement. There were many

---

[196] Petit, *Charles de Valois*, pp. 81-86; *H.F.*, xx, 587, 672; Martène, *Thesaurus*, III, 58.

[197] Langlois, *Philippe III*, pp. 104-5.

[198] Digard, I, 52; see ibid., II, 238, for the treaty between Philip and Sancho promising Murcia to the la Cerda (1288).

opportunities to intervene in Castile, especially during the disturb-
ances that followed the death of Sancho IV in 1295 and continued
throughout the minority of Ferdinand IV. The king of Aragon
encouraged risings in favor of Alfonso de la Cerda,[199] but Philip
took no interest in these plans. He remained a little suspicious of
Aragonese intentions (as was shown by his reluctance to give up
the Val d'Aran), and he wanted Castilian aid, or at least neutrality,
in the long, drawn-out war of Aquitaine.[200] He had nothing to
gain and a great deal to lose by becoming involved in the complicated problems of Castile. He was quite willing to give Alfonso
an honorable position in his court and a generous pension,[201] but
he would not lift a finger to help him acquire a kingdom in Spain.

APPENDIX

The French Armies

One cannot write of the French army, because there was no continuing body of soldiers and officers always ready for combat.
There was a continuing high command—the Constable, two
Marshals, and the master of the arbalesters (chief of infantry)—
but these men were not full-time professional soldiers. The Constable and the Marshals were great officers of the crown; they
could sit in the Parlement or in Council (as Marshal Jean de Grez
did when the ordinance giving Marigny control of royal finance
was adopted),[1] or they could be used as envoys, as Constable
Gaucher de Châtillon was in Flanders.[2] Nevertheless, they did

---

[199] Ibid., I, 270, n. 2. See Finke, ed., *Acta Aragonensia*, I, 450, for letters
from James of Aragon urging Philip to aid Alfonso de la Cerda (July 1300).

[200] Instructions to French envoys sent to discuss a marriage treaty with
Sancho in 1294 told them to ask for military and naval aid in the war of
Aquitaine (Digard, II, 294).

[201] Alfonso had a pension of 4,000 l.t. (*J.T.P.*, nos. 598, 2464, 4322, 5414);
he was still drawing this in 1316 (Fawtier, ed., *Comptes du Trésor*, no.
2718). In *J.T.P.*, no. 2464, Alfonso was called "rex Castelle," but this was
in 1299 and must have been a courtesy title; Philip had other things on his
mind then. For Alfonso's later years see H. F. Delaborde, "Un arrière petit-
fils de Saint Louis," in *Mélanges Jules Havet* (Paris, 1895), pp. 414-19. Alfonso was definitely excluded from the Castilian throne in 1295, but he
received, lost, and regained some lordships in Spain. He died in Spain in
1333.

---

[1] Boutaric, "Documents inédits," pp. 209-13; cf. Borrelli de Serres, *Recherches*, III, 54. The Constable was on the Parlement lists of 1296 and 1307.
[2] Funck-Brentano, *Philippe le Bel en Flandre*, pp. 434, 566, 602, 634.

spend a large part of their time on military affairs or on problems that might require a military solution. The accounts of Gaucher de Châtillon that are listed in Mignon's inventory are all connected with war or threat of war.[3] The masters of the arbalesters, such as Jean de Burlas, Thibaud de Chepoy, or Pierre de Galard, had less to do with high politics and were primarily concerned with military or police operations. It was Jean de Burlas, for example, who arrested Bishop Bernard Saisset.

Above these men who were officially concerned with the army were the princes of the blood—Charles of Valois, Louis of Evreux, and Robert of Artois. Gui, count of Saint-Pol, and his brother Jacques de Châtillon were not princes of the blood, but they were related to the queen; both held high commands in Flanders. Beneath such men were nobles who had high rank in their own provinces and long experience in and some aptitude for warfare. Béraud de Mercoeur, constable of Champagne, was the most prominent member of this group. He led troops in Flanders and was made captain of Lyon in 1310. Unfortunately, when he could not fight the king's enemies he was apt to fight neighbors or the king's friends, and he was often in disfavor at court.[4]

Another interesting example of a professional soldier is Robert de Wavrin, lord of Saint Venant. Though he was a Fleming and a chamberlain of the count of Flanders, he served Philip in Aquitaine and acted as governor of the duchy from September 1298 to June 1300. He then commanded a body of troops in Flanders and fought for Philip the Fair in the crucial battle of Mons-en-Pévèle. He was richly rewarded by the king with rents worth 1,000 l.t. a year.[5]

The southern seneschals, who were nobles, were also qualified for army commands. They were certainly helpful in raising troops and, at times, in bringing them to the theater of combat. But when Guichard de Marzi and Blayn Loup of Toulouse and Henri d'Elise of Carcassonne were called "captains of Gascony" or of Aquitaine, were they acting as army commanders?[6] Probably they were, in effect, military governors. They had troops at their disposal, but there was very little fighting in Aquitaine while they

---

[3] Mignon, nos. 2634-50.

[4] Funck-Brentano, *Philippe le Bel en Flandre*, pp. 438, 450; Mignon, nos. 2608, 2644; *J.T.P.*, no. 3635; *H.F.*, xxiv, *181.

[5] Funck-Brentano, *Philippe le Bel en Flandre*, pp. 262-63; *C.R.*, ii, no. 25450; Mignon, no. 2355; *J.T.P.*, nos. 571, 1528, 3757, 5417.

[6] Mignon, nos. 2340, 2394, 2430.

were captains. This is not to disparage the military abilities of the seneschals; most of them were quite capable of crushing local uprisings. But the only seneschal who became a career officer was Jean de Burlas, seneschal of Carcassonne, 1285-1287, governor of the duchy of Aquitaine, 1294-1298, and master of the arbalesters, 1287(?)-1302.[7]

Below such experienced commanders would come the nobles who were willing to serve in two or three campaigns but who had no desire to spend long years as officers in the army. The careful accounts kept by Jean l'Archévêque, acting seneschal of Toulouse, give a good sample of this group. He lists 82 nobles of his district who served, often with a company of their sergeants, in three different campaigns in Gascony. Of these, only 11 went on all three expeditions, and 15 served in only one. The vast majority, 56, felt that two campaigns were enough to satisfy their honor and their duty to the king.[8] Although there was some decline in the overall size of the Toulouse contingent from the first to the third army,[9] individual nobles were quite erratic in their choice of when to serve. Some came to the first and second armies, some to the first and third, and some to the second and third. If this were the attitude of nobles who were, so to speak, on the front line, who were paid good wages, and who ran little danger (casualties in the war of Aquitaine were very low), one can imagine the problems faced by the government in finding company commanders in other districts and for the much bloodier Flemish war. One can also see problems of organization. If there were no permanent or, at least, continuing companies (as there were during the Hundred Years' War), if noble leaders came and went as they chose, how could the operations of an army be coordinated?

The sergeants, or foot soldiers, were the largest part of most French armies, but little is known about their command structure. Again, using the accounts of Jean l'Archévêque, it is clear that some nobles brought their own groups of foot soldiers with them and presumably commanded them directly. More often, however,

[7] *H.F.*, xxiv, *222, *254; Mignon, no. 2349; *J.T.P.*, no. 675n; *C.R.*, i, no. 12780. Thibaud de Chepoy, who succeeded Jean de Burlas as master, was briefly (1298) seneschal of Agenais (*H.F.*, xxiv, *220), but this was a post in territories occupied by the French army.

[8] *C.R.*, ii, nos. 26568-776.

[9] The number of constabularies (companies of infantry) was 100 in the first army, 59 in the second, and 44 in the third (ibid., nos. 26365-567).

the records refer to "constabularies," or companies, recruited village by village and commanded by a constable, who drew 2 s.t.
a day, twice the wage of an ordinary foot soldier. These constabularies could be quite large—one of 150 men is mentioned as
forming part of the garrison of La Réole in Gascony in 1302.[10]
This was unusual; in the south a constabulary of 50 seems to have
been the standard. There were 50 men in another company at
La Réole, and when the garrison of Aigues-Mortes was reinforced
in 1302, there were three constabularies of 49, 55, and 45 men,
respectively.[11] In Flanders the groups seem to have been smaller.
There is a fairly complete account of the garrison of Béthune
in 1303 that gives yearly pay for each constabulary. Assuming that
the size of groups engaged in garrison duty would not change
very much during a year and that each man drew about 18 l.t.
a year (36 l.t. for the constables), the companies would have had
20 to 25 men each.[12] In Flanders in 1299 the count of Forez had
25 men under one constable,[13] exactly the number that seems to
have been the standard for the constabularies of Béthune.

Thus the infantry constables were, to use modern terminology,
noncommissioned officers of some importance. When they were
performing garrison duty they were clearly under the orders of
the commander of the town. In field operations the link between
the constables and the top command is uncertain. The master of
the arbalesters could command mounted troops as well as infantry,
and his aide, the clerk of the arbalesters, was a paymaster. In any
case, there were so many constabularies in any army that one
man could not have given orders directly to each group. For
example, the Toulouse region sent about 100 constabularies to the
"first army" that invaded Gascony.[14] There were a large number
of Italian crossbowmen in the French army in Flanders; they
may have been directly under the master of the arbalesters, but
in that case he could not have had direct control of all the French
infantry. Probably one or more of the French constabularies were
assigned to the "comitiva" of each knight or baron, as in the case
of the count of Forez, but this would mean that the infantry
could not be maneuvered as a group. If true, this would have been
a serious weakness and would explain some of the problems of the

[10] Ibid., I, no. 12861.
[11] Ibid., nos. 12864, 13872, 13874-76.
[12] Ibid., nos. 5986-92, 5996.   [13] *J.T.P.*, no. 4104.
[14] See above, note 9.

French army. At Courtrai, for example, it is clear that infantry and cavalry operations were not coordinated and that the commander, the count of Artois, did not or could not withdraw his infantry before ordering a cavalry charge. The same problem appeared at Mons-en-Pévèle, where the infantry, under Thibaud de Chepoy, master of the arbalesters, was given little cavalry support and was driven back.[15]

Every able-bodied man in France was liable for military service to defend the realm. This was implied early in the reign and was made explicit in general summonses after 1300.[16] Of course, Philip did not want universal military service; he could not have supplied or maneuvered an army of several hundred thousand men. Anyone who had the money could buy exemption from service, and most men, including most of the nobles, did so. On the other hand, some nobles wanted to have combat experience (and pay), and a community that bought off service still had to furnish or pay for a certain number of troops. Philip did need more troops than any of his predecessors, especially during the period when he had to keep large garrisons in Aquitaine and a field force in Flanders, and he did try to increase the size of his forces. How large were the French armies during these years of crisis? There are no complete figures for any one of the major expeditions; one can only extrapolate from fragmentary and incomplete accounts. Perhaps, with a maximum effort, Philip may have been able to put 30,000 men in the field at one time and at one place, but such concentrations were rare. A mobile force of 5,000 to 10,000 men was probably more common. As for garrisons, their forces increased and decreased depending on the political situation, and it is nearly impossible to estimate how many men were tied down in purely defensive positions. Thus at one point (no date given, but certainly in a time of peace) the garrisons in Flanders were token forces—four horsemen and four foot soldiers at Lille, for example.[17] But in 1303-1304 the *bailliage* of Mâcon alone was supporting nine constabularies, plus 100 sergeants under Hugues de Toissi and several men-at-arms (certainly over 300 men in all), for the garrison of Béthune.[18]

Garrisons in Aquitaine also varied in size. Thus in about 1301

[15] J. Petit, "Thibaut de Chepoy," *Le Moyen Age*, x (1897), 229. In an earlier, successful action, Thibaud's division was mostly cavalry, with only about 90 foot soldiers (ibid., p. 228).

[16] Strayer and Taylor, pp. 56-64; *Ord.*, I, 345, 350, 546, 383, 391.

[17] *C.R.*, II, nos. 26989-27011.   [18] Ibid., I, nos. 5985-99.

the garrison of St. Emilion comprised 1 knight, 11 squires, and 50 sergeants.[19] In a less placid time for Aquitaine (1299) there were 32 sergeants at Ste. Livrade, 256 at Moissac, and 50 at Villefranche.[20] When the population of Bordeaux seemed restless in the same year, the garrison was increased by four bannerets, 23 knights, 227 squires, and 192 sergeants. The low proportion of foot soldiers is probably owing to the fact that this was an emergency and that horsemen could be brought up more rapidly. This is a good example of the unstructured and loosely organized groups that made up the French army. No contingent served more than 15 days, and one group of sergeants was sent home before it arrived at Bordeaux.[21] With such fluctuations, about all that can be said is that between 1293 and 1305 some thousands of men must have been tied up in garrisons.

As for the field armies, there is one fairly complete account of the mounted men ("armeures de fer") who were with Charles of Valois when he overran Flanders after the expiration of the truces in 1299.[22] The scribe gives a total of 1,563 men with full armor. The figure may be a little high, as it includes some men who were attached to Valois's contingent of 240 but who were also listed separately. It is also evident from the receipts given by the paymasters that, as in Aquitaine, some knights and squires served only briefly in the army of occupation and departed as soon as the success of the operation was assured. On the other hand, the men-at-arms of Gui of Saint-Pol were explicitly omitted, and a man of his rank would have had a following of at least 100, and probably more. Thus in the first phase of the operation, when Valois was overawing the Flemings and occupying the entire county, he must have commanded one of the largest armies that Philip ever raised, at least 1,650 mounted men. If we accept this figure, how many foot soldiers should be added to arrive at the grand total? They were certainly more numerous than the horsemen, but how much more numerous?

We know the exact composition of a small force raised by the acting *bailli* of Mâcon for a demonstration against the archbishop of Lyon in 1304. There were 17 knights, 113 men-at-arms, and 2,188 foot soldiers.[23] This would give a proportion of almost 17 foot to 1 horseman. But this was a small affair; no one served

---

[19] Ibid., II, nos. 26987-88.

[20] *J.T.P.*, no. 4237.

[21] *C.R.*, II, nos. 25448-507.

[22] Ibid., nos. 27022-133.

[23] Ibid., I, nos. 6004-5.

more than a few days, and it is fairly certain that some of the
men-at-arms of the *bailliage* were absent on duty in Flanders.

The Toulouse records of Jean l'Archévêque, however, give an
even higher percentage of foot soldiers. Jean listed only "nobles,"
which may have excluded many men-at-arms, but the dispropor-
tion is striking—about 100 constabularies in the first army, 59 in
the second, and 44 in the third, and only 82 nobles for all three.
Even if constabularies were smaller than the average of 50 mentioned above, and even if each of the nobles were accompanied
by several men-at-arms[24] it is hard to bring the figure down to a
level much below that of the Mâcon expedition. Here again it
is true that there was little fighting and that foot soldiers, at 1 s.t.
a day, were cheaper than knights at 10 s.t. a day and about as useful for garrison duty in small towns and villages.

On the other hand, the plan of Benedetto Zaccharia, Philip's
admiral, for a raid on England gives a different ratio. He proposed
a fleet of 16 ships and 4 galleys, manned by 4,800 armed sailors.
The vessels were to carry 400 knights and 400 men-at-arms.[25]
Here the proportion is 6 marines to 1 (potentially) mounted man;
in an actual attack it would have been lower, since some sailors
would have had to stay with the ships. But the admiral was planning a raid, not a conquest, and too many foot soldiers would have
slowed down a quick strike. It is interesting, however, to see that
he thought that a force of a little over 5,000 men could seriously
disconcert the English.

A different, but still low, ratio is given in summonses to Languedoc in 1304—2,016 men-at-arms and 17,850 infantry.[26] Here again
the slow rate of travel of men on foot may explain their relatively
small number. Philip was having trouble getting his army together; he had had to postpone the date of assembly at Arras three
times, from 19 May to 22 July.[27] He could not wait for slow-
moving infantry; one wonders, with Funck-Brentano, how many
of these southerners ever arrived in Flanders.

---

[24] Certain men are listed as "de societate" of a noble, and not as sergeants
(Ibid., II, nos. 26627, 26707, 26726, 26747).

[25] Boutaric, "Documents inédits," pp. 112-19.

[26] Funck-Brentano, *Philippe le Bel en Flandre*, pp. 463-64; *H.L.*, x, col.
439; *H.F.*, XXIII, 792-95. Funck-Brentano gives only 7,330 infantry, but the
source used in *H.F.*, XXIII, is fuller. Even this source gives no sergeants for
Périgord and Rouergue, so the overall ratio may have been 10 to 1, as
it was in Toulouse and Carcassonne.

[27] Funck-Brentano, *Philippe le Bel en Flandre*, p. 463.

The chroniclers, even the best informed, tend to exaggerate the size of armies and are not very precise about their composition. Thus Valois's 1,550 men-at-arms in 1300 become 6,000 in the *Chronique artésienne*. The same writer gives the French force at Courtrai as 10,000 mounted men and 10,000 arbalesters. In late 1302, he believed, Philip had 16,000 men; his contemporary at Ghent said 20,000. Both figures seem high; this was less than two months after Courtrai. In the summer of 1303 the estimate was 6,000 men-at-arms and 30,000 foot, almost certainly too high, though the proportions are reasonable.[28] Funck-Brentano thought that Philip had 60,000 men at Mons-en-Pévèle, but he had little evidence for this figure.[29] Altogether, the numbers given by the chroniclers simply mean that French armies were very large by the standards of their time.

My own guess may be no better than that of Funck-Brentano. Taking the one sure figure for a large army, the 1,550 "armeures de fer" of Valois in 1300, and allowing at least 100 more for the count of Saint-Pol, I have estimated that there were 10, and perhaps 15, foot soldiers for every mounted man. This is the pattern for armies that did little fighting but that had to be dispersed over wide areas in order to prevent scattered resistance after a region had been occupied. If these assumptions are correct, then Valois had about 17,000 to 26,000 men. I would prefer the lower figure. If this can be accepted, then the armies at Courtrai and at Mons-en-Pévèle were probably somewhat larger. Given the problems of finance and logistics, I find it hard to believe that Philip ever had more than 30,000 men concentrated in one theater of war. The peak was probably reached at Mons-en-Pévèle.

[28] Ibid., pp. 339, 409, 433, 450.   [29] Ibid., pp. 465, 473.

VI. The King and His People

Philip the Fair accomplished much, but in doing so he put heavy strains on the loyalty of his subjects. In asserting his authority over all France and in defining the boundaries of the France in which his authority was to be accepted, he had to fight expensive wars and impose general taxes to pay for those wars. He had to increase the number of royal officials and encourage them to intervene in the affairs of prelates, barons, and towns. He had to risk a direct attack on the authority and the person of the pope. Nobody liked taxation; many people found the bureaucracy oppressive; there was some uneasiness about the conflict with Boniface VIII. Yet opposition to royal policy never led to unmanageable violence, and Philip gained most of his objectives without the use of force. This was just as well, since he had little force on which to rely—no standing army and only a small and scattered police force (the sergeants). Raising an army took a considerable amount of time, effort, and money, and military victories did not always lead to quick and decisive solutions. What was gained by force had to be preserved by force; it was relatively easy to overrun Aquitaine, but very expensive to keep garrisons there year after year. Thus, when Philip felt that he had to use force against his two strongest vassals—the king of England and the count of Flanders—he gained very little in return for vast expenditures. He acquired some useful border territories (notably Lille), but he solved none of the basic problems that had caused the wars. Aquitaine and Flanders remained virtually autonomous, and the wars had to be renewed in the reigns of his successors. On the other hand, where little or no force was used, the gains were solid: an increase in revenues, general recognition of royal sovereignty in judicial matters, and virtual control over the French Church.

To achieve these results, it is obvious that there had to be a continuous exchange of opinions between the king and his people. Philip and his ministers worked hard to persuade the country that royal policy was wise, lawful, and necessary. The politically conscious part of the population worked just as hard to prove that the king's demands were unreasonable, illegal, and not warranted by the circumstances. The usual result was a compromise, but it should be noted that any compromise favored the king, since it meant a departure from the status quo. If he took a lump sum instead of a tax assessed at a specific rate, or if he shared the income from a tax with a great lord (for example, the duke of Burgundy),[1] he was still collecting revenues that he had not had before. If he made a *paréage* with a southern bishop, setting up a common court in which he had a share in the appointment of officials and the profits of justice, he was still gaining rights in a district that had been a virtually independent ecclesiastical principality.[2] If he issued a reforming ordinance limiting arbitrary actions by his officials, he received in return tacit recognition of the greatly expanded area within which his officials could operate.[3]

It is easier to describe this process of compromise and accommodation in general terms than to explain why it worked so successfully in particular cases. The main lines of royal propaganda are clear enough; they appear in ordinances, administrative regulations, court decisions, diplomatic correspondence, political tracts, and sermons. The king of France is unique among European rulers. Annointed with oil brought from Heaven, healer of the sick, heir of Charlemagne and of St. Louis, he has a sacred character. He holds his kingdom directly from God; he acknowledges no earthly superior; he is emperor in his realm.[4] All subjects within this realm (and its boundaries were being defined with greater and greater precision) owe obedience and service to the king. Obedience means, above all else, accepting the king as final and supreme judge. Service means military service or its equivalent in money (and even, in some extreme statements, all private possessions, if needed for the common welfare).[5] Defense of the realm is the highest obligation of all subjects, and this is

---

[1] Boutaric, *La France sous Philippe le Bel*, p. 260.

[2] See, for example, *Ord.*, XI, 396-403 (Mende), VI, 343-47 (Le Puy), both in 1307.

[3] For example, the ordinance of 1303 for reform of the realm (*Ord.*, I, 357) assumes in articles 25 and 29 that anyone can appeal from a lord's court to the king's Court.

[4] See my article, "France: The Holy Land, the Chosen People, and the Most Christian King," pp. 302-3, and the sources cited there.

[5] Ibid., p. 301, n. 2. This theory was based on the Code, lib. VII, tit. 87: "omnia sunt principis quantum ad defensionem et tuitionem."

especially true in the case of France, because France is distinguished for its piety and support of the Church. To be willing
to die for one's fatherland is a religious duty.[6]

This was the official doctrine, and if one could be sure that it
was also the actual political creed of Philip's subjects, then it
would have been sufficient to justify most of Philip's activities.
The real problem is to determine how much of the doctrine was
accepted, or even understood, by the people of France. The evidence on political attitudes and beliefs is not good even for the
upper classes, and it is almost nonexistent for the poorer (and
larger) part of the population. Court sermons, the self-serving
protestations of Nogaret, the political pamphlets of Pierre du
Bois and his anonymous contemporaries are almost useless for
determining popular attitudes. These writers were either preach-
ing to the converted or trying to sell official doctrine to the upper
classes in France or to the pro-French faction in the papal curia.
Works by independent writers, such as the lawyer Pierre Jame
of Montpellier[7] or the philosopher Henri de Gand[8] (both of
whom supported the king's right to take taxes), probably come
closer to expressing actual opinion, but it is only the opinion of
the learned. The chroniclers and writers of satirical poems, like
Geoffroi de Paris,[9] are a step lower, both in the social and in the
intellectual scale, but they tend to reflect clerical opinion and the
opinion of the Paris area. The best evidence of political attitudes
that cut across class lines and regional differences comes from the
reactions of individuals and groups to royal initiatives. There
is abundant proof of the dislike of taxation by all classes: the

[6] Dupuy, pp. 309, 310; Kantorowicz, pp. 249-54.

[7] *Aurea practica libellorum* (Cologne, 1575), pp. 274-79, 280-81. Note
that, while admitting the king's right to tax, Pierre thinks that he has exercised it unjustly at times.

[8] See Georges de Lagarde, "La philosophie sociale d'Henri de Gand et
Godefroi de Fontaines," *Archives d'histoire doctrinale et littéraire du Moyen
Age*, XIV (1943-1945), 96, 100, 111. According to Henri de Gand, one should
die for one's fatherland, as Christ died for us (Philip used this idea in a
letter to the clergy of Tours in 1305, A.N., J 350, no. 5), and all subjects
must contribute for the common good. Most scholars of the period agreed
with this statement; see Gaines Post, *Studies in Medieval Legal Thought:
Public Law and the State, 1100-1322* (Princeton, 1964), pp. 284, 287-89, 300,
451.

[9] Geoffroi was annoyed by all taxation, but especially by taxes on the
Church (*H.F.*, XXII, 97, 118).

protests of the count of Foix[10] or the abbot of Dunes,[11] the acts
of provincial Church councils,[12] the attempts of towns to evade
or at least to diminish the sums to be paid,[13] and actual armed
resistance in certain areas.[14] There is also good evidence of resentment against royal officials (especially the sergeants): the
accusations carefully drawn up by Guillaume le Maire, bishop
of Angers,[15] the reform ordinances of 1303 and 1304, which attempted to calm down protests,[16] the grievances collected by the
enquêteurs, and the restrictions imposed on royal officials after
complaints made in the king's own courts.[17] The records of the
courts are especially helpful in determining reactions to the king's
attempts to extend and define his authority. Some of them, such as
the long, drawn-out suit between the king and the bishop of
Mende over their rights in the Gévaudan, turn into veritable
treatises on political theory.[18] A rough count of the cases heard

[10] B.N., ms. Doat 176, fols. 1 ff. (1294), fol. 172 (1296); *H.L.*, x, 341
(1297).

[11] Someone at Dunes collected protests against tenths asked of the abbot
of Clairvaux, the abbot of Dunes, and other Cistercian abbots (*Codex
Dunensis*, pp. 112, 114, 159, 169, 209, 253, 294, 510).

[12] For a discussion of the acts of provincial councils seeking to moderate
or to gain concessions for grants of tenths see Strayer and Taylor, pp. 25-
41. Resistance was especially strong in 1305.

[13] Ibid., pp. 51-53, 68-69, 71.

[14] There was violence in Langres and Chaumont in 1296 (Mignon, nos.
1292 and 1327). An attempt to collect a subsidy in Toulouse in 1303 was
abandoned and fines for disobedience remitted (Baudouin, ed., *Lettres
inédites*, no. 176). A small army of sergeants had to be hired to collect
from "rebels in Champagne" the aid for knighting Louis of Navarre, 1314
(Longnon, ed., *Documents*, III, 136-39).

[15] *Le livre de Guillaume le Maire*, pp. 322 ff., 335 ff., 358-60, 364-66. On
p. 322 the sergeants are called "ministri tartarei."

[16] *Ord.*, I, 357 ff., 403 ff. (for the Church). For the many copies and
variants of the ordinance for the Church see Strayer and Taylor, pp. 38-40.

[17] See *Olim*, II, for an ordinance on *mainmorte* and goods of deceased
foreigners and bastards, made by the Parlement after "graves clamores"
against the collectors, 1301 (p. 456), for a rebuke of the excessive zeal of
collectors of confiscated Jewish debts, 1310 (p. 506), and for an ordinance
by Parlement regulating the behavior of officers of the Châtelet in order
to stop their "extorsions et outrageuses prises," 1313 (p. 587).

[18] Most of the documents on the Gévaudan case were published by Roucaute and Saché, eds., *Lettres de Philippe le Bel relatives au pays de Gévaudan*. The arguments of the lawyers were published (in part) by Maisonobe, "Mémoire relatif au paréage de 1307." This partial publication takes
up 607 pages.

in the Parlement during the reign indicates that more than two-fifths of them involved royal officials. In some cases they had simply intervened to help settle disputes among private persons or corporations, but they could also be plaintiffs arguing that the king's rights were being infringed or defendants accused of over-stepping their authority. Both kinds of lawsuits reveal a great deal about the attitudes of the population.

Finally, there is the evidence provided by the assemblies that Philip called when he was undertaking risky or unprecedented operations. Here again it is necessary to reason backwards. If Philip called an assembly, it was because he feared that his plans might be disliked or misunderstood, and the arguments used in the assemblies give some idea of the kinds of opposition that he feared. There was no idea of obtaining formal consent from an assembly, so its composition could be quite flexible. As long as there were enough people from enough regions to ensure that information about the reasons for the royal decision would be disseminated widely, it did not matter which individuals attended or what communities were represented. Just as in England, where some sheriffs found many boroughs to send representatives to Parliament and some only one or two, so in France some provinces sent procurators from mere villages, while others sent them from only the larger towns. For example, in 1308 Poitou was repre-sented only by Poitiers, while the Orléanais sent men from Orléans and 12 other communities, including insignificant places such as Millençai and Alluies.[19] The assemblies were exercises in propaganda, not in constitutionalism. As far as they had any position in the structure of government, they were extraordinary meetings of the king's Court. Full forms of procuration were required, and many of the procurations empowered the delegates to attend a "parlamentum." Some procurations had been prepared earlier for other purposes (one was four years old); others gave the delegates power to transact other business while they were at court.[20] Doubtless, most of those who attended realized that they were not going to a session of *the* Parlement, in the nar-row sense of the word, but their position was not very different from that of procurators in the royal court of justice. In one way it was worse: they had no way of presenting their views officially,

[19] See the lists published by Boutaric, *La France sous Philippe le Bel*, pp. 439-48.

[20] Picot, pp. 609, 622, 647, 698, 708.

though doubtless their presence forced royal spokesmen to make their statements seem convincing. Legally, however, the procurators were present only to hear the decisions of the king and his councillors. Reasons for the decisions would be given, but the procurators were bound by the decisions, whether they liked them or not. Then they were to report the decisions, and the reasons for the decisions, to their communities. In short, the assemblies were a way of obtaining publicity for and a moral commitment to royal policies.

The large assemblies of the reign heard reasons for the attack on Boniface VIII, the arrest of the Templars, and, in 1314, the tax for the renewed war with Flanders. There were smaller assemblies of town representatives in 1308, 1313, and 1314 to discuss the coinage, a subject that was of great concern to the bourgeoisie.[21] Regional assemblies were also called, usually to discuss taxation. The nobles of Beaucaire met in 1295, the nobles of Toulouse in 1304, the nobles and (separately) the towns of Carcassonne in 1304, the towns of Beaucaire in 1304, the nobles of Normandy and the nobles of Champagne in the same year.[22] Local assemblies were used in Flanders to gain acceptance of the onerous peace treaty of 1305 and in the Lyonnais in 1307 to ratify the annexation of Lyon.[23] Finally, as Bisson has pointed out, the "day" of each *bailliage* and *sénéchausée* in the Parlement brought together leading men of each province. They certainly heard explanations of royal policy; they may have consulted one another (as the procurators of towns protesting the marriage aid probably did in 1309-1310); they could be consulted by royal officials, as Norman notables present at the Parlement were in 1313.[24] Attendance at the Parlement was an educational experience, if not always an enjoyable one.

The pattern is fairly clear. Philip felt that he needed to make a special effort to explain his policies to his subjects when he was interfering with the Church or imposing taxes. At the local level,

[21] *Ord.*, i, 449, 519, 548. In 1314 there were men from 43 towns, all of some importance (Auch and Moissac perhaps marginal) and well distributed (4 from Normandy, 10 from the northeast, 12 from Languedoc, etc.).

[22] Strayer and Taylor, pp. 46, 67-71.

[23] Bonnassieux, pp. 96-105; Funck-Brentano, *Philippe le Bel en Flandre*, pp. 513-15.

[24] T. N. Bisson, "Consultative Functions in the King's Parlements," *Speculum*, XLIV (1969), 367-71; B.N., ms. fr. 8764, fol. 1 (consultation on a point of Norman law).

he needed support when he annexed or asserted his authority over areas that had been virtually autonomous. He was certainly right about the unpopularity of taxation and about Flemish dislike of the treaty of Athis. On the other hand, he may have worried too much about opposition to his attacks on Boniface and on the Temple. Transfer of loyalty from the Church to the king had gone further than Philip realized. In contrast to other countries, there was little support for the Templars in France; Philip's charges were accepted wholeheartedly by prelates like Guillaume le Maire who had criticized other royal policies.[25] The assembly of 1308 may have convinced a few doubters, but its real purpose was to show the pope that the people were united behind their king. As for Boniface, he had few supporters; the clergy did not rally to his defense, and the nobility and the bourgeoisie, with few exceptions, supported the king. The Paris meetings on Boniface were followed up by the dispatch of commissioners throughout the country to secure adhesions to the accusations against the pope.[26] The commissioners convoked clergy, nobles, and representatives of towns and villages to their meetings and received almost unanimous support. Granting that it was hard to disagree with an emissary of the king and that the charges were worded so that it was difficult to believe that the pope was totally innocent, it is still surprising that there were so few objections. There was moral pressure but little physical coercion; the Dominicans, the lawyers, and the officials of Montpellier who refused to adhere to the king's accusation were threatened but not actually punished.[27] Pressure and threats were scarcely necessary. As was to happen again and again in the future, the French were so sure of their own orthodoxy and so convinced that they were "the

---

[25] Le livre de Guillaume le Maire, p. 472.

[26] Picot, Documents relatifs aux Etats Généraux sous Philippe le Bel, printed the records of these local meetings. See especially pp. 194-97 for royal letters to the clergy, nobility, and laity of 21 dioceses, asking them to adhere to the charges against Boniface, and the Table des documents, pp. 831, 833-46, listing adhesions from all parts of France.

[27] Ibid., pp. 191, 481-82. Montpellier, or, rather, the semi-independent part of Montpellier held by the king of Majorca, was the only place where there was large-scale resistance. The Dominicans were ordered to leave France, the others were ordered to appear before the king; but there is no evidence to show that either order was enforced. The abbot of Cîteaux resigned rather than support the charge against Boniface, but he was replaced, quite peacefully, by Henri, abbot of Jouy, who had been one of Philip's Treasurers (Gallia Christiana, IV, cols. 998-99).

principal column of the Church" that they saw no harm in a violent disagreement with a pope.

In summing up the scattered evidence, it is clear first of all that the "royal religion," the belief that the French king was a semi-sacred personage, was accepted everywhere, even beyond the boundaries of the kingdom. For example, the lists of the people suffering from scrofula who were touched and supposedly healed by the king show that belief in the "royal miracle" had spread far beyond the old domain and into neighboring countries.[28] And if one believed in the miracle, then it was hard to deny the king's other claims to sanctity. The people, like their king, saw no conflict between the royal religion and the Catholic faith. Such beliefs gave Philip a tremendous advantage; it was difficult to oppose a ruler who had received evident marks of divine favor and who was unquestionably a pious Christian. Direct attacks on the character and ability of the king were rare (which is one reason why Bernard Saisset's remarks about Philip's stupidity cut so deeply). The usual way of criticizing royal policy was to say that the king was being misled by evil and corrupt advisers—but what was to be done when the saintly king persisted in using unscrupulous officials? The usual answer was to ask for reform ordinances and the appointment of *enquêteurs-réformateurs*. Philip was quite ready to agree to such requests, since neither procedure required permanent changes in policy. Thus the reform ordinance of 1304 canceled recent requests for amortization payments by the Church; but within a few years heavy payments for amortization were again demanded.[29]

Glorifications of France as a holy land, the center of piety, learning, and chivalry,[30] had a less universal appeal than invocations of the royal religion. They may have had some effect on the clergy and on the upper classes of the old royal domain, but probably meant little to the poor and the uneducated or to those who still felt a strong attachment to their own province. Many

---

[28] Marc Bloch, *Les rois thaumaturges* (Paris, 1961), pp. 105-109 (based on the accounts of Renaud de Roye, published in *H.F.*, XXII, 545-65). Patients came from Brittany, Toulouse, Bordeaux, and Bigorre, from Lorraine and Savoy, from Spain, and even from Italy (at least 16).

[29] *Ord.*, I, 382, 403; see the discussion in Strayer and Taylor, pp. 36-40, on relaxation of rules about amortization. In 1314 Prouille paid 1,800 l.t. and Fontfroide 1,637 l.t. for amortization (A.N., JJ 50, fol. 28, no. 40, fol. 64, no. 99).

[30] See my "France."

subjects of the king of France did not live in "France," at least not as they defined it. To the inhabitants of Languedoc, "France" was still the Ile de France. In Toulouse, Carcassonne, and Beaucaire the king's own officials spoke of sending messengers to "France."[31] It is evident that Philip worried about the loyalty of the south. He sent *enquêteurs* there more frequently than to any other part of the realm; he paid special attention to it in his reform ordinances, and he visited it himself when it was disturbed by the activities of the Inquisition and the demands of tax collectors. Philip must have known that Nogaret's vision of a French fatherland that included the south was the vision of a convert to a new religion. Nothing indicates that many of Nogaret's fellow southerners shared his views.[32] All around the Ile de France were other provinces with their own customs and their own dialects, none of them, perhaps, quite as distinctive as those of Languedoc, but still not "French." Even Burgundy, ruled by a branch of the Capetian family and near to Paris both geographically and linguistically, had its own identity—one that persisted through the rest of the Middle Ages.

On the other hand, while the idea of France as a nation could hardly have existed, and while the idea of France as a complex of concordant cultures was just beginning to take shape, the idea of France as a political unit had some validity. There was a *regnum Francie* with definite borders (at least in theory); one was either in this *regnum* or out of it. If one was "in regno et de regno," then one had to recognize the "superiority" and the competence of the king as the final judge.[33] These principles were generally accepted, though there could be disputes about their exact meaning. Very few people who were in the *regnum* wanted to be out of it; they simply wanted it to bother them as little

[31] *C.R.*, I, nos. 9727, 21943, 13013, 13900, 13908.

[32] Emmanuel LeRoy Ladurie, *Montaillou, village occitan* (Paris, 1975), p. 442, speaking of the upper Ariège (but to some extent of all of Occitania) in the early fourteenth century: "remarquable est l'absence, dans le Sabarthès, des émanations du monde 'français' . . ."; "le rayonnement humain, migratoire et culturel des pays 'français' est très faible."

[33] "Mémoire relatif au paréage," p. 521: "omnia que sunt infra fines regni sui sint domini regis, saltim quoad protectionem et altam jurisdictionem. . . ." In demanding service in 1294 from Montpellier (held by the king of Majorca), the royal procurators said that Montpellier was "in regno et de regno et quoad superioritatem omnis ressorti et feudi et omnia jura regalia . . ." (*B.N.*, ms. lat. 9192, fol. 54v). The seneschal repeated this almost word for word.

as possible. In fact, since the kingdom of France was the strongest political unit in western Europe, and since its leaders were held in high esteem, there were some advantages, both material and psychic, in being part of that kingdom. The idea that there was an obligation to defend the *regnum* could be accepted, even by people who would never have said that they were "French."

Respect for the king and attachment to the realm would, by themselves, have generated support for Philip in his clashes with the pope. The phrases about the king being "emperor in his realm" and "recognizing no temporal superior" were not new and probably had little direct influence on anyone outside the small circle of the learned. Nevertheless, they described a basic change in attitudes. The political leadership of the papacy had collapsed; the dream of a united western Christendom had vanished. Political decisions were going to be made by secular authorities, and interference by the Church was going to be resented. Boniface VIII was quite right when he said that the laity had always been hostile to the clergy, and the background reasons for conflict were as sharp as ever in Philip's day—conflicts of jurisdiction, the questions of the liability of trading and married clerks to pay tolls and municipal taxes, the arrest and punishment of criminous clerks, the collection and appropriation of tithes. The emphatic assertion of the king's independent position and the loss of respect for papal leadership reinforced all these old animosities. As usual, the stronger the faith, the more that was expected of the ministers of the faith, and these expectations had not been satisfied. A very large part of the population was willing to believe the worst of the clergy, even of the pope. And an even larger part was delighted when the king insisted that the clergy contribute to the defense of the realm. As the clergy of Reims told the pope, they were held in contempt by laymen because they had been forbidden to grant a tenth to aid the king, and the only way to regain respectability was to remove the prohibition.[34]

To put it another way, though the arguments of political theorists reached only a few ears, there was general agreement that the king was responsible for the welfare and the security of the realm. He did not need outside help in performing his duties, and he could not permit outside interference. But if the king were responsible for the general welfare, then he had to be given the

---

[34] The French Church cannot defend itself "a nostrorum, quorum non deest copia, persecutione continua emulorum . . ." (Dupuy, *preuves*, p. 26).

same latitude of discretion that had formerly been allowed the pope. The faith would not suffer if the king opposed papal interference in France, for no one could doubt Philip's complete orthodoxy, but the kingdom might suffer if the pope were allowed to interfere. Thus, although there was some criticism of the king's treatment of the French clergy, there was practically no criticism of his dealings with the court of Rome. Some people must have been shocked by the attack at Anagni, but they have left no record of their feelings. Chroniclers who were filled with indignation over internal royal policies accepted the official version of Anagni without question: Boniface VIII got what he deserved.[35]

What was true of relations with the pope was true of relations with other foreign rulers; nobody had, or at least nobody wanted to express, any opinions on these matters. The war with England, the war with Flanders, and the negotiations with German princes and Spanish kings were completely the king's business. One might criticize the conduct, but not the necessity, of a war. Thus it was easy to convince the assembly of 1314 that a campaign against Flanders was necessary, but there was bitter criticism when Marigny ended the campaign with an inconclusive truce.

It was over internal affairs that the dialogue between ruler and subjects became most intense, and therefore left most traces in the records. Philip needed more money than any of his predecessors; he wanted to increase the jurisdiction of his courts; he wanted to make ordinances, especially on economic problems, that would be enforced everywhere in the realm. Taxes were hard to accept in a country where taxes had never been paid before. Many people were troubled by interference with neighborhood courts, especially those who drew a profit from the courts. Even men who had no proprietary interests to protect had to balance the chance of better administration of justice in royal courts against the certainty of greater expenses and delays. Nobody liked the restrictions on exports, the manipulation of the currency, or the rigorous ordinances regulating possession of foreign coins and precious metals that were necessary if the king were to profit from the manipulation. Many people were annoyed by the laws that required substantial payments if land were transferred from nobles to clerics or commoners: the nobles might lose a sale; the clerics might find it expensive to accept a gift; the commoners might find investment in land unprofitable. Besides these griev-

[35] See Ruiz, "Reaction to Anagni."

ances against policies, there were complaints against the way in which the policies were enforced. Royal officials could be too rigid in interpreting the law, taking advantage of technicalities in order to gain more money for the king. They could be too harsh in securing obedience, for example, by putting a horde of "eaters" (*comestores*) into property taken into the king's hand— men who would consume a year's store of provisions in a few weeks.[36] Royal officials could be corrupt, perhaps not as often as was generally believed, but often enough to justify general suspicion of their honesty.

From all levels of society came protests against the internal policies of the king and the behavior of his officials. Great lords like the count of Foix and the king of Majorca,[37] influential bishops like Guillaume le Maire of Angers,[38] urban officials, chroniclers, and even rural communities[39] complained that rights and privileges were being ignored and that services or payments that were not due were being required. The more ill-tempered opponents added that, even if there were legitimate reasons for the demands for money, most of the sums collected were lost by the inefficiency or corruptness of royal officials.[40] These complaints were not purely verbal; there was sporadic rioting against taxation in

[36] Le livre de Guillaume le Maire, pp. 359-60; H.L., x, col. 299; Baudouin, ed., Lettres inédites, nos. 5, 17, 54, 139.

[37] H.L., IX, 145, 148, 255, 283, X, cols. 258-64, 285, 287, 289, 328-33, 370-72, 376, 405-7, 453, 485 (complaints of the count of Foix); B.N., ms. lat. 9192, fols. 51, 53, 54, 55v, 59, 62, 71v, etc. (protests by agents of the king of Majorca).

[38] Le livre de Guillaume le Maire, pp. 322-30, 353-59.

[39] The consuls of Montpellier joined in all the protests of the king of Majorca and often initiated protests of their own (B.N., ms. lat. 9192). See also Baudouin, ed., Lettres inédites, nos. 137, 141-44, 156-57, 160, 171 (complaints of consuls of Toulouse); Archives anciennes de la Ville de St. Quentin, nos. 188, 211, 214, 224 (complaints of mayor and council of St. Quentin); A.N., J 892, no. 3, J 896, nos. 8, 9, 25, 29, J 1024, no. 38, J 1029, no. 2, J 1031, nos. 7, 8, 9, J 1034, nos. 46, 47 (complaints of small communities in the south). There are many more examples in all these categories.

[40] Le livre de Guillaume le Maire, pp. 360, 364. Geoffroi de Paris claimed that the king's evil servants got most of the taxes on the Church and that most of the goods of the Jews were kept by the king's men (H.F., XXII, 97, 119). Geoffroi also said that the king demanded much but received little because his agents were corrupt—"de cent solz n'avoit que un denier" (Six Historical Poems of Geoffroi de Paris, ed. W. H. Storer and C. A. Rochedieu, University of North Carolina Studies in Romance Languages, no. 16 [Chapel Hill, 1960], pp. 66-67).

Champagne and in the bishopric of Langres.[41] Languedoc was said to be on the verge of rebellion in 1303.[42] In 1292 the lower classes in Rouen, angered by a sales-tax, broke into the house of the receiver and besieged the men holding the Exchequer.[43] There are many other examples of attacks on royal officials.[44]

Still, for over ten years (1294-1305) Philip and his officials were able to impose policies that were greatly disliked. The currency was overvalued in spite of increasing protests from the landed classes, whose real income naturally fell. "Good money" was not restored until 1306. General taxes were collected in seven of these years, and the last of the great taxes (the levy of 1304) produced more income than any royal tax taken down to the crisis of 1356.[45] Amortization and *nouveaux acquêts* (payments for transfer of noble land to clergy and commoners) was being collected at a high rate. Quarrels over rights of jurisdiction between the king and some of his prelates and nobles continued. All this while, Philip was very near to being beaten by the Flemings and very near to being excommunicated by the pope.

The fact that Philip could press so hard in such dangerous circumstances proves that the royal religion was more than a court cult. The people did revere their king, even when he was following policies that they disliked. Philip's success also demonstrates the flexibility and political skill of the government. Careful negotiation and timely compromise calmed most of the people who were offended by the king's demands. As I showed in my study of Philip's taxation, as long as taxpayers admitted their liability, they were often able to make their own terms wih the collectors.[46]

[41] In 1296 there were "plures recusias a collectoribus qui voluerunt levare dictam quinquagesimam in ballivia calvimontis," and the same tax could be collected in the bishopric of Langres only "per vim et violentiam armorum" (Mignon, nos. 1327, 1292).

[42] *H.F.*, xx, 675 (Chronicle of St. Denis).

[43] Ibid., p. 575; *Olim*, ii, 356.

[44] See *Olim*, iii: the men of Nant who had resisted the collectors of the last subsidy were amerced in 1308 (p. 260); the abbot and monks of Nerlac attacked with arms a royal sergeant guarding a property in the king's hand (before 1308) (p. 265); the men of Montbrison attacked collectors of a subvention at some date before April 1309 (p. 362); the royal *prévôt* of Laon was injured in a riot by the men of Châlons-sur-Marne, who were protesting a royal ordinance restoring "good money" (p. 610). Attacks on royal sergeants are too numerous to list.

[45] Henneman, pp. 352-53.

[46] Strayer and Taylor, pp. 45, 50-55, 62, 68.

The first tax imposed by the king, a sales-tax of a penny in the pound, was commuted to lump-sum payments by many towns. Paris, for example, paid 12,500 l.t. a year for eight years.[47] The southern provinces usually changed property- or income-taxes into hearth-taxes, and the southern towns often went one step further and settled for a lump-sum payment.[48] During the period of greatest strain, the collectors were told to ignore the official rate and make the best terms they could with the inhabitants of their districts. Nobles were conciliated with a share of up to 50 percent of the taxes paid by their men. The clergy were conciliated by the grant of privileges, notably the great privilege of 1304, which was a reward for the grant of a double tenth. For laymen in general there was an important ordinance for reform in 1303 and special grants to Toulouse and Carcassonne in 1304.[49]

In short, Philip was well aware that taxation was unpopular, and he did his best to disarm the opposition. He and his officials were increasingly willing to negotiate with individuals who objected to the kind of tax or the amount of tax that had been decreed. This process of negotiation reached its peak in 1304,[50] and it is significant that the subvention of 1304 was the most productive of all of Philip's taxes.

Nevertheless, the fact that such extensive negotiations were necessary in 1304 was a warning to Philip that he had better give his subjects a respite. After the king had gained his chief objectives—recognition of his sovereignty in Aquitaine and an alliance with England, an advantageous peace with Flanders, and the election of a friendly pope—he was very cautious about imposing new taxes. He did try to extend to subjects not directly under the king the customary aid for marrying his daughter (ordained in 1309), but he allowed those who felt aggrieved by these demands to compromise with his agents or to argue their case in the Parlement.[51] He made a similar attempt to expand the aid for knighting his oldest son (1313) but again did not push his claim with any

---

[47] Ibid., pp. 12-13.   [48] Ibid., pp. 51, 54-55, 68.

[49] Ibid., pp. 50, 62 (instructions to collectors), 47, 48, 54 (nobles), 39-40 (clergy); *Ord.*, I, 357 (for the realm), 392-94, 399, 402 (for Toulouse and Carcassonne).

[50] Strayer and Taylor, pp. 66-72.

[51] *Olim*, II, 508; A.N., J 356, nos. 1-14, JJ 42A, fols. 97-97v, no. 72. Professor Elizabeth A. R. Brown is preparing a study of this aid and the aid for knighting Louis of Navarre. She very kindly allowed me to read her first draft of this monograph.

great energy,[52] probably because he was trying at the same time to impose a general tax to pay for a renewal of the war with Flanders. This tax, in turn, was not pushed very hard, and it was completely canceled when a truce was made.[53] It was only in the last year of the reign, when the Flemish war broke out again, that Philip made a real effort to collect a tax that might have ranked with those of 1303 and 1304. He was clearly uneasy about this decision; he took the unusual step of calling a meeting of representatives of the towns to hear an explanation of the need for a tax. Philip's uneasiness was justified. As soon as a new truce with Flanders was made, a clamor arose for the cancellation of the tax. Philip had some justification for continuing to collect the subvention. He had raised an army that had invaded Flanders, and this was an expensive operation; but for once in his life he had misjudged the temper of his people. Leagues were formed demanding the revocation of the tax, and, in what was almost the last act of his life, Philip accepted their demands.[54]

This one failure should be balanced against ten years of remarkable success. The French (unlike the English) had never paid general taxes before. Philip persuaded them that they should pay taxes, and he collected substantial sums during both the Gascon and the Flemish wars. He showed great skill in modifying the rate and type of taxation to meet the objections of his subjects. The cancellation of the tax of 1314 was an episode; the establishment of a tax system was permanent.

Philip was less successful in securing acquiescence to another financial policy: manipulation of the currency. By overvaluing his coins, especially the *gros tournois*, he made enormous profits from his mints, probably more than he made from general taxation.[55] But this overvaluation hurt everyone who had a fixed

[52] Petit et al., pp. 128, 131-32; Longnon, ed., *Documents*, III, 138, 140, 141.

[53] *H.F.*, XXII, 140; Ménard, *Histoire de Nismes*, II, *preuves*, pp. 12, 17; *C.R.*, II, no. 27496 (account of a collector in Toulouse: "De subventione levavimus 471 l. 12 s. 6 d.t. . . . . Nichil plus levavimus, quia habuimus preceptum de cessando").

[54] Strayer and Taylor, pp. 83-87; Artonne, pp. 18-21, 164-65; *Ord.*, I, 580 (the cancellation of the tax, no date, but between 16 November, when the tax was merely suspended in some places, and 29 November, when Philip died).

[55] Borrelli de Serres, *Recherches*, II, 445-46, 549, and App. D 1. Borrelli estimates that in 1299 the profit from the mints was over 1,200,000 l.t. I have estimated that the most profitable tax, the subvention of 1304, brought

income, and especially those who were dependent on fixed rents for land—that is, the nobility, the clergy, and a considerable part of the bourgeoisie. Some bankers were able to make a profit on exchange transactions, and peasants who paid money rents were certainly better off. But bankers were unpopular, and peasants had no political influence. The articulate sections of the population were outraged. There was little that the king could do to mollify the opposition. He could not explain that inflation was easier to arrange than taxation, first, because he probably did not think in these terms, and, second, because to admit that inflation was only disguised taxation would have made it more difficult to collect taxes. He could not increase the wages of one of the most disgruntled groups, the nobles serving in the army, because this would have consumed most of the profit from the overvaluation. He had no way of increasing fixed incomes of the rest of the nobility and of the clergy, even if he had so desired. Given the limited administrative resources of the government, he could not have fixed prices at a prewar figure. Data are scanty, but grain prices seem to have risen about in proportion to the overvaluation of the currency, while wages remained constant.[56]

A real dialogue between the king and his subjects on the currency problem was thus impossible. The propertied classes simply demanded, over and over again, a return to the "good money of St. Louis." The king could only promise that he would make the change as soon as he could. The clergy insisted strongly on "good money" when they made their grants to the king in 1303 and 1304, and Benedict XI reiterated their demands.[57] The nobility were equally insistent. A Sienese banker wrote to his home office in 1305 that as soon as peace was made with Flanders, the prelates and the barons were going to force Philip to reform the currency.[58]

---

in about 735,000 l.t., and this was in currency that was more overvalued than that of 1299.

[56] Strayer, "Costs and Profits of War," pp. 288-89.

[57] Strayer and Taylor, pp. 35, 38, 40, 100, 102; Mignon, no. 796 (a two-year tenth granted by Benedict XI "pro reductione monete ad suum pondus debitum et antiquum").

[58] The Council that approved the tax of 1304 insisted that the king reform the currency by November—and these councillors were devoted servants of the king (Ord., I, 383, 408). A similar demand was made by the towns of the bailliage of Rouen on 1 May 1304 (Boutaric, ed., "Docu-

The Sienese banker proved to be a good prophet. "Good money" was restored in 1306. As might have been (but apparently was not) expected, the sudden change caused a new set of problems. People who had leased property or contracted debts during the period of overvalued currency now found themselves bound to pay their creditors in coins that had only one-third of their former value. There were riots in Paris; at one point Philip was forced to take refuge in the strongly fortified house of the Templars.[59] The story that it was on this occasion that the king became aware, and therefore covetous, of the enormous wealth of the Temple is patently absurd. Philip could not have used the Temple as his bank for many years without having some idea of its resources. But it was a humiliating experience for a ruler so conscious of his dignity, and Philip may have felt that his bankers could have done a better job in preparing for the dangers of the transition period.

Unrest subsided after royal ordinances scaled down debts contracted during the time of overvalued currency.[60] Philip was very cautious after this experience. He tampered with the currency only once more in his reign. The variation was slight: in 1311 a small coin was overvalued by 20 percent, but again there was a storm of protest, and Philip retreated in 1313.[61] One can hardly speak of public opinion in the early fourteenth century, but for centuries the people of western Europe had been very sensitive to changes in the currency, and many rulers had given them guarantees of a stable coinage. In Normandy, for example, the duke had given up his right to alter the currency in return for a payment of 12 d. from each nonnoble household every three years.[62] Philip must have been aware of this tradition, and he certainly had been concerned by the criticisms of the "weak mon-

---

ments inédits," no. 21). For the banker's letter, see Paoli and Piccolomini, eds., *Lettere volgari del secolo xiii*, in Vol. cxvi of *Scelta di curiosità letterarie inedite o rare*, pp. 71-72.

[59] *H.F.*, xxi, 27,619. There was also a riot at Laon (*Olim*, iii, 610).

[60] *Ord.*, i, 444, 446, 456.

[61] The trick consisted in striking a coin worth only a penny *tournois* and giving it the value of a penny *parisis*. Since the old ratio between *tournois* and *parisis* was 5 to 4, a buyer should have paid 1¼ pennies *tournois* for an object worth 1 penny *parisis*. See *Ord.*, i, 477, 525. As one chronicler put it, "tournois et parisis eurent un pris."

[62] Tardif, *Coutumiers de Normandie*, ii, 40. See Thomas N. Bisson, *Conservation of Coinage* (Oxford, 1979).

ey" of the early 1300s. He had had to risk disapproval during the years of crisis, but there was less need to take such a risk in 1311. Still, as in the case of taxation, it was the innovation, not the final retreat, that set a precedent. Philip had shown that tampering with the currency did not create unbearable problems with the privileged classes and that it did provide a means of meeting extraordinary expenses. His successors followed his example.

Next to the financial demands of the crown (and often closely associated with them), the behavior of royal officials caused the largest number of complaints. The king's men were accused of exceeding their authority, of ignoring group and individual privileges, of enforcing royal rights in such a heavy-handed way that they collected more than was actually owed the king, and of accepting bribes and practicing extortion. As in the case of taxation, the complaints came from all classes. Prelates, barons, and towns protested that their rights of justice were being ignored, that services were being demanded that were not owed, and that royal ordinances were being enforced in areas where the king had no authority, for example, in Montpellier.[63] Peasant communities complained that they were forced to pay enormous fines for failure to give service or to pay servile dues (*casalgia*) to the king.[64] Commissions to recover lost or overlooked royal rights were common, and every time they were issued they caused bad feeling and often prolonged litigation.

Payments for transferring land to the Church or to nonnobles caused problems for all classes. It was recent, but accepted, law that the king could demand compensation when land held of him passed to religious establishments or to *roturiers*, since this deprived him of military service and the profits of relief and wardship.[65] But there could be arguments about the value of the land, its status before the gift or sale, and the status of the purchaser

[63] B.N., ms. lat. 9192, is almost entirely concerned with the protests of the town against the demands of royal officials; see, for example, fols. 9-12, and the long list of complaints on fols. 51-52v (published in *H.L.*, x, cols. 422-26). See also *Le livre de Guillaume le Maire*, in which Guillaume, bishop of Angers, registered his grievances.

[64] A.N., J 896, J 1031, J 1034.

[65] The basic ordinance was in 1275, but Philip the Fair made it much more rigid in 1291-1292 and increased the amounts to be paid, for example, from three years' income to six years' income for land bought by the Church that had been held directly of the king (*Ord.*, I, 303, 323). To make things worse, the new rates were doubled for Périgord, Rouergue, Carcassonne, and Beaucaire. Naturally, resentment was greatest in these districts.

(since nobility was not yet clearly defined). Complicating these problems was the fact that the king was very free with grants of exemption. Most men with connections at court could easily secure priviliges allowing them to give land for pious purposes without payment.[66] Nonnoble royal officials (even petty officers in the provinces) were allowed to acquire noble land freely or for minimum fines.[67] In painful contrast, at the same time that exemptions were pouring out of Paris, the provinces were full of royal agents trying to discover who owed how much for amortization and *nouveaux acquêts* (acquisitions by nonnobles). The *enquêteurs* were often asked to investigate these problems; so were seneschals and other high-ranking officials. Even a great lord of the Council, Hugues de la Celle, who was the virtual viceroy of Saintonge and Poitou, spent much of his time seeing that the fines were properly assessed and collected.[68] Perhaps the most annoying combination of functions came when collectors of taxes were told to insist at the same time on fines for *nouveaux acquêts*. This was very nearly blackmail, since willing payment of the tax might cut down the amount of the fine. A particularly shocking example of this practice came in 1309, when Philip was trying to collect the aid for marrying his daughter from men who were not his immediate subjects, a practice of very doubtful legality. In both Quercy and in Saintonge-Poitou the collectors were also taking payments for *nouveaux acquêts*.[69] The trick worked quite

[66] See the grants listed under the headings "amortissements" and "acquisitions par les non-nobles" in the index to Fawtier's *Registres*. There are over 400 free amortizations. Considering that there are only 2,288 documents in the registers, this shows how easy it was to obtain such a grant; about one-fifth of the royal letters recorded there are amortizations.

[67] It is not surprising that Philippe le Convers, godson and favorite of the king received many exemptions (Fawtier, et al., eds., *Registres*, nos. 356, 1220, 1470, 1478). It is also understandable that bankers like the Chauchats and the Gaytes, who performed many financial operations for the king, received privileges (ibid., nos. 539, 730). But Philippe des Fontaines, *viguier* of Toulouse, Gui de Noys, ex-procurator of Bourges, Guillaume Gendrat, keeper of the seal of St. Pierre-le-Moutier, Guillaume Faure, royal *avocat* of Saintonge, and Raymond Rigaud, judge of Millau, were not very important officials, and yet all of them were allowed to acquire noble lands freely (ibid., nos. 1212, 1466, 1474, 1608, 1995).

[68] *Archives historiques du Poitou*, XI, nos. 33-34 and p. 65n; Fawtier, et al., eds., *Registres*, index under Hugues de la Celle, "commissaire aux francs-fiefs et nouveaux acquêts" (47 entries).

[69] A.N., J 356, nos. 7, 8, 14 (for Périgord-Quercy). Hugues de la Celle was *enquêteur*, collector of fines for *nouveaux acquêts*, and collector of the

successfully in Saintonge-Poitou, where Hugues de la Celle received the astonishingly large sum of 19,000 l.t. for the marriage aid, an amount about equal (allowing for the deflation of 1306) to what the two *sénéchaussées* had paid for the much more legitimate war tax of 1304.[70] The results for Quercy are unknown.

There was certainly grumbling about fines for amortization and *nouveaux acquêts* (it was a grievance of the towns of Quercy in 1309), but only the clergy were able to do much about the problem. They were better organized than the laity, and when Philip bypassed the pope and asked for direct grants of tenths by the French Church, they were in a strong bargaining position. In 1304, when the king was in great need of money, he gave permanent exemption from amortization payments for land acquired for church buildings or cemeteries. This had been a special grievance of the clergy, since such land produced no income to compensate for the fine. In addition, Philip freely amortized all acquisitions up to 1304, though nothing was said about payments already made.[71] These concessions proved to be more helpful than they appeared; the bishops paid relatively little for amortization in the years immediately following 1304, and the monasteries no more than 200 to 500 l.t. at a time. By the end of the reign, however, large payments began to reappear, for example, 1,800 l.t. from Prouille and 1,637 l.t. from Fontfroide in 1314.[72] Once again Philip had shown that he was sensitive to the opinion of a politically active group, and once again he had shown that he knew how to make concessions that conciliated his critics without abandoning his principles.

---

marriage aid in Saintonge-Poitou (*Archives historiques du Poitou*, xi, 65-66, 68-70; Mignon, nos. 1573-75).

[70] See Mignon, no. 1575, for the marriage aid. Saintonge-Poitou paid 46,000 l.t. in 1304, worth about 15,500 l.t. in the money of 1309-1310 (H.F., xxi, 566). But La Marche and Angoumois were specifically included in the payment of Saintonge-Poitou for the marriage aid, since they were then in the king's hand; they would have paid less in 1304, when they were under thir own count. Also Hugues may have included fines for *nouveaux acquêts in his total*; La Rochelle paid 4,500 l.t. for *nouveaux acquêts* and exemption from the marriage aid (A.N., JJ 46, fol. 136v, no. 246 [published in *Archives historiques de la Saintonge*, xii (1884), no. 35]).

[71] *Ord.*, i, 382, 406; Strayer and Taylor, pp. 38-40, 101.

[72] A.N., JJ 50, fol. 28, no. 40 (Prouille), fol. 64, no. 99 (Fontfroide). Prouille was definitely out of favor; it was the one monastery that paid a really large fine in the years of peace—500 l. toulousain (1,000 l.t.) in 1309 (A.N., JJ 41, fol. 38, no. 59).

There is a considerable difference between Philip's treatment of the clergy and his treatment of bourgeois and peasant acquirers of noble land. There was no perceptible slackening of pressure on these classes at any time, and a noticeable increase in the number and size of payments in the last few years of the reign. Part of this increase was owing to the activity of Hugues de la Celle, who squeezed the bourgeois of Saintonge-Poitou unmercifully.[73] But Hugues was not responsible for one of the largest fines on record, a payment of 4,500 l.t. by Mirepoix and 44 other communities, obtained by Alain de Lamballe and Aimeri du Cros, who were almost as active in Carcassonne as Hughes was in Poitou.[74]

The difference is not surprising. Philip did respect the Church (after his own fashion), but he had little respect for the bourgeoisie, and even less for the peasants. Moreover, the nonnobles did not have the permanent organization that the Church enjoyed in its provincial and national councils; they had to form ad hoc alliances to bring any pressure to bear. This was done with some success in Quercy in 1309[75] and apparently by small communities in Carcassonne in 1314,[76] but not in Saintonge-Poitou, where Hugues de la Celle was able to avoid collective settlements. Elsewhere, cases were too scattered to have made organized opposition possible. The citizens of Toulouse were able to prove that they had the right to acquire noble land freely,[77] but they were unusually privileged. In most cases, each individual and each community had to make the best bargain they could with the king's men.

Most of the chroniclers and many churchmen were convinced that royal officials were corrupt and oppressive. Oppressive they

[73] See the references in notes 68 and 70 above. But although Hugues took many fines, few of them were over 100 l.t., and only one (La Rochelle) was over 1,000 l.t.

[74] A.N., JJ 50, fol. 3v, no. 2 (in 1314). Besides the 4,500 l.t. from the Mirepoix group, they also took 1,000 l.t. from Lapenne and eight other communities (A.N., JJ 50, fol. 17, no. 18), and 1,637 l.t. from Fontfroide (see note 72 above). Apparently there was pressure to raise money for the Flemish war.

[75] A.N., J 356, nos. 7, 8, 14. Toulouse gained a respite, pending inquiry, in 1305 but won a partial exemption only in 1324. (Philippe Wolff, "La noblesse toulousaine," in Ph. Contammine, ed., La noblesse au Moyen Age [Paris, 1976], p. 170.)

[76] See note 74 above. The total sums were large, but the 5,500 l.t. was spread over 54 communities, almost exactly 100 l.t. per village.

[77] Ord., xi, 390 (25 January 1298 [n.s.]).

were, as will be shown below, though it must be remembered that what seemed to a subject to be oppression might seem to the king to be laudable zeal. The charge of corruption is more difficult to document, especially for the higher members of the government. Certainly the men closest to the king profited enormously from gifts, pensions, and (for the clerks) ecclesiastical benefices, but taking advantage of the king's favor can scarcely be called corruption. Philippe le Convers (Philippe de Villepreux) had a large income from his benefices; with this and with some not very large gifts from the king he was able to build up sizable holdings in Normandy.[78] Yet the forest administration, which Philippe headed, was one of the best-managed branches of the government, and there is no indication that Philippe increased his wealth by misusing his official position.[79] Vast sums of money passed through the hands of the commanders of the royal armies, but almost all of it was spent for legitimate purposes. There are not only detailed accounts of expenditures but also hundreds of receipts given by individual knights and squires.[80] There was undoubtedly low-level graft in securing supplies for the army (and for the navy), but the chief complaint against the purveyors was not that they were embezzling the king's money but that they were taking provisions without paying for them.[81] Philip's

[78] Pegues, pp. 132-34.

[79] Pegues, p. 138, thinks that there were shortages in Phillippe's accounts, but the entries in Mignon (nos. 2245-48, 2257, 2259) seem to be no more than the normal arrears that occur in all such accounts. Any officer working in the field had to keep back some money for current expenses. The final account by his executor (3 November 1328) has Philippe owing 1,233 l. and the Treasury owing him 891 l.t. (ibid., no. 2257). This is normal; most *baillis* kept a working balance of about 500 l.t. instead of sending all receipts to the Treasury.

[80] Many such receipts may be found in B.N., mss. Clairembault nos. 14, 35, 63, 55, 57.

[81] In asking for a new subvention the king promised immediate payment for supplies (*Ord.*, I, 370), but in three months the king had to ask owners of food to accept promises of future payment (A.N., JJ 36, no. 73). The same thing happened in 1304, and some food was seized by force (A.N., JJ 36, no. 74). In 1299 sergeants in the *bailliage* of Sens were not only commandeering supplies but also taking bribes to let subjects escape such seizures (*Olim*, III, 17). In 1302 the king had to order the seneschal of Toulouse to pay for some wine that had been seized so that further complaints could be avoided (B.N., ms. Clairembault 210, no. 25). Purveyors of army supplies were accused of graft in Carcassonne in 1302 (*H.L.*, x, col. 414). The king himself was worried in 1302 about his purveyors in

financial officers were not popular, but none of them, from Biche and Mouche through the Templars to Marigny, was blatantly dishonest in handling the king's money. Lesser men may have been guilty of small peculations, but, unless there was a gigantic conspiracy to alter all the accounts, receipts and expenditures match so closely that there could not have been any large-scale looting of the Treasury. The king did not always spend his money wisely, but he knew how his money was spent.

What was true of the financial offices was true of other branches of the government. The decisions of the Parlement show few signs of corrupt influence,[82] and no contemporary suggested that the judges could be bribed. The Council seems to have been equally honest. Its members, especially those sent on missions abroad, received (and at times gave) presents to foreign rulers. This practice was considered perfectly respectable then (and for centuries thereafter), and in most cases it is clear that a present did not corrupt the judgement of the recipient. Yves de Loudéac may have been an exception, but I have suggested above that the king had already decided to surrender the Val d'Aran and that Yves saw no harm in taking a present from the king of Aragon in return for a recommendation that he knew would be approved.[83] Yves certainly could not have believed that a very minor councillor like himself could have swayed the opinions of the great lords of the Council; he must have known that he was doing what Philip wanted.

At the local level the record is less clean. Royal officials of all ranks, from seneschals to sergeants, were frequently accused, and occasionally convicted, of misconduct in office. The *enquêteurs*, though they often seem to have been too interested in recovering royal rights, did not entirely forget their original duty of receiving complaints against royal officials. They were well aware that there could be abuses of power, and they were willing to accept accusations from men of very low status—Norman peasants or southern village communities.[84] Although the machinery for col-

---

Senlis, who, he says, took horses, carts, and food that the army never received (A.N., JJ 36, fol. 12, no. 38).

[82] A rare example of corruption is the case (1314) of Guillaume Boucel, a king's clerk and a *rapporteur* of *enquêtes*. He took bribes for giving litigants information about their cases (*Olim*, II, 590). This, however, would not necessarily have led to a corrupt judgement. See above, pp. 216-17.

[83] See above, p. 29.

[84] Formeville, pp. 517-28; C.R., I, nos. 12734-42 (Carcassonne, 1303).

lecting complaints was reasonably efficient, convictions were rare and punishments light. Some men, such as Pierre Peitavi, *juge-mage* of Carcassonne, were simply demoted; Pierre became a district judge.[85] Others were fined and removed from office, but even such punishments were not always definitive. Guichard de Marzi, dismissed as seneschal of Toulouse and fined for "excès" in 1301, returned to favor and ended his career as a member of the Parlement and (a crowning irony) as an *enquêteur*.[86] The case of Pierre Roche, judge of Minervois, has already been mentioned: condemned in 1310, pardoned and ennobled in 1314, executed in 1318. He must have taken graft on a large scale; his property, confiscated after his death, was sold for 11,000 l.t.[87] But he was one of the very few royal officials to suffer such a fate.

At the very lowest level—sergeants, forest guards, and other minor officers—there was, inevitably, a certain amount of petty graft. No government has ever been successful in eradicating this sort of corruption, and yet this kind of corruption touches the largest part of the population and creates the most widespread resentment. Langlois collected some typical complaints against the sergeants in his article on the *enquêteurs*.[88] Guillaume le Maire, bishop of Angers, complained bitterly about these "ministri tartarei."[89] But, as was the case with higher officials, the most usual punishment was an amercement or an order to return money or goods that had been wrongfully exacted. Very few sergeants were dismissed from office. This leniency did less harm to relations between the king and his people than might have been expected. No one expected these minor officials to be very honest, and a good many people knew that the agents of the great barons were no better than those of the king. Guillaume le Maire, for

[85] Strayer, *Gens de justice*, pp. 104-5, 194.

[86] *H.F.*, xxiv, *262; *H.L.*, x, col. 384; A.N., JJ 46, fol. 132, no. 238. However, the *bailli* of Amiens, Hugues de Filains, who was removed from office and fined for corruption in 1311, never held office again; see *Olim*, iii, 578, 669. In 1303 the king had to encourage his *enquêteurs* in Carcassonne to do their duty in spite of rumors that no royal official would lose his job because of the *enquête* and that any accusers of officials would be punished (*H.L.*, x, col. 411).

[87] See above, p. 207.

[88] Langlois, "Doléances recueillies par les enquêteurs," pp. 64-86. See also Formeville, "Réformateurs."

[89] *Le livre de Guillaume le Maire*, p. 322. They are worse than wolves (p. 365).

example, had just as much trouble with the sergeants of Charles of Valois as he did with those of the king.[90] Nothing could be gained by exchanging the lordship of a baron for that of the king, and at least the king had a procedure for receiving complaints against dishonest officials.

Another mitigating factor was that the complainants were not always in the right, and some of them must have known it. A good many cases of apparent extortion turn out to be cases of distraint, that is, goods were seized to force their owners to pay money owed to the king. Admittedly, distraints were often made in an unnecessarily harsh, and even brutal way, but the profits went to the king and not to the official. A famous case is that of the raid made through Toulouse by Pierre de Latilly and Raoul de Breuilly in 1297-1298. They were to search out and collect all sums owed to the king, especially by the men of the towns and villages of the region. The regular procedure seems to have been to send in sergeants, arrest or threaten to arrest some leading men, seize goods of recalcitrant debtors, evict their families, and cause such trouble that the consuls in the end would promise to pay large sums (thousands of pounds in most cases and over 48,000 l.t. in all) in order to be cleared of all possible debts to the king. There are more complaints about this raid than about any other action by royal officials.[91] The protests were so great that an investigation was ordered, and the detailed testimony that was taken persuaded the king that a mistake had been made. Raoul and Pierre denied using unnecessary violence, but they did not deny that pressure had been used in order to obtain payments and promises of payments. Philip abolished *casalagium* (the principal excuse for the fines) in return for an annual payment of a sou for each sextariate of land, and he canceled all penalties imposed by Latilly and Breuilly.[92] But even in this case the king's

[90] Ibid., pp. 332, 335, 341, 349, 391.

[91] They accounted for well over 4,000 l.t. from these sources (Mignon, nos. 2392-93). The total mentioned in the complaints is 48,200 l.t.! (A.N., J 892, nos. 3, 3 bis, J 896, nos. 8, 9, 25, 29, 34, 37, 40, J 1024, no. 38, J 1029, no. 2, J 1031, nos. 7, 8, 9, 10, J 1033, nos. 9, 10, 11, 38, J 1034, nos. 46, 47.) This is an astonishing figure, and one wonders whether anyone ever expected it to be collected. The whole *sénéchaussée* of Toulouse was assessed only 79,479 l.t. for the heavy tax of 1304 (Mignon, no. 1549), and inflation had gone much further in 1304 than it had in 1298. But even though the fines were canceled, they had caused great indignation in the area.

[92] B.N., ms. Doat 156, fols. 81-85.

agents had not asked the money for themselves (though their sergeants had doubtless extorted some payments for favorable treatment). As a result, the repudiation of their acts did not harm the career of either man. Latilly became one of Philip's closest advisers, was made bishop of Châlons in 1313, and succeeded Nogaret as Keeper in the same year. Raoul de Breuilly was an older man who had been in royal service at least since 1278, when he was *bailli* of Caux. He sat in the Parlements of 1299 and 1300 and then probably retired. The inquiry helped to calm the people of the Toulousain by redressing their immediate grievances, but they cannot quickly have forgotten the extreme aggressiveness of the king's officials. It is not surprising that this is the region that was said to have been on the edge of revolt in 1303.

Nevertheless, excessive zeal in collecting royal revenues is the exact opposite of corruption, and one wonders why the charges of dishonesty were so widely accepted. Granting that the evidence is not as complete as it might be, it is still difficult to find large sums of money disappearing or turning up in the wrong hands. Even expense accounts—the great refuge of the semi-honest official—do not seem padded. They were carefully audited; some items were questioned or disallowed, but no great sums were involved.[93] In fact, Philip's upper-level officials seem to have been remarkably honest, by medieval standards. It is noteworthy that, even in court intrigues, charges of corruption were not commonly used. Guichard of Troyes was the one official whose career was ruined by accusations of taking a bribe, and Guichard was probably innocent.[94] Nogaret was accused of using wrongful methods to make the king rich, not himself.[95] Latilly, who had handled a great deal of money in his day, was accused of murder, not embezzlement. Even Marigny could not be convicted on charges of malversation; it took some very dubious evidence about the practice of magic and sorcery to bring him

[93] At the end of an expense account of Guillaume de Plaisians it is noted that his wages for the period when he was traveling at the king's expense should be deducted (*C.R.*, 1, no. 6694, footnote). Gilles de Remy charged 20 l. 7 s.p. for his robes on a trip to Rome (no. 6697); the footnote asks whether he also drew his money for "pallia" (robes) at court at the same time. Or, to take a less conspicuous person, the payment of 15 l.t. by the seneschal of Carcassonne to a messenger sent to France is questioned because the seneschal had already entered a lump sum of 78 l. 5 s. for messengers in his expense account (ibid., nos. 12938, 12952 and footnote).

[94] See the Appendix to Chapter IV.

[95] See above, Chapter I, note 75.

to the gallows.[96] In short, one could profit from being in the service of the king without having to steal his money, and the higher the rank, the less need there was to be dishonest.

It seems probable that the real difficulty for the chroniclers and other writers who expressed the opinion of the middle groups in each class (lesser nobles, middle clergy, middle bourgeoisie) was that the king had taken a great deal of money from his subjects and had gained very little in return. The war of Aquitaine had cost well over a million pounds; the result was a temporary, though useful, alliance with England and a not very meaningful or profitable recognition of Philip's position as overlord of the duchy. The war with Flanders must have been at least as expensive as the war of Aquitaine (the accounts are less complete), and it did bring some profit—a large indemnity (never fully paid) and the annexation of Lille and Douai. On the other hand, while the alliance with England was still firm at the end of the reign, it was evident by 1313 that the Flemings had not accepted their defeat and that new campaigns in Flanders would be necessary. Money-fiefs (pensions, in effect) to the prelates and princes of the Empire had assured their neutrality, if not their help, in the wars with England and Flanders and had also prevented any violent reaction to the annexation of small territories along the border and to the completion of the process of making Lyon a French city.[97] But Philip had gained no real influence on major developments in German politics, and the total cost of the pensions was far greater than the income from the annexations. Thus it is not surprising that the constantly repeated question of the chroniclers was: Where did all the money go? The king has had his tenths and his fiftieths, his sales-taxes and his aids, the wealth of the Jews, the Templars, and the Lombards, and yet he still needs more.[98] Ordinary people did not understand how expensive

---

[96] Petit, *Charles de Valois*, pp. 151-53; Favier, *Marigny*, pp. 209-14.

[97] Lyon, *From Fief to Indenture*, pp. 213-14; Kern, ed., *Acta Imperii*, nos. 90, 114, 148, 152, 157, 279, 303, 307, 309.

[98] Geoffroi de Paris puts this speech in the mouths of the barons (*H.F.*, XXI, 153):

> Or as tu eu la centiesme
> Et puis après le cinquantiesme
> Et pris tant de subventions! . . .
> Rois, encores as tu eu
> Au moins l'ont ta gent receu
> Des Templiers et l'argent et l'or
> Que doit estre en ton trésor

the new type of warfare was, with larger armies, well-paid soldiers (especially the nobles), and longer campaigns. All that they could see was that Philip had taken millions of pounds for defense of the realm, and yet the realm was still not secure. The obvious conclusion was that corrupt officials had pocketed most of the money. This conclusion certainly had something to do with the opposition to taxation that smouldered throughout the reign and blazed into organized resistance in 1314.

Complaints about corruption were easy to believe, especially as they had some foundation in fact. Minor officials were numerous, ubiquitous, and not very honest. Higher officials had higher standards, but they were also more visible: one corrupt seneschal or judge could give a bad reputation to the administrative staff of a whole district. But corruption usually harmed only the poor and the politically impotent part of the population. The most dangerous complaints came from prelates, barons, and towns, who were not greatly worried about corruption. Their grievance was that royal officials persistently disregarded their privileges, their customs, and their rights of jurisdiction. Such complaints could lead to war, as in the case of Aquitaine and Flanders, to rebellion, as in the case of Béreud de Mercoeur (normally a loyal supporter of the king),[99] and to urban riots, as in the case of Amiens.[100] One of Philip's most difficult political tasks was to settle such disputes with the privileged classes without engaging in endless

---

Des Juis et des usuriers
Et des Lombarz les granz deniers
Tostes et tailles as levées
Qui toute ont esté paiées
De ta fille le marriage
Un tel ne semblable outrage
Onques mes nul temps ne levèrent
Les roys qui avant toi regnèrent. . . .

The Church was hurt by collection of the tenths, but the king received little of the money; most of it was kept by his servants (ibid., p. 97).

In his exasperation after the defeat at Courtrai the king was inclined to agree with his critics; he said that the collectors of the subvention in Senlis had taken much and given him little (A.N., JJ 36, fol. 12, no. 38).

[99] Béraud's grievance was that the paréage with the bishop of Mende interfered with his rights of justice in the Gévaudan (Roucaute et Saché, eds., Gévaudan, pp. 94-95, 203-6, 210 [1309]), but by 1311 he was back in favor and was captain of the royal troops in the region of Lyon (A.N., JJ 42A, fol. 118v, no. 129).

[100] Olim, III, 197.

police operations on the one hand or impairing the royal dignity on the other. He was ready to use force when it was necessary; fortunately, there was enough respect for the king and enough fear of his power so that force was not often necessary. A few demonstrations sufficed. The war of Aquitaine showed that Philip would fight his most powerful vassal in order to preserve his rights; the campaign against Béraud de Mercoeur in 1309 showed that even a noble who had been (and was to be again) an influential councillor would not be spared if he offended the royal dignity. Usually, however, conflicts of jurisdiction between the king and his prelates and barons led to legal, not military, combats, and these, in turn, often ended in compromises. Many of the southern bishops and abbots settled their disputes by making a *paréage* with the king (for example, the abbots of Sarlat and St. Papoul, the prior of St. Oriens of Auch, the bishops of Cahors, Le Puy, Mende, and Viviers). Some of the lesser barons did the same, but the greater men tried to wear down the government by protests, appeals, and other delaying tactics. The king of England and the count of Foix were both good at this game, but the record was surely set by the king of Majorca, lord of Montpellier (or, rather, by his agents in the town). Every attempt to apply royal ordinances in Montpellier was resisted; every ruling against local privileges was challenged; as soon as one excuse for exemption was denied, another was invented.[101] It was an interesting game, played without much bad feeling on either side. The net result was that the king of France preserved his rights in theory, but in practice allowed Montpellier a good deal of leeway in complying with his demands.

Towns that did not have a great baron as their immediate lord were far more vulnerable, whether they were in the royal domain, or in a *paréage*, or subject to a prelate. Philip had no great fear of or respect for French towns (Flemish towns, as he learned, were rather different). The royal capital of Paris was a model of what a town should be—ruled directly by royal officials, always ready to pay its taxes, seldom engaging in the great urban sport of rioting. Philip was very angry when other towns failed to follow this example. He imposed heavy amercements on towns that were guilty of disobedience or that showed contempt for established authorities. Rouen had to pay 30,000 l.t. to regain its rights of self-government, which had been forfeited for a riot against

[101] See note 63 above.

royal fiscal agents in 1292. Carcassonne, which in 1304 had carried its protests against the Inquisition to the edge of treason, was supposed to pay 60,000 l.t.; at least 20,000 l.t. was collected.[102] To give only a few other examples, Beauvais was amerced 10,000 l.p. and Amiens 20,000 l.p. in 1306, Cahors 3,000 l.t., Castelnaudary 4,000 l.t., and Montbrison 5,000 l.t. in 1309, and Laon 10,000 l.t. in 1311.[103] One can see why Philip did not have a good reputation with the chroniclers, most of whom wrote in urban centers. One can also see how little Philip cared about urban opinion and how much less willing he was to compromise with the bourgeoisie than with prelates and barons. Even when he agreed to remit an amercement in return for a grant that was technically a free gift (as he did for Rouen and Carcassonne), he was not renouncing his right to inflict similar punishments in the future, though he may have salved the pride of the town fathers.

In most disputes between the royal government and its subjects neither side used force, and there was ample opportunity to discuss the merits of the case, sometimes at great length. The aggrieved subject could complain to the king that his rights (or those of his community) were being infringed by the actions of a royal official, and the king, or a member of the Council acting in his name, could order the official to desist, to moderate his demands, or to investigate the complaint. The clergy were especially successful in using this informal procedure by petition, as a glance at the documents collected by Baudouin for Toulouse and by Roucaute and Saché for the Gévaudan will show. The line between such petitions and formal court proceeding was not very distinct. The plaintiffs used the same verbs—"conquestus est," "significavit"—and the result was often the same. The court might suggest that "letters of grace" (much like the answer to a petition) be requested, or it might order an inquest. In the latter case, the chief difference was that a direct order by the king to a seneschal or *bailli* to investigate could speed up procedure; it

---

[102] A.N., JJ 41, fol. 90v, no. 152 (Rouen, 1309); *H.L.*, x, cols. 473-75 (Carcassonne, 1309).

[103] *Olim*, III, 163 (Beauvais, 1306), 197 (Amiens, 1306), 299 (Cahors, 1309), 324 (Castelnaudary, 1309), 362 (Montbrison, 1309), 366 (former officials of Périgueux, 1309), 610 (Laon, 1311). Note the clustering in 1309. This was when the king was trying to collect the marriage aid; the amercements may have been a substitute in the case of towns that denied their liability.

took longer to complete an inquest ordered by the Parlement. On the other hand, if the recipient of a royal mandate to redress or investigate a grievance protested the order or gave an unfavorable report after an inquest, the case would probably be reopened in a royal court and some time would have been lost. In either event, the men who advised the king on petitions had also had some experience in the Parlement, so that there would not be much difference between their opinion and a formal judgement of the High Court. Under Philip's sons such men were in fact formally included in the Parlement lists as "maîtres des requêtes de l'hôtel." The title and the degree of specialization that it implies did not exist under Philip the Fair, but the connection between serving in the Parlement and advising on petitions did.

If petitions did not elicit satisfactory answers, or if it seemed that petitioning conceded too much show of right to the government's action, then a formal lawsuit would be instituted. In a typical case, a royal official would send an order or a summons to a subject and the subject would deny the validity of the act. After a certain amount of procedural sparring, the case would go to a royal court, where further delaying tactics could be used. The final step would be an appeal to Paris, but there could be further argument as to whether the appeal should be granted, whether the aggrieved party should ask for "letters of grace" (a waiver or a compromise of royal claims) or "letters of justice" (a definite ruling by the Parlement). If the latter course were chosen, it might be some years before a decision was rendered, and in some cases no decision at all is recorded. Thus, with good lawyers and a little influence at court, a case could be kept open for several decades. The first attempt to subject the county of Gévaudan (held by the bishop of Mende) to royal jurisdiction was made in 1269; the case was settled in principle by a compromise, the *paréage* of 1307, but the nobles of the county objected to the terms of the *paréage*, and their objections were overcome only in 1341.[104]

Not all cases lasted this long, but, on the whole, the government tried to avoid hasty and one-sided decisions. This was a successful way of defusing potentially dangerous conflicts; in the long run, changing circumstances, the death of a claimant, or

---

[104] Michel, pp. 181, 454-58; Roucaute et Saché, eds., *Gévaudan*, pp. 174-95 (text of the *paréage*), 202-8 (protests of the nobles and final settlement in 1341).

sheer fatigue made it relatively easy to arrange a compromise. Conversely, when decisions came quickly and possible compromises were rejected, as in the cases of Aquitaine and Flanders in the 1290s, one can be almost certain that Philip had decided that war was the only way of ending the dispute. Normally, however, the policy of delay and compromise was more effective. In the first place, delay was possible only if the game were played according to the king's rules, by working through his officials in his courts or by appealing directly to him for grace. Either course was a recognition of royal sovereignty. By nagging his subjects into using his courts to defend their rights, Philip achieved one of his principal objectives: recognition of his position as supreme and final judge of all inhabitants of the realm. Appeals for grace also recognized the king's supreme power, especially his power to supersede his own courts. In most cases subjects were given much of what they asked, as long as they accepted royal supremacy. Usually they were allowed to keep many of their rights of local government. As was pointed out above, Philip could not have ruled all of France directly, and such an idea probably never entered his head. It would have offended his sense of the fitness of things; the barons were meant to carry part of the burden of administration. It would also have offended his common sense; he simply did not have the manpower or the administrative structures to take over all the details of local government.

Thus there was a tacit agreement between the king and the possessing classes to seek their rights and to settle their disputes by peaceful means—by lawsuits or by compromises that would avoid or terminate lawsuits. Neither the king nor his subjects were entirely satisfied with this arrangement. Philip was obviously annoyed by the fact that his own courts could be used to hamper his own officials and to cause interminable delays in enforcing his claims to income or to jurisdiction. This is why he sent out, from time to time, commissioners with extraordinary powers to recuperate royal rights, as in the raid of Pierre de Latilly and Raoul de Breuilly.[105] From the subject's point of view, due judicial process was hard to accept when sergeants enforcing court orders were guilty of excessive violence or undue seizure and wastage of property. The sergeant's life was not always a happy one; they were abused and beaten by indignant subjects,

---

[105] They were "destinati pro juribus domini nostri conservandis et requirendis" (A.N., J 896, no. 29, J 1024, no. 38).

but these reactions were usually kept within tolerable limits. At the worst, they led to local riots, not to the collapse of royal authority in a district. The punishments inflicted for contempt of court or disobedience to royal officers seldom upset the division of power between the king and local authorities. Amercements and *amendes honorables* were more common than loss of jurisdiction, and amercements were often reduced after proof of good behavior. Thus the count of Foix, who drove off royal guards (killing one) from a monastery over which he claimed jurisdiction, was fined, ordered to surrender two castles, and required to make a pilgrimage to the Holy Land (1290). But his help was needed in the war of Aquitaine; he proved to be a faithful supporter of the king, and, little by little, all penalties were remitted.[106] Even the towns, where some of the worst riots took place, usually lost their rights of self-government only for limited periods. They would have to pay a price to redeem their liberties, but they did regain them; Rouen, for example, lost its commune in 1292 but bought back many of its rights in 1294 and regained almost all of them in 1309.[107]

By emphasizing the availability of legal remedies, the government succeeded in cooling off some of the grievances of its subjects. However, confidence in the courts was not unlimited, especially when it came to dealing with complaints against royal officials. There was a feeling that the king's men stuck together, that to accuse one official to another was at best useless and at worst dangerous, because it could lead to reprisals by the accused and his friends. St. Louis had begun the practice of sending out *enquêteurs* to remedy this lack of confidence, and his grandson continued the custom.

Unfortunately, there was a considerable difference between the *enquêteurs* of St. Louis and those of Philip the Fair. As we have seen, over half of them were themselves government officials (often high officials), and none of them was as independent and impartial as St. Louis's men had been. Even worse, they were often used primarily to recuperate royal rights rather than to punish royal officials. A blatant example of this practice may be seen in the commision of Jean d'Auxois and Nicolas de Luzarches for Languedoc in 1305; they were to collect subsidies and amortizations as well as punish royal officials.[108] These men in effect,

---

[106] *H.L.*, IX, 148-49, X, cols. 260-67.   [107] A.N., JJ 41, fol. 90v, no. 152.
[108] *H.L.*, X, col. 447; *Cartulaire de Prouille*, I, no. 126.

were being asked to reinforce local officers in their task of squeezing as much as they could out of the people, rather than to protect the people against those officials. Even when the *enquêteurs* were "bons hommes et loyaulx," the minor officials were supported by their superiors, and the superiors in turn by the "collateraulx du roy," who would then have the *enquêteurs* recalled. Then the local officials, reassured, would commit more wrongs than before. Such, at least, was the opinion of one critic of the system,[109] and the king himself seems to have agreed that such evils were possible. On 6 March 1303 he wrote to the *enquêteurs* in Carcassonne that the seneschal and other royal officials were trying to prevent inhabitants of the *sénéchaussée* from bringing accusations against them. They were asserting that they would soon be restored to office, that earlier *enquêtes* had not resulted in any penalties, and that accusers would be punished as soon as the *enquêteurs* departed. Some officials were seeking support from members of the king's Household. Philip ordered the *enquêteurs* to do their duty, and perhaps they did. At least the seneschal, Gui Chevrier, was replaced, but he received an equally important post as seneschal of Poitou and remained in royal service until his death.[110]

Nevertheless, faith in the *enquêteurs* persisted, and one of the complaints against Philip in 1314 was that he had not sent them out frequently enough. The complaint was justified. During the first 12 years of the reign there were only 9 missions, and many parts of the country were not visited at all (Vermandois, Bourges, Mâcon, Beaucaire, for example). Then came the period of greatest strain, the quarrel with Boniface VIII and the defeat of Courtrai. The number of missions increased markedly—at least 17 in the years 1300-1304. The south, which was the most restive part of the country, was visited during every one of these years, and often 2 or 3 groups were working there. The north and center did not receive quite so much attention, but every district had at least one chance to voice its complaints. Then came the period of relaxation of tensions, and the use of *enquêteurs* dropped off sharply; only 14 missions were sent out in the period 1305-1314 (including one to Gascony and one to Navarre). What was worse, this is precisely the period when some *enquêteurs* were

---

[109] Formeville, "Réformateurs," p. 507.

[110] Philip's letter is in *H.L.*, x, col. 411. On Gui Chevrier see F. Maillard, "Gui Chevrier," *Bibliothèque de l'Ecole des Chartes*, CXIII (1955), 195.

encouraged to concentrate on recovering royal rights and revenues. It is not surprising that Louis X found it expedient to send out 21 groups of *enquêteurs* during his brief reign (November 1314–June 1316). The fact that his subjects wanted the *enquêteurs* in their districts shows that the institution had not become completely perverted or completely useless.[111] Some officials, especially minor officials, were punished by the *enquêteurs*, and some wrongfully seized property was returned. Probably more important were the psychological effects. Grievances could be voiced to men who presumably had the king's ear. Oppressive officials were put on the defensive; they might not be punished, but they could be humiliated by having their misdeeds discussed in public. Probably the *enquêteurs* could do little to bring about a lasting improvement in local administration, but they did act as a safety valve for pent-up resentments.

It is significant that in the crisis year of 1303, when the *enquêteurs* were particularly active, Philip issued a great reforming ordinance.[112] Some of the articles dealt with purely administrative problems: rulings of the Parlement were to be enforced without appeal, *enquêtes* were to be judged within two years, no *bailli* or seneschal was to be a member of the Parlement, assizes were to be held every two months, men living in regions of customary law could have their cases judged by written law if the matter in dispute lay in a written-law district (articles 12, 13, 16, 26, 59). The rights and jurisdiction of the Church were to be protected against overzealous royal officials (articles 1-8). The greatest number of articles, however, dealt with the complaints of laymen against the king's agents. The old rules forbidding *baillis* and seneschals to profit from their offices by acquiring lands, rents, and prebends for themselves or their children in the lands that they administered were repeated. They were also ordered to punish lesser officials who misbehaved and to accept nothing from them (articles 15, 18, 38-55). As for these lesser officials—*prévôts*, *bayles*, and keepers of the seals of local royal courts—they were to be carefully chosen and were not to abuse their power by taking graft, wasting property seized by court order, assessing unreasonable amercements, or allowing people to buy immunity from all amercements for a lump sum (articles 10, 11, 19, 23, 28, 29).

This ordinance shows that the king and his Council were aware

[111] Artonne, pp. 123-24.   [112] *Ord.*, I, 357 ff.

of most of the grievances of subjects against royal officials. Its one weakness was that it was more specific about possible misdeeds of seneschals or *baillis* than it was about misbehavior of *prévôts* and sergeants. Nevertheless, if it could have been enforced, it would have eased some of the resentment that built up during the last years of the reign. It clearly was not enforced at the lower levels of administration. In the protests of 1314-1315 not much was said about seneschals and *baillis*, but there were bitter complaints about *prévôts* and sergeants. Doubtless these minor officials could never have been completely reformed, but a little more attention might have been given to their conduct in the relatively peaceful years that followed the end of the Flemish war. The decreased use of *enquêteurs* in this period probably had something to do with the failure to improve the behavior of local officials. Nevertheless, the movement of 1314 was not caused by misdeeds of minor officials but by upper-class resentment against royal policy in taxation and in relations with Flanders. There is nothing to show that sergeants and *prévôts* were any more oppressive after 1303 than before. It was useful to add complaints against minor officials to other grievances, but those complaints by themselves would never have shaken the royal government.

To sum up, Philip did not seek popularity, but he did desire domestic tranquility, and during all but the last months of his reign he was reasonably successful in obtaining it. If politics is the art of the possible, then he was a good politician. He seldom allowed his firm belief in royal supremacy to interfere with the necessity of keeping the support of the politically conscious people of the realm. If his rights were recognized in theory, he was willing to make any reasonable compromise in putting them into practice. An individual or a community could negotiate about the form or the amount of a tax as long as it was admitted that a tax was due. A conflict over jurisdiction could be settled on generous terms as long as the lord admitted that final appeals ran to the king's Court. Subjects who felt that the king (or his officials) were claiming rights or property unjustly had complete freedom to oppose these actions in the courts, and the courts (especially the Parlement) did not always rule in the king's favor. It sufficed that by using the king's courts, the king's supremacy was openly admitted.

Philip also recognized the fact that public opinion, or at least the opinion of the possessing classes, had to be conciliated at times by extraordinary measures. The *enquêteurs* were not regular or permanent officials. They were used for the most part in areas where discontent seemed to be reaching dangerous levels or where the king's authority was not fully accepted (for example, Gascony). Royal propaganda was normally spread through documents sent out from the central government or through the statements of local officials. When these outlets seemed inadequate, Philip called meetings of representatives of the propertied classes or sent his agents to local meetings in order to explain his policies. He seems to have understood that he could not push equally hard on all fronts at the same time. When the confrontation with Boniface VIII reached its peak, he began to ease pressure on the French Church and granted privileges to his prelates that he had refused before. When he seized the goods and debts of the Jews, he accepted the demands of the landed classes for a restoration of "good money." He was ruthless toward the Templars, but quite conciliatory in trying to collect the aid for marrying his daughter. It is true that his rights to a kingdom-wide marriage aid were very doubtful, but his case against the Temple was no better. It was simply easier to make people believe in the guilt of the Temple than in their duty to pay the aid.

Philip never succeeded in allaying the smouldering resentment against his officials; neither did his successors. But here one must make some distinctions. The minor officers who made arrests and seizures could never have been popular, but no one expected them to be any better than they were. At the other extreme, the men who were promoted rapidly and who became royal favorites would have been hated as upstarts even if they had been completely upright as officials. This was the fate of Biche and Mouche, of Flote, of Nogaret and Marigny. But the career officials, men who served 25, 30, or 40 years, men who worked for four or five successive kings, as did Pierre de Chalon, must have had some competence and some sense of duty. It is hard to believe that Pierre de Ferrières could have remained as seneschal of Rouergue for 14 years (1306-1320) if he had been thoroughly hated by the people of his district, or that Aimeri du Cros could have served in Carcassonne for 20 years (10 as judge, 1302-1311, 10 as seneschal, 1311-1321) if he had been blatantly oppressive and corrupt. Below this level there were viscounts and *viguiers* who held their office for many years;[113] above it were the men who served in

---

[113] Strayer, "Viscounts and Viguiers," pp. 227-28.

minor posts for many years but who gradually worked their way up to the top, such as the notary Ami d'Orléans (1301-1329), who eventually became a judge in the Parlement.[114] It is true that one of Philip's admirable (and at times annoying) qualities was his loyalty to the men who served him. He would not abandon Nogaret when to do so would have greatly facilitated reconciliation with the papacy. He rehabilitated Guichard de Marzi after Guichard had been deprived of his seneschalship by the *enquêteurs* (a rare enough occurrence to make one believe that Guichard must have been guilty of serious offenses).[115] But Philip's favor could not have protected his servants after his death, and the remarkably large number of his officials who still held positions in the reigns of his sons, and even in the time of Philip VI, is a testimony to their competence, if not to their character. Moreover, appointment to office by Philip the Fair was no guarantee of a lifetime job. Granting that some men, notably the well-educated lawyers who became judges in the south, may have found royal service tedious and unprofitable, there are still too many officials who served less than 10 years to allow one to believe that all these resignations were voluntary. There must have been some sifting out of the very incompetent and very unpopular officials. Not enough of them were removed to allay all discontent, but perhaps enough of them were removed to keep the discontent from boiling over.

In any case, it was not opposition to the king's servants but opposition to the king's policies that caused the one serious challenge to royal authority during Philip's reign: the formation of the leagues in 1314. This episode is not easy to understand. Philip did nothing in 1313-1314 that he had not done before, and he was asking rather less in the way of taxes than he had in 1303 and 1304. Perhaps he had lost some of his political skill; he reacted slowly and clumsily to grievances that he had dealt with easily in earlier years. A man of 46 was old in those days, and Philip may have been ailing during the last months of his life. Certainly his judgement seems to have been impaired. His daughters-in-law may have been guilty of adultery, but there were better ways of dealing with the problem than to make a public spectacle of the execution of their lovers. The king's sons were humiliated, and the image of a semisacred royal dynasty was tarnished. Marigny was probably the ablest of all the king's servants, but it might have been wiser to let him exercise his skills behind the scenes. The

---

[114] Guillois, pp. 239-40.   [115] *H.L.*, x, cols. 528-29.

official concentration of all financial operations in his hands and his prominent role in negotiations with Flanders irritated the great lords of the Council, notably Charles of Valois, and deprived the king of some support. Philip's (or Marigny's) policy toward Flanders in 1314 was probably wise, but it could be made to seem cowardly or, at best, vacillating. There is no evidence to show that the king made any great effort to refute this impression.

The final blow was Philip's unwillingness to suspend the war tax of 1314 once a truce with Flanders had been made. The principle of *cessante causa* had been fully recognized in 1313, and it was not wise to contradict such a recent precedent. There had been perfectly legitimate expenses for the army in 1314, and Philip probably could have arranged a compromise that would have given him enough money to meet most of those expenses. (In practice, this is fairly close to what actually happened. Louis X never returned the part of the tax that had been collected before Philip ordered the levy canceled, and in some districts this left him with fairly large sums of money—about 116,000 l.t. in all.)[116] But Philip offered no compromise and stubbornly refused to cancel the tax. Only after the nobles of Champagne, Burgundy, and the northeast had formed leagues against him, only when he was a dying man did he order that "ladite subvention cesse du tout."[117] As long as he had any vigor, he rebuffed the demands for cancellation.

The crisis of 1314 was aggravated by the king's mistakes, but it seems likely that there would have been a crisis even if Philip had played his cards perfectly. It is instructive to compare the year 1314 with the year 1300. Flote, who was the king's chief adviser in 1300, was certainly no more popular than Marigny. The war with England had ended in a truce that had not given Philip much profit. A truce with Flanders had expired on 6 January, and a French army had occupied the county without much trouble. By May the count had surrendered, and the fighting was over. Garrisoning Flanders was expensive, but so was garrisoning Aquitaine (which the French still held), and since Edward I had accepted a truce and Guy of Flanders had surrendered, one could hardly say that France was in a state of war. The principle of *cessante causa* had been recognized in the 1290s;[118] if it had been

---

[116] Strayer and Taylor, pp. 87-88.

[117] Ibid., pp. 86-87; Artonne, pp. 21-24; *Ord.*, I, 580.

[118] Strayer and Taylor, pp. 26-28, 31, 41 (collections of tenths from the Church to cease if peace or truce is made), 67-68, 71 (collection of the

applied as strictly in 1300 as the nobles wanted it applied in 1314, there should have been no taxation after the middle of the year (at the latest). But the fiftieth of 1300 was collected throughout the year with no difficulty. No one objected that war had ceased, no one asked for a refund of money paid in after the end of May.[119] Obviously there was a change in attitudes between 1300 and 1314.

It appears that Philip's errors in the last year of his reign merely provided an excuse for venting long-accumulated resentments. Taxation was the immediate cause of the formation of the leagues, but the charters granted by Louis X give more space to other grievances. They do state that taxes were to be taken only when the "arrière-ban" had been summoned, in time of necessity, and for the common welfare. They were to cease if peace were made. These provisions simply emphasized already accepted (if sometimes violated) rules, namely, the theory that taxes were a substitute for universal military service and the principle of *cessante causa*.[120] These rules could be stated briefly because they were well understood. The larger part of every charter was taken up with highly technical provisions meant to protect local customs and jurisdictions and to restrain abuses of power by royal officials (especially the *prévôts* and the sergeants). *Enquêteurs* were to be sent out to put an end to arbitrary and illegal acts by the king's men. The Norman charter tried to define exactly the limits on the activities of royal officials and to protect Norman law by forbidding appeals from the highest Norman court (the Exchequer) to the Parlement. The precision of the Norman charter made it more useful and longer-lived than those granted to other areas, but the message was the same.[121] There had been too much interference in local affairs, too much disregard of local custom, too much manipulation of legitimate royal rights to gain illegitimate increases in the king's income and power.

---

lay subvention of 1304). See Elizabeth A. R. Brown's article, "Cessante Causa," pp. 565-87.

[119] Strayer and Taylor, pp. 53-55. It is true that the principle of *cessante causa* had been emphasized only for the clergy and not for laymen up to 1300 and that the subvention of 1300 was levied at a very low rate. But much of this subvention was collected and accounted for long after all hostilities had ceased (Mignon, nos. 1268-70, 1276, 1280, 1290, 1296, 1299, 1302, 1321, etc.).

[120] *Ord.*, 1, 552, 566, 569, 579-80; Artonne, pp. 105-6.

[121] Artonne, pp. 108-19.

In short, the movement of 1314 suggests that the politically conscious part of the population was a little weary after years of pressure from above, even though that pressure had been exerted with some caution. No government, however good, can remain popular for nearly 30 years, and Philip's government was far from being as good as it might have been. The king had tried to be reasonable and accommodating, especially in dealing with his prelates and barons, but he had not gained the reputation for absolute probity that his grandfather had enjoyed. Philip was respected, but respect for royal majesty could not make subjects forget the arrogant behavior of some seneschals and *baillis* or the violence and peculations of lesser officials. The leagues were saying that it was time for a change, a change back to the good days of St. Louis.

One other factor must be mentioned with some caution. After 1300 the economy of France (and of much of western Europe) became unstable. The rapid growth in population, production, and income that had marked the thirteenth century was coming to an end. In Normandy there is some evidence that a depression had begun. Income from market taxes and from mills was declining, and land values were decreasing.[122] The fairs of Champagne were becoming less attractive as centers of international trade and finance. Granting that this was largely a result of war with Flanders, changes in trade routes, and new business techniques, the decline of the fairs deprived France of a certain amount of income and working capital. Mistreatment and mistrust of the Lombards delayed the development of a replacement for the Champagne money market in France. War diverted money from the more productive to the less productive elements of the population, from urban centers and the richer agricultural regions to the poorer nobles and peasants.[123] France was not heavily dependent on foreign trade, but foreign trade was certainly not flourishing. Italian merchants who bought licenses to export wool were never able to fulfill their contracts, and customs dues provided very little income.[124]

The evidence is scattered and incomplete, but it suggests that the French economy was at best stagnating. There were more

[122] Strayer, "Economic Conditions in Upper Normandy at the End of the Reign of Philip the Fair," in *Economies et sociétés au Moyen Age. Mélanges offerts à Edouard Perroy* (Paris, 1973), pp. 283-96.

[123] Strayer, "Costs and Profits of War," pp. 274-76, 290-91.

[124] Strayer and Taylor, pp. 15-16.

people to share the pie in 1300 than in 1250, but the pie was growing no larger. Such a situation would explain the extreme sensitivity of the population to royal financial policies. If the king wanted a larger income than his grandfather had enjoyed, and if the gross national product was not increasing, then any demand for taxes and any act by a royal official that caused a loss of money or of potential income would seem oppressive. A salestax of a penny in the pound, 1/240, seems light to us, but the chroniclers damned it bitterly.[125] Quarrels over rights of jurisdiction may often have been motivated by pride, but it is also true that the loss of a few pounds of income from a court might be a serious matter for a poor lord. Fines for amortization bore heavily on all the possessing classes. One of the great gains made by the nobles of Languedoc during the agitation of 1314-1315 was to obtain the right to amortize their lands freely.[126] In short, if the economic situation was worse in 1314 than in 1294, then it is easy to understand why there was more organized resistance to taxation and other financial demands at the end of the reign rather than at the beginning.

On the other hand, the precarious state of the economy may help to explain why Philip's dealings with the Church caused little resentment at any time and why the clergy took little part in the movement of 1314. The more the clergy paid, the less other classes had to pay, and the more control the king had over the Church, the surer he was of receiving tenths and annates. There were, of course, other forces at work. Political crusades had hurt the reputation of the Church, and in attacking the emperor, the papacy had had to recognize the growing authority of the kings. Nevertheless, as the bishops of France admitted, their failure to contribute to national defense in 1296 made them unpopular.[127] The failure, in turn, could be blamed on the pope, as could the suspension of payments of a tenth in 1301. There was always some latent anticlericalism among the laity, a feeling that the clergy did little to deserve their wealth and power. This feeling would be stronger in a period of economic difficulties.

This attitude persisted even after the death of Boniface. The few chroniclers who complained about the oppression of the clergy certainly did not reflect the opinion of most laymen. The

[125] Ibid., pp. 11-13; H.F., xx, 577, 662, xxi, 205.
[126] H.L., x, col. 548.
[127] Dupuy, pp. 26-27; Digard, I, 269.

nobles were more inclined to quarrel with the clergy over rights of jurisdiction than to give them support. The bishop of Mende, like several other prelates, found it preferable to share his rights with the king through a *paréage* rather than to try to defend them against his nobles.[128] The bourgeoisie tried to imitate the king and to force the clergy (or at least clerks engaged in business) to contribute to local taxes.[129] No doubt quarrels among members of the possessing classes would have occurred in any case, but a deteriorating economic situation made such quarrels more frequent and more bitter. The result was that the clergy played only a minor role in the leagues of 1314. As landholders they received the same benefits as lay lords, but very few of their specific grievances as clergy were remedied. They were still liable to the payment of tenths and annates, and none of the guarantees, however imperfect, that put some restraints on lay taxation applied to these ecclesiastical levies.

Accumulated resentments and economic insecurity may explain the movement of 1314, but neither the resentments nor the economic insecurity had reached the heights that they were to attain later in the century. The importance of the leagues and of the charters that they obtained should not be overestimated. The existence of the leagues does not prove that Philip's efforts to gain the support of his subjects had been an utter failure. The charters did not condemn the administrative system that had developed in Philip's reign; they simply tried to purge it of abuses that had long been recognized. The protesters did not try to destroy the bureaucracy. Marigny was executed, Latilly was driven from office, and a few of Marigny's closest associates lost their property. Otherwise there were no sudden changes. New men gradually rose in rank as older men died or retired, but the courts and councils of the 1320s were still full of men who had served Philip the Fair. There was no sharp change in policy. Internally, the administration developed along quite predictable lines; externally, the war with Flanders had to be renewed, and the old frictions with England led to another occupation of the duchy of Aquitaine. But it is difficult to find a real turning point in French history until well into the reign of Philip VI.

This continuity is some indication that Philip had been success-

---

128 Strayer, "La noblesse du Gévaudan," pp. 66-69.

129 *Olim*, II, 312, 325, III, 129, 633; Ménard, *Histoire de Nismes*, I, *preuves*, pp. 105, 114; F. Castets et J. Berthelé, *Archives de la ville de Montpellier* (Montpellier, 1895), I, pt. 2, nos. 3189-91, 3193-3200, 3206, 3275-81.

ful in his attempt to bind the realm together through allegiance to the king. Another indication of his success is that the kingdom went through a period of disputed successions (1316-1328) without being torn apart by civil war. Loyalty to the king was not very strong in many parts of France, but it was stronger than any competing loyalty. Even Languedoc, suspicious of the north as it was, could see no alternative to accepting the rule of the king who was recognized in Paris. As long as the ruler could keep internal strife at a minimum, prevent foreign invasion, and preserve his reputation as a dispenser of justice, much could be forgiven him. No one ever spoke of the good times of Philip the Fair as they did of the good times of St. Louis, but people who lived through the crises of the Hundred Years' War might well have done so. There were no civil wars in Philip's reign, no notable acts of treason, no executions of famous men, no plunderings of towns and villages. Philip drew heavily on the political capital accumulated by his ancestors, but he also replenished it. He was king of all France in a way that none of his predecessors had been. He had forced the most independent lords—the king-duke of Aquitaine, the counts of Flanders and of Bar, the southern bishops—to recognize his superiority. His courts, and especially the High Court that was the Parlement, retained their reputation for justice and made that justice available to more subjects than ever before. Provincial loyalties were still strong, but some men were beginning to see a vision of a *patria* that was the kingdom of France.

The one thing that his people could not forgive was Philip's financial policy. If he could have run his government on the revenues that St. Louis had enjoyed—a course urged on him by some of his critics—he would have had a better reputation. Or, since this was clearly impossible, if Philip had made a better case for his early taxes, resentment might not have built up to the level that it did. Philip could never have been popular—he lacked the warm personal qualities of his grandfather—but if he could have secured more understanding of his financial problems, he might have been remembered as an unusually able administrator. As it was, he received very little credit for his achievements, and a great deal of blame for his mistakes.

Bibliography

Actes et comptes de la commune de Provins. Edited by Maurice Prou and Jules d'Auriac. Provins, 1933.

Arbois de Jubainville, Henri d'. *Histoire des ducs et comtes de Champagne*. 7 vols. Troyes, 1859-1869.

Archives anciennes de la Ville de St. Quentin. Edited by Emmanuel Lemaire. St. Quentin, 1888-1910.

Archives de la ville de Montpellier. Edited by F. Casters and J. Berthelé. Montpellier, 1895.

Archives historiques de la Saintonge, XII (1884).

Archives historiques du Poitou, XI (1881), XIII (1883).

Archives municipales d'Agen. Published by A. Magen and G. Tholin. Villeneuve-sur-Lot, 1876.

Artonne, André. *Le mouvement de 1314 et les chartes provinciales de 1315*. Paris, 1912.

Barraclough, G. "Edward I and Adolf of Nassau." *Cambridge Historical Journal*, VI (1940), 225-62.

Baudon de Mony, Charles. "La mort et les funérailles de Philippe le Bel d'après un compte rendu à la cour de Majorque." *Bibliothèque de l'Ecole des Chartes*, LVIII (1897), 11-12.

Baudouin, Adolphe, ed. *Lettres inédites de Philippe le Bel*. Paris, 1887.

Bautier, R. H. "Guillaume de Mussy." *Bibliothèque de l'Ecole des Chartes*, CV (1944), 64-98.

Beaumanoir, Philippe de. *Coutumes de Beauvaisis*. Edited by Amédée Salmon. Paris, 1899-1900.

Beaumont de Lomagne. *Le livre juratoire de Beaumont de Lomagne*. Edited by G. Babinet de Rencogne and F. Mouleng. Montauban, 1888.

Beaurepaire, Charles de. *De la vicomté de l'eau de Rouen*. Paris, 1856.

Bémont, Charles. *Rôles Gascons*. 3 vols. Paris, 1896-1906.

Benton, John F. "Philip the Fair and the *Jours* of Troyes." *Studies in Medieval and Renaissance History*, VI (1969), 281-344.

Bessin, Guillaume. *Concilia Rotomagensis Provinciae*. 2 vols. Rouen, 1727.

Bigwood, Georges. "La politique de la laine en France sous les règnes de Philippe le Bel et ses fils." *Revue belge de philologie et d'histoire*, XV (1936), 79-102, 429-57, XVI (1937), 95-129.

———. "Un relevé de recettes." In *Mélanges d'histoire offerts à Henri Pirenne*, pp. 31-42. Brussels, 1926.

Bisson, T. N. *Conservation of Coinage*. Oxford, 1979.

———. "Consultative Functions in the King's Parlements." *Speculum*, XLIV (1969), 353-73.

Blackley, F. D., and Hermansen, G., eds. *The Household Book of Queen Isabella*. Edmonton, 1971.

Bloch, Marc. *Les rois thaumaturges*. Paris, 1961.

Boase, T.S.R. *Boniface VIII*. London, 1933.

Bonnassieux, Pierre. *De la réunion de la Lyon a la France*. Lyon, 1875.

Borrelli de Serres. *Recherches sur divers service publics du XIIIᵉ au XVIIᵉ siècle*. 3 vols. Paris, 1895-1909.

———. *Les variations monétaires sous Philippe le Bel*. Chalon-sur-Saône, 1902. (Extracted from *Gazette numismatique française* [1902], pp. 246-425.)

Boulet, M. "Les Gayte et les Chauchat de Clermont." *Revue d'Auvergne*, XXVIII–XXX (1911-1913).

Boutaric, Edgard, ed. *Actes du Parlement de Paris*. 2 vols. Paris, 1863-1867.

———. *Clément V, Philippe le Bel et les Templiers*. Paris, 1874. (Also in *Revue des questions historiques*, X [1871].)

———. *La France sous Philippe le Bel*. Paris, 1861.

———. "Notices et extraits de documents inédits relatifs à l'histoire de France sous Philippe le Bel." *Notices et extraits*, XX, pt. 2 (1861).

Brown, Elizabeth A. R. "Cessante Causa and the Taxes of the Last Capetians: The Political Applications of a Philosophical Maxim." *Studia Gratiana* [*Post Scripta*], XV (1972), 565-88.

———. *Customary Aids and Royal Finance*. Forthcoming.

———. "Philip IV and Fair, of France." In *Encyclopedia Britannica*, 15th ed. (1974).

———. "Royal Salvation and the Needs of State in Late Capetian France." In William C. Jordan, Bruce McNab, and Teofilo F. Ruiz, eds., *Order and Innovation in the Middle Ages: Essays in Honor of Joseph R. Strayer*, pp. 365-83. Princeton, 1976.

———. "Taxation and Morality in the Thirteenth and Fourteenth Centuries: Conscience and Political Power and the Kings of France." *French Historical Studies*, VIII (1973), 1-28.

Brugier-Roure, L. *Cartulaire de l'oeuvre des église, maison, pont et hospitaux du Saint-Esprit.* Academie de Nimes, *Mémoires,* 7th ser., XII (1889), annexe.

Brussel, Nicolas. *Nouvel examen de l'usage général des fiefs.* 2 vols. Paris, 1727.

Carolus-Barré, L. "Les baillis de Philippe III le Hardi." *Annuaire-Bulletin de la Societe de l'Histoire de France* (1966-1967), pp. 109-244.

———. "L'organization de la jurisdiction gracieuse à Paris." *Le Moyen Age,* LXIX (1963), 417-35.

Cartulaire de Notre-Dame de Prouille. Published by Jean Guiraud. 2 vols. Paris, 1907.

Cazelles, Raymond. *La société politique et la crise de la royauté sous Philippe de Valois.* Paris, 1958.

Chaplais, Pierre. "La souveraineté du roi de France et le pouvoir legislatif en Guyenne au début du XIVe siècle." *Le Moyen Age,* LXIX (1963), 449-69.

Cheyette, F. "La justice et le pouvoir à la fin du Moyen Age Français." *Revue historique de droit français et étranger* (1962), pp. 373-94.

Codex Dunensis. Edited by J.B.M.C. Kervyn de Lettenhove. Brussels, 1875.

Compagni, Dino. *Cronica.* Edited by Isidoro del Lungo. Florence, 1902.

Compayré, A. *Etudes historiques et documents inédits sur l'Albigeois.* Albi, 1841.

Coussemaker, Ed. *Documents historiques sur la Flandre Maritime.* In *Bulletin du Comité Flamend de France,* Vols. V, VI. Lille, 1870.

Cuttino, George. *English Diplomatic Administration 1259-1339.* 2d ed. Oxford, 1971.

Delaborde, H. F. "Un arrière petit-fils de Saint Louis." In *Mélanges Jules Havet,* pp. 414-19. Paris, 1895.

Delcambre, E. "Recueil de documents inédits relatifs aux relations du Hainaut et de la France de 1280 à 1297." Académie Royale de Belgique, *Bulletin de la Commission Royale d'Histoire de Belgique,* XCII (1928).

———. *Les relations de la France avec le Hainaut.* Mons, 1930.

Delisle, Léopold. "Guillaume d'Ercuis." In *Histoire littéraire,* XXXII (1898), 154-71.

———. *Mémoire sur les opérations financières des Templiers.* Paris, 1889.

De Vic, Claude, and Vaissette, Jean-Joseph. *Histoire générale de Languedoc, avec des notes et les pièces justificatives.* Rev. ed. by A. Molinier et al. 16 vols. Toulouse, 1872-1904.

Dessales, L. *Histoire du Périgord.* 3 vols. Périgueux, 1883-1886.

Digard, Georges. *Philippe le Bel et le Saint-Siège de 1285 à 1304.* 2 vols. Paris, 1936.

Disputatio inter clericum et militem. Edited and translated by Norma N. Erickson. *Proceedings of the American Philosophical Society,* CXI (1967), 288-309.

Dossat, Yves. "Une tentative de réforme administrative dans la sénéchaussée de Toulouse en 1271." *Bulletin philologique et historique (jusqu'à 1610) du Comité des travaux historiques et scientifiques* (1964), pp. 505-15.

Du Bois, Pierre. *De recuperatione terre sancte.* Edited by Charles-Victor Langlois. Paris, 1891.

―――. *Summaria brevis.* Edited by Hellmut Kämpf. Leipzig, 1936.

Dubrulle, H. *Cambrai à la fin du moyen âge.* Lille, 1903.

Duby, Georges. *La société aux XIe et XIIe siècles dans la région mâconnaise.* Paris, 1953.

Ducoudray, Gustave. *Les origines du Parlement de Paris.* 2 vols. Paris, 1902.

Dupont-Ferrier, G. *Gallia Regia ou l'état des officiers royaux des bailliages et des sénéchaussées de 1328 à 1515.* 6 vols. Paris, 1942-1965.

Dupuy, Pierre. *Histoire du différend d'entre le pape Boniface VIII et Philippes le Bel. . . .* Paris, 1655.

Egidius Columna seu Romanus. *De regimine principum.* Rome, 1607.

Favier, Jean, ed. *Cartulaire et actes d'Enguerran de Marigny.* Paris, 1965.

―――. *Un conseiller de Philippe le Bel. Enguerran de Marigny.* Mémoires et documents publiés par la Société de l'Ecole des Chartes, XVI. Paris, 1963.

―――. "Les légistes et le gouvernement de Philippe le Bel." *Journal des Savants* (April-June 1969), pp. 92-108.

Fawtier, Robert. "L'attentat d'Anagni." *Mélanges d'archéologie et d'histoire, Ecole Française de Rome* (1948), pp. 153-79.

―――, ed. *Comptes du Trésor (1296, 1316, 1384, 1477).* Recueil des historiens de la France, Documents financiers, II. Paris, 1936.

―――. *L'Europe occidentale de 1270 à 1380.* Pt. 1. Vol. VI, pt. 1 of Gustave Glotz, ed., *Histoire générale.* Paris, 1940.

————, et al., eds. *Registres du Trésor des Chartes.* Vol. I: *Règne de Philippe le Bel.* Paris, 1958.

Fawtier, Robert, and Maillard, François, eds. *Comptes royaux 1285-1314.* 3 vols. Recueil des historiens de la France, Documents financiers, III. Paris, 1953-1956.

Finke, Heinrich, ed. *Acta Aragonensia.* 3 vols. Berlin, 1908-1922.

————. *Aus den Tagen Bonifaz VIII. Funde und Forschungen.* Münster, 1902.

————. *Papsttum und Untergang des Templerordens.* 2 vols. Münster, 1907.

————. "Zur Charakteristik Philipps des Schönen." *Mitteilungen des Instituts für Osterreichische Geschichtsforschung,* XXVI (1905), 201-24.

Foedera, conventiones, literae. . . . Edited by Thomas Rymer. New ed. by A. Clarke, F. Holbrook, and J. Caley (covering only the years 1069-1383). 4 vols. London, 1816-1869.

Formeville, H. de. "Réformateurs envoyés dans la bailliage de Caen vers l'an 1300." *Mémoires de la Société des Antiquaires de Normandie,* 2d ser., IX (1851), 517-28.

Fournier, P. *Le royaume d'Arles et Vienne 1138-1378.* Paris, 1891.

Funck-Brentano, Frantz, ed. *Annales Gandenses.* Paris, 1896.

————, ed. *Chronique artésienne.* Paris, 1889.

————. "Document pour servir à l'histoire des relations de la France et l'Allemagne." *Revue historique,* XXXIX (1889), 326-48.

————. *Philippe le Bel en Flandre.* Paris, 1897.

————. "Philippe le Bel et la noblesse Franc-Comtoise." *Bibliothèque de l'Ecole des Chartes,* XLIX (1888), 5-40, 238-53.

Gallia Christiana in provincias ecclesiasticas distributa. 16 vols. Paris, 1715-1865.

Gaudemet, Jean. *La collation par le Roi de France des bénéfices vacants en régale.* Paris, 1935.

Geoffroi de Paris. *Six Historical Poems.* Edited by W. H. Storer and C. A. Rochedieu. University of North Carolina Studies in Romance Languages, no. 16. Chapel Hill, 1960.

Germain, Alexandre, ed. *Cartulaire de l'Université de Montpellier.* 2 vols. Montpellier, 1890-1912.

————. *Histoire de la commune de Montpellier.* 3 vols. Montpellier, 1851.

Gervaise du Bus. *Le roman de Fauvel.* Published by Arthur Lanfors. Paris, 1914-1919.

Giry, Arthur. *Manuel de diplomatique.* Paris, 1925.

Glénisson, Jean. "Les enquêteurs-réformateurs de 1270 à 1328." Thèse dactylographé, École des Chartes, 1946.

Gras, P. "Les évêques de Chalon." *Mémoires de la Société pour l'histoire du droit et des institutions des anciens pays bourguignons* . . . , xv (1953), 20 ff.

Gravier, H. "Essai sur les prévôts royaux." *Revue historique de droit français et étranger,* xxvii (1903), 649-53, 661-64.

Grün, A. "Notices sur les Archives du Parlement de Paris." In Boutaric, ed., *Actes du Parlement de Paris,* i.

Grunzweig, A. "Les incidences internationales des mutations monétaires de Philippe le Bel." *Le Moyen Age,* lix (1953), 117-72.

Guenée, Bernard. *Tribunaux et gens de justice dans le bailliage de Senlis (1380-1450).* Paris, 1963.

Guérout, Jean, ed. *Registres du Trésor des Chartes.* Vol. II: *Règnes des fils de Philippe le Bel.* Pt. 1: *Règnes de Louis X le Hutin et de Philippe V le Long.* Paris, 1966.

Guilhiermoz, Paul. *Enquêtes et procès.* Paris, 1892.

Guillaume le Maire. *Le livre de Guillaume le Maire.* Edited by Célestin Port. In *Collection de documents inédits. Mélanges historiques,* ii. Paris, 1877.

Guillois, André. *Recherches sur les maîtres des requêtes de l'hôtel des origines à 1350.* Paris, 1909.

Haberg, H. *Taxae pro Communibus Servitiis.* Studi e Testi 144. Vatican, n.d.

Henneman, John Bell. *Royal Taxation in Fourteenth Century France: The Development of War Financing 1322-1356.* Princeton, 1971.

Herbomez, A. "L'annexation de la Mortagne à la France." *Revue des questions historiques,* liii (1893), 27-55.

———. *Philippe le Bel et les Tournaisiens.* Brussels, 1892. (Extracted from *Bulletin de la commission royale d'histoire de Belgique,* 5th ser., iii, 1893.)

Histoire littéraire de la France. Paris, 1733- .

Höfler, C. "Rückblick auf P. Bonifatius VIII." *Abhandlungen der historische Klasse der Königlich Bayerischen Akademie,* iii. Munich, 1843.

Holtzmann, Robert. *Wilhelm von Nogaret.* Freiburg-im-Breisgau, 1898.

Jame, Pierre. *Aurea practica libellorum.* Cologne, 1595.

Jassemin, H. *La Chambre des Comptes de Paris.* Paris, 1933.

Jusselin, M. "Les 'Presidenz à Paris' au temps des derniers Capétiens." *Bibliothèque de l'Ecole des Chartes*, xcii (1931), 277 ff.

Kantorowicz, Ernst H. *The King's Two Bodies: A Study in Mediaeval Political Theology*. Princeton, 1957.

Kern, Fritz. "Die abtreten des linken Maasufers an Frankreich durch Albrecht I." *Mitteilungen des Instituts für Osterreichische Geschichtsforschung*, xxxi (1910), 558-81.

———, ed. *Acta Imperii Angliae et Franciae (1267-1313)*. Tübingen, 1911.

———. *Die Anfänge der französischen Ausdehnungspolitik bis zum Jahre 1308*. Tübingen, 1910.

Kleinclausz, A. *Histoire de Lyon*. Lyon, 1939.

Komefort, J. de. "Le Rhône . . . frontière des Capétiens au XIIIe siècle." *Revue historique*, clxxxi (1929), 74-89.

Lacoste G. *Histoire générale de Quercy*. 2 vols. Cahors, 1883-1886.

Lafforgue, P. *Histoire de la ville d'Auch*. Auch, 1851.

Lagarde, Georges de. "La philosophie sociale d'Henri de Gand et Godefroi de Fontaines." *Archives d'histoire doctrinale et littéraire du Moyen Age*, xiv (1943-1945), 96 ff.

Langlois, Charles-Victor. "Autographes nouveaux de Guillaume de Nogaret." *Journal des Savants* (1917), p. 323.

———. "Doléances recueillies par les enquêteurs de S. Louis et les derniers Capétiens directs." *Revue historique*, c (1900), 74 ff.

———. "Geoffroi du Plessis, protonotaire de France." *Revue historique*, lxvii (1889), 74 ff.

———. "Notices et documents relatifs à l'histoire de France au temps de Philippe le Bel." *Revue historique*, lx (1896).

———, ed. "Les papiers de Guillaume de Nogaret et de Guillaume de Plaisians au Trésor des Chartes." *Notices et extraits*, xxxix, pt. 1 (1909), 211 ff.

———. "Pons d'Aumelas." *Bibliothèque de l'Ecole des Chartes*, lii (1891), 259-64, 673-76.

———. "Registres perdus des archives de la Chambre des Comptes de Paris" (and Appendix II, "Le livre rouge"). *Notices et extraits*, xl (1916), 33 ff.

———. *Le règne de Philippe III le Hardi*. Paris, 1887.

———. *St. Louis, Philippe le Bel et les derniers Capétiens directs*. Vol. III, pt. 2 of E. Lavisse, *Histoire de France*. Paris, 1911.

———, ed. *Textes relatifs à l'histoire du Parlement de Paris*. Paris, 1888.

Lauer, Ph. "Une enquête au sujet de la frontière française dans le Val d'Aran sous Philippe le Bel." *Comité des travaux historiques et scientifiques. Bulletin de la section de géographie*, xxxiv (1919), 24 ff.

Lazard, L. "Les revenus tirés des juifs de France (XIIIe siècle)." *Revue des études juives*, xv (1887).

Lea, Henry Charles. *History of the Inquisition in the Middle Ages*. 3 vols. New York, 1888.

Leber, C. *Collection des meilleurs dissertations . . . relatifs à l'histoire de France*. 20 vols. Paris, 1838.

Leclerq, Jean. "Un sermon prononcé pendant la Guerre de Flandre." *Revue du Moyen Age Latin*, i (1945), 165-72.

Lehugeur, Paul. *Histoire de Philippe le Long, Roi de France 1316-1322*. Vol. I: *Le règne*. Paris, 1897. Vol. II: *Le mécanisme du gouvernement*. Paris, 1931.

Le Roux de Lincy. *Histoire de l'hôtel de ville de Paris*. Paris, 1846.

Le Roy Ladurie, Emmanuel. *Montaillou, village occitan*. Paris, 1975.

Limburg-Stirum, Thierry de. *Codex diplomaticus Flandriae*. Bruges, 1879-1889.

Lizerand, Georges. *Clément V et Philippe IV le Bel*. Paris, 1910.

———. *Le dossier de l'affaire des templiers*. Paris, 1923.

———. "Philippe le Bel et l'empire au temps de Rodolphe de Habsbourg." *Revue historique*, cxlii (1923), 189 ff.

Longnon, Auguste, ed. *Documents relatifs au comté de Champagne et de Brie, 1172-1362*. 3 vols. Paris, 1901-1914.

Lugge, M. *Gallia und Frankreich im Mittelalter*. Bonn, 1960.

Lyon, Bryce D. *From Fief to Indenture*. Cambridge, Mass., 1957.

McIlwain, C. H. *The Growth of Political Thought in the West*. New York, 1932.

Mahul, J. Alphonse, ed. *Cartulaire et archives des communes de l'ancien diocèse . . . de Carcassonne*. 7 vols. Paris, 1857-1885.

Maillard, François, ed. *Comptes royaux (1314-1328)*. 2 vols. Recueil des historiens de la France, Documents financiers, iv. Paris, 1961.

———. "Gui Chevrier." *Bibliothèque de l'Ecole des Chartes*, cxiii, (1955), 194-96.

———. "Mouvements administratifs des baillis et des sénéchaux sous Philippe le Bel." *Bulletin philologique et historique* (jusqu'à 1610) *du Comité des travaux historiques et scientifiques* (1959), pp. 407-30.

Marca, Peter de. *De Concordia sacerdotii et imperii.* Frankfurt, 1708.

Marrone, J., and Zuckerman, C. "Cardinal Simon of Beaulieu." *Traditio,* XXXI (1975), 195-222.

Martène. *Thesaurus novus anecdotorum.* 5 vols. Paris, 1717.

Martin-Chabot, E., ed. *Les archives de la cour des comptes, aides et finances de Montpellier.* Paris, 1907.

———. "Contribution à l'histoire de la famille Colonna." *Annaire-Bulletin de la Société de l'Histoire de France,* LVII (1920), 137 ff.

Maubourguet, J. M. *Le Périgord Méridionale.* Cahors, 1926.

Meijers, E. M. *Etudes d'histoire de droit.* 3 vols. Leyden, 1959.

———. *Responsa doctorum Tholosanorum.* Haarlem, 1938.

"Mémoire relatif au paréage de 1307." Edited by Abel Maisonobe. *Bulletin de la Société d'Agriculture, Industrie, Sciences et Arts du Département de la Lozère* (Mende, 1896).

Ménard, Léon. *Histoire civile, ecclésiastique et littéraire de la ville de Nismes.* 7 vols. Paris, 1744-1758.

Ménestrier, P. le. *Histoire de la ville de Lyon.* Lyon, 1696.

Michaëlsson, K. *Le livre de la taille de Paris: l'an 1296.* Göteborg, 1958.

Michel, Robert. *L'administration royale dans la sénéchaussée de Beaucaire au temps de Saint Louis.* Paris, 1910.

Mignon, Robert. *Inventaire d'anciens comptes royaux dressé par Robert Mignon sous le règne de Philippe de Valois.* Edited by Charles-Victor Langlois. Recueil des historiens de la France, Documents financiers, I. Paris, 1899.

Morel, Octave. *La grande chancellerie royale.* Paris, 1900.

Monumenta Germaniae Historica: Constitutiones et acta publica imperatorum. Vols. III, IV. Berlin, 1926- .

Les Olim, ou registres des arrêts rendus par la cour du roi. . . . Edited by Arthur Beugnot. 3 vols. in 4 parts. Paris, 1839-1848.

Ordonnances des roys de France de la troisième race. . . . Edited by Eusèbe-Jacob de Laurière et al. 22 vols. Paris, 1723-1849.

Ozanam, D. "Les receveurs de Champagne." In *Recueil . . . Clovis Brunel,* II, 342 ff. Paris, 1955.

Paoli, C. "Documenti di ser Ciappelleto." *Giornale storico della letterature Italiana,* V (1885), 344 ff.

Paoli, C., and Piccolomini, E., eds. *Lettere volgari del secole XIII.* Bologna, 1871. In Vol. CXVI of *Scelta di curiosità letterarie inedite o rare.*

Pegues, Franklin J. *The Lawyers of the Last Capetians*. Princeton, 1962.

Perrichet, L. *La grande chancellerie de France*. Paris, 1912.

Perrot, E., ed. *Arresta communia Scacarii*. Caen, 1910.

———. *Les cas royaux*. Paris, 1910.

Petit, Joseph. *Charles de Valois*. Paris, 1900.

———. "Thibaut de Chepoy." *Le Moyen Age*, x (1897), 224-39.

Petit, Joseph, et al. *Essai de restitution des plus anciens mémoriaux de la Chambre des Comptes de Paris*. Paris, 1899.

Picot, Georges, ed. *Documents relatifs aux Etats Généraux sous Philippe le Bel*. Paris, 1901.

Piquet, Jules. *Des banquiers au Moyen Age. Les Templiers*. Paris, 1939.

Piton, Camille. *Les Lombards en France et à Paris*. 2 vols. Paris, 1891-1892.

Poquet du Haut-Jussé, B. A. "Le second différend entre Boniface VIII et Philippe le Bel." In *Mélanges Albert Dufourg*, pp. 73-168. Paris, 1932.

Post, Gaines. *Studies in Medieval Legal Thought: Public Law and the State, 1100-1322*. Princeton, 1964.

Powicke, Frederick Maurice. *The Thirteenth Century, 1216-1307*. Oxford, 1953.

Prestwich, Michael. *War, Politics and Finance under Edward I*. Totowa, N.J., 1972.

Processus super zelo. Edited by C. Höfler. In *Abhandlungen der historische Klasse der Königlich Bayerischen Akademie der Wissenschaften*, iii. Munich, 1843.

Recueil des historiens des Gaules et de la France. Edited by Martin Bouquet et al. 24 vols. Paris, 1738-1904.

Redoutey, J. P. "Le comté de Bourgogne de 1295 à 1314." *Mémoires de la Société pour l'histoire de droit et des institutions des anciens pays bourguignons . . .* , fasc. 33 (1975-1978), 7-35.

———. "Philippe le Bel et la Franche-Comté." *Cahiers de l'association interuniversitaire de l'Est*, no. 19 (1979), 207-31.

Regestum Clementis Papae V. By monks of the Order of St. Benedict. 10 vols. Rome, 1885-1892.

Registre de Benoît XI. Edited by Ch. Granjean. Paris, 1905.

Les registres de Boniface VIII. Edited by Georges Digard, M. Faucon, and Antoine Thomas. Paris, 1907-1939.

Les registres d'Honorius IV. Edited by Maurice Prou. Paris, 1888.

Les registres de Nicholas IV. Edited by Ernest Langlois. Paris, 1886-1891.

Reglá Campistol, Juan. *Francia. La Corona de Aragon y la Frontera Pirenaica. La luche por el Valla de Arán*. 2 vols. Madrid, 1951.

Regné, J. *Histoire du Vivarais*. 2 vols. Largentière, 1914-1921.

Richard, Jean. *Les ducs de Bourgogne et la formation du duché du XIe au XIVe siècle*. Publications de l'Université de Dijon, XII. Paris, 1954.

Rigault, Abel. *Le procès de Guichard, évêque de Troyes*. Paris, 1896.

Rossignol, E. A. *Monographies communales du département du Tarn*. Toulouse, 1864-1866.

Roucaute, Jean, and Saché, Marc, eds. *Lettres de Philippe le Bel relatives au pays de Gévaudan*. Mende, 1897.

Ruiz, Teofilo. "Reaction to Anagni." *Catholic Historical Review*, LXV (1979), 385-401.

Saige, G., ed. *Documents historiques relatifs à la Vicomté de Carlat*. Monaco, 1900.

———. *Les juifs de Languedoc*. Paris, 1881.

Samenek, V. "Neue Beiträge zu den Regesten König Adolfs." *Akademie der Wissenschaften in Wien, Philologische-Historische Klasse, Sitzungsberichte*, CCXIV, Band 2.

Scholz, Richard. *Die Publizistik zur Zeit Philipps des Schönen*. Stuttgart, 1903.

Schwalm, Jakob. "Beiträge zur Reichsgeschichte des 14. Jahrhunderts." *Neues Archiv*, XXV (1900), 564 ff.

———. "Reise nach Frankreich." *Neues Archiv*, XXIX (1904), 571 ff.

Soudet, F. *Ordonnances de l'Echiquier de Normandie*. Rouen and Paris, 1929.

Stengel, E. *Avignon und Rhens*. Weimar, 1930.

Strayer, Joseph R. *Administration of Normandy under St. Louis*. Cambridge, Mass., 1932.

———. "La clientèle du Parlement de Paris sous Philippe le Bel." *Revue historique de droit français et étranger* (1975), pp. 166-67.

———. "The Costs and Profits of War." In H. A. Miskimin, D. Herlihy, and A. L. Udovitch, eds., *The Medieval City*, pp. 269-91. New Haven, 1977.

———. "The Crusade against Aragon." *Speculum*, XXVIII (1953), 102-13. Reprinted in *Medieval Statecraft*, pp. 107-22.

———. "Defense of the Realm and Royal Power in France." In *Studi in onore di Gino Luzzato*, I, 289-96. Milan, 1949. Reprinted in *Medieval Statecraft*, pp. 291-99.

———. "Economic Conditions in the County of Beaumont-le-Roger, 1261-1313." *Speculum*, XXVI (1951), 277-87. Reprinted in *Medieval Statecraft*, pp. 13-27.

———. "Economic Conditions in Upper Normandy at the End of the Reign of Philip the Fair." *Economies et sociétés au Moyen Age. Mélanges offerts à Edouard Perroy*, pp. 283-96. Paris, 1973.

———. "Exchequer and Parlement under Philip the Fair." In *Droit privé et institutions regionales. Etudes historiques offertes à Jean Yver*, pp. 655-62. Rouen, 1976.

———. "France: The Holy Land, the Chosen People, and the Most Christian King." In Theodore K. Rabb and Jerrold E. Seigel, eds., *Action and Conviction in Early Modern Europe: Essays in Memory of E. H. Harbison*, pp. 3-19. Princeton, 1969. Reprinted in *Medieval Statecraft*, pp. 300-314.

———. *Les gens de justice du Languedoc sous Philippe le Bel.* Toulouse, 1970.

———. "Italian Bankers and Philip the Fair." In D. Herlihy, R. S. Lopez, and V. Slessarev, eds., *Economy, Society, and Government in Medieval Italy: Essays in Memory of Robert L. Reynolds*, pp. 113-21. Kent, Ohio, 1969. Reprinted in *Medieval Statecraft*, pp. 239-47.

———. "The Laicization of French and English Society in the Thirteenth Century." *Speculum*, XV (1940), 76-86. Reprinted in *Medieval Statecraft*, pp. 251-65.

———. *Medieval Statecraft and the Perspectives of History: Essays by Joseph R. Strayer.* Edited by John F. Benton and Thomas N. Bisson. Princeton, 1971.

———. "La noblesse du Gévaudan et le paréage de 1307." *Revue du Gévaudan*, n.s., XIII (1967), 66-72.

———. "Notes on the Origin of English and French Export Taxes." *Studia Gratiana*, XV (1972), 399-422.

———. "Philip the Fair—A 'Constitutional' King." *American Historical Review*, LXII (1969), 18-32. Reprinted in *Medieval Statecraft*, pp. 195-212.

———. "Pierre de Chalon and the Origins of the French Customs

Service." In *Festschrift Percy Ernst Schramm*, I, 334-39. Wiesbaden, 1964. Reprinted in *Medieval Statecraft*, pp. 232-38.

———. *The Royal Domain in the Bailliage of Rouen*. Princeton, 1936. 2d ed. London, 1976.

———. "Viscounts and Viguiers under Philip the Fair." *Speculum*, XXXVIII (1963), 242-55. Reprinted in *Medieval Statecraft*, pp. 213-31.

Strayer, Joseph R., and Taylor, Charles H. *Studies in Early French Taxation*. Cambridge, Mass., 1939.

Sturler, J. de. *Les relations politiques et les échanges commerciaux entre Brabant et l'Angleterre*. Paris, 1936.

Tanon, L. *Justices des églises de Paris*. Paris, 1883.

Tardif, E. J., ed. *Coutumiers de Normandie*. Vol. II. *La Summa de legibus Normannie*. Rouen and Paris, 1896.

Teulet, Alexandre, et al., eds. *Layettes du Trésor des Chartes*. 5 vols. Paris, 1863-1909.

Thomas, Louis. "La vie privée de Guillaume de Nogaret." *Annales du Midi*, XVI (1940), 161-98.

Varin, Pierre. *Archives administratives de la ville de Reims*. 2 vols. Paris, 1839-1853.

———. *Archives legislatives de la ville de Reims*. Paris, 1840.

Verlaguet, P. A., ed. *Cartulaire de l'abbaye de Silvanès*. Archives historiques du Rouergue, I. Rodez, 1910.

Viard, Jules. "La cour au commencement du XIVe siècle." *Bibliothèque de l'Ecole des Chartes*, LXXVII (1916), 3-16.

———, ed. *Les journaux du Trésor de Charles IV le Bel*. Paris, 1917.

———, ed. *Les journaux du Trésor de Philippe IV le Bel*. Paris, 1940.

Vuitry, Adolphe. *Etudes sur le régime financier de la France avant la Révolution de 1789*. New ser. 2 vols. Paris, 1883.

Waquet, H. *Le bailliage de Vermandois*. Paris, 1919.

Wenck, Karl. *Clemens V und Heinrich VII*. Halle, 1882.

———. "Französische Werbungen um die deutsche Königskrone." *Historische Zeitschrift*, LXXXVI (1901), 253-69.

———. *Philipp der Schöne von Frankreich—seine Persönlichkeit und das Urteil der Zeitgenossen*. Marburg, 1905.

Willemsen, Carl. "Der Kampf um das Val d'Aran." *Spanische Forschungen der Görresgesellschaft. Erste Reihe. Gesammelte Aufsätze zur Kulturgeschichte Spaniens*, 6 Band, pp. 157 ff.

Wolff, Ph. "Achets d'armes pour Philippe le Bel dans le région Toulousaine." *Annales du Midi*, LXI (1948-1949), 84-91.

———. "La noblesse Toulousaine." In Ph. Contamine, ed., *La noblesse au Moyen Age*, pp. 153-74. Paris, 1976.

Wood, Charles T. *The French Apanages and the Capetian Monarchy 1224-1328*. Cambridge, Mass., 1966.

———. "*Regnum Francie*, a Problem in Capetian Administrative Usage." *Traditio*, XXIII (1967), 117-47.

Index

accounting periods, 144
Adinolfo di Papa, 278
Adolf of Nassau, 320, 322, 346, 347, 355
adultery of king's daughters-in-law, 19, 417
advocates, royal, 126
aid for knighting, 84-85, 109, 154, 177, 343, 393
aid for marriage, 84, 86-87, 108-9, 154, 160, 234, 287, 385, 393, 398, 399, 409, 416
Aigues-Mortes, 375
Aimeri du Cros, 54-55, 57, 91, 400, 416
Alain de Lamballe, 91, 92, 94, 95, 98, 400
Albert of Austria (Habsburg), 260, 275, 316, 322, 324, 346-47
Albi: bishops of, 159, 298; diocese of, 14, 155
Albigensians, 260
Alfonse de Rouvrai, 18, 54, 60, 89, 92, 93, 227
Alfonso III, king of Sicily, 368, 369
Alfonso X of Castile, 371
Alfonso de la Cerda, 391-92
Alluies, 384
Almont, castle of, 118
Amanieu d'Albret, 201
Amaury de la Charmoye, 184, 185
amercements, 155, 177, 201, 202, 231, 233, 409, 412
Ami d'Orléans, 72-73, 338, 417
Amiens, 155, 229, 407, 409
amortization, 91, 109, 131, 138, 155, 235, 236, 238, 240, 245, 248, 256-58, 387, 390, 392, 397, 398-99, 400, 412; exemptions from, 398
Anagni, 12, 35, 278, 280-81
André Porcheron, 303, 304
Angers, diocese of, 155, 258, 273
Anjou, county of, 192, 369
annates, 154-55, 164, 257-58, 280

Anseau de Morgneval, 170
Ansel de l'Isle, 58
Antequam essent clerici, 253
appeals, 138-39, 197-201, 203, 204-6, 220, 228, 229, 245, 247, 317, 362
Aquitaine, 101, 148, 192, 201, 317, 319-20, 323-24, 325, 373-74, 376-77, 380
Aragon, 10, 27-30, 368-69, 371
arbalesters: clerk of, 165, 166, 167, 168; master of, 265, 340, 373, 375, 376
Arles, kingdom of, 347, 366-67
Armagnac, count of, 202, 205
army, French, 315, 372-79; size, 375-79; supplies, 168, 170, 172, 400-401. *See also* wages, of armed forces
Arnaud de Proboleno, 117
Arnoldo Deghi. *See* Noffo Dei
Arnoul Mellin, 93
Arnoul de Wisemale, 144
Arras, conference of, 343, 344
arrêt, 219, 222
Artois: count of, 45; county of, 192. *See also* Robert, count of Artois
assemblies, 33, 109, 110-11, 159, 245, 271-72, 275-76, 277, 286, 384-86, 416
assizes, 123, 199, 203-4, 205, 414
Athis, treaty of, 337, 340, 342, 386
Ausculta fili, 2, 238, 260, 267-69, 270-71, 274
Autun, bishop of, 276, 359, 360
Auvergne, 42-43, 44, 51, 103, 114, 351
Avignon, 293, 366

bailli, baillis, 11, 41, 43-44, 46, 56, 103, 111, 112, 123, 132, 142, 204, 206, 208, 214, 414-15
bailliages, 100-101, 103, 142
banishment, 232
Bar: count of, 316, 320, 322, 340-41; county of, 164, 315, 320, 352, 359, 360

Library of Congress Cataloging in Publication Data

Strayer, Joseph Reese, 1904-
    The reign of Philip the Fair.

    Bibliography: p.
    Includes index.
    1. Philippe IV, le Bel, King of France, 1268-1314.
    2. France—History—Philip IV, 1285-1314.
    3. France—Kings and rulers—Biography.   I. Title.
DC92.S83   944'.024'0924   [B]   79-3232
ISBN 0-691-05302-2
ISBN 0-691-10089-6 lib. pbk.